Of Courts and Constitutions

The essays which appear in this volume have been written to pay tribute to the Hon Mr Justice Nial Fennelly, Judge of the Supreme Court of Ireland, and former Advocate General at the European Court of Justice, on the occasion of his retirement.

The overall theme of the book is the relationship between European Union law and national law, and the role of courts in defining that relationship. The book consists of four main parts – the structure and functioning of the European Court of Justice, material issues of European Union law, aspects of Irish law and transversal issues of national and European law. The contributors are all past and present members of the European bench, members or former members of the Irish judiciary or Bar and/or experts in European Union law, many of whom have worked with Mr Justice Fennelly during his long and distinguished career at the Bar and on the bench.

Of Courts and Constitutions

Liber Amicorum in Honour of Nial Fennelly

Edited by

Kieran Bradley, Noel Travers and Anthony Whelan

·HART·
PUBLISHING
OXFORD AND PORTLAND, OREGON
2014

Published in the United Kingdom by Hart Publishing Ltd
16C Worcester Place, Oxford, OX1 2JW
Telephone: +44 (0)1865 517530
Fax: +44 (0)1865 510710
E-mail: mail@hartpub.co.uk
Website: http://www.hartpub.co.uk

Published in North America (US and Canada) by
Hart Publishing
c/o International Specialized Book Services
920 NE 58th Avenue, Suite 300
Portland, OR 97213-3786
USA
Tel: +1 503 287 3093 or toll-free: (1) 800 944 6190
Fax: +1 503 280 8832
E-mail: orders@isbs.com
Website: http://www.isbs.com

Hart Publishing is an imprint of Bloomsbury Publishing plc.

British Library Cataloguing in Publication Data
Data Available

ISBN: 978-1-84946-665-3

Typeset by Criteria International, Quito, Ecuador
Printed and bound in Great Britain by
CPI Group (UK) Ltd, Croydon CR0 4YY

Foreword

MARY MCALEESE*

IT IS A GREAT pleasure for me personally to provide the foreword for this *Liber Amicorum* in honour of Mr Justice Nial Fennelly. Nial Fennelly has been a leading light on the Irish legal scene, both as a practitioner and a judge, for over forty years. While a recent *Irish Times* profile, describing him as 'a calm, courteous and experienced jurist', accurately evoked some of his many personal qualities, it hardly begins to reflect his influence and standing as a lawyer.

Nial Fennelly was called to the Irish Bar in 1966, after taking a Masters' degree in economics at University College Dublin, a background which was to serve him well in later life. He became a Senior Counsel in 1981, and served as Chairman of the Bar Council in 1990 and 1991. He also served as Chairman of the Legal Aid Board, from which position he resigned in protest in 1989 at a lack of government funding. That resignation was not in vain, as the civil legal aid scheme was finally put on a statutory footing in 1995. His willingness to devote time and energy to promoting access to justice for those who might otherwise be denied a fundamental right, and to representing his colleagues at the Bar, typifies a generosity of spirit that Nial has shown throughout his professional career.

In January 1995, Nial was appointed an Advocate General at the European Court of Justice, the first (and, to date, only) Irish lawyer to occupy this distinguished post. Busy though he was in that demanding role, he always had time for visiting academics like me with a bunch of law students in tow as we toured the European institutions. The appointment allowed him to shine on another, and rather different, stage though one with which he was already quite familiar from his work at the Bar. Even after returning to Ireland, he has maintained his keen interest in European law, and has worked hard to promote greater understanding and awareness of EU and European human rights law in Ireland, particularly in his role as Chairman of the Irish Centre for European Law from 2002 until 2009. I recall with particular fondness the warm reception I received from Nial when I addressed the Centre, as its patron, at its twentieth anniversary conference in November 2008. He has also long served as the President of the Irish Society for European Law, which organised the extremely successful FIDE Congress which took place in Dublin in May 2004.

I first met Nial while I was teaching in Trinity College Dublin in the late 1970's. Even then, we shared interests in several areas, including EU law, access

* Former President of Ireland

to justice and professional legal education. I was therefore particularly gratified that, on a crisp October morning in 2000, it fell to me to appoint him a judge of the Supreme Court, following his return from Luxembourg at the end of his mandate as Advocate General. In both these capacities, he has produced Opinions and judgments which will continue to be cited for many years to come, displaying both the authority to convince and the courage to dissent, as need be.

In an essay written early on in his term as Advocate General and published in a prestigious American law journal, Nial Fennelly wrote that:

> The object of all interpretation lies in the true intention of the lawmakers, whether they be framers of a constitution or a treaty, legislators, or drafters of secondary legislation. Its pursuit at the Court of Justice of the European Communities demands of the common lawyer a readiness to set sail from the secure anchorage and protected haven of "plain words" and to explore the wider seas of purpose and context.

I think it would be widely accepted that Nial has set sail on many legal journeys during his illustrious career and explored with distinction, skill and adroitness many, often turbulent, legal seas. The breadth, quality and diversity of the contributions to this *Liber Amicorum* marking his retirement from the bench are a testimony to the influence that he has had on the development of Irish and EU law. Therefore, I highly commend this timely volume to legal scholars and practitioners alike, confident that it is richly deserving of its all-encompassing title, 'Of Courts and Constitutions'. The contributions it contains reflect in numerous ways the many fine qualities of the remarkable person whom they most deservingly honour.

December 2013

Preface

THAT SO MANY of his past and present colleagues, collaborators and friends have been so willing to contribute to this *Liber amicorum* is a mark of the esteem in which Nial Fennelly is held, in Ireland and in the wider world of European law. Apart from the authors represented here, a number of others were only prevented from contributing a chapter by pressing work commitments: dayjob *oblige*. It is clear that the encomia of former President Mary McAleese in her generous foreword to the present volume are very widely shared.

The chapters are rich in variety and, fittingly for one who has served in the highest courts at the European and the national level, cover a vast gamut of legal topics from each of these legal orders and where they interact. For the purposes of presentation, these are divided into four parts, though certain issues and judgments put in an appearance in more than one part. The first part covers the functioning of the European Court of Justice, including the evolution of the Union judicature over six decades, as well as Union law principles of interpretation in the area of civil procedure, the special procedures the Court has adopted to ensure the speedy administration of justice in particular circumstances, and the question of the obligation of the lower Union courts to follow the case law of their respective higher courts, so-called 'vertical precedent'.

A second part covers different aspects of material EU law. It starts with two chapters which deal with the Court's response to ensuring judicial protection of individual rights in the highly sensitive area of asset freezing on foot of decisions of the UN Sanctions Committee. There follow contributions on certain highly topical areas of material law: the treatment of arbitration in the Union's private international law, the impact on the rule of law of the Union's reaction to the financial crisis, the development of new regulatory techniques for facilitating the functioning of the internal market, the long and difficult road to unitary patent protection and market regulation in the electronic communications industries.

The section on Irish law sees two well-placed observers revisit the *Crotty* doctrine, which has obliged successive governments, in political fact if not necessarily in law, to hold referendums on the major acts of EU Treaty reform, in the light of the recent *Pringle* litigation in the Irish Supreme Court. Two other chapters examine the influence Mr Justice Fennelly has had in quite diverse areas of Irish law: the reasons-giving requirement in administrative law, and the law on 'missing evidence'. The topic of remedies for unconstitutionality is also subjected to thorough examination.

A final, quite heterogeneous, section examines issues at the intersection of European and national law. The topics include the enforcement of competition law in national courts and the adequacy of damages as a remedy in public procurement law; the mutual interaction of the European legal order and those of the common law jurisdictions; comparative reflections on principles for the protection of fundamental rights in the Irish Constitution and the Union Charter; the Europeanisation of the reasons-giving requirement, the right of child citizens and their third country parents to remain on the national territory, and the defence of the core values in the German Constitution in the context of deeper European integration. Finally, one chapter explores some of the legal and philosophical issues which arise when a judge switches allegiance from an international court to a national court, or vice versa.

Contents

Contributors

Kieran Bradley, Judge of the European Union Civil Service Tribunal; *référendaire* in the chambers of Advocate General Nial Fennelly (1995–2000)

Frank Clark, Judge of the Supreme Court of Ireland and adjunct Professor at Trinity College, Dublin

Anthony J Collins, Judge of the General Court of the European Union

Michael M Collins, Senior Counsel, Law Library, Dublin

Cathryn Costello, Andrew W Mellon Associate Professor in International Human Rights and Refugee Law, at the Refugee Studies Centre, University of Oxford, and Fellow of St Antony's College

Catherine Donnelly, Barrister in the Law Library, Dublin and Blackstone Chambers, London. Associate Professor and Fellow of Trinity College, Dublin.

David Edward, Professor Emeritus, University of Edinburgh; Judge of the European Court of Justice (1992–2004)

Nicholas J Forwood, Judge at the General Court of the European Union

Paul Gallagher, Senior Counsel, former Attorney General of Ireland

Hugh Geoghegan, former Judge of the Supreme Court of Ireland (2000–2010)

Wolfgang Heusel, Director of the Academy of European Law, Trier, Germany

Herwig C H Hofmann, Professor of European and Transnational Public Law, Jean Monnet Chair; University of Luxembourg – Faculty of Law, Economics and Finance – Centre for European Law

Gerard Hogan, Judge of the High Court of Ireland

Ronan Keane, former Chief Justice of Ireland (2000–2004); former Judge of the Supreme Court of Ireland (1996–2000)

John MacMenamin, Judge of the Supreme Court of Ireland

José Carlos de Carvalho Moitinho de Almeida, former Judge of the European Court of Justice (1986–2000)

Muireann Noonan, Barrister, Law Library, Dublin; office manager in the chambers of Advocate General Nial Fennelly (1995–1997)

Aindrias Ó Caoimh, Judge of the European Court of Justice

Donal O'Donnell, Judge of the Supreme Court of Ireland.

Diarmuid Rossa Phelan, Senior Counsel, Law Library, Dublin; Fellow, Trinity College, Dublin

Vassilios Skouris, President of the Court of Justice of the European Union

Giuseppe Tesauro, Judge of the Italian Constitutional Court. Advocate General at the European Court of Justice (1988–1998)

Noel J Travers, Barrister, Law Library, Dublin; *référendaire* in the chambers of Advocate General Nial Fennelly (1995–2000) and in the chambers of Judge Bo Vesterdorf, President of the (then) Court of First Instance of the EC (2000–2003)

Melchior Wathelet, Advocate General at the European Court of Justice. Judge of the European Court of Justice (1995–2003)

Anthony Whelan, Acting Director for Electronic Communications Networks and Services, European Commission; *référendaire* in the chambers of Advocate General Nial Fennelly (1995–2000)

PART I: THE STRUCTURE AND FUNCTIONING OF THE EUROPEAN COURT

1

The Evolution of the Judicial Architecture of the European Union and its Procedural Implications

VASSILIOS SKOURIS*

INTRODUCTION

NIAL FENNELLY WAS the first Irish lawyer to be appointed as Advocate General at the European Court of Justice (ECJ), where he served from 1995 to 2000. As Advocate General his opinions dealt with several areas of EU law and, although I did not have the pleasure of working directly with him on specific cases, I came to appreciate the clarity of his opinions and the pragmatic and convincing nature of his reasoning. Upon leaving the ECJ in 2000, he continued to serve the EU system of administration as a Judge of the Supreme Court of Ireland. In fact, he brilliantly illustrated the role of the national judge as judge of the European Union in his contribution to the book published recently by the ECJ on the occasion of its 60th anniversary.[1]

Given the wide range of areas where Nial Fennelly has contributed in the evolution of EU law, I have chosen a more general topic for my contribution to this *Liber amicorum*. The focus of this article will be the evolution of the judicial architecture of the European Union and its procedural implications. In the pages that follow, I will endeavour to briefly present the history of the judiciary of the EU from its very beginning until today, to analyse its transformation over the years and to examine both the reasons that led to the successive reforms of the EU judicial system and the procedural consequences of those reforms.

* President, Court of Justice of the European Union

[1] See N Fennelly, 'The National Judge as Judge of the European Union', in A Rosas, E Levits, Y Bot (eds), *The Court of Justice and the Construction of Europe : Analyses and Perspectives on Sixty Years of Case-law* (The Hague, TMC Asser, 2013), 61.

A BRIEF HISTORY

In order to get a better sense of how the judicial architecture of the EU has evolved over the years, one has to go back to the very beginning of the European Communities and the creation of the Court of Justice of the European Coal and Steel Community (ECSC Court). This will necessarily bring us back to December 1952, some 61 years ago, when the Judges and Advocates General of the ECSC Court were being sworn in. At that time the Court, with seven Judges and two Advocates General, was a revolutionary judicial institution because it was supranational and permanent, and enjoyed mandatory jurisdiction. These characteristics have not changed over the years and they still define the judicial system of the EU.

Nevertheless, the ECSC Court of 1952 was significantly different from what the Court is today. Firstly, it had the luxury of time. To illustrate that fact, it is necessary to note that one of the first decisions of the ECSC Court was to define specific periods when the Court would not be in session, known as the judicial holidays, which were much more generous than they are today.

Secondly, the Rules of Procedure were also tailored for a Court that had the luxury of time and would not expect an immense workload. One of the characteristics of the Rules of Procedure included the preparation of a report for the hearing summarising the case and arguments of the parties. This document would be read aloud by the reporting judge at the beginning of each hearing. The full text of the opinion of the Advocate General and of the judgment was also read out during a public hearing.

Thirdly, the Court was not composed solely of jurists. Given the limited scope of the ECSC Treaty, the composition of the Court included an economist and a trade unionist.

In 1953, the first full calendar year of the existence of the Court, a mere four cases were introduced and all four were subsequently withdrawn. The first case which led to a judgment was introduced at the beginning of 1954. From that point, the number of cases introduced increased at an extremely slow rate until 1958 when the Court received 43 cases. There were 99 new cases in 1963, 131 in 1973, 217 in 1982 and 244 in 1989. Since then, the number of new cases introduced before the Court has increased every year. There are three reasons for this. First, the ECSC was complemented by the European Economic Community (EEC) and the European Atomic Energy Community (Euratom). In other words, the scope of the Court's competences became significantly wider. Second, the membership of the European Communities had doubled by the mid-1980s, with 12 Members States instead of six. Third, the Court progressively gained more trust amongst Member States, national courts with regard to the preliminary reference procedure, and private individuals.

THE CREATION OF THE COURT OF FIRST INSTANCE

By the mid-1980s, it had become apparent that the Court of Justice could not handle its caseload in an efficient and effective way due to the fact that incoming cases were increasing in number and complexity. The surge of the popularity of the preliminary reference procedure and the multiplication of the official languages of the European Communities, coupled with the Court's multilingual regime, made it almost impossible for the Court to deliver judgments within reasonable time limits.

It was at that point that the European legislature decided for the first time to consider a structural reform of the judicial architecture of the European Communities. Hence, the Single European Act provided a legal basis for the creation of a Court of First Instance which would have jurisdiction at first instance for certain categories of cases introduced by private individuals and undertakings.

Following negotiations which lasted for almost two years, the Court of First Instance was created at the end of 1988. It comprised one judge per Member State and had rather limited jurisdiction over cases brought by private individuals and undertakings in the field of Competition Law. The Treaty of Maastricht later provided for the possibility to transfer all the direct actions to the Court of First Instance and thus further categories of cases were transferred in 1993, 1994 and 2004.

The creation of the Court of First Instance was instrumental in the effort to maintain the efficiency of the European justice system. Nevertheless, it was not the result of a systematic and thoughtful reflection on the desirable judicial architecture of the European Union. Rather, it was a simple and pragmatic solution which made the European judiciary more efficient by alleviating the workload of the Court of Justice, and therefore improving the system qualitatively by adding a level of jurisdiction, following the example of national judiciaries.

However, in light of the future massive enlargement of the Union which was being planned, it became clear by the end of the 1990s that the entire judicial architecture of the European Union had to be reconsidered.

THE TREATY OF NICE

Reconsideration and reform was instigated by one of the most influential treaties that the European justice system has experienced to this day, the Treaty of Nice.[2] The reforms introduced by this Treaty had a twofold objective: to maintain the consistency of the jurisprudence in light of the enlargement, and to improve the efficiency of the European judiciary.[3] These objectives were to be met by four

[2] Entered into force on 1 February 2003. In effect, it amended the Maastricht Treaty and the Treaty of Rome so as to reform the institutional structure of the European Union to take account of eastward expansion.

[3] V Skouris, 'De nouveaux défis pour la Cour de justice dans une Europe élargie' (2008) *ERA Forum* 101.

key innovations in relation to the organization and internal functioning of the Court.

The first one was the provision of two distinct options for the evolution of the judicial architecture of the European Union. On the one hand, the Treaty of Nice abolished the rule of 'one judge per Member State' in the Court of First Instance,[4] thus permitting an increase in the number of judges in this court.[5] On the other hand, it provided a legal basis for the creation of specialised tribunals which could exercise jurisdiction, at first instance, over cases in particular fields of European law. The jurisdiction for appeals against the judgments of these specialised courts was vested in to the Court of First Instance.

The second was the formation of the Grand Chamber of the Court of Justice which comprised initially 11, then 13 and finally 15 judges. In essence, the Grand Chamber became the body which hears the cases considered to be the most important. As a result of this development, the Full Court, now composed of 28 judges, would only sit on rare occasions. In this respect, it is important to take into account that the Court has been developing its case-law for more than 60 years. Consequently, legal issues that could justify a formation of 28 judges are not likely to occur with any frequency.

The third major innovation introduced by the Nice Treaty was the election of the Presidents of the Chambers of five judges for a mandate of three years, rather than one year.[6] This longer period of time, coupled with the fact that the judges, including the President and Vice President of the Court, sit on cases bought before the Grand Chamber, confers on the Presidents of these Chambers a crucial institutional role within the Court.[7] In my view, this particular innovation was of extreme importance. In a Court of 28 judges, sitting in 10 different formations, it is essential to ensure the coherence of the case law. The presence of the President and the Vice-President of the Court along with a minimum of three Presidents of Chambers in all the cases brought before the Grand Chamber is likely to guarantee the required coherence. Additionally, the fact that each President of Chamber sits on all the cases brought before his or her Chamber is also important in that respect.

The fourth and last innovation of the Treaty of Nice concerns the role of the Advocate General. Although the Treaty of Nice maintained the principle of 'one judge per Member State', it did not provide for an increase in the number of Advocates General. Therefore, there was a risk of considerable procedural delays due to a 'bottlenecking' effect at the stage of the intervention of the Advocate General. For that reason, the Nice Treaty introduced for the first time the possibility of the Court rendering judgments without an opinion from the Advocate General on cases where no new points of law are raised.[8] It is

[4] The court was renamed the 'General Court' in accordance with the Treaty of Lisbon.

[5] See Art 224(1) EC, now Art 19(2), second subpara, TEU, and Art 254(1) TFEU.

[6] Art 16(1) of the Statute of the Court of Justice of the European Union (hereinafter 'Court Statute').

[7] Ibid, Art 16(2).

[8] Art 20(5), Court Statute.

important to stress that this possibility would not only speed up the process on a large number of cases but would also ease the workload of the Advocates General. Taking into account the well-established practice of responding to certain requests for a preliminary ruling by way of a simple order (and therefore without an opinion by the Advocate General), one cannot help but notice an important change in the role of the Advocate General. Effectively, Advocates General present opinions on fewer cases and consequently, they concentrate on the more important cases brought before the Court.

THE ENLARGEMENTS

The aforementioned measures were all designed to reform the European justice system in order to ensure its efficient functioning within an enlarged European Union. One can now say with confidence that these reforms fulfilled their purpose. Nevertheless, the three successive enlargements of the European Union, in 2004,[9] 2007[10] and 2013, and the organisational changes that they entailed for the Court, have had a transformative effect on the system as a whole. The arrival of 26 new judges with their *cabinets* (private offices), that is 13 judges at the ECJ and 13 judges at the General Court, in addition to the significant increase in the number of staff of the institution, illustrates that the Court changed profoundly after 2004.

On an organisational level, the arrival of the new judges made it necessary to increase the number of judicial chambers. Thus, the ECJ now comprises five chambers of five judges and five chambers of three judges. The General Court, on the other hand, is composed of nine chambers of three judges. On an administrative level, the staff currently exceeds 2000 employees and its organisational chart is divided into five directorates-general, ten directorates and 48 units.[11]

Finally, the greatest challenge these enlargements represented for the Court was the increase in the number of the official languages of the European Union, and consequently of the potential languages in which cases can be conducted. Moreover, the present number of language combinations has risen to over 500.

[9] See Documents concerning the accession of the Czech Republic, the Republic of Estonia, the Republic of Cyprus, the Republic of Latvia, the Republic of Lithuania, the Republic of Hungary, the Republic of Malta, the Republic of Poland, the Republic of Slovenia and Slovak Republic to the European Union, and in particular: Art 13 of the Act concerning the conditions of accession [2003] OJ L236/1 37 and [2003] OJ C227E/1.

[10] See Documents concerning the accession of the Republic of Bulgaria and Romania to the European Union and in particular Art 10 of the Protocol concerning the conditions and arrangements for admission, [2005] OJ L157/1, 32.

[11] See the Abridged Organisational Chart of December 2010 in Court of Justice of the European Union, *Annual Report 2012*, 256.

THE CREATION OF THE EUROPEAN UNION CIVIL SERVICE TRIBUNAL – FURTHER TRANSFER OF COMPETENCES TO THE GENERAL COURT

In addition to the changes in the organisation and operation of the Court introduced by the Treaty of Nice and the aforementioned enlargements, it is worth noting that two reforms in the judicial structure of the European Union have been carried out via the modification of the Court Statute and acts of secondary legislation.

In 2004, some of the competences of the Court of Justice were transferred to the General Court, which thus acquired jurisdiction over certain actions for annulment and for illegal failure to act brought by the Member States.[12] It is also worth noting that the Treaty of Nice has also provided the possibility of transferring to the General Court jurisdiction to hear certain categories of preliminary references.[13]

Moreover, in October 2005 a new 'judicial panel' was established at the Court. The European legislature made use of the possibility of creating a specialised court introduced by the Treaty of Nice for the first time. The European Union Civil Service Tribunal was given jurisdiction at first instance in any dispute between the Union and its officials and staff.[14] Its decisions are subject to appeal before the General Court. Consequently, the European Union disposes of two courts of appellate review. Unquestionably, it rests with the Court to ensure the preservation of the unity and consistency of Union law through the extraordinary review procedure.[15] However, it is essential to highlight that this procedure does not represent a third degree of jurisdiction, but rather an exceptional judicial procedure which the Court can follow if First Advocate General so proposes.

THE REFORMS OF THE COURT'S WORKING METHODS

Along with all the reforms and changes set out above, the Court has adopted in the last decade a series of internal measures with regard to its working methods in order to render them more effective and to reverse the trend in the increase of procedural delays. The most important of those measures consists of setting up a more rigorous monitoring system concerning the Court's judicial work, as well as the adoption of a stricter approach with regard to the extensions of time limits for submitting pleadings in the context of direct actions and appeals. The effects of these measures have been considerable and are clearly visible in the judicial statistics of the Court, which are constantly improving.

A final reference should be made regarding the adoption of a more selective policy concerning the publication of decisions in the European Court Reports according to their importance for the development of European Law. However, the text of those decisions which are not published in the Reports will still

[12] See Art 51(a), Court Statute.
[13] See ex-Art 225(3) EC, now Art 256(3) TFEU.
[14] See Annex I, Court Statute.
[15] Art 62 of and Annex I to the Court Statute.

be accessible to the public via the Court's website in the available languages. In addition, the ECJ has recently decided to publish its Reports in electronic format, thus making them available to the public quickly.

THE TREATY OF LISBON

The observations outlined and explained so far concern the recent past of the Court of Justice. At present, it is significantly influenced by the entry into force of the Treaty of Lisbon on 1 December 2009.[16] The stated aim of the Treaty, as set out in its preamble was 'to complete the process started by the Treaty of Amsterdam and by the Treaty of Nice with a view to enhancing the efficiency and democratic legitimacy of the Union and to improving the coherence of its action.' Democratic legitimacy, transparency and efficiency of the European Union were at the core of this Treaty. The judicial system of the European Union was not affected by this development since its essential features had already been defined by the Treaty of Nice.[17] Nonetheless, this does not imply that the entry into force of the Treaty of Lisbon did not constitute a significant challenge for the Court of Justice.

It should be noted that the jurisdiction of the Court now extends to the law of the European Union in its entirety, unless the Treaties provide otherwise.[18] Thus, the ECJ is vested with general jurisdiction to give preliminary rulings in the area of freedom, security and justice, as a result of the disappearance of the pillars, and the repeal by the Treaty of Lisbon of Articles 35 EU and 68 EC which imposed restrictions on its jurisdiction.

On the one hand, in relation to police and judicial cooperation in criminal matters, the jurisdiction of the ECJ in preliminary rulings has become obligatory, and is no longer subject to a declaration by each Member State recognising that jurisdiction and specifying which national courts may request a preliminary ruling.[19] Transitional provisions nevertheless provide that such full jurisdiction will not apply until five years after the entry into force of the Treaty of Lisbon.[20]

On the other hand, in relation to visas, immigration, asylum and other policies related to the free movement of persons (in particular, judicial cooperation in civil matters, as well as recognition and enforcement of judgments), any national court or tribunal[21] can henceforth request preliminary rulings.[22] Additionally, the Court has jurisdiction to rule on measures taken on grounds of public policy in connection with cross-border controls.[23]

[16] The Court's name was officially changed from the 'Court of Justice of the European Community' to the 'Court of Justice', and the 'Court of First Instance' was officially changed to the 'General Court'.

[17] M Dougan, 'The Treaty of Lisbon 2007: Winning Minds, not Hearts' (2008) 45 *CML Rev* 673.

[18] See Art 19 (1) TEU; K Lenaerts, 'Challenges Facing the European Court of Justice after the Treaty of Lisbon' (2010) *Revista Romana de Drept European* 20.

[19] Repeal of Art 35 EU, except for para 5 of this Art, which is now Art 276 TFEU.

[20] See Art 10 of Protocol No 36 on transitional provisions; Dougan (n 17) 682.

[21] Previously only higher courts were entitled to make such references.

[22] Repeal of Art 68(1) EC

[23] Repeal of Art 68(2) EC.

It should also to be emphasised that the Charter of Fundamental Rights of the European Union becomes a binding legal act with the same legal value as the Treaties.[24] This conversion of the Charter is the logical consequence of the constant evolution of the jurisprudence and legislation, and consequently contributes towards the prominence and better protection of fundamental rights within the European Union.

The introduction of a legally binding Bill of Rights for the Union is certainly a vital step forward in the process of European integration which confirms, deepens and improves its democratic legitimacy. Apart from reaffirming a pre-existing system of protection of fundamental rights, it adds to the achievement of a level of transparency, clarity and legal certainty which is of paramount importance in the field of fundamental rights.

However, the conversion of the Charter into a binding legal text does not resolve all the problems relating to the effective protection of fundamental rights which may arise. A multitude of sources of law with overlapping fields of application (national Constitutions, the Charter of Fundamental Rights, the ECHR) can be the source of confusion for private individuals, lawyers and judges.[25] The range of protected rights and the level of protection can vary from one text to another. Therefore, the risk of conflicting case law between the ECJ on the one hand, and national supreme courts and the ECtHR on the other, exists. In any event, the Treaty of Lisbon expressly states[26] that the Union is to accede to the ECHR. This element is likely to render the European judicial architecture slightly more complex.

Finally, it is necessary to mention that in the sensitive area of common foreign and security policy (CFSP), the Court, by way of exception, has jurisdiction to monitor the delimitation of the Union's competences with respect to those of the CFSP, the implementation of which must not affect the exercise of the Union's competences or the powers of the institutions in respect of the exercise of the exclusive and shared competences of the Union.[27] Simultaneously, the Court has jurisdiction for annulment actions brought against decisions providing restrictive measures against natural or legal persons which are adopted by the Council in connection, for example, with the freezing of assets of terrorist suspects.[28] It should be noted that the number of these particular cases, which are brought at first instance before the General Court, has increased significantly due to the recent events in Northern Africa and the Middle East.

Moreover, the possibility of a significant increase in the number of cases brought before the courts of the European Union is also related to the important procedural reforms introduced by the Treaty of Lisbon. The most important of these consists of simplifying and relaxing the conditions for the admissibility

[24] See Art 6(1) TEU.

[25] V Skouris, 'Introducing a Bill of Rights of the European Union – Can Three Parallel Systems of Protection of Fundamental Rights Coexist Harmoniously?' A Blankenagel, I Pernice and H Schulze-Fielitz (eds), *Verfassung im Diskurs der Welt – Liber Amicorum für Peter Häberle zum siebzigsten Geburtstag* (Tübingen, Mohr Siebeck, 2004) 273.

[26] See Art 6(2) TEU.

[27] See Art 24(1), second sub-para, TEU, Art 40 TEU and Art 275 TFEU.

[28] See Art 275(2) TFEU.

of actions brought by individuals against regulatory acts of the institutions, bodies, offices and agencies of the European Union. In particular, natural or legal persons may henceforth bring proceedings against a regulatory act it if they are directly affected by, and if the act does not require implementing measures.[29] Consequently, such persons no longer have to demonstrate that they are individually concerned.

NEW COMPETENCES ARISING FROM THE FISCAL COMPACT AND THE ESM TREATY

Although it only entered into force recently,[30] the Treaty of Lisbon was not the last stage in the transformation of the Court. The current financial crisis, and the measures taken by the European Union and the Eurozone to tackle it, reserve an important new role for the Court; the so-called Fiscal Compact[31] and the ESM Treaty[32] introduce new and specific competences for the Court.

At the core of the Fiscal Compact is the rule that national budgets must be balanced or in surplus. Article 8(1) stipulates that the European Commission is invited to present in due time to the Contracting Parties a report on the provisions adopted by each of them in compliance with the balanced budget rule. If the European Commission, after having given the Contracting Party concerned the opportunity to submit its observations, concludes in its report that such Contracting Party has failed to comply with this rule, the matter will be brought to the Court of Justice of the European Union by one or more Contracting Parties.[33] Contracting Parties are also able to bring such matters to the Court, independently and separately from the Commission's report. In both situations, the judgment of the Court of Justice shall be binding on the parties to the proceedings, which shall take the required measures to comply with the judgment within a period set by the Court of Justice. Furthermore, the Fiscal Compact provides for an enforcement mechanism including pecuniary sanctions imposed by the Court in case of non-compliance of a Contracting Party with such a judgment.

The ESM Treaty reserves a role for the Court which is less radical and far-reaching compared to that of the Fiscal Compact. The Board of Governors of the ESM is competent to decide on any dispute arising between an ESM Member and the ESM, or between ESM Members, in connection with the interpretation and application of the ESM Treaty, including any dispute about the compatibility of the decisions adopted by the ESM with this Treaty. If an ESM Member contests the decision referred to in the previous paragraph, the

[29] See Art 263(4) TFEU.

[30] 1 December 2009.

[31] Treaty on Stability, Coordination and Governance in Economic and Monetary Union, http://european-council.europa.eu/media/639235/st00tscg26_en12.pdf. It entered into force on 1 January 2013.

[32] Treaty establishing the European Stability Mechanism, 2 February 2012, at http://www.european-council.europa.eu/media/582311/05-tesm2.en12.pdf.

[33] See Art 260 TFEU.

dispute shall be submitted to the Court of Justice whose judgement shall be binding on the parties in the procedure.

THE IMMEDIATE FUTURE

The new competences conferred upon the European judiciary especially by the Treaty of Lisbon, the Fiscal Compact and the ESM Treaty reflect the increasing caseload of the European Courts and will continue to do so in the coming years. Hence, the requirement for an effective handling of cases in a reasonable period of time is likely to be a constant challenge. As far as the ECJ is concerned, this challenge is particularly important in the context of preliminary rulings since the procedure before the Court entails the suspension of the proceedings before the national courts. With regard to the General Court, the rights and interests of individuals are almost always directly in question.

The measures adopted by the ECJ and the General Court during the last decade have borne fruit to the extent possible. Nevertheless, the General Court is now in a critical position with an unprecedented increase in the number of new cases; for instance, the number of new cases exceeded 700 in 2011 and will most likely exceed 750 in 2013. As regards the ECJ, although the current situation remains satisfactory, it is necessary to take into account the prospects of a constant increase in the number of cases brought, following, in particular, the enlargements of 2004, 2007 and 2013 and the entry into force of the Treaty of Lisbon. It is in this context that the Court has recently submitted a series of proposals to the legislative authorities of the Union[34] to amend its Statute[35] and to recast its Rules of Procedure.[36]

The most important proposed amendment is the increase in the number of judges of the General Court by 12. Following a lengthy internal consultation procedure, the Court concluded that the adoption of internal measures alone would not suffice to resolve the efficiency problems related to the increase caseload of the General Court. An increase in staff was deemed essential.

This consideration led the Court to opt for an increase in the number of the judges of the General Court instead of establishing a new specialised court, namely a court with jurisdiction to hear and determine direct actions in the area of trade marks. In particular, the Court considered that the cases representing the highest workload for the General Court consist of economic disputes relating to competition law and state aid. Trade marks cases, on the other hand, are treated by the General Court in a simplified way within a relatively reasonable period of time.

Moreover, conscious of the fact that the number of Advocates General could not possibly remain at the pre-Enlargement levels without compromising the

[34] Under Arts 281, second para, and 253, sixth para, TFEU concerning Statute and the Rules of Procedure, respectively.

[35] Interinstitutional file 2011/0901 (COD), 7 April 2011.

[36] The new Rules of procedure were adopted on 25 September 2012 and entered into force on 1 November 2012: [2012] OJ C337/1.

efficient treatment of cases, the Court has also recently proposed an increase in the number of Advocates General by three. This proposal was accepted by the legislative authorities of the European Union and the first of the additional Advocates General will be sworn in before the end of the year.

Finally, as mentioned above, the Court has recently proposed a general recast of its Rules of Procedure. This initiative aims to simplify the procedure, to adapt the Rules of Procedure to the case law and the current practices and to improve its structure and its legibility. The Court's proposal was adopted one year ago and, although it is too early to comprehensively evaluate this reform, the flexibility and efficient structure of the new Rules is already producing some noticeable results.

CONCLUSION

The judicial architecture of the Court has changed extensively in the last two decades as have the procedure of the Court and the variety of the cases brought before it. Since its establishment in 1952, the European judicial system has been able to adapt to the changing circumstances and to advance efforts for European integration. Indeed, it could be argued that historically the Court has become accustomed to changes and reforms. Beginning as a single Court of seven Judges and two Advocates General, it has evolved into a judicial structure comprising three courts, 74 judges and Advocates General, working in 24 languages and employing more than 2000 staff occupying 200,000 square meters of buildings in the city of Luxembourg. Without a doubt, the history of the judicial system has been a course of innovative evolution.

Since the European Union is in a constant state of change, its judicial system can only follow the same path. As former Advocate General Francis Jacobs rightly states: 'The goal should surely be to preserve what is best in the existing system… while seeking to adapt the system by such changes as are essential to enable its best features to continue to function.'[37] It could be argued that this philosophy carries with it an element of realism. Change is needed to remedy the drawbacks of a system but at the same time its finest features should remain. It is via this mode that the Court has been able to survive.

Throughout this period, the Court has proven to be vigilant and ready to adapt to new circumstances. However, the advancement of the European integration process and in particular, the enhancement of judicial protection at the European level compel the Court to be both responsive to changes in circumstances and proactive, in order to avoid a possible decline in quality and effectiveness of the EU system for the administration of justice. In this difficult task, maintaining efficient procedures and proposing the necessary reforms ahead of time is of paramount importance. In this respect, the Court has always found staunch allies in the political and legislative authorities of the European Union as well as in the academic world and amongst practitioners.

[37] F Jacobs, 'The Court of Justice in the Twenty-First Century: Challenges Ahead for the Judicial System'. in Rosas et al (n 1) 51.

2

L'interprétation par la Cour de justice de l'Union du droit européen de procédure civile

JOSÉ CARLOS DE CARVALHO MOITINHO DE ALMEIDA*

I. INTRODUCTION

LES MÉTHODES QUE la Cour de justice de l'Union utilise pour interpréter le droit européen de procédure civile méritent les réflexions qui suivent en hommage à l'ancien avocat général *Nial Fennelly*. Elles auront pour objet, en particulier, la jurisprudence relative aux trois règlements qui constituent l'épine dorsale de la matière, les règlements Bruxelles I[1] et II,[2] ainsi que les conventions de Bruxelles[3] et de Lugano.[4]

Dans ce domaine, la Cour se sert des méthodes qu'elle emploie pour interpréter le droit primaire et le droit dérivé. S'agissant de la convention de Bruxelles, elle ignore ainsi les articles 31 et suivants de la convention de Vienne sur le droit des traités.[5]

L'interprétation fournie par la Cour de la convention de Bruxelles vaut également dans le domaine du règlement Bruxelles I lorsqu'il s'agit de

* Ancien juge de la Cour de justice.

[1] Règlement du Conseil relatifs à la compétence, la reconnaissance et l'exécution des décisions en matière civile et commerciale (n°44/2001, du 22 décembre 2000, JO L 12 du 16 janvier 2001, p 1), qui a été remplacé par le règlement n°1215/12, du Parlement européen et du Conseil du 12 décembre 2012 (JO L 351 du 20 décembre 2012, p.1) qui s'applique à partir du 10 janvier 2015, mais du 10 janvier 2014 quant aux articles 75 et 76 (article 81).

[2] Règlement du Conseil relatifs à la compétence, la reconnaissance et l'exécution des décisions en matière matrimoniale et en matière de responsabilité parentale (n°2201/2003, du 27 novembre 2003, JO L 338 du 23 décembre 2003, p 1).

[3] La convention de Bruxelles de 1968 concernant la compétence judiciaire, la reconnaissance et l'exécution des décisions en matière civile et commerciale (JO L 299 du 31 décembre 1972, p 32) a précédé le règlement n°44/2001 mais est encore applicable dans certains territoires appartenant à la France et aux Pays Bas.

[4] La convention de Lugano sur la compétence judiciaire, la reconnaissance et l'exécution des décisions en matière civile et commerciale du 27 novembre 2008 (JO L147 du 10 juin 2009, p 1) a remplacé celle de 1988 et lie les États membres de l'Union ainsi que la Suisse, l'Islande et la Norvège.

[5] B Hess, *Europäisches Zivilprozessrecht* (C F Müller, Heidelberg, 2010), 149, pt 44.

dispositions qui peuvent être qualifiées d'équivalentes.[6] C'est le principe de continuité, évoqué au 19e considérant dudit règlement.[7]

II. INTERPRÉTATION AUTONOME

Les notions employées par les règlements mentionnés sont, en règle générale, interprétées de manière autonome, sans prendre en considération les notions semblables des droits nationaux notamment celles de la *lex causae*. Si dans l'affaire *Tessili* de 1976,[8] la Cour a considéré que la question de savoir si les notions employées par la convention de Bruxelles doivent être interprétées de manière autonome dépend de l'analyse de chaque affaire, la jurisprudence postérieure aux années 1980 observe que l'interprétation autonome s'impose *dans la mesure du possible*,[9] condition qui ne figure plus dans les arrêts rendus depuis 2005.[10] Cette interprétation s'appuie sur les exigences d'assurer la pleine efficacité de la convention de Bruxelles dans la perspective des objectifs de l'article 220 du traité CEE[11], de promouvoir la sécurité juridique[12] et de l'application uniforme du règlement Bruxelles.[13] L'objectif du traité d'Amsterdam de créer un espace de liberté de sécurité et de justice et le transfert du traité UE vers le traité CE du régime permettant l'adoption de mesures relevant du domaine de la coopération judiciaire dans les matières civiles ayant une incidence transfrontalière, attestent la volonté des États membres d'ancrer de telles mesures dans l'ordre juridique communautaire et de consacrer ainsi le principe de leur interprétation autonome.[14]

[6] Entre autres, les arrêts du 2 juillet 2009, SCT Industri, C-111/08, pt 22 et du 10 septembre 2009, German Graphics, pt 27, respectivement, Rec. p. I-5655 et p. I-8421. Voir également les arrêts du 19 avril 2011, F-XTex SAI, C-213/10, pt 23, du 21 juin 2012, Wolf Naturprodukte/SEWAR, C-514/10, pt 26, et l'arrêt du 26 avril 2012, Česká spořitelna , C-419/10, pt 27.

[7] Voir le 34 ème considérant du nouveau règlement.

[8] Arrêt du 6 octobre 1976, 12/76, Rec. p. 1473, pt 11.

[9] Entre autres, l'arrêt du 27 septembre 1988, Kalfelis, 189/87, Rec. p. 5565, pt 10.

[10] Entre autres, les arrêts du 20 janvier 2005, Engler, C-27/02, pt 33, du 7 décembre 2010, Peter Pammer, C-585/08 et C-144/09, pt 53, respectivement, dans le Rec. p. I-481 et p.I-12527. Voir également les arrêts du 6 septembre 2012, Daniela Mühlleitner, C-190/11, pt 28, du 25 octobre 2012, Ritrama SpA, C-133/11, pt 30, du 14 mars 2013, C-419/11, n 6, point 25, et du 16 mai 2013, Melzer, C-228/11, pt 34. Les dispositions du droit de l'Union, en règle générale, qui ne comportent pas un renvoi exprès au droit des États membres doivent recevoir une interprétation autonome – arrêts du 18 octobre 2007, Österreichisches Rundfunk, C-195/06, pt 24, Rec. p. I-8817, du 20 octobre 2011, Interedil, C-396/09, pt 42 et du 22 novembre 2012, Bank Handlowy w Warszawie SA, C-116/11, pt 49, ainsi que la jurisprudence y citée.

[11] Entre autres, les arrêts du 13 juillet 1993, Mulox, C-125/92, pt 10 et du 28 septembre 1999, GIE Groupe Concorde, C-440/97, pt 11, respectivement, Rec. p.I-4075 et p.I-6307.

[12] Arrêts du 10 avril 2003, Pugliese, C-437/00, pt 16 et du 23 avril 2009, Draka, C-167/08, pts 25 et 26 respectivement, Rec., p.I-3573 et p.I-13477. Voir également l'arrêt du 7 février 2013, Refcomp SpA, C-543/10, pt 39.

[13] Entre autres, les arrêts du 6 mars 2008, Nordania, C-98/07, pt 17 et du 2 avril 2009, A, C-523/07, pt 34, respectivement, Rec. p. I-1281 et p.I-2805. Voir également l'arrêt Refcomp SpA, n 12, pt 18. Ainsi qu'il a été observé, l'interprétation autonome comporte en outre deux autres avantages: pour les opérateurs économiques, la réduction des frais et la sécurité juridique, pour les juridictions nationales dont la tâche est facilité par des notions communes – A-L Calvo Caravaca et J Carrascosa González, *Derecho Internacional Privado, vol I* (Comares, Granada, 2010) 109, pt 13, 4.

[14] Arrêt du 8 novembre 2005, Leffler, C-443/03, pt 45, Rec. p.I-9611. Il s'agissait d'interpréter l'article 8, paragraphe 1 du règlement n°1348/2000, du Conseil, du 29 mai 2000, relatif à la signification et

III. RECONSTITUTION DE LA VOLONTÉ DU LÉGISLATEUR

Sans la même force des autres méthodes d'interprétation,[15] la Cour s'appuie souvent sur la volonté du législateur. À cet effet, elle mentionne les travaux préparatoires[16] ainsi que les rapports sur la convention de Bruxelles,[17] la convention de Lugano[18] et le règlement Bruxelles II.[19] Les rapports explicatifs de la convention de Bruxelles peuvent être employés pour interpréter le règlement Bruxelles I pour autant que le texte et la teneur du règlement coïncident avec ceux de la convention.[20]

Les considérants font partie intégrante des actes respectifs et constituent des moyens d'interprétation particulièrement importants.[21]

Parfois, les actes de droit dérivé sont accompagnés de déclarations du Conseil, inscrites aux procès-verbaux. De telles déclarations ne peuvent pas être retenues comme moyen d'interprétation lorsque leur contenu ne trouve aucune expression dans le texte ou dans la teneur de la disposition en cause.[22] Mais elles peuvent être prises en considération pour corroborer l'interprétation faite sur la base d'autres moyens.[23]

à la notification dans les États membres des actes judiciaires et extrajudiciaires en matière civil et commerciale, adopté dans le cadre de ladite coopération et remplacé par le règlement du Parlement européen et du Conseil n°1393/2007, du 13 novembre 2007, JO L324, du 10 décembre 2007, p 79.

[15] J Kropholler et J von Hein, Europäisches *Zivilprozessrecht, Kommentar zu EuGVO, Lugano-Übereinkommen 2007, EuVTVO, EuMVVO et EuGFVO* (RIW, Francfort, 2011) 59, pt 76. T Henninger, *Europäisches Privatrecht und Methode* (Tübingen, Mohr Siebeck, 2009) 296, observe que cette méthode ne joue qu'un rôle accessoire.

[16] Entre autres, les arrêts du 22 mai 2008, Glaxosmithklein, C-462/06, pt 24 (est invoquée ici une proposition concernant le règlement Bruxelles I), du 23 avril 2009 et Falco, C-533/07, pt 54 (travaux préparatoires du même règlement), respectivement, Rec. p. I-3968 et p.I-3327, ainsi que l'arrêt du 7 décembre 2010, C-585/08 et C-144/09, *préc*, pts 73 et 82 (procédure législative).

[17] Entre autres citent le rapport Jenard, les arrêts du 26 mai 1981, Rinkau, 157/80, pt 6, du 4 février 1988, Hoffmann, pt 21, du 6 février 2002, Italian Leather, C-80/00, pt 48 et du 15 novembre 2012, Gothaer Allgemeine Versicherung, C-456/11, pts 34 et 37, respectivement, Rec. p.1391, p.645 et p.499. Le rapport Schlosser est cité notamment par les arrêts du 11 août 1995, Ampersand Software BV, C-432/93, pt 28, du 17 novembre 1998, Van Uden, C-190/89, pt 32 et du 9 novembre 2011, Corek Maritime, C-387/98, pt 19, respectivement, Rec. p.I-2269, p.I-7091 et p. I-5337. Le rapport Almeida Cruz, Desantes Real, Jenard est cité notamment par les arrêts du 9 janvier 1997, Petrus Wilhelmus Rutten, C-383/95, pt 20 et du 17 avril 1999, Unibank, C-260/97, pt 20, respectivement, Rec. p. I-57 et p.I-3715.

[18] Arrêt rendu dans l'affaire Unibank n 17, pt 16.

[19] Arrêt du 17 juillet 2009, Bianca Purrucker, C-256/09, pts 84 et 85, Rec. p. I-11163. Ces rapports sont parfois ignorés. Ainsi, l'arrêt du 15 janvier 1985, Erich Rösler, 241/83, Rec. p. 99 a considéré comme relevant de la compétence exclusive de l'État où est situé l'immeuble (article 16, point 1 de la convention de Bruxelles) les litiges concernant le recouvrement de loyers, contrairement à l'interprétation préconisée dans le rapport Jenard.

[20] Conclusions de l'avocat général Kokott dans l'affaire Prism Investments BV, C-139/10, n 66 ci-dessous, pt 31. Tel n'était pas le cas dans cette affaire. La Cour n'a pas pris en considération les rapports explicatifs de la convention de Bruxelles lesquels, sans préciser, admettaient que le recours prévu à l'article 36 pouvait se baser sur le fait que la créance avait déjà été satisfaite – arrêt du 13 octobre 2011.

[21] M Frisch, *Die Richtlinienkonforme Auslegung nationalen Rechts* (Schüling, Munich, 2000) 25 b.

[22] Entre autres, les arrêts du 26 février 1991, Antonissen, C-292/89, pt 18, du 29 mai 1997, VAG Sverige AB, C-329/95, pt 23 et du 27 février 2007, P. Segi, C-355/04, pt 60, respectivement, Rec. p. I-745, p.I-2675 et p.I-1655. Les travaux préparatoires doivent se matérialiser dans le texte même de l'instrument juridique en cause – arrêt du 8 novembre 2005, Leffler, C-443/03, n14 ci-dessus, pt 48.

[23] Arrêt du 7 novembre 2010, C-585/08 et C-144/09, Peter Pammer, n 10 ci-dessus, pt 74.

IV. INTERPRÉTATION TEXTUELLE

L'interprétation textuelle présente des difficultés particulières compte tenu de l'existence de multiples versions linguistiques, souvent divergentes. D'abord, dans le cadre du droit primaire,[24] et, après, dans celui du droit dérivé,[25] la Cour estime qu'une interprétation uniforme s'impose. En cas de divergence, les autres méthodes d'interprétation sont employées, si nécessaire.[26]

Dans le domaine de la convention de Bruxelles, cette jurisprudence est amplement suivie. Dans l'arrêt *De Bloos*, elle a pris en considération les versions allemande et italienne et observé que l'article 5,1 ne saurait être interprété comme se référant à n'importe quelle obligation découlant du contrat en cause, mais vise seulement l'obligation contractuelle qui sert de base à l'action judiciaire;[27] dans l'arrêt *Effer*, après avoir constaté des différences dans les versions linguistiques, la même disposition a été interprétée en ce sens qu'elle est applicable à des litiges ayant pour objet l'appréciation de l'existence des éléments constitutifs du contrat lui-même;[28] dans l'arrêt *Gubish*, la Cour observe que même si la version allemande de l'article 21 ne distingue pas expressément entre les notions d'« objet » et de « cause », elle doit être comprise dans le même sens que les autres versions linguistiques qui connaissent toutes cette distinction. Il s'ensuit que la notion de litispendance, visée audit article, recouvre le cas dans lequel une partie introduit une demande devant une juridiction d'un État contractant cherchant l'annulation ou la résolution d'un contrat de vente international, alors qu'une demande de l'autre partie visant à l'exécution du même contrat est pendante devant une juridiction d'un autre État contractant;[29] dans l'arrêt *Lancray*, toutes les versions sont prises en considération en ce sens que l'article 27, point 2 exige que la notification soit régulière et effectuée en temps utile;[30] dans l'arrêt *Danvaern*, malgré l'ambiguïté de la version danoise, l'article 6, point 3 est interprété en ce sens qu'il s'applique exclusivement à des demandes tendant au prononcé d'une condamnation distincte; [31] et, dans l'arrêt *Mietz*, la Cour s'est appuyée sur l'expression *instalment credit terms* de la version anglaise, pour interpréter l'article 13, premier alinéa, point 1 en ce sens qu'il ne s'applique pas à un contrat portant sur la fabrication d'un objet mobilier corporel dont le prix serait payé en plusieurs versements et la propriété transférée après le dernier.[32]

[24] Arrêts du 16 décembre 1960, Humblet, 6/60, pt 16, du 12 novembre 1969, Stauder, 29/69, pt 4 et du 6 octobre 1982, CILFIT, 283/81, pt 18, respectivement, Rec. p. 545, p. 419 et p. 3415.

[25] Entre autres, les arrêts du 27 octobre 1977, Bouchereau, 30/77, pt 14 et du 20 novembre 2001, Aldona Malgorzata, C-268/99, pt 47, respectivement, Rec. p. 1-999 et p. I-8615.

[26] Henninger, n 15, p. 281.

[27] Arrêt du 6 octobre 1976, 14/76, pt 12, Rec. p. 1497.

[28] Arrêt du 4 mars 1982, 38/81, pt 7, Rec. p.825.

[29] Arrêt du 8 décembre 1987, 144/86, pts 14 et 19. En ce sens, voir aussi l'arrêt du 6 décembre 1994, Tatry, C-406/92, Rec. p. I-439.

[30] Arrêt du 3 juillet 1990, C-305/88, pt 16, Rec. p. I-2725.

[31] Arrêt du 13 juillet 1995, C-341/93, pt 17, Rec. p. I-2053.

[32] Arrêt du 27 avril 1999, C-99/96, pt 31, Rec. p. I-2277.

V. RECOURS AU SYSTÈME

Le recours au système est une méthode fréquente d'interprétation. La Cour tient compte d'autres dispositions du même acte ou d'actes différents ainsi que des principes généraux pour aboutir à un résultat cohérent. Elle utilise aussi des éléments externes tels que le droit comparé ou des traités.[33] La convention de Bruxelles et, maintenant, le règlement Bruxelles I sont des exemples de l'importance de cette méthode.

À titre d'exemple, le recours à d'autres dispositions du même acte a eu lieu dans l'arrêt *Zelger*: la relation entre les articles 5, point 1 et 17 de la convention de Bruxelles permet d'exclure du domaine d'application de ce dernier des conventions portant sur le lieu où l'obligation a été ou doit être exécutée, matière qui relève du droit national;[34] dans l'arrêt *Kalfelis*, l'exigence d'une connexité entre les différentes demandes pour l'application de l'article 6, point 1 de la convention de Bruxelles a été déduite du principe de la compétence des juridictions de l'État du domicile du défendeur qui sans une telle exigence pourrait être remis en question;[35] et, dans l'arrêt *Falco*, la Cour s'est fondée sur l'article 5, point 1 sous c) et a) du règlement Bruxelles I pour écarter la qualification comme contrat de fourniture de services le contrat, par lequel le titulaire d'un droit de propriété intellectuelle concède à son cocontractant le droit de l'exploiter en contrepartie du versement d'une rémunération.[36]

Le recours à d'autres textes est fréquent. Ainsi, dans l'arrêt *Arcado*, l'article 10 de la Convention de Rome sur la loi applicable aux obligations contractuelles a été utilisé en appui de l'interprétation de l'article 5, point 1 de la convention de Bruxelles, en ce sens que constitue « matière contractuelle » un litige fondé sur la rupture abusive d'un contrat d'agence dont l'objet est le versement d'une indemnisation compensatoire;[37] dans l'arrêt *Sonntag*, la notion de « travailleur », au sens de l'article 48 du traité CE, telle qu'interprétée par la Cour, a été prise en considération pour qualifier comme « matière civile», au sens de l'article 1er, premier alinéa de la convention de Bruxelles, une action judiciaire contre un enseignant d'une école publique visant l'indemnisation du préjudice causé à un élève du fait de la violation fautive du devoir de vigilance;[38] l'arrêt *FBTO* s'est appuyé sur un considérant d'une directive en matière d'assurance automobile obligatoire pour confirmer l'interprétation des articles 9, paragraphe premier sous b) et 11, paragraphe 2 de la convention en ce sens que la personne lésée peut intenter directement une action contre l'assureur devant le tribunal du lieu où elle est domiciliée dans un État membre,

[33] A Bredimas, *Methods of Interpretation and Community Law* (Elsevier Science, Amsterdam, 1979) pp 43 et seq, D Simon, *L'interprétation judiciaire des traités d'organisations internationales, Morphologie des conventions et fonction juridictionnelle* (éditions A Pedone, Paris, 1981) pp 350 et s., H Kutscher, 'Alcune tesi sui metodi d'interpretazione del diritto comunitario del punto di vista di un giudice', (1976) *Rivista di diritto Europeo*,13.

[34] Arrêt du 17 janvier 1980, 56/79, pts 3 et 4, Rec. p. 89.

[35] N 9 ci-dessus, pts 7-9.

[36] Arrêt du 23 avril 2009, C-533/07, pts 42-43, Rec. p. I-3327.

[37] Arrêt du 8 mars 1998, 9/87, pt 15, Rec. p. 1539.

[38] Arrêt 21 avril 1993, C-172/91, pt 29, Rec. p. I-1963.

lorsqu'une action directe est possible et l'assureur est domicilié dans un État membre;[39] et, dans l'arrêt *St. Paul's Dairy*, la Cour a estimé que ne relève pas de la notion de « mesures provisoires ou conservatoires » la demande d'audition de témoins dans le but de permettre au demandeur d'évaluer l'opportunité d'une action éventuelle, de déterminer le fondement d'une telle action et d'apprécier la pertinence des moyens pouvant être invoqués dans ce cadre. Une telle demande pourrait être utilisée pour échapper aux règles prévues au Règlement (CE) n°1206/2001, du Conseil, du 28 mai 2001, relatif à la coopération entre les juridictions des États membres dans le domaine d'obtention de preuves, en matière civile et commerciale.[40]

La jurisprudence relative à des notions figurant dans un acte communautaire peut s'étendre à des notions identiques figurant dans d'autres actes,[41] à moins que les domaines couverts justifient des régimes différents. C'est le cas de la notion de « prestation de services », figurant à l'article 5, point 1, second tiret du règlement Bruxelles I, laquelle ne peut pas être interprétée à la lumière de la jurisprudence relative à la même notion au sens de l'article 50 du traité CE (article 57 du traité sur le fonctionnement de l'Union européenne), ou des directives en matière de TVA, ce qui serait incompatible avec l'exigence de l'interprétation restrictive des règles de compétences spéciales, reviendrait à contourner l'intention du législateur communautaire et affecterait l'effet utile dudit article 5, point 1, sous c) et a).[42]

Le principe de la cohérence entre le droit communautaire des conflits et le règlement Bruxelles I est mentionné au septième considérant des règlements Rome I et Rome II.[43] Des notions dans leur essence semblables doivent faire l'objet

[39] Arrêt du 13 décembre 2007, C-463/06, pt 29, Rec. p. I-11321.

[40] Arrêt du 28 avril 2005, C-104/03, pt 23, Rec. p. I-3481. Dans un arrêt postérieur, la Cour a précisé que cette jurisprudence est inapplicable lorsque l'audition des témoins a été demandée par la juridiction compétente sur le fond – du 6 septembre 2012, Lippens, e.a.,C-170/11.

[41] Ainsi, la jurisprudence relative à la notion d'ordre public dans le domaine du règlement Bruxelles I (article 32, paragraphe 1er) s'applique dans le domaine d'application du règlement (CE) du Conseil, du 29 mai 2000, relatif aux procédures d'insolvabilité (JO L160, p.1) – arrêt du 2 mai 2006, Eurofood, C-341/04, points 63 et 64, Rec. p. I-3813. Et, dans le domaine du règlement de Bruxelles II, la jurisprudence selon laquelle il n'y a aucune raison pour accorder à un jugement, lors de son exécution, des droits qui ne lui appartiennent pas dans l'État d'origine ou des effets qu'un jugement du même type rendu directement dans l'État requis ne produirait pas – arrêt du 26 avril 2012, Health Service Executive, C-92/12 PPU, point 142.

[42] Arrêt du 23 avril 2009, C-533/07, n 36, pts 33 et s. Dans le domaine du règlement Bruxelles II, la notion de « résidence habituelle » figurant dans d'autres domaines du droit de l'Union ne peut pas être transposée dans le cadre de l'appréciation de la résidence habituelle des enfants au sens de l'article 8, paragraphe 1er du règlement – arrêt du 21 avril 2009, AC-523/07, pt 36, Rec. p. I-10141. Et relève de la notion de « matières civiles » (article 1, premier paragraphe) une décision de prise en charge immédiate et de placement d'un enfant en dehors de son foyer d'origine, lorsque que cette décision a été adoptée dans le cadre de règles de droit public relatives à la protection de l'enfance – arrêt du 27 novembre 2007, C, C-435/06, Rec. p. I-10141. Notion qui a une portée différente de celle figurant au règlement Bruxelles I où la distinction par rapport aux matières de droit public se base sur l'exercice de pouvoirs d'autorité – entre autres, l'arrêt du 15 février 2007, Lechouritou, C-292/05, Rec., p.I-1519.

[43] Règlements du Parlement européen et du Conseil n°593/2008, du 17 juin 2008, sur la loi applicable aux obligations contractuelles et n°864/2007, du 11 juillet 2007, relatif à la loi applicable aux obligations extracontractuelles, respectivement, JO L 177 du 4 juillet 2008, p 6, et JO L 199 du 11 juillet 2007, p 40.

de la même interprétation, à moins que les particularités de la réglementation concernée s'y opposent.[44] Il convient d'observer que selon le 17e considérant du règlement Rome I, les notions de « prestation de services » et de « vente de biens » doivent recevoir la même interprétation que celle retenue pour l'application de l'article 5 du règlement Bruxelles I et le 24e considérant du même règlement mentionne, à propos de l'article 6, une déclaration conjointe du Conseil et de la Commission relative à l'article 15 du même règlement.

Les principes généraux qui se dégagent de l'ensemble des systèmes de droit nationaux sont également pris en considération. Ils ont été invoqués, p.ex., pour considérer que ne relèvent pas de la notion de « matière civile et commerciale » (article 1er de la convention de Bruxelles) des litiges opposant une autorité publique à une personne privée, lorsque la première agit dans l'exercice de la puissance publique,[45] pour interpréter la notion d'« infraction involontaire », figurant à l'article II du protocole annexé à la convention, en ce sens qu'elle se réfère à toute infraction dont la définition légale n'exige pas, expressément ou par la nature du délit qu'elle définit, l'existence du chef du prévenu de l'intention de commettre l'action ou l'omission pénalement sanctionnée,[46] et en appui de l'interprétation selon laquelle l'action intentée par un État en vue de l'exécution d'un contrat de droit privé de cautionnement, relatif à une dette fiscale, peut relever de la notion de « matière civile et commerciale » et, ainsi, du domaine d'application de la convention.[47]

Le recours au système peut également s'étendre à des conventions internationales. Ainsi, l'article 2, paragraphe 2 de la convention des Nations unies du 14 juin 1974 sur la prescription en matière de vente internationale de marchandises, confirme l'interprétation selon laquelle sont à qualifier comme des contrats de vente les contrats dont l'objet est la livraison de marchandises à fabriquer ou à produire, à moins que la partie qui effectue la commande n'ait à fournir une partie essentielle des éléments essentiels à cette fabrication ou production, des contrats qui relèvent, par conséquent, de l'article 5, point 1 sous b), premier tiret du règlement Bruxelles I.[48] Et la Cour de justice s'est appuyée sur la jurisprudence de la Cour européenne des droits de l'homme pour interpréter l'article 8, paragraphe 1er du Règlement n°1348/2000 précité[49] en ce sens que le destinataire de la notification d'un acte introductif d'instance ne peut pas en refuser la réception en invoquant que les annexes n'étaient pas

[44] Kropholler et von Hein n 15, p 57, pt 74.

[45] Arrêt du 14 octobre 1976, Eurocontrol, 29/76, pts 3–5, Rec. p. 1541.

[46] Arrêt 21 avril 1993, C-172/91, n 38 ci-dessus, pts 13–15.

[47] Arrêt du 15 mai 2003, TIARD, C-266/01, pt 27, Rec., p.I-4867. Voir encore les arrêts du 15 février 1989, Paul Humbert, 32/88, pt 21 et du 10 mars 1992, Paul Duffryn, C-214/89, point 26, respectivement, Rec. p. 341 et p.I-1745. Dans le premier, en appui de l'interprétation des articles 5 et 2 de la convention de Bruxelles en ce sens que ce dernier est applicable en matière de contrat de travail, lorsque l'obligation du travailleur d'effectuer les activités convenues a été ou doit être accomplie en dehors du territoire des États contractants; dans le deuxième, pour considérer que les exigences de forme posées par l'article 17 de la convention pour les clauses attributives de juridiction se trouvent remplies, lorsqu'une telle clause figure dans les statuts d'une société et que ces statuts sont déposés en un lieu auquel l'actionnaire peut avoir accès ou figurent dans un registre public.

[48] Arrêt du 25 février 2010, Keysafety, C-381/08, pt 37, Rec. p. I-1059.

[49] N 14.

traduites dans la langue de l'État requis, dès lors que l'acte est suffisant pour permettre au défendeur de faire valoir ses droits.[50]

Enfin, l'interprétation du droit dérivé de manière à assurer le respect du droit primaire ainsi que des droits fondamentaux et des principes généraux de l'ordre juridique communautaire[51] est une méthode d'interprétation qui relève de l'interprétation systématique.[52]

VI. L'INTERPRÉTATION TÉLÉLOGIQUE

La Cour de justice privilégie l'interprétation téléologique.[53] Les objectifs poursuivis par le législateur communautaire soit résultent de l'acte concerné soit de l'interprétation de celui-ci.

S'agissant du règlement Bruxelles I, l'objectif de la libre circulation des décisions (6e considérant) est invoqué, p.ex., dans l'arrêt *Hoffmann*, pour considérer que la reconnaissance doit avoir comme effet d'attribuer aux décisions l'autorité et l'efficacité dont elles jouissent dans l'État où elles ont été rendues;[54] dans l'arrêt *Axa Versicherung*, pour interpréter l'article 71 en ce sens que les conventions y mentionnées ne sauraient porter atteinte aux principes qui sous-tendent la coopération judiciaire au sein de l'Union[55] et dans l'arrêt *Gothaer Allgemeine Versicherung*, pour imposer une interprétation large de la notion de « décision » susceptible d'être reconnue ou exécutée.[56] Dans plusieurs arrêts, la référence à cet objectif est implicite.[57]

L'objectif de la création d'un système de compétences clair et prévisible (11e considérant) est souvent pris en considération. Ainsi, dans l'arrêt *Color Drack*, pour interpréter l'article 5, point 1, sous b), premier tiret en ce sens qu'en cas de pluralité de lieux de livraison il faut entendre par lieu d'exécution le lieu qui assure le lien de rattachement plus étroit entre le contrat et la juridiction compétente,[58] et dans l'arrêt *Falco* précité pour interpréter la notion de « prestation de services ».[59] Fréquemment, la Cour, sans mentionner le considérant, invoque l'objectif de la sécurité juridique « qui consiste à renforcer la protection juridique des personnes établies dans l'Union européenne, en permettant à la fois au demandeur d'identifier facilement la juridiction qu'il peut saisir et au défendeur de prévoir

[50] Arrêt du 8 mai 2008, Ingenieurbüro Michael Weiss und Partner GbR, C-14/07, pt 91, Rec. p. I-3367.

[51] Arrêt du 26 juin 2007, L'ordre des barreaux francophones et germanophobes e.a., C-305/05, point 28, ainsi que la jurisprudence citée, Rec. p. I-5305.

[52] T Henninger, n 15 ci-dessus, p 284, et P Franzina, *La giurisdizione in materia contrattuale, L'art.5 n.1 del regolamento n.44/2001/CE nella prospettiva della armonia delle decisioni* (Walters Kluwer Italia, Milan, 2006) p 80.

[53] En règle générale, l'interprétation téléologique est décisive – H Schak, *Internationales Zivilverfahrensrecht* (Beck Verlag, Munich, 2010) p 34, pt 96.

[54] N 17, pt 10.

[55] Arrêt du 4 mai 2010, C-533/08, pts 49 et 54, Rec. p. I-1736.

[56] N 17, pt 27.

[57] Entre autres, l'arrêt du 11 mai 2000, Maxicar, C-38/98, pt 26, Rec. p. I-2973.

[58] Arrêt du 7 mai 2007, C-386/05, pt 19, Rec. p. I-3699.

[59] N 36 ci-dessus, pt 5.

raisonnablement celle devant laquelle il peut être attrait».[60] C'est ainsi que la doctrine du *forum non conveniens*, développée par les tribunaux écossais et admise en Angleterre ainsi qu'aux Etats-Unis,[61] a été jugée incompatible avec le règlement Bruxelles I.[62]

Le 12e considérant justifie les fors spéciaux en raison du lien étroit entre la juridiction et le litige ou en vue de faciliter une bonne administration de la justice. La Cour de justice estime que cet objectif, auquel se réfère également le 15e considérant, est un objectif qui doit être pris en compte dans l'interprétation du règlement Bruxelles I.[63]

Le principe de la confiance réciproque dans l'administration de la justice est mentionné aux 16e et 17e considérants et au préambule de la convention de Bruxelles. Dans le domaine de celle-ci, il a été pris en compte, dans l'affaire *Turner*, pour juger inadmissible le prononcé d'une injonction par laquelle une juridiction d'un État membre interdit à une partie à la procédure d'introduire ou de poursuivre une action en justice devant une juridiction d'un autre État membre (*anti-suit injunctions*) [64] et pour considérer que relève du domaine d'application

[60] Entre autres, l'arrêt du 25 octobre 2012, C-133/11, n 10, point 33 et la jurisprudence y citée. Dans l'arrêt du 16 mai 2013, C-228/11, n 10 ci-dessus, pt 35, cet objectif est de nouveau mentionné en appui de l'interprétation de l'article 5, point 3, selon laquelle cette disposition ne permet pas d'établir une compétence juridictionnelle à l'encontre d'un coauteur du dommage qui n'a pas agi dans le domaine de la compétence territoriale de la juridiction demandée. La Cour a ainsi décidé contrairement à la doctrine qui soutenait une opinion différente, appuyée sur le §830 de la BGB allemande, et faisait valoir, d'une part, que le lieu du fait dommageable peut souvent être situé dans une place financière *Off Shore*, et, d'autre part, que le risque de *forum shopping* est inexistant étant donné que la loi applicable est prévue à l'article 4, point 1 du règlement Rome II – Kropholler et von Hein, n 15 ci-dessus, p 218, pt 83b.

[61] L Collins et al (eds) *Dicey, Morris & Collins – The Conflict of Laws, I*, 13th edn (Sweet & Maxwell, Londres, 2004) p 465, pt 12-007.

[62] Arrêt du 1er mars 2005, Owusu, C-281/02, point 41, Rec. p. I-1383. Mais cette doctrine est admise, à titre exceptionnel, par le règlement Bruxelles II, pour des raisons tenant à l'intérêt supérieur de l'enfant (article 15, paragraphe 1er).

[63] Arrêt du 25 octobre 2012, C-133/11, n 10, pt 34 et arrêt du 1er décembre 2011, Eva-Maria Painer, C-145/10, point 77.

[64] Arrêt du 27 avril 2004, Turner, C-159/02, pts 24 et seq, Rec. p. I-3565. Cet arrêt, ainsi que l'arrêt rendu dans l'affaire C-281/02, n 62 font l'objet de critiques: il s'agit de domaines qui n'entrent pas nécessairement en conflit avec les textes de référence et dans lesquels le droit européen peine à fournir des solutions communes – JS Bergé, 'Dynamique interprétative de la Cour de justice et codification européenne du droit international privé', *in* M Fallon, P Lagarde et S Poillot-Peruzzetto (eds) *La matière civile et commerciale, socle d'un code européen de droit international privé*, (Dalloz, Paris, 2009) 164, pt 7. Néanmoins, cette jurisprudence se fonde sur des arguments solides. En ce qui concerne la doctrine du *forum non conveniens*, elle est incompatible avec le principe de la sécurité juridique (prévisibilité du for) et la protection des demandeurs assurée par des fors spéciaux serait fortement compromise – P Mankowski, *in* T Rauscher, *Europäisches Zivilprozess und Kollisionsrecht, EuZPR/EuIPR, Brüssel I -VO, LuggÜbk* (Sellier, Munich, 2011) 156, pt 15, Geimer, *in* Geimer/Schütze, *Europäisches Zivilverfahrensrecht* (Beck Verlag, Munich, 2010) 127, pts 70–73. En faveur du rejet de la théorie du *forum non conveniens* mais critique du raisonnement de la Cour – P de Vareilles-Sommières, 'La compétence internationale de l'espace judiciaire européen', en *Vers de nouveaux équilibres entre ordres juridiques, Mélanges en honneur de Hélène Gaudemet-Tallon* (Dalloz, Paris, 2008) p 413. Quant aux *anti-suit injunctions*, souvent utilisées dans quelques États membres pour assurer le respect de clauses attributives de juridiction ou de conventions d'arbitrage, elles ne respectent pas la souveraineté des juridictions des autres États membres et produiraient le chaos si plusieurs de ces juridictions assumaient une telle compétence et rendaient des décisions contradictoires – P Mankowski, *op cit*, p 163, pt 20a. Dans sa résolution du 2 septembre 2003, l'Institut de droit international admet, sous certaines conditions, la doctrine du *forum non conveniens* ainsi que les *anti-suit injunctions*.

de cette convention l'action juridictionnelle, intentée par une personne physique à l'encontre d'un autre État membre, visant à obtenir la réparation du préjudice subi par les ayants droit des victimes des agissements de forces armées de cet État dans le cadre d'opérations de guerre, sur le territoire de l'État du for.[65] Dans le domaine d'application du règlement Bruxelles I, ce principe a notamment été utilisé pour considérer que le juge saisi d'un recours prévu aux articles 43 et 44 ne peut refuser une déclaration constatant la force exécutoire d'une décision pour un motif autre que ceux indiqués aux articles 34 et 35.[66]

Le respect des droits de la défense, mentionné aux 18e et 19e considérants et garanti à l'article 47 de la charte des droits fondamentaux, est souvent invoqué. Par exemple, dans le domaine de la convention de Bruxelles, la Cour s'y est appuyée pour interpréter l'article 27, point 2 en ce sens que le juge requis, lorsqu'il examine si la notification a eu lieu en temps utile, peut tenir compte de circonstances exceptionnelles, intervenues après la notification régulière.[67] Dans le domaine du règlement Bruxelles I, la protection des droits de la défense a servi pour interpréter l'article 26, paragraphe 2 en ce sens qu'une juridiction compétente au titre du règlement ne saurait poursuivre valablement la procédure, dans le cas où il n'est pas établi que le défendeur a été mis à même de recevoir l'acte introductif d'instance que si toutes les mesures nécessaires ont été prises pour permettre à celui-ci de se défendre;[68] pour admettre que le juge de l'État requis pouvait appliquer la clause de l'ordre public du fait que le juge de l'État d'origine a refusé au défendeur, domicilié sur le territoire du premier, le droit de se faire défendre sans comparaître personnellement[69] et pour définir les conditions d'admissibilité d'ordonnances qui d'une part, interdisaient au défendeur, à titre provisoire, de disposer de certains de ses avoirs et, d'autre part, lui enjoignaient de divulguer des informations relatives à certains de ses biens ainsi que des documents en sa possession, sous peine de ne pas pouvoir se défendre.[70]

« S'agissant de contrats d'assurance, de consommation et de travail, il est opportun de protéger la partie la plus faible au moyen de règles de compétence plus favorables à ses intérêts que ne sont les règles générales » (13e considérant). Cet objectif a été notamment pris en compte, même dans le domaine d'application de la Convention de Bruxelles dont le préambule n'y fait pas référence, pour exclure des règles de compétence en matière d'assurances les litiges entre un réassureur et un réassuré[71] et un appel en garantie entre assureurs, fondé sur un cumul d'assurances;[72] pour considérer valide une clause de prorogation de compétence,

[65] Arrêt du 15 février 2007, C-292/05, n 42, pt 44.

[66] Arrêt du 13 octobre 2011, C-139/10, Prism Investments, pt 27, Rec. p. I-9511. Le principe de la confiance légitime a aussi été rappelé au point 40 de l'arrêt du 6 septembre 2012, Trade Agency, C-619/10. La Cour a cependant considéré que le respect des droits de la défense exige que le juge saisi d'un recours contre la décision constatant la force exécutoire d'une décision rendue par défaut et accompagnée du certificat prévu à l'article 54, où le défendeur faisait valoir qu'il n'avait pas reçu notification de l'acte introductif d'instance, est compétent pour vérifier la concordance entre les informations figurant dans ledit certificat et les preuves.

[67] Arrêt du 11 juin 1985, Debaecker, 49/84, pt 31, Rec. p. 1779.

[68] Arrêt du 17 novembre 2011, Hypotečni banka a.s., C-327/10, pt 52.

[69] Arrêt du 28 mars 2000, Krombach, C-7/98, pt 44, Rec. p. I-1935.

[70] Arrêt du 2 avril 2009, Gambazzi, C-394/07, pts 37 et seq, Rec. p. I-2563.

[71] Arrêt du 13 juillet 2000, Group Josi, C-412/98, pt 64, Rec. p. I-5925.

[72] Arrêt du 26 mai 2005, GIE, C-77/04, pts 17–18, Rec. p. I-4509.

introduite dans un contrat d'assurance conclu entre un assureur et un preneur d'assurance, stipulée par ce dernier lui-même et en faveur de tiers (il suffit que la forme écrite exigée par l'article 17, premier alinéa, sous a) de la convention de Bruxelles soit respectée dans les relations entre assureur et preneur d'assurance);[73] pour juger qu'une clause attributive de juridiction n'est pas opposable à un tiers assuré qui ne l'a pas souscrite,[74] que les personnes lésées peuvent intenter une action contre l'assureur devant le tribunal du lieu où elles sont domiciliées et bénéficier ainsi du for prévu à l'article 9, paragraphe 1, sous b) du règlement Bruxelles I[75] et que l'article 15, paragraphe 1, sous c) du même règlement est applicable même si le contrat conclu entre le consommateur et le professionnel n'est pas conclu à distance.[76] La Cour de justice tient compte d'autres objectifs pas mentionnés aux considérants du règlement Bruxelles I, notamment le principe de sécurité juridique dont le domaine d'application est au-delà de l'exigence d'un système de compétences clair et prévisible, à laquelle il est souvent lié. Ainsi, ce principe, considéré comme un principe général de l'ordre juridique communautaire, et les objectifs poursuivis par la convention impliquent l'égalité et l'uniformité des droits que les personnes lésées tirent de celle-ci et exigent que, dans le cadre d'un pourvoi en cassation, la juridiction saisie se déclare d'office incompétente en cas de violation de l'article 16 (compétences exclusives), nonobstant une règle de procédure nationale qui limite l'examen aux moyens invoqués par les parties.[77] Et, dans l'arrêt *Italian Leather*, a été jugée incompatible avec le principe de sécurité juridique la reconnaissance d'une mesure provisoire inconciliable avec une décision juridictionnelle rendue dans l'État requis.[78] Un autre objectif, celui d'éviter un déni de justice, est souvent invoqué. Il légitime, dans certaines conditions, des sanctions à l'égard de personnes qui adoptent un comportement dilatoire qui aboutirait, en fin de compte, à un déni de justice[79] et justifie qu'un jugement par défaut puisse être prononcé dans le cas où l'acte introductif d'instance a été signifié par voie de publication selon le droit national.[80]

[73] Arrêt du 14 juillet 1983, Gerling, 201/82, pt 17, Rec. p. I-2503.

[74] Arrêt du 12 mai 2005, Société industrielle et financière du Peloux, C-112/03, pt 40, Rec. p. I-3707.

[75] Arrêt du 13 décembre 2007, C-463/06, n 39 ci-dessus, pt 28.

[76] Arrêt du 14 septembre 2012, C-190/11, n 10 ci-dessus, pt 42.

[77] Arrêt du 15 novembre 1983, Duijnstee, 288/82, pts 13 et seq, Rec. p. 3663. Cet arrêt est considéré comme un exemple du principe de l' « interprétation la plus favorable à l'intégration » – A Staudinger, *in* T Rauscher, n 64, p 62, pt 40. Il convient d'observer que la jurisprudence postérieure vérifie si la législation nationale prive de son effet utile la règle communautaire en cause – voir VII ci-dessous. S'agissant de droits conférés par l'ordre juridique communautaire, le droit national de procédure s'applique sous réserve du principe d'équivalence et dès lors que la protection de ces droits ne soit pas impossible ou s'avère excessivement difficile (principe d'effectivité) – entre autres, les arrêts du 14 décembre 1995, Peterbrook, C-312/93, pt 14 et van Schijndel et van Veen, C-430/93, pt 15 et du 7 juin 2007, van der Weerd e.a., C-222/05 à C-225/05, pt 33, respectivement, Rec. p. I-4599, 4705 et 4232. Voir aussi, dans le domaine de la protection des consommateurs contre des clauses abusives insérées dans des contrats non négociés (Directive n°93/13), l'arrêt du 14 juin 2012, Banco Español de Crédito, C-618/10, pts 53 et seq, ainsi que les conclusions de l'avocat général Trstenjak dans cette affaire et la jurisprudence y citée. Le principe d'effectivité apparaît lié à l'exigence de la pleine effectivité des règles de droit communautaire dans plusieurs arrêts – entre autres, l'arrêt du 15 juillet 2010, C-256/09, n 19 ci-dessus, point 99 ainsi que la jurisprudence y citée, Rec. p. I-1163.

[78] Arrêt du 6 juin 2002, C-80/00, n17, pt 51, dans le domaine de la convention de Bruxelles.

[79] Arrêt du 2 avril 2009, C-394/07, n 70, pt 31.

[80] Arrêt du 15 mars 2012, G, C-292/10, pt 56. Voir aussi l'arrêt du 17 novembre 2011, C-327/10, *préc*, pt 51.

Le principe de la confiance réciproque est aussi mentionné au 21e considérant du règlement Bruxelles II. La Cour de justice en tient compte pour ne pas admettre l'opposition à l'exécution d'une décision certifiée ordonnant le retour de l'enfant illicitement retenu, au motif que la juridiction de l'État membre d'origine aurait violé l'article 42 du règlement Bruxelles I. L'appréciation de l'existence d'une telle violation relève exclusivement de la compétence de la juridiction de l'État membre d'origine.[81]

VII. LE RECOURS À L'EFFET UTILE

Le recours à l'effet utile est une manifestation spéciale de l'interprétation téléologique.[82] Dans un style plus décisionnaire que déductif,[83] la Cour s'est servie de l'effet utile pour admettre l'effet direct des décisions[84] et l'effet direct vertical des directives[85] ainsi que la primauté du droit communautaire sur le droit national, antérieur ou postérieur.[86] Parfois, elle invoque la « pleine efficacité » du droit communautaire, notamment pour exiger l'adoption de mesures provisoires en vue de garantir l'efficacité d'une décision juridictionnelle postérieure[87] et admettre la responsabilité civile découlant de la violation du droit communautaire, imputable à un État.[88] Ainsi qu'il a été observé, s'agissant du droit primaire l'effet utile opère à trois niveaux: pour éviter un résultat absurde ou impropre, pour conférer aux traités un minimum d'efficacité ou pour leur attribuer une efficacité maximum.[89]

Dans le domaine de la convention de Bruxelles et du règlement Bruxelles I, le recours à l'effet utile est plus modéré, ce qui se justifie par la nature des règles de procédure en cause qui impliquent de fortes exigences de sécurité juridique et ne se prêtent pas à une interprétation constructive.[90] En règle générale, il est accompagné d'une interprétation appuyée sur le texte ou le contexte, sur les objectifs poursuivis par la réglementation en cause ou sur des principes qui président à l'interprétation des instruments juridiques mentionnés.

Par exemple, la juridiction saisie d'un recours contre une décision constatant la force exécutoire d'une décision rendue par défaut est compétente pour vérifier

[81] Arrêt du 22 décembre 2010, Joseba Andoni Aguirre Zarraga, C-491/10 PPU, pt 70, Rec. p. I-1427.

[82] Kropholler et von Hein, n 15, p.61, pt 78.

[83] R Streinz, 'Der « effet utile» der Rechtsprechung des Gerischtshofs der Europäischen Gemeinschaften', en ODue/M Lutter/J Schwarze, *Festschrift für Ulrich Everling*, vol II (Baden-Baden, 1995) 1507.

[84] Arrêt du 6 octobre 1970, Franz Grad, 9/70, pt 5, Rec., p. 825.

[85] Arrêt du 4 décembre 1974, Van Duyn, 41/74, pt 12, Rec., p. 1337.

[86] Arrêt du 9 mars 1978, Simmenthal, 106/77, pt 20, Rec., p. 629.

[87] Arrêt du 19 juin 1990, Factortame, C-213/89, pt 21, Rec., p.I-2433.

[88] Arrêt du 28 mai 1991, Francovich, C-6/90 et 9/90, pt 33, rec., p. I-5357.

[89] P Pescatore, 'Monisme, dualisme et « effet utile » dans la jurisprudence de la Cour de justice de la Communauté européenne', *in* N Colneric, D Edward, J-P Puissochet, D Ruiz-Jarabo, *Une communauté de droit: Festschrift für Gil Carlos Rodríguez Iglesias* (Berlin, Berliner Wissenschafts-Verlag, 2003), 340.

[90] Hess, n 5, p 173, pt 90, observe à cet égard que seulement à titre exceptionnel la Cour a interprété de manière constructive la convention de Bruxelles.

la concordance entre les informations figurant au certificat prévu à l'article 54 du règlement Bruxelles I et les preuves. Limiter l'étendue des pouvoirs du juge requis, dans cette phase, reviendrait à vider de tout effet utile le contrôle que ce même juge doit effectuer, notamment en vue d'assurer le respect des droits de la défense visé par le règlement et énoncé au considérant 18 de celui-ci.[91] Le contrat par lequel le titulaire d'un droit de propriété intellectuelle concède à son cocontractant le droit d'exploiter en contrepartie du versement d'une rémunération n'est pas un contrat de fourniture de services au sens de l'article 5, point 1, sous b) du même règlement. Élargir le champ d'application de cette disposition reviendrait à contourner l'intention du législateur communautaire et affecterait l'effet utile dudit article 5, point 1 sous c) et a). Il s'agit d'une compétence spéciale qui doit faire l'objet d'une interprétation restrictive.[92] L'article 5, point 3 de la convention de Bruxelles doit être interprété en ce sens que l'expression « lieu où le fait dommageable s'est produit » vise à la fois soit le lieu où le dommage est survenu soit le lieu de l'évènement causal qui est à l'origine de ce dommage. L'option pour ce dernier lieu aurait pour effet d'amener, dans un nombre appréciable de cas, une confusion entre les chefs de compétence prévus par les articles 2 et 5, point 3 de la convention, de manière que cette dernière disposition perdrait pour autant son effet utile.[93]

Enfin, l'application des règles de procédure nationales, lorsqu'elle est admissible, ne saurait porter atteinte à l'effet utile de la convention de Bruxelles ou du règlement Bruxelles I. Une telle atteinte aurait lieu dans le cas du rejet d'une demande en garantie (article 6, point 2 de la convention) fondée sur le fait que les tiers appelés en cause résidaient dans un autre État contractant,[94] ou sur l'exigence, prévue par le droit national, d'un lien de connexité au-delà du nécessaire pour éviter un détournement de for,[95] ainsi que d'une procédure nationale qui empêche une juridiction d'un État membre d'exercer les compétences qui lui sont attribuées en vertu du règlement.[96]

L'arrêt *Leffler*[97] a été considéré comme un changement par rapport à l'attitude restrictive de la Cour de justice à l'égard de l'interprétation du droit européen de procédure civile.[98] Certes, contrairement à ce qui avait été décidé dans un arrêt précédant[99] et à des travaux préparatoires qui démontreraient la volonté de certaines délégations que ne soit pas affecté le droit procédural national, la Cour a interprété l'article 8, paragraphe 1er du Règlement n°1348/2000[100] en ce sens

[91] Arrêt du 6 septembre 2012, Trade Agency, C-619/10, pt 45.

[92] Arrêt du 23 avril 2009, C-533/07 n 36 ci-dessus, pts 37 et 43.

[93] Arrêts du 30 novembre 1976, Mines de potasse d'Alsace, 21/76, pt 20, du 7 mars 1995, Shevill, C-68/93, pt 22 et du 16 juillet 2009, Zuid-Chemie, C-189/08, point 31, respectivement, Rec. p. 1735, p. I-415 et p. I-6917.

[94] Arrêt du 15 mai 1990, Hagen, C-365/88, pt 20, Rec. p. I-1845.

[95] Arrêt du 26 mai 2005, C-77/04, n 72 ci-dessus, pt 35.

[96] Arrêt du 10 février 2009, C-185/07, Allianz SpA et Generali Assicurazioni Generali SpA contre West Tankers Inc., Rec. p. I-663, pt 24.

[97] Arrêt du 8 novembre 2005, C-443/03, n 14.

[98] Hess n 5, p.177, pt 99. Cet auteur admet, cependant, que la Cour ne s'est pas trop éloignée des règles d'interprétation – p.176, pt 98.

[99] Arrêt du 3 juillet 1990, C-305/88, n 30, point 29.

[100] N14 ci-dessus.

que lorsque le destinataire a refusé la notification d'un acte, au motif que celui-ci n'a pas été rédigé dans une langue officielle de l'État membre requis ou dans une langue que le destinataire comprend, l'expéditeur a la possibilité d'y remédier en envoyant la traduction demandée. Mais le recours à l'effet utile[101] s'intègre dans un ensemble d'arguments, fondés sur le contexte, la finalité et la nature du règlement qui ne s'écartent pas des règles d'interprétation. D'abord, le formulaire attestant l'accomplissement ou non-accomplissement de la notification, établi conformément à l'article 10, n'inclut pas le refus de l'acte en raison de la langue utilisée, comme motif possible de défaut de signification ou de notification, mais prévoit cette mention dans un poste différent; ensuite, à supposer qu'il ne puisse jamais être remédié à l'absence de traduction, l'expéditeur ne prendrait jamais le risque de signifier un acte non traduit, ce qui va à l'encontre de l'objectif poursuivi par le règlement d'assurer la rapidité de la transmission des actes; quant à la jurisprudence précédente, elle concerne un instrument juridique d'une autre nature qui, à la différence du règlement, ne visait pas à établir un système de signification et de notification intracommunautaire; enfin, les travaux préparatoires décrits par un commentateur ne se sont pas matérialisés dans le texte même du règlement.[102] Il convient d'observer que le nouveau règlement prévoit expressément la possibilité de remédier au défaut de traduction.[103]

Le recours à l'effet utile, dans le domaine du règlement Bruxelles II, apparaît lié à la protection de l'intérêt de l'enfant. Ainsi, dans l'arrêt *Inga Rinau*, la Cour a estimé que la force exécutoire d'une décision certifiée doit être immédiatement constatée, nonobstant l'existence d'incidents procéduraux admis par le droit national de l'État membre où l'enfant est illicitement retenu. Une interprétation différente viderait le règlement de son effet utile. Elle observe, à cet égard, que le risque du retard « est d'autant plus à pondérer que, en ce qui concerne les enfants en bas âge, le temps biologique ne peut être mesuré selon des critères généraux, vu la structure intellectuelle et psychologique de tels enfants et la rapidité avec laquelle celle-ci évolue ». En appui de cette interprétation sont invoqués certains articles du règlement.[104] Et, dans l'arrêt *Health Service Executive*, elle considère que l'effet utile et le bon fonctionnement du règlement, dont les dispositions visent à parvenir à des solutions efficaces, exigent que la décision de la juridiction de l'État membre requis soit prise avec une célérité particulière, sans que le recours porté contre une telle décision puisse avoir un effet suspensif.[105] Nous sommes ici déjà devant une jurisprudence constructive puisque les articles 31 (exigence d'un bref délai), 28, paragraphe 1er (les décisions rendues dans un État membre sont mises en exécution après avoir été déclarées exécutoires dans l'État membre requis) et 20 (les mesures provisoires cessent d'avoir effet lorsque que la juridiction de l'État membre compétent pour connaître du fond a pris les mesures qu'elle estime appropriée) sur lesquels l'arrêt s'est également appuyé ne suffisent pas pour étayer l'interprétation faite. L'intérêt supérieur de l'enfant a été déterminant.

[101] Pt 48

[102] Pts 41, 42, 47 et 48.

[103] Règlement n°1393/2007, n 11 ci-dessus, article 8, paragraphe 2.

[104] Arrêt du 11 juillet 2008, C-195/08 PPU, points 81 à 85, Rec. p. I-5271.

[105] Arrêt du 26 avril 2012, C-92/12 PPU, n 41, pts 211 et 129.

VIII. CONCILIATION D'OBJECTIFS

Parfois, les objectifs poursuivis se trouvent en conflit. Il est alors nécessaire de les concilier ce qui peut aboutir à des résultats souvent imprévisibles.[106] Ainsi, dans l'arrêt *Trade Agency Ltd*, la Cour a estimé que le juge requis peut, conformément aux articles 45, paragraphe 1 et 34, point 2 du règlement Bruxelles I, contrôler les informations figurant au certificat prévu à l'article 54, ce que la protection des droits de la défense exige ainsi que l'effet utile de cette dernière disposition, principes qui doivent prévaloir sur la confiance réciproque dans la justice au sein de l'Union européenne.[107] S'agissant d'une décision rendue par défaut et dépourvue d'appréciation, la restriction au droit à un procès équitable qui en résulte peut être justifiée si la mesure nationale en cause répond effectivement à un but d'intérêt général (bonne administration de la justice) et ne constitue pas une atteinte manifeste et démesurée au droit fondamental précité. À cet égard, il incombe à la juridiction nationale d'apprécier, notamment, si et dans quelle mesure la partie défenderesse a eu connaissance de l'exposé détaillé des conclusions du demandeur ainsi que les voies de recours dont la première a disposé après le prononcé de la décision afin d'en demander la modification ou le retrait. Le droit de recours doit pouvoir être exercé de manière utile et effective.[108] Cette jurisprudence se trouve dans la même ligne des arrêts *Eurofood*,[109] et *Gambazzi*.[110] Et nous avons vu comment, dans l'arrêt *Ingenieurbüro Michael Weiss*, la Cour a défini les principes auxquels doit obéir la conciliation entre le droit à un procès équitable et les exigences d'efficacité et de rapidité de la transmission des actes de procédure nécessaires à une bonne administration de la justice.[111]

Il convient d'observer que l'appréciation qui incombe ainsi aux juridictions de renvoi n'est pas facile, notamment lorsqu'elles doivent vérifier si le recours prévu dans le droit national est *utile* et *effectif*. Il s'avère pourtant difficile de définir avec précision les conditions auxquelles doivent se soumettre les règles de compétence de manière à assurer le respect des droits fondamentaux.[112]

[106] Hess n 5, ci-dessus, p.171, pt 85.

[107] Arrêt du 6 septembre 2012, C-619/10, *préc*, pts 40 à 46.

[108] Ibid, point 60.

[109] Arrêt du 5 mai 2006, C-341/04, pt 66, Rec. p. I-3813. La Cour observe que dans une procédure d'insolvabilité, le droit pour les créanciers ou leurs représentants de participer à la procédure dans le respect du principe d'égalité d'armes revêt une importance particulière. Toute restriction à ce droit doit être dûment justifiée et entourée de garanties procédurales donnant aux personnes concernées une possibilité effective de contester les mesures adoptées dans l'urgence. Les procédures d'insolvabilité font l'objet du règlement du Conseil n°1346/2000, du 29 mai 2000, JO L160, p 1.

[110] Arrêt du 2 avril 2009, C-394/07, n 70, pts 40 et s. Était en cause ici l'exclusion de la partie défenderesse de la procédure du fait qu'elle n'avait pas entièrement satisfait, dans le délai imparti, aux obligations fixées par une ordonnance (*unless order*).

[111] N 47, point 5.

[112] P Franzina, n 52, p 96.

IX. INTERPRÉTATION STRICTE DES RÈGLES DE COMPÉTENCES SPECIALES OU QUI FONT EXCEPTION AU SYSTÈME DE COMPÉTENCES

Les dispositions de la convention de Bruxelles et du règlement Bruxelles I qui prévoient des compétences spéciales sont d'interprétation stricte en ce sens qu'elles ne permettent pas une interprétation allant au-delà des hypothèses envisagées de manière explicite.[113] Ce principe s'applique également aux règles qui font exception au système de compétences, notamment l'article 20 du règlement Bruxelles II (mesures provisoires).[114] Il convient d'observer que la jurisprudence n'est pas systématiquement restrictive.[115]

X. ABUS DE DROIT

L'objectif d'éviter les détournements de for est toujours présent dans la jurisprudence communautaire. Il explique, notamment, l'exigence d'un lien de rattachement réel entre l'objet des mesures provisoires sollicitées et la compétence territoriale de l'État du juge saisi[116] ou d'un lien de connexité entre les différentes demandes formées à l'abri de l'article 6, point 1 de la convention de Bruxelles de sorte à éviter que le requérant se serve d'une demande dirigée contre plusieurs défendeurs, à seule fin de soustraire l'un de ces défendeurs aux tribunaux de l'État où il est domicilié,[117] ainsi que l'application de l'article 22, point 4 du règlement Bruxelles I (article 16, point 4 de la convention) quel que soit le cadre procédural dans lequel la validité d'un brevet est soulevée, que ce soit par voie d'action ou par voie d'exception, lors de l'introduction de la demande ou à un stade plus avancé de celle-ci. Cette interprétation permet d'éviter que le demandeur soit en mesure, par la simple formulation des conclusions de sa

[113] Voir, entre autres, les arrêts du 1er décembre 2001, C-145/10, pt 74, du 6 septembre 2012, C-190/11, *préc*, pt 27, du 14 mars 2013, C-419/11, pt 26, et du 16 mai 2013, C-228/11, pt 24, *préc*, ainsi que du 11 avril 2013, Land de Berlin, C-645/11, pt 41.

[114] Arrêts du 23 décembre 2009, Jasna Detiček, C-403/09 PPU, pt 38, Rec. p. I-12153 et du 26 avril 2012, C-92/12 PPU n 41, pt 130.

[115] P Franzina, n 52, p 107. L'auteur évoque, à cet égard, deux arrêts: du 30 novembre 1976, Mines de potasse d'Alsace, 21/76, Rec. p. 1735; et du 13 juillet 2006, Reisch Montage, C-103/05, Rec. p. I-6827. Dans le premier, l'expression « lieu où le fait dommageable s'est produit » figurant à l'article 5, point 3 de la convention de Bruxelles a été interprétée en ce sens qu'elle vise, à la fois, le lieu où le dommage est survenu et le lieu de l'évènement causal; dans le deuxième, l'article 6, point 1 de la même convention a été considéré applicable lorsque l'action intentée contre le défendeur domicilié dans l'État du for serait inadmissible en application de la loi nationale (recouvrement d'une dette contre un débiteur en état de faillite): interprétation large, contraire à celle préconisée par l'avocat général, qui se prête à de justes critiques et exige un contrôle d'éventuels abus autrement dispensable – S Leible in Rauscher n 64, p 305, point 10f et H Gaudemet-Tallon, *Compétence et exécution des jugements en Europe, Règlement 44/2001: Conventions de Bruxelles (1968) et de Lugano (1988 et 2007)*, 4ième edn, (Paris, LGDJ, 2010) p 257.

[116] Arrêt du 17 novembre 1998, Van Uden, C-391/95, pt 40, Rec. p. I-7091. Des obstacles au *forum shopping* sont ainsi créés dans le domaine de la protection juridique provisoire – Hess, n 5, p 175, pt 93.

[117] Arrêts du 27 septembre 1988, 189/87, n 9, pts 8 et 9, et du 27 octobre 1998, C-51/97 Réunion européenne, pt 47, Rec. p.I-6511. Ce lien de connexité est aujourd'hui expressément prévu (article 6, point 1 du règlement Bruxelles I).

demande, de contourner le caractère impératif de la règle de compétence posée audit article.[118]

XI. L'INTERPRÉTATION DE LA CONVENTION DE LUGANO

Conformément à l'article 1er, paragraphe 2, du Protocole n°2 de la convention de Lugano (2007) « [t]out tribunal appliquant et interprétant la présente convention tient dûment compte des principes définis par toute décision pertinente rendue par les tribunaux des États liés par la présente convention et par la Cour de justice des Communautés européennes concernant la ou les dispositions en cause ou toute disposition similaire de la convention de Lugano de 1988 et des instruments visés à l'article 64, paragraphe 1er, de la présente convention ». Cette obligation n'implique pas que les tribunaux soient liés par la jurisprudence d'autres États; ils doivent en tenir compte, mais sont libres de ne pas suivre les principes y consacrés tout en exposant les motifs du dissentiment.[119]

Conformément au préambule, l'obligation en cause s'étend à la jurisprudence de la Cour de justice relative à des dispositions semblables de la convention de Bruxelles et du règlement Bruxelles I. Ainsi, la Cour suprême fédérale allemande (*Bundesgerichtshof*) a interprété les articles 9 et 11 de la convention de Lugano (2008) à la lumière de l'arrêt *FBTO*[120] et considéré qu'en l'espèce la personne lésée pouvait demander directement l'assureur du responsable. En effet, l'action directe était prévue soit par la loi suisse soit par la loi allemande.[121] Mais elle n'existe pas lorsqu'il s'agit de décisions fondées sur une interprétation systématique qui se réfèrent à des dispositions inapplicables dans l'État en cause[122] ou sur des notions qui doivent être appréciées à la lumière de valeurs particulières à un État, comme la notion d'ordre public.[123] La formule « tout tribunal » inclut la Cour de justice.[124]

En vue d'assurer une interprétation uniforme, l'article 3 du protocole n°2 établit que la Commission mettra en place un système d'échanges d'informations ouvert au public relatif à des décisions rendues par des tribunaux de dernière

[118] Arrêts du 13 juillet 2006, GAT, C-4/03, pts 24 et 27, Rec. p. I-6509, et du 12 juillet 2012, Solvay, C-616/10, pts 44 et 45. Mais cette solution peut donner lieu à certains abus – Rapport de la Commission sur l'application du règlement de Bruxelles I, du 21 avril 2009 (voir COM(2009) 174, final), point 3.4.

[119] C Kohler, 'Trois défis: la Cour de justice des Communautés européennes et l'espace judiciaire européen en matière civile', en G Venturini et S Bariatti, *Nuovi Strumenti del diritto internazionale privato, Liber Fausto Pocar*, I (Milan, Giuffrè, 2009) p 581.

[120] Arrêt du 13 décembre 2007, C-463/06 n 39.

[121] Arrêt du 23 octobre 2012, Versicherungsrecht, 2013, p 73.

[122] Kropholler et von Hein, n 15, p. 80, pt 111. C'est le cas des dispositions des règlements Rome I et Rome II – Hess, n 5, p 199, point 33. Mais il faut procéder autrement lorsque la référence à un acte communautaire se limite à confirmer une interprétation déjà faite. Ainsi, la directive n°2000/26, en matière de responsabilité civile résultant de la circulation automobile, invoquée au point 29 de l'arrêt du 13 décembre 2007, C-463/06 n 9.

[123] Ainsi, dans l'arrêt du 2 avril 2009, C-394/07 n 70, la Cour de justice n'a pas pris en considération une décision du Tribunal fédéral suisse relative à la compatibilité avec l'ordre public des décisions en cause (points 36 à 38).

[124] C Kohler, n 119, Kropholler et von Hein, n 15, p 81, pt 112.

instance et par la Cour de justice, ou particulièrement importantes, passées en force de chose jugée, en application de la convention ainsi que de la convention de Bruxelles, du règlement Bruxelles I ou d'autres instruments mentionnés à l'article 64, paragraphe 1er. Le greffier de la Cour effectue une sélection des affaires revêtant un intérêt particulier et les décisions respectives peuvent être consultées dans le site de la même institution.[125]

Un comité existe, prévu à l'article 4, qui élabore un rapport annuel avec l'analyse de la jurisprudence particulièrement importante, accessible aux intéressés dans le site de l'*Office fédéral de la justice* suisse.[126]

XIII. CONCLUSION

La jurisprudence foisonnante[127] de la Cour de justice de l'Union dans le domaine des règles européennes de procédure civile dont nous venons d'analyser les méthodes d'interprétation, à l'instar de celle des juridictions suprêmes de certains États membres, ne mentionne pas les sources d'information utilisées. Le droit comparé, souvent examiné dans les conclusions des avocats généraux, dans les prises de position de la Commission ou dans des notes de recherche, joue néanmoins un rôle très important.[128] Souvent, la règle de droit choisie n'est pas celle qui correspond au dénominateur commun des droits des États membres, mais plutôt à l'objectif de l'intégration européenne.[129]

Comme nous avons vu, la Cour utilise les méthodes classiques d'interprétation, fréquemment de manière cumulative, dans une dynamique qui mène à la constitution d'un droit autonome de dimension européenne.[130] Elle se garde, toutefois, d'interprétations constructives susceptibles de compromettre la sécurité juridique, exigence particulière des règles européennes de procédure civile. Certes, dans des cas exceptionnels, ce *self restraint* n'a pas été respecté. Les intérêts en cause justifiaient en l'espèce l'interprétation faite.

Cette jurisprudence qui n'est pas à l'abri de critiques, parfois suivie par le législateur communautaire,[131] parfois écartée,[132] occupe largement la doctrine

[125] http://curia.eu/comm/redoc/convention/fr/index.htm?56, 17.

[126] http://www.bj.admin.ch/content/bj/fr/home/themen/wirtschaft/ internationales_privatrecht/ lugue 2007.html.

[127] J-S Bergé, n 64 ci-dessus, p 158, pt 2.

[128] T Henninger, n 15 ci-dessus, p 293.

[129] Ibid, p 294.

[130] J-S Bergé, n 64 ci-dessus, p 160.

[131] Ainsi, l'exigence de connexité qui figure à l'article 6, paragraphe 1er du règlement Bruxelles I, n'était pas prévue à l'article 6, paragraphe 1er de la convention de Bruxelles mais résultait de la jurisprudence de la Cour – n 114 ci-dessus.

[132] La Cour interprétait l'article 27, paragraphe 2 de la convention de Bruxelles en ce sens qu'une décision ne devrait pas être reconnue si l'acte introductif d'instance n'avait pas été notifié régulièrement au défendeur, indépendamment du fait que celui-ci avait eu connaissance de la décision rendue et n'avait pas fait usage des voies de recours – arrêt du 12 novembre 1992, Minimalet, C-123/91, point 21, Rec., p.I-5661. Cette interprétation donnait lieu à des abus et était justement critiquée par la doctrine –Geimer, *in* Geimer/Schütze, Europäisches Zivilverfahrensrecht, n 64 ci-dessus, p 651, pts 76 et s. L'article 34, paragraphe 2 du règlement Bruxelles I n'exige plus que la décision soit régulière. D'autres exemples peuvent être mentionnés comme la reformulation du

dans les États membres ainsi que les juridictions respectives. Son rôle déterminant dans la consolidation des textes communautaires est indiscutable.

texte de l'article 5 de la convention de Bruxelles pour mettre fin aux hésitations jurisprudentielles – J-S Bergé, *Dynamique interprétative de la Cour de justice et codification européenne du droit international privé*, cit, p 162, n 64.

3

Accelerated Procedures before the European Court of Justice

MELCHIOR WATHELET*

I. INTRODUCTION

THE RULES OF PROCEDURE of the Court of Justice[1] (the Rules) make available to referring courts three mechanisms which can accelerate[2] the pace of proceedings where such measures are necessary for the prompt administration of justice. These mechanisms are: (i) the expedited procedure for preliminary rulings under Articles 105–106 of the Rules and the expedited procedure for direct action under Articles 133–136 of the Rules; (ii) the urgent preliminary ruling procedure under Articles 107–114 of the Rules; and (iii) priority treatment under Article 53(3) of the Rules. The purpose of this essay in honour of former Advocate General Nial Fennelly is to examine the conditions under which such procedures are granted and the effect they have on the duration of the cases in which they are applied.

In order to make this comparison possible, it was necessary to look at the number of cases in which the expedited and urgent procedures have been applied for, the number of such requests which were rejected as well as the duration of the cases in which these procedures were applied. The data regarding the expedited procedure go back to 2004 whereas the data regarding the urgent procedure go back to 2008, when such procedures were first introduced. This implies that the expedited procedure has a larger pool of cases than the urgent procedure. This fact should be taken into account when comparing the figures concerning these procedures. The same considerations apply to cases where priority treatment was granted. One should take into account that the data collected on this acceleration mechanism go back to 1995 and that the statistics below concern only the cases to which priority

*Advocate General at the European Court of Justice.

[1] See Rules of Procedure of the Court of Justice of 25 September 2012 [2012] OJ L265/1.

[2] Unless used in relation to Article 104a of the old Rules of Procedure (Rules of Procedure of the Court of Justice of the European Communities of 19 June 1991, [1991] OJ L176/7, and [1992] OJ L383 (corrigenda), as subsequently amended), the term is used in its ordinary meaning.

treatment was granted, thus excluding those for which priority treatment was requested but not granted.

It is worth noting at the outset that the urgent and expedited procedures as well as priority treatment are not the only procedural means which accelerate the pace of proceedings. Other measures that may have that effect include the decision to proceed without a hearing (Article 76(2) of the Rules) and/or without an opinion from the Advocate General (Article 59(2) of the Rules and Article 20 of the Court's Statute) as well as the decision to reply to a request for a preliminary ruling by reasoned order (Article 99 of the Rules). However, the present essay does not examine these procedural mechanisms because their primary aim is not accelerate the pace of proceedings but to alleviate the burden of the Court's workload.

This essay first deals with the legal regime applying to the expedited procedure (section II), the urgent procedure (section III) and priority treatment (section IV).[3] It then proceeds to compare the impact that these means of acceleration have on the adjudication of cases pending before the Court (section V). The analysis of this data shows that while the expedited and urgent procedures considerably accelerate the pace of proceedings it is doubtful that priority treatment has any meaningful impact on it. It also shows that over the years the Court has resorted to these means of acceleration with considerable reserve, making use of them only where it was necessary to do so.

II. THE EXPEDITED PROCEDURE (ARTICLES 105–106 AND 133–136 OF THE RULES)

The expedited procedure is a set of rules which, by way of derogation from the ordinary procedure, accelerate the pace of proceedings before the Court. It is available for both preliminary rulings (Articles 105–106 of the Rules) and direct actions (Articles 133–136 of the Rules). Under the expedited procedure for preliminary rulings, the President immediately fixes the date for the hearing and sets a deadline for the submission of written observations by the interested persons referred to in Article 23 of the Court's Statute. That deadline may be not less than 15 days.[4] The President may also restrict the matters the parties may address in their written observations to the essential points of law raised by the request for a preliminary ruling.[5]

The expedited procedure for direct actions is very similar to that for preliminary rulings. While the expedited procedure for preliminary rulings may be granted at the request of the referring court or tribunal, the expedited procedure for direct actions may be granted at the request of the applicant or the defendant.[6] The other party will be heard before such a request is

[3] This essay represents the Court's practice as it stood up to 22 October 2013. Orders regarding the means of acceleration in question issued after that date have not been taken into account.

[4] Ibid, Art 105 (2)–(3).

[5] Ibid, Art 105(3) in fine.

[6] See Rules, Art 133(1).

granted.[7] Unless otherwise decided by the President, the written phase of the proceedings is restricted to the filing of the application initiating proceedings and the defence.[8] As to the oral part of the procedure, and without prejudice to the rules regarding the introduction of new pleas in law or new evidence, a party may supplement its arguments and produce evidence at the hearing provided it can give reasons for the delay in producing such further arguments or evidence.[9]

The expedited procedure is the continuation of the so-called 'accelerated procedure' which was first introduced in 2000 by the insertion of Article 104a to the Rules of 1991[10] and the expedited procedure which was also introduced in 2000 by the insertion of Article 62a to the Rules of 1991.[11] The accelerated and expedited procedures under the Rules of 1991 effectively covered all proceedings brought before the Court. Indeed, Article 104a made it clear that the accelerated procedure could be granted '[a]t the request of the national court' and hence applied only to requests for preliminary rulings, whereas Article 62a stipulated that the expedited procedure could be granted '[o]n application by the applicant or the defendant'. The expedited procedure therefore applied to all other types of proceedings. The possibility offered by Article 62a has been used twice in direct actions.[12]

Despite the difference in the types of proceedings covered, the expedited and accelerated procedures were in fact subject to the same standard of urgency. In the case of Article 62a, the expedited procedure was available 'where the particular urgency of the cases require[d] the Court to give its ruling with the minimum delay', whereas Article 104a referred to 'circumstances [establishing] that a ruling on the question put to the Court is a matter of exceptional urgency'. Although the term urgency was qualified in the one instance as 'particular' and in the other as 'exceptional', there has been no instance where the President of the Court acknowledged any difference as to the high standard of urgency that had to be met.

The Rules depart from Articles 62a and 104a of the Rules of 1991 as they provide a different formulation of the standard of urgency which must be met. Thus the expedited procedure is available 'where the nature of the case requires that it be dealt with within a short time'.[13] Despite the different wording, the standard of proof remains the same. The referring court is required to show that the treatment of the case within a short period of time is necessary in order to avoid a risk that could be incurred if the ordinary procedure were applied.[14] Past

[7] Ibid.

[8] Ibid, Art 134(1).

[9] Ibid, Art 135(2).

[10] See Amendments to the Rules of Procedure of the Court of Justice of the European Communities of 16 May 2000 [2000] OJ L122/43, Art 1(9).

[11] See Amendments to the Rules of Procedure of the Court of Justice of the European Communities of 28 November 2000 [2000] OJ L322/1, Art 1(4).

[12] See Order of the President of 13 February 2004 in Case C-27/04, *Commission v Council* [2004] ECR I-6649; Order of the President of 13 July 2012 in Case C-286/12, *Commission v Hungary*.

[13] See Rules, Art 105(1) and Art 133(1).

[14] See Order of the President of 21 November 2005 in Case C-385/05, *Confédération générale du travail and others* [2007] ECR I-611.

practice shows that such a finding has been made in cases where there was a risk of irreversible consequences that might not be avoided using the ordinary procedure, which were of significance on a European level, or where the main proceedings before the referring court were expedited. In this respect, it is worth noting that it has been held that the degree of difficulty of a case, which could even turn out to be manifestly inadmissible, has no bearing on the element of urgency that has to be established.[15]

With regard to the risk of irreversible consequences that might not be avoided by using the ordinary procedure, the President of the Court has acknowledged the existence of such a risk in: (a) cases concerning the deprivation of personal liberty;[16] (b) cases that could affect an individual's right to family life;[17] and (c) cases where the length of the ordinary procedure could be such as to render the enjoyment of EU rights ineffective[18] or the granting of an effective remedy practically impossible.[19]

Regarding the significance of the case on a European level, the President of the Court has decided to apply the expedited procedure in instances where the case at hand raised an issue of interpretation in an essential and sensitive area of EU law and policy or where the proper functioning of a specific area of EU policy could be affected. Such a finding has been made in cases concerning the economic and monetary union, the European arrest warrant, the fight against terrorism and asylum, immigration and external border control.[20] Particular regard should be paid to the *Pringle* case which concerned Ireland's participation in the European Stability Mechanism. In that case, the President of the Court decided to apply the expedited procedure on the basis of the gravity and urgency of the economic situation of the Eurozone.[21]

A request to apply the expedited procedure has been granted in instances where urgency arose due to the very short time frame provided by national law and in which the referring court had to reach a decision.[22] Thus, in the *E & F* case the Oberlandesgericht Düsseldorf had already fixed a hearing before it for the period between 11 March 2010 and 31 August 2010 and thanks to the application of the expedited procedure the Court's judgment was delivered on 29 June 2010.

[15] See Order of the President of 26 February 2010 in Case C-40/10, *Commission v Council* [2010] ECR I-12043.

[16] See Order of the President of 22 February 2008 in Case C-66/08, *Kozłowski* [2008] ECR I-6041; Order of the President of 1 March 2010 in Case C-550/09, *E and F* [2010] ECR I-6213; Order of the President of 30 September 2011 in Case C-329/11, *Achughbabian* [2011] ECR (not yet reported).

[17] See Order of the President of 17 April 2008 in Case C-127/08, *Metock and others* [2008] ECR I-6241; Order of the President of 15 July 2010 in Case C-296/10, *Purrucker* [2010] ECR I-111 63; Order of the President of 9 September 2011 in Case C-256/11, *Dereci and others* [2011] ECR I (not yet reported).

[18] See Order of the President of 12 May 2010 in Case C-149/10, *Chatzi* [2010] ECR I-8489.

[19] See Order of the President of 13 July 2012 in Case C-286/12 (n 8 above).

[20] See Order of the President of 13 February 2004 in Case C-27/04 C-27/04 ; Order of the President of 22 February 2008 in Case C-66/08, *Kozlowski* (n 12 above); Order of the President of 1 March 2010 in Case C-550/09, *E and F* [2010] ECR I-6213; Order of the President of 12 May 2010 in Jointed Cases C-188/10 and C-189/10, *Melki and Abdeli* [2010] ECR I-5667.

[21] See Order of the President of 4 October 2012 in Case C-370/12, *Pringle*.

[22] See Order of the President of 1 March 2010 in Case C-550/09, *E and F* (n 12 above); Order of the President of 12 May 2010 in Jointed Cases C-188/10 and C-189/10, *Melki and Abdeli* (n 16 above).

Similarly, in the *Melki and Abdeli* case, the French Cour de cassation had three months to decide whether to refer the case to the Conseil constitutionnel by means of a special procedure for the review of the compatibility of a statute with the Constitution (*question prioritaire de constitutionnalité*). Thanks to the application of the expedited procedure, the Court handed down its ruling on 22 June 2010, ie 67 days after the receipt of the request for a preliminary ruling by the Court's registry. It was thus possible to assist the national courts in their respective tasks within the stringent time limits prescribed by national law.

Finally, in one instance the fact that a significant amount of time had already been spent by the national court on a case seems to have played some role in the decision granting the expedited procedure.[23]

III. THE URGENT PRELIMINARY RULING PRODCEDURE (ARTICLES 107–114 OF THE RULES)

First introduced in 2008,[24] the urgent procedure is a set of rules which, by way of derogation from the ordinary procedure, accelerates the pace of proceedings before the Court in relation to requests for preliminary rulings. The Court may grant it at the request of the referring court or may apply it ex officio, which to date has only occurred once.[25]

Like the ordinary procedure for requests for preliminary rulings, the urgent procedure normally comprises a written and oral phase, although the former may be omitted in cases of extreme urgency.[26] However, the duration of the various steps in the written, oral and post-hearing phase of the procedure is significantly reduced. Under Article 109(2) of the Rules, the Court may set a tight time limit within which the parties may lodge written observations and specify the maximum length of such observations.

It is worth noting in this respect that, unlike the ordinary procedure for requests for preliminary rulings, the parties to the urgent procedure are limited. Article 109(1) thus limits the right to participate in the urgent procedure to the parties in the main proceedings, the Member State from which the reference is made, the European Commission and the institution which adopted the act whose validity or interpretation is in dispute.

In view of the urgency of the procedure, the hearing follows as soon as possible after the end of the written phase and the Advocate General produces his or her View within the shortest timeframe possible with the judgment following immediately thereafter.

Due to the exceptional nature of this procedure which requires the Court to deal with the proceedings immediately, eligibility for this procedure is limited by two conditions. The first of these requirements provided by Article 107(1) of the

[23] See Order of the President of 15 July 2010 in Case C-296/10, *Purrucker* (n 13 above).

[24] See Amendments to the Rules of Procedure of the Court of Justice of the European Communities of 15 January 2008, [2008] OJ L24/39, Art 104b.

[25] See Case C-491/10 PPU *Aguirre Zarraga* [2010] ECR I-14247.

[26] See Rules, Art 111.

Rules is that the reference for a preliminary ruling should relate to at least one of the areas covered by Title V of Part Three of the Treaty on the Functioning of the European Union titled 'Area of Freedom, Security and Justice'. The urgent procedure thus concerns policies on border checks, asylum and immigration, judicial cooperation in civil and criminal matters and police cooperation.

The second condition is that of urgency imposed by Article 107(2) of the Rules. Although the term 'urgency' is not defined in the Rules, there is little doubt that it is designed to catch those cases where it is expedient to hear and decide them immediately in order to avoid some grave or irreversible consequence that the application of the ordinary procedure might give rise to. Even though the decision of the designated chamber of the Court as to the urgency of the case is not a public document,[27] the reasons for which the application for the urgent procedure has been granted are clearly stated in the judgment of the Court in all such cases.

The Court has thus accepted that there is an urgent matter to be decided in cases where: (a) a person has been deprived of his or her liberty and the judgment of the Court could affect the duration of such deprivation,[28] or (b) there is a risk of irreparable harm to a child's relation with one of his parents where the other parent has on his or her own initiative taken custody of the child.[29] There was also one instance where the Court applied the urgent procedure because the issue to be decided would affect the health and safety of a child[30] and another instance where the number of similar cases pending before the referring court was one of the reasons the request to apply the urgent procedure was granted.[31]

IV. PRIORITY TREATMENT (ARTICLE 53(3) OF THE RULES)

Although priority treatment is not in itself a type of procedure different to the ordinary procedure, its application is meant to accelerate the pace of proceedings. Article 53(3) of the Rules provides that '[t]he President [of the Court] may in special circumstances decide that a case be given priority over others'. Although this facility existed under Article 55(2) of the old Rules,[32] the

[27] See Rules, Art 108.

[28] See Case C-296/08 PPU, *Santesteban Goicoechea* [2008] ECR I-6307; Case C-388/08 PPU, *Leymann and Pustovarov* [2008] ECR I-8983; Case C-357/09 PPU, *Kadzoev* [2009] ECR I-11189; Case C-61/11 PPU, *El Dridi* [2011] ECR I-3015; Case C-83/12 PPU, *Vo*, judgment of 10 April 2012; Case C-192/12 PPU, *West*, judgment of 28 June 2102 ; Case C-278/12 PPU, *Adil*, judgment of 19 July 2012 ; Case C-168/13 PPU, *F*, judgment of 30 May 2013; Case C-383/13 PPU, *G and R* judgment of 10 September 2013.

[29] See Case C-195/08 PPU, *Rinau* [2008] ECR I-5271; Case C-403/09 PPU, *Detiček* [2009] ECR I-12193; Case C-211/10 PPU, *Povse* [2010] ECR I-6673; Case C-400/10 PPU, *McB* [2010] ECR I-8965; Case C-491/10 PPU, *Aguirre Zarraga* (n 21 above); Case C-497/10 PPU, *Mercredi* [2010] ECR I-14309; Case C-155/11 PPU, *Mohammad Imran* [2011] ECR I-5095.

[30] See Case C-92/12 PPU, *Health Service Executive*.

[31] See Case C-278/12 PPU, *Adil* (n 24 above).

[32] See Rules of Procedure of the Court of Justice of the European Communities of 19 June 1991, [1991] OJ L176/7, and [1992] OJ L383 (corrigenda), as subsequently amended.

Rules themselves do not contain a clear definition of what priority treatment actually entails. The Court's practice however shows that priority treatment effectively engages a best-efforts obligation on the part of the Court to respect its internal deadlines. There is thus no derogation from the rules governing the ordinary procedure before the Court. Unlike the expedited and the urgent procedure which, today, may apply only to requests for preliminary rulings, priority treatment can be granted to any type of proceedings brought before the Court.

V. A COMPARISON OF THE URGENT PROCEDURE, THE EXPEDITED PROCEDURE AND PRIORITY TREATMENT

The first thing one might wish to know about each of the above procedures is their length. It is thus interesting to note that since 2008, the urgent procedure was applied in 18 cases, the duration of the procedure being on average 55.33 days. Since 2004, the expedited procedure was applied in 11 cases, the average duration of each case being 151.36 days. Since 1995, priority treatment was applied in 58 cases which lasted on average 570.05 days. Given that the urgent procedure has existed since 2008 and in order to provide a better comparison with the other two means of acceleration, it is meaningful to look at the average duration of priority treatment since 2008. This brings the average to 515.78 days, which shows a gain of about two months over the years.

These figures not only establish the urgent and expedited procedures as truly accelerated procedures, but they also raise an interesting question regarding their duration. While these figures show that the expedited procedure lasts on average three times longer than the urgent procedure, this prima facie delay could be explained by the fact that the urgent procedure is subject to a truncated procedure and that it relates to a narrowly confined area of the law over which the Court has accumulated considerable experience over the past years.

It is also useful to compare these figures with the general performance of the Court in all cases pending before it. The Court's annual report for the year 2012 shows that for the period 2008–2012 requests for preliminary rulings lasted on average 492.6 days, direct actions 543.6 days and appeals from the General Court 472.6 days, the overall average being approximately 503 days.[33] These figures establish the urgent and expedited procedures as truly accelerated procedures, whereas priority treatment turns out not to make a significant difference to the duration of the case.

[33] See Court of Justice of the European Union, *Annual Report 2012: Synopsis of the work of the Court of Justice, the General Court and the Civil Service Tribunal* (Luxembourg, Office for Official Publications of the European Union, 2013) 104.

In terms of statistics, it is also of interest to note the rate of success of requests for the application of urgent and expedited proceedings.[34] Requests for the urgent procedure have been granted to 17 out of 28 applications, whereas the President decided to apply it on his own initiative in only one instance, in the *Aguirre Zarraga* case.[35] This brings the rate of success of the application for an urgent procedure to 62.06% (excluding the *Aguirre Zarraga* case) or 60.71% (including it). By comparison to these figures, the rate of success of applications for an expedited procedure is rather low. Such requests were granted in 11 out of 65 applications, the rate of success thus being approximately 16.92%.[36]

One might have expected that the success rate of requests to apply the urgent procedure would have been much lower than that concerning the expedited procedure, given the fact that the former applies to a narrow area of EU law, namely the Area of Freedom, Security and Justice, and it has existed for a shorter period of time. Indeed there is no obvious explanation as to why the rate of success of applications for the urgent procedure has so far turned out to be almost 4 times higher than the rate of success of applications for the expedited procedure.

One plausible explanation might the nature of the cases in which urgency has been proven to exist. Indeed eight out of the 18 cases where the urgent procedure was applied, ie 44.44%, concerned the health and safety of children[37] or the risk of irreparable harm to a child's relation with its parents.[38] Another five of the 18 cases, ie 27.77%, concerned the European arrest warrant,[39] four cases, ie 22.22%, concerned the return of third State national and the application of criminal sanctions to them,[40] and one case, ie 5.5%, concerned the Schengen Borders Code.[41]

[34] It was not possible to identify the number of applications for priority treatment made to the Court. In any event, priority treatment remains in the discretion of the President which he can accord at his own initiative without an application of the parties to that effect.

[35] See Case C-491/10 PPU *Aguirre Zarraga* (n 21 above).

[36] The exceptional nature of the urgent and expedited procedure becomes all the more so clear by looking at the figures regarding the procedural treatment of requests for preliminary rulings generally. During the period 1 January 2008 to 30 September 2013, the Court closed 3,436 cases out of which 1,950 were requests for preliminary rulings. In particular, the Court adjudicated 778 requests for preliminary rulings by holding a hearing, requesting and receiving an opinion from the Advocate General and by handing down a judgment. It handed down judgment in 212 requests for preliminary rulings without a hearing and an opinion, whereas it handed down a reasoned order in 241 requests for preliminary rulings without a hearing and an opinion. It treated 124 requests for preliminary rulings by means of judgment without a hearing but after requesting and receiving an opinion from the Advocate General, whereas it adjudicated 393 requests for preliminary rulings by means of judgment with a hearing but without an opinion from the Advocate General. No reasoned order was handed down in requests for preliminary rulings where there was a hearing or an opinion.

[37] See Case C-92/12 PPU, *Health Service Executive*.

[38] See Case C-195/08 PPU, *Rinau* (n 25 above); Case C-403/09 PPU, *Detiček* (n 25 above); Case C-211/10 PPU, *Povse*(n 25 above); Case C-400/10 PPU, *McB* (n 25 above); Case C-491/10 PPU, *Aguirre Zarraga* [(n 21 above); Case C-497/10 PPU, *Mercredi* (n 25 above); Case C-155/11 PPU, *Mohammad Imran* (n 25 above).

[39] See Case C-296/08 PPU, *Santesteban Goicoechea* (n 24 above); Case C-388/08 PPU, *Leymann and Pustovarov* (n 24 above); Case C-105/10 PPU, *Gataev and Gataev* (removed from the register by Order of the President of the Third Chamber of 3 April 2010); Case C-192/12 PPU, *West* (n 24 above) ; Case C-168/13 PPU, *F* (n 24 above) .

[40] See Case C-357/09 PPU, *Kadzoev* (n 24 above); Case C-61/11 PPU, *El Dridi* (n 24 above); Case C-83/12 PPU, *Vo* (n 24 above); Case C-383/13 PPU, *G and R* (n 24 above); .

[41] See Case C-278/12 PPU, *Adil* (n 24 above).

The picture looks slightly different with regard to the expedited procedure, where four out of the 11 cases, ie 36.36%, concerned third State nationals and their right to stay in a Member State or their return to their home country,[42] two cases, ie 18.18%, concerned the right of custody of children and parental leave,[43] another two cases, ie 18.18%, related to the Stability Pact and the European Stability Mechanism,[44] one case, ie 9.09%, concerned the European arrest warrant,[45] one case concerned equality at work,[46] and one case concerned measures adopted in the context of the fight against terrorism.[47]

This shows that there is a certain overlap between the urgent and expedited procedures regarding the subject-matter of the cases. Such matters include issues of parental responsibility, the return of third State nationals and the European arrest warrant. One might think that this could be simply the result of a referring court requesting the application of the expedited procedure if its application for an urgent procedure fails. This is not, however, the case. Out of the 10 cases where the request of the referring court for the application of the urgent procedure was not granted, in only one instance did that court request the application of the expedited procedure (which was granted).[48]

The frequent granting of an expedited or urgent procedure in those matters reflects the affinity of the two procedures in terms of the degree of urgency that has to be demonstrated, be it urgency within the meaning of Article 107(2) of the Rules or expediency ('where the nature of the case requires that it be dealt with within a short time') within the meaning of Articles 105(1) and 133(1) of the Rules. It is not of course argued that these two standards should be treated as identical. Rather the difference between the two of them should be one of degree. Thus, for example, in cases concerning the deprivation of personal liberty, the Court requires a demonstration that the individual's personal liberty is at risk or that the judgment of the Court could put an end to the deprivation of his or her liberty.[49]

By contrast, in cases where the Court's judgment has no impact on the individual's personal liberty, including cases where the individual is not detained, the urgent procedure will normally not be granted.[50] It should however be clarified that the case-law of the Court in this respect is not entirely consistent. There are

[42] See Case C-127/08, *Metock and others* (n 13 above); Joined Cases C-188/10 and C-189/10, *Melki and Abdeli* (n 16 above); Case C-256/11, *Dereci and others* (n 12 above); Case C-329/11, *Achughbabian* (n 12 above).

[43] See Case C-149/10, *Chatzi* (n 14 above); Case C-296/10, *Purrucker* (n 13 above).

[44] See Case C-27/04 (n 8 above); Case C-370/12, *Pringle* (n 17 above).

[45] See Case C-66/08, *Kozłowski* [2008] ECR I-6041 (n 12 above).

[46] See Case C-286/12, *Commission v Hungary* (n 8 above).

[47] See Case C-550/09, *E and F* (n 12 above).

[48] See Order of the President of 30 September 2011 in Case C-329/11, *Achughbabian* (n 12 above).

[49] See Case C-296/08 PPU, *Santesteban Goicoechea* (n 21 above) para 33; Case C-388/08 PPU, *Leymann and Pustovarov* (n 21 above) para 38; Case C-357/09 PPU, *Kadzoev* (n 24 above) para 32; Case C-61/11 PPU, *El Dridi* (n 24 above) para 27); Case C-83/12 PPU, *Vo* (n 24 above) para 31; Case C-192/12 PPU, *West* (n 24 above) para 33; Case C-278/12 PPU, *Adil* (n 24 above) para 34; Case C-168/13 PPU, *F* (n 24 above) para 31; Case C-383/13 PPU, *G and R* (n 24 above) para 25.

[50] See Case C-123/08, *Wolzenburg* [2009] ECR I-9621; Joined Cases C-261/08 and C-348/08, *Zurita García and Choque Cabrera* [2009] ECR I-10143; Case C-175/11, *HID and BA* ; Case C-329/11, *Achughbabian* (n 12 above).

cases where the individual concerned was in custody and despite the fact that the Court's judgment would not result in his release, the urgent procedure was nonetheless granted.[51] In any event, it should be noted that it is clear from the case-law that detention per se is not enough to found a request for the urgent procedure but rather there has to be a possibility that the Court's judgment might either lead to the release of the individual concerned or preclude his detention. This is demonstrated by the fact that the Court refused to apply the urgent procedure in a case where the justification put forward by the referring court was that the decision to detain the third-State national in question would soon expire.[52]

With regard in particular to cases where questions concerning an individual's liberty, such as European arrest warrant cases or those on the return of third State nationals, the mere fact that the Court's judgment will have no bearing on their personal liberty does not suffice to ensure that a case, which failed to meet the standard of urgency required for an urgent procedure, automatically qualifies for the expedited procedure. An independent finding of urgency must be made for the expedited procedure to apply. This is evidenced by the fact that out of three such cases where the Court did not grant an urgent procedure[53] only one case qualified for the expedited procedure.[54]

Thus, in the *Achughbabian* case, the finding of the degree of urgency necessary to expedite the case consisted in the fact that, although Mr Achughbabian had already been set free, several other individuals were in the same position as he, and their continued deprivation of liberty or release would depend on the outcome of the case before the Court. By contrast, in the *Kita* case, where the Court's ruling would not in any way have affected the detention of Mr Kita and there was no prospect of his qualifying for earlier release from custody, the request for the application of the expedited procedure was rejected. Similarly, in the *Pontini* case the prolonged duration of criminal proceedings before the domestic courts, as well as the delay in the notification of the request for a preliminary ruling by the referring court, counted significantly against the granting of the request for the expedited procedure.

Be that as it may, it is of interest to note that, unlike those that have qualified for the urgent procedure, some of the cases which have qualified for the expedited and accelerated procedures concerned important political issues which warranted the Court's immediate attention due to their wider significance for the European Union. Such instances include an annulment action brought by the Commission against the Council's decision not to take the action recommended by the Commission against France and Germany with regard to the latters' alleged failure to observe their obligations under the so-called Stability Pact.[55]

[51] See, eg, Case C-168/13 PPU, *F* (n 24 above).

[52] See Case C-514/13, *Bouzalmate* (pending).

[53] See Case C-375/08, *Pontini and others* [2010] ECR I-5767; Case C-264/10, *Kita* (removed from the register by Order of the President of 19 October 2010); Case C-329/11, *Achughbabian* (n 12 above).

[54] See Order of the President of 30 September 2011 in Case C-329/11, *Achughbabian* (n 12 above).

[55] See Case C-27/04, (n 8 above).

In the same vein, it is unsurprising that the Commission's infringement action against Hungary, concerning the latter's plan to force a certain number of judges, prosecutors and notaries to retire by lowering the age of compulsory retirement, was granted expedited treatment. As the President of the Court ruled, an expedited procedure was warranted because if the ordinary procedure were applied and the Court were to find that Hungary's actions breached EU law it would have been impossible to provide an effective remedy for the judges, prosecutors and notaries who would have in the meantime been affected by the Hungarian measure in question.[56]

Another case with a high political profile, where the accelerated procedure was granted, concerned Ireland's participation in the European Stability Mechanism and the question whether through such participation Ireland assumed obligations contrary to the TFEU. In granting the expedited procedure, the President of the Court considered the emergency situation that the Eurozone was facing as a result of the sovereign debt crisis, and the need to resolve any doubts as to the validity of the European Stability Mechanism Treaty in the shortest timeframe possible, as sufficient reasons to grant the expedited procedure.[57]

This shows that, contrary to the urgent procedure, which concerns cases where there is a risk of irreparable harm to an individual if the proceedings take their normal course, the expedited procedure has been also used to accelerate the pace of proceedings in cases of political and economic significance for the European Union.

Another reason that applications for the expedited procedure are rejected more often than for the urgent procedure might be that the referring courts often fail to justify their request properly. It seems that the referring courts often limit the reasons for which an expedited procedure should be granted to the interest of the parties to have their dispute resolved in a timely manner, and the financial risk that the parties might encounter depending on the outcome of the case. The President of the Court has consistently held that, although the referring court may succeed in demonstrating the importance of the case, this kind of reasoning does not establish the degree of urgency required by Articles 105(1) and 133(1) of the Rules.[58]

[56] See Case C-286/12, *Commission v Hungary* (n 8 above).

[57] See Order of the President of 4 October 2012 in Case C-370/12, *Pringle* (n 17 above) para 8.

[58] See, eg, Order of the President of 7 May 2004 in Joined Cases C-154/04 and C-155/04, *Alliance for Natural Health and others* [2005] ECR I-6451; Order of the President of 24 September 2004 in Case C-344/04, *IATA and ELFAA* [2006] ECR I-403; Order of the President of 18 March 2005 in Case C-11/05, *Friesland Coberco Dairy Foods* [2006] ECR I-4285; Order of the President of 23 March 2007 in Case C-12/07, *Autostrada dei Fiori and AISCAT* [2007] ECR I-162; Order of the President of 8 November 2007 in Case C-456/07, *Mihal* [2008] ECR I-79; Order of the President of 29 September 2008 in Case C-375/08, *Pontini and others* (n 49 above); Order of the President of 21 September 2009 in Case C-241/09, *Fluxys* [2010] ECR I-12773; Order of the President of 23 October 2009 in Case C-69/09 P, *Makhteshim-Agan Holding and others v Commission* [2010] ECR I-10; Order of the President of 16 March 2010 in Case C-3/10, *Affatato* [2010] ECR I-121; Order of the President of 16 March 2010 in Case C-20/10, *Vino* [2010] ECR I-148; Order of the President of 1 October 2010 in Joined Cases C-411/10 and C-493/10, *NS* [2011] ECR I (not yet reported); Order of the President of 29 November 2010 in Case C-416/10, *Križan and others* ; Order of the President of 1 July 2011 in Case C-248/11, *Nilaş and others* ; Order of the President of 14 December 2011 in Cases C-478/11 P to C-482/11 P, *Gbagbo v Council* ; Order of the President

In addition, the mere reference to the multitude of similar cases that may be pending before the national courts or the number of individuals who may be affected by the outcome of the case is not in and of itself grounds to justify the application of the expedited procedure.[59] Despite the many Orders finding that the numbers of individuals that may be affected by the Court's response to the request for a preliminary ruling is not decisive with regard to the urgency criterion, in the *Achughbabian* case the Court has granted the request to apply the expedited procedure on the sole basis that, although its ruling would not affect the personal liberty of the individual concerned, who had already been released, the status of several other individuals hinged on its ruling.[60] In this sense, this prima facie inconsistency might reflect some kind of higher standing that personal liberty may have vis-à-vis other values of the European legal order.

An application for an expedited procedure has, unsurprisingly, failed where it is clear from the file that the national authorities are not in any particular rush. For example, in one instance the Bulgarian authorities took a decision which was notified to the interested party only several months later.[61] On another occasion the domestic court did not appear to have to decide the case within a tight deadline,[62] or the case was pending before it for two years before it submitted a request for a preliminary ruling to the Court.[63] In the same fashion, a request for an expedited procedure will not be granted if the referring court is required to decide a matter within an unrealistic deadline which has already expired by the time the request for a preliminary ruling has reached the Court.[64]

No similar comparison with respect to the reasons for which requests for priority treatment have been granted or rejected can be drawn for two main reasons. First, priority treatment may be effectively granted to any kind of case

of 8 March 2012 in Case C-6/12, *P* ; Order of the President of 10 April 2013 in Case C-26/13, *Kásler and others* (pending); Order of the President of 30 September 2013 in Case C-282/13, *T-Mobile Austria GmbH* (pending).

[59] See, eg, Order of the President of 24 October 2005 in Case C-330/05, *Granberg* [2007] ECR I-9871; Order of the President of 21 September 2006 in Jointed Cases C-283/06 and C-312/06, *KÖGÁZ and others* [2007] ECR I-8463; Order of the President of 25 September 2006 in Case C-368/06, *Cedilac* [2007] ECR I-12327; Order of the President of 3 July 2008 in Case C-201/08, *Plantanol* [2009] ECR I-8343; Order of the President of 3 December 2008 in Joined Cases C-403/08 and C-429/08, *Football Association Premier League and others* [2011] ECR I-9083; Order of the President of 3 December 2008 in Case C-439/08, *VEBIC* [2010] ECR I-12471; Order of the President of 19 October 2009 in Case C-310/09, *Accor* [2011] ECR I-8115; Order of the President of 23 October 2009 in Case C-240/09, *Lesoochranárske zoskupenie* [2011] ECR I-1255; Order of the President of 31 January 2011 in Case C-573/10, *Micşa* [2011] ECR I-101; Order of the President of 8 September 2011 in Joined Cases C-356/11 and C-357/11, *O and S* ; Order of the President of 10 January 2012 in Case C-534/11, *Arslan*; Order of the President of 5 October 2012 in Case C-394/12, *Abdullahi* (pending); Order of the President of 8 January 2013 in Case C-400/12, *MG* (pending); Order of the President of 28 June 2013 in Case C-140/13, *Altmann and others* (pending).

[60] See Order of the President of 30 September 2011 in Case C-329/11, *Achughbabian* (n 12 above).

[61] See Order of the President of 25 November 2011 in Case C-528/11, *Halaf.*

[62] See Order of the President of 10 October 2011 in Case C-300/11, *ZZ.*

[63] See Order of the President of 8 September 2011 in Joined Cases C-356/11 and C-357/11, *O and S.*

[64] See Order of the President of 3 April 2007 in Case C-33/07, *Jipa* [2008] ECR I-5157.

regarding any kind of issue. Indeed, priority treatment has been granted to a larger number of cases covering a much wider range of issues where the much higher threshold of urgency in the urgent and expedited procedures could not be met. For example, priority treatment has been granted to cases relating to animal health, the environment, the advertising of tobacco products, the interpretation of the 6th VAT directive, jurisdiction in insolvency proceedings etc. Second, the reasoning behind the decision to grant priority treatment is not recorded in the Court's judgment or in a separate order issued by the President, as is the case for applications for the urgent and expedited procedures. The wide range of areas in which priority treatment was granted reveals however that it constitutes in effect a useful and flexible tool that the Court may use at its discretion and on an ad hoc basis in order to accelerate the process of adjudication, where necessary. One should not lose sight however of the fact that, as has been shown above, priority treatment comes nowhere close to the same speed of acceleration as the urgent and expedited procedures.

VI. CONCLUSION

The urgent procedure, the expedited procedure and the priority treatment collectively constitute the Court's main tools to accelerate the pace of proceedings pending before it. Although the three procedures are not available for all types of cases before the Court, they provide for three progressive types of acceleration. When compared with the Court's general performance, the figures of the average duration of each of these procedures cited above show that the urgent and expedited procedures provide for a significant acceleration of the proceedings. By contrast, priority treatment does not seem to make a difference, thus leading one to question its *raison d'être*. It is clearly arguable that the process of adjudication would not suffer any considerable impact by the abolition of priority treatment.

Be that as it may, this Article shows that the Court has exercised its discretion to apply the urgent and expedited procedures in a conservative manner to accelerate the pace of proceedings only where strictly necessary. The prime candidates for acceleration appear to have been cases where there the application of the ordinary procedure would result in irreversible consequences for the individual concerned. The Court's practice shows that the best cases for the making of such a finding are those where personal liberty is at risk, or where the custody of children is disputed and the prolongation of proceedings could result in the child's failure to develop a relationship with one of his or her parents.

4

Vertical Precedent at the Court of Justice of the European Union: When Push Comes to Shove

KIERAN BRADLEY*

INTRODUCTION

MUCH HAS BEEN written about the practice of the Court of Justice[1] as regards the precedential value of its own decisions.[2] Indeed, the volume of commentary on the subject appears to stand in inverse proportion to the number and pertinence of the indications which may be garnered from the Treaty or the judgments of the Court of Justice. Happily, while an Advocate General, Nial Fennelly made a significant contribution to that commentary in his Opinion in *Merck v Primecrown*,[3] where he was proposing

*Judge at the European Union Civil Service Tribunal, writing in a private capacity. The present chapter is a much-reworked version of a presentation made at the Faculty of Law of the University of Sydney on 25 March 2013. My best thanks are due to my *référendaire* Roberto Schiano, and to a number of unnamed colleagues, for their helpful comments on an earlier version of this text; responsibility for any errors remains with the author alone.

[1] Since the Lisbon Treaty, the Union's judicial institution is properly known as the 'Court of Justice of the European Union' (CJEU), while 'Court of Justice' (ECJ) designates the uppermost tier of the judicial hierarchy; the other two tiers are the 'General Court', and the 'Civil Service Tribunal'. The term 'Union judicature' is used to designate the CJEU, though of course national courts at all levels are an essential part of that judicature (see Opinion 1/09 *European Patent Court Agreement* [2011] ECR I-1137).

[2] According to Toth, academic treatment and judicial treatment of the subject 'reveals a remarkable degree of disagreement on virtually every aspect of the question', of which he provides a comprehensive overview: AG Toth, 'The Authority of Judgments of the European Court of Justice: Binding Force and Legal Effects' (1985) 4 *YEL* 1, 2. See, more recently, A Arnull, 'Owning up to fallibility: precedent and the Court of Justice' (1993) 30 *CML Rev* 247; JJ Barceló, 'Precedent in European Community Law' in DN MacCormick and RS Summers (eds) *Interpreting Precedents – A comparative study* (Ashgate, Dartmouth, 1997), 407; J Komarek, *Reasoning with Previous Decisions: Beyond the Doctrine of Precedent*, LSE Law Society and Economy Working Papers 8/2012, and T Tridimas, 'Precedent and the Court of Justice: A Jurisprudence of Doubt?' in J Dickson and P Eleftheriadis, *Philosophical Foundations of EU Law'* (Oxford, OUP, 2012) 307.

[3] Joined cases C-267/95 and C-268/95 *Merck & Co Inc and Ors v Primecrown Ltd and Ors* [1996] ECR I-6285, hereinafter *Merck v Primecrown*; see also in this volume N Travers, 'From *Merck v*

that the Court radically modify its long-established interpretation of the impact of patents on the free movement of goods. He noted that the supreme courts of the two common law jurisdictions of the Union,[4] though wedded to the notion of legally binding precedent or 'stare decisis', as 'the normal, indeed almost universal, procedure', were prepared to depart from an earlier ruling

> where it appears to be clearly wrong ... However desirable certainty, stability and predictability of law may be, they cannot ... justify a court of ultimate resort in giving a judgment which they are convinced, for compelling reasons, is erroneous [or where] too rigid adherence to precedent may lead to injustice in a particular case and also unduly restrict the proper development of the law. [5]

It was obvious, he opined, that, though not bound as a matter of principle, 'the Court should, as a matter of practice, follow its previous case-law except where there are strong reasons for not doing.' He based this conclusion on the grounds that many important aspects of Union law were 'judge-made' and that the preliminary ruling procedure sought to ensure the uniform application of Union law. After reviewing a handful of judgments where the Court of Justice had openly overruled, or at least materially qualified, the scope of its previous rulings, the Advocate General suggested that the Court would depart from earlier judgments 'which may have been based on an erroneous application of a fundamental principle of [Union] law, which interpret a Treaty provision as applicable to situations which are properly outside its scope, or which result in an imbalance between differing principles, such as the free movement of goods and the protection of intellectual and commercial property'.[6]

The question which Advocate General Fennelly so succinctly examined may be dubbed 'horizontal precedent', that is, the extent to which a court is obliged, as a matter of law, to follow its own previous judgments. On the other hand, the matter of 'vertical precedent' in Union law, that is, the extent to which the lower courts of the Union judicature, the General Court and Civil Service Tribunal, are obliged to follow judgments of their respective higher court(s) has been largely ignored; a recent, and otherwise helpful, study consigned the subject to a single footnote providing references to two of the three relevant provisions of the Court's Statute.[7] Yet such an obligation, if it existed, would have even more impact on the outcome of the decisions of these courts than would a doctrine of binding precedent for the Court of Justice. As a court of final resort, the ECJ can, in effect, decide in a given case whether or not to follow its own previous

Stephar to the Unitary Patent Regulation and Court: Reflections on the incremental development of an EU patent law and legal system'.

[4] For convenience, the term 'Union' and 'General Court' are used throughout in preference to 'Community' and 'Court of First Instance' in defiance of chronology, except where confusion would otherwise arise.

[5] *Merck v Primecrown* (n 3), paras 138–146, pp 6343–6347.

[6] His analysis has in turn been taken up by at least one well-advised academic commentator: A Arnull, *The European Union and its Court of Justice* 2nd ed (Oxford, OUP, 2006), 630–1.

[7] Tridimas (n 2), 307, fn 4. The CJEU Statute, which applies to all three courts, is set out at Protocol No 3 to the TEU and TFEU; an up-to-date version is available on the Court's webside, http://curia.europa.eu.

judgments; in theory, it could even decide, like the House of Lords did in the century up to 1966, that it would be bound strictly to follow its own case law, however erroneous it considered that case law to be.[8]

The possible application of a doctrine of vertical binding precedent in the Union legal order is one of fundamental, not to say existential, importance for the courts concerned. It affects the court's conception of its own role. Where bound by a doctrine of stare decisis, a major part of the court's role in deciding a case is to determine whether or not there is a binding precedent and, if so, whether there is any reason which would justify not following it. A court not so bound must, on the other hand, determine the law, and, though it may draw inspiration from past judgments, may nonetheless not simply base its own decision entirely on the authority of such judgments. The application of some form of strict stare decisis would also have an impact on the expectations of the parties which appear before the court; obviously, where there already exists an established precedent, the chances of success of a potential litigant depend, in large part, on whether or not that court is obliged to follow such a precedent.

The question arises for consideration in the first place because of the general ethos of almost unquestioning respect for the decisions of the higher courts of the Union, which in turn reflects the clearly hierarchical structure of the Union judicature, with an appeal on a point of law lying to the Court of Justice from a decision of the General Court, and to the General Court in respect of decisions of the Civil Service Tribunal. In some jurisdictions at least the adoption of a doctrine of vertical precedent appears to have come about largely because of the establishment of different layers of jurisdiction in a judicial pyramid.[9] The fact that the judgments of the Court of Justice have a certain precedential value for the courts of the Member States could give support to the idea of an equivalent binding effect on the lower courts of the Union. In a major comparative study of the subject of precedent, one author suggests that the ECJ 'appears to be developing, at least in a de facto sense, a doctrine of *stare decisis*, although employing a continental methodology and style that focuses on the rules and principles articulated in the cases, rather than on the cases themselves in their factual settings'.[10] When authorising the Union legislature to set up specialised courts, the Treaty of Nice also introduced an express obligation on the Courts of the Union to respect the 'unity [and] consistency of Union law' and a special procedure to review compliance with this obligation. The question of the binding character of the case law of the higher Union courts arises in this context too, particularly as the Court of Justice itself regularly refers to the notion of a judicial 'precedent'.

[8] See *Beamish v Beamish* (1859–61) 9 HLC 274, and *London Street Tramways v London County Council* [1898] AC 375; the 1966 Practice Statement reversing this position was itself unprecedented ([1966] 3 All ER 77).

[9] JC Dobbins, 'Structure and Precedent' (2010) 108 *Michigan Law Review* 1453.

[10] JJ Barceló (n 2) 433; see also *Cristina*, text to n 64 below.

WHAT WERE THE TREATY AUTHORS THINKING OF?

The 'Original Understanding': Approaches to Precedent in (some of) the Founding Member States

Unlike the Statute of the International Court of Justice (ICJ), the Union Treaties (and the Community Treaties before them) do not provide any indication of the sources of law which the Court of Justice should apply. In particular, the Treaty authors did not feel obliged to stipulate that '[t]he decision of the Court has no binding force except between the parties and in respect of that particular case', nor that, subject to this proviso, 'judicial decisions' could constitute a 'subsidiary means for the determination of rules of law'.[11] Clearly the Statute had to cater for the participation in the work of the ICJ of judges and lawyers from States Parties from the common law tradition, for whom stare decisis is an article of faith, as well as those from other jurisdictions who reject so binding a form of precedent. [12]

Given the civil law traditions of the original six Member States, such a clarification in the Union Treaties would in any case have been supererogatory. The flavour of French thinking on case law ('*jurisprudence*'), generally considered to have exercised a preponderant influence in the design of the first European Court of Justice, may be gleaned from Robespierre's rallying cry: '[t]he word "*jurisprudence*" must be expurgated from the French language; in a country which has a Constitution and legislation, *jurisprudence* is nothing more than law-making.'[13] This view was reflected in more moderate terms in the Code Civil, Article 5 of which prohibits judges – the prohibition is directed at the judges individually, not just the courts – from providing general or abstract rulings in deciding the cases before them. As a result, 'judicial decisions are not a source of law in France. Strictly speaking, they never create legal rules ... It is never enough ... simply to refer to a prior judicial decision'.[14] This mistrust of precedent applied as much to judgments of the highest courts for civil, criminal and administrative matters, the *Cour de cassation* and the *Conseil d'Etat*, as to the lower courts amongst themselves. The lower courts are thus free not to follow judgments of the higher courts, though of course there is always a risk of their decisions being overturned on appeal:

> Because higher court precedents do not bind, lower courts can offer 'legitimate resistance' to them. The refusal of lower courts to follow a ruling of the Cour de cassation has sometimes led the latter to reconsider its views and to come up with a different solution.[15]

[11] Respectively Articles 59 and 38(1)(d) ICJ Statute.

[12] The European Convention on Human Rights, which also preceded the first European Community Treaty, restricts the jurisdiction of the Court it established to 'matters concerning the interpretation and application of the Convention and the Protocols thereto' (Art 32).

[13] Speech to the *Assemblée constituante*, 18 November 1790 (author's translation).

[14] R David (trans M Kindred), *French Law* (Baton Rouge, Louisiana State University Press, 1972) 181.

[15] J Bell, *Judiciaries within Europe: a comparative review* (Cambridge, CUP, 2006) 71.

Similarly in Germany, '[j]udicial decisions are authoritative as interpretations of the law, but not authorities in their own right. Judges are free to depart from precedents when circumstances change or [when] they think it right to do so'.[16] One lower court famously refused on 160 occasions to follow an interpretation of asylum law given by a superior administrative court, though, in Germany as elsewhere, 'precedents carry substantial weight'.[17] Similarly '[i]n Italy, there are no generally recognized rationales for treating precedents as formally binding, since the precedent is not ascribed any formal binding force'.[18]

While it is difficult to draw very reliable conclusions from what the Treaties do not say, it is clear that the imposition of a system of binding precedent on the Union judicature would be a significant departure both from the practice followed in the Member States in their own legal orders, and from international practice. At the very least, the Treaty authors might have been expected to provide some indication that this was indeed their intention.

Treaty Indications: The Shared Duty to Ensure 'the Law is Observed'

The principal indication in the Union Treaties, which has remained essentially unchanged since Article 31 ECSC,[19] is currently set out in the second sentence of the first sub-paragraph of Article 19(1) TEU. This provides that the Court 'shall ensure that in the interpretation and application of the Treaties the law is observed.' It would be difficult to overstate the importance of this provision for the development of the Union's legal order over the years. It is, in effect, the Treaty foundation for the bold jurisprudence of the Court of Justice which defines the relationship between the Union and the national legal orders, on which the Treaty was, if not actually silent, at least far from forthcoming. Under the powers vested in it by this provision, the Court has interpreted 'the law' as embracing inarticulate structural imperatives, such as the direct effect of Treaty provisions, the liability in damages of Member States for their failure properly to apply Union law and, most importantly, the primacy of Union law. In turn, this admonition against judicial passivity led the Court to develop the material law of the common market at a time when the legislature was unwilling or unable to carry out its policy-making duties under the Treaty. On a few rare occasions, the Court relied on this statement of its general duty in order to escape the limits on the wording of the jurisdictional clauses of the Treaty, in pursuit of a higher legal ideal such as the rule of law or the intended balance in decisional powers between the Union institutions. The use of the term 'the law' also gave the Court the springboard to develop a case law in favour of legal protection of fundamental rights which the Treaty had not foreseen in terms.[20]

[16] Ibid 140.

[17] Bell (n 15) 141.

[18] M Taruffo, 'Precedent in Italy' in DN MacCormick and R Summers (n 2) 141, 165.

[19] Later Art 164 EEC and latterly Art 220, first para, EC.

[20] The literature on the role of the Court in the development of the Union's legal order is vast, and it would be invidious to select one or a few references; these may be found in any case in the standard textbooks on EU law.

For present purposes, it is important to note that under Article 19(1) TEU the duty and power to ensure that 'the law is observed' is conferred equally and indivisibly on all three levels of Union court.[21] Indeed, in this regard the old Article 220 EC was somewhat more specific, in conferring the duty and power on the ECJ and the Court of First Instance 'each within its jurisdiction'. In other words, Article 19(1) TEU did not, as conceivably it might have, confer this duty on the sole Court of Justice, and confer a lesser duty and power on the lower courts; in particular it did not impose on them a specific obligation to comply with rulings of the higher court(s). Moreover, according to the 1988 Council decision establishing the then Court of First Instance, [22] the new court was charged with exercising 'the jurisdiction conferred on the Court of Justice by the Treaties', implying that it was to operate within its areas of competence under the same conditions as regards precedent as the Court of Justice.

Structural Considerations

As noted above, the Union judicature now comprises three levels of jurisdiction, in line with the judicatures of many Member States:[23] the Court of Justice, the General Court and specialised courts which are 'attached to the General Court to hear and determine at first instance certain classes of action or proceeding brought in specific areas'. To date, only one such specialised court, the Civil Service Tribunal, has been established. An appeal is available from 'decisions' – including orders bringing a case to an end – of the General Court to the Court of Justice, and from the Civil Service Tribunal to the General Court, in each case 'on points of law only'.[24] The grounds on which such an appeal may succeed are defined as a 'lack of competence ... a breach of procedure before [the Court] which adversely affects the interests of the applicant as well as the infringement of Union law' by the lower court.[25]

The CJEU Statute expressly requires the lower court to comply with a decision of the higher court in three situations. Firstly, where the Court of Justice finds that an action which has been lodged with its Registrar falls within the jurisdiction of the General Court[26] and refers the action to that court, the General Court 'may not decline jurisdiction'. Similarly when the Court of Justice quashes a judgment of the General Court and refers the case back to that court, the General Court is then 'bound by the decision of the Court of Justice

[21] Under Art 19(1) TEU, '[t]he Court of Justice of the European Union shall include the Court of Justice, the General Court and specialised courts'.

[22] Art 3(1), Council Decision 88/591/ECSC, EEC, Euratom, OJ 1988 L319/1.

[23] See also in this volume V Skouris, 'The Evolution of the Judicial Architecture of the European Union and its Procedural Implications'.

[24] Respectively Arts 256, second para, and 257, third para, TFEU. No appeal lies from a decision of the General Court on appeal from the Civil Service Tribunal (but see the Review procedure, below).

[25] Respectively Art 58, first para, and Art 11(1), Annex I, CJEU Statute.

[26] For convenience, reference will be made here to the General Court only; similar provisions apply to the Civil Service Tribunal.

on points of law'. Finally, the General Court is also so bound when the Court of Justice, in a review procedure, remits an appeal judgment to it.[27]

While the existence of hierarchical judicial structures means that the decisions of the higher courts are almost always followed in practice, this does not necessarily imply that the lower court is bound by a doctrine of strict precedent. Again the practice of the Member States shows that such structures can operate perfectly well without the need for vertical stare decisis.

Under a system of stare decisis, a lower court may issue a so-called 'critical concurrence', that is, a judgment which follows, but criticises, a previous ruling with which it is obliged by law to comply.[28] A court of the Union judicature has no such luxury and, save where the Treaty vests a decision of another court with binding authority, must in all circumstances decide in accordance with its own conception of 'the law'.

ON THE PRECEDENTIAL EFFECT OF PRELIMINARY RULINGS

The *Locus Classicus*: *Da Costa*

Article 267 TFEU,[29] which governs the powers and duties of the national courts with regard to preliminary rulings, does not expressly indicate the extent to which the rulings of the Court are binding on national courts. In *Da Costa*, the Court was in effect invited to rule on the precedential value of its judgment in *Van Gend en Loos*, which had been handed down just two weeks before the hearing in *Da Costa*.[30] On the grounds that the substantive questions put by the national court in *Da Costa* were identical to those in the earlier case, the Commission had argued at the oral hearing that there was no need to answer the *Da Costa* reference which, it contended, should be 'dismissed for lack of substance'. It is unclear from the case report precisely why the Commission had taken such a position, which prima facie contradicted the terms of the Treaty; then as now, national courts of final instance are obliged to request a preliminary ruling from the Court where 'a decision on the question is necessary to enable [the national court] to give judgment'. It may be, if one might be allowed to speculate, that the Commission felt that the judgment in *Van Gend en Loos*, adopted by the slimmest margin imaginable,[31] was 'as good as it gets', and that the Commission was concerned that the Court might be tempted not to treat *Van Gend en Loos* as a precedent and hence reconsider its strikingly bold decision in the earlier case.

[27] Respectively Art 54, second para, Art 61, second para, and Art 62b, first para, CJEU Statute.

[28] EH Caminker, 'Why Must Inferior Courts Obey Superior Court Precedents?' (1994) 46 *Stanford Law Review* 817, 863.

[29] Formerly Art 177 EEC and latterly Art 234 EC.

[30] Joined Cases 28-30/62 *Da Costa en Schaake NV and Ors v Netherlands Inland Revenue Administration* [1963] ECR 31, and Case 26/62 NV *Algemene Transport – en Expeditie Onderneming van Gend & Loos v Netherlands Inland Revenue Administration* [1963] ECR 1.

[31] It is well known that three of the seven judges supported the position proposed by the Advocate General in *Van Gend en Loos* denying Art 12 EEC direct effect.

If that were the case, the Opinion of Advocate General Lagrange would have brought the Commission cold comfort at best. He suggested that the *Van Gend en Loos* judgment had no binding effect on later disputes: '[however] important the [Court's prior] judgment ... the golden rule of *res judicata* must be preserved: it is from the *moral* authority of its decisions, and not from the legal authority of *res judicata* that a jurisdiction like ours should derive its force'.[32] In the result, however, he did not even examine the substantive questions put in *Da Costa*, but proposed that the Court provide exactly the same answers as it had in *Van Gend en Loos*.

The Court took a different approach again as regards the binding effect of *Van Gend en Loos*. While the referring court was a court of final instance and hence, according to the terms of what is now Article 267 TFEU, obliged in principle to request a preliminary ruling, the Court held that

> [T]he authority of an interpretation ... already given by the Court may deprive the obligation of its purpose and thus empty it of its substance. Such is the case especially when the question raised is materially identical with a question which has already been the subject of a preliminary ruling in a similar case.[33]

The Court hinted that the authority of a preliminary ruling could extend to courts in other Member States; the purpose of this procedure was to ensure 'unity of interpretation of [Union] law within the ... Member States'. That said, the Court also underlined the fact that a national court was always entitled to request a second preliminary ruling if it so wished, and concluded that it (the Court) was therefore obliged to answer the second batch of requests from the national court. It did so by reproducing the answers it had provided in *Van Gend en Loos* and holding that the questions posed in the instance case were identical and that 'no new factor [had] been presented to the Court'.

Extending the Authority of Preliminary Rulings: *CILFIT* and *Foto-Frost*

In confirming and refining the scope of the obligation of national courts of final instance to refer questions for a preliminary ruling in *CILFIT*,[34] the Court extended the potential authority of its judgments. Thus a previous Court ruling, whatever the procedural setting in which this was delivered, on the point of law at issue before the national court was sufficient to obviate the need for that court to refer the matter to the ECJ.[35] Whereas *Da Costa* allowed the application of an identical ruling provided in essentially identical circumstances, *CILFIT* allowed the extrapolation of a legal solution adopted in one set of procedural circumstances to a different, but legally pertinent, set of circumstances. In so

[32] Opinion in *Da Costa* (n 20) (emphasis in original), 42.

[33] Judgment in *Da Costa* (n 20), 38.

[34] Case 283/81 *C.I.L.F.I.T. v Ministry of Health* [1982] ECR 3415.

[35] The same dispensation from the obligation to refer was recognised where 'the correct application of [Union] law [was] so obvious as to leave no scope for any reasonable doubt', under the so-called '*CILFIT* criteria'.

doing, the Court necessarily based its reasoning the idea that a judgment could have authority beyond the four corners of the dispute which had generated it.

The Court has also interpreted Article 267 TFEU to mean that it has a monopoly of the authority to annul acts of the Union institutions; a national court which has serious doubts regarding the validity of such an act may not annul it, but must refer the question to the ECJ. This is so even for courts which are not courts of final instance and are hence not otherwise obliged to refer questions of Union law to the Court of Justice.[36]

What is significant is that the Court did not base its reasoning in these cases on some notion that its judgments are inherently blessed with binding precedential value, but relied instead on an interpretation of the relevant Treaty provisions. The precedential value of a preliminary ruling is not such as to deprive the national court of the possibility of re-submitting to the Court a question it has already answered, which is indeed the reason the Court has been able to revise its position in certain of the judgments mentioned by Advocate General Fennelly in *Merck v Primecrown*. The reasoning of the Court of Justice in this regard is solidly based on Treaty provisions; it would make little sense to oblige national courts of last instance to refer questions of Union law to the Court if the ruling were not binding, particularly as lower national courts are not even obliged to refer such questions. The Treaty authors clearly intended that preliminary rulings provided to national courts of last instance would benefit from the natural authority of such courts in the legal orders of the Member States, even where they did not operate a system of binding precedent. The qualified stare decisis of preliminary rulings also explains why the Member States are given the possibility of submitting observations on requests for preliminary rulings from courts in other Member States.

UNITY, CONSISTENCY AND THE REVIEW PROCEDURE: SOMETHING NEW UNDER THE SUN?

The Review Procedure

The review procedure which was established, along with the possibility of setting up specialised courts, by the Treaty of Nice is truly an extraordinary judicial proceeding in the European Union constellation; the Treaty enjoins the Court to use it only 'exceptionally'.[37] It allows the Court of Justice to review two categories of General Court decision: decisions on appeal from specialised courts, and preliminary rulings. As no jurisdiction has (as yet) been conferred on the General Court to provide such rulings, the procedure has only ever been applied to judgments on appeals from the Civil Service Tribunal. The review procedure is not an appeal, and it may not therefore be initiated by the parties;

[36] Case 314/85 *Foto-Frost v Haputzollamt Lübeck-Ost* [1987] ECR 4199.

[37] See now Art 256(2) and (3) TFEU and Arts 62–62b CJEU Statute for the review procedure, and Art 257 TFEU for the 'specialised courts', formerly 'judicial panels'.

in theory it falls outside the scope of effective judicial protection per se, and may be considered a proceeding in the interests of the law. That said, where it is applied, the parties, along with the Member States and the Commission and, according to the circumstances, other institutions or Union bodies, may present legal argument, both in writing and, if the Court so decides, orally. More importantly, the review may lead to the appeal judgment's being set aside and the case being either remitted to the General Court (and thence possibly to the Civil Service Tribunal) or decided by the Court of Justice itself; the effect on the interests of the parties is therefore equivalent to that of an appeal.

The review procedure is initiated by the Court of Justice operating under a double filter: the Court may only act on the basis of a proposal to this effect by the First Advocate General, and only if it agrees with the latter's assessment that the appeal judgment poses a 'serious risk [that] the unity or consistency of Union law [is] affected'. The procedure thus operates rather like certiorari in the United States Supreme Court, though the Court of Justice decides whether or not to review by a majority of the judges in the chamber responsible, rather than by minority decision as in its American counterpart.[38] In practice, the Court of Justice adopts a first decision on the basis of the case file forwarded by the General Court that it is necessary to review the appeal judgment and setting out the matters to be reviewed and, after hearing the parties, a second judgment reviewing the appeal judgment on the merits.

While it certainly provides a useful backstop in relation to direct actions, where appeal judgments of the General Court in highly specific areas of Union law may occasionally raise questions with wider implications, the review procedure would arguably come into its own in respect of preliminary rulings of the General Court; not only is there is no possibility of an appeal from such rulings, but all the courts (and indeed other public authorities) of the Member States would be expected to comply with the General Court's ruling.[39] Indeed, it could be argued that it is precisely because the General Court is not formally obliged to follow the rulings of the Court of Justice that such a procedure is particularly appropriate, given that it is intended to safeguard the same values as a system of binding precedent, the 'unity' and the 'consistency' of Union law.

'Unity' and 'Consistency' of Union Law

It is not clear what precisely is intended by the terms 'unity' and 'consistency' in this context; though they are used elsewhere in the Treaty,[40] they could hardly be

[38] In fact, the number of review procedures to date (3) as a percentage (1.5%) of the total number of appeal judgments handed down by the General Court (2007–2013: 197) is slightly higher than that of cases in which certiorari is accepted by the Supreme Court in a normal year, about 1%.

[39] For this reason, the ruling would only take effect after the expiry of the deadlines for initiating the review procedure: Art 62b, CJEU Statute.

[40] The Council and High Representative for foreign policy are to 'ensure the unity, the consistency and effectiveness' of the Union's action in this area (Art 26(2), second subpara, TEU).

described as terms of art. One dictionary definition of 'unity' is '[t]he quality or fact of being one body or whole ... [d]ue interconnection and coherence of the parts', while 'consistency' is defined as 'the agreement of parts or elements with each other'; [41] semantically in any case, the terms are not far apart.

It is also unclear why the English text of the relevant Treaty provisions does not refer to 'coherence', rather than 'consistency', as do some of the other language versions of the relevant phrase.[42] The two terms are arguably not identical in meaning: an interpretation of a legal provision could be coherent with other, previous, interpretations, in that they can be reconciled in the framework of a larger whole, without necessarily being consistent, in the sense that the two interpretations are in agreement with each other. In other words, 'coherence' and 'consistency' appear to posit different tests of the degree to which a later interpretation need accord with an earlier one.

Be that as it may, the notion of coherence/consistency has also been introduced into the proportionality test with which Member States must comply in certain circumstances, for example in order to justify a restriction on a Treaty freedom. Such a restriction may only be considered 'appropriate for securing attainment of the [national] objective relied upon only if it genuinely reflects a concern to attain that objective in a consistent and systematic manner'.[43] The test seeks to reconcile judicial review with the margin of appreciation enjoyed by the Member States: 'coherence is designed to object to rules which are found to be self-contradictory or, at least, manifestly inappropriate without questioning the legitimate scope left to Member States by Union law'.[44]

Review Judgments and 'Precedents' under Union Law

The Court of Justice showed a distinct reluctance, in its first two judgments under the review procedure, to define the notion of 'unity [and] consistency of Union law'. At first instance in *M v EMEA*, the Civil Service Tribunal had rejected an application for annulment as manifestly inadmissible, without examining the merits of the case. On appeal, the General Court had not merely set aside the judgment, but had itself ruled on the merits, as it is entitled to do under the CJEU Statute 'where the state of the proceedings ... permits'; in particular, it awarded the applicant compensation for non-material damage.

The review procedure[45] was here limited to the compensation award by the General Court. The Court of Justice first established a number of errors of law in the appeal judgment under review, and identified four factors which it

[41] *Shorter Oxford English Dictionary* 5th edn (Oxford, OUP, 2002).

[42] eg '*cohérence*' '*coerenza*', '*Kohärenz*' and '*coherencia*' in French, Italian, German and Spanish, respectively.

[43] Joined Cases C-171/07 and C-172/07 *Apothekerkammer des Saarlandes and Ors v Saarland and Ors* [2009] ECR I-4171, para 42.

[44] T von Danwitz, 'Thoughts on Proportionality and Coherence in the Jurisprudence of the Court of Justice' in Cardonnel et al (eds), *Constitutionalising the EU Judicial System – Essays in honour of Penilla Lindh* (Oxford, Hart, 2012), 367, 381.

[45] Case C-197/09 RX-II [2009] ECR I-12033.

considered were relevant to the question of whether the General Court had put unity or consistency at risk:

- the appeal judgment was the first occasion on which the General Court had ruled on the merits of a case which the Civil Service Tribunal had dismissed as inadmissible without examining the merits and it 'could therefore constitute a precedent for future cases';
- the General Court had 'departed from the established case-law' of the Court of Justice;
- the procedural rules which the General Court misinterpreted were applicable generally, rather than being confined to the area of staff regulations law, and
- the rules in question were set out in provisions of primary law, *in casu* the CJEU Statute, and hence 'occupy an important position in the [Union] legal order'.

On the basis of these four points, 'considered as a whole', the Court held that the appeal judgment affected 'the unity and the consistency of [Union] law', without distinguishing between these two notions. The case was remitted back to the General Court as regards the damages claim, which in turn remitted it to the Civil Service Tribunal.

Of the Court's four indicators of a risk to unity or consistency, the first two are particularly noteworthy in the present context. As the 'precedent' in the first point concerned a decision of the General Court in appeal proceedings, the Court seems to be using the term as meaning an example which the General Court itself might follow in the future, rather than in the sense of a precedent which would bind the Civil Service Tribunal. Moreover, the reference to the General Court's departing from the case law could be seen as shorthand for its failure properly to interpret the rule laying down the conditions under which it may decide the merits of an appeal case whenever the first instance judgment has been set aside, which the Court of Justice had established in some detail earlier in the judgment.

The Court relied on the same four risk indicators in the second review judgment, which concerned the notion of a 'reasonable deadline' for initiating court proceedings where the relevant statutory provisions had not determined any rule in this regard.[46] On this occasion, the Court was much exercised by the fact that the General Court had not followed previous case law of both the Court and the General Court itself, and had thereby contravened the principle of effective judicial protection under Article 47 of the Charter and Article 6 of the ECHR. Noting that 'the members of staff concerned ... were entitled to expect that the General Court would simply apply that case-law', the Court concluded that the appeal judgment affected the consistency of Union law. Once again, however, the strictures of the review court should not be read as indicating that the General Court is in some way bound by a rigorous doctrine of precedent; the notion of a 'reasonable deadline' applies in such circumstances where there

[46] Case C-334/12 RX-II *Review Arango Jaramillo*, judgment of 28 February 2013.

is no rule of positive law, and is hence defined exclusively in the case law of the Union Courts.

In *Strack*, however, the Court abandoned the 'four factors' test.[47] It held that, by failing to take account of the European Union Charter of Fundamental Rights ('the Charter') in interpreting the relevant provisions of the EU Staff Regulations, the appeal judgment adversely affected the unity of European Union law. By not applying the Charter in these circumstances, the appeal judgment undermined, in effect, the recognition of its Treaty status. More generally, as suggested by Advocate General Kokott, 'the unity of Union law is adversely affected, in particular, where the General Court has misconstrued rules or principles of EU law which have particular importance'.[48] The appeal judgment at issue was also held to affect the consistency of Union law; by ruling that measures governing working conditions did not cover the organisation of working time, and in particular the rules on paid leave, the General Court had ignored the contrary ruling of the Court of Justice in the 'Working Time' case.[49] It thus appears that 'the consistency of European Union law is adversely affected where the General Court has misconstrued existing case-law of the European Union courts.'[50]

The Court of Justice has indicated extra-judicially that the review procedure is 'not ... an appropriate tool for ensuring consistency of case-law other than in relation to important issues of principle.'[51] It follows that '[one] or more errors, even glaring errors, do not necessarily affect the unity *or* consistency of European Union law'.[52] Indeed, the Court has held that 'it is now solely for the Civil Service Tribunal and the General Court of the European Union to develop the case-law in matters relating to the civil service'.[53] While, as Advocate General Kokott crisply noted, 'this does not mean [these courts] have been given "carte blanche" ... to develop the case-law [on staff matters] ... without concern for the compatibility of that case-law with other areas of EU law',[54] the Court has in effect acknowledged the absence of a strict obligation to comply with its case law in this particular area.

NON-BINDING PRECEDENT IN ACTION: FOUR JUDGMENTS AND A TREATY AMENDMENT

That the system of non-binding precedent works well in practice may be illustrated by a number of examples from the case law of the General Court and the Civil Service Tribunal.

[47] Case C-579/12 RX II, *Review Commission v Strack*, judgment of 19 September 2013.

[48] View in *Review Commission v Strack*, para 75.

[49] Case C-84/94 *United Kingdom v Council* [1996] ECR I-5755.

[50] AG Kokott, View in *Strack* , n 48 above.

[51] Explanatory note to the draft amendments to the CJEU Statute submitted by the Court to the European Parliament and the Council, Luxembourg, 28 March 2011, 9.

[52] View of AG Mengozzi, *Review Arango Jaramillo*, para 69 (emphasis in original).

[53] Case C-17/11 RX, *Petrilli Review Proposal* [2011] ECR I-229, para 4; the Court decided not to review an appeal judgment which allegedly contravened previous General Court case law on liability for damages in staff law.

[54] N 48, para 63.

Intention to Harass? *Q v Commission*

In 2004, the EU Staff Regulations were amended to include an express prohibition on 'psychological harassment' in the workplace, also known as 'mobbing' or, in more familiar terms, bullying. The definition of the prohibited conduct requires, inter alia, 'acts that are intentional and that may undermine the personality, dignity or physical integrity of any person'. In its case law prior to the 2004 reforms, the General Court had ruled that the alleged victim had to 'prov[e] he was subjected to conduct aimed, objectively, at discrediting him or at deliberately impairing his working conditions'; it adopted the same position in 2007 in *Lo Giudice v Commission*, when it first interpreted the new provision.[55] When the question of the statutory definition of psychological harassment came before the Civil Service Tribunal (Tribunal), the precedent was clear, and under a system of stare decisis would have been more or less unarguable.

The Tribunal took a different view.[56] On the basis of the wording of the relevant provision, it deduced that there was no requirement that the conduct complained of be committed with the intention of undermining the personality, dignity or integrity of the victim, but that '[i]t is sufficient that such reprehensible conduct, provided it was committed intentionally, led objectively to such consequences'. For the Tribunal, a contrary interpretation – that is, the interpretation espoused repeatedly by the General Court in the past – would 'depriv[e] the provision of any useful effect, on account of the difficulty of proving the malicious intent of the perpetrator of an act of psychological harassment' in all but the rarest cases, as 'the alleged harasser is careful to avoid any conduct which could indicate his intention to discredit his victim or to impair the latter's working conditions'. The Tribunal was also able to rely on the definition of 'harassment' provided in the general law of the Union,[57] which it interpreted as being intended to ensure 'adequate judicial protection', an objective which could not be attained if the victim had to show intention to harass, rather than conduct which was objectively capable of having that effect. Moreover, it was 'hardly ... likely' that the legislature would adopt a different, and markedly less protective, standard for harassment in the case of Union officials than that which applied generally.

The previous case law was dispatched briefly; some of the judgments relied on were pre-2004 and hence not directly germane to the new provision, while the Tribunal considered that it was 'not apparent from [*Lo Giudice*] that the [General] Court [ ] expressly intended to interpret Article 12a(3) of the Staff Regulations as making the malicious intent of the alleged harasser a condition for the existence of psychological harassment'. Though the Commission appealed against the judgment, to its credit it did not seek to challenge the Tribunal's interpretation of the conditions under which an official could establish bullying at the workplace.[58]

[55] Case T-154/05 [2007] ECR-SC I-A-2-00203 and II-A-2-01309; the case had been commenced before the Civil Service Tribunal was operational, and had not been transferred to the Tribunal.

[56] F-52/05 *Q v Commission* [2008] ECR-SC I-A-1-409 and II-A-1-2235.

[57] Council Directive 2000/78/EC of 27 November 2000 establishing a general framework for equal treatment in employment and occupation [2000] OJ L303/1.

[58] Case T-80/09 P *Commission v Q* [2011] ECR II-4313.

Obligation to Give Reasons for Resiling a Temporary Contract: *Landgren*

The cards were more heavily stacked against any temptation to innovate in *Landgren*,[59] where the Tribunal had to contend with a judgment of the Court of Justice which was almost thirty years old, interpreting a statutory provision which had not been amended since. The question was whether an institution[60] which wished to terminate a contract of indefinite duration which it had concluded with a member of the temporary staff was obliged to state the reasons for its decision. The answer provided by the Court in 1977 [61] was abundantly clear; the justification for the termination was to be found in the temporary nature of the employment relationship itself, which was fundamentally different from that between the institution and an official, and the employer was therefore under no obligation to provide reasons for the termination of the contract.

Though acknowledging the fundamental difference between the legal position of permanent officials and that of other agents, the Tribunal nonetheless relied on

> the development of the law concerning the protection of workers against dismissal and the abusive recourse to successive fixed-term employment contracts or relationships and of the [Union] case-law itself as to the requirement of a formal statement of the reasons on which [a contested] act ... is based.[62]

In regard to the first, the Tribunal was able to call in aid a variety of measures of social protection adopted both within and outside the Union legal order, including the 1999 Council Directive on fixed-term work, international standards protecting workers from unfair dismissal, and the 2000 Charter of Fundamental Rights of the European Union. The Tribunal concluded that 'there is no overriding reason to exclude members of the temporary staff ... from protection against unjustified dismissal' and that such protection implied a concomitant obligation on the employing institution to notify the agent of the reasons for his dismissal. Moreover, the Tribunal continued, 'the recognition of [such] an obligation ... does not prevent the [employer] enjoying broad discretion in regard to dismissal, and review by the [Union] Courts is therefore confined to ensuring there has been no manifest error or misuse of powers'.

This time the defendant institution did challenge on appeal the Tribunal's novel finding on the requirement to provide reasons, though not specifically on the grounds that the Tribunal had offended against any duty to comply with existing precedent. Once again, the General Court upheld the judgment of the Tribunal, albeit for reasons which were slightly different, though no less convincing. The appeal court stressed the 'general and essential principle

[59] Case F-1/05 *Landgren v European Training Foundation* [2006] ECR-SC I-A-1-123 and II-A-1-459.

[60] In fact, the defendant was an agency rather than an institution per se, but the legal question is the same.

[61] Case 25/68 *Schertzer v European Parliament* [1977] ECR 1729; the proceedings had been suspended for several years pending the outcome of different proceedings before the national courts.

[62] On the legal requirement to provide reasons in different contexts, see D O'Donnell 'Nial Fennelly: *Mallak* and the Rule of Reasons', and C Donnelly 'Transparency, Reasons and the Europeanisation of Public Law', both in the present volume.

that the administration must give reasons for its decision', to which a broad exception such as the appellant was relying on 'could only be the result of the express and unequivocal will of the [Union] legislature which is not evident in' the relevant statutory provisions. It therefore 'interpreted' the existing case law as not requiring that the employee be provided with a formal statement in the dismissal decision, but holding that the decision must be based on valid grounds to which the employee must have access.[63]

When Precedents Clash: *Cristina*

That it is not always simple for a lower court to benefit from the wisdom of prior decisions of the higher courts, even where it wishes to do so, is illustrated by *Cristina*.[64] The applicant was a candidate in an open competition to join the EU civil service, who had been refused admission to the tests on the ground that she did not have the necessary qualifications. On 11 July 2011, she lodged a complaint under the Staff Regulations to challenge the selection board's decision excluding her from the competition; the following day, for reasons which do not appear from the case report, she brought legal proceedings against the Commission before the Civil Service Tribunal. The Commission objected that the action was inadmissible, as the complaint procedure had not been completed.

Under long-established case law, an unhappy competition candidate is not required to follow the administrative complaint procedure before initiating legal proceedings, as other litigants are obliged to do; the thinking is that the institution may not in any case amend the decision of a selection board, which is wholly independent, and that in these circumstances following the complaint procedure would be pointless. The question in the present case was whether the candidate who nonetheless chooses to launch such a procedure is then obliged to await the outcome, or whether he may also initiate legal proceedings in parallel. The applicant was able to point to judgments of the Court of Justice and the General Court from 1978 and 1990 respectively, admitting an annulment action in essentially identical circumstances to the instant case, while the Commission relied on a much more recent judgment of the General Court holding expressly that an action commenced before the administrative complaint had been completed was inadmissible.

Borrowing a leaf from the book of common law, the Tribunal distinguished the more recent judgment of the General Court rather than confront the appeal court head-on on this point. On a close analysis, the Tribunal found that the General Court had held in its judgment that the complaint and the annulment

[63] It has been argued that the Court should have reviewed the *Landgren* appeal judgment, but was unable to do so because the First Advocate General made no such proposal: P Iannuccelli in A Tizzano and P Iannuccelli, 'Premières application de la procédure de "réexamen" devant la Cour de justice de l'Union européenne', in N Parisi et al (eds), *Scritti in onore di Ugo Draetta*, (Naples, Editoriale Scientifica, 2011) 733, 746–748.

[64] Case F-66/11 *Cristina v Commission*, judgment of 20 June 2012.

action there at issue concerned different Commission decisions and had different purposes; as a result, the legal proceedings had not been preceded by an administrative complaint. If this was the ratio decidendi, 'there was no need for the General Court to declare premature an action for annulment brought before the pre-litigation administrative procedure … was concluded', and the General Court's finding in this regard was therefore in effect obiter; as the recent judgment 'relates to factual and legal situations which are significantly different from those in the present case, it cannot be regarded as relevant in this instance'.

Individual Concern and Effective Judicial Protection: *Jégo-Quéré*

The *Cristina* litigation only arose in effect because the General Court had not followed a prior judgment of the Court of Justice. A more dramatic and telling example of its independence of spirit is provided by the *Jégo-Quéré* saga, where the application of the consistent, not to say immutable, case law of the Court of Justice on the *locus standi* of individuals over a forty-year period would, in the view of the General Court, have left the applicants with no means of legal redress.

The applicants in *Jégo-Quéré*[65] sought to challenge the validity of a Union measure of general scope, *in casu*, a Commission regulation setting a minimum mesh size for fishing nets being used in waters south of Ireland; to do so, they needed to show the Regulation affected them individually, that is 'by reason of certain attributes which are peculiar to them or by reason of circumstances in which they are differentiated from all other persons and by virtue of these factors distinguishes them individually just as in the case of the person addressed', under the so-called *Plaumann* test.[66] Unable to do so, the applicants contended they had no means of effective judicial protection, and that the Union was thereby failing to respect a fundamental right guaranteed under Union law and the European Convention of Human Rights.

The General Court first considered, and rejected, two other possible means of indirectly challenging the validity of the regulation, that is, a request for a preliminary ruling by a national court and an action in damages: the first because it would require the applicants to break the law in order to get to court, and the second because it would not allow the Court full review of the validity of the measure, which would in any case remain in place even if the action were successful. The General Court came what it described as 'the inevitable conclusion' that the Treaty no longer guaranteed the right to an effective judicial remedy. It therefore proposed a revised definition of the notion of 'individual concern', which would be established if the applicant could show that the measure of general scope affected his legal position 'in a manner which is both definite and immediate.'

The Court of Justice was quick to respond; in giving judgment in an unrelated case just under three months later,[67] which happened to pose a similar question

[65] Case T-177/01 *Jégo-Quéré v Commission* [2002] ECR II-2365.

[66] Case 25/62 *Plaumann v Commission* [1963] ECR 95, 107.

[67] Case C-50/00 P *Unión de Pequeños Agricultores v Council* [2002] ECR I-6677; judgment was pronounced on 25 July, some weeks into the judicial vacation.

of the effectiveness of judicial protection under the Treaty,[68] it re-stated the *Plaumann* test for individual concern, and held that where 'that condition is not fulfilled, a natural or legal person does not, under any circumstances, have standing to bring an action for annulment of a regulation.' Though not unsympathetic to the concerns raised by the General Court, the Court of Justice considered that it could not ignore the requirement of individual concern and that 'it is for the Member States to establish a system of legal remedies and procedures which ensure respect for the right to effective judicial protection'. In particular, the admissibility of an annulment action before the Courts of the Union could not depend on the vagaries of the respective procedural laws of the Member States, some of which would have allowed persons in the same position as the applicants a remedy. The Court subsequently quashed the judgment in *Jégo-Quéré*, though making no reference to the fact that the General Court had not followed the test laid down in *Plaumann.*[69]

The saga has a kind of happy ending, however, in terms of the development of Union law and the effectiveness of the judicial protection provided by the Union Courts; indeed, it may be that this is exactly what the Court of Justice had intended by putting the ball in the Member States' court, given that by the summer of 2002 a convention charged with drawing up a Constitution for Europe was in full swing. By not following a clear, and clearly relevant, precedent, the General Court had drawn attention to what it considered to be a lacuna in 'the complete system of judicial protection' which the Court of Justice had first declared in the landmark *Les Verts* judgment,[70] and which both Courts relied upon in their respective judgments in this case. As a result, the Constitution, and subsequently the Lisbon Treaty, extended the scope of annulment proceedings to include those by persons whose legal position is directly affected by a regulatory act which does not entail implementing measures.[71] At the same time, though merely the consecration of an existing principle, the Member States were enjoined to 'provide remedies sufficient to ensure effective legal protection in the fields covered by Union law'.[72]

CONCLUSIONS

If the Treaty provides little by way of explicit instruction regarding vertical precedent in the Union's legal order, the reasons for following judgments of a higher court are obviously myriad and solid, notably equal treatment of equal situations, efficiency of the judicial process, stability and predictability in legal

[68] In *Jégo-Quéré*, the General Court had relied on the Opinion AG Jacobs had presented in *Unión de Pequeños Agricultores*.

[69] Case C-263/02 P [2004] ECR I-3425; in the relevant part of its judgment, the Court refers exclusively to *Unión de Pequeños Agricultores*, which had been handed down after the first instance judgment in *Jégo-Quéré*, rather than to *Plaumann*.

[70] Case 294/83 *Parti écologiste 'Les Verts' v European Parliament* [1986] ECR 1339.

[71] Respectively Art III-365(4), Constitution for Europe, and Art 263, fourth para, TFEU.

[72] Respectively Art I-29(1), second subpara, Constitution for Europe, and Art 19(1), second subpara, TFEU.

relations, respect for judicial authority, and most important of all, because the lower court will usually have no doubt that the earlier judgment is correct. As a matter of practice then, lower courts follow rulings of the higher courts; in the EU judicature, as elsewhere, '[t]he doctrine of [vertical] precedent is so deeply ingrained in judicial practice and consciousness that its dominance has rarely been questioned'.[73] The issue remains however, of what to do when push comes to shove, that is, when the lower court is profoundly convinced that, on an issue within its own specific field of law,[74] the judgment of the higher court does not provide a just solution in the instant case.

In this regard, there is much wisdom in the approach of the General Court, which is particularly well placed to have a balanced view on the matter, being both a court of first instance and an appeal court. In its judgment in *Kadi III*, it had to deal with arguments criticising the ruling of the Court of Justice in *Kadi II* concerning the intensity and extent of judicial review of asset-freezing decisions,[75] criticisms which the General Court viewed as 'not entirely without foundation,' and which were very similar to those the General Court had itself previously taken on the matter. On the one hand, it noted that 'in the context of the present proceedings, the General Court is not bound under Article 61 of the Statute of the Court of Justice[76] by the points of law decided by the Court of Justice in its judgment in *Kadi*'. On the other hand, the General Court took into account the particular circumstances of the case – the fact that in its earlier judgment the Court of Justice had annulled a judgment of the General Court – as well as structural considerations, and in particular 'the appellate principle itself and the hierarchical judicial structure which is its corollary'. The General Court concluded that 'in principle it falls not to it but to the Court of Justice to reverse precedent in that way'.[77] Whether or not it formally binds the lower courts of the Union, *Kadi III* provides invaluable guidance on the question of vertical precedent at the CJEU, complementing that of Advocate General Fennelly on horizontal precedent in *Merck v Primecrown*.

[73] Caminker (n 28), 817.

[74] It is hardly to be expected that a lower court, particularly a specialist tribunal, would challenge a ruling of the higher court(s) on a matter of general application, such as rules of judicial procedure; within the EU judicature, the Review procedure would provide the necessary corrective.

[75] See also in this volume D Edward 'Due Process, Judicial Protection and the *Kadi* saga' and NJ Forwood, 'Closed Evidence in Restrictive Measures Cases: A Comparative Perspective'.

[76] This provides that, when a matter is referred back to it after its judgment has been quashed, the General Court is bound by the points of law on which the Court of Justice has ruled.

[77] Case T-85/09 *Yassin Abdullah Kadi v European Commission* [2010] ECR II-5177, paras 112, 121 and 123; the judgment was upheld as to the result on appeal, Joined Cases C-584/10 P, C-593/10 P and C-595/10 P, *European Commission and Ors v Kadi*, judgment of 18 July 2013.

PART II: MATERIAL ISSUES OF EUROPEAN UNION LAW

5

Due Process, Judicial Protection and the Kadi *Saga*

DAVID EDWARD*

A COMMENTARY ON the dissenting judgment of Mr Justice Fennelly in *Equality Authority v Portmarnock Golf Club and Others*[1] refers to it as 'a plainly clever judgment that is unconcerned with protesting its cleverness'.[2] Indeed it is. For example:

> It is, moreover, a matter of simple common sense that the principal purpose of Portmarnock Golf Club is the playing of golf. When the far-seeing founding members of Portmarnock came together in 1894 and led to the establishment of what is now the first and greatest of Irish golf clubs, what was their purpose if it was not the establishment of a golf club? Clearly, the answer is 'none'. Any other answer would be preposterous.[3]

When he was one of the Advocates General of the European Court of Justice Nial Fennelly delivered many plainly clever opinions that were unconcerned with protesting their cleverness. They were straightforward, easy to read and, at least as far as I was concerned, always (or almost always) right.

Sadly, as an Advocate General from one of the 'small' Member States, his term of office was limited to six years, but Luxembourg's loss was Ireland's gain. His judgments in the Supreme Court carry the same imprint of a precise judicial mind concerned to identify the real issue in a case and to find an acceptable solution, consistent with common sense. In particular, they are constantly imbued with a concern for due process and procedural fairness, as in the *Portmarnock* case:

> Another issue raised by the Club and canvassed at the hearing of the appeal was the position of the Masonic Order under the legislation. I find it objectionable that the interests of a body which is not before the Court and not represented should

* Professor Emeritus, University of Edinburgh; Judge of the European Court of Justice (1992–2004).

[1] *Equality Authority v Portmarnock Golf Club* [2009] IESC 73.

[2] D O'Connell, 'No "ladies" need apply – Equality Authority v Portmarnock Golf Club,' *Village Magazine,* December 2009.

[3] N 1, para 58.

> be debated at all. In any event, whether that or any other club or body is treated correctly under the legislation is, to my mind, also utterly irrelevant to the legal issue before the Court. [4]

In the common-law countries, due process and procedural fairness have been the recurring theme in the historic proclamations of fundamental rights from Magna Carta onwards: the right to be heard; the right to trial within a reasonable time; the right of the accused to be confronted with accusers and witnesses; protection against arbitrary search and seizure, and so on. The underlying principles have been developed over centuries by the case-law of the courts, and Jean-Pierre Warner, the first Advocate General from a common-law country, brought them firmly into EU law with his Opinion in *Transocean Marine Paint*.[5]

Due process and procedural fairness were at the core of what Advocate General Bot called 'the saga of the *Kadi* cases'. But the *ultimate ratio* decidendi (if there be such a thing[6]) is not very easy to identify and analysis is complicated by nuances of difference between the French and English texts.

What, at the end of the day, was the outcome of the saga? In particular, what do the principles of due process and procedural fairness require in cases that raise security concerns about full disclosure to those, like Mr Kadi, who are alleged to have been involved in terrorism? How far can the principle of judicial protection compensate for what may be lacking? These highly topical questions have been overshadowed in discussion of wider questions raised by the *Kadi* saga, such as the relationship between EU law and international law.

Using nomenclature which seems to have become conventional, the cases will be referred to as *Kadi I* (the judgment of the Court of First Instance in 2005);[7] *Kadi II* (the judgment of the Court of Justice in 2008 setting aside the judgment in *Kadi I*);[8] *Kadi III* (the judgment of the General Court in 2010);[9] and *Kadi IV* (the judgment of the Court of Justice in July 2013 in the appeal from *Kadi III*).[10]

I. *KADI I* – THE FACTS

The underlying facts can be stated fairly shortly. Beginning in 1999, the Security Council of the United Nations adopted a series of measures designed to stop Afghanistan being used as a safe haven for terrorism, and established a Sanctions Committee to ensure that the measures were implemented. The measures to be taken by States included the freezing of 'funds and other financial assets of

[4] N 1, para 75.

[5] Case 17/74 *Transocean Marine Paint v Commission* [1974] ECR 1063 at pp 1088 *ff.*

[6] 'With the possible exception of the legal term "malice", … the most misleading expression in English law' *per* AL Goodhart, 'Determining the *Ratio Decidendi* of a Case' (1930) XL *Yale Law Journal* 161, 162.

[7] Case T-315/01 *Kadi v Council and Commission* [2005] ECR II-3649.

[8] Joined Cases C-402 and 415/05 P *Kadi and Al Bakaraat v Council and Commission* [2008] ECR I-6351.

[9] Case T-85/09 *Kadi v Commission* [2010] ECR II-5177.

[10] Joined Cases C-584, 593 and 595/10 P *Commission v Kadi*, judgment of 18 July 2013.

Usama Bin Laden and individuals and entities associated with him as designated by the [Sanctions Committee]'.

The Council of the European Union adopted a Regulation providing that '[a]ll funds and other financial assets belonging to any natural or legal person, entity or body designated by the … Sanctions Committee and listed in Annex I shall be frozen.'[11]

Annex I contained the list of those affected by the freezing of funds, and the Commission was empowered to amend the list on the basis of determinations made by the Security Council or the Sanctions Committee.

On 21 October 2001, the Sanctions Committee added the name of Mr Kadi to its list, and on the same day the Commission added his name to the list in Annex I, with the result that his assets were frozen.[12] The Security Council subsequently adopted resolutions providing for relaxation of the freezing regime in limited circumstances, including the possibility of individuals making representations through their national authorities to the Sanctions Committee ('de-listing procedure'). The Council of the EU adopted a further Regulation for that purpose.[13]

II. *KADI I* – THE GENERAL COURT

In *Kadi I,* Mr Kadi sought annulment of the Council and Commission Regulations which had the effect of freezing his assets, principally on the ground that he had been arbitrarily deprived of rights of property without a fair, or indeed any, hearing and with no right to judicial review. This, he said, constituted a breach of his fundamental rights. The Council and Commission did not dispute that Mr Kadi had not been allowed any hearing, contending that they had no discretion in the matter since they were bound, under the Charter of the United Nations,[14] to comply with the Resolutions of the Security Council.

The Court of First Instance (now General Court) comprehensively rejected Mr Kadi's arguments. It held that the EU was bound by Community law (quite apart from international law) to implement the resolutions of the Security Council; that there had, in any event, been no arbitrary deprivation of a right of property nor any breach of the right to be heard since there was provision

[11] Council Regulation (EC) No 467/2001 of 6 March 2001 prohibiting the export of certain goods and services to Afghanistan, strengthening the flight ban and extending the freeze of funds and other financial resources in respect of the Taliban of Afghanistan, and repealing Regulation (EC) No 337/2000 [2001] OJ L67/1, Art 2.

[12] Commission Regulation (EC) No 2062/2001 of 19 October 2001 amending, for the third time, Council Regulation (EC) No 467/2001 prohibiting the export of certain goods and services to Afghanistan, strengthening the flight ban and extending the freeze of funds and other financial resources in respect of the Taliban of Afghanistan and repealing Regulation (EC) No 337/2000, [2001] OJ L277/25.

[13] Council Regulation (EC) No 561/2003 of 27 March 2003 amending, as regards exceptions to the freezing of funds and economic resources, Regulation (EC) No 881/2002 imposing certain specific restrictive measures directed against certain persons and entities associated with Usama bin Laden, the Al-Qaida network and the Taliban [2003] OJ L82/1.

[14] Arts 24(1), 25, 48(2) and 103.

for resort (albeit indirect) to the Sanctions Committee; and, as regards the availability of judicial protection, that it was not open to the Community courts to review decisions of the Security Council or the Sanctions Committee.

III. *KADI II* – THE ADVOCATE GENERAL

In *Kadi II*, Advocate General Poiares Maduro affirmed the right and obligation of the Court, notwithstanding the terms of the UN Charter, to uphold fundamental rights within the Community legal order in relation to the Community act freezing Mr Kadi's assets. As he said, '[t]he only novel question is whether the concrete needs raised by the prevention of international terrorism justify restrictions on the fundamental rights of the appellant that would otherwise not be acceptable'.[15]

As to the right of property, he said that '[c]learly, the indefinite freezing of someone's assets constitutes a far-reaching interference with the peaceful enjoyment of property.'[16]

He then dealt fairly briefly with the right to be heard,[17] and concentrated his fire on the lack of effective judicial protection:

> The appellant has been listed for several years in Annex I to the contested regulation and still the Community institutions refuse to grant him an opportunity to dispute the grounds for his continued inclusion on the list. They have, in effect, levelled extremely serious allegations against him and have, on that basis, subjected him to severe sanctions. Yet, they entirely reject the notion of an independent tribunal assessing the fairness of these allegations and the reasonableness of these sanctions. As a result of this denial, there is a real possibility that the sanctions taken against the appellant within the Community may be disproportionate or even misdirected, and might nevertheless remain in place indefinitely. The Court has no way of knowing whether that is the case in reality, but the mere existence of that possibility is anathema in a society that respects the rule of law.
>
> Had there been a genuine and effective mechanism of judicial control by an independent tribunal at the level of the United Nations, then this might have released the Community from the obligation to provide for judicial control of implementing measures that apply within the Community legal order. However, no such mechanism currently exists.[18]

IV. *KADI II* – THE COURT OF JUSTICE

In its judgment in *Kadi II*, the Court of Justice drew an important distinction between judicial review of the acts of the institutions of the UN and review of those of the EU, and emphasised that

[15] Para 46.
[16] Para 47.
[17] Para 51.
[18] Paras 53 and 54.

> in circumstances such as those of these cases, the review of lawfulness thus to be ensured by the Community judicature applies to the Community act intended to give effect to the international agreement at issue, and not to the latter as such.[19]

Thus the Court did not, as it might have done, rest its decision on the supremacy, in international law, of the fundamental rights enshrined in the Universal Declaration of Human Rights even as against acts of the UN institutions.

In 2006 (after the judgment in *Kadi I* but before the judgment in *Kadi II*), the Security Council had put in place a 're-examination procedure' before the Sanctions Committee. The Court held in *Kadi II* that this was not an adequate substitute for judicial review because (i) the procedure was in essence diplomatic and intergovernmental; (ii) the applicant had no right to be heard; (iii) the applicant had no right of access, even restricted access, to the evidence justifying his appearance on the list; and (iv) if the Committee rejected the application, it was not bound to give reasons.

The Court therefore concluded:

> It follows from the foregoing that the Community judicature must, in accordance with the powers conferred on it by the EC Treaty, ensure the review, *in principle the full review*, of the lawfulness of all Community acts in the light of the fundamental rights forming an integral part of the general principles of Community law, including review of Community measures which, like the contested regulation, are designed to give effect to the resolutions adopted by the Security Council under Chapter VII of the Charter of the United Nations.[20]

The words italicised in the quotation ('in principle the full review') have given rise to substantial confusion and misunderstanding discussed below.

On the facts of the case, the Court held that 'the rights of the defence, in particular the right to be heard, and the right to effective judicial review of those rights, were patently not respected'.[21]

There then follows a passage where 'the rights of defence, in particular the right to be heard' and 'effective judicial protection' appear to be treated as two sides of the same coin. Thus:

> [t]he effectiveness of judicial review, which it must be possible to apply to the lawfulness of the grounds (*motifs*) on which, in these cases, the name of a person or entity is included in the list forming Annex I to the contested regulation and leading to the imposition on those persons or entities of a body of restrictive measures, means that the Community authority in question is bound to communicate those grounds to the person or entity concerned, so far as possible, either when that inclusion is decided on or, at the very least, as swiftly as possible after that decision in order to enable those persons or entities to exercise, within the periods prescribed, their right to bring an action.
>
> Observance of that obligation to communicate the grounds is necessary both to enable the persons to whom restrictive measures are addressed to defend their rights in the best possible conditions[22] and to decide, with full knowledge of the relevant facts,

[19] Para 286.

[20] Paras 322–326 (emphasis added).

[21] Para 334.

[22] It is not clear whether the French '*dans les meilleurs conditions possibles*' should be understood to mean 'in the best possible conditions in any circumstances' or 'in the best conditions possible in the particular circumstances of the case'. The difference may be important.

> whether there is any point in their applying to the Community judicature ..., and to put the latter fully in a position in which it may carry out the review of the lawfulness of the Community measure in question which is its duty under the EC Treaty.[23]

However, it becomes clear that the two concepts (rights of defence and judicial protection), although related, are not two sides of the same coin.

On the one hand, the Court held that there was no right to be told in advance before one's name was entered on the list, nor to be heard before that measure was taken, since 'such measures must, by their very nature, take advantage of a surprise effect'. Moreover,

> with regard to a Community measure intended to give effect to a resolution adopted by the Security Council in connection with the fight against terrorism, overriding considerations to do with safety or the conduct of the international relations of the Community and of its Member States may militate against the communication of certain matters to the persons concerned and, therefore, against their being heard on those matters.[24]

On the other hand,

> that does not mean, with regard to the principle of effective judicial protection, that restrictive measures such as those imposed by the contested regulation escape all review by the Community judicature once it has been claimed that the act laying them down concerns national security and terrorism.
>
> In such a case, it is none the less the task of the Community judicature to apply, in the course of the judicial review it carries out, techniques which accommodate, on the one hand, legitimate security concerns about the nature and sources of information taken into account in the adoption of the act concerned and, on the other, the need to accord the individual a sufficient measure of procedural justice (see, to that effect, the judgment of the European Court of Human Rights in *Chahal* v. *United Kingdom*[25]).[26]

The reference to available 'techniques' becomes clearer if one refers to the judgment of the ECtHR in *Chahal*, which held that the form of judicial review available in England was inadequate:

> Because the Secretary of State invoked national security considerations as grounds for his decisions to deport Mr Chahal and to detain him pending deportation, the English courts' powers of review were limited. They could not themselves consider the evidence on which the Secretary of State had based his decision that the applicant constituted a danger to national security or undertake any evaluation of the Article 3 (art. 3) risks. Instead, they had to confine themselves to examining whether the evidence showed that the Secretary of State had carried out the balancing exercise required by the domestic law.[27]

The 'technique' suggested to overcome this objection was one adopted in Canada:

[23] N 8, paras 336 and 337.

[24] N 8, paras 338–342.

[25] *Chahal v United Kingdom*, ECtHR, 15 November 2006, Reports of Judgments and Decisions 1996-V, para 131.

[26] *Kadi II* n 8, paras 343–344.

[27] *Chahal*, n 25, para 143.

> Under the Canadian Immigration Act 1976 (as amended by the Immigration Act 1988), a Federal Court judge holds an in camera hearing of all the evidence, at which the applicant is provided with a statement summarising, as far as possible, the case against him or her and has the right to be represented and to call evidence. The confidentiality of security material is maintained by requiring such evidence to be examined in the absence of both the applicant and his or her representative. However, in these circumstances, their place is taken by a security-cleared counsel instructed by the court, who cross-examines the witnesses and generally assists the court to test the strength of the State's case. A summary of the evidence obtained by this procedure, with necessary deletions, is given to the applicant.[28]

Thus, it appears that, while the rights of defence (or at any rate the normal due process rights of the individual) may have to give way before 'legitimate security concerns', the individuals affected can nevertheless be given a 'sufficient measure of procedural justice' through 'effective judicial protection'. Such protection may be afforded by allowing the judge to see (and to assess) what the affected individual may not see. A similar line of thought recurs in *Kadi IV*, where the Court refers to 'the task of the Court of the European Union before whom the secrecy or confidentiality of that information or evidence is no valid objection'.[29]

Having raised the possibility of overcoming security objections by special techniques, the Court reverted to infringement of the rights of defence in Kadi's case. The Court held that:

> Because the Council neither communicated to the appellants the evidence used against them [*les éléments retenus à leur charge*] to justify the restrictive measures imposed on them nor afforded them the right to be informed of that evidence [*prendre connaissance desdits éléments*] within a reasonable period after those measures were enacted, the appellants were not in a position to make their point of view in that respect known to advantage. Therefore, the appellants' rights of defence, in particular the right to be heard, were not respected.[30]

The Court then brought together rights of defence and judicial protection in this way:

> In addition, given the failure to inform them of the evidence adduced against them [*les éléments retenus à leur charge*] and having regard to the relationship ... between the rights of the defence and the right to an effective legal remedy [*recours juridictionnel effectif*], the appellants were also unable to defend their rights with regard to that evidence [*au regard des dits éléments*] in satisfactory conditions before the Community judicature, with the result that it must be held that their right to an effective legal remedy has also been infringed.
>
> Last, it must be stated that that infringement has not been remedied in the course of these actions. Indeed, given that, according to the fundamental position adopted by the Council, no evidence of that kind may be the subject of investigation [*vérification*] by the Community judicature, the Council has adduced no evidence to that effect.
>
> The Court cannot, therefore, do other than find that it is not able to undertake the review of the lawfulness of the contested regulation in so far as it concerns the

[28] N 8, para 144.
[29] *Kadi IV*, n 11, para 125.
[30] *Kadi II*, n 9, para 348.

> appellants, with the result that it must be held that, for that reason too, the fundamental right to an effective legal remedy which they enjoy has not, in the circumstances, been observed.[31]

This passage implies that judicial protection is cognate to, but conceptually different from, rights of defence. The point being made is that judicial review can operate only if there is something susceptible of review, so judicial protection can be given only if the individual affected has a means of bringing the matter before a judicial authority (a legal remedy). It may be that the outcome will be a decision that there has been no infringement of the rights of defence: judicial protection is concerned with the right to have that matter considered and determined by a court.

The Court then considered the claim of infringement of Mr Kadi's rights of property and concluded that:

> The contested regulation, in so far as it concerns Mr Kadi, was adopted without furnishing any guarantee enabling him to put his case to the competent authorities, in a situation in which the restriction of his property rights must be regarded as significant, having regard to the general application and actual continuation of the freezing measures affecting him.[32]

V. TWO LINGUISTIC PROBLEMS

Before moving on to *Kadi III*, it is necessary to deal in more detail with two linguistic problems raised by the judgment in *Kadi II*. They concern two phrases in the English text: first, 'the review, in principle the full review, of lawfulness'; and, second, 'the evidence adduced against them', used together with the word 'investigate'. It has to be borne in mind that, while the judgment was almost certainly drafted in French, the authentic languages of the case were English and Swedish.

(1) As regards the first problem, the use of expressions such as 'full review', 'marginal review' and 'restricted review' suggests that they refer to well-defined and well-understood (and presumably mutually exclusive) legal categories. But experience shows that the nature and scope of judicial review does not lend itself to easy categorisation.

In the French text of *Kadi II*, the expression used is '*un contrôle, en principe complet, de la légalité*'. The Swedish text refers to '*en i princip fullständig kontroll*' ['complete review']. The German text is even more emphatic: '*eine grundsätzlich umfassende Kontrolle der Rechtsmäßigkeit*' ['in principle, an all-embracing review'].

The Italian text refers to '*un controllo, in linea di principio completo, della legittimità*'. This is inconsistent with an argument later advanced by the Advocate General in *Kadi IV* that a distinction should be drawn between '*en principe*' (in principle) and '*par principe*' (as a matter of principle). The Italian

[31] N 9, paras 349–351.
[32] N 9, para 369.

phrase '*in linea di principio*' clearly means the latter rather than the former. In any event, while it may be true that the judgment in *Kadi II* was drafted and deliberated in French, the authentic languages of the case were English and Swedish, so logic-chopping about French prepositions is, with respect, both technically and legally inept.

Comparing the different language texts, it is difficult to imagine that any rational reader of the judgment in *Kadi II* could suppose that the words 'full review' were intended to mean other than what they say.

(2) The second linguistic problem concerns the distinction between the English 'evidence adduced against someone' and the French '*éléments retenus à charge*'.

In English, particularly in the context of the common-law system, the word 'evidence' has very specific connotations. Evidence may be written or oral, coming from an identifiable source, and it will be tested for relevance, admissibility, credibility and reliability. Where it is said, in the English text of the judgment, that the individual has 'the right to be informed of that evidence' and, later, that the evidence 'may be the subject of investigation', this would be taken by a common lawyer to mean that the individual has the right to be informed, not simply of the allegation against him, but that he or she is entitled to an independent investigation of the underlying evidential basis for that allegation.

The French expression '*éléments retenus à charge*' does not have the same connotation. In the German text, the expression is rendered '*welche Umstände ihnen zur Last gelegt werden*' [what circumstances are charged against him]. Almost exactly the same phraseology as in the German is found in the archaic English of the King James Bible: 'They laid to my charge things that I knew not'.[33] Comparison of these texts suggests that the Court, in referring to '*éléments retenus à charge*', intended to refer only to the allegations made against Mr Kadi and not to their evidential basis.

A requirement that a judicial authority should be able to 'verify' or 'check' [*vérifier*, *überprüfen*] the allegations against someone in order to justify listing is rather different from a requirement (implied by the English text) that the authority should be able to 'investigate' and then (presumably) assess the reliability of their evidential basis.

This linguistic confusion helps to explain the difference of approach between the General Court in *Kadi III* and the Court of Justice in *Kadi IV*.

VI. EVENTS FOLLOWING *KADI II*

Shortly before the Court's decision in *Kadi II* (3 September 2008), the Security Council had, on 30 June 2008, adopted Resolution 1822 (2008) which took note of the challenges to the listing procedure and made some modifications to that procedure. In particular, it provided for the release to the person affected of a 'statement of reasons' for listing. This was followed by Resolution 1904 (2009)

[33] *Psalm* 35.11. See also *Romans* 8.33 : ' Who shall lay anything to the charge of God's elect?'.

which provided that the Sanctions Committee was to be assisted by an 'Office of the Ombudsperson' who would carry out investigations and report to the Committee on requests for delisting. (The powers of the Ombudsperson were later increased.)

On 8 September 2008, the Sanctions Committee was asked, as a matter of urgency, to make available the summary of reasons for Mr Kadi's listing. This was provided on 21 October 2008 and communicated to Mr Kadi the following day. Mr Kadi was given rather less than three weeks to submit observations.

The reasons given for Mr Kadi's listing were in brief:[34]

- that he was the founding trustee and directed the activities of a Foundation which operated under the umbrella of an organisation that was the predecessor of, and was subsequently absorbed into, Al-Qaeda;
- that he appointed to manage the Foundation a person with close links to Usama bin Laden. notably in the training of Tunisian mujahidin;
- that the Foundation provided logistical and financial support to a mujahidin battalion in Bosnia and Herzegovina;
- that Mr Kadi was a major shareholder in a Bosnian bank where planning sessions for an attack against a US facility in Saudi Arabia may [sic] have taken place; and
- that he owned several firms in Albania through which money was funneled to extremists and in some cases received working capital from Usama bin Laden.

On 10 November 2008, Mr Kadi submitted his observations in which, as summarised by the General Court, he:

- requested the Commission to disclose the evidence supporting the assertions and allegations made in the summary of reasons and also the relevant documents in the Commission's file;
- requested a further opportunity to make representations on that evidence, once he had received it; and
- attempted to refute, providing evidence in support of his refutation, the allegations made in the summary of reasons, in so far as he was able to respond to general allegations. [35]

In particular Mr Kadi pointed out that criminal proceedings against him in Switzerland, Turkey and Albania had been dropped.

On 28 November 2008, without further communication with Mr Kadi, the Commission adopted a new Regulation[36] renewing his inclusion in Annex 1 of the Council Regulation giving effect to the Security Council listing. The preamble stated:

> After having carefully considered the comments received from Mr Kadi in a letter dated 10 November 2008, and given the preventive nature of the freezing of funds and

[34] Following the summary in the judgment of the Court of Justice in *Kadi IV*, n 11, paras 141–148.
[35] *Kadi III,* para 55.
[36] Regulation (EC) No 1190/2008, [2008] OJ L 322/25.

economic resources, the Commission considers that the listing of Mr Kadi is justified for reasons of his association with the Al-Qaeda network.

On 8 December 2008, the Commission replied to Mr Kadi. The text of the Commission's letter is not quoted anywhere in full. The clearest summary of its contents is in the Advocate General's Opinion in *Kadi IV*:[37]

- in providing him with the summary of reasons and inviting him to comment on them, the Commission had complied with the judgment of the Court of Justice in *Kadi II*;
- the judgment of the Court of Justice in *Kadi II* did not require that the Commission disclose the further evidence requested;
- as the relevant Security Council resolutions required 'preventative' asset freezing, the freezing must be supported, with respect to the requisite evidentiary standard, by 'reasonable grounds, or a reasonable basis, to suspect or believe that the individual or entity designated is a terrorist, one who finances terrorism or a terrorist organisation';
- the letter from Mr Kadi confirmed his participation in the decisions and activities of the Muwafaq Foundation and his links with Mr Ayadi, who was part of a contact network with Usama bin Laden; and
- the dropping of the criminal proceedings in Switzerland, Turkey and Albania had no bearing on the relevance of his inclusion on the list drawn up by the Sanctions Committee, which may be based on information from other United Nations Member States. In addition, those decisions to drop proceedings were taken within the framework of criminal proceedings, which have different standards of evidence from those applicable to Sanctions Committee decisions, which are preventative in nature.

The Commission concluded that the listing of Mr Kadi was justified by his association with the Al-Qaeda network. It enclosed a statement of reasons identical to the summary of reasons previously sent, together with the text of the Regulation adopted on 28 November, drawing attention to the possibility for him to challenge that regulation before the General Court and to submit at any time a request to the Sanctions Committee to have his name removed from the list.

Against that background, by an action raised on 26 February 2009, Mr Kadi sought annulment of the Regulation adopted on 28 November 2008.

In the interim, the General Court had issued three judgments involving the People's Mojahedin Organization of Iran (PMOI) in which it dealt with the appropriate level of judicial review in such cases.[38] In the last of them, the Court said that:

the judicial review of the lawfulness of a decision to freeze funds extends to the assessment of the facts and circumstances relied on as justifying it, and to the evidence

[37] N 11, para 27.

[38] Case T-228/02 *Organisation des Modjahedines du peuple d'Iran v Council* [2006] ECR II-4665, '*OMPI*', paras 154, 155 and 159; Case T-256/07 *People's Mojahedin Organization of Iran v Council* [2008] ECR II-3019, '*PMOI I*', paras 141 to 143; and Case T-284/08 *People's Mojahedin Organization of Iran v Council* [2008] ECR II-3487, '*PMOI II*', paras 74 and 75.

> and information on which that assessment is based … The Court must also ensure that the right to a fair hearing is observed and that the requirement of a statement of reasons is satisfied and also, where applicable, that the overriding considerations relied on exceptionally by the Council in order to justify disregarding those rights, are well founded.[39]

VII. *KADI III* – THE GENERAL COURT

Before the General Court, Mr Kadi called for an 'intensive and anxious' standard of judicial review, basing his arguments on the judgment of the Court of Justice and the Opinion of the Advocate General in *Kadi II* and the Judgments of the General Court in the PMOI cases. The Commission, the Council and the intervening Member States sought, in effect, to revisit the judgment in Kadi II, protesting that 'full review' would be unworkable and inconsistent with the UN listing system.

In its judgment, the General Court considered these submissions in some detail, and concluded that

> once there is acceptance of the premiss, laid down by the judgment of the Court of Justice in *Kadi* , that freezing measures such as those at issue in this instance enjoy no immunity from jurisdiction merely because they are intended to give effect to resolutions adopted by the Security Council under Chapter VII of the Charter of the United Nations, the principle of a full and rigorous judicial review of such measures is all the more justified given that such measures have a marked and long-lasting effect on the fundamental rights of the persons concerned.[40]

The Court then dealt shortly and severely with the situation in which Mr Kadi had been placed. The essence of the Court's reasoning is in these paragraphs:

> In the context of a judicial review which is 'in principle the full review' of the lawfulness of the contested regulation in the light of the fundamental rights (judgment of the Court of Justice in *Kadi* , paragraph 326) and in the absence of any 'immunity from jurisdiction' for that regulation (*Kadi*, paragraph 327), the arguments and explanations advanced by the Commission and the Council – particularly in their preliminary observations on the appropriate standard of judicial review in the present case – quite clearly reveal that the applicant's rights of defence have been 'observed' only in the most formal and superficial sense, as the Commission in actual fact considered itself strictly bound by the Sanctions Committee's findings and therefore at no time envisaged calling those findings into question in the light of the applicant's observations.
>
> By the same token, the Commission, notwithstanding its statements at recitals 4 to 6 in the preamble to the contested regulation, failed to take due account of the applicant's comments and as a result he was not in a position to make his point of view known to advantage.
>
> Furthermore, the procedure followed by the Commission, in response to the applicant's request, did not grant him even the most minimal access to the evidence

[39] *PMOI II*, n 38, para 74.
[40] *Kadi III*, para 151.

> against him. In actual fact, the applicant was refused such access despite his express request, whilst no balance was struck between his interests, on the one hand, and the need to protect the confidential nature of the information in question, on the other (see, in that regard, the judgment of the Court of Justice in *Kadi*, paragraphs 342 to 344).
>
> In those circumstances, the few pieces of information and the imprecise allegations in the summary of reasons appear clearly insufficient to enable the applicant to launch an effective challenge to the allegations against him so far as his alleged participation in terrorist activities is concerned.
>
> That is the case, taking as a particularly telling but in no way unique example, of the allegation, not otherwise substantiated and thus irrefutable, that the applicant was a shareholder in a Bosnian bank in which planning sessions against a United States facility in Saudi Arabia 'may have' taken place.[41]

The Court went on to hold that

> The General Court cannot, therefore, do other than find that it is not able to undertake a review of the lawfulness of the contested regulation, with the result that it must be held that, for that reason too, the applicant's fundamental right to effective judicial review has not, in the circumstances, been observed (see, to that effect, the judgment of the Court of Justice in *Kadi*, paragraph 351).
>
> Consequently, it must be held that the contested regulation was adopted without any real guarantee being given as to the disclosure of the evidence used against the applicant or as to his actually being properly heard in that regard, and it must therefore be concluded that the regulation was adopted according to a procedure in which the rights of the defence were not observed, which has had the further consequence that the principle of effective judicial protection has been infringed (see, to that effect, the judgment of the Court of Justice in *Kadi*, paragraph 352).[42]

For these and other reasons, the General Court annulled the Commission's Regulation of 28 November 2008.

VIII. *KADI IV* – THE ADVOCATE GENERAL

The judgment of the General Court was delivered on 30 September 2010, and appeals were lodged by the Council, the Commission and the United Kingdom on 10 December 2010. On 5 October 2012, the Sanctions Committee, following the advice of the Ombudsperson, decided to delist Mr Kadi, and on 11 October 2012 his name was removed by the Commission from Annex I to Regulation of 881/2002.

Nevertheless, the hearing in the appeals went ahead on 16 October 2012, since there was a continuing interest in the outcome for the reasons explained subsequently by Advocate General Bot and affirmed by the Court in *Abdulrahim v Council and Commission.*[43]

[41] Paras 171–174.

[42] Paras 183–184.

[43] Case 239/12 P *Abdulrahim v Council and Commission,* Opinion delivered on 22 January 2013; judgment of 28 May 2013. And see the Opinion in *Kadi IV,* para 42.

In his Opinion in *Kadi IV*, the Advocate General first sought to explain that the Court's reference to 'full review' in *Kadi II* meant 'precisely the opposite of the one adopted by the General Court'.[44] The reasoning of this passage is unconvincing, not to say (*pace* Pope Francis) jesuitical. Indeed, it is significant that, in its judgment in *Kadi IV*, the Court did not seek to make any such apologia but simply repeated the words of *Kadi II*.[45] The point may perhaps best be left for judicial hermeneutists to torment their students.

Nevertheless, *ex malo bonum*. The Advocate General pointed out that

> As the Ombudsperson has acknowledged, the judgment of the Court of Justice in *Kadi* led to the establishment of the Office of the Ombudsperson, which has made it possible to raise the quality of the list considerably. It would be paradoxical if the Court failed to take account of the improvements to which it has directly contributed, even though the Office of the Ombudsperson is not a judicial body.[46]

The next part of the Opinion sets out the Advocate General's own preferred approach which involves making a distinction between (a) a 'normal' review of the 'external' lawfulness of the contested regulation, and (b) a 'limited' review of its 'internal' lawfulness.[47]

A normal review of external lawfulness implies 'a strict review of compliance with essential procedural requirements and of the existence of a procedure which respects the rights of the defence'. In this particular context, that will involve a 'rigorous review' of

> whether [the contested act] was adopted in a procedure which respected the rights of the defence. In particular, it must ascertain whether the reasons [*motifs*] for listing were communicated to the person concerned, whether those reasons are sufficient to permit him to defend himself properly, whether he was able to submit his comments to the Commission and whether the latter took them adequately into consideration. …
>
> By contrast, in the context of the contested regulation, the requirement of a procedure which respects the rights of the defence does not extend so far as to require the EU institutions to obtain from the Sanctions Committee all the information or evidence [*tous les éléments d'information ou de preuve*] which was available and then to transmit it to the listed person so that he can submit his comments on its relevance.[48]

The second of these paragraphs illustrates the second linguistic problem discussed above, since, in the case of this Opinion, we are rightly concerned with the language in which it was written. *Éléments d'information* are not the same as *éléments de preuve*, and the distinction is brought out clearly enough in the distinction between 'information' and 'evidence' in the English text. However, the problem arises again in a subsequent paragraph, where the Advocate General says:

> I take the view that the references made by the Court of Justice in its judgment in *Kadi* to the need for listed persons to be communicated the 'evidence adduced against them' or 'used against them' relate only to the communication of a sufficiently detailed

[44] Opinion in *Kadi IV*, para 61.
[45] Judgment in *Kadi IV*, para 97.
[46] Opinion, para 83.
[47] Para 95.
[48] Paras 97–8 and 103.

> statement of reasons, but not to the communication of the evidence or information held by the Sanctions Committee in support of the listings decided by it.[49]

The statement makes perfectly good sense in the original French but is little short of nonsense in English. However, the point is not central to the Advocate General's reasoning on the issue of 'limited review of internal lawfulness', where he says:

> I consider that the different components of the substantive lawfulness of an EU act giving effect to decisions of the Sanctions Committee must ... be limited to ascertaining the existence of a manifest error.
>
> That is the case, first, with the review of the accuracy of the facts claimed. ... Since the substantive accuracy of the facts must be presumed to have been established by the Sanctions Committee, only a manifest error in the factual finding made is capable of leading to the annulment of the implementing act.
>
> The same holds, second, for the review of the legal classification of the facts. In my view, the EU judicature must simply ascertain that the Commission did not commit a manifest error when it took the view, in the light of the statement of reasons, that the legal conditions permitting the adoption of a freezing measure were satisfied.
>
> Lastly, with regard to the review of the content of the contested act, the review by the EU judicature must be limited, in view of the broad discretion enjoyed by the Sanctions Committee in determining whether inclusion on the list is appropriate, to ascertaining that the listing is not manifestly inappropriate or disproportionate in the light of the importance of the objective pursued, namely the fight against international terrorism.
>
> In summary, the review performed by the EU judicature of the internal lawfulness of EU acts giving effect to decisions taken by the Sanctions Committee must not, in principle, call into question the merits of the listing, except in cases where the implementation procedure for that listing within the European Union has highlighted a flagrant error in the factual finding made, in the legal classification of the facts or in the assessment of the proportionality of the measure.[50]

The Advocate General then went on to apply his criteria to the facts of the case, and concluded, as is obvious, that the reasoning of the General Court was vitiated by errors of law because, in essence, the Court had required from the Commission more than the Commission had provided or indeed could have provided.

IX. *ZZ V HOME SECRETARY*

Shortly before giving judgment in *Kadi IV*, the Court gave judgment in *ZZ v Home Secretary*, a reference from the Court of Appeal of England and Wales.[51] The case concerned the interpretation of Article 30(2) of Directive 2004/38/EC,[52]

[49] Para 114.

[50] Opinion, paras 105–110.

[51] Case 300/11, *ZZ v Secretary of State for the Home Department*, judgment of 4 June 2013.

[52] Directive 2004/38/EC of the European Parliament and Council of 29 April 2004 on the right of citizens of the Union and their family members to move and reside freely within the territory of the Member States [2004] OJ L158/77.

which provides that, where a Member State takes a decision to restrict the freedom of movement and residence of Union citizens,

> the persons concerned shall be informed, precisely and in full, of the public policy, public security or public health grounds on which the decision taken in their case is based, unless this is contrary to the interests of State security.

The United Kingdom had put in place a system analogous to the Canadian system referred to in *Chahal* (quoted above) where material regarded as confidential on security grounds could be tested by a 'special advocate' without being disclosed to the individual concerned. The question in the case was whether this system was compatible with Article 30(2), read in the light of Article 47, of the Charter of Fundamental Rights, which enshrines the right to an 'effective remedy before a tribunal' – ie effective judicial protection.

In answer to the question referred, the Court set out the procedural rules by which effective judicial protection can be guaranteed. These formed the basis of the subsequent judgment in *Kadi IV* and are in essence the following:

1. The person concerned must be able to ascertain the reasons upon which the decision taken in relation to him is based, either by reading the decision itself or by requesting and obtaining notification of those reasons.
2. The parties to a case must have the right to examine all the documents or observations submitted to the court for the purpose of influencing its decision, and to comment on them.
3. If precise and full disclosure is opposed on grounds of State security, the competent court must have at its disposal and apply techniques and rules of procedural law which accommodate both legitimate State security considerations and the need to ensure sufficient compliance with the person's procedural rights, such as the right to be heard and the adversarial principle [*le principe du contradictoire*].
4. To that end, Member States must (i) provide for effective judicial review of (a) the existence and validity of the alleged reasons of State security and (b) the legality of the decision taken and (ii) prescribe techniques and rules relating to that review. These rules must enable the court to examine all the grounds and the related evidence on the basis of which the decision was taken.
5. A *court* must be entrusted with verifying whether the reasons of State security stand in the way of precise and full disclosure of the grounds on which the decision in question is based and of the related evidence. There is no presumption that the reasons invoked by a national authority exist and are valid.
6. If the court concludes that State security does not stand in the way of precise and full disclosure, the competent national authority will be given the opportunity to disclose the missing grounds and evidence to the person concerned. If that authority does not authorise their disclosure, the court will proceed to examine the legality of the decision on the basis solely of the grounds and evidence which have been disclosed.

7. If, on the other hand, State security does stand in the way of disclosure, judicial review must be carried out by a procedure which strikes an appropriate balance between the requirements of State security and those of the right to effective judicial protection, while limiting any interference with the exercise of that right to that which is strictly necessary. That procedure must ensure, to the greatest possible extent, that the adversarial principle is complied with, in order to enable the person concerned to contest the grounds on which the decision in question is based and to make submissions on the evidence relating to the decision.
8. Where disclosure of the underlying evidence is liable to compromise State security in a direct and specific manner (for example endangering the life, health or freedom of persons or revealing the methods of investigation specifically used by the national security authorities), the court must assess whether and to what extent the restrictions on the rights of the defence are such as to affect the evidential value of the confidential evidence.
9. In summary, the court must, first, ensure that the person concerned is informed of the essence of the grounds which constitute the basis of the decision in a manner that takes due account of the necessary confidentiality of the evidence and, second, draw the appropriate conclusions from any failure to inform him.[53]

X. *KADI IV* – THE COURT OF JUSTICE

In its judgment in *Kadi IV*, the Court referred briefly, and without further comment, to its judgment in *Kadi II* including the use of the phrase 'in principle, full review'. The discussion of the principles to be applied is headed simply 'The extent of the rights of the defence and of the right to effective judicial protection'. To a considerable extent, the judgment applies by analogy the principles laid down in *ZZ*, taking into account the special characteristics of the UN listing procedure and the changes that had been made to it since *Kadi II*.

Recognising the soundness of the maxim that the law does not require the impossible (*lex non cogit ad impossibilia*), the Court said:

> In proceedings relating to the adoption of the decision to list or maintain the listing of the name of an individual in Annex I to Regulation No 881/2002, respect for the rights of the defence and the right to effective judicial protection requires that the competent Union authority disclose to the individual concerned the evidence against that person *available to that authority* and relied on as the basis of *its* decision, that is to say, at the very least, the summary of reasons provided by the Sanctions Committee... .[54]

The Court then laid particular stress on the requirement to 'ensure that the individual is placed in a position in which he may effectively make known his views on the grounds advanced against him' and 'the obligation to examine, carefully and impartially, whether the alleged reasons [in the summary of

[53] *ZZ*, paras 53–68.
[54] Judgment in *Kadi IV*, para 111 (emphasis added).

reasons] are well founded, in the light of those comments and any exculpatory evidence provided with those comments'. That may involve going back to the Sanctions Committee and, through that Committee, to the Member State which proposed the listing of the individual concerned. Moreover,

> without going so far as to require a detailed response to the comments made by the individual concerned, the obligation to state reasons laid down in Article 296 TFEU entails in all circumstances, not least when the reasons stated for the European Union measure represent reasons stated by an international body, that that statement of reasons identifies the individual, specific and concrete reasons why the competent authorities consider that the individual concerned must be subject to restrictive measures.
>
> ...
>
> The effectiveness of the judicial review guaranteed by Article 47 of the Charter also requires that, as part of the review of the lawfulness of the grounds which are the basis of the decision to list or to maintain the listing of a given person, ... the Courts of the European Union are to ensure that that decision ... is taken on a sufficiently solid factual basis. That entails a verification of the [facts alleged][55] in the summary of reasons underpinning that decision ... with the consequence that judicial review cannot be restricted to an assessment of the cogency in the abstract of the reasons relied on, but must concern whether those reasons, or, at the very least, one of those reasons, deemed sufficient in itself to support that decision, is substantiated.[56]

Applying by analogy the criteria set out in *ZZ* (above), the Court held that the reasoning of the General Court was defective in relation to four of the allegations against Mr Kadi, but well founded in rejecting as insufficiently detailed and specific the allegation that he owned several firms in Albania through which money was funneled to extremists and in some cases received working capital from Usama bin Laden.[57]

The Court then looked again at the other four allegations. In each case, the Court focused, not simply on the text of the summary of reasons, but also on the explanations given by Mr Kadi and the basis on which the Commission had rejected them. The outcome was that

> none of the allegations presented against Mr Kadi in the summary provided by the Sanctions Committee are such as to justify the adoption, at European Union level, of restrictive measures against him, either because the statement of reasons is insufficient, or because information or evidence which might substantiate the reason concerned, in the face of detailed rebuttals submitted by the party concerned, is lacking.

So, although the reasoning of the General Court was held to have been wrong in respect of four out of five allegations, the result – annulment of the Commission Regulation – was held to have been correct.

[55] For no obvious reason, the English text uses the expression 'allegations factored'. The French text reads *faits allégués*.

[56] Paras 114–116 and 119.

[57] Para 141.

XI. CONCLUSION

The *Kadi* saga illustrates a feature of any system based on case-law – namely, that a durable principle of general application rarely emerges from a single judgment. The first statement is often too broad or has been stated in such a way as to lead to unintended consequences or erroneous inferences as to what the court intended. The first statement of principle will be explained, refined or even abandoned in favour of a better. The EU system, based on the case-law of the Luxembourg courts, is no different in this respect.

The problem with which the General Court and the Court of Justice were faced at the beginning of the *Kadi* saga was quite novel. The UN listing system was manifestly deficient as regards due process and procedural fairness, and it did not offer judicial protection in any form. The Court of Justice was surely right in *Kadi II* to draw attention to this deficiency, and to insist on the obligation of the judiciary to ensure minimum standards of due process and procedural fairness even in the face of risks of terrorism. That is essentially what judicial protection, as a distinct principle of law, is about. Moreover, the stand taken by the Court led to some significant improvements in the UN procedure, albeit still lacking in full judicial protection.

The ensuing problems arose from the introduction of five words ('in principle, the full review'). With hindsight, the words were unnecessary. But it is questionable whether, without them, and the head-to-head confrontation between the General Court and the Advocate General that ensued, the principles set out in *ZZ*, and applied in *Kadi IV*, would have emerged so clearly.

One important lesson of the saga is that attempts to classify and distinguish different standards or levels of judicial review without regard to the facts and circumstances of the instant case are quite as likely to lead to confusion and misunderstanding as to the efficient discharge of judicial business. It is not without cause that judges like Nial Fennelly prefer to assess the facts of the case before them in the light of their own conception of fairness and common sense.

6

Closed Evidence in Restrictive Measures Cases: A Comparative Perspective

NICHOLAS J FORWOOD*

I. INTRODUCTION

COUNTERTERRORISM AND OTHER restrictive measures cases have become increasingly prominent before EU courts in recent years. Stemming from CFSP action, restrictive measures targeting individuals, groups or entities have led the Union judge to balance the legitimate purposes of counterterrorism and other external relations policies with fundamental rights, in particular the right to a fair hearing and the right to an effective remedy. These cases have in that sense provided unique opportunities for the EU courts to clarify the nature and scope of judicial review in the Union's legal order. The first 'generation' of cases, epitomised by the *Kadi I*[1] and *PMOI*[2] judgments, focused on the procedural guarantees required for those targeted by smart sanctions. EU Courts annulled a number of decisions entailing restrictive measures as a result of breaches of fundamental principles of Union law, including the right to a fair hearing, the obligation to state reasons and the right to effective judicial protection. As a consequence, the procedures leading to the adoption of restrictive measures were amended in order to entitle the persons, groups or

* Judge at the General Court of the European Union. I would like to express sincere thanks for their help in preparing this contribution to my *référendaire* Stanislas Adam, and to Trent Buatte, a former *stagiaire* and Dean Acheson Scholar, whose research on the relevant provisions of US law and practice has been of the greatest value both for this contribution and in aiding my general understanding of the ways in which the US courts have addressed problems similar to those now faced by the EU courts.

[1] Joined Cases C-402/05 P and C-415/05 P, *Kadi and Al Barakaat International Foundation v Council and Commission* ('*Kadi I*') [2008] ECR I-6351; see also Case T-306/01, *Yusuf and Al Barakaat Foundation v Council and Commission* [2005] ECR II-3533 and Case T-315/01, *Kadi v Council and Commission* [2005] ECR II-3649.

[2] Case T-226/02, *Organisation des Modjahedines du peuple d'Iran v Council* ('*PMOI I*') [2006] ECR II-4665.

entities concerned, in essence: first, to receive notice of their initial inclusion on a sanctions list and a statement of the reasons for that inclusion; second, to have an opportunity to make known their observations on their listing, after it has become effective; and third, to have the opportunity to be heard prior to the adoption of subsequent decisions maintaining restrictive measures.[3]

While procedural issues have certainly not disappeared in more recent cases, for instance concerning the minimum degree of clarity and precision required in the summary of reasons notified to the targeted person, group or entity, a second generation of cases has now arisen, where the Union judge, in addition to strictly procedural issues, is called upon to verify that there was sufficient substantive justification for adopting the restrictive measures under scrutiny. This new generation of cases poses important challenges for EU courts. The first concerns the availability of closed evidence. If they are to be in a position to examine such pleas effectively, Union judges should, as a matter of principle, have access to the administrative file so as to be able to make an overall assessment of the evidence on which the challenged decision was based. However, restrictive measures cases, particularly but not exclusively in the field of counterterrorism measures, are characterised by the frequent reliance of the EU authorities on material of a security sensitive nature. For that reason, the authority holding that material may be unwilling to disclose it to the Court, or even, at least in the manner usual in EU administrative practice, to the decision maker itself. That in turn raises the sensitive and controversial issue of the 'handling' of closed evidence, namely whether, and how, the EU judge, when asked judicially to review such a decision, should be able to judge such cases on the basis of confidential material which, though it has not been disclosed to the targeted person, group or entity, is clearly relevant to that decision, and of how such a review can be reconciled with respect for the rights of the defence in the course of judicial proceedings.

It is these issues that I would like to address in the present contribution, as a testimony of Nial Fennelly's continued interest in judicial review in the Union's legal order. The objective is not to propose solutions to what could be perceived as a systemic impasse following the *Kadi II* judgment of the Court of Justice regarding the so-called UN restrictive measures against Al-Qaeda and the Taliban.[4] Rather, the purpose will be to shed some light on the main parameters that ought to be taken into account when discussing those issues in the future, and in building an appropriate framework both for the adoption and renewal of smart sanctions decisions, and in ensuring that such decisions are subject to an effective judicial review which assures a correct balance between the competing interests at stake. In doing so, I believe that some useful conclusions can be drawn from a comparison between the sanctions regimes

[3] See in particular Council Regulation (EU) No 1286/2009 of 22 December 2009 amending Regulation (EC) No 881/2002 imposing certain specific restrictive measures directed against certain persons and entities associated with Usama Bin Laden, the Al-Qaeda network and the Taliban ([2009] OJ L 346/42).

[4] Joined Cases C-584/10 P, C-593/10 P and C-595/10 P, *Commission and others v Kadi ('Kadi II')*, Judgment of 18 July 2013.

in the EU and the parallel regimes in the United States involving the use of security sensitive material.

II. THE EU COURT AFTER *KADI II* AND THE NEED FOR CLOSED EVIDENCE PROCEDURES

There are, broadly, four distinct types of EU smart sanctions cases: first, those in which the Council or Commission, acting under Regulation (EC) No 881/2002, directly implements Security Council resolutions against UN listed supporters of terrorism;[5] second, those in which the Council, acting under Regulation (EC) No 2580/2001, includes individuals or groups on EU sanctions lists based on a decision related to terrorist activity that will have been adopted by the competent authority, normally in a Member State;[6] third, nuclear proliferation cases involving the adoption, under Regulation (EC) No 423/2007, of restrictive measures against individuals and entities suspected of providing support to nuclear proliferation activities;[7] and fourth, 'political' sanctions aimed at individuals associated with particular regimes in foreign countries where the EU finds that such sanctions are appropriate.[8] Regardless of the sanction regime under review, it results from EU case law that individuals, groups and entities subject to sanctions are entitled, at minimum, to be given notice of their inclusion on a sanctions list and the reasons for that inclusion, as well as an opportunity to make known their observations on the measures concerned.[9] Upon review, the EU courts have to assess whether the reasons supporting the listing and notified to the individual or entity are 'sufficiently detailed and specific' and 'whether the accuracy of the facts relating to the reason concerned has been established'.[10]

In *Kadi II*, the Court of Justice made it clear that the EU courts must conduct a substantive, although limited, review of the underlying factual basis for the initial listing decision, if such argument is made by the applicant. In order to ensure the right of effective judicial review, they should determine, based on the information disclosed,[11] whether the decision to list an individual, group or entity was 'taken on a sufficiently solid factual basis'.[12] According to the judgment, judicial review is to entail a verification of the allegations factored in the summary of reasons underpinning the challenged decision, with the consequence that it cannot be restricted to an assessment of the cogency in the

[5] See eg *Kadi I* and *Kadi II*.

[6] See eg Case T-256/07, *People's Mojahedin Organisation of Iran v Council* ('*PMOI II*') [2008] ECR II-3019; Case T-348/07, *Al-Aqsa v Council* [2010] ECR II-4575.

[7] See eg Joined Cases T-246/08 and T-332/08, *Melli Bank v Council* [2009] ECR II-2629; Case T-496/10, *Bank Mellat v Council*, judgment of 29 January 2013.

[8] See eg Case C-417/11 P, *Council v Bamba*, judgment of 15 November 2012; Case T-383/11, *Makhlouf v Council*, judgment of 13 September 2013.

[9] See *Kadi II*, n 4 above, para 135.

[10] Ibid.

[11] Ibid, paras 127–28, on using information disclosed to the court.

[12] Ibid, n 4 above, para 119 (citing *Al-Aqsa*, n 6 above, para 68).

abstract of the reasons relied on, but must concern whether those reasons, or, at the very least, one of those reasons, deemed sufficient in itself to support that decision, are substantiated. To that end, the Court continued, it is for the EU courts, in order to carry out that examination, to request the competent European Union authority, when necessary, to produce information or evidence, whether confidential or not, relevant to such an examination. Most importantly, the Court added:

> [I]f the competent European Union authority finds itself unable to comply with the request by the Courts of the European Union, it is then the duty of those Courts to base their decision solely on the material which has been disclosed to them, namely, in this case, the indications contained in the narrative summary of reasons provided by the Sanctions Committee, the observations and exculpatory evidence that may have been produced by the person concerned and the response of the competent European Union authority to those observations. If that material is insufficient to allow a finding that a reason is well founded, the Courts of the European Union shall disregard that reason as a possible basis for the contested decision to list or maintain a listing.[13]

While making it clear that EU courts must conduct a searching, substantive review of the evidence underpinning the Council's reasons for imposing sanctions on individuals, that part of the judgment does not address explicitly the issues of what information is likely, in practice, to be made available to the court, and how it may be used. The Court acknowledged however that, given the sensitive nature of counterterrorism sanctions, access to information at the basis of restrictive measures may be limited.[14] Hence, the EU authority need not produce all of the evidence underpinning the challenged decision, but must provide the court with enough evidence to support the restrictive measure under scrutiny.[15]

As the Court pointed out, protecting sources and methods of intelligence information 'may [moreover] preclude the disclosure of some information or some evidence to the person concerned'. While the ECJ did not elaborate on what 'techniques'[16] could be used to strike the balance between the need for sufficient information to exercise judicial review and the protection of other legitimate interests, it has, in its *Kadi II* and *ZZ* judgments,[17] suggested a basic process for evaluating the need for closed evidence, to be used both by EU Courts and the courts of the Member States in similar contexts. First, the relevant authority (EU or Member State) should offer reasons to the court as to why it cannot disclose certain information or evidence to the other party.[18] It would then be for the court to conduct an independent examination of the information available and determine if the reasons for nondisclosure are 'well founded'.[19] If the court finds the reasons unfounded, and the relevant authority maintains its refusal to disclose,

[13] Ibid, paras 119–123.
[14] Ibid, para 125.
[15] Ibid, para 122.
[16] Ibid, para 122.
[17] Case C-300/11, *ZZ*, judgment of 4 June 2013.
[18] *cf Kadi II*, n 4 above, para 126; *ZZ*, para 61.
[19] Ibid, para 126.

the court will disregard the material, and shall determine the lawfulness of the listing measure based only on material disclosed to the other party.[20] If, however, the court finds the reasons for non-disclosure well founded, it may consider the closed evidence without revealing it to the other party.[21]

In the latter situation, however, it will be necessary for the Court to strike the appropriate balance between the requirements attached to the right to effective judicial protection, in particular respect for the principle of an adversarial process, and those flowing from the security of the EU or its Member States or the conduct of their international relations.[22] Although the Court did not elaborate on what might meet this standard, it did suggest that 'a summary outlining the information's content or that of the evidence in question' might be satisfactory.[23] Ultimately, though, the Court emphasised that it is up to the courts of the EU to assess whether and to what extent disclosure of information is necessary,[24] suggesting a case-by-case analysis.

Thus, the *Kadi II* decision leaves the door open with respect to closed evidence in two important ways. First, courts can, provided certain conditions are met, consider closed evidence when evaluating the reasons underlying a particular listing. It remains to be seen, of course, whether the Union's authorities competent to adopt the restrictive measures are in possession of such evidence at all and, even if that is the case, whether they are in a position to hand it over to the Union judge. That latter aspect is likely to be particularly problematic in the context of restrictive measures resulting from prior decisions of the sanctions' committee of the United Nations, such decisions being adopted on the basis of an essentially diplomatic process. Second, once in possession of the closed evidence, the courts should decide if and to what extent disclosure is necessary to ensure that the protection of national security interest does not overly burden a party's right to an adversarial process. In *Kadi I*, the ECJ made it clear that national security concerns cannot outweigh fundamental freedoms such as the right of the defence; EU institutions must ensure that the process by which they list individuals on assets-freezing lists does not impede unjustifiably civil liberties.[25] Thus, any procedures the EU Courts adopt to handle the issue of classified or closed evidence must also respect the targeted individual, group or entity's fundamental right to make an effective defense, a right which normally includes the right to confront the evidence adduced against the accused.

It should be emphasised in that connection that any procedural changes allowing for the use by the General Court of material that is not disclosed to the principal parties will require, as a necessary first step, modification of the current Rules of Procedure of that court. In their current form, subject only to two limited exceptions (provision of documents to interveners, and verification of the confidential nature of documents for which access has been sought under Regulation 1049/2001), the Rules of Procedure include a general rule that

[20] Ibid para 127.
[21] Ibid, para 128.
[22] Ibid.
[23] Ibid, para 129.
[24] Ibid (citing *ZZ* n 17, para 67).
[25] *Kadi I* n 1 above, para 284 (citing Case C-112/00 *Schmidberger* [2003] ECR I-5659, para 73).

the General Court shall take into consideration only those documents which have been made available to the lawyers and agents of the parties and on which they have been given an opportunity of expressing their views (Article 67(3) RP).

At the time of writing, the General Court, together with the Court of Justice, is considering how this rule, reflecting a broad conception of the adversarial principle, should best be modified in order to provide for the procedural possibilities to balance legitimate security interests with the right of the targeted person, group or entity to be heard, along the lines of the *Kadi II* and *ZZ* judgments. While the precise outcome is as yet unknown, not least since the proposed changes will require approval by the Council, the upcoming changes should provide the procedural framework within which the General Court will have to operate. The remainder of this contribution is therefore focussed on how other jurisdictions, within Europe and the US, have dealt with this issue, in an attempt to inform that debate and foster effective and appropriate solutions in the EU legal order.

III. GUIDANCE FROM THE EUROPEAN COURT OF HUMAN RIGHTS

The European Court of Human Rights has ruled on numerous 'closed evidence' cases over the past seventeen years. The Court has addressed the use of closed evidence, in the context of cases involving anonymous witnesses, withholding evidence concerning confidential informants, and special advocates.[26] In *Jasper*, for example, the ECtHR expressly held that the 'entitlement to disclosure of relevant evidence is not an absolute right [for the accused]'.[27] According to the Strasbourg court, although judicial systems must always seek to uphold the defendant's rights to a fair trial, such rights must be weighed against competing interests 'such as national security or the need to protect witnesses at risk of reprisals or keep secret police methods of investigation of crime'.[28] Thus, that court held, '[i]n some cases it may be necessary to withhold certain evidence from the defence so as to preserve the fundamental rights of another individual or to safeguard an important public interest'.[29] However, any court procedures excluding the defendant from viewing certain evidence are subject to a test of proportionality, the court being

[26] See, eg, *Doorson* (use of anonymous witness and *in camera* review of witness statements that defence counsel was not allowed to cross-examine); *Rowe and Davis v United Kingdom* [GC] no 28901/95, ECHR 2000 II, para 61 (appellate UK court considered evidence from prosecution not shown to the defence, although defence was allowed to make arguments about disclosure); *Fitt v United Kingdom* [GC], no 29777/96, ECHR 2000 II, para 45 (ex parte hearing to not disclose prosecution evidence of statements from witness that could reveal confidential sources); *V v Finland* no. 40412/98, 24 April 2007, para 75 (police sought to withhold information about the monitoring of defendant's mobile phone). See also *Van Mechelen and Others v the Netherlands*, judgment of 23 April 1997, Reports 1997-III; *S.N v Sweden*, no. 34209/96, § 47, ECHR 2002-V; *Botmeh and Alami v United Kingdom*, no. 15187/03, judgment of 7 June 2007, § 37; *Edwards and Lewis v United Kingdom* [GC], nos. 39647/98 and 40461/98, §§ 46–48, ECHR 2004; *Chahal v United Kingdom* [GC], judgment of 15 November 1996, Reports of Judgments and Decisions 1996-V), paras 130, 131, 144.

[27] *Jasper v United Kingdom*, [GC], no. 27052/95 (2000), para 52.

[28] Ibid.

[29] Ibid, para 52.

required to counterbalance the adopted procedures with any difficulties caused to the defence.[30] The ECtHR has repeatedly used this 'counterbalancing' test as the yardstick by which it measures the legality of evidence exclusion procedures adopted by national courts.[31]

Most recently, the Strasbourg court has applied this test in the context of the UK's 'special advocate' system to handle classified evidence in certain terrorism cases. Under the special advocate system, UK courts appoint counsel to represent the interests of a party against the State when all or part of the evidence against him cannot be disclosed for national security reasons. Special advocates must be pre-cleared to view classified information. They may communicate with the party they represent any time before viewing the classified material but not afterwards. Upon review, the Strasbourg court held that the special advocate 'could perform an important role in counterbalancing the lack of full disclosure and the lack of a full, open, adversarial hearing'.[32] The sufficiency of the special advocate's system of protection of the rights of the defence must be assessed on a case-by-case basis.[33] The court has suggested in that regard that, even in cases in which the majority of the evidence is unavailable for the accused, 'sufficiently specific' allegations in the open material can nonetheless safeguard his defence rights if they enable him and his representatives to provide the special advocate with information to refute those specific allegations.[34] The court mentioned in this connection the Canadian evidence system where the party is provided with a detailed summary of the case against him,[35] suggesting that a summary of classified evidence, subject to a test of proportionality, can possibly meet the requirement of an effective remedy in Article 13 ECHR.

It results equally from the ECtHR's case-law, however, that at least in the criminal setting, a conviction cannot be based 'solely or to a decisive extent' on closed evidence[36] and that access to material of a nature 'vital' to the outcome of the proceeding should be granted in principle.[37]

Based on these assumptions, Advocate General Sharpston concluded, in her opinion in the *PMOI II* case, that procedures allowing the General Court to review closed evidence are 'essential'.[38] Building upon the reasoning in *A. and Others v United Kingdom*, AG Sharpston described as follows the 'irreducible minimum requirement':

> [I]n order for the requirements of the Convention to be satisfied, it is necessary that as much information about the allegations and evidence against each applicant be disclosed as is possible without compromising national security or the safety of others, that the party concerned be provided with sufficient information about the allegations

[30] Ibid.

[31] See eg *Doorson*, n 26 above, para 72: *A and Others v United Kingdom* [GC], no 3455/05, para 205; *Chahal* n 26 above, para 130.

[32] *A. and Others*, n 31, para 220.

[33] Ibid.

[34] Ibid, para 220.

[35] Ibid, para 210.

[36] *Doorson*, n 26 above, para 76.

[37] *See McMichael v United Kingdom*, paras 78–82.

[38] Opinion of AG Sharpston, *PMOI II*, n 6 above, para 239.

against him to enable him to give effective instructions to the special advocate and that any difficulties caused to the defendant by a limitation on his rights [be] sufficiently counterbalanced by the procedures followed by the judicial authorities.[39]

Although arising in a different context, the ECJ's case-law on restrictive measures examined above already mirrors the ECtHR's analysis in closed evidence cases. For instance, the Court in *Kadi II* acknowledged that national security concerns might prevent the full disclosure of evidence to a party or his/her representatives.[40] The *Kadi II* judgment also calls for a balancing of the defendant's fair trial rights with the legitimate security interests of Member State governments in keeping certain information confidential, echoing the 'counterbalancing' test applied by the ECtHR. Finally, both courts seem to suggest that a sufficiently specific summary of allegations against the defendant may appropriately strike this balance.[41]

IV. COMPARISONS TO UNITED STATES PROCEDURES

Challenges to terrorism listings in the United States fall under two distinct statutory regimes. The International Emergency Economic Powers Act (IEEPA) and Executive Order 13,224 provide for the listing of individuals as 'specially designated global terrorists', the listing regime being managed by the Department of Treasury. The Anti-Terrorism and Effective Death Penalty Act of 1996 (AEDPA) allows the Secretary of State to designate groups or entities as 'foreign terrorist organisations'. Although the designation process is different under the two statutes, both regimes are subject to the same confidential evidence procedures and a similar standard of judicial review before US federal courts.[42] Finally, it may be instructive to look at the use of secret evidence in criminal cases in the United States.

A. The International Emergency Economic Powers Act and Executive Order 13,224

The IEEPA authorises the President of the United States 'to declare a national emergency when an extraordinary threat to the United States arises that originates in substantial part in a foreign state' and 'block property subject to US jurisdiction'.[43] The President is authorised to:

[I]nvestigate, block during the pendency of an investigation, regulate, direct and compel, nullify, void, prevent or prohibit, any acquisition, holding, withholding, use, transfer, withdrawal, transportation, importation or exportation of, or dealing in, or exercising

[39] Ibid, at para 245 (internal quotations omitted).
[40] Ibid, para 125.
[41] Ibid, para 129.
[42] See, eg, *Kadi v Geithner*, No. 09-0108 (D.D.C. 19 March 2012); *People's Mojahedin Org. of Iran v Dep't of State*, 327 F3d 1238 (DC Cir 2003).
[43] 50 USC § 1701 *et seq*.

> any right, power, or privilege with respect to, or transactions involving, any property in which any foreign country or a national thereof has any interest by any person, or with respect to any property, subject to the jurisdiction of the United States [...].[44]

After the events of September 11, 2001, the President issued Executive Order 13,224[45] on the basis of his authority under the IEEPA and the United Nations Participation Act.[46] The Executive Order declared a national emergency with respect to 'grave acts of terrorism and threats of terrorism' on September 11 and the 'continuing and immediate threat of further attacks on United States nationals or the United States'. Executive Order 13,224 ordered the blocking of property of twenty-seven specifically designated terrorists and terrorist organisations[47] and authorised the Secretary of the Treasury to designate additional persons whose property or interests in property should be blocked, where the Secretary finds that such persons 'act for or on behalf of' or are 'owned or controlled by' designated terrorists, or 'assist in, sponsor, or provide [...] support for' or are 'otherwise associated with them'.[48] The Treasury Secretary has delegated his powers under EO 13,224 to the Office of Foreign Asset Control (OFAC) within the Department of Treasury.[49] OFAC, supported by various intelligence bodies in the United States, investigates suspected persons and adopts an administrative decision based on a classified and unclassified administrative record. Persons designated pursuant to the Executive Order are referred to as 'specially designated global terrorists' (SDGT).[50]

The IEEPA does not expressly allow for judicial review. However, considering that designation decisions are taken by an executive agency of the US federal government, individuals can challenge such designation pursuant to the Administrative Procedures Act (APA).[51] Federal courts consistently apply the APA standard of judicial review to OFAC designations so long as the designation is considered final.[52] The APA requires that the Court 'hold unlawful and set aside agency action, findings, and conclusions' that are 'arbitrary, capricious, an abuse of discretion, or otherwise not in accordance with law'.[53] The scope of review under the 'arbitrary and capricious' standard is intentionally narrow: a court is 'not to substitute its judgment for that of the agency'.[54] The agency's decisions are entitled to a 'presumption of regularity',[55] and although 'inquiry

[44] 50 USC § 1702(a)(1)(B).

[45] 66 Fed Reg 49,079 (23 September 2001) (hereinafter 'EO 13,224').

[46] See 22 USC § 287c.

[47] See EO 13,224 § 3.

[48] Ibid, §§ 1(c)–(d).

[49] 31 CFR § 594.802.

[50] See 31 CFR § 594.310.

[51] See 5 USC § 702: '[a] person suffering legal wrong because of agency action, or adversely affected or aggrieved by agency action within the meaning of a relevant statute, is entitled to judicial review thereof'. This applies so long as the agency determination is considered "final" and there is no other adequate remedy in a court' (at § 704).

[52] See, eg, *Kadi v Geithner*, n 42 at page 8; *Holy Land Found for Relief & Dev v Ashcroft*, 333 F3d 156, 162 (DC Cir 2003).

[53] 5 USC § 706(2)(A).

[54] *Motor Vehicle Mfrs. Assn of US, Inc v State Farm Mut Auto Ins Co*, 463 US 29, 43 (1983).

[55] *Citizens to Preserve Overton Park, Inc v Volpe*, 401 US 402, 415 (1971).

into the facts is to be searching and careful, the ultimate standard of review is a narrow one'.[56] This means that the federal district court must be satisfied that the agency has 'examine[d] the relevant data and articulate[d] a satisfactory explanation for its action including a rational connection between the facts found and the choice made'.[57] The district court, then, 'must consider whether the decision was based on a consideration of the relevant factors and whether there has been a clear error of judgment'[58]

Although courts grant substantial deference to OFAC decisions according to the APA, this does not render them immune from challenge. At least two federal courts have held that OFAC violated procedural due process rights in designating individuals or groups as SDGTs.[59] For example, in the *Al Haramain Islamic Foundation (AHIF)* case, the Ninth Circuit Court of Appeals held that OFAC violated an Oregon-based Islamic education corporation's due process rights by failing to provide it with an adequate statement of reasons for its investigation. Mirroring EU principles of fair hearing and the rights of the defence, due process requires notice 'reasonably calculated, under all the circumstances, to apprise interested parties of the pendency of the action and afford them an opportunity to present their objections'.[60] AHIF did not challenge the lack of pre-decision notice, which has been repeatedly upheld by US courts, but rather the lack of adequate notice and reasons in a four-year period after the initial assets-freezing in 2004.[61] In four years, OFAC had never directly notified the corporation any reasons for its listing and only ever came close with one press statement about the listing. The court held that this notice was both 'untimely and incomplete' because it came seven months too late and only contained one, unexplained reason for the listing.

Similarly, in *KindHearts*, the District Court for the Northern District of Ohio faced a parallel fact pattern and also found a violation of due process for failure to provide adequate notice and opportunity to be heard to the organisation concerned. In that case, OFAC blocked that entity's assets but gave no statement of reasons until thirty-four months after the block was imposed pending investigation, and approximately eighteen months after its provisional determination to designate.[62] According to that court, '[c]onstitutionally sufficient notice should give the party an understanding of the allegations against it so that it has the opportunity to make a meaningful response,'[63] and OFAC's failure to provide any reasons at all clearly failed to meet this standard.[64]

[56] Ibid, at 416.

[57] *Alpharma, Inc v Leavitt*, 460 F3d 1, 6 (DC Cir 2006).

[58] *Citizens to Preserve Overton Park*, 401 US at 416.

[59] See *Al Haramain Islamic Found., Inc v US Dep't of Treasury*, 686 F3d 965, 985 (9th Cir 2012) (concluding that OFAC violated an SDGT's due process rights by failing to provide sufficient notice of reasons behind designation); *KindHearts for Charitable Humanitarian Dev, Inc v Geithner*, 647 F. Supp. 2d 857, 897 (ND. Ohio 2009) (finding that OFAC's asset blocking denied an SDGT its due process rights to notice and an opportunity to be heard).

[60] *United Student Aid Funds, Inc v Espinosa*, 559 US 260 (2010).

[61] *Al Haramain Islamic Found, Inc v US Dep't of Treasury*, n 59 above.

[62] *KindHearts for Charitable Humanitarian Dev, Inc v Geithner*, n 59 above, at 903.

[63] Ibid, at 901.

[64] Ibid, at 904–08.

B. The Anti-Terrorism and Effective Death Penalty Act

The AEDPA empowers the Secretary of State to designate an entity as a 'foreign terrorist organisation' (FTO).[65] This designation allows the Treasury Department to freeze any funds the organisation has on deposit with any financial institution in the United States,[66] to exclude representatives of the organisation from entering the United States,[67] and to impose criminal penalties on anyone who 'knowingly provides material support or resources' to such organisations.[68]

If the Secretary of State decides to designate a group under AEDPA, he must report his intention to the Speaker and Minority Leader of the House of Representatives, the Senate President *pro tempore*, the Majority and Minority Leaders of the Senate, and members of certain congressional committees, each via a classified statement.[69] The State Department must also create an administrative record of the reasons supporting the designation, which can include both classified and unclassified information.[70] The government need not disclose the classified information to the FTO but must disclose the information to a court upon judicial review.[71] Once the Secretary of State notifies Congress of the designation, OFAC can freeze all of that group's assets held or controlled by a US financial institution.[72] Designation as an FTO lasts indefinitely and can only be revoked by an Act of Congress or by the Secretary of State.[73]

A designated FTO may seek judicial review of the Secretary of State's action in the D.C. Circuit no later than thirty days after publication of its designation or the response to a revocation petition.[74] Upon judicial review, the Court of Appeals for the D.C. Circuit examines only the administrative record created during the designation process.[75] Unlike the IEEPA, the AEDPA contains an explicit provision on the standard of judicial review to be used by federal district courts in reviewing the State Department's designation decision The AEDPA empowers courts to 'hold unlawful or set aside' any decision if it was 'arbitrary, capricious, an abuse of discretion, or otherwise not in accordance with law', 'contrary to [a] constitutional right,' 'in excess of statutory jurisdiction, authority, or limitation,' or 'lacking substantial support in the administrative record'.[76] Thus, the standard of review under the AEDPA mirrors the 'arbitrary and capricious' standard applied by courts in IEEPA cases. Courts also apply the same level of deference to the executive's fact-finding as in APA cases,[77] and

[65] 8 USC § 1189 (2000)
[66] 18 USC § 2339B(a)(2) (2000).
[67] 8 USC § 1182(a)(3)(B)(i)(IV) & (V) (2000).
[68] 18 USC § 2339B(a)(1).
[69] Ibid, § 1189(a)(2)(A)(i).
[70] 8 USC § 1189(a)(3)(A)–(B).
[71] Ibid, § 1189(a)(3)(B).
[72] Ibid, § 1189(a)(2)(C).
[73] Ibid, § 1189(a)(4)(A)
[74] Ibid, § 1189(c)(1).
[75] Ibid, § 1189(c)(2).
[76] Ibid, § 1189(c)(3)(A)–(D).
[77] See, eg, *Nat'l Council of Resistance of Iran v Dep't of State*, 251 F3d 192, 209 (DC Cir 2001); *People's Mojahedin Org. of Iran v Dep't of State*, n 42 above.

will uphold FTO designations so long as there is 'substantial support [for it] in the administrative record'.[78]

Such judicial deference is once again not unlimited, however. For example, the Court of Appeals for the D.C. Circuit recently held that the State Department violated the procedural due process rights of the People's Mojahedin Organisation of Iran (PMOI) when it did not provide the group with sufficient notice of the reasons behind its designation as an FTO.[79] In FTO cases, the Secretary of State is required to notify a listed entity 'of the unclassified material upon which [s]he propose[d] to rely' and to allow the alleged FTO 'to present, at least in written form, such evidence as [it] may be able to produce to rebut the administrative record or otherwise negate the proposition that' it is an FTO.[80] In the PMOI case, PMOI had already been designated an FTO and the Department of State sought to re-designate them as such; however, PMOI was only notified after its re-designation and although it was allowed to submit its own evidence supporting delisting, it was not given the opportunity to rebut unclassified portions of the Department of State record.[81] The Court of Appeals for the D.C. Circuit held that this violated PMOI's due process rights under the Fifth Amendment because it was entitled to notice and comment procedures *before* re-designation.[82]

C. Secret Evidence in Terrorist Designation Cases

In both IEEPA and AEDPA cases, the designated person or entity is entitled to view the *unclassified* administrative record against them but not *classified* portions therein. Both statutes provide that classified information is not subject to discovery but is subject to disclosure in *ex parte* and *in camera* review.[83] Thus, US law establishes a system whereby the judge, in determining whether the entire agency record is 'arbitrary or capricious', may review both classified and unclassified information without revealing classified information to the plaintiff.

This system necessarily places the plaintiff at a disadvantage.[84] However, US courts have balanced the plaintiff's interest in confronting the evidence adduced against him with national security interests of the executive branch.[85]

[78] 8 USC § 1189(c)(3).

[79] *People's Mojahedin Org of Iran v US Dep't of State*, 613 F3d 220, 227 (DC Cir 2010) (per curiam).

[80] Ibid (citing *NCRI I*, 251 F3d at 209).

[81] Ibid, n 79 above.

[82] Ibid, at 228.

[83] 8 USC § 1189(a)(3)(B) ('[c]lassified information shall not be subject to disclosure for such time as it remains classified, except that such information may be disclosed to a court *ex parte* and *in camera* for purposes of judicial review . . .'); 50 USC § 1702(c) ('if the determination was based on classified information . . . such information may be submitted to the reviewing court *ex parte* and *in camera*.').

[84] *See Kadi v Geithner* n 42 above, at page 34 ('[t]he Court fully acknowledges and is sympathetic to Kadi's argument that he is at somewhat of a disadvantage in being unable to review the whole administrative record, in particular the classified record.'); *see also Islamic Am Relief Agency v Unidentified FBI Agents*, 394 F Supp 2d 34, 45 (D.D.C. 2005).

[85] *See Nat'l Council of Resistance of Iran*, n 77, 208; *Holy Land Found for Relief & Dev v Ashcroft*, n 52, 162.

The President and executive branch have primacy 'in controlling and exercising responsibility over access to classified information,'[86] and courts have been unwilling to disturb this balance of power by allowing uncleared plaintiffs access to classified information. What is more, federal courts have consistently held that the IEEPA and AEDPA's use of *ex parte* and *in camera* review does not violate plaintiff's due process rights.[87] According to US courts, due process requires 'the disclosure of *only* the unclassified portions of the administrative record'.[88] Courts have arrived at this finding because, according to the Supreme Court, the due process clause of the US Constitution 'requires only that process which is due under the circumstances of the case'.[89] Given that challenges to SDGT and FTO designations inherently involve sensitive national security or foreign policy information, federal courts have held that the process due to plaintiffs challenging their designation does not include the right to access classified information contained in the administrative record.[90]

A recent example of a US court's review of both classified and unclassified information is the March 2012 decision of the US District Court for the District of Columbia in *Kadi v Geithner*. Sheikh Yassin Abdullah Kadi, the same man who has successfully challenged his inclusion on terrorism lists before the UN and the ECJ, challenged his designation as an SDGT pursuant to the IEEPA. Mr Kadi challenged the evidentiary basis for his designation as violating the APA and also challenged the OFAC designation process as violating various provisions of the US Constitution.[91] In examining Mr Kadi's claim that OFAC's decision to list him as an SDGT was 'arbitrary or capricious,' the district court reviewed 2800-pages of classified and unclassified material in the administrative record, 'extensive submissions Kadi made to OFAC during the reconsideration process,' and arguments Mr Kadi made before the court.[92] Mr Kadi challenged OFAC's use of confidential information to support his designation, but the district court dismissed this claim in a preliminary order of 30 March 2010 denying Mr Kadi's motion to preclude the government's reliance on such evidence.[93] In its March 2012 decision dismissing all of Mr Kadi's claims, the court also reiterated that its consideration of classified evidence did not violate the plaintiff's due process rights.[94]

[86] *Holy Land Found*, n 52, 162 (citing *Nat'l Council of Resistance of Iran*, n 77, at 208).

[87] *Kadi v Geithner* n 42 above, at pages 34–35; *Holy Land Found*, n 52 above, 164; *People's Mojahedin Org. of Iran v Dep't of State*, n 42, 1242; *Nat'l Council of Resistance of Iran*, n 77, 208–09 (holding that the 'opportunity to be heard at a meaningful time and in a meaningful manner' does not include access to the classified record).

[88] *People's Mojahedin Org of Iran v Dep't of State*, n 42, 1242 (emphasis original); *see also Kadi v Geithner* n 42 above, at page 35.

[89] *People's Mojahedin Org of Iran v Dep't of State*, n 42, 1242 (D.C.Cir.2003) (citing *Morrissey v Brewer*, 408 US 471, 481 (1972)).

[90] *Holy Land Found*, n 52, 164.

[91] See *Kadi v Geithner,* n 42 above (asserting violations of the Fifth Amendment Due Process and Takings clauses; First Amendment freedoms of speech and association; Fourth Amendment prohibition on unlawful search and seizure; Article I Sec 9 prohibition on bills of attainder; and a general Constitutional claim against the IEEPA as overly broad and vague).

[92] Ibid, at page 12.

[93] *Kadi v Geithner* n 42 above, at page 14.

[94] Ibid, at pages 34–35.

The district court also distinguished between the classified and unclassified information under review. It first analysed evidence in the voluminous unclassified record and concluded that the unclassified portions 'taken as a whole' 'confirm Kadi's close involvement [...] in the financing of terrorist activities'.[95] The court then stated that the classified information *corroborated* information in the unclassified record: 'although the Court cannot cite to any specific information in the classified record, the Court's careful review confirms that there is substantial evidence in the record before OFAC that Kadi was involved, through Muwafaq, in providing financial support for terrorists'.[96] Thus, the US court did not rely solely on classified evidence and instead primarily relied on unclassified information that was substantiated by the classified record.

D. Secret Evidence in US Criminal Cases

(i) Admissibility Procedure under CIPA

Although US counterterrorism statutes expressly permit courts to review classified information *ex parte* and *in camera*, it is important to note that the United States has also established a system enabling courts to consider classified information in criminal proceedings. The Classified Information Procedures Act (CIPA) provides criminal procedures permitting a trial judge to rule on the relevance or admissibility of classified information in a secure setting. Congress enacted CIPA in 1980 in response to the growing problem of 'graymail,' in which criminal defendants threatened to disclose classified information throughout trial proceedings in an effort to force the government to drop charges against them.[97] CIPA was intended to balance competing, legitimate interests: the government's interest in protecting sensitive and classified information that could compromise national security, and the defendant's interest in obtaining and using exculpatory evidence.[98] Although originally intended to allow criminal defendants to use classified information in their case-in-chief, courts have extended CIPA to allow the government to submit substitutions for its own evidence. CIPA thus authorises the court to permit the government to propose redactions to classified information or admit summaries of classified information. In the case of terrorism prosecutions, courts will typically issue 'protective orders' preventing disclosure to the defendant and the public.[99] The court may permit such procedures if the

[95] *Kadi v Geithner* n 42 above, at page 24. This section only analysed Mr Kadi's involvement in the Muwafaq organisation The Court conducted a similar analysis over 11 pages regarding his involvement with Wa'el Julaidan, Chariq Ayadi, Muhammad Salah, Osama bin Laden, and other SDGTs: ibid, at pages 23–33.

[96] Ibid, page 24; see also ibid page 34: ('the information relied on by OFAC that Kadi attacks as unsubstantiated is further supported by the classified record, which confirms Kadi's financial transactions and relationships with SDGTs.').

[97] See *United States v Rezaq*, 134 F3d 1121, 1142 (DC Cir 1998).

[98] Ibid.

[99] See 18 USC app. 3, §3.

government submits a written statement explaining why the defendant is not entitled to the redacted information. The court may review this evidence *ex parte* and *in camera*.[100]

There are three basic steps the parties and courts follow under CIPA. First, if either side intends to disclose sensitive or classified information in its case, it must provide the court and other party with pre-trial written notice.[101] The notice must 'include a brief description of the classified information'[102] and 'must be *particularised*, setting forth *specifically* the classified information which the defendant reasonably believes to be necessary to his defence'.[103] Second, the government may then petition the court for a hearing 'to make all determinations concerning the use, relevance, or admissibility of classified information that would otherwise be made during the trial or pre-trial proceedings' known as a 'Section 6(a) hearing'.[104] The court conducts this determination *in camera* and *ex parte* upon submission of an affidavit from the Attorney General stating that disclosure of such national security information would damage the United States' national security. At the section 6(a) hearing, the court is to hear the arguments of both sides and then rule whether the classified information identified by the defence is relevant under the Federal Rules of Evidence.[105] However, the court's inquiry does not end there because the court must also determine whether the information is not just relevant but also *admissible*. The Court therefore must also determine whether the evidence is not 'cumulative, prejudicial, confusing, or misleading',[106] such that it should be excluded under the rules of evidence. At the conclusion of the section 6 (a) hearing, the court must state in writing the reasons for its determination as to each item of classified information.[107]

Finally, if the court rules any classified information to be admissible, section 6(c) of CIPA permits the government to propose unclassified substitutes for that information. The court determines whether the government's substitution proposal should be permitted based on whether the 'statement or summary will provide the defendant with substantially the same ability to make his defence as would disclosure of the specific classified information.'[108] Consequently, there is a basic fairness test applied to every substitution proposal under CIPA. CIPA explicitly approves redactions, stipulations, and substitutions. Entire classified documents may be admitted into evidence in redacted form.[109] Substitutions

[100] Ibid, §4.

[101] Ibid, § 5(a).

[102] Ibid.

[103] *United States v Collins*, 720 F2d 1195, 1199 (11th Cir 1983) (emphasis added). See also *United States v Smith*, 780 F.2d 1102, 1105 (4th Cir 1985) (*en banc*). It is noteworthy that if the notice is not specific enough, not given in enough time before trial, or the defendant attempts to admit evidence not mentioned in the initial notice, the evidence can be excluded: see 18 USC app 3, § (b); *United States v Badia*, 827 F2d 1458, 1465 (11th Cir. 1987); *United States v Smith*, ibid, 1105; ('[a] defendant is forbidden from disclosing any such information absent the giving of notice').

[104] 18 USC app 3, § 6(a).

[105] See Fed R Evid 401.

[106] *United States v Wilson*, 750 F2d, 9.

[107] 18 USC app. 3, § 6(a).

[108] Ibid, § 6(c).

[109] See *United States v Passaro*, 577 F3d 207, 220 (4th Cir 2009).

and stipulations may be admitted to the jury when both parties agree to it or when the court determines that neither party can contradict the substitution.[110] There is no firm consensus on whether CIPA authorises only substitutions, stipulations, and redactions, and consequently courts have been creative in approving prosecutors' proposals.[111]

Regardless of their form, procedures under CIPA must also be constitutional and cannot infringe on the defendant's Fifth Amendment and Fourteenth Amendment rights to confront the evidence against him. In one specific terrorism case, the D.C. circuit court ruled that Guantanamo Bay detainees have a right to access secret evidence where that evidence is both relevant and material to their claims.[112] It is for the court to assess the evidence against these criteria and determine whether any classified information is 'actually inculpatory'.[113] The court did, however, add that alternatives to full disclosure such as substitution or redaction could preserve the classified information while simultaneously offering sufficient constitutional guarantees to the claimants.[114]

(ii) Securing Classified Information under CIPA

In addition to the foregoing provisions, CIPA addresses the practical need to protect classified information in the possession of courts during criminal proceedings. Pursuant to CIPA § 9, Supreme Court Chief Justice Burger issued procedural rules intended to safeguard classified information against disclosure.[115] Those rules require:

- the appointment of a 'Court Security Officer' to supervise security measures in any criminal case or appeal therefrom involving classified information;
- the identification of secure quarters within the courthouse where proceedings involving classified information will take place;
- security clearances for court personnel with access to classified information; clearances can only be given to personnel for whom access to the information is 'necessary for the performance of an official function';
- specific procedures for the storage, custody and transmittal of classified information within the court;

[110] See *United States v Salah*, 462 F Supp 2d 915, 917–24 (ND Ill 2006) (allowing substitutions to be read to the jury that neither party could contradict); *United States v Marzook*, 435 F Supp 2d 708, 749 (ND Ill 2006) (approving such stipulations).

[111] See, eg, *United States v North*, 713 F Supp 1442 (DDC 1989) (combining multiple unclassified documents to hide their classification levels); *United States v Marzook*, 412 F Supp 2d 913, 923–28 (ND Ill 2006) (allowing intelligence agents to testify from a separate courtroom via a live video feed and using pseudonyms); *United States v Zettl*, 835 F.2d 1059, 1063 (4th Cir 1987) (witness and jury were allowed to see the full classified document and the witness could refer to it in 'codes' such that the jury could follow along); *United States v Rosen*, 487 F Supp 2d 703 (ED Va 2007) (witness and jury allowed to see classified document, but defendant and public only saw substitutions and redactions).

[112] *Al Odah v United States*, 559 F3d 539 (DC Cir 2009).

[113] Ibid at 545.

[114] *Al Odah v United States*, n 112 above, 546.

[115] See Security Procedures Established Pursuant to Pub L 96-456, 94 Stat 2025, by the Chief Justice of the United States for the Protection of Classified Information, at paras 1–15, reprinted following 18 USCA app 3, § 9.

- the creation of operating procedures for handling classified information; and
- the establishment of procedures for disposal of classified information.[116]

Importantly, '[a] security clearance for justices and judges is *not required*,' but the judge may ask to be cleared. The rules do not require background checks of jurors but instruct the trial judge to 'consider a government request for a cautionary instruction [...] regarding the release or disclosure of classified information'.[117]

(iii) Cleared Counsel under CIPA

In addition, the rules authorise the government to investigate 'the trustworthiness of persons associated with the defence'.[118] In terrorism cases, courts have required that the disclosure of classified information be limited to defence counsel who have passed a formal security clearance and have prohibited defence counsel from disclosing the information to the defendant.[119] In effect, these protective orders allow cleared counsel to review classified discovery materials, while blocking the defendant from seeing the materials and possibly passing sensitive information on to confederates. CIPA does not specifically authorise the cleared-counsel process and 'counsel's eyes-only' protective orders. Nonetheless, courts have inherent power to structure the discovery process,[120] and it is widely recognised that 'CIPA vests district courts with wide latitude'[121] to restrict the defendant's access to classified discovery materials in terrorism cases, in effect supplementing CIPA. In this way, CIPA protective orders essentially operate in a broadly similar, though not identical, way to special advocates in the U.K. — a cleared representative can argue on behalf of the defendant at evidentiary hearings but cannot disclose confidential information to the defendant or his counsel.

The case of *Abu Ali* before the US Court of Appeals of the Fourth Circuit is an example of how the cleared counsel process works. In that case, the US government brought nine criminal charges against Ahmed Omar Abu Ali, a dual American and Saudi citizen, related to his affiliation with al-Qaeda in Saudi Arabia and attempt to carry out terrorist attacks in the United States. At the federal trial court level, the government sought to admit classified evidence in its case-in-chief.[122] The government filed a CIPA section 4 motion seeking to protect two classified documents and two 'secret witnesses'. Upon a request by the US Attorney General, the district court then held an *in camera* review

[116] Ibid, paras 2–4, 7–11.

[117] Securitiy Procedures, n 115 above, para 6.

[118] Ibid, para 5.

[119] See, eg, *United States v Moussaoui*, No 01-cr-00455, 2002 WL 1987964, at page 1 (ED Va 29 August 2002); *United States v Bin Laden*, No 98-cr-01023, 2001 WL 66393 (*Bin Laden II*), at page 2 (SDNY 25 January 2001); *United States v Bin Laden*, 58 F Supp 2d 113, 116–17 (SDNY 1999).

[120] See Fed R Crim P 16(d)(1): ('At any time the court may, for good cause, deny, restrict, or defer discovery or inspection, or grant other appropriate relief').

[121] *United States v Abu Ali*, 528 F3d 210, 247 (4th Cir 2008).

[122] This is therefore an example of a reverse-CIPA case in which the government rather than the accused seeks to use classified evidence in its case.

of the classified information and made a formal finding that release of the information would harm US national security. Because neither Abu Ali nor his counsel was granted a security clearance, the court appointed an attorney to act as 'CIPA-cleared counsel' for Abu Ali.[123] Although Abu Ali and his counsel were not present during the *in camera* CIPA hearing, his CIPA-cleared counsel made substantive arguments about the evidence on Abu Ali's behalf and 'conducted a thorough and unrestricted cross-examination' of the two 'silent witnesses'.[124] The cleared counsel was able to confer with and take instructions from Abu Ali and his other counsel but not allowed to reveal to them any classified information. Moreover, the court considered objections from Abu Ali's uncleared counsel about the constitutionality of their and their client's exclusion from the proceeding.[125] The court overruled the motion and admitted the evidence at trial. The jury was allowed to see a full unredacted version of the documents and deposition while Abu Ali and his uncleared counsel were only privy to slightly redacted versions.[126]

On appeal, Abu Ali argued that the CIPA procedure applied by the District Court violated his Sixth Amendment rights under the Confrontation Clause.[127] The appellate court rejected most of Abu Ali's constitutional claims and upheld the 'cleared counsel' procedure through a similar analysis as in the *Kadi II* judgment of the ECJ. First, the court applied a balancing test to determine whether and to what extent the defendant should have access to classified information. While the court can consider the government's compelling interest in national security, 'this interest cannot override the defendant's right to a fair trial'.[128] Mirroring the balancing test applied by the ECJ in *Kadi II*, US trial courts are 'required to balance the public interest in nondisclosure against the defendant's right to prepare a defence', '[a] decision on disclosure of such information [being] depend[ent] on the particular circumstances of each case, taking into consideration the crime charged, the possible defences, the possible significance of the [evidence,] and other relevant factors'.[129] Second, the court explained that the Supreme Court has held that in order for court procedures to comply with the Fifth and Sixth Amendments, courts must conduct a two-step investigation. In a first step, the district court must conduct an independent assessment of the information to be withheld from the defendant. If that information is 'relevant and material to the defence,' then the information *must* be admitted and disclosed to the defendant.[130] If the government cannot propose adequate substitutions or redactions to preserve the defendant's rights, 'the

[123] *Abu Ali*, n 121 above, 249.

[124] Ibid, at 251.

[125] Ibid, at 251–52.

[126] Ibid 252.

[127] The Confrontation Clause of the Sixth Amendment to the United States Constitution provides that 'in all criminal prosecutions, the accused shall enjoy the right…to be confronted with the witnesses against him'.

[128] *Abu Ali*, n 121 above, 248. *Fernandez*, 913 F2d at 154; *United States v Moussaoui*, 382 F3d 453, 466 n18 (4th Cir 2004).

[129] *Smith*, n 103 above, 1107.

[130] *Moussaoui*, n 128 above, 476; *Smith* n 103 above, 1110.

government must decide whether it will [continue to] prohibit the disclosure of the classified information; if it does so, the district court must impose a sanction, which is presumptively dismissal of the indictment'.[131] The result is to produce, at least in US criminal proceedings, a situation which is broadly similar to that envisaged by the ECJ in paragraph 127 of its judgment in *Kadi II*.

Most importantly, the court in *Abu Ali* expressly ruled that the CIPA cleared counsel procedure strikes an 'appropriate balance' between the government's national security interest and the defendant's right to a fair trial without infringing any constitutional rights.[132] Indeed, '[a] defendant and his counsel, if lacking the requisite security clearance, *must* be excluded from hearings that determine what classified information is material and whether substitutions crafted by the government suffice to provide the defendant adequate means of presenting a defence and obtaining a fair trial'.[133] The court found that although Abu Ali and his uncleared counsel were excluded from the *in camera* review of classified information and his cleared counsel was not allowed to relate any classified information to Abu Ali, the cleared counsel's ability to make motions and cross-examine witnesses was an adequate safeguard for Abu Ali's constitutional rights.

In a similar case, the District Court for the Eastern District of Virginia found that appointing a cleared counsel, even against the will of a defendant, offered sufficient constitutional guarantees.[134] In that case, Mr Moussaoui represented himself (*pro se*) against criminal charges of terrorism and conspiracy. However, Mr Moussaoui was denied a security clearance and was thus ineligible under CIPA to review classified evidence against him. The court specially appointed a 'standby counsel' who represented Mr Moussaoui's interests during *in camera* review of classified information. The court expressly held that this procedure did not violate Mr Moussaoui's Fifth and Sixth Amendment rights to make an effective defence.

Similarly, in the *Bin Laden* case, the District Court for the Southern District of New York ruled that using CIPA-cleared counsel in *in camera* proceedings while precluding the defendant and his ordinary counsel to see classified evidence did not violate the (1) right to counsel; (2) the right to confront witness and evidence; (3) the right to be present at critical proceedings; (4) the right to assist in the preparation and presentation of his defence; and (5) the due process right to present an effective defence.[135] Although a defendant is usually 'permitted to review items which have been produced in discovery,' that right, held the Court, is not absolute and must be balanced against the government's national security interests.[136] The court applied a balancing test similar to that reflected in *Kadi II*: 'the Court will, in determining the relevance and materiality of classified information, bear in mind that defence counsel have not been able to consult

[131] *Abu Ali*, n 121, 248; *Smith*, n 103 above, 1110.

[132] Ibid, n 121, 254.

[133] Ibid.

[134] *United States v Moussaoui*, n 119, para 1.

[135] *Bin Laden II*, n 119 above, *aff'd sub nom. In re Terrorist Bombings of US Embassies in E Africa*, 552 F3d 93 (2d Cir. 2008).

[136] Ibid, at page 4.

with the Defendant to the extent they would have preferred'.[137] The court expressly held that CIPA-cleared counsel strikes this balance appropriately and does not violate any of the defendant's constitutional rights.[138] Moreover, the court importantly stated, 'the Defendant's exclusion from the [CIPA] hearing [...] is not unconstitutional'.[139]

However, there is one primary constitutional limit US courts apply to the use of classified evidence: confidential evidence to which the defendant does not have access cannot be the sole basis for conviction.[140] CIPA was designed to allow cleared parties and the court to review classified evidence *in camera* before trial in order to determine how or if the evidence should be admissible at trial. Thus, '[a] defendant's right to see the evidence that is tendered against him *during* trial [...] does not necessarily equate to a right to have classified information disclosed to him *prior* to trial'.[141] Against that background, it is a violation of the defendant's rights to a fair trial, to confront the evidence against him, and to make a proper defence if the jury is privy to the classified information but the defendant is not.[142] Thus, in *Abu Ali*, the Fourth Circuit Court of Appeals held that although the CIPA-cleared counsel procedure *before trial* was constitutional, the jury's access to confidential information *at trial* was unconstitutional.[143] The circuit court reasoned as follows:

> If classified information is to be relied upon as evidence of guilt, the district court may consider steps to protect some or all of the information from unnecessary public disclosure in the interest of national security and in accordance with CIPA, which specifically contemplates such methods as redactions and substitutions so long as these alternatives do not deprive the defendant of a fair trial. However, the government must at a minimum provide the same version of the evidence to the defendant that is submitted to the jury. We do not balance a criminal defendant's right to see the evidence which will be used to convict him against the government's interest in protecting that evidence from public disclosure. If the government does not want the defendant to be privy to information that is classified, it may either declassify the document, seek approval of an effective substitute, or forego its use altogether. What the government cannot do is hide the evidence from the defendant, but give it to the jury. Such plainly violates the Confrontation Clause.[144]

Therefore, although the government may request summaries, redactions, or substitutions, the defendant's ultimate guilt or innocence cannot be determined by information to which he does not have access. However, in the event, the

[137] *Bin Laden II*, n 119 above.

[138] Ibid, page 4.

[139] *Bin Laden II*, n 119 above, page 7.

[140] *Abourezk v Reagan*, 785 F2d 1043, 1060 (D.C.Cir.1986) ('[i]t is therefore a firmly held main rule that a court may not dispose of the merits of a case on the basis of *ex parte, in camera* submissions'); *Abu Ali*, n 121, 245.

[141] *Abu Ali*, n 121 above, 245.

[142] 'CIPA provides district courts wide discretion to evaluate and approve suitable substitutions to be presented to the jury. CIPA does not, however, authorise courts to provide classified documents to the jury when only such substitutions are provided to the defendant': see *Abu Ali*, n 121 above, 255.

[143] *Abu Ali*, n 121 above, 253.

[144] N 121 above, 255.

Fourth Circuit Court of Appeals in the *Abu Ali* case found this violation of a civil liberty to be 'harmless error' not warranting a remand or retrial.[145]

V. CONCLUSION

Going beyond strictly procedural issues, the second generation of terrorism cases will involve EU Courts in substantive judicial assessments of the evidence on the basis of which the restrictive measures under scrutiny have been adopted. As is clear from the *Kadi II* judgment, the right to effective judicial protection requires, in this context, that EU Courts be in a position to verify that the competent authorities in the EU have made no material error of assessment when adopting the restrictive measures. The Court therefore rejected an abstract conception of judicial review that would have been limited to verifying that procedural requirements have been met and that the applicant has not been able to rebut the elements contained in the statement of reasons. However, such substantive judicial review, entailing the assessment of secret evidence, raises at least two important challenges for EU Courts.

First, there is a delicate but important issue of mutual trust within the EU itself. It is by no means certain that, at the present stage of development of EU integration, every Member State would accept to share within the Council all secret evidence originating from its intelligence services, or to submit such evidence to the Commission or the Court. After all, under Article 346(1)(a) TFEU, no Member State shall be obliged to supply information the disclosure of which it considers contrary to the essential interests of its security. That provision *prima facie* applies also to limit the powers of the EU Courts to require such material contrary to the wishes of that Member State. The fact that the rules of procedure of the EU Courts currently contain no specific provisions allowing for confidential treatment of such material makes the present situation even more acute, and in need of an urgent solution.

The US system of handling classified evidence in terrorist cases offers food for thought on how EU courts may move forward with sanctions cases. In some respects, the American system can be considered as a more complete and effective one. US federal courts have applied uniform principles of *in camera* and *ex parte* rules to classified evidence review in criminal cases for over three decades. Moreover, federal statutes allowing the government to place 'blocking orders' (restrictive measures) against alleged supporters of terrorism expressly allow courts to view classified information at their discretion. It is interesting to observe, in that connection, that the way in which US courts apply the Classified Information Procedures Act in criminal cases closely resembles the UK special advocate system, the ECHR compatibility of which has been confirmed recently

[145] *Abu Ali*, n 121 above, 257: ('[i]n sum, while the district court violated Abu Ali's Sixth Amendment right to confront the evidence against him by submitting the unredacted versions of the documents, instead of the redacted substitute versions, to the jury as evidence at trial, we are satisfied that the error was harmless beyond a reasonable doubt.').

by the European Court of Human Rights in *A. and Others v United Kingdom*. Under both schemes, the court appoints a pre-cleared counsel to review classified information and advocate on the defendant's behalf. Both systems are intended not only to preserve the defendant's right to a fair trial but also to preserve the confidentiality of sensitive security information. There is however one important difference. In the United Kingdom, the special advocates cannot communicate with the client once they have seen classified information, whereas appointed counsel in the United States may maintain communication with the client even after seeing classified information. Moreover, the United Kingdom (as well, I understand, as some other European states) requires that the *judge* in each case be granted a security clearance in order to review classified evidence. In the US, on the other hand, all federal judges are deemed to be trustworthy and do not need to undergo a security clearance to obtain access to secret information. On this point at least, the Court of Justice in the *Kadi II* judgment also seems to favour the US approach that judges should not be required to obtain a security clearance, as a matter of principle.[146]

Of course, national intelligence information rests at the heart of continued individual sovereignty over national security and defence. Classified information is confidential because it not only contains sensitive information about informants and intelligence networks but also because it contains information about *methods* of gathering intelligence. Whatever the status of judges, it will clearly be vital in this context that EU Courts put in place procedures for the handling of closed evidence that overcome Member States' distrust in that field, and the US procedural practice may provide useful guidance on this point.

A second challenge concerns the difficulty for EU institutions to obtain classified information through the UN or third countries in the context of smart sanctions decided by the UN's Al-Qaeda Sanctions Committee. For the most part, intelligence information leading to a UN listing comes from third countries. This means that, as is recognised explicitly in the *Kadi II* judgment, a diplomatic process should be initiated whereby the third country concerned accepts to communicate confidential information to an EU institution, following which that information is presented to the Court. There is ample reason to have doubts that such system could work in practice. Even assuming that EU courts were to adopt measures protecting closed evidence, it may simply be unlikely that they will ever obtain the primary evidence supporting the initial listing before the UN Security Council.

If these difficulties do indeed prove insurmountable, attention may focus again on the role of the Ombudsperson of the Security Council's 1267 Committee,

[146] See *Kadi II* n 4 above, para 125 (emphasis added):

In such circumstances, it is none the less the task of the Courts of the European Union, *before whom the secrecy or confidentiality of that information or evidence is no valid objection*, to apply, in the course of the judicial review to be carried out, techniques which accommodate, on the one hand, legitimate security considerations about the nature and sources of information taken into account in the adoption of the act concerned and, on the other, the need sufficiently to guarantee to an individual respect for his procedural rights, such as the right to be heard and the requirement for an adversarial process.

Judge Kimberley Prost. Created in 2009 amidst a barrage of challenges to UN listings, the ombudsperson now acts in a quasi-judicial capacity, reviewing applications by individuals to be delisted, conducting a substantive review of evidence against them, conducting interviews, and ultimately deciding whether, under the 'totality of the circumstances', the person's continued listing is justified. The ombudsperson's recommendation to delist can only be rejected by a consensus vote of the Al-Qaeda Sanctions Committee. At least one State has signed an agreement to share classified information with the ombudsperson while another eleven States have agreed to do so on an *ad hoc* basis. Meanwhile, the United States 'has expressed willingness, and demonstrated an ability, to share confidential information on an *ad hoc* basis',[147] although it has not so far signed a formal agreement to that effect. While these agreements do not solve all the problems of access to secret evidence for EU Courts, they do demonstrate that certain States may be willing, under certain conditions, to share confidential information with some judicial or quasi-judicial bodies. The conclusion of information-sharing agreements with third countries could be, in that context, the only way of enabling EU courts in the future to conduct in a proper manner the investigative review contemplated in the *Kadi II* judgment.

As ever, however, the devil will be in the detail. The challenge now is for all interested parties, Courts, legislators, EU institutions and Member States, to work together to devise robust solutions to these and similar problems which, while taking account of all the fundamental interests involved, will provide fair and balanced mechanisms for substantive judicial review of restrictive measures.

[147] *See* http://www.unorg/en/sc/ombudsperson/accessinfo.shtml.

7

The Arbitration Exception and the Revised Brussels Regulation

MICHAEL M COLLINS*

COURTS DO NOT need arbitration but arbitration needs courts, albeit in comparatively limited areas. Courts are needed to resolve disputes over the appointment of an arbitrator or requests for interim relief such as orders freezing a party's assets or other temporary injunctive relief. Most significantly of all, the court mechanism is required for resolving disputes about the recognition and enforcement of arbitration awards. In addition, there are certain disputes which occupy a sort of twilight zone between the court process and arbitration, most notably disputes about the validity of an arbitration agreement and the extent to which the arbitrator is competent to adjudicate on the validity of the agreement under which he or she has been purportedly appointed. Most states consider the arbitrator can decide the issue but there are varying views on the extent to which that decision is subject to review by a court. The United Nations Convention on the Recognition and Enforcement of Foreign Arbitral Awards (New York Convention) says nothing about the extent of the review which may be carried out by a court when examining the validity of an arbitration agreement. The UNCITRAL Model Law on International Commercial Arbitration (UNCITRAL Model Law), while acknowledging in Article 16(1) that the arbitral tribunal may rule on its own jurisdiction, makes provision under Article 16(3) for review by a court of the arbitrator's jurisdiction.[1]

But, for the most part, arbitration and courts proceed quite separately. Arbitration is fundamentally a party-driven process where the parties choose the law, the forum and the arbitrator. In the case of European Union (EU) law, the intersection between EU law as applied and administered through courts and arbitration has historically been even more limited. Quite early on, the

* Senior Counsel, Law Library, Dublin

[1] At time of writing, judgment is awaited from the US Supreme Court in Case 12-138 *BG Group PLC v Republic of Argentina* as to whether a jurisdictional ruling by arbitrators on whether a precondition to arbitration under a Bilateral Investment Treaty has been satisfied can be subject to *de novo* review by the federal courts. This is the first investment arbitration case to come before the US Supreme Court.

European Court of Justice (ECJ) took the view that the critical preliminary reference procedure from a 'court or tribunal of a Member State'[2] did not extend to references from an arbitrator, even one sitting in a Member State and applying the procedural or substantive law of a Member State.[3]

There was therefore and still is no direct mechanism by which issues of EU law arising in an arbitration can be the subject of rulings by the ECJ although if and when an arbitral award comes before a national court for recognition or enforcement it is possible in an appropriate case for the national court to refer a question to the ECJ.

EU law, though permeating vast areas of economic, commercial and social life in the EU, has by and large respected the autonomy of the arbitral process and has historically stayed away from it. This finds particular expression in Article 1(2)(d) of Council Regulation (EC) No. 44/2001 of 22 December 2000 on Jurisdiction and the Recognition and Enforcement of Judgments in Civil and Commercial Matters (Brussels Regulation)[4] which provides, in deceptively simple terms, that the 'Brussels Regulation shall not apply to ... arbitration', which is commonly referred to as the arbitration exception or the arbitration exclusion. Given that some reliance on courts is a necessary adjunct to the arbitral process, it was always likely that the apparent starkness of the arbitration exception in the Brussels Regulation was going to give rise to some difficulties of interpretation. The arbitration exception, although not specifically discussed in the reports which led up to the Brussels Regulation, had been the subject of comment in the Jenard Report[5] on the Brussels Convention which preceded the Brussels Regulation. The Jenard Report justified the arbitration exception on the grounds that there were a number of existing international agreements on arbitration governing issues such as jurisdiction, recognition and enforcement, and it was envisaged at the time that there would be a European Convention providing for a uniform law on arbitration. Similarly, the Schlosser Report[6] pointed to the fact that all Member States had signed the New York Convention. It was envisaged that the New York Convention would govern jurisdictional and enforcement issues with regard to arbitrations, and the Brussels Convention (and later the Brussels Regulation) would govern such issues in the context of court proceedings in Member States.

Nonetheless, the Schlosser Report acknowledged the possibility that the arbitration exception could be construed in two quite different ways, a difference which, as in so many such cases, reflected a difference between common law and civil law traditions. One interpretation, favoured by the United Kingdom, was that all disputes which the parties had agreed should be resolved by arbitration

[2] See Art 267 TFEU.

[3] Case 102/81 *Nordsee Deutsche Hochseefischerei GmbH v Reederei Mond Hochseefischerei Nordstern AG* [1982] ECR 1095.

[4] [2001] OJ L12/1.

[5] P Jenard, 'Report on the Convention on Jurisdiction and the Recognition and Enforcement of Judgments in Civil and Commercial Matters' [1979] OJ C59/1.

[6] P Schlosser, 'Report on the Convention and the Accession of the Kingdom of Denmark, Ireland and the United Kingdom of Great Britain and Northern Ireland to the Convention on Jurisdiction and the Recognition and Enforcement of Judgments in Civil and Commercial Matters and to the Protocol of its Interpretation by the Court of Justice', [1979] OJ C59/72.

must include secondary disputes connected with the arbitration, and therefore all such disputes including such secondary disputes were excluded from the operation of the Brussels Convention.

A more narrow interpretation favoured by the civil law countries was that the exception only applied where the issue of arbitration was the main issue before the court. If, for example, the court had to decide on the validity of an arbitration agreement as something which was merely incidental to the question of whether the court had jurisdiction, the Convention rules would apply.

An obvious issue which needed to be resolved was whether the Convention governed jurisdictional rules for matters ancillary to arbitration proceedings such as the appointment of arbitrators, determining the seat of the arbitration or extending time limits. Such an issue arose in *Marc Rich & Co AG v Società Italiana Impianti PA*[7] in a dispute between an Italian company and a Swiss company under a contract containing an English arbitration clause. Faced with proceedings in Italy initiated by the Italian company for money due, the Swiss company sought to commence arbitration proceedings in London. It applied for an order appointing an arbitrator in response to which the Italian company argued that the arbitration issue was linked to the underlying substantive dispute and was therefore within the Brussels Convention. As such, the Italian Court, as the court first seised, was argued to be the court which could exclusively decide whether the dispute was governed by the arbitration clause.

The ECJ relied on the traditional rationale for the arbitration exception as being the existence of various international agreements governing arbitration including the New York Convention whose

> rules … must be respected not by the arbitrators themselves but by the courts of the contracting States … It follows that, by excluding arbitration from the scope of the [Brussels] Convention on the ground that it was already covered by international Conventions, the Contracting Parties intended to exclude arbitration in its entirety, including proceedings brought before national courts.[8]

The Court stated that

> Article 1(4) of the [Brussels] Convention must be interpreted as meaning that the exclusion provided for therein extends to litigation pending before a national court concerning the appointment of an arbitrator, even if the existence or validity of an arbitration agreement is a preliminary issue in that litigation.[9]

Thus, despite the fact that the Italian Court was the court first seised of the dispute, the Swiss company was still entitled to apply to the English Court for the appointment of the arbitrator. This conclusion was generally regarded as supportive of arbitration and in conformity with the principle of autonomy of arbitral proceedings.

The question of whether provisional measures applied for by a party to an arbitration were governed by the Brussels Convention was considered by

[7] Case C-190/89 [1991] ECR I-3855.
[8] Ibid, para 18.
[9] *Marc Rich* n 7 above, para 29.

the ECJ in *Van Uden Maritime BV v Kommanditgesellschaft in Firma Deco Line*.[10] A Dutch company commenced an arbitration in the Netherlands against a German company pursuant to arbitration clause in their contract but also applied to the Dutch Court for an order directing an interim payment by the German company pursuant to the Netherlands Arbitration Act and in reliance on Article 24 of the Brussels Convention,[11] which states:

> Application may be made to the courts of a Contracting State for such provisional, including protective, measures as may be available under the law of that State, even if, under this Convention, the courts of another Contracting State have jurisdiction as to the substance of the matter.

In an important passage which foreshadowed later controversies, the ECJ emphasised that the question of whether the provisional measures fell within the scope of the Brussels Convention depended not on the nature of the provisional measures themselves but rather on the nature of the rights which they served to protect, ie the rights at issue in the substantive dispute:

> It must therefore be concluded that where, as in the case in the main proceedings, the subject matter of an application for provisional measures relates to a question falling within the scope *ratione materiae* of the Convention, the Convention is applicable and Article 24 thereof may confer jurisdiction on the court hearing that application even where proceedings have already been, or may be, commenced on the substance of the case and even where those proceedings are to be conducted before arbitrators.[12]

A key distinction, in the Court's view, was the distinction between proceedings ancillary to arbitration proceedings (such as the appointment or dismissal or arbitrators, extension of time limits for making awards and so forth), which were excluded from the scope of the Convention, and proceedings which were not in principle ancillary to arbitration proceedings but were parallel to such proceedings as measures of support to protect a wide variety of substantive rights which did not concern arbitration as such. Thus, the national court did have jurisdiction to grant provisional measures in principle notwithstanding the arbitration exception although the Court set out limitations on the type of provisional measures which could be granted.[13]

Thus it was that, when the interface between arbitration and the Brussels Regulation created by the existence of parallel proceedings came to be

[10] Case C-391/95 [1998] ECR I-7091.

[11] Article 31, Brussels Regulation.

[12] *Van Uden* n 10 above, para 34.

[13] The ECJ noted that the very nature of an order for interim payment of a sum of money might pre-empt the decision on the substance of the case. If a plaintiff could obtain such an order before the national court where it is domiciled despite the fact that this court might not normally have jurisdiction under the Brussels Convention, and if the plaintiff then sought to have that order recognised and enforced in the defendant's state, the jurisdictional rules of the Convention could be circumvented. Accordingly, the ECJ stated (ibid, para 47) that

> interim payment of a contractual consideration does not constitute a provisional measure within the meaning of Article 24 unless, first, repayment to the defendant of the sum awarded is guaranteed if the plaintiff is unsuccessful as regards the substance of his claim and, second, the measure sought relates only to specific assets of the defendant located or to be located within the confines of the territorial jurisdiction of the court to which application is made.

considered in *Allianz Spa Generali Assicurazioni Generali v West Tankers Inc*,[14] it was the characterisation of the nature of the dispute which lay at the heart of the decision.

West Tankers is a much discussed case whose facts are well known. An Italian company chartered a ship from a ship owner (West Tankers) under a charter party which contained an English arbitration clause. Following a collision in Syracuse with a pier owned by the Italian company, the Italian company recovered from its insurer up to the limit of its cover and commenced English arbitration proceedings against West Tankers for the balance of its loss. The insurer (which, of course, subrogated to the rights of the Italian company by virtue of having paid out on the insurance policy) brought proceedings in Italy against West Tankers who maintained that the Italian Court lacked jurisdiction because of the arbitration agreement. West Tankers sought an anti-suit injunction from the English courts to restrain the insurer from pursuing its proceedings in Italy.

The House of Lords[15] was clearly of the view that the English courts had jurisdiction to grant such an injunction given that it appeared to follow from the *Marc Rich* case that the arbitration exception in the Brussels Regulation covered both arbitration proceedings and legal proceedings in relation to arbitration. However, the ECJ considered that since the Italian Court was the court first seised of proceedings in relation to the dispute, it was for that court to determine the validity of the arbitration agreement, since to permit otherwise would undermine the jurisdictional structure and effectiveness of the Brussels Regulation. Reconciling this conclusion with the arbitration exception depends critically on how the dispute before the Italian Court is characterised.

The decision in *West Tankers* was highly controversial, argued by many to undermine the autonomy of the arbitral process by failing to properly interpret the arbitration exception in Article 1(2)(d) of the Brussels Regulation. To understand why the *West Tankers* decision was so controversial, it is necessary to first consider two earlier decisions of the ECJ. In *Erich Gasser GmbH v MISAT*[16] a jurisdictional conflict arose between the Austrian and Italian courts. The Italian purchaser commenced court proceedings in Italy for breach of contract against the Austrian supplier who in turn commenced proceedings in Austria for money due and owing on the basis of an exclusive jurisdiction clause giving the Austrian courts jurisdiction. This raised a potential conflict between the policy of upholding the effectiveness of choice of law clauses and the *lis pendens* rule of the Brussels Convention that jurisdiction rests with the court first seised (which would therefore have to examine the exclusive jurisdiction clause and then, if satisfied as to its validity, decline further jurisdiction in favour of the contractually chosen court). Although Advocate General Léger (in an argument similar to that favoured by the English Court of Appeal in *Continental Bank*

[14] C-185/07 [2009] ECR I-663.

[15] [2007] All ER (D) 249.

[16] Case C-116/02 [2003] ECR I-14693. Although not an anti-suit injunction case, it is helpful to understanding the subsequent decision in *Turner v Grovit* Case C-159/02 [2005] ECR I-3565, discussed below.

NA v Aeakos Compania Naviera SA)[17] argued that at least in cases where the exclusive jurisdiction clause was clear, the chosen court should be regarded as the court 'first seised' and therefore an exception to the ordinary 'first in time' rule, the ECJ held that the latter rule set out in Article 21 of the Convention trumped the Article 17 claim to jurisdiction by virtue of the exclusive jurisdiction clause:

> From the clear terms of Article 21 it is apparent that, in a situation of lis pendens, the court second seised must stay proceedings of its own motion until the jurisdiction of the court first seised has been established and, where it is so established, must decline jurisdiction in favour of the latter ...
>
> [The fact that it is claimed that the second court has jurisdiction by virtue of the jurisdiction clause and Article 17 of the Convention] is not such as to call in question the application of the procedural rule contained in Article 21 of the Convention, which is based clearly and solely on the chronological order in which the courts involved are seised.
>
> Moreover, the court second seised is never in a better position than the court first seised to determine whether the latter has jurisdiction. That jurisdiction is determined directly by the rules of the Brussels Convention which are common to both courts and may be interpreted and applied with the same authority by each of them ...
>
> In those circumstances, in view of the disputes which could arise as to the very existence of a genuine agreement between the parties, expressed in accordance with the strict formal conditions laid down in Article 17 of the Brussels Convention, it is conducive to the legal certainty sought by the Convention that, in cases of lis pendens, it should be determined clearly and precisely which of the two national courts is to establish whether it has jurisdiction under the rules of the Convention. It is clear from the wording of Article 21 of the Convention that it is for the court first seised to pronounce as to its jurisdiction, in this case in the light of a jurisdiction clause relied on before it, which must be regarded as an independent concept to be appraised solely in relation to the requirements of Article 17 ...[18]

The fact that the court first seised might take a very long time to come to its conclusion on the jurisdictional issue and therefore to a large extent subvert the contractual intention of the parties who had chosen a different court could not, in the view of the ECJ, alter the interpretation of the Convention even if the proceedings had been launched in the slow jurisdiction with precisely the objective of torpedoing the resolution of the dispute in the contractually chosen court. The United Kingdom had argued for a bad faith exception but this would seem to be unworkable as running entirely contrary to the principle of mutual trust which, as explained by the ECJ, fundamentally underpins the jurisdictional structure of the Brussels regime:

> Second, it must be borne in mind that the Brussels Convention is necessarily based on the trust which the Contracting States accord to each other's legal systems and judicial institutions. It is that mutual trust which has enabled a compulsory system of jurisdiction to be established, which all the courts within the purview of the Convention are required to respect and as a corollary the waiver by those States of the right to apply their internal rules on recognition and enforcement of foreign

[17] [1994] 1 WLR 588.

[18] Case C-116/02 [2003] ECR I-14693, paras 42, 47–48, 51.

> judgments in favour of a simplified mechanism for the recognition and enforcement of judgments. It is also common ground that the Convention thereby seeks to ensure legal certainty by allowing individuals to foresee with sufficient certainty which court will have jurisdiction.[19]

This principle of mutual trust was reiterated by the ECJ in the context of an anti-suit injunction in *Turner v Grovit*.[20] In response to constructive dismissal proceedings brought by the plaintiff in England, the defendant brought proceedings in Spain, which proceedings were held by the English Court to have been brought in bad faith and for the purpose of harassing and oppressing the plaintiff. He applied for an anti-suit injunction to prevent the defendant from pursuing the Spanish proceedings but on a reference from the House of Lords, the ECJ took the view that anti-suit injunctions were inconsistent with the jurisdictional architecture of the Convention:

> However, a prohibition imposed by a court, backed by a penalty, restraining a party from commencing or continuing proceedings before a foreign court undermines the latter court's jurisdiction to determine the dispute. Any injunction prohibiting a claimant from bringing such an action must be seen as constituting interference with the jurisdiction of the foreign court which, as such, is incompatible with the system of the Convention.
>
> Notwithstanding the explanations given by the referring court and contrary to the view put forward by Mr. Turner and the United Kingdom government, such interference cannot be justified by the fact that it is only indirect and is intended to prevent an abuse of process by the defendant in the proceedings in the forum State. Insofar as the conduct for which the defendant is criticised consists in recourse to the jurisdiction of a court of another Member State, the judgment made as to the abusive nature of that conduct implies an assessment of the appropriateness of bringing proceedings before a court of another Member State. Such an assessment runs counter to the principle of mutual trust which, as pointed out in paragraphs 24 to 26 of this judgment, underpins the Convention and prohibits a court, except in special circumstances which are not applicable in this case, from reviewing the jurisdiction of the court of another Member State.
>
> Even if it were assumed, as has been contended, that an injunction could be regarded as a measure of a procedural nature intended to safeguard the integrity of the proceedings pending before the court which issues it, and therefore as being a matter of national law alone, it need merely be borne in mind that the application of national procedural rules may not impair the effectiveness of the Convention … However, that result would follow from the grant of an injunction of the kind at issue which, as has been established in paragraph 27 of this judgment, has the effect of limiting the application of the rules on jurisdiction laid down by the Convention …
>
> Consequently, the answer to be given to the national court must be that the Convention is to be interpreted as precluding the grant of an injunction whereby a court of a Contracting State prohibits a party to proceedings pending before it from commencing or continuing legal proceedings before a court of another Contracting State, even where that party is acting in bad faith with a view to frustrating the existing proceedings.[21]

[19] Ibid para 72.
[20] Case C-159/02 [2005] ECR I-3565.
[21] *West Tankers* n 14 above, para 27–29 and 31.

West Tankers was not a case of a clash between the courts of competing jurisdictions, but rather a clash between arbitration proceedings and court proceedings where the anti-suit injunction was prayed in aid of that very distinction.[22] The failure of the arbitration exclusion to preserve the jurisdiction of the English Court to determine that the arbitration agreement was valid and that the Italian company should be restrained from continuing with the Italian proceedings rests almost entirely on the ECJ's characterisation of the issue of the validity and effect of the arbitration agreement as being merely incidental to the substantive matter of the dispute before the Italian Court. Once the nature of the dispute is so characterised, the conclusion that a court, such as the Italian Court, seised of jurisdiction for a claim for damages in tort under Article 5(3) of the Brussels Regulation is the appropriate court to rule on its own jurisdiction follows inexorably. Given that characterisation, then

> a preliminary issue concerning the applicability of an arbitration agreement, including in particular its validity, also comes within its scope of application ... the verification, *as an incidental question*, of the validity of an arbitration agreement which is cited by a litigant in order to contest the jurisdiction of the Court before which he is being sued pursuant to the Brussels Convention, must be considered as falling within its scope.[23]

When making the reference in *West Tankers*, Lord Hoffmann in the House of Lords characterised the right at issue as the contractual right to have the dispute determined by arbitration. Accordingly, the subject matter of the dispute before the Italian Court was viewed by the House of Lords as arbitration in which case the Brussels Regulation should have no application:

> The basic principles by which the [Brussels] regulation allocates jurisdiction, giving priority (subject to exceptions) to the domicile of the defendant, are entirely unsuited to arbitration, in which the situs and governing law are generally chosen by the parties on grounds of neutrality, availability of legal services and the unobtrusive effectiveness of the supervisory jurisdiction. There is no set of uniform Community rules which Member States can or must trust each other to apply.[24]

It is not to the judgment of the ECJ, but rather to the opinion of Advocate General Kokott that one must turn to find a discussion of the distinction between the common law approach that the arbitration exception extends to secondary disputes connected with the arbitration and the civil law view that it only covers proceedings before national courts which refer to actual arbitration proceedings about to be started, in progress or concluded:

> The crucial difference between the two approaches is therefore that the arbitration exception is understood broadly in the first view; as soon as it is claimed that there is an arbitration agreement, all disputes arising from the legal relationship are subject exclusively to arbitration, irrespective of the substantive subject matter. Only the arbitral body and the courts of the seat of arbitration are entitled to examine jurisdiction.

[22] The anti-suit injunction is, of course, an *in personam* remedy directed to the party, rather than the foreign court.

[23] *West Tankers* n 14 above, para 26, emphasis added.

[24] [2007] All ER (D) 249, para 12.

> The opposite view takes account first and foremost of the substantive subject matter. If that subject matter falls within [the Brussels Regulation], a court which in principle has jurisdiction thereunder is entitled to examine whether the exception under Article 1(2)(d) applies and, according to its assessment of the effectiveness and applicability of the arbitration clause, to refer the case to the arbitral body or adjudicate on the matter itself.
>
> The wording of Article 1(2)(d) of [the Brussels Regulation] does not give any clear indication as to which interpretation should be preferred. It can be concluded from the use of the term 'arbitration', however, that that means not only the actual arbitration proceedings but also related proceedings before the national courts can be excluded from the scope of the Regulation.[25]

Despite this acknowledgement that national court proceedings which are related to the arbitration proceedings come within the arbitration exception, she nonetheless concluded that if the related question (for instance, as to the applicability of the arbitration clause) arose as a preliminary issue in proceedings which raised the substantive subject-matter of the dispute (presumably by way of contrast with proceedings set up to formulate the arbitration-related issue as a standalone issue), then the arbitration exclusion no longer applied:

> The existence and applicability of the arbitration clause merely constitute a preliminary issue which the court seised must address when examining whether it has jurisdiction. Even if the view were taken that that issue fell within the ambit of arbitration, as a preliminary issue it could not change the classification of the proceedings, the subject matter which falls within the scope of the Regulation. It can be left undecided here how proceedings which concern similar findings in the main case should be evaluated.[26]

Notwithstanding Advocate General Kokott's focus on 'classification', there is, however, a danger in making the classification or characterisation of the proceedings conclusive as to the outcome of the jurisdiction issue, since characterisation is often a matter of form rather than substance. In one sense all jurisdictional disputes, whether involving court or arbitral proceedings, are merely ancillary to or derivative from some other underlying substantive dispute. It is difficult to discern guidance from *West Tankers* as to where the dividing line is to be drawn for the purpose of the arbitration exclusion in Article 1(2)(d) of the Brussels Regulation. But one anchor to which it may be useful to cling is the fact that an arbitration clause in a contract is not merely one clause in

[25] *West Tankers* n 14 above, Opinion of Advocate General Kokott, paras 43–45.

[26] Ibid paragraph 54. See also *National Navigation Co v Endesa Generacion SA* [2010] 2 All ER (Comm) 1243 where the Court of Appeal held that a Spanish judgment that an arbitration clause was not incorporated into a bill of lading was a judgment within the scope of the Brussels Regulation and had to be recognised for all purposes including English proceedings brought by the defendant seeking a stay of the Spanish proceedings on the basis of the purported arbitration clause. Moore-Bick LJ referred to the *Marc Rich* case as supporting the following conclusions (at 1268):

> (a) that when deciding whether the Regulation applies it is necessary to examine the nature of the proceedings rather than individual issues to which they give rise; (b) whether the Regulation applies depends on the essential subject matter of the dispute; (c) the essential subject matter of the dispute is not determined by the nature of a preliminary issue, even if the nature of that issue differs from that of the principal dispute; and (d) that therefore some issues which, viewed in isolation, would fall outside the Regulation may, if they arise as a preliminary issue, have to be treated as falling within the Regulation and vice versa.

a contract. It is a severable agreement in its own right which may or may not be governed by the same law as governs the substantive contract in which it is located and in respect of which damages may be claimed if one party suffers loss (such as costs) by virtue of having to defend court proceedings brought by the other party in breach of the arbitration agreement.[27] Thus, if a party brings an application before a court seeking to enforce the arbitration agreement (or to persuade the court that the arbitration agreement is invalid) it seems curious, to say the least, that the question of whether the whole jurisdictional apparatus of the Brussels Regulation applies to such an application depends upon the procedural mechanism by which the issue is brought before the court.

The decision in *West Tankers* also highlights what appears to be a conflict between the New York Convention and the Brussels Regulation. Article II(3) of the New York Convention obliges the court of a Contracting State, when seised of an action in a matter in respect of which the parties have made an arbitration agreement to refer the parties to arbitration 'unless it finds that the said agreement is null and void, inoperative or incapable of being performed.' Yet, such a court, if faced with the fact that one of the parties, in breach of the arbitration agreement, has commenced proceedings in another State governed by the Brussels Regulation, would find itself powerless to give effect to its obligation under Article II(3) of the New York Convention.

West Tankers is, of course, confined in its effect to parties within the contracting states. In a series of subsequent decisions[28] culminating in the decision of the UK Supreme Court in *UST-Kamenogorsk Hydropower Plant JSC v AES Ust-Kamenorgorsk Hydropower Plant LLP*[29] the English courts have confirmed that they still have jurisdiction to grant anti-suit injunctions restraining court proceedings brought in violation of an arbitration agreement in jurisdictions outside the Brussels Regulation regime, even where arbitration proceedings have not been commenced or even proposed. The decision was essentially based on a construction of the relevant English statutory provisions governing the jurisdiction of the English court under certain provisions of the English Senior Courts Act 1981 and the Arbitration Act 1996. Lord Mance considered and rejected the proposition that the effect of *West Tankers* was to restrict the power of the court to grant anti-suit injunctions in a worldwide context. Referring to the argument that the Arbitration Act 1996 in some way limited the power arising under section 37 of the Senior Courts Act 1981 to injunct foreign proceedings begun or threatened in breach of an arbitration agreement he stated:

> On the contrary, it would be astonishing if Parliament should, silently and without warning, have advocated or precluded the use by the English court of its previous well established jurisdiction under section 37 in respect of foreign proceedings commenced

[27] See, for example, *Union Discount Co v Zoller* (2002) 1 All ER 693; *Starlight Shipping Co v Allianz Marine & Aviation Versicherungs AG* [2013] All ER (D) 71.

[28] See, for example, *Shashoua v Sharma* [2009] All ER (D) 64; *Midgulf International Ltd v Groupe Chimique Tunisien* [2010] All ER (D) 144.

[29] [2014] 1 All ER (Comm) 1.

> or threatened in breach of the negative aspects of an arbitration agreement ...Yet a regime under which the English court could no longer enforce the negative rights of a party to a London arbitration agreement by injunctive relief restraining foreign proceedings would have been, and would have been seen, as a radical diminution of the protection afforded by English law to parties to such an arbitration agreement. It would have aroused considerable interest and, no doubt, concern. The only sensible inference is that the drafters of the Act never contemplated that it could or would undermine the established jurisprudence on anti-suit injunctions.
>
> It was only later that the Court of Justice in Luxembourg restricted the use of such injunctions; and then only in relation to foreign proceedings in the area covered by the Brussels/Lugano regime and on the basis of a mutual trust affirmed to exist between courts within that regime. The interest and concern that this aroused witnesses to the interest that would have been aroused had the Bill or 1996 Act been seen as having such any radical intention or effect in relation to courts worldwide. The *West Tankers* case... suggests that it did not occur to anyone until this case that it did.[30]

The *West Tankers* saga itself continues to surprise. Despite the court proceedings, the arbitration continued and in 2008 the arbitral panel found that West Tankers were not liable to pay anything to the insurers despite the fact that the proceedings in Italy were still pending (with the possibility of the Italian court arriving at an opposite conclusion to that reached by the arbitrators). The ship owners then applied to the English court to have the arbitrators' award made a judgment or order of the court notwithstanding that the award was in the form of a negative declaration, ie that the ship owners were not liable to the insurers. Both the High Court and the Court of Appeal held[31] that the court had jurisdiction in an appropriate case to give leave for the arbitral award to be entered as a judgment, notwithstanding its nature as a negative declaration, because such a judgment could make a positive contribution to securing the material benefit of the award. For example, Article 34(3) of the Brussels Regulation provides that a 'judgment shall not be recognised if it is irreconcilable with a judgment given in a dispute between the same parties in the Member State in which recognition is sought.' Thus, if the Italian court were ultimately to hold against West Tankers and if the insurers sought to enforce such judgment in England, they would face the difficulty that such judgment would be irreconcilable with the judgment already given by the English court enforcing the arbitral award, albeit only in declaratory terms. The torpedo of the Italian proceedings may thus be in fact defused.

In yet another twist, the English Commercial Court ruled in *West Tankers Inc vAllianz SpA*[32] that notwithstanding that the Brussels Regulation precluded the court from granting an anti-suit injunction, the arbitral tribunal had jurisdiction to make an award of damages against the Italian company for breach of the arbitration agreement by commencing the proceedings in Italy.

[30] Ibid paragraphs 58 and 59. See also *Claxton Engineering Services Limited v TXM Olaj-És Gázkutató Ktf (No. 2)* [2011] 2 All ER (Comm) 128, holding that the court has jurisdiction to grant an injunction restraining a party from pursuing an arbitration in another EU Member State as the Brussels Regulation applies to court proceedings, not to arbitration proceedings, albeit that such an anti-arbitration injunction would generally only be granted in exceptional circumstances.

[31] *West Tankers Inc v Allianz SpA* [2012] All ER (D) 127.

[32] [2012] All ER (D) 166.

These jurisdictional complexities and others, such as the problem of parallel proceedings where one of the proceedings is outside the Brussels/Lugano jurisdictions,[33] gave increased impetus to proposed revisions of the Brussels Regulation. Article 73 of the Regulation required that within five years the European Commission should present to the European Parliament, the Council and the Economic and Social Committee a report on the application of the Regulation with proposals for any recommended changes. In fulfilment of this obligation in September 2007 the Report on the Application of Regulation Brussels I,[34] known as the Heidelberg Report, was published based on an empirical study in 24 Member States. Although most responses did not favour including arbitration in the Brussels Regulation, the report made a number of recommendations for reform, which included deleting the arbitration exclusion to bring court proceedings relating to arbitration (but not arbitration proceedings themselves) within the Regulation. Following a further report,[35] a Green Paper[36] and a report from an international expert group on the relationship between arbitration and the Regulation, the Commission published its proposed amendments to the Regulation on 14 December 2010.[37] After further consultations and further revisions to the proposals, the European Parliament and the Council approved a final recast version of the Brussels Regulation (the "recast Regulation") which was published on 20 December 2012.[38] It entered into force on 9 January 2013 but will only apply to court proceedings in the EU from 10 January 2015.

The recast Regulation contains a variety of changes most of which are beyond the scope of this chapter. Apart however from the impact on the arbitration exception (discussed below) there is an important change to the current rules on exclusive jurisdiction clauses aimed at resolving, at least in the context of court proceedings, the problem of the Italian torpedo. Where there is an exclusive jurisdiction clause nominating the court of a Member State as the chosen court, the court of that country is given priority to determine the validity of the agreement and the extent to which the agreement applies to the dispute pending before it.[39] Thus, even if another court is first seised of the dispute, that

[33] See, for example, Case C 281/02 *Owusu v Jackson* [2005] ECR I-138; *Goshawk Dedicated Ltd v Life Receivables Ireland Ltd* [2008] IEHC 90.

[34] B Hess, T Pfeiffer, P Schlosser, *Report on the Application of Regulation Brussels I in the Member States,* (Study JLS/C4/2005/3, 2nd edn (Munich/Oxford/Baden Baden, CH Beck/Hart/Nomos, 2008).

[35] Report from the Commission to the European Parliament, the Council and the European Economic and Social Committee on the Application of Council Regulation (EC) No 44/2001 on Jurisdiction and the Recognition and Enforcement of Judgments in Civil and Commercial Matters, 21 April 2009, COM(2009) 174 final.

[36] Green Paper on the Review of the Council Regulation (EC) No 44/2001 on Jurisdiction and the Recognition and Enforcement of Judgments in Civil and Commercial Matters, 21 April 2009, COM(2009) 175 final.

[37] European Commission, 'Proposal for a Regulation of the European Parliament and of the Council on jurisdiction and the recognition and enforcement of judgments in civil and commercial matters', COM (2010) 748 final.

[38] Regulation (EU) No 1215/2012 of the European Parliament and of the Council of 12 December 2012 on jurisdiction and the recognition and enforcement of judgments in civil and commercial matters (recast) [2012] OJ L351/1.

[39] Ibid, recital 22 and Arts 29 – 34.

court must stay its proceedings until the court of the jurisdiction chosen in the agreement declares it has no jurisdiction under the agreement.[40] In other words, in this situation the first in time rule is reversed. However, this new rule does not apply to non-exclusive jurisdiction clauses or to jurisdiction clauses which seek to confer jurisdiction on a non-Member State (although there are provisions which give Member States a discretion to take into account proceedings pending before a non-Member State).[41]

Despite the recommendation in the Heidelberg Report that the arbitration exclusion be removed and variations on this theme proposed by the Commission the debate was won by those who insisted that the arbitration exclusion should be retained in its entirety and Article 1(2)(d) remains in the recast Regulation. Furthermore, Recital 12 in the recast Regulation contains a number of statements which, while not directly reflected in the substance of the recast Regulation, give significant support to the arbitration exclusion and at least partially undo some of the effects of the *West Tankers* decision.

Recital 12 defines the scope of the arbitration exception by setting out certain categories of proceedings and judgments which fall outside the scope of the recast Regulation. Thus the Regulation does not apply to any action or ancillary proceedings relating to matters such as the establishment of an arbitral tribunal, the powers of arbitrators, the conduct of an arbitration procedure or any other aspects of such a procedure. This gives express recognition to what had been the general understanding of what sort of arbitration related ancillary proceedings fell outside the Brussels Regulation. Similarly the recital makes clear that the Regulation does not apply to any action or judgment concerning the annulment, review, appeal, recognition or enforcement of an arbitral award.

The courts of a Member State when seised of a matter in respect of which the parties have entered into an arbitration agreement are expressly empowered to refer the parties to arbitration, to stay or dismiss the proceedings, or to examine whether the arbitration agreement is null and void, inoperative or incapable of being performed (wording which directly and consciously reflects Article II(3) of the New York Convention), in accordance with the court's national law.

Clearly, this is intended to ensure that a court faced with proceedings apparently in breach of an arbitration agreement has full jurisdiction to adjudicate on the validity of the arbitration agreement and either refer the parties to arbitration or not as the case may be. Furthermore, Recital 12 continues:

> A ruling given by a court of a Member State as to whether or not an arbitration agreement is null and void, inoperative or incapable of being performed should not be subject to the rules of recognition and enforcement laid down in this Regulation, regardless of whether the court decided on this as a principal issue or as an incidental question.

Assume Ireland is the chosen seat under the arbitration agreement but one party commences court proceedings in France. Even where the French court is first seised of the dispute and rules on the validity or invalidity of the arbitration

[40] Reg (EU) No 1215/2012, n 37 above, Art 31(2).
[41] Ibid, recital 24 and Arts 33 and 34.

agreement, the Irish court would no longer be obliged by virtue of the recast Regulation to decline jurisdiction or be bound by the French court ruling. It could proceed to determine the issue of validity itself (although there could of course be various discretionary reasons as to why the Irish court might decline to entertain jurisdiction). To this extent at least it can be said that the recast Regulation has reversed *West Tankers*.

What, however, if the French court decides the arbitration agreement is invalid and proceeds to determine the substance of the underlying dispute? Such a decision would appear to be a decision governed by the recast Regulation and therefore enforceable in accordance with that Regulation. Subject to the effect of the New York Convention, the Irish court would at first sight have to recognise and enforce the French judgment in Ireland even if the Irish court considered that the arbitration agreement was binding. Thus Recital 12 states:

> … where a court of a Member State, exercising jurisdiction under this Regulation or under national law, has determined that an arbitration agreement is null and void, inoperative or incapable of being performed, this should not preclude that court's judgment on the substance of the matter from being recognised or, as the case may be, enforced in accordance with this Regulation. This should be without prejudice to the competence of the courts of the Member States to decide on the recognition and enforcement of arbitral awards in accordance with the [New York Convention], which takes precedence over this Regulation.

The latter sentence is particularly noteworthy. As noted earlier, one of the problems flowing from the *West Tankers* decision is the potential conflict between a court's obligation under Article II(3) of the New York Convention to refer the parties to arbitration save in very limited circumstances and that court's obligation to recognise the judgment of the court of another Member State on the merits under the Brussels Regulation even if procured in the teeth of an arbitration agreement considered binding by the first court. The recast Regulation is unambiguous that in the event of conflict, the New York Convention takes priority. It is not just Recital 12 which states this. Article 73(2) provides that the 'Regulation shall not affect the application of the 1958 New York Convention' which, interpreted in light of the more express acknowledgment in the recital, seems fairly clear.

And yet, the silence on anti-suit injunctions is deafening. The New York Convention says nothing about them and despite the intense debate that followed *West Tankers* and the fact that the recast Regulation clearly seeks to address the issues arising, the latter is equally silent. The inference is, at the very least, arguable that the refusal to expressly sanction anti-suit injunctions means that the recast Regulation does not contemplate them as legitimate judicial tools. This is more understandable when one recalls that anti-suit injunctions have their origin in early 19th century English common law cases preventing the ecclesiastical courts from expanding their jurisdiction[42] whereas

[42] See C Ambrose, 'Can Anti-Suit Injunctions Survive European Community Law?' [2003] 52 *ICLQ* 401, 404. The common law view is well expressed by Lord Justice Millett in *Aggeliki Charis Compania Maritima SA v Pagnan SpA (The Angelic Grace)* [1995] 1 Lloyd's Rep 87 at 96:

civil law jurisdictions see such injunctions as directed against the foreign court, a violation of national sovereignty and offensive to international comity.

Notwithstanding the improved clarity brought by the recast Regulation, the underlying conflict still rumbles on. The primacy given to the New York Convention surely means that an arbitral award must be upheld if not invalidated on any of the limited grounds set out in the Convention despite the indication in Recital 12 that a judgment of another Member State on the merits must be enforced even if given in breach of an arbitration agreement. If so, there would, or perhaps should, seem to be no objection in principle to an anti-suit injunction issued by the court of the seat of arbitration stopping the party to the arbitration agreement from commencing court proceedings in any other jurisdiction. It remains to be seen whether this argument will prevail over the combination of civil law antipathy to anti-suit injunctions and the silence of the recast Regulation on the point.

As in so many areas, public policy may be the oil that enables the imperfectly interlocking mechanisms of the New York Convention and the Brussels Regulation to grind together without causing undue gnashing of teeth. Article 45(1)(a) of the recast Regulation provides that recognition of a judgment shall be refused if such recognition is manifestly contrary to the public policy of the Member State addressed. All Member States are signatories to the New York Convention and it seems plausible that most will recognise the enforcement of valid arbitral awards as a key component of their jurisdiction's public policy.

In the context of the New York Convention, public policy does not just mean anything and everything that may count as public policy in the State concerned. The national public policy in question has to be essential to the forum State's legal system and be consistent with applicable international principles. Thus in *Brostrom Tankers v Factorias Volcano*[43] the Irish High Court enforced a Norwegian arbitration award at the behest of a Swedish claimant against a Spanish company notwithstanding the argument of the Spanish company (which was insolvent and under Court protection in Spain) that to do so would give the Swedish company preferential treatment over its other creditors which, it was argued, would be contrary to public policy. The Irish High Court stated that the 'caselaw and the textbook writers make it clear that the public policy defence to an enforcement application is one which is of a narrow scope. It extends only to a breach of the most basic notions of morality and justice.'[44]

In circumstances where the recognition and enforcement of arbitral awards is an obligation under the New York Convention and having regard to the

> If an injunction is granted it is not granted for fear that the foreign court may wrongly assume jurisdiction...but on the surer ground that the defendant promised not to put the plaintiff to the expense and trouble of applying to that court at all...a jurisdiction which he had promised not to invoke and which was his own duty to decline...the time has come to lay aside the ritual incantation that this is a jurisdiction which should only be exercised sparingly and with great caution.

[43] [2004] 2 I.R. 191.
[44] Ibid, para 28.

fundamental importance of the autonomous nature of arbitral proceedings, it is likely that such recognition would qualify as domestic public policy for the purposes of the New York Convention. If so, the same would surely apply in the case of the Brussels Regulation, recast or otherwise. For a Member State court faced with a conflict between a valid arbitral award and a contrary foreign judgment, the logical solution would seem to be that recognition or enforcement of the foreign judgment would be contrary to the State's public policy.

Courts may not need arbitral processes but they continue to dance with each other in increasingly complex arabesques. No longer strangers in the night, they are certainly doing more than exchanging glances.

8

The Financial Crisis, Banking Union and the Rule of Law

PAUL GALLAGHER*

1. Since 2008 the European Union (Union) has been engulfed by a financial and economic crisis. The crisis has threatened the survival of the Euro and some would argue has threatened the survival of the Union project, at least in its present form. The severity and extent of the crisis has been such that it has in fact undermined fundamental objectives of the Treaty on European Union (TEU) and the Treaty on the Functioning of the European Union (TFEU).
2. The fundamental objectives of the Union are contained in Article 3 TEU. Amongst those objectives are the promotion of the well-being of the peoples of the Unions;[1] the sustainable development of Europe based on balanced economic growth and price stability; a highly competitive social market economy aiming at full employment and social progress; and the promotion of social justice and solidarity between generations and amongst Member States.[2] The attainment of these objectives which are core Union values has been significantly undermined in many Member States and particularly within many Euro Area Member States. Many Member States have experienced very high unemployment, a halt to or reversal of social progress, the undermining of economic and social cohesion and a disruption of solidarity between generations. There has also been a marked deterioration in the solidarity amongst Member States.
3. There has been widespread dissatisfaction and criticism of the Union's response to this existential crisis. For many Member States on the periphery of the Euro Area there is very considerable dissatisfaction with what is perceived as being the failure of Union institutions to take decisive and effective action to resolve the crisis. On the other hand in some of the non-periphery Euro Area States there are strident complaints that many of the

* SC, former Attorney General of Ireland.
[1] Art 3(1) TEU.
[2] Art 3(3) TEU.

actions taken by Union institutions to address the crisis go beyond the Treaties and have no valid legal basis. This has led many commentators to contend that Union efforts to resolve the crisis have infringed the Rule of Law and that this is destructive of the Union and undermines the very basis on which Member States ceded significant sovereignty to the Union.[3]

4. These rival criticisms raise an issue of the utmost importance which goes to the core of the Union project and to its very legitimacy. If, on the one hand, the existing legal structures are not used when they ought to be to protect the Union's citizens, this amounts to a fundamental failure of the Union and undermines its objectives. On the other hand, if the Union has exceeded its legal authority, the Rule of Law on which the Union is based has been undermined. If the Union exercise powers which have never been conferred upon it, this also undermines its democratic legitimacy and contravenes the principle of conferral[4] which is not only central to the Treaties,[5] but is also central to the future development of the Union. In this paper I will consider this issue by reference to some of the Union's major policy responses to the crisis and I will examine whether it can be said that the Union has respected the Rule of Law during this period.
5. The phrase 'The Rule of Law' was, according to Professor Lawson, coined by Professor A.V. Dicey.[6] However the modern understanding of the Rule of Law, which differs from that of Dicey, is that the concept embraces a number of principles which include accessibility of laws, protection for rights, adequacy of adjudication procedures and compliance by government and public institutions and States with the law.[7] In the present context the principle which is of central relevance is that which requires public bodies to abide by the law and to exercise the powers conferred on them in good faith for the purpose for which those powers were conferred. In modern democratic societies there is a presumption, or at least an expectation, amongst citizens that the government and public bodies will act in accordance with the law. Transferred to a European level there is a presumption or expectation that Union institutions will act in a similar fashion.
6. In recent decades a philosophy of relativism has intruded into the legal domain. Relativism applied in a legal sphere suggests that legal analysis and justification can properly be influenced by social and political agendas. This in turn leads to a belief that there is no correct legal conclusion or at least no

[3] See R Vaubel, 'The Breakdown of the Rule of Law at EU level: Implications for the Reform of the European Court of Justice', http://www.vwl.uni-mannheim.de/vaubel/pdf-Dateien/TheBreakdown12.04.13.pdf (April 2013); L Zanzinger, *The ESM. A breach of the Treaties? – The Value of European law on the Eurocrisis* (Munich, GRIN Publishing GmbH, http://www.grin.com/en/e-book/215125/the-esm-a-breach-of-the-treaties, 2013: consulted 10 January 2014); P-A Van Malleghem, '*Pringle*: The Paradigm Shift in the European Union's Monetary Constitution' (2013) 14 *German Law Journal* 141.

[4] Art 5 TEU.

[5] G de Búrca and B de Witte, 'The delimitation of Powers between the EU and its Member States' in A Arnull and D Wincott, *Accountability and Legitimacy in the European Union* (Oxford, OUP, 2003).

[6] FH Lawson, 'The Oxford Law School 1850–1965 (Oxford, Clarendon Press, 1968) 72.

[7] See T Bingham, *Lives of the Law* (Oxford, OUP, 2011) 10–11.

unanimity as to what that correct conclusion might be and therefore that that rationale is sufficient, in order to justify a particular action, to base it on some legal rationale even if that rationale is deficient in its reasoning or legal logic. This philosophy undermines the Rule of Law because it undermines the power of legal constraint and equates respect for the Rule of Law with the existence of some legal justification for a particular course of action, notwithstanding that the legal justification lacks coherent reasoning and is based on legal analysis which cannot withstand detailed scrutiny. This philosophy has become more manifest in recent times. At a European level when rival bodies of lawyers or commentators advance wholly conflicting views with regard to the legal validity of measures, it is frequently the case that these legal views are in turn influenced by different and opposing agendas.

7. Unless we subscribe to the principle that there is one correct interpretation of the law even though that interpretation may be difficult to ascertain in any given case and may be subject to some uncertainty pending resolution by the ultimate deciding body (such as the Court of Justice at the Union level), we run the risk that adherence to the Rule of Law means little more than adherence to a stateable legal interpretation. This in turn releases from governments and public bodies from many of the constraints which is the Rule of Law is designed to impose.
8. On the other hand, those charged with making decisions can rarely be certain that the legal basis relied upon is beyond legitimate dispute. Frequently the more important the decision, and the more challenging and novel the problem which it is intended to address, the greater the uncertainty over whether its validity will ultimately be upheld by the courts. If however no decision is made because doubts exist as to its legal validity this would paralyse the effective functioning of government and public institutions and, in a European context, the effective functioning of Union institutions and would result in the failure to exercise necessary powers even though the decision being considered may be legally valid. In such circumstances not to act because of legal doubts could do untold damage and would, in effect, deprive citizens of the benefit of legal provisions which in fact address the problem that requires remediation.
9. It follows that the application of the Rule of Law must therefore permit on the part of those exercising the relevant power (or making the relevant decisions) something less than legal certainty as to the legal validity of the power or the decision. It is difficult to articulate a comprehensive definition of what level of legal certainty is required before a decision can be made consonant with respect for the Rule of Law. It would suggest that the appropriate approach is to require that a reasonable legal basis does exist for the exercise of the power or for the making of the decision, even if there are real grounds for challenging their legality. Such an approach respects the Rule of Law while permitting the effective functioning of institutions and the discharge of obligations by those who have the responsibility for decision-making and taking action.

10. It is noteworthy that some of those who have complained that Union institutions have not respected Treaty constraints in relation to the European Stability Mechanism (ESM) maintain their criticism of the ECM despite the decision of the Court of Justice (ECJ) in the case of *Pringle v Ireland*.[8] Such criticism is misplaced. In any legal order there must be some institution charged with determining legal disputes, and the rulings of those institutions form a vital part of the Rule of Law at least where those rulings are properly reasoned and arrived at through adherence to proper procedures. In considering whether Union institutions acted in accordance with the Rule of Law as thus defined, it is important, as *Pringle* demonstrates, to consider the circumstances in which Union actions took place because those circumstances are in fact relevant to an examination of the legal validity of the measures considered.
11. In an essay in the *Columbia Law Review* in 1935, Felix Cohen lamented '[t]he divorce of legal reasoning from questions of social fact and ethical value.' The law, Cohen concluded, should not be a self-referring construct but 'a social process, a complex of human activity, with cause and effect, with the past and the future.'[9] There is much to be said for Cohen's view. Legal reasoning entirely divorced from social realities can result in the law being perceived as being out of touch with reality. The reasoning of the ECJ has, historically, never been divorced from the realities being confronted by the Union (and former Community). This is an important factor which is relevant in considering the Union's compliance the Rule of Law during its greatest crisis since its foundation.
12. What is now known as the 'Great Recession' began in 2007 in the US with the collapse of the subprime mortgage market.[10] A serious deterioration of the financial markets and financial liquidity ultimately resulted in the collapse of Lehman Brothers on 15 September 2008, which in turn triggered the collapse of a number of the major credit institutions in the US and caused major instability in credit institutions throughout Europe necessitating enormous government support for the domestic financial system in many Member States. That government support in turn triggered the sovereign debt crisis which in turn impacted on the ability of Member States to control fiscal imbalance.
13. Former Chairman of the Federal Reserve Ben Bernanke described what occurred as a recession accompanied by a financial near collapse. Yves Mersch[11] stated there were important similarities between banking

[8] Zanzinger (n 3); Case C-370/12, judgment of 27 November 2012.

[9] FS Cohen, 'Transcendental Nonsense and the Functional Approach', (1935) 35 *Columbia Law Review* 809, 814 and 844.

[10] See AS Blinder, *After the Music Stopped* (London, Penguin, 2013) 91.

[11] Member of the Executive Board of the European Central Bank; keynote speech 'Towards a European Bankning Union, Bridge Forum Dialogue, Luxembourg 30 September 2013, http://www.ecb.europa.eu/press/key/date/2013/html/sp130930_1.en.html, and a further keynote speech 'Economic and legal limits of Central Banking', IMFS Conference on Monetary and Financial Stability, Frankfurt-am-Main 26 November 2013, http://www.ecb.europa.eu/press/key/date/2013/html/sp131126.en.html (both consulted 10 January 2014).

developments and the evolution of the crisis across the Atlantic. He stated that when systemic risk materialised in 2007/2008 the world was struck by a sudden systemic financial crisis, unprecedented when measured by financial losses and fiscal costs, unprecedented when measured by its geographical reach, and also unprecedented when measured by the collapse in worldwide trade, economic output and financial activity. The world was on the brink of a global financial meltdown. That is a reality which it would be difficult for a any court to ignore.

14. The fiscal and financial crisis in the Euro Area made manifest the critical gaps in the architectural structure of the Euro. The deterioration of balance sheets and the reversal of capital flows has forced very sharp economic contractions and financial market fragmentation resulting in borrowing costs of sovereigns and national private sectors diverging widely and persistently with adverse sovereign-bank-real economy consequences in the Euro area.[12] Yves Mersch also acknowledged[13] the deficiencies in the existing institutional framework. It is those deficiencies which the current and proposed measures now seek to remedy.
15. In this context it has become apparent that the cession of monetary sovereignty to the Union in a legal context which prevents the ECB from acting to regulate liquidity and interest rates in capital markets by making large scale purchases of government bonds (ie from engaging in quantitative easing) and the lack of a banking union together with the disparities in the fiscal policies of Euro Area States has meant that the Euro was structurally unable to withstand serious financial shocks.[14] The problem has been exacerbated by the absence of any exit mechanism from the Eurozone and the legal and financial uncertainties that would occur were a Euro Area Member State to attempt to leave the Euro. All of these circumstances created an environment in which Union action was necessary in order to protect Union objectives and to prevent the occurrence of widespread alienation, among Union citizens, from the Union and its institutions.
16. Before examining the legality of some specific measures introduced by the Union to address the crisis, and consequently the Union's adherence to the Rule of Law, it is necessary to consider the broader legal framework within which any proper analysis of legal validity must take place. The ECJ as the ultimate legal decision-maker is central to that framework. An argument about the legal validity of particular measures which ignores the legal approach of the ECJ developed through more than fifty years of jurisprudence ignores a crucial aspect of legal validity. Union institutions in introducing legislative measures and in making decisions consider not only the wording of the Treaties but also the likely interpretative approach of the ECJ. That interpretative approach can be gleaned from an analysis of

[12] R Goyal et al, *A Banking Union for the Euro Area*, IMF Staff Discussion Note (Washington DC, February 2013) SDN/113/01.

[13] Speech of 26 November 2013 (n 11).

[14] T Mayer, *Europe's Unfinished Currency – The Political Economics of the Euro* (London, Anthem Press, 2012) 2.

the ECJ's legal decisions and the well-established principles of construction consistently used by the ECJ. In this regard it is important to acknowledge from the beginning that the Treaty documents, like most constitutional documents do not provide in a clear way the answers to some of the central questions of EU law. Neither do they always provide a clear legal basis for the development of that law. The ECJ's historical decision-making demonstrates a willingness to fill in some of the gaps especially where this is necessary to protect the Union. Recognition of this approach is vital to any assessment of the legal validity of the Union's acts. The approach is exemplified by a number of important decisions of the Court of Justice.

17. It must be recollected that the ECJ's foundational ruling on direct effect in *Van Gend en Loos* established that the then European Community constituted a 'new legal order of international law for the benefit of which states [had] limited their sovereign rights, albeit within limited fields'. [15] According to the Court, Community law not only imposed obligations on individuals but was also intended to confer upon them rights which became part of their legal heritage. Those rights arose not only where they were expressly granted by the Treaty but also by reason of obligations which the Treaty imposed in a clearly defined way upon individuals as well as upon Member States and the Institutions of the Community. This legal conclusion was nowhere expressly provided in the European Economic Community Treaty (EEC Treaty) which did not deal with the legal effect of Community Law within a Member State. However it is now accepted that the *Van Gend* judgment was crucial to the development of the European project and its laws. It is noteworthy that the ECJ in arriving at its conclusion did not limit itself to a textual interpretation of the EEC Treaty.

18. In *Costa v ENEL*, the ECJ held that the new legal order of the then EEC was autonomous. It concluded that '[b]y creating a Community of unlimited duration, having its own institutions, its own personality, its own legal capacity and capacity of representation on the international plane and ... real power stemming from a limitation of sovereignty or a transfer of powers from the Member States to the Community, the Member States [had] limited their sovereign rights.' [16] The integration in the laws of each Member State of provisions which derive from the Community made it impossible for the Member States to accord precedence to unilateral and subsequent measures over a legal system accepted by them on the basis of reciprocity. Again this conclusion was not based on any express wording contained in the Treaty, but was arrived at following a process of legal interpretation which was not limited to the text of the Treaty. This decision too was critical to the legal foundations not only of the European Community but of the Union as we know it today. Those decisions, which declare principles which were not expressly authorised by the Treaties could in fact be said to have

[15] Case 26/62 *NV Algemene Transport – en Expeditie Onderneming van Gend & Loos v Netherlands Inland Revenue Administration* [1963] ECR 1 [1963] ECR 1, 12.

[16] Case 6/64 [1964] ECR 585, 593.

democratised the Community because it made individuals central to the legal structure and ensured that litigation by natural and legal persons would have a profound effect on the development of EC Law and ultimately EU Law.

19. The legal revolution effected by *Van Gend en Loos* and *Costa v ENEL* was further developed in *Simmenthal* [17] which held that national courts were not only obliged to give effect to Community law, but that they were also precluded from giving effect to any domestic law which might prevent its enforcement. These decisions demonstrate above all else that in determining the legality of Union measures it is not sufficient to conduct some arid textual analysis of the Treaty provision. A much broader approach to interpretation is required in which the teleological approach is of considerable importance.[18]
20. The ECJ has not confined itself to asserting the primacy of EU laws over national laws. In more recent times it has asserted the primacy of EU law over implementing measures of resolutions of the United Nations[19] and thus the development of EU law continues in a way not wholly dependent on textual analysis. These more recent decisions demonstrate the continued state of development of EU Law and the continued willingness of the ECJ to address current problems in a manner that does not accord primacy to the literal interpretation.
21. The ECJ has historically been prepared, in exceptional cases, to fill the gaps in the legal system. In the *Les Verts*[20] case, the ECJ accepted that, although the European Parliament was not mentioned in the EC Treaty among the institutions whose measures might be challenged in court, it had jurisdiction to hear and determine an action for annulment brought against a resolution adopted by the European Parliament. The Court assumed that the Treaty intended to establish 'a complete system of legal remedies and procedures designed to permit the Court of Justice to review the legality of measures adopted by the institutions'. The Court has also consistently used the teleological method of interpretation including using it to prevent unacceptable results. In the second *Schlüter* case,[21] the Court accepted that the adoption of MCAs by the Council despite the fact that there was 'no adequate provision in the common agricultural policy for adoption of urgent measures necessary to counteract the monetary situation [in question].'
22. The Court's interpretative approach over the years has referred expressly to the objective of 'an ever closer union',[22] and also to the principles of loyal

[17] Case 106/77 *Amministrazione delle Finanze dello Stato v Simmenthal SpA* [1978] ECR 629.

[18] See G de Burca and JHH Weiler (eds), *The European Court of Justice* (Oxford, OUP, 2001) 45.

[19] Joined Cases C-402/05 P and C-415/05 P *Kadi and Ors v Council and Commission* [2008] ECR 1-6351 and Joined Cases C-399/06 P and C-403/06 P *Hassan v Council and Commission* [2009] ECR I-11393.

[20] Case 294/83 *Parti écologiste 'Les Verts' v European Parliament* [1986] ECR 1339.

[21] Case 9/73 *Carl Schlüter v Hauptzollamt Lörrach* [1973] ECR 1135, 1152.

[22] See eg Case C-105/03 *Criminal proceedings against Mario Pupino* [2005] ECR I-5282, para 41.

cooperation and interpretation which apply the integrationist objective of the Treaty Preamble to the specific interpretative problem in the case. It is not unrealistic therefore to expect that the Court in examining the legal validity of any measure adopted to combat the financial instability generated by the present crisis will be inclined towards an interpretation which supports the Union rather than an interpretation which is likely to undermine it. The Court has also consistently taken into account the objectives of the EU legal order which include the values of that order and the general principles of EU Law.[23]

23. Gerard Conway in *The Limits of Legal Reasoning and the European Court of Justice* [24] concludes that the ECJ relies more frequently on the purposive or teleological approach to interpretation than the literal or originalist approach to a greater extent than most other courts. He concludes that the ECJ has shown a marked tendency towards a meta-teleological approach which involves the Court emphasising the purposes of the EU Treaty order at a very high level of systemic unity. According to Conway, this has favoured and enhanced the tendency towards future integration and harmonisation in Union law.
24. It is in the above legal context that the legality of some of the most significant and controversial measures introduced by Union Institutions to combat the financial crisis need to be assessed. On 9 May 2010, in an extraordinary meeting of the ECOFIN Council, the European Council decided to create the European Financial Stabilisation Mechanism (EFSM) based on Article 122(2) TFEU and the European Financial Stability Facility (EFSF) based on an intergovernmental agreement of Eurozone Member States to provide financial assistance. This decision was made in the context of the Greek financial crisis. The resulting EFSM and European Financial Stability Facility (EFSF) were vital in addressing the financial crisis in Ireland in November 2010.[25] They were also used to provide financial assistance to Portugal in April 2011 and the EFSF (but not the EFSM) was subsequently used to provide funding as part of the second financial assistance programme for Greece in March 2012.
25. Council Regulation EU No 407/2010 established the EFSM.[26] This regulation was based on Article 122(2) TFEU which provides:

> Where a Member State is in difficulty or is seriously threatened with severe difficulties caused by natural disasters or exceptional occurrences beyond its control, the Council and a proposal from the Commission may grant, under certain conditions, Union financial assistance to the Member State concerned. The President of the Council shall inform the European Parliament of the decision taken.

[23] See G Beck *The Legal Reasoning of the Court of Justice of the EU* (Oxford, Hart Publishing Company, 2013) 323.

[24] Cambridge, CUP 2012, 212

[25] This was the first time that the EFSM and EFSF were called upon to provide financial support and it was done in the context of joint EU-IMF Financial Assistance Package; See further discussion of this topic, CD Zimmermann, *A Contemporary Concept of Monetary Sovereignty* (Oxford, OUP 2013).

[26] [2010] OJ L118/1.

26. The Recitals to the EFSM Regulation recount that such difficulties 'may be caused by a serious deterioration in the international and economic and financial environment.' It also noted that the deepening of the financial crisis had led to a severe deterioration of the borrowing conditions of several Member States beyond a level which could be explained by economic fundamentals and, if that situation was not addressed as a matter of urgency, it could present a serious threat to the financial stability of the European Union as a whole.
27. The EFSM Regulation provided for Union financial assistance to take the form of a loan or of a credit line which was to be subject to strict financial conditionality as provided for by Article 3 of the Regulation, including the approval of an adjustment programme prepared by the beneficiary Member State to meet the economic conditions attached to the Union's financial assistance. The measure was clearly provisional in nature. Article 9 required the Commission to forward to the Economic and Financial Committee and the Council every six months a report on the implementation of the Regulation and on 'the continuation of the exceptional occurrences that justify the adoption of this Regulation.'
28. The argument that Article 122(2) TFEU did not provide a legal basis for the EFSM is not legally correct. It is based on a contention that the threat to Member States was not based on 'exceptional occurrences beyond [their] control.' This contention ignores the economic reality. The collapse of credit markets and bank liquidity following the start of the Great Recession in 2007 gave rise to a contagion effect which brought the US and Union financial systems to near collapse which in turn impacted greatly on Member States economies. There were undoubtedly other causes of fiscal imbalance in many Member States which were due to failures on the part of those Member States, but the existence of these other causes does not detract from the simple fact that a serious threat to the financial and economic stability of Member States was caused by exceptional occurrences beyond their control. The imposition of strict conditionality by the requirement of prior approval of the Member State's adjustment programme, addresses those causes that are attributable to the failures of the individual Member States. The provisional nature of the EFSM further emphasised that its necessity was related to exceptional occurrences.
    The legality of the EFSF has also being challenged. The EFSF Framework Agreement (EFSF Agreement) was entered in order to provide financial support to Euro Area Member States in conjunction with the IMF with the aim of safeguarding the financial stability of the Euro Area as a whole and of its Member States. It was concluded outside the framework of the Treaties and there was no express prohibition in the Treaties preventing the Euro Area Member States entering into such an agreement. The EFSF Agreement did not involve the Union assuming any liability contrary to Article 125 TFEU.
29. The preamble to the EFSF Agreement recorded that the ECB analysis recognised the existence of exceptional financial market circumstances and

risks to financial stability. Financial assistance was subject to agreement on a Memorandum of Understanding which required strict financial conditionality. The EFSF was also envisaged as being a temporary measure. Despite the absence of an express prohibition it was contended that the EFSF was prohibited by the TFEU and intruded on the Union's exclusive competence in the area of monetary policy.[27] It is now clear from the ECJ's decision in *Pringle* that a stability mechanism cannot be considered as monetary policy and therefore that objection (which was one of the principal objections of the EFSF) has no validity.

30. The ECJ in *Pringle* further confirmed that Article 136(3) TFEU was not the legal basis for the Member States' authority to conclude the European Stability Mechanism ('the ESM Treaty') and stated that concluding this treaty fell within their residual competence. It is true that the Court implied that the amendment was significant to the extent that it ensured that the mechanism would operate in a way which would comply with Union law, but that of course is quite different from saying that the amendment was legally necessary. It is clear that the strict conditionality of the ESM Treaty was critical to the *Pringle* judgment, and of course this strict conditionality was something that had already been recognised both in the EFSM and the EFSF.
31. The decision in *Pringle* addresses (at least by implication) a number of the legal objections that were made to the EFSM and EFSF. Prior to the decision in *Pringle*, it was however clear that on any view there was a sound legal basis for the introduction of these necessary measures even if arguments could properly be made challenging their legal validity. Furthermore the price of inaction would have been horrendous and would have been borne by Union Citizens. Inaction would also have undermined the Union project because it would have demonstrated that its legal structures were incapable of addressing the greatest threat to that project since its inception. If the Union institutions had failed to take the necessary emergency action at the time the consequences for the stability not only of the relevant Member States but of the Euro Area as a whole could have been disastrous. This could have led to an undermining not only of the Euro but also of the European Union. Those who suggest that no action should have been taken because of doubts about legal validity not only ignore the significant legal basis for these measures, but adopt an approach to the question of legality that ignores much of the Court's jurisprudence and in particular its approach to interpretation.
32. It is generally recognised that no other economic activity touches upon so many aspects of our lives as banking does. The systemic threat to banks in so many Member States became a systemic threat to the economies of those Member States. The need for a banking union underpinned by a single supervisory mechanism and a single resolution mechanism is obvious. The President of the European Council Herman Van Rompuy[28] has

[27] Art 3(1)(c) TFEU.

[28] 'Towards a Genuine Economic and Monetary Union', Brussels, 26 June 2012, http://www.astrid-online.it/Riforma-de/GOVERNANCE/COMPLETING/Van-Rompuy_EU-Council-Presentation_28_06_13.pdf (consulted 10 January 2014).

acknowledged that the financial crisis revealed structural shortcomings in the institutional framework for financial stability. The general consensus is that these structural shortcomings can only be addressed through a banking union which provides an integrated financial framework while preserving the unity and integrity of the single market in the field of financial services. As Yves Mersch has stated[29] it is not possible to partake in a strong single market and strong single currency with weakly coordinated national fiscal policies, economic policies and financial arrangements. The efficacy of the transmission of monetary policy is impaired by the existence of national regulation supervision and resolution systems. There is therefore a general consensus as to the need for a Banking Union comprising a Single Supervisory Mechanism (SSM), a Single Resolution Mechanism (SRM) and a Deposit Guarantee System.

33. The necessity therefore for the proposed SSM and SRM is obvious. However both of these measures have also been greeted with significant legal objection particularly the SRM. As far as the SSM is concerned, Article 127(6) TFEU specifically provides for the conferral on the ECB of tasks concerning policies relating to the prudential supervision of credit institutions and other financial institutions with the exception of insurance undertakings. Notwithstanding this explicit Treaty basis, objections were made to the SSM on various grounds and in particular on the ground that combining monetary policy and supervision creates unavoidable conflicts of interest for the ECB. However the inescapable legal fact is that the monetary and supervisory roles are conferred by the TFEU on the ECB and with the correct structures those risks can, in any event, be greatly reduced. The risk of a potential conflict therefore cannot be used as a ground for invalidating the SSM. There is accordingly no sound basis for contending that the creation of the SSM is unlawful.

34. There is no explicit Treaty basis for the SRM. The present legislative proposal is based on Article 114 TFEU. Article 114 TFEU permits the introduction of measures designed to achieve the objectives set out in Article 26 TFEU, namely measures with the aim of establishing or ensuring the functioning of the internal market. The Commission's Explanatory Memorandum for the proposed SRM states that the proposal aims to preserve the integrity and enhance the functioning of the internal market, and that uniform application of a single set of resolution rules together with access to a single European Resolution Fund by a central authority would restore the orderly functioning of the European banking markets and would remove obstacles to the exercise of the fundamental freedoms and avoid significant distortion of competition at least in Member States which share the supervision of credit institutions at the European level. This Commission statement is backed up by the substantial evidence of the effect on the internal market in the last number of years of differential resolution mechanisms in different Member States. The measure is fully supported by the ECB[30] and also by

[29] N 11 above.

[30] See Opinion of the European Central Bank, 6 November 2013, ECB document CON/2013/76.

many statements of members of the ECB Executive Board which recognise the central role which the measure would have in strengthening the single market.[31] Mr Jorg Asmussen[32] recently stated that the ECB considered the SRM to be an indispensible pillar of the Banking Union and stated: '[t]he Banking Union should be about strengthening the internal market, rather than fragmenting. Both the single currency and the single market are key pillars of growth and prosperity in Europe.'

35. The ECJ when considering the entitlement to rely on Article 114 TFEU applies a number of fundamental legal principles which can be summarised as follows:
    a. A mere finding of disparities between national rules and the abstract risk of infringement of fundamental freedoms or distortions of competition is not sufficient to justify the choice of Article 114 TFEU as a legal basis.[33] Nor is it sufficient that a measure has an incidental effect on harmonisation. The Union legislature is only entitled to have recourse to Article 114 TFEU in particular where there are differences between national rules which are such as to obstruct the fundamental freedoms and thus have a direct effect on the functioning of the internal market.
    b. Reliance can be placed on Article 114 where obstacles to trade resulting from the divergent development of national law are likely to emerge and the measure is designed to prevent those obstacles emerging.[34]
    c. Article 114 can be used to establish a centralised decision-making process to bring about approximation provided this decision-making process is determined and circumscribed precisely in the legislation.[35] The very adoption of a decision by the centralised decision-maker may in itself be regarded as a harmonising measure.[36]
    d. The issue of whether the harmonisation should be achieved through a Directive addressed to the Member States or through a centralised decision procedure is a matter for the political assessment of the legislature.[37]
    e. The Regulation must apply uniformly throughout the Member States and cannot permit of any derogation.
    f. The Regulation must not infringe fundamental rights and in this particular context, property rights.

[31] Mersch (n 11 above).

[32] Member of the Executive Board of the ECB, at the Danske Bank Financial Forum 2013, Stockholm, 5 November 2013, http://www.bis.org/review/r131106a.htm (consulted 10 January 2014).

[33] Case C-58/05 *The Queen, on the application of Vodafone Ltd and Others v Secretary of State for Business, Enterprise and Regulatory Reform* [2010] ECR I-4999.

[34] Case C-491/01 *The Queen v Secretary of State for Health ex parte British American Tobacco (Investments) Ltd and Imperial Tobacco Ltd* [2002] ECR I-11453.

[35] Case C-66/04 *United Kingdom of Great Britain and Northern Ireland v European Parliament and Council of the European Union* [2005] ECR I-10553.

[36] Ibid.

[37] *Vodafone* (n 33) para 42.

In addition to the above general principles the Court will assess legal validity by reference to the form and structure of the proposed regulation including the structure of the decision-making and the proposed basis of the SRM Fund so as to ensure that they are consistent with the Treaties.

36. The present SRM proposal meets those requirements. While some concerns have been expressed by the Council Legal Service in its second opinion about other aspects of the SRM and their compatibility with Treaty provisions,[38] there is no reason in principle why those issues are not capable of being addressed in order to ensure the necessary legal robustness.

37. Many commentators have called for Treaty change prior to the introduction of the SSM and SRM in order to provide a 'proper' legal basis for them. In this context it is of course worth remembering that there were also significant legal objections to the ESM Treaty and many of those objecting also called for Treaty change. In December 2010 a political decision was made to amend the TFEU by adding a third paragraph to article 136 of the Treaty to explicitly permit the granting of required financial assistance subject to strict conditionality pursuant to a stability mechanism to be established by Treaty if indispensible to safeguarding the stability of the Euro area as a whole. The decision was undoubtedly influenced not just by political considerations but also by legal uncertainty surrounding the ESFM and EFSF. It is somewhat ironic that the amendment of the TFEU and the conclusion of the ESM Treaty was in breach of EU Law and violated *inter alia* Article 125 TFEU. These contentions were rejected in *Pringle*. The decision of the ECJ in *Pringle* confirms the general interpretative approach of the ECJ described above and provides additional confidence that crisis containment measures can be devised within existing Treaty structures. The *Pringle* decision also provides strong confirmation of the Union's adherence to the Rule of Law during the financial and economic crisis.

38. In conclusion in introducing these measures descrived above the Union institutions have respected the Rule of Law. While valid criticisms can be made about the Union institutions' delayed reaction to the financial and economic crisis those institutions have now properly availed of the existing legal framework to devise and implement important responses to that crisis. Not to have acted becaused of legal objections to which there was a strong legal response would have deprived Union citizens of the benefit of a stable Euro and would have postponed indefinitely the creation of a sound banking framework which is essential to achieving the Union's objectives. The Union's decisions and actions certainly respected the test suggested in paragraph 9 above. Those who criticise the Union's actions would do well to remember that law is not just an abstract discipline. Legal decisions can impact hugely on people's lives and well-being. Those charged to govern and make decisions are obliged to discharge their functions. In making decisions they do not have the benefit of the detailed analysis and argument

[38] Opinion of 15 October 2013, http://interactive.ftdata.co.uk/docCloud/templates/onePageAttr.html?p=802602-cls-banking-union (consulted 10 January 2014).

and presentation of rival views which characteristic of a court hearing or the opportunity for long reflection and consideration. The application of the Rule of Law must recognise these realities or otherwise it transforms from being a necessary restraint in a democratic society to a straitjacket which prevents vital action necessary for the preservation of that society

9

The Internal Market in a Context of Deepening Integration – Long on Content and Short on Modes of Delivery?

HERWIG CH HOFMANN*

Abstract

This contribution takes one of Advocate General Fennelly's most influential Opinions during his time at the European Court of Justice – the Opinion in Case C-376/98 known as *Tobacco advertising I* – as a starting point to look at developments in the internal market legislation of the European Union since. It thereby explores the diversifying limits to integration by harmonisation of national law for the 'establishment and functioning of the internal market' (Article 114 TFEU) by the adoption of substantive and procedural 'measures' under EU law in the past decade and a half.

I. INTRODUCTION

THE EUROPEAN UNION'S (EU) internal market is an 'area without internal frontiers in which the free movement of goods, persons, services and capital is ensured' (Article 26 TFEU) inter alia by the possibility for the EU legislature to adopt 'measures' for its establishment and functioning (Article 114 TFEU). Defining the outer limits of this legal basis[1] for the adoption of 'measures' has always been a complex task, but it has

* Professor of European and Transnational Public Law, Jean Monnet Chair; University of Luxembourg – Faculty of Law, Economics and Finance – Centre for European Law (herwig.hofmann@uni.lu).

[1] On this notion in EU law generally, see K Bradley,'Powers and procedures in the EU Constitution: Legal bases and the Court' in P Craig and G de Búrca (eds), *The Evolution of EU Law* 2nd edn (Oxford, OUP, 2011) 85.

become more so in the past decade and a half, not least because of two main factors. The first is that regulation which is relevant for the establishment and the functioning of the internal market can rarely be completely disassociated from the regulation of other policy areas. Product rules, for example, will also have an influence on health, safety and environmental standards. Free movement of services and workers, as well as rules on the establishment of businesses and self-employed persons will have an immediate influence on matters such as social security systems and labour policies, professional qualifications and education, to name just a few. This means that balancing economic rights with social and political rights is a key feature of regulation of the internal market.[2] The second contributing factor to the difficulties of defining the limits to the Union's power to adopt internal market legislation is an increasing diversification of the forms of 'measures', in the context of the steady transformation of the EU from an organisation primarily engaged in legislative action into an organisation increasingly active in the field of the administrative implementation of Union law.

In the area of internal market regulation, therefore, there are many hard cases on the reach of internal market-related legislative powers of the Union. In this chapter, I will outline some of the major developments of the past decade and a half in this field starting with Advocate General (AG) Fennelly's Opinion in 2000 in *Tobacco advertising* I[3] on issues of the definition of the possible extent of legislative 'measures' and the limits thereof in the context of the principle of conferral, expanding and explaining *Titanium dioxide*[4] and laying the foundations of *Alliance for Natural Health*.[5] In this chapter I will discuss these cases also regarding the concepts of subsidiarity and proportionality which were further explored in *Vodafone*,[6] *Smoke flavourings*,[7] *ENISA*[8] and, more recently, *Short selling*.[9] I will add a different dimension by looking at the notion of 'measures' not only from a substantive and legislative angle, but additionally review the issue of the limits on the legislature's discretion in this regard from their structural, institutional and implementing perspective. I will discuss the various parameters of the limits of legislative powers for the harmonisation of the internal market, first, from the more traditional angle of the limits of legislative measures adopted by the EU (I), before turning to the question of using the internal market related powers to establish structural and procedural

[2] S Weatherill, 'Free Movement of Goods' (2012) 61 *ICLQ* 541, 545.

[3] Opinion of 15 June 2000 in Case C-376/98 *Germany v Parliament and Council (Tobacco advertising I)* [2000] ECR I-8423.

[4] Case C-300/89 *Commission v Council* [1991] ECR I-2867.

[5] Joined Cases C-154/04 and C-155/04 *The Queen, on the application of the Alliance for Natural Health and Others v Secretary of State for Health and National Assembly for Wales* [2005] ECR I-6451.

[6] Case C-58/08 *Vodafone and Others* [2010] ECR I-4999.

[7] Case C-66/04 *UK v Parliament and Council (Smoke flavorings)* [2005] ECR I-10553.

[8] Case C-217/04 *UK v Parliament and Council (ENISA)* [2006] ECR I-3771.

[9] Opinion of AG Jääskinen of 12 September 2013 in Case C-270/12 *UK v Council and Parliament (Short selling)*, judgment of 22 January 2014. The Opinion is discussed by H Marjosola, 'Case C-270/12 (UK v Parliament and Council) – Stress Testing Consitutional Resiliance of the Powers of EU Financial Supervisory Authorities' (2014/02) *EUI Law Working Papers*.

measures coordinating Member State implementation of EU law (II). These discussions are brought together in a new generation of cases starting with *Short selling* (III), which I will discuss briefly before drawing some conclusions from the diverse developments in EU internal market legislation for the future of Union powers (IV).

II. LIMITS OF LEGISLATIVE 'MEASURES' HARMONISING MEMBER STATE LAW

Limitations on the legislative powers of the Union are to be found first and foremost in the three basic principles of Union competence listed in Article 5 TEU: the principle of the limited attribution of powers to the Union, generally known as the principle of conferral; the principle of subsidiarity; and the principle of proportionality of Union action.[10]

1. Conferral

One of the cornerstones of the definition of the notion of conferral was given by AG Fennelly's Opinion in *Tobacco advertising I*,[11] on the basis of which the Court famously clarified and re-stated that a legislative act which is based on Article 114 TFEU may not simply reduce or eliminate regulatory differences between the Member States. Teleologically speaking, Article 114 TFEU is not available in order to level regulatory differences between the Member States without restriction. Instead, a measure under Article 114 TFEU must actively contribute in some way or another to the creation or functioning of the internal market. This has been heralded as a 'momentous' ruling,[12] since in it the European Court of Justice (ECJ)[13] for the first time concluded that a legislative act of the EU harmonising national legislation was ultra vires the rules of what is now Article 114 TFEU as breaching the principle of conferral.

The case concerned the highly controversial first Directive on tobacco advertising.[14] According to its preamble, the Directive sought to approximate national laws on products and services which until then had traditionally been used as media for advertising tobacco and tobacco products. These included newspapers and magazines, goods such as umbrellas and perfumes, as well as services such as broadcasting and sports events. Divergent national rules on the treatment of such goods and services were addressed by the Directive in a

[10] Article 5 TEU.

[11] N 3 above.

[12] Weatherill (n 2 above), 547.

[13] The abbreviation 'ECJ' refers to the Court of Justice, part of the Union's judicial institution, the Court of Justice of the European Union; ECJ is therefore to be understood as opposed to the General Court, the former Court of First Instance.

[14] Directive 98/43 of the European Parliament and of the Council of 6 July 1998 on the approximation of the laws, regulations and administrative provisions of the Member States relating to the advertising and sponsorship of tobacco products [1998] OJ L213/9.

way which, to many commentators, appeared to be driven predominantly by the intention to combat smoking and thus to be oriented towards consumer health protection. The Treaty provisions on public health at the time of the adoption of the contested *Tobacco advertising I* directive in Article 167(6) TFEU, however, explicitly excluded, and continue to exclude even now, 'any harmonisation of the laws and regulations of the Member States'. In the absence of a legal basis for measures harmonising in the field of health, the Directive was designed as a measure for the approximation of rules for the single market which, as is required by Article 114(3) TFEU, attempt to ensure a high level of health protection.

The choice of legal basis under the principle of conferral is an area to which the ECJ applies full judicial review. The choice is based on what the Court refers to as objective criteria, clarifying that this choice is not a matter which falls within the political discretion of the decision-maker. This is the context in which the Court, following AG Fennelly, and enforcing the concept of the limited attribution of powers to the Union, found that Article 114 TFEU is not linked to a specific policy matter but, under its functional approach, must be reviewed by assessing the 'objective requirements of the internal market'.[15] These include in particular, 'the concrete internal market benefits claimed for the measure'[16] as a 'test of the reality of the link between such measures and the internal-market objectives.'[17] Effectively, prohibiting activity within a sector without harmonising Member State laws concerning that sector or the remaining legal activity therein cannot, in the words of Advocate General Fennelly, be said to facilitate the exercise of the fundamental freedoms in the internal market, or 'remove distortions of completion in the sector in question.'[18]

By contrast, Advocate General Fennelly explains that in order to be within the scope of application of Article 114 TFEU, measures approximating Member State laws would have to satisfy a two-step test: they 'should be specific to the sector, however widely drawn, and should not be merely incidental'.[19] Advocate General Fennelly thereby applied and clarified the approach adopted in *Titanium dioxide* under which the distortion of competition leading to a harmonising measure had to be 'appreciable'.[20] Given that in the view of the Advocate General and the Court the Directive did not have a sufficiently appreciable and merely incidental effect on the conditions of the internal market, it violated the principle of conferral for want of a proper legal basis in the Treaties.[21]

Applying these criteria, the Court in *Alliance for Natural Health* confirmed that it is not *per se* forbidden to ban the marketing of a product in the context of a measure adopted under Article 114 TFEU.[22] The case concerned a

[15] Case C-376/98 *Germany v Parliament and Council (Tobacco advertising I)* [2000] ECR I-8423, para 58.
[16] Ibid.
[17] N 15, para 89.
[18] N 3, para 58.
[19] N 3, para 91.
[20] N 4, para 23.
[21] N 3, para 116.
[22] N 5, paras 38–40.

legislative act containing certain prohibitions on the marketing of products which had not been cleared for human consumption. At the same time, the contested measure ensured that those products which had been approved under the system established for their control could freely circulate throughout the internal market. But apart from the fact that the measure in *Alliance for Natural Health*, unlike that in *Tobacco advertising I*, actually created conditions for free movement of food additives within an internal market, the measure differed as regards the definition of the relevant market for product or services. This is relevant for the definition of when an actual or potential distortion of competition can be found. The definition of such market is often only undertaken implicitly by the Courts. Openly addressing this definition would be preferable in that it might well contribute to further clarification of the reasoning behind a judgment.

According to the principle of conferral, the legality of legislative 'measures' under Article 114 TFEU in today's case law of the ECJ therefore contains the following key criteria:[23] Article 114 TFEU cannot be used to erase all forms of disparities between national rules.[24] Instead, disparities between national regulatory approaches, in order to qualify, must be found to 'obstruct' the fundamental freedoms in a specific sector, and thus have a direct and not merely incidental effect on the functioning of the internal market or the conditions of competition therein.[25] On the basis of this finding, Article 114 TFEU can also be used to remove existing or prevent likely appreciable future obstructions.[26] Article 114 TFEU can also be used as legal basis for subsequent updates and adaptation of legislative acts originally based on Article 114 TFEU, when necessary to accommodate new circumstances or technical and scientific developments.[27] Within these limits, there is legislative discretion in relation to the method of approximation most appropriate for achieving the desired result.[28] The Union legislature is obliged to balance various interests and societal values 'once the competence is triggered by the need to harmonise a particular field' in the context of Article 114 TFEU.[29]

[23] See for an overview especially K Lenaerts, 'The European Court of Justice and Process–oriented Review', *College of Europe, Research Paper in Law* 1/2012, 4. See for criticism of this set of criteria eg S Weatherill, 'The Limits of Legislative harmonization Ten Years after *Tobacco Advertising*: How the Court's Case Law has become a "Drafting Guide"', (2011) 12 *German Law Journal* , 827, 827. In his view, the use of these criteria risks becoming part of a circular pattern which relies on 'approved but reliably vague vocabulary'.

[24] Opinion of AG Miguel Poiares Maduro of 1 October 2009 in *Vodafone* (n 6) para 1: 'this is not a provision intended to give to the Community a general power of regulation over the internal market'.

[25] Judgment in *Tobacco advertising I* (n 15 above) paras 84 and 106.

[26] Case C-301/06 *Ireland v Parliament and Council (Data retention)* [2009] ECR I-593, para 64.

[27] Case C-491/01 *British American Tobacco (Investments) and Imperial Tobacco (Tobacco advertising II)* [2002] ECR I-11453, paras 77 and 78; Case C-374/05 *Gintec* [2007] ECR I-9517, para 29.

[28] Eg *Smoke flavourings* (n 7 above), para 43.

[29] Maduro (n 24 above) para 8. Obviously high levels of protection of values protected by Union law including those listed in Article 114(3) TFEU must be ensured – see eg *Alliance for Natural Health and Others* (n 5 above) para 30.

2. Proportionality and Subsidiarity

One of the reasons for the definition by the ECJ of detailed limits on the use of Article 114 TFEU under the principle of conferral is that the choice of legal basis is subject to full judicial review. By contrast, the review of the exercise of the powers once conferred is more limited, given that the Court must take account of the existing broad legislative discretion of the EU legislature in these matters which requires some more or less pronounced judicial self-restraint.

In the context of this review, the Court has developed in the past few years a key instrument which is based on the fact that review of compliance with the principles of subsidiarity and particularly of proportionality is based on a certain degree of information about the motivation for the legislative choice and potential alternatives which had not been adopted in the process. This has led the Court to oscillate between exercising restraint and undertaking an increasingly more stringent review of compliance with legislative procedures, incidentally having an effect on the legislative substance also. [30]

One key step in this direction was *Vodafone*,[31] in which various mobile telephone operators challenged the legality of an EU regulation on roaming charges which had been based on what today is Article 114 TFEU.[32] This regulation had the effect of capping the fees that telephone service operators could charge their customers for cross-border calls within the internal market. The Commission's impact assessment study had found that mobile phone operators were using national licences which allowed for service provision within specific territories of individual Member States to charge customers who were moving within the internal market exorbitant fees which often stood in no relation to the cost associated with providing this service.

Reviewing the legality of the legislation capping the fees, Advocate General Maduro in *Vodafone* suggested a new kind of procedure-based review of compliance with the principle of proportionality. He suggested taking into account the institutions' impact assessment reports to analyse whether the legislature had complied with the requirements of the Court's proportionality test, especially whether the legislature had reviewed whether there were regulatory alternatives which were less onerous with regard to the applicants' rights. He was satisfied with compliance with the proportionality test inter alia on the ground that the legislature had analysed, prior to adopting the Regulation, the relevant alternative means of achieving the objective under Article 114 TFEU, and had not found solutions which were less onerous for the applicants' rights than the solutions chosen by the Union legislature in the Regulation.[33] The ECJ confirmed the Opinion in its judgment, establishing that the Regulation was aimed at bringing to an end an activity which was detrimental to the provision

[30] See eg A Alemanno and A Meuwese, 'Impact Assessment of EU Non-Legislative Rulemaking: The Missing Link of "New" Comitology', (2013) 19 *European Law Journal* 76.

[31] N 6.

[32] [2007] OJ L171/32, amended by Regulation No 544/2009, [2009] OJ L167/12 (enlarging the scope of application to SMS and data roaming).

[33] Maduro (n 24), paras 38–40.

of mobile telephone services within the internal market, and that it was thereby genuinely aimed at improving the conditions for the establishment and functioning of the internal market.[34] The distortions of competition arose from the fact that telephone companies were essentially exploiting to the disadvantage of the consumers the territorially exclusive licences which Member States had accorded to them. In doing so, the Court followed the 'procedural' approach to proportionality-review proposed by Advocate General Maduro.[35]

The ECJ has applied this procedure-based approach to the review of the principle of proportionality, making reference to impact assessment studies by the institutions, in *Afton Chemicals* [36] and *Luxembourg v Commission*.[37] Lenaerts, himself a judge at the ECJ though writing in a personal capacity, comments that under the *Vodafone* approach, the ECJ 'applies the principle of proportionality in a procedural fashion' by focussing not on the regulatory substance of the measure but on whether the institutions showed that they 'had examined different regulatory options and assessed their economic, social and environmental impact' before adopting a legislative act.[38] This approach so far developed for the review of proportionality could potentially also be applied for review of compliance with the principle of subsidiarity. This has, as far as I can see, so far not been done.

III. ARTICLE 114 TFEU AND STRUCTURAL MEASURES – *QUI PEUT LE PLUS, PEUT LE MOINS* ?

Whilst the decision on the allocation of regulatory powers which was addressed in *Tobacco advertising I* was, at the end of the day, one of the transfer of legislative power *tout court*, the possibilities of what could be understood as a 'measure' under Article 114 TFEU have since been expanded.[39] It has branched out into two related sub-issues: one is the question of the degree of 'Europeanisation' of the implementation of a policy through sub-legislative measures, the other is the question of whether instead of wholesale legislative harmonisation more cooperative and sovereignty-preserving means could be identified.[40]

Two 'post-*Tobacco advertising I*' cases illustrate this change in nature and perception of integration. *Smoke flavourings*[41] and *ENISA*[42] are both disputes concerning the extent and limits of the powers conferred on the Union under what was Article 95 EC, now Article 114 TFEU.[43] They each raise the question

[34] N 6, para 32.
[35] N 6, referring to the impact assessment report in paras 45, 55, 58 and three times in para 65.
[36] Case C-343/09 *Afton Chemical Limited* [2010] ECR I-7027.
[37] Case C-176/09 *Luxembourg v European Parliament/Commission* [2011] ECR I-3727.
[38] Lenaerts, n 23 above, 7.
[39] See eg, with great detail, H-H Herrnfeld, AEUV Artikel 114, in J Schwarze (ed) *EU-Kommentar*, 3rd edition (Baden-Baden, Nomos, 2012) 1421–1476.
[40] See, eg *Smoke flavourings* (n 7) and *ENISA* (n 8) which will be discussed in greater detail later in this paper.
[41] N 7.
[42] N 8.
[43] Comments in the literature on these two judgements have included worries that they might 'inflame the perennial tensions underlying the division of competence between the Community

of resorting to European agencies and, in *Smoke flavourings*, also that of using a comitology procedure as means to reduce the 'hard' legislative approach to harmonisation, and achieve legislative goals through the use of forms of integrated administration.

In *ENISA*, the UK relied essentially on the illegality of using (what is now) Article 114 TFEU as the legal basis for adopting structural 'measures' instead of the 'straightforward' approximation of the rules of the Member States. In this case, the structural measure was the creation of the European Network and Information Security Agency ('ENISA') as an EU agency with its own legal personality and designed to advise Member States on matters related to safety of information networks. Similarly, in *Smoke flavourings* the UK incidentally challenged the use of what is now Article 114 TFEU as the legal basis for the empowerment of an EU agency – the European Food Safety Authority – to participate in a procedure provided by law to establish a market authorisation for certain food additives referred to as smoke flavourings. In the absence of general regulatory powers of the Union in the area of the internal market, in the UK's view, Article 114 TFEU merely intended to confer powers for the adoption of measures directed at the Member States. Under this view, the creation of multiple-step regulatory procedures failed to harmonise national law directly and was thus illegal.[44] Similarly, in *ENISA*, the UK contested the legality of the regulation establishing ENISA as a 'measure' under Article 114 TFEU.[45] The UK argued that the creation of an agency to improve the conditions of the exchange of information within the internal market could not be regarded as a measure designed to approximate Member State law, since it was not aimed directly at addressing the conditions of competition in a specific policy field.

The Court's judgements in *Smoke flavourings* and *ENISA* are noteworthy specifically because they do not follow the applicant's approach of portraying the possibilities of EU law in terms of a two-level model, in which the EU may exclusively legislate and Member States must maintain all implementing powers. In *Smoke flavourings*, the ECJ held by contrast that the Union legislature enjoyed discretion 'as regards the harmonisation technique most appropriate for achieving the desired result'.[46] This may include cases 'where the Community

and the Member States' and have the 'potential to enliven concerns about the magnitude of the Community's competence': K Gutman, Case note on Case C-66/04, *Smoke Flavourings*; Case C-436/03, *SCE*; and Case C-217/04, *ENISA*, (2006/2007) 13 *Columbia Journal of European Law* 147, 182. For further critical reviews of the cases, especially with respect to the principle of conferral see A Epiney, 'Anmerkung zu C-217/04, (2007) *Neue Verwaltungsrechts Zeitschrift*, 1012; M Ludwigs, 'Artikel 95 als allgemeine Kompetenz zur Regelung des Binnenmarktes oder als "begrenzte Einzelermächtigung"?', (2006) *Europäische Zeitschrift für Wirtschaftsrecht*, 417.

[44] The UK acknowledged that establishing a detailed decision-making procedure with a regulatory committee procedure assisting and supervising the Commission, whose decisions are prepared with input from the European Food Safety Agency established a procedure which could result in harmonisation of national law. That, according to the argument, was too far removed to be acceptable under Art 95 EC.

[45] Reg EC 460/2004 of the European Parliament and Council of 10 March 2004, [2004] OJ L77/1. The UK argued that Art 308 EC, requiring unanimity in the Council, would have been the correct legal basis for such a measure.

[46] N 7 paras 45 and 46.

legislature establishes the detailed rules for making decisions at each stage of such an authorisation procedure, and determines and circumscribes precisely the powers of the Commission as the body which has to take the final decision'.[47]

AG Kokott's Opinion had stressed this latter point by entering into a detailed analysis of the principles of proportionality and subsidiarity comparing different possible regulatory approaches in the case. These consisted of, on the one hand, a multi-step procedure for establishing a list of marketable smoke flavouring food additives, which consisted of a comitology committee procedure for decision-making in combination with scientific analysis prepared by the European Food Safety Authority. She compared this with, on the other hand, a more traditional notion, generally referred to as 'executive federalism'. This consists of harmonising legislation on the European level and implementation by the Member States, combined with the obligation of mutual recognition on the Member States regarding administrative decisions within the internal market. In the long term the latter solution, she reasoned, could not only lead to conflicts between Member States to the disadvantage of the internal market. It also risks restricting the competences of the Member States 'just as much' as the solution chosen by the Regulation, and 'would at the same time make the procedure for the authorisation of smoke flavourings considerably clumsier and if anything reduce the rights of participation of manufacturers'.[48]

In *ENISA*, the ECJ rejected the UK's claim and recognised the validity of the contested Regulation. It held that, first, the addressees of 'measures' are not exclusively the Member States. Second, the objective of the Regulation, 'to improve the conditions for the establishment and functioning of the internal market'[49] by creating a 'body responsible for contributing to the implementation of a process of harmonisation' where 'the adoption of non-binding supporting and framework measures seems appropriate,' was in conformity with Article 114 TFEU.[50] Third, echoing the requirements developed in *Tobacco advertising I*, the Court found that the tasks conferred on such a body must be 'closely linked to the subject matter of approximation of laws'.

To these criteria, one might also add, in the words of the judgment in *Tobacco advertising I*, the requirement that the measure 'genuinely have as its object to improve the conditions for the establishment and functioning of the internal market',[51] by preventing or eliminating an actual or potential 'appreciable distortion of competition' or 'the emergence of future obstacles to trade resulting from multifarious development of national laws'.[52] In view of the Court, in a field of complex and rapidly developing technical circumstances the creation of an agency providing technical advice facilitated the implementation of EU

[47] N 7 para 49.

[48] Opinion of Advocate General Kokott in *Smoke flavorings* (n 7 above) para 47.

[49] N 8 above, para 42, with reference to *Smoke flavourings*.

[50] N 8 above, paras 44 and 45. The Court explains that '[s]uch is the case in particular where the Community body thus established provides services to national authorities and/or operators which affect the homogenous implementation of harmonising instruments and which are likely to facilitate their application.'

[51] N 15, para 84.

[52] Ibid para 86.

law, and thereby made a real contribution to the achievement of the internal market.[53] 'Low-intensity approximation' in the form of establishing an agency providing advice to national bodies who remain free to exercise their discretion and adopt different measures than the ones proposed, is possible,[54] in this context, under an *'a maiore ad minus'* argument. Applying an approach based on administrative cooperation in order to achieve technically sound solutions, while at the same time devising a sovereignty-preserving measure,[55] appeared to the ECJ to give effect to the principles of subsidiarity and proportionality. Therefore, although the principle of conferral remains the basis of the rule of law and the control of whether the Union has acted within its competencies, for the delimitation of EU law, conferral needs to be understood in the context of an integrated legal system, for the most part in the form of executive networks with participants from the Member States, the Union institutions and private parties.[56] Interestingly, the development of a system of decentralised yet cooperative administrative structures historically goes hand in hand with the emergence of subsidiarity as a constitutional notion.[57]

IV. MEASURES MATURING – SHORT SELLIING DELEGATION?

The Court of Justice recently added a layer to these considerations in *Short selling*.[58] The case concerns predominantly the validity of an EU legislative provision, that is, Article 28 of the EU regulation on short selling and certain aspects of credit default swaps,[59] and also addresses the creation of the European Securities and Markets Authority (ESMA) on the basis of Article 114 TFEU. ESMA is one of the three EU agencies established in 2011 to support the surveillance of key financial actors within an Economic and Monetary Union.[60] Article 28 of the Regulation vests ESMA with powers to intervene inter alia by adopting binding legal acts addressed to individuals, in the event of threats to the orderly functioning or the stability of financial markets or the financial system in the EU. These may contain injunctions to comply with various

[53] N 8, paras 60–66. It needs to be added that in *ENISA*, the ECJ did not agree with AG Kokott's Opinion. AG Kokott had argued that Art 95 EC was not the correct legal basis for measures which are not closely related to the approximation of national law. In this way, she argued, it was immaterial whether the measure finally adopted 'had less of an effect on national competences than a genuinely approximating measure' (Opinion of AG Kokott (n 8) para 39).

[54] N 8, paras 25 and 38.

[55] Especially when compared with full-scale detailed regulation for transposition in Member States under a more traditional two-level model.

[56] M Egeberg, 'Europe's Executive Branch of Governments in the Melting Pot: An Overview' in M Egeberg (ed), *Multilevel Union Administration* (London, Palgrave, 2006) 1.

[57] HCH Hofmann, 'Conflicts and Integration: Revisiting *Costa v ENEL* and *Simmental II*' in M Maduro and L Azoulai (eds), *The Past and the Future of EU Law* (Oxford, Hart, 2010), 66.

[58] Case C-270/12 *UK v Council and Parliament (Short Selling)*, judgment of 22 January 2014.

[59] Regulation (EU) No 236/2012 of the European Parliament and of the Council of 14 March 2012 on short selling and certain aspects of credit default swaps [2012] OJ L86/1.

[60] Regulation (EU) No 1095/2010 of the European Parliament and the Council of 24 November 2010 establishing a European Supervisory Authority (European Securities and Markets Authority) [2011] OJ L 331/1.

disclosure requirements and a prohibition against entering into certain types of transactions, namely those commonly known amongst market participants as 'short selling'.[61] The UK claimed *inter alia* that Article 114 TFEU was an invalid legal basis for authorising EMSA to impose prohibitions on short selling under Article 28 of the Regulation. This would not only constitute a breach of the limits on delegation to agencies set by the Court in the *Meroni* judgment of the early days of European integration.[62] It would also be *ultra vires* Article 114 TFEU, as that provision does not allow for the delegation of individual regulatory decisions overriding those taken by national authorities.[63]

Short selling thereby combines the various strands of the ongoing debate about the limits of Article 114 TFEU – the questions of substance and procedure, and regarding which structural measures can be adopted as 'measures' for the approximation of the conditions on the internal market. Accordingly, AG Jääskinen's Opinion looked at the limits of Article 114 TFEU as a legal basis in two respects: first, for the adoption of a structural measure such as the creation of ESMA as an EU agency, and second, for the substantive question of whether ESMA could be vested with the power to adopt measures prohibiting certain market activities such as short selling, even in cases in which the supervisory authorities of the Member State saw no reason to intervene. Instead of considering the preliminary question of the legality of the creation of an agency vested with these powers, the Court, by contrast, mixes the questions of the empowerment of the agency with that of its creation.

Regarding the creation of an agency such as ESMA on the basis of Article 114 TFEU, the Court had established *inter alia* in *ENISA* and *Smoke flavourings* that Article 114 TFEU allows not only for the adoption of measures addressed at Member States but also for the creation of structures under EU law such as agencies. The Advocate General found that creating ESMA and conferring on it the power to regulate short selling activities was in fact undertaken in view of the divergences in Member State rules. The EU legislature claims that this was one of the causes of the market volatility which had led to the financial crises since 2008. Given the legislative discretion in this field, in view of the Advocate General, there should be no objection in principle 'to the establishment of ESMA and the regulation of its tasks and powers on the basis of Article 114 TFEU'.[64] The Court, by discussing the matter principally in the context of delegation of powers outside of Articles 290 and 291 TFEU, implicitly concurred with that approach.[65]

The second question concerning ESMA's power to adopt individual measures on the basis of Article 28 of the Regulation is more problematic.

[61] Article 28 (1)(b) and (2)(a) of Regulation (EU) No 236/2012 of the European Parliament and of the Council of 14 March 2012 on short selling and certain aspects of credit default swaps [2012] OJ L86/1.

[62] Case 9/56 *Meroni v High Authority* [1957 and 1958] ECR 133. The case concerned the legality of delegation of powers from the High Authority of the European Coal and Steel Community to bodies established under Belgian law.

[63] N 58 above, paras 28–34, 89 and 90.

[64] N 9 above, paras 32–34.

[65] N 58 above, paras 78–86.

Whether the conferral of powers to regulate and prohibit certain types of trades on financial markets falls within the scope of Article 114 TFEU can be judged against the criteria of 'whether or not the decisions of the agency concerned either contribute or amount to internal market harmonisation, in the sense this notion is used in EU law.'[66] For the Advocate General, it was not the fact of ESMA having been granted the power to impose a prohibition on, or lay down conditions related to, short selling, which would render the powers vested in ESMA ultra vires with regard to Article 114 TFEU. Instead, the Advocate General, siding with the applicant Member State, found Article 28 of the Regulation conferring powers on ESMA to be objectionable because it allowed to 'lift implementation powers ... from the national level to the EU level when there is disagreement between ESMA and the competent national authority or between national authorities'.[67] In his view, this did not comply with the three most central criteria for the application of Article 114 TFEU requiring approximation of Member State law: first, whether the emergence of obstacles to the conditions of competition on the internal market is 'likely', and the measure was designed to prevent these obstacles; second, whether the measure would 'genuinely' improve the conditions on the internal market,[68] and, third, whether the emergence of obstacles to the conditions of competition on the internal market was 'closely linked to the subject matter of the acts approximating' the Member State provisions.[69]

The Court, however, dismissed the Advocate General's view that a harmonisation measure under Article 114 TFEU, such as Article 28 of the Regulation, should only allow for the adoption of a general regulatory measure such as establishing standards for national agencies.[70] It found that 'general laws alone may not be sufficient to ensure the unity of the market,'[71] especially in view of the fact that measures under Article 114 TFEU did not necessarily have to be addressed at the Member States. After all, the idea of a close relation between disturbances on the financial markets and certain market behaviour seems to be a necessary pre-condition for action of the agency under Article 28 of the Regulation. Therefore, the action of an EU agency intervening vis-à-vis individuals could still be deemed the approximation of the Member State provisions in the core sense of Article 114 TFEU. The Court had little to say about whether the prohibition of an activity such as short selling would fall foul of the conditions for the regulation of the internal market established by *Tobacco advertising I* and *Alliance for Natural Health* which required some sort of market to remain regulated. It simply referred to the necessity of creating a 'common regulatory framework with regard to

[66] N 9, para 36.
[67] Ibid, paras 50 *et seq*.
[68] Opinion, n 9, para 46, with reference to *Tobacco advertising I* (n 3).
[69] *Tobacco advertising I* (n 15) paras 84–86; *ENISA* (n 8) para 44.
[70] N 58, para 45; A Orator, 'Die unionsrechtliche Zulässigkeit von Eingriffsbefugnissen der ESMA im Bereich von Leerverkäufen', (2013) *Europäische Zeitschrift für Wirtschaftsrecht* 852.
[71] N 58, para 106.

requirements and powers relating to short selling and credit default swaps'.[72] However, from the context of the judgment it would appear that the Court assessed that an exceptional and occasional banning of certain specific market activity was consistent with the requirements of Article 114 TFEU. Whether the prohibition of one activity was part of the regulation of a greater market, or simply limited the scope of a specific one, was not openly discussed. The issue of the reach of powers under Article 114 TFEU and the necessity of there remaining a market to be regulated will therefore continue to be an open issue in the future. The strict criteria set up by *Tobacco advertising* in the context of setting the limits of internal market harmonisation this regard, seem to have been an exception of clarity.

At the end of the day, the judgment in *Short selling*, which following the Opinion of Advocate General Jääskinen, could have become another milestone in the developing case law on Article 114 TFEU, does not live up to expectations. It will not be remembered for its necessary definition and explanation of Article 114 TFEU. It might instead, rather sadly, become cited for its quite unwarranted expansion of the *Meroni* doctrine. Prior to this case, the Court had consistently applied *Meroni* only to specific cases of sub-delegation of powers by the institutions.[73] The Advocate General had convincingly dissected the principles contained in *Meroni* which were also generally applicable beyond that limited scope.[74] But the Court, seemingly eager to follow the lead of the pleas of the applicant Member State, instead of simply ignoring a false lead and leaving *Meroni* aside, as it had for example in *ENISA* and *Smoke flavouring* but also in *Schräder v CPVO*,[75] in *Short selling* discusses questions of when the delegation of discretionary powers is too broad to be permissible. Lacking any definition of what it understands as 'discretionary powers', instead of clarifying the issue the Court in *Short selling* further confuses the matter of delegation under EU law. In so doing, it has opened the door wide open to litigation arising from a host of different notions of discretion, stemming both from considerations on procedure and the extent of judicial review, as well as from matters of substance. It would have been far better to have left *Meroni* to rest in the well-deserved peace of the Court's archives.

[72] Ibid, para 114.

[73] See with further detail, HCH Hofmann and A Morini, 'Constitutional Aspects of the Pluralisation of the EU Executive through "Agencification"', (2012) 36 *European Law Review*, 419, 423–426.

[74] N 9, paras 61–64.

[75] Without discussing *Meroni* or equating the discretion exercised by the Community Plant Variety Office (CVPO) with the quasi-legislative discretionary powers of the type discussed in *Meroni*, the General Court held in *Schräder* that an agency, such as the CPVO, can be entrusted with the exercise of administrative discretion, including a certain margin of appreciation. As a result it did not subject the exercise of a power requiring complex scientific and technical appraisals to 'strict review in the light of objective criteria', but accepted the limited nature of judicial review of certain agency decisions in the field akin to trade mark law (Case T-187/06 *Schräder v CPVO* [2008] ECR II-3151, para 63, confirmed on appeal in C-38/09 P *Schräder v CPVO* [2010] ECR I-3209; cf judgment in *Short selling*, n 3 above, para 41).

V. THE NEW FRONTIERS OF INTERNAL MARKET LEGISLATION?

This overview of some of the main cases on the limits of legislation under Article 114 TFEU decided in the last decade and a half illustrate the dynamic development of the Union. It is moving away from a traditional two-level legal system, with the Union legislating and the Member States implementing and towards an integrated legal system linking the various levels through ever more procedural cooperation in implementation. In this process, Article 114 TFEU continues to be an important legal basis, not least for the reason that the internal market remains at the heart of the European integration project. The last few years have seen a reinforcement of earlier trends towards deeper integration, though not predominantly in the sense of ever more matters being addressed by EU legislation. On the contrary, the use of EU agencies as coordinators of the activities of the Member States in implementing EU policies might even be seen as a means of replacing the need at the EU level for increasingly detailed legislation harmonizing Member State law. This predominantly competence-friendly and subsidiarity-enhancing approach has been accepted by the Court of Justice in the context of what might be described as an '*a maiore ad minus*' approach.

The new frontier, it appears with *Short selling,* is how far the agencies may be empowered to adopt measures vis-à-vis market participants and other individuals, when the agency exercises regulatory powers normally reserved to national regulators. *Short selling* allows the conferral of regulatory powers in the internal market on a body created on the basis of Article 114 TFEU, which powers are to be used *ad hoc* and selectively. But what *Short selling* gives with one hand, it takes away with the other by limiting the possibilities of delegation to an agency because it relies on an ill-defined and altogether quite woolly definition of 'discretionary powers'. These questions thus straddle the borders of the past developments of defining the limits for using Article 114 TFEU for general legislative measures, as well as the limits of its use for structural 'measures'. The combination of structural, individual and general measures will require a new set of limits which have not so far been defined in the case law. Additionally, it would appear from the discussion of the matter in this chapter, that the question of the distortion of conditions of competition might require further development. Which conditions of competition in which markets need to be addressed appears to be a worthwhile topic of further reflection – perhaps more so than the mode of delivery of the 'measure' for approximation on which cases such as *ENISA, Smoke flavourings* and *Short selling* had concentrated. The suggestion might be, to use the language of financial markets, to go long on content and short on modes of delivery.

10

From Merck v Stephar *to the Unitary Patent Regulation and Court: Reflections on the Incremental Development of an EU Patent Law and Legal System*

NOEL J TRAVERS*

I. INTRODUCTION

A PATENT IS a legal right conferred in respect of a specific invention and entitling the inventor to prevent others from making, using or selling the invention for the duration of the patent. One of the earliest known patents was granted by King Henry VI to Flemish-born 'John of Utynam' in 1449, conferring a 20-year monopoly for a method of making stained glass, required for the windows of Eton college, which was previously unknown in England.[1] The description of this early patent reflects the core features of the patent systems that developed over the following centuries in most western legal systems. That only John of Utynam could supply such stained glass windows to Eton college all those centuries ago illustrates the tension that continues to be created in Europe by the territorial nature of national patent rights in the modern era, where the European Union has undertaken for its citizens to establish an internal market comprising an area without internal frontiers in which the free movement inter alia of goods and services is ensured. In seeking to reconcile the apparently irreconcilable internal market imperative of free movement with the territoriality of national intellectual property rights (IPRs), the Court of Justice of the European Union developed the concept of the 'specific subject-matter' of such rights. Although the balance struck by the Court has been subject to

* Barrister-at-Law, Bar of Ireland.

[1] See the Opinion of Advocate General Jacobs, at para 19, in Case C-377/98 *Netherlands* v *European Parliament and Council* [2001] ECR I-7079 (discussed below) for the example.

criticism, particularly as regards patent rights, there can be little doubt that it provided the impetus for many of the legislative developments that followed. This essay concentrates on the development of what may now be described as nascent EU patent law.

While the developments in the field of patent law have been incremental, given that the starting point comprised effectively a *tabula rasa* just over a generation ago, and that one is now looking at the likely creation of a unified patent court to apply the new 'European patent with unitary effect', which has been created under the enhanced cooperation procedure between 25 Member States, the slow pace of such developments does not diminish their significance.[2] As it is not feasible in an essay of this nature to consider all of the many relevant developments in detail, the focus of this contribution will be on the Court, which, assisted by some seminal opinions from its Advocates-General (including Nial Fennelly), has had a major influence on the development of EU patent law.

II. SPECIFIC SUBJECT-MATTER OF PATENTS

A. Background

Advocate General Fennelly addressed in *Merck v Primecrown* the interface between the free movement of goods rules under the EC Treaty and patent protection in national law.[3] The context was the discrepancies between the Member States regarding the scope of patent protection provided to pharmaceutical products and preparations. Traditionally, the patentability of pharmaceutical products was exceptional. Only Ireland and the United Kingdom have recognised the patentability of such products since the early part of the twentieth century (initially by way of case law subsequently confirmed in legislation), with most other European states following suit (mostly via legislative amendments) progressively from the late 1960s onwards after legislative recognition in Germany in the early 1960s. In Italy, recognition became possible because of a judgment of the *Corte costituzionale* in March 1978 declaring unconstitutional a 1939 law that excluded patentability of pharmaceutical products and processes for their manufacture. The (then) still relatively new Member States, Spain and Portugal, which had acceded to the Community in 1986, extended patent protection to manufacturing processes only but not to pharmaceutical products themselves. On joining the Community, they undertook, like Greece before them (but with effect from 8 October 1992), to accede to the European Patent Convention and to extend patent protection to pharmaceutical products, subject only to a short

[2] See Regulation (EU) No 1257/2012 of the European Parliament and of the Council of 17 December 2012 implementing enhanced cooperation in the area of the creation of unitary patent protection (discussed below), [2012] OJ L361/1.

[3] See the Opinion of 6 June 1996 in Joined Cases C-267/95 and C-268/95 *Merck & Ors v Primecrown & Ors* [1996] ECR I-6285.

three-year transitional period from the date such products became patentable in Spain and Portugal.[4] This obligation was reiterated in the 1990s in the Agreement on Trade-Related Aspects of Intellectual Property Rights ('the TRIPs Agreement'), constituting Annex 1C to the Agreement establishing the World Trade Organisation ('the WTO Agreement'), which was signed at Marrakesh on 15 April 1994.[5] Article 27(1) of the TRIPs Agreement provides that any invention, whether a product or a process, which is new, involves an inventive step and is capable of industrial application, is patentable, provided only that it belongs to a field of technology.

In its recent decision in *Daiichi Sankyo v DEMO*, the Court has confirmed that this provision covers pharmaceutical products.[6] The case is more significant for its treatment of the issue whether, since the entry into force of the Treaty of Lisbon on 1 December 2009, the subject of patentability is a shared Member State/Union competence in the field of the internal market. Contrasting Article 207(1) TFEU on the 'Common Commercial Policy' ('CCP') with the comparable provision in force when the TRIPs Agreement was concluded, namely Article 113 EC, the Court emphasised that, the 'commercial aspects of intellectual property' had not been mentioned in Article 113 EEC. Based on this 'significant development of primary law,' the Court held that the distribution of the competences between the Union and its Member States must be examined on the basis of the amended Treaty, such that neither Opinion 1/94[7] (where the Court established in relation to Article 113 of the EC Treaty which provisions of the TRIPs Agreement fell within the then Community's exclusive CCP competence), nor its 1997 judgment in *Merck Genéricos – Produtos Farmacêuticos*[8] (wherein it defined the dividing line between the obligations under the Agreement assumed by the Union and those that remained the responsibility of Member States), was material for determining to what extent the Agreement, as from the entry into force of the TFEU on 1 December 2009, fell within the Union's exclusive CCP competence.[9] The Court held that as the TRIPs Agreement has a specific link with international trade, it now falls within the exclusive competence of the Union.

Spain and Portugal also undertook to adjust their patent laws to make them 'compatible with the principles of free movement of goods and with the level of

[4] Convention on the Grant of European Patents signed at Munich on 5 October 1973.

[5] Approved by Council Decision 94/800/EC of 22 December 1994 concerning the conclusion on behalf of the European Community, as regards matters within its competence, of the agreements reached in the Uruguay Round multilateral negotiations (1986–1994) ([1994] OJ L336/1).

[6] Case C-414/11, judgment of 18 July 2013. The Court held (at para 64) that 'it is clear that pharmacology is regarded by the contracting parties to the TRIPs Agreement as a field of technology within the meaning of Article 2,' and that it follows 'from Article 70(8) of the TRIPs Agreement, a transitional provision dealing with the situation in which 'a Member does not make available as of the date of entry into force of the WTO Agreement patent protection for pharmaceutical ... products commensurate with its obligations under Article 27' (which provides that, in that situation, the WTO member in question must at least provide, as from that date, 'a means by which applications for patents for such inventions can be filed'), that 'Article 27 of the TRIPs Agreement includes the obligation to make inventions of pharmaceutical products patentable.'

[7] [1994] ECR I-5267.

[8] Case C-431/05 [2007] ECR I-7001.

[9] Case C-414/11, n 6 above, at para 48.

protection of industrial property attained in the Community.'[10] Amongst those principles was the interpretation of Article 30 EEC on the free movement of goods (now Article 34 TFEU) expounded by the Court in its seminal judgment in *Merck v Stephar*.[11] In *Merck v Stephar*, it held that Article 30 EEC fell to be interpreted as preventing the proprietor of a patent for a medicinal preparation, who sells the preparation in one Member State where patent protection exists and then markets it in another where there is no such protection, from availing himself of the right conferred by the patent laws of the first Member State to prevent the marketing there of such a preparation where it is imported from the other Member State. At issue was the parallel importation into the Netherlands from Italy of batches of a pharmaceutical product to the marketing of which Merck, the patentee in the Netherlands, had consented in Italy although unable to obtain patent protection there: this was initially because of the 1939 Italian law precluding same and then, following the abovementioned Constitutional Court judgment in March 1978, because of a lack of novelty. Under *Merck v Stephar* a patentee could lose the benefit of patent protection even in a case where it had had no opportunity to benefit from it. This sent shock waves through the pharmaceutical sector and was the subject of some forceful academic critique.[12] The Court disregarded what might have been viewed as a reasonable application of the derogation from the free movement rules contained in Article 36 EEC (now Article 36 TFEU) regarding 'the protection of industrial and commercial property' in favour of a highly integrationist construction of the principle of free movement that applied a near-absolutist variant of the international exhaustion doctrine.

B. Genesis of Exhaustion Doctrine

The genesis for the exhaustion doctrine in Community law was the early decision in *Parke, Davis v Probel*,[13] where Parke Davis' Dutch licensee had invoked its Dutch-registered patents to prevent imports into the Netherlands of products protected thereunder but manufactured in Italy by a third party at a time when it could not obtain patent protection for its inventions there.[14] The questions referred focused on competition law and whether the use of the Dutch patent law to prevent the imports would amount to a breach of Articles 85 and 86 EEC (now Articles 101 and 102 TFEU), considered with Articles 36 EEC and 222 EEC (now Articles 36 and 345 TFEU). The Court, noting that the variations between the different legislative systems regarding

[10] See para 1 of Protocols 8 and 19, respectively, to the Acts of Accession of Spain and Portugal.

[11] Case 187/80 *Merck v Stephar and Exler* [1981] ECR 2063.

[12] See, eg, G Marenco and K Banks, 'Intellectual Property and Community Rules of Free Movement: Discrimination Unearthed' (1990) 15 *EurLRev* 247, V Korah, *EC Competition Law and practice*, 3rd edn (1994), 193, and W Koch, 'Article 30 and the Exercise of Industrial Property Rights to Block Imports' (1986) *Fordham Corp L Int* 605.

[13] [1968] ECR 55.

[14] It owned patents for the product in all the then Member States save Italy, and had assigned a different licensee in each country.

IPRs 'are capable of creating obstacles both to the free movement of the patented products and to competition within the common market,' held that 'prohibitions and restrictions on imports' could be justified under Article 36 EEC 'on grounds of the protection of industrial property,' provided they did not 'constitute a means of arbitrary discrimination or a disguised restriction on trade between Member States.'[15] Thus, the existence/exercise distinction came into being, which the Court was later to use to reconcile the prohibition on invoking national IPRs with the stipulation articulated in what is now Article 345 TFEU that the Treaty shall 'in no way prejudice the rules in Member States governing the system of property ownership'. In *Parke Davis*, the exercise of rights under Dutch law to prevent the imports of the protected product was justifiable did not arise, as the imports were not produced by it or with its consent in Italy.

The defining moment regarding the conflict between the freedom of movement of goods objective and the territoriality of national IPRs came several years later in 1971 in the copyright case of *Deutsche Grammophon v Metro* concerning sound recordings (records).[16] Deutsche Grammophon ('DG') sought to maintain higher prices in Germany through the imposition of minimum-resale-price obligations on its German retailers. Supplies to Metro, a discount supermarket chain, had been discontinued consequent upon its breaching this obligation, but it managed to obtain the records in question from an undertaking in a third country that had acquired them from DG's French subsidiary. DG sought an order to prevent Metro from marketing those records. The referring court asked whether granting the order would infringe Community law. The Court held that such rights could only be exercised to prevent imports where this was 'justified for the purpose of safeguarding rights which constitute the specific subject matter of such property.'[17] As regards the exercise of rights in circumstances such as those of the main proceedings, the Court then held that if a national IPR:

> is relied upon to prevent the marketing in a Member State of products distributed by the holder of the right or with his consent on the territory of another Member State on the sole ground that such distribution did not take place on the national territory, such a prohibition, which would legitimise the isolation of national markets, would be repugnant to the essential purpose of the Treaty, which is to unite national markets into a single market.[18]

An EC law variation of the concept of 'exhaustion' of rights had, thus, effectively been developed long before that term was used. That concept, as Advocate General Fennelly later observed in his opinion in *Merck v Primecrown*, bore little resemblance to the Dutch and German laws which largely inspired it, whereunder the marketing abroad of a patented product, even with the patentee's consent, did not deprive the patentee of its right to oppose imports

[15] [1968] ECR 55, p 71.
[16] Case 78/70 [1971] ECR 487.
[17] Ibid, para 11.
[18] N 16, para 12.

of such products as infringements of its national patent.[19] The Court, however, took a very different view in *Merck v Stephar*.[20]

C. Defining the Specific Subject-matter of Patent Rights

The Court first defined in 1974 in *Centrafarm v Sterling Drug* the specific subject-matter of a patent as being:

> the guarantee that the patentee, to reward the creative effort of the inventor, has the exclusive right to use an invention with a view to manufacturing industrial products and putting them into circulation for the first time, either directly or by the grant of licences to third parties, as well as the right to oppose infringements.[21]

Thus, national patent legislation providing that a patentee's right is not exhausted when its patented product is marketed by it in another Member State amounts to a restriction on trade. It held that such a restriction could be justified, but only as regards 'a product coming from a Member State where it is not patentable and has been manufactured by third parties without the consent of the patentee.'[22]

It was arguable that *Sterling Drug* applied only where parallel patents existed in both the exporting and the importing Member States, although the language of the judgment was also open to the construction later put on it in *Merck v Stephar*.[23] In such a case, the patentee has enjoyed a guaranteed exclusivity at the point of first marketing a particular batch of a protected product. It would, thus, have had the opportunity of obtaining monopoly profits in the exporting Member State before its national rights in the importing Member State could be said to be exhausted. The question whether the conditions cited by the Court in *Sterling Drug* were cumulative was decided in *Merck v Stephar*. In essence, the Court held that they were not, and that consent to marketing of protected product even without the benefit of patent protection sufficed to exhaust patent rights: 'the substance of a patent right lies essentially in according the inventor an exclusive right of first placing the product on the market.'[24] It thus attached more importance to marketing consent than to monopolistic rights, as it considered that the first marketing right 'enables the inventor, by allowing him a monopoly in exploiting his product, to obtain the reward for his creative effort without, however, guaranteeing that he will obtain such a reward in all circumstances.'[25] The Court assumed that this right would suffice to permit an appropriate remuneration for the inventive activity underlying the development of the protected product. The appropriateness of this assumption underlay the referring court's request in *Merck v Primecrown* for a reconsideration of the

[19] N 3, para 93, fn 101, of the Opinion
[20] N 11.
[21] Case 15/74 *Centrafarm & Adriaan de Peijper* v *Sterling Drug* [1974] ECR 1147, para 9.
[22] Ibid, para 11,
[23] N 11.
[24] N 11, para 9.
[25] N 11, para 10.

Merck v Stephar ruling. It was central to Advocate General Fennelly's opinion in *Merck v Primecrown* recommending reconsideration of *Merck v Stephar*: he opined that a right conferred by a national patent cannot be exercised and, consequently, cannot be exhausted by an act of marketing in a Member State which recognises no patent right in the product.[26]

Advocate General Fennelly essentially considered that a patentee should be given one opportunity to release the patented goods under the monopolistic conditions of a patent right. Noting that national patent laws traditionally permit patentees to compartmentalise national markets by relying upon their national IPRs in one country to preclude parallel imports of units of the product marketed from another so as to seek to extract monopoly profits in each controlled marketplace, and recognising that 'such discriminatory treatment could not be tolerated in a Community whose fundamental aims include the establishment of a single market without internal frontiers', he nevertheless considered *Merck v Stephar* went further 'by applying the same treatment to imports not so controlled.'[27] He was unconvinced that seeking to restrict imports when 'the products concerned were marketed voluntarily in another Member State without the benefit of patent protection' constituted an arbitrary restriction on intra-Community trade, and that the effect of *Merck v Stephar* was 'to export not merely the product but also the commercial consequences of the legislative choice made by the exporting State to the importing State because the patentee has made a commercial choice to sell the product even in a less protected environment,' such that it could 'favour commercially irrational decisions to withhold products from the markets of such States.'[28]

This approach could arguably facilitate creating free-market conditions in two ways: by encouraging governments to put an end to price-control schemes, on the one hand, and, on the other, to help free-market forces to prevail over price differences that exist despite free-market conditions.[29] The Court declined to reconsider the rationale underlying *Merck v Stephar*, because it considered that the exercise by a patentee of its rights under the laws of one Member State to prevent marketing of a patented product in that state when the patented product has been brought into circulation in another Member State by the patentee, or with its consent, could not be reconciled with the freedom of movement of goods for which the Treaty provides. The Court's concern clearly remained with compartmentalisation within the single market: 'if a patentee could prohibit the importation of protected products marketed in another Member State by him or with his consent, he would be able to partition national markets and thereby restrict trade between the Member States.'[30] However, central to this conclusion that it had not been 'wrong' in its assessment in *Merck v Stephar* regarding 'the

[26] See, in particular, paras 94–99, 106, 110 and 115 of the Opinion, n 3 above.

[27] Para 107 of the Opinion, n 3.

[28] N 3, para 108.

[29] See, in this respect, C Heath (1999) 'Parallel imports and international trade', World Intellectual Property Organization Report, at www.wipo.int/edocs/mdocs/sme/en/atrip_gva.../atrip_gva_99_6.pdf.

[30] N 3, judgment, para 36.

balance between the principle of free movement of goods in the Community and the principle of protection of patentees' rights', even where, 'as a result of striking that balance, the right to oppose importation of a product may be exhausted by its being marketed in a Member State where it is not patentable', was its continuing view that the specific subject-matter of a patent right cannot extend beyond a voluntary act of marketing.[31]

The effect of *Merck v Primecrown* is that the consensual pursuit of profit, even without the benefit of a monopoly right, anywhere in the single market operates to exhaust, throughout the rest of the single market, the specific subject-matter of a patentee's right in respect of patent-protected products. Nothing short of a legal obligation to market, such as pursuant to a compulsory licence, would permit the patent proprietor thereafter to resist, based on national IPRs rights in other Member States, parallel imports from the state where first marketing occurred.[32] The argument that ethical obligations may compel patentees to provide supplies of protected pharmaceuticals to Member States where they are needed, even if they are not patentable, was readily dismissed as a justification for precluding parallel imports of such supplies into other Member States: 'such considerations are not, in the absence of any legal obligation, such as to make it possible properly to identify the situations in which the patentee is deprived of his power to decide freely how he will market his product.'[33]

D. Protection Regarding Unauthorised Samples of Protected Product

Shortly after *Merck v Primecrown*, the Court considered, in *Generics v Smith Kline*, a prohibition under Dutch patent law on the making and submission of samples of medicinal products as part of marketing authorisation applications during the term of a patent protection by persons other than the patentee.[34] Comparable provisions are contained in most national patent laws.[35] The purpose of the advance application was to enable Generics to market generic equivalents of the patent-protected product or process immediately following the expiry of the relevant patents. Smith Kline, the patentee, obtained an injunction preventing Generics from marketing such products using the manufacturing process for a period of 14 months following the date of expiry of the patents in

[31] N 3, para 37.

[32] In Case 19/84 *Pharmon v Hoechst* [1985] ECR 2281, the Court held (at para 26) that a patent proprietor could prevent the importation and marketing (in that case into the Netherlands) of products manufactured pursuant to a compulsory licence (in the case in the United Kingdom) in order to protect the substance of its Dutch patent rights, which the Court had defined as 'according the inventor an exclusive right of first placing on the market so as to allow him to obtain a reward for his creative effort.'

[33] *Merck v Primecrown*, n 3, at para 53. Agreeing with the view expressed by Advocate General Fennelly on this issue (see particularly para 157 of his Opinion), the Court held that '[s]uch considerations are, at any rate in the present context, difficult to apprehend and distinguish from commercial considerations. Such ethical obligations cannot, therefore, be the basis for derogating from the rule on free movement of goods laid down in *Merck*.'

[34] Case C-316/95 [1997] ECR I-3929.

[35] See, in this respect, paras 37 to 49 of the Opinion of Advocate General Jacobs, n 34.

question based on evidence that, if Generics had waited to apply for its product registrations until after the expiry of the patent, it would not have obtained marketing authorisations, given the average actual duration of the registration procedure in the Netherlands, for a further 14 months. Could the patentee effectively extend the term of the patent in respect of protected products authorised before the cut-off dates for the application of Council Regulation (EEC) No 1768/92 of 18 June 1992 concerning the creation of a supplementary protection certificate for medicinal products?[36]

The Court identified an obstacle to trade (even though no actual imports were involved in the dispute in the main proceedings) in the impediment to potential imports of generic medicinal products from other Member States during the waiting period that follows the filing of a marketing-authorisation application after the expiry of the patent. Referring to *Merck v Stephar*, it held that such an obstacle could be justified, because prohibiting the production and use of samples for obtaining a marketing authorisation came within the specific subject-matter of the patent right provided 'such samples have been used without the direct or indirect consent of the patentee.'[37] Concerning Generics' argument that a prohibition on the sale of products until after expiry of the patent was disproportionate, given the alternative remedies of damages or cancellation of the marketing authorisations, the Court held that the 'moratorium' imposed on Generics by the injunction, insofar as it seeks to place the patentee 'in the position in which it would, in principle, have been had its rights been respected, cannot in itself be held to be a disproportionate form of reparation.'[38] It also held that the fact that the 14-month period exceeded the maximum period authorised by Community legislation[39] for the procedure for granting a marketing authorisation could not, in circumstances where it corresponded 'to the actual average duration of such a procedure in the Member State concerned', be relied upon 'by an infringer as against the proprietor of the patent in order to obtain a shorter prohibition period', since '[t]he contrary view would amount ... to accepting the risk of favouring the infringer over the victim of the infringement.'[40]

Generics v Smith Kline demonstrates that real substance to the specific subject-matter of a patent remains under the concept developed in *Merck v Stephar*. The Court's finding that the free movement rules do not require that the infringement remedy available to a patentee in such circumstances should

[36] [1992] OJ L182/1. Regulation No 1768/92 (which is discussed below), as amended, was repealed and codified by Regulation (EC) No 469/2009 of the European Parliament and of the Council of 6 May 2009 concerning the supplementary protection certificate for medicinal products (Codified version).

[37] N 34, para 20.

[38] N 34, para 28.

[39] Article 7 of Council Directive 65/65/EEC of 26 January 1965 on the approximation of provisions laid down by law, regulation or administrative action relating to proprietary medicinal products (OJ, English Special Edition 1965, 20), read in conjunction with Article 4(c) of Council Directive 75/319/EEC of 20 May 1975 on the approximation of provisions laid down by law, for the procedure for granting a marketing authorisation ([1975] OJ L147/13).

[40] Paras 30 and 32, judgment, n 34.

be limited to the duration of the term of its monopoly right emphasises the autonomy of the concept of specific subject-matter. The Court may have been influenced by the fact that Generics would have a discrete remedy against the authorities responsible for the delay exceeding 12 months in granting authorisation, but agreed with Advocate General Jacobs that any such delay could not be invoked as a basis for challenging the duration of the injunction granted in the main proceedings.[41]

III. SUBSTANTIVE EU PATENT LAW

A. Background

Prior to the adoption of Regulation 1257/2012 on the creation of unitary patent protection, there was no general substantive harmonisation at EU level of national patent laws.[42] This contrasts with procedural law, where a significant degree of harmonisation was achieved by Directive 2004/48/EC of the European Parliament and of the Council of 29 April 2004 on the enforcement of intellectual property rights,[43] whose objective is 'to ensure a high, equivalent and homogenous level of protection in the internal market' of rights, whether based on national or European law.[44] The Directive, which has been described as the 'centrepiece of intellectual property protection in the EU,'[45] regulates in a horizontal manner the civil and administrative sanctions that are available in the Member States for infringements of intellectual property rights.

The lack of non-sector specific substantive harmonisation prior to the adoption of Regulation 1257/2012 is unsurprising for several reasons. Firstly, the original Treaties, even as amended, lacked a specific legal basis for such legislation until the Treaty of Lisbon came into effect on 1 December 2009. The latter provides such a legal basis in Article 118 TFEU.[46] Secondly, an important degree of harmonisation of national law, by means of harmonising some central notions of patent law, had been achieved by means of the 1963 'Strasbourg Patent Convention' of the Council of Europe.[47] Although the Strasbourg Convention ultimately entered into

[41] Para 68 of the Opinion, n 34.

[42] N 2.

[43] [2004] OJ L195/16.

[44] See, in particular, recital 10 to the Directive and Article 2(1) thereof.

[45] See A Kur and T Dreier, *European Intellectual Property Law* (Edward Elgar, Cheltenham, 2013) 67.

[46] Article 118(1) TFEU provides that the European Parliament and the Council, 'in the context of the establishment and functioning of their internal market' and acting pursuant to the ordinary legislative procedure, 'shall establish measures for the creation of European intellectual property rights to provide uniform, protection of intellectual property rights throughout the Union and for the setting up of centralised Union-wide authorisation, coordination and supervision arrangements.' A special legislative procedure, under which the Council acts unanimously after consulting the European Parliament, applies under Article 118(2) TFEU in respect of 'the language arrangements for the European intellectual property rights'.

[47] Convention on the Unification of Certain Points of Substantive Law on Patents for Invention of 27 November 1963, Council of Europe, Treaty Series, No 47.

force only on 1 August 1980, it influenced the development of patent laws across Europe, especially regarding the critical criteria for establishing patentability.[48] Thus, under Article 1, the contracting parties committed themselves to granting patents 'for any inventions which are susceptible of industrial application, which are new and which involve an inventive step' and not to grant patents to inventions that fail to 'comply with these conditions.' Unlike the Convention on the Grant of European Patent signed in Munich on 5 October 1973 (the 'EPC'), which adopts very similar substantive criteria, the Strasbourg Convention did not establish an independent system for granting European patents. Furthermore, the success of the EPC, which is founded on an international convention establishing an international organisation, the European Patent Organisation ('EPO'), which is ultimately controlled by the contracting parties (through the Administrative Council, one of the two organs of the EPO under Article 4 of the EPC), reduced the willingness of the Member States to agree to legislation at EU level.[49] The EPC's general success may principally be attributed to the fact that patent titles granted by the EPO follow a single application, examination and registration procedure and comprise bundles of national patents whose territorial scope comprises the EPC member countries designated in the application.[50] By selecting only some countries, patent applicants can implement flexible patenting strategies and save significant translation and other costs. Moreover, obtaining patent protection for the Member States with larger economies, such as France, Germany, Italy, the United Kingdom, and perhaps also the Netherlands and Spain, can be sufficient to secure de facto EU-wide protection.

Nevertheless, in two sensitive and economically important areas, that is, the pharmaceutical and agro-chemical sectors, agreement was reached on granting supplementary patents protection: the first in 1992 through Regulation No 1768/92, which entered into force on 2 January 1993, and the second through Council Regulation (EC) No 1610/96 of the European Parliament and the Council of 23 July 1996 concerning the creation of a supplementary protection certificate for plant protection products, which entered into force on 8 February 1997.[51] Both Regulations were adopted on the internal market legal basis of Article 100a EEC (later Article 95 EC and now Article 114 TFEU) and are substantively similar as regards the conditions and mechanisms for obtaining a supplementary protection certificate ('SPC').[52] Furthermore, in the controversial

[48] Under Article 9(2), the Convention entered into force three months after the date of deposit of the eighth instrument of ratification or acceptance. This occurred three months after Germany's ratification on 30 April 1980. Ireland was, in fact, the first Member State of the Council of Europe to ratify the Convention when it ratified it on 25 January 1968. France ratified the Convention on 27 February 1980, which followed Switzerland's and the United Kingdom's respective ratifications on 9 and 16 November 1977. Under Article 13(1), the Convention remains in force indefinitely.

[49] The Court does not have jurisdiction to interpret the provisions of the EPC, since, unlike the Member States, the European Union has not acceded to that convention The Court confirmed this in Case C-493/12 *Eli Lilly v Human Genome Sciences*, Judgment of 12 December 2013, para 40.

[50] All Member States and currently 10 non-EU States, including the EFTA States and Turkey, are parties to the EPC.

[51] [1996] OJ L198/30.

[52] The Court rejected a challenge to the validity of the legal basis of Regulation No 1768/92 in Case C-350/92 *Spain v Council* [1995] ECR I-1985, holding that preventing the heterogeneous

field of biotechnical inventions, substantive harmonisation of national patent laws was achieved by Directive 98/44/EC of the European Parliament and the Council of 6 July 1998 on the legal protection of biotechnological inventions.[53]

B. Extending the Term of Specific Patent Rights

The SPC regulations address the problem encountered by patentees of pharmaceutical and plant protection products because of the delays involved in obtaining regulatory approval, namely marketing authorisations, to place products protected by such patents on the market. At issue are medicinal products for human or animal use, on the one hand, and herbicides, fungicides and insecticides on the other. The first six recitals of Regulation No 1768/92 are highly instructive as regards its motivation and objective.[54] They are designed to re-establish a sufficient period of effective protection of the basic patent by permitting the holder to enjoy an additional period of exclusivity on the expiry of that patent, which is intended to compensate, at least in part, for the delay to the commercial exploitation of his invention by reason of the time which has elapsed between the date on which the application for the patent was filed and the date on which the first marketing authorisation in the European Union was granted. They do this by allowing the patentee to apply for an extension to the usual period of national patent protection in respect of market-authorised, patent-protected products.

As regards pharmaceutical products, the extension is now calculated, under Article 13 of the codified Regulation No 469/2009, by reference to the period which elapsed between the date upon which the application for a basic patent was lodged and the date upon which the first authorisation to place the product on the market in the EU was granted.[55] However, it was not possible to apply for such protection if the first authorisation to place the product at issue on the market was obtained before 1 January 1985 (as was the case with the products involved in *Generics v Smith Kline*), or before accession in the case of Member States acceding after the entry into force of the original regulation, Regulation No 1768/92.[56]

An SPC does not extend the duration of the patent itself, but only the protection for the product that is the subject of a marketing authorisation. It creates a distinct and *sui generis* form of intellectual property right, rather than simply extending the term of existing patents. The SPC, however, is closely

development of national laws that could affect the establishment and functioning of the internal market came within the legislative competence conferred by Article 100a EEC.

[53] [1998] OJ L213/13 ('the Biotechnology Directive').

[54] See now recitals 2 to 7 in the codified regulation, Regulation (EC) No 469/2009. Similar recitals are contained in recitals 2 to 9 of Regulation 1610/1996.

[55] Article 13 of the original Regulation No 1768/92 contained substantially the same rules.

[56] See Article 19(1) of Regulation No 1768/92 (now repealed), whereunder an earlier date (1 January 1982) was originally provided regarding Belgium and Italy while a later one was prescribed for Germany and Denmark (1 January 1988).

connected with the national systems under which the underlying patent was initially granted, since it extends the duration of the exclusive right conferred by that patent. In substantive terms, an SPC can only be granted if a basic patent protects a product, and the protection conferred by a certificate must remain within the limits of that conferred by the basic patent.

This was illustrated by the Court's answer to the third question referred in the abovementioned *Daiichi Sankyo v DEMO* case. There, the protection conferred by the patent at issue expired on 20 June 2006, but was extended by an SPC such that Daiichi Sankyo continued to benefit from protection until 2011. DEMO was granted marketing authorisations by the competent Greek authorities (in September 2008 and July 2009) to place generic medicinal products produced with the active ingredient protected by the patent at issue on the market under its own name 'Talerin'. In September 2009, Daiichi Sankyo brought proceedings seeking, inter alia, the cessation of all marketing of Talerin by DEMO, which ultimately resulted in the preliminary reference. The third question asked essentially whether a patent obtained following an application claiming the invention both of the process of manufacture of and of the pharmaceutical product as such, but granted solely in relation to the process (as in 1986 only the former was possible under Greek patent law), must, by reason of the rules set out in Articles 27 and 70 of the TRIPs Agreement, be regarded, from the date of entry into force of that agreement, as covering the invention of the pharmaceutical product.[57] The Court held that there is no obligation under the TRIPs Agreement requiring WTO members to convert claimed inventions into protected inventions. This response is interesting in the light of the Court's statement over 16 years earlier in *Merck v Primecrown* that 'the situations addressed by the ruling in Merck are set to disappear since pharmaceutical products are now patentable in all the Member States.'[58] The refusal to reconsider its *Merck v Stephar* ruling in that case, insofar as it considered that issues created by the different approaches to the patentability of pharmaceutical products were set to disappear, was based on a somewhat precipitate assessment.

An SPC normally has a maximum lifetime of 5 years, but the total combined duration of market exclusivity of a patent and SPC cannot exceed 15 years. By virtue of Article 4 of the Regulation No 469/2009, the concept of a 'product' is central to the determination of the protection conferred by a certificate. Thus, SPCs extend the monopoly period for a 'product' (active ingredient or a combination of active ingredients) that is protected by a patent and considerable debate has arisen concerning the definition of 'product' and whether a product is protected by the patent upon which an SPC application is based. In the early *Farmitalia* case[59] concerning whether a German marketing authorisation related only to a single salt of a free base protected by the basic patent (in circumstances

[57] The TRIPs Agreement was ratified by the Hellenic Republic with effect from 9 February 1995. Pharmaceutical products had only became patentable in Greece from 8 October 1992, when the reservation within the meaning of Article 167(2)(a) of the EPC made in 1986 regarding such products by Greece, upon its ratification of the EPC, expired in accordance with Article 167(3) thereof.

[58] N 3 above, at para 39.

[59] Case C-392/97 *Farmitalia Carlo Erba Srl* [1999] ECR I-5553.

where a medicinal product with equivalent properties could probably be manufactured from different salts of this free base), or whether (as contended by Farmitalia) the scope of protection of the basic patent extended by implication to all such salts, Advocate General Fennelly gave an opinion establishing the foundations for the purposive approach that has subsequently been adopted by the Court in construing Regulation No 1768/92 and its successor.

Recognising that 'the term 'product' is open to a number of possible interpretations, none of which can be excluded on purely textual grounds,' Advocate General Fennelly opined that one had 'to look to the scheme and objectives of the SPC Regulation for further assistance,' in which respect he considered that 'the SPC Regulation is intended ... to confer an additional compensatory period of protection for pharmaceutical inventions,' and that it 'would not achieve this aim if it were interpreted as providing for SPC protection limited to the narrow category of authorised medicinal products, or to the invention set out in the patent claims.'[60] Focusing on the marketing authorisation itself, he observed that it would 'almost inevitably name the active constituent by reference not to the parent compound but to its salt or ester,' and recommended to the Court that it construe 'an active ingredient as being the pharmacologically active free base or parent compound underlying a medicinal product which is subject to a marketing authorisation.[61] He proposed a broad interpretation to the Court whereunder the certificate should be granted in the same terms as the patent claims, and opined that such an approach:

> would have the advantage of establishing a uniform criterion for the grant of a certificate, which could not easily be arrived at on the basis of the scope of protection of the basic patent, and of permitting national competent authorities to grant certificates without having to engage in an inquiry into the likely additional scope of protection of the patent and of the certificate, which is alien to their normal function [and would] preserve the normal division of functions between those authorities and the national courts, permitting the latter to decide the ultimate scope of protection of a certificate worded in terms of the patent claims on the basis of the same principles of national law as are applied to the patent itself.

The Court agreed and held that the scope of an SPC may encompass more than just the single form of the active ingredient that is included in the medicinal product authorised for sale. It ruled that:

> where an active ingredient in the form of a salt is referred to in the marketing authorisation concerned and is protected by a basic patent in force, the certificate is capable of covering the active ingredient as such and also its various derived forms such as salts and esters, as medicinal products, in so far as they are covered by the protection of the basic patent.[62]

More recently in *Novartis v Actavis*, the Court was asked to consider whether marketing a medicinal product containing the active ingredient protected by the

[60] Paras 25 and 29 of the Opinion, n 59.
[61] Ibid, para 35.
[62] Case C-392/97 [1999] ECR I-5572, para 21.

patent at issue, in combination with another active ingredient not so covered, after the expiry of the patent would comprise the marketing of a product other than that protected by the underlying patent, such that an SPC should not be granted. The Court held that an SPC could be granted provided the underlying patent would have enabled the patentee to oppose the marketing of a medicinal product containing the protected active ingredient in combination with one or more other active ingredients.[63]

The issue of the scope of Regulation 1768/92 (and now of Regulation 469/2009) has been revisited several times by the Court, which has consistently adopted a broad interpretation thereof. This may be illustrated by reference to two further recent rulings. Firstly, in *Neurim Pharmaceuticals v Comptroller-General of Patents*, the Court addressed a reference regarding a European patent concerning a formulation of melatonin, the natural hormone, which had been developed on the basis of research, which had allowed Neurim to discover that appropriate formulations of melatonin could be used as a medicine for insomnia.[64] Having obtained a European patent concerning its formulation, Neurim applied for a European marketing authorisation to market that formulation in the form of a medicinal product for human use, which it obtained from the European Commission in June 2007 when the underlying patent had just five years to run. It then applied in the United Kingdom for an SPC, basing its application on the marketing authorisation it had just obtained. The United Kingdom Intellectual Property Office refused and, ultimately, on appeal several questions were referred to the European Court.

The first and third questions asked whether the provisions of Articles 3 and 4 of the Regulation were to be interpreted as precluding in such a case the grant of an SPC for the product application that was protected by the patent and the subject of the second marketing authorisation. Citing the 'fundamental objective of the SPC Regulation' as being 'to ensure sufficient protection to encourage pharmaceutical research, which plays a decisive role in the continuing improvement in public health,'[65] the Court referred to the explanatory memorandum for the proposal for the regulation and, by analogy, its judgment in *Medeva*.[66] It held that a patent protecting a new application of a new or known product may, in accordance with Article 2 of Regulation 469/2009, enable an SPC to be granted, and, in that case, in accordance with Article 5 thereof, 'the SPC confers the same rights as conferred by the basic patent as regards the new use of that product, within the limits laid down by Article 4 of that regulation.'[67] The marketing of a new medicinal product commercially exploiting a new therapeutic application of an active ingredient will enable its proprietor to obtain an SPC, provided that the SPC application is within the limits of the protection conferred by the basic patent relied upon for the

[63] Case C-442/11, Order of 9 February 2012.
[64] Case C-130/11, Judgment of 19 July 2012.
[65] Ibid, para 22, citing in particular its case law in Case C-322/10 *Medeva* [2011] ECR I-12051, para 30, and Case C-422/10 *Georgetown University and Others* [2011] ECR I-12157, para 24.
[66] Case C-322/10, para 32.
[67] *Neurim Pharmaceuticals*, n 64 at para 24.

purposes of the SPC application, that is, provided the SPC covers only the new use of the active ingredient covered by the patent.

Secondly, the ruling in *Eli Lilly v Human Genome Sciences* illustrates that the Court's broad approach to interpreting the scope for SPCs is influenced by its consciousness of the underlying purpose of encouraging pharmaceutical research.[68] Reiterating the key role played by the claims for the purpose of determining whether a product is protected by a basic patent within the meaning of that provision, the Court held that an active ingredient not identified in the claims of a basic patent by means of a structural, or functional, definition cannot be considered to be protected within the meaning of Article 3(a) of Regulation 469/2009. However, the refusal of an SPC application for an active ingredient not specifically referred to by the patent relied upon in support of an SPC application may be justified – in circumstances such as those in the main proceedings where Eli Lilly had brought an action seeking a declaration that any SPC application relying, for its legal basis, on the Human Genome Sciences patent at issue would be invalid – 'where the holder of the patent in question has failed to take any steps to carry out more in-depth research and identify his invention specifically, making it possible to ascertain clearly the active ingredient which may be commercially exploited in a medicinal product corresponding to the needs of certain patients'.[69] To grant an SPC in such circumstances, notwithstanding the patentee failure to invest in research regarding that aspect of its original invention, would undermine the Regulation's objective.

C. Biotechnology Directive

The Biotechnology Directive was based on Article 100a EEC (now Article 114 TFEU) as an internal market measure. The rationale that motivated its framers emerges clearly from recitals 1 to 3 in its extensive preamble comprising 56 recitals. Chapter I (comprising Articles 1 to 7) of the Directive is entitled 'Patentability'. Article 1 requires Member States to protect 'biotechnological inventions' under national patent law. No definition of such inventions is provided, but it is clear from Article 3(1) that the concept essentially comprises inventions concerning 'a product consisting of or containing biological material or a process by means of which biological material is produced, processed or used'. 'Biological material' is defined as 'any material containing genetic information and capable of reproducing itself or being reproduced in a biological system' in Article 2(1)(a). Under Article 3(2), biological material which is isolated from its natural environment or produced by means of a technical process may be the subject of an invention even if it previously occurred in nature, whilst Article 5(2) provides similarly that an element isolated from the human body or otherwise produced by means of a technical process, including the sequence or partial sequence of a gene, may constitute a patentable invention, even if the structure of that element is identical to that of a natural element.

[68] Case C-493/12, n 49.
[69] Ibid, at para 43.

Articles 4 to 6 provide that the following may not be patented: (i) plant and animal varieties; (ii) essentially biological processes for the production of plants or animals; (iii) the human body, at the various stages of its formation and development, and the simple discovery of one of its elements, including the sequence or partial sequence of a gene; and (iv) inventions the commercial exploitation of which would be contrary to *ordre public* or morality. Article 6(2) provides the following non-exhaustive examples of exploitation that would be considered contrary to *ordre public* or morality: (a) processes for cloning human beings; (b) processes for modifying the germ line genetic identity of human beings; (c) uses of human embryos for industrial or commercial purposes; and (d) processes for modifying the genetic identity of animals which are likely to cause them suffering without any substantial medical benefit to man or animal, and animals resulting from such processes.

Chapter II (comprising Articles 1 to 7) deals with the 'Scope of protection'. Under Article 8(1), the substantive patent protection for biological material 'possessing special characteristics as a result of the invention' extends 'to any biological material derived from that material through preparation or multiplication in an identical or divergent form and possessing those same characteristics', while Article 8(2) provides comparable protection for process patents. Under Article 9, the protection also extends to material in which the product is incorporated and in which the genetic information contained therein 'performs its function'.

The validity of the Biotechnology Directive was challenged by the Netherlands relying on six discrete pleas, some of which (particularly the first, second and sixth pleas) raised essentially constitutional or formal issues relating to the adoption of the Directive.[70] However, the legal-basis plea that the Directive was incorrectly based on Article 100a EEC (now Article 114 TFEU) raised a substantive patent law issue; whether, by providing for an alleged 'patent on life', the Directive had created a new intellectual property right. Advocate General Jacobs pointed out in his opinion that the essence of the Netherlands' objection to the Directive was to the notion that plants, animals and parts of the human body may be patentable, because they considered that the right to a patent in the field of biotechnology should be limited to biotechnological processes and not extended to the products deriving therefrom, such that plants and animals, including genetically modified plants and animals, and human biological material would not be patentable.[71]

The Court had little hesitation in finding that the Biotechnology Directive was a proper internal-market measure appropriately based on Article 100a EEC. Noting that the national provisions predating the Directive were most often taken from the EPC, it held that the differing interpretations to which those provisions were open as regards the patentability of biotechnological inventions were 'liable to give rise to divergences of practice and case law prejudicial to the proper operation of the internal market', and that when the Directive was

[70] Case C-377/98 *Netherlands v European Parliament and Council*, n 1 above.

[71] See para 10 of the Opinion

adopted 'marked differences with significant consequences were already apparent between certain national laws on specific points such as the patentability of plant varieties and that of the human body'.[72] The Netherlands also argued that the Directive was not an appropriate measure for the approximation of Member States laws, since it created a new type of property right distinct in several respects from the rights covered by existing patent law. In this respect, the Netherlands referred, inter alia, to the fact that the Directive concerns products previously excluded from patentability in certain Member States and to the fact that protection for which it provides, under Articles 8 and 9 in particular, extends beyond specific biological material to biological material obtained from it by reproduction or multiplication. In response, confirming the then Community's competence to harmonise national laws in the field of IPRs based on Article 110a EEC, the Court held that, '[t]he patents to be issued under the Directive are national patents, issued in accordance with the procedures applicable in the Member States and deriving their protective force from national law', and that, '[a]s the creation of a Community patent is neither the purpose nor the effect of the Directive, it does not introduce a new right which would require recourse to the [further powers] legal basis afforded by Article 235 of the Treaty [now Article 352 TFEU]'.[73]

In rejecting the third plea, the Court held that Article 6 of the Directive, by precluding the patentability of inventions whose commercial exploitation would be contrary to *ordre public* or morality, exacerbated existing legal ambiguities and breached the principle of legal certainty, that this provision was 'a well known one in patent law and appears inter alia in the relevant international legal instruments, such as the EPC' and, that, in any event, Member States' scope for manoeuvre was limited, 'since the Directive limits the concepts in question, both by stating that commercial exploitation is not to be deemed to be contrary to ordre public or morality merely because it is prohibited by law or regulation, and by giving four examples of processes or uses which are not patentable'.[74] In this respect, the Court concluded that the Directive gives guidelines for applying the concepts at issue that otherwise do not exist in the general law on patents.

Regarding the Netherlands' contention that the patentability of isolated parts of the human body provided for by Article 5(2) of the Directive reduced living human matter to a means to an end, thereby undermining human dignity, the Court held that the right to ensure that the Union's institutions respect in the acts they adopt the fundamental right to human dignity was a general principle of Union law.[75] Reviewing the Directive, the Court held that human dignity was respected because Article 5(1) provides that the human body at the various stages of its formation and development cannot constitute a patentable invention. Thus, while an element of the human body may be part of a product

[72] At paras 16–17.

[73] At paras 24 to 25, referring to para 59 of Opinion 1/94 of 15 November 1994, [1994] ECR I-5267.

[74] At paras 38–39.

[75] Article 2 of the TEU now expressly provides that the Union is, inter alia, founded on the value of respect for human dignity.

which is patentable, 'it may not, in its natural environment, be appropriated' and 'the protection envisaged by the Directive covers only the result of inventive, scientific or technical work, and extends to biological data existing in their natural state in human beings only where necessary for the achievement and exploitation of a particular industrial application'.[76] Furthermore, Article 6 provides '[a]dditional security' by 'excluding from patentability, processes for cloning human beings, processes for modifying the germ line genetic identity of human beings and uses of human embryos for industrial or commercial purposes', such that, 'as regards living matter of human origin, the Directive frames the law on patents in a manner sufficiently rigorous to ensure that the human body effectively remains unavailable and inalienable and that human dignity is thus safeguarded'.[77]

The strict approach subsequently adopted by the Court in interpreting the scope of the patent protection permitted by the Biotechnology Directive has given teeth to the limitations to patentability of biotechnological material it identified in *Netherlands v Council*. The first preliminary reference concerning the interpretation of the Directive only occurred seven years later in *Monsanto Technology v Cefetra*.[78] It raised one of the key concerns with biotechnological patents, *ie* the 'non-obviousness' of the scope of application of biological material at the time of gene sequencing. Under Article 5(3) of the Directive, 'the industrial application of a sequence or partial sequence of a gene must be disclosed in the patent application', but it was unclear whether this meant that the scope of patent protection conferred is limited to the specific function so disclosed. At issue was an end product (soy meal produced from a genetically modified plant containing a protected DNA sequence) imported into the Netherlands from Argentina, where Monsanto did not hold a patent, and marketed in the Union in a form where the modified gene did not perform the function for which it was patented, *ie* making the plant resistant to herbicides.[79] It was clear that the patented product could perform that function if it was extracted from the end-product and inserted into a cell of a living organism.[80] Monsanto, however, sought an injunction based on Article 16 of Regulation No 1383/2003 prohibiting infringement of its European patent in all countries in which it was valid. Cefetra contended that since the DNA present in the soy meal no longer performed its function therein, Monsanto could not oppose the marketing of the meal solely on the ground of the DNA presence. The Court, following Advocate General Mengozzi, agreed that the patentability for which

[76] At paras 73 and 75.

[77] Paras 76–77.

[78] Case C-428/08 [2010] ECR I-6765.

[79] Three consignments of the soya meal had been detained at Amsterdam port by the Dutch customs authorities pursuant to Council Regulation (EC) No 1383/2003 of 22 July 2003 concerning customs action against goods suspected of infringing certain intellectual property rights and the measures to be taken against goods found to have infringed such rights; [2003] OJ L196/7. The consignments were tested by Monsanto, which found that they contained the presence of its protected gene sequence.

[80] See in this respect R Clark, S Smyth and N Hall, *Intellectual Property Law in Ireland*, 3rd edn (London, Bloomsbury, 2010), p 71.

the Directive provides is limited to where the patented material continues to perform its function. It held that Article 9 of the Directive did not extend protection to a patented DNA sequence that is unable to perform the specific function for which it was patented, and emphatically declared that: 'a DNA sequence such as that at issue in the main proceedings is not able to perform its function when it is incorporated in a dead material such as soy meal'.[81] The judgment provides a strong indication that the scope of patent protection for gene or partial gene sequences is limited thereby allaying many of the initial fears as to potential overreach of the monopolising effect of permitting the patenting of such sequences. It remains unclear if the same approach will be adopted if the conflict concerns third-party use of a function performed by the protected gene sequence that differs from that disclosed in the patent application claim.[82]

The second question referred asked whether Article 9 of the Directive effects an exhaustive harmonisation of the protection it confers, with the result that it precludes national patent legislation from offering absolute protection to the patented product as such, regardless of whether it performs its function in the material containing it. Unsurprisingly in the light of its interpretation of Article 9, the Court replied that the harmonisation was exhaustive. Drawing on a review of recitals 3, 5 to 7 and 8 to 13 in the preamble to the Directive, the Court held that 'the Community legislature intended to effect a harmonisation which was limited in its substantive scope, but suitable for remedying the existing differences and preventing future differences between Member States in the field of protection of biotechnological inventions', that the harmonisation agreed was 'aimed at avoiding barriers to trade' and represents 'a compromise between the interests of patent holders and the need for proper functioning of the internal market', and that, consequently, 'the harmonisation effected by Article 9 of the Directive must be regarded as exhaustive'.[83]

The Court's simultaneously strict and dynamic approach in *Monsanto* to the interpretation of the Biotechnology Directive is also evident in its *Brüstle v Greenpeace* ruling concerning stem cell patenting.[84] The backdrop to the reference from the German *Bundesgerichtshof* in *Brüstle* was the decision of the Enlarged Board of Appeal of the EPO in the *WARF* case concerning a cell culture comprising primary embryonic stem cells capable of in vitro fertilisation. At issue was, inter alia, the interpretation of Rule 28(c) of the Implementing Regulation, which corresponds with Article 6(2) of the Directive. In support of its application for a European patent, the applicant contended that the use of human embryos to make the embryonic stem cell cultures did not amount to use 'for industrial or commercial purposes'. Upholding the earlier EPO examining division's decision to refuse a patent, the Enlarged Board found that a claimed new or inventive product must first be made before it can be used. However, making the claimed product, even where there is an intention to use it for further

[81] At para 48.
[82] See, in this respect, Kur and Dreier, n 45 above, at p 135.
[83] At paras 55 to 57 and 60.
[84] Case C-34/10 *Brüstle v Greenpeace* [2011] ECR I-9821.

research, remained, in its view, excluded 'commercial or industrial exploitation of the invention' of the cultures.[85]

Unlike *WARF*, the German patent whose validity was challenged by Greenpeace in *Brüstle* did not concern cell cultures as such but their use for medical purposes. Furthermore, the production of the cell cultures did not require totipotent cells which exist in their original state for a few days after fertilisation and whose main characteristic is that each of them has the capacity to develop into a complete human being, but only pluripotent stem cells (that is cells that are able to differentiate into any type of cell or body tissue necessary for the harmonious development of the foetus's organs) of human origin that are removed at an early stage of development following the fertilisation of an ovum by a sperm. The referring court sought clarification of how, and by whom, the term 'human embryos' in Article 6(2)(c) of Biotechnology Directive is to be defined. Notwithstanding the absence of consensus on the issue in 1998, when the Directive, after considerable delay and various drafts (none of which sought to define the term 'human embryo'), was adopted, the Court held that its objective of promoting the internal market by removing obstacles to trade and research caused by differences in national legislation and case-law between the Member States regarding the concept of a human embryo, required it to be considered as 'an autonomous concept' of EU law that fell to be 'interpreted in a uniform manner throughout the territory of the Union'.[86] The Court drew support for this conclusion from the fact that, whilst Article 6(1) gives national courts and authorities 'a wide discretion in applying the exclusion from patentability of inventions whose commercial exploitation would be contrary to ordre public and morality, Article 6(2) allows the Member States no discretion with regard to the unpatentability of the processes and uses which it sets out, since the very purpose of this provision is to delimit the exclusion laid down in Article 6(1)'.[87] Regarding the meaning to be given to the concept of human embryo, the Court held that, notwithstanding the highly sensitive nature of the definition and the 'multiple traditions and value systems' in the Member States, it had to 'restrict itself to a legal interpretation of the relevant provisions of the Directive'.[88] Having reviewed those provisions and its interpretation of Article 5(1) in *Netherlands v Council*, the Court held the 'context and aim of the Directive' show that 'the Union legislature intended to exclude any possibility of patentability where respect for human dignity could thereby be affected',

[85] See Case G2/06 *Stem Cells v WARF*, OJ EPO, May 2009, p 306, at para 25. The Court refers to this ruling in *Brüstle v Greenpeace*, at paras 45 and 51.

[86] *Brüstle v Greenpeace*, para 26.

[87] Ibid, para 29.

[88] Para 30. In this respect, the Court followed the advice of Advocate General Bot who opined (at paras 39–40 and 45 of his Opinion) that it is 'on the question of the definition of an embryo that the main points of different philosophies and religions and the continual questioning of science meet', that the Court should not 'decide between beliefs or to impose them' but decide a 'difficult' but 'exclusively legal in nature' question In this respect, the criticism of the Court by W Cornish, D Llewelyn and T Alpin, *Intellectual Property: Patents, Copyright, Trade Marks and Allied Rights*, 8th edn (London, Sweet & Maxwell, 2013), that, by its strict approach to patentability, it 'appears to have absorbed the teachings of the Roman Catholic church on the subject' (at p 907) would appear to ignore both the wording of the judgment and the recommendation made by Advocate General Bot.

such that 'the concept of 'human embryo' within the meaning of Article 6(2)(c) of the Directive must be understood in a wide sense'.[89] It concluded that 'any human ovum must, as soon as fertilised, be regarded as a 'human embryo' within the meaning and for the purposes of the application of Article 6(2)(c) of the Directive, if that fertilisation is such as to commence the process of development of a human being', and that this classification applies to 'a non-fertilised human ovum into which the cell nucleus from a mature human cell has been transplanted and a non-fertilised human ovum whose division and further development have been stimulated by parthenogenesis', because, although not the subject of fertilisation as such, they are 'capable of commencing the process of development of a human being just as an embryo created by fertilisation of an ovum can do so'.[90]

The capacity for commencing the process of development of a human being is therefore critical for determining whether stem cells fall within the concept of a human embryo under Article 6(2). The approach was shared by Advocate General Bot who opined that the concept of a human embryo is engaged 'from the fertilisation stage to the initial totipotent cells and to the entire ensuing process of the development and formation of the human body', including 'the blastocyst'.[91] In contrast to the Court, he excluded pluripotent embryonic stem cells 'taken individually' from the concept, because they do not in themselves have the capacity to develop into a human being.[92] However, the Court recognised that it remained for national courts in individual cases, '[a]s regards stem cells obtained from a human embryo at the blastocyst stage', to ascertain 'in the light of scientific developments, whether they are capable of commencing the process of development of a human being'.[93]

The Court also confirmed that the Biotechnology Directive does not regulate the use of human embryos for scientific research, but only the patentability of biotechnological inventions. However, such research use, where it 'constitutes the subject-matter of the patent application cannot be separated from the patent itself and the rights attaching to it', with the result, having regard to recital 42, that the exclusion in Article 6(2)(c) covers the use of human embryos for purposes of scientific research, with the exclusive exception of use for therapeutic or diagnostic purposes which is applied to the human embryo and is useful to it.[94] As Advocate General Bot opined, an 'invention must be excluded from patentability … where the application of the technical process for which the patent is filed necessitates the prior destruction of human embryos or their use as base material, even if the description of that process does not contain any reference to the use of human embryos'.[95]

[89] Para 34.
[90] Paras 35–36.
[91] Para 115 of the Opinion
[92] Ibid, para 116
[93] Para 37.
[94] Para 43.
[95] Para 117 of the Opinion

IV. UNITARY PATENT PROTECTION AND A UNIFIED PATENT COURT

It is beyond the scope of this essay to consider the long and tortuous path that has led, after almost 30 years of endeavor, to the adoption, under the enhanced cooperation procedure and currently in respect of 25 Member States, of Regulation 1257/2012 providing for the creation of unitary patent protection.[96] Suffice it to note that in a seminal judgment on the scope of enhanced cooperation, as it is now provided for in the EU and FEU Treaties, in *Spain and Italy v Council*,[97] the Court upheld the underlying use of enhanced cooperation by the Council for the adoption of Regulation 1257/2012 based on Article 118 TFEU.[98] The Court held, inter alia, (rejecting the annulment actions and agreeing with Advocate General Bot) that, although rules on intellectual property are essential in order to maintain undistorted competition on the internal market, they do not, for that reason 'constitute "competition rules" for the purpose of Article 3(1)(b) TFEU' falling within the exclusive competence of the Union as provided for in Article 3(1)(b) TFEU, and, thus, as outwith the scope of Title III on 'Enhanced Cooperation' of Part Six of the TFEU by virtue of Articles 20(1) TEU and 329(1) TFEU. Instead, the creation of European IPRs providing uniform referred to in Article 118 TFEU falls within an area of shared, non-exclusive competence, to which the enhanced cooperation procedure may be applied.[99] Another of the applicants' pleas was that the creation of a unitary patent covering only part of the Union would be likely to damage the existing degree of uniformity (flowing from the requirement that Member States' patent legislation must be compatible with the provisions of the EPC) rather than improve it. The Court rejected this plea holding that: 'European patents granted in accordance with the rules of the EPC do not confer uniform protection in the Contracting States to that convention but rather, in every one of those States, guarantee protection whose extent is defined by national law', while '[i] n contrast, the unitary patent contemplated by the contested decision would confer uniform protection in the territory of all the Member States taking part in the enhanced cooperation'.[100] It concluded that the proposed unitary patent would 'be advantageous in terms of uniformity, and so of integration, compared to the situation created by the operation of the rules laid down by the EPC'.[101] The level of unitary protection ultimately achieved by Regulation 1257/2012 (discussed briefly below) is significantly diminished by comparison with that envisaged in Decision 2011/167/EU authorising the enhanced cooperation,

[96] See n 2 above. For a discussion of the path to Regulation 1257/2012, see, eg: Kur and Dreier, n 45, pp 149 to 155; F Dehousse, 'The Unified Court on Patents: The New Oxymoron of European Law', Egmont Paper No 60 – The Royal Institute for International Relations, Brussels, October 2013; and H Ullrich, 'Harmonising patent law: the untamable Union patent', Max Planck Institute Paper 2012, No 3.

[97] Joined Cases C-274/11 and C-295/11, judgment of 16 April 2013.

[98] Council Decision 2011/167/EU of 10 March 2011 authorising enhanced cooperation in the area of the creation of unitary patent protection, [2011] OJ L76/53.

[99] See paras 21 to 25 of judgment and paras 58 to 60 of the Opinion

[100] At para 62.

[101] At para 63.

whereunder the aim (see recital 7 thereto) was stated to be the creation of 'a unitary patent, providing uniform protection throughout the territories of the participating Member States'. However, Regulation 1257/2012 does not provide for the creation of such a patent as a matter of EU law. Having regard to the Court's reasoning in *Spain and Italy v Council* a doubt as to the Regulation's validity as a measure based on Article 118 TFEU cannot therefore be excluded. A challenge to the validity of the Regulation has been brought by Spain wherein this important issue may be addressed by the Court.[102]

Regulation 1257/2012 entered into force on 20 January 2013 but will only apply, that is have legal effect, under Article 18(2) thereof (assuming it is not annulled by the Court in Spain's pending challenge) from the date of entry into force of the Agreement on the Unified Patent Court signed on 13 January 2013 ('UPCA'). However, the latter will not occur until at least 13 Contracting Member States to that agreement (it is an international agreement between Member States) have ratified it. A further precondition for the application of Regulation 1257/2012 is that the ratifications of the UPCA must include those of the three Member States which had the most patents in force in 2012 (*ie* Germany, France and the United Kingdom). Assuming these conditions are met, the applicability of Regulation 1257/2012 is then subject to the additional proviso that, by then, the necessary preliminary amendments to Regulation (EU) No 1215/2012 of the European Parliament and of the Council of 12 December 2012 on the jurisdiction and recognition of judgments in civil and commercial matters concerning its relationship with the EPCA have been adopted.[103] Consequently, it seems unlikely at the time of writing (December 2013) that the Regulation 1257/2012 will apply (assuming its validity is upheld by the Court) for several years.

Furthermore, even after its entry into effect, it is not unlikely that considerable variations could persist in the application of Regulation 1257/2012. Thus, under Article 18(2) thereof, the unitary patent protection thereunder 'shall have unitary effect only in those Member States in which the Unified Patent Court has exclusive jurisdiction with regard to European patents with unitary effect at the date of registration'. This would appear to preclude unitary effect as regards all Member States participating in the enhanced cooperation under which the Regulation was adopted, but which do not ratify the UPCA, as well as in such of those states as do ratify the UPCA as regards all patents registered there before the dates of their respective ratifications of that agreement. This would appear to be a recipe for the creation of ongoing transitional issues and related litigation for many years.

The objective of Regulation 1257/2012 is to provide (as Article 1(2) thereof declares), by way of a regional patent treaty for the purposes of Article 142 of the EPC, for what is described as a European patent with unitary effect ('EPUE') in all Member States participating in the Regulation, where it is requested by

[102] See Case C-146/13 *Spain v European Parliament and Council* (pending), where one of Spain's pleas is that the Regulation lacks a legal basis because it does not introduce measures guaranteeing the uniform protection envisaged in Article 118 TFEU.

[103] [2012] OJ L351/1.

the patentee, and provided an entry to that effect is made in a special register (that is 'the Register for unitary patent protection' as defined under Article 2(e) of the Regulation), which is to be kept by the EPO. Under Article 18(6) of the Regulation, such requests may be made regarding 'any European patent granted on or after the date of application of this Regulation'. Under Article 3(1), the Regulation provides that a patent granted by the EPO with the same set of claims in all participating Member States 'shall benefit from unitary effect' in all those states provided its 'unitary effect' has been registered. It shall also therein, under Article 3(2), have 'unitary character', provide 'uniform protection' and have 'equal effect', although it may be licensed in all or part of the territories of the participating Member States. Article 3(3) provides that the unitary effect shall be deemed not to have arisen to the extent that the European patent 'has been revoked or limited'. Under Article 5(1), an EPUE shall confer on the patentee the right to prevent third parties committing infringing acts throughout the participating Member States. However, under Article 5(3), the acts against which the patent provides protection 'shall be those applied to the European patents with unitary effect in the participating Member State whose national law is applicable to the European patent with unitary effect as an object of property in accordance with Article 7'.

Article 7 of Regulation 1257/2012 is important. Under the heading, 'Treating [an EPUE] as a national patent', it reveals the very limited, yet complex, nature of the substantive harmonisation achieved by Regulation 1257/2012. Thus, under Article 7(1) to (3), an EPUE patent 'is to be treated in its entirety and in all participating Member States as a national patent of the participating Member State in which that patent has unitary effect'. The latter is to be the state in which the patentee was resident or had its principal place of business when the application was filed, or, failing that, the state in which where it has a place of business or, further failing that, as in Germany a German patent (Germany being the Member State where the EPO has its headquarters). It seems that the Regulation, if it comes into effect, will graft unto a European patent title granted by the EPO, and having effect as a national patent right of the participating Member State where the applicant resides (or is deemed to reside or have its business), unitary patent effect throughout all participating Member States, notwithstanding that (under Article 7(4)) 'it shall not be dependent on any entry in a national patent register'. Thus, if, for instance, Regulation 1257/2012 comes into effect and Ireland ratifies the UPCA, one would have the phenomenon of patents which are deemed to be Irish patents having have unitary effect throughout the participating Member States but which may not be registered in Ireland, but only with the EPO in the Register for unitary patent protection.

An overview of Regulation 1257/2012 (which is all this essay can attempt) would not be complete without a comment on Article 6. Concerned with 'Exhaustion of the rights conferred by [an EPUE]', it provides that the rights conferred by an EPUE 'shall not extend to acts concerning a product covered by that patent which are carried out within the participating Member States in which that patent has unitary effect after that product has been placed on the market in the Union by, or with the consent of, the patent proprietor, unless there are legitimate grounds for the patent proprietor to oppose further commercialisation of the product'.[104] There is no explanation in the recitals of what such 'legitimate grounds' might be. However, the provision appears to presage the existence of circumstances where the specific subject-matter of an EPUE may not be exhausted in respect of protected products put on the market with the patentee's consent. It is difficult to reconcile this provision on its face with *Merck v Stephar*. It could not, of course, as secondary legislation, seek to restrict the *Merck v Stephar* principle, which (as discussed above) is based on primary law, namely the Court's interpretation of (what are now) Articles 34 and 36 TFEU. Short of an amendment of the Treaties, only the Court could reconsider the principles it enunciated in *Merck v Stephar*. As it declined Advocate General Fennelly's express and considered invitation to do so over 17 years ago in *Merck v Primecrown*, it seems unlikely that it would be inclined to do so now by reference to Article 6 of Regulation 1257/2012.

Given the international nature of the system of courts envisaged by the UPCA and the fact that it provides that the envisaged Unified Patent Court ('UPC') will have jurisdiction not only in respect of disputes regarding the EPUE but also in respect of those concerning European patents validated in the participating Member States, it is difficult to conceive of it as an EU court system. However, the UPC will be a court common to the Member States that are party to the UPCA and, under Article 1 thereof, will be 'subject to the same obligations under Union law as any national court of the Contracting Member States'. Under Article 6(1), the UPC 'shall comprise a Court of First Instance, a Court of Appeal and a Registry'. Article 7 provides that the envisaged 'Court of First Instance' of the UPC 'shall comprise a central division as well as local and regional divisions' and that: 'The central division shall have its seat in Paris, with sections in London and Munich'. Local divisions will, in general, be set up in a Contracting Member State 'upon its request in accordance with the Statute' and will be capped at a maximum of four local divisions per Member State. Contrariwise, a regional division 'shall be set up for two or more Contracting Member States, upon their request in accordance with the Statute', the Contracting Member States involved will designate the division's seat but it 'may hear cases in multiple locations'. Under Article 9, the Court of Appeal shall have its seat in Luxembourg. Article 9(1) provides that: 'Any panel of the Court of Appeal shall sit in a multinational composition of five judges' and 'shall sit in a composition of three legally qualified judges who are nationals of different Contracting Member States and two technically qualified judges with qualifications and experience in the field of technology concerned'. Thus, while the legally qualified judges will have to be nationals of Contracting Member States, technically qualified judges may be nationals of other Member States or third countries.

Under Article 32(1) of the UPCA, the UPC will have exclusive jurisdiction in, inter alia, actions for actual or threatened infringements of patents and SPCs

[104] Article 29 of the UPCA contains a virtually identical provision as regards European patent titles granted by the EPO.

and related defences, actions for declarations of non-infringement of patents and SPCs, actions for provisional and protective measures and injunctions and counterclaims for revocation of patents and for declaration of invalidity of SPCs.[105] Furthermore, it will be required, under Article 20 of the UPCA, to 'apply Union law in its entirety' and to 'respect its primacy', while Article 21 of the UPCA envisages close cooperation between it and the Court so as 'to ensure the correct application and uniform interpretation of Union law, as any national court, in accordance with Article 267 TFEU in particular'.

If the UPC is established, it will clearly be hybrid in character; an international court operating in at least several Member States that will be a court or tribunal of the Member States who ratify the UPCA for the purpose of Article 267 TFEU. Thus, it will be subject ultimately to the control of the Court regarding application of EU law in respect of disputes regarding the EPUE and in respect of those concerning European patents validated in a Member State(s) where the dispute gives rise to issues of EU law. The Court will continue not to have jurisdiction to interpret in such preliminary references either the EPC (as the Union will not be acceding to it), or the UPCA, which is an international agreement between certain Member States and, as such, outwith the Court's jurisdiction under Article 267 TFEU.[106] The Court would, of course, have jurisdiction to provide the UPC (or indeed national courts) with all the criteria it (or they) may require for the interpretation of EU law to enable it (or they) to assess in a particular case whether provisions of the UPCA are compatible with EU law.[107]

Given the general exclusion of jurisdiction for the Court to interpret the UPCA, the inclusion therein of many substantive patent law provisions is unsatisfactory. Thus, provisions on the right to prevent direct and indirect uses of inventions are contained in Articles 25 and 26 of the UPCA; Article 27 deals with limitations of the effects of patents; Article 28 with rights based on prior use of inventions; Article 29 with (as discussed above in connection with Article 6 of Regulation 1257/2012) the exhaustion of the rights conferred by a European patent; while, finally, Article 30 deals with the effects of SPCs. It would have been more appropriate to include these provisions within Regulation 1257/2012, or otherwise within the formal scope of EU law, thereby bringing them within the preliminary-reference jurisdiction of the Court under Article 267 TFEU. The fact that they comprise provisions of international law will probably create doubts and uncertainties regarding their relationship with both EU law and national law, and perhaps also as regards their relationship with the EPC. These doubts and uncertainties will, almost inevitably, give rise to litigation, but in circumstances where there will be no ultimate over-arching interpretative role for the Court.

[105] Under Article 30(2), '[t]he national courts of the Contracting Member States shall remain competent for actions relating to patents and supplementary protection certificates which do not come within the exclusive competence of the Court'.

[106] See Case C-132/09 *Commission v Belgium* [2010] ECR I-8695, para 43.

[107] See Case C-370/12 *Pringle v Ireland*, Judgment of 27 November 2012, at para 80, and Case C-489/09 *Vandoorne* [2011] ECR I-225, para 25.

V. CONCLUSION

It is possible now to speak of an embryonic EU patent law. Clearly, many issues remain that will need to be worked out and resolved regarding the application of the EPUE and its relationship with national law and the EPC. There will also be significant issues of a substantive patent and constitutional law nature, both at EU and national level, to which the creation of the envisaged international UPC system will likely give rise.[108] Notwithstanding these numerous difficulties, the adoption of Regulation 1257/2012 represents, after almost 30 years in gestation, a first (albeit tentative) concrete step towards substantive harmonisation at EU law level of national patent law. It seems likely that the Court will continue to play, especially by way of answering preliminary references from national courts and, in future, from the UPC (if it is established), a key role in the further developments that will almost inevitably follow. It will endeavour to interpret Regulation 1257/2012 in a way that renders it as effective as possible. Nevertheless, challenging times lie ahead for patent lawyers. They will (to the extent that they may have been able to date largely to ignore EU law) have to adapt in the medium term to the likely reality of a hybrid unified patent court system dealing with many of the most important patent disputes in Europe, and applying EU law, the EPC, the UPCA and other relevant principles of international law, as well as national law, and where appropriate (or necessary in the case of the envisaged Court of Appeal of the UPC) making preliminary references regarding EU law issues arising from potentially numerous eclectic sources of applicable law to the Court with regard to EU patent law, and in the words of the folk singer, 'the times are a changing'.

[108] In Ireland, for instance, it seems likely that a constitutional referendum to permit the State to ratify the EPCA will be required, having regard to the significant transfer of judicial competence in favour of the UPC in relation to patents and SPC disputes that the agreement envisages. That the UPC will be hybrid in character as discussed above would not seem capable of reconciling it with Article 34, in particular, of the Constitution of Ireland on the 'Courts'. Ireland, it should be recalled, already amended its constitution, following a constitutional referendum approved by the People, by way of the Eleventh Amendment of the Constitution Act 1989, which inserted a provision into Article 29.4 of the Constitution expressly to permit Ireland to ratify the 'Protocol on the Settlement of Litigation concerning the Infringement of Community Patents' adopted at the 1985 Luxembourg conference on the Community Patent Convention signed in Luxembourg on 15 December 1975. As that Protocol was not adopted by all the Member States and so never entered into force, the Eleventh Amendment of the Constitution Act 1989 became effectively redundant in Irish constitutional law. It was finally repealed by the Twenty-eighth Amendment of the Constitution Act 2009, the enactment of which followed the referendum held on 2 October 2009 wherein the Irish People approved (at the second time of asking) the ratification by Ireland of the Treaty of Lisbon as well as the deletion of the provision inserted by the 1989 Act regarding the litigation protocol to the Community Patent Convention.

11

Market Regulation in Network Industries: Subsidiarity, Convergence and the Single Market in the Digital Age

ANTHONY WHELAN*

AS WITH OTHER network industries such as energy, the story of the building of the internal market for electronic communications in Europe is one both of market liberalisation and of market integration – and the achievements in the two areas are not always equal. In the case of telecommunications (now known as electronic communications in the relevant legal instruments), innovative use was made of the competition powers under the Treaty, in particular what is now Article 106 TFEU.[1] The period of gradual market opening and experimentation in the 1990s used both competition instruments and sector-specific legislation, some of it very prescriptive.[2] This period ended with the adoption in 2002 of a regulatory framework composed of several directives and a decision.[3] That legislation was further reviewed in 2007–9.

*Acting Director for Electronic Communications Networks and Services, European Commission; *Référendaire* in the chambers of Advocate General Nial Fennelly, 1995–2000.

[1] Commission Directive 90/388/EEC of 28 June 1990 on competition in the markets for telecommunications services [1990] OJ L192/10, amended several times up to 1999 and replaced by Commission Directive 2002/77/EC of 16 September 2002 on competition in the markets for electronic communications networks and services [2002] OJ L249/21.

[2] eg Regulation (EC) No 2887/2000 of the European Parliament and of the Council of 18 December 2000 on unbundled access to the local loop [2000] OJ L336/4.

[3] Directive 2002/21/EC of the European Parliament and of the Council of 7 March 2002 on a common regulatory framework for electronic communications networks and services [2002] OJ L108/33; Directive 2002/20/EC of the European Parliament and the Council of 7 March 2002 on the authorisation of electronic communications networks and services [2002] OJ L108/21; Directive 2002/19/EC of the European Parliament and of the Council of 7 March 2002 on access to, and interconnection of, electronic communications networks and associated facilities [2002] OJ L108/7; Directive 2002/22/EC of the European Parliament and of the Council of 7 March 2002 on universal service and end users' rights relating to electronic communications networks and services [2002] OJ L108/51; Directive 2002/58/EC of the European Parliament and of the Council of 7 March 2002 concerning the processing of personal data and the protection of privacy in the electronic communications sector [2002] OJ L201/37; Decision No 676/2002/EC of the European Parliament and the Council of 7 March 2002 on a regulatory framework for radio spectrum policy in the European Community [2002] OJ L108/1.

That regulatory framework contains a number of key features – these include generally applicable rules on matters such as authorisation of operators (based on general authorisation to the extent possible) and protection of end-users (sector-specific rules going beyond general consumer protection, and with a strong accent on enhancing competition through contract termination and switching possibilities), as well as provisions that inevitably require assessments by an administrative authority, eg on imposition on dominant operators of ex ante remedies in markets which are durably uncompetitive, on individual authorisation of use of scarce radio spectrum, or on nomination of a provider of a universal service (where such a scheme is chosen by the national legislator).

This regulatory system has been built on the founding premise of there being (one or more) national regulatory authorities (NRAs) in each Member State, entrusted with the relevant tasks, resources and powers, with guaranteed independence as regards at least some of these tasks. Having legislated by co-decision, the Union level is active thereafter in this system through the Commission, which, in addition to using its general enforcement powers under the Treaty to pursue failures by Member States to transpose or correctly apply any of the relevant rules, has some specific functions. These include:

- adoption of implementing measures regarding certain procedural or technical matters (eg network security, compulsory standards, technical harmonisation of radio spectrum use);[4]
- review of NRAs' draft market analysis measures, with a power to require withdrawal of measures as far as concerns market definition and assessment of significant market power (dominance) and a power to recommend withdrawal of proposed remedies, where the measure could impede the internal market or would be incompatible with Union law;[5]
- issuing recommendations on the markets which are considered to require *ex ante* regulation by NRAs (imposition of remedies on operators with significant market power in order to address durable competition problems which cannot be adequately addressed by the application of competition law);[6]
- issuing recommendations on the harmonised application of the provisions of the Directives to address divergences which could create a barrier in the internal market; in certain areas, in particular *ex ante* regulation of markets, the Commission may subsequently adopt a binding decision to address 'inconsistent implementation of general regulatory approaches'.[7]

[4] Arts 13a, 17, Directive 2002/21/EC of the European Parliament and of the Council of 7 March 2002 on a common regulatory framework for electronic communications networks and services [2002] OJ L108/33 (hereafter Framework Directive); Art 4, Decision No 676/2002/EC of the European Parliament and the Council of 7 March 2002 on a regulatory framework for radio spectrum policy in the European Community [2002] OJ L108/1 (hereafter Radio Spectrum Decision).

[5] Respectively Art 7, 7a, Framework Directive.

[6] Art 15, Framework Directive.

[7] Art 19, Framework Decision.

In addition, the 2009 Review saw the creation of a new entity, the Body of European Regulators of Electronic Communications (BEREC) – a small Union entity with legal personality performing support functions, the BEREC Office, and BEREC itself, which does not have legal personality, and which gathers the independent NRAs under a Chair elected from among the heads of its members. BEREC is intended to promote cooperation among NRAs and between NRAs and the Commission, to ensure the consistent application of the framework through common approaches or guidelines, assistance to individual NRAs, and opinions on draft Commission measures; and to advise the Commission and, on request, the Council and the European Parliament.[8]

The framework seeks to foster convergence with a range of requirements that the NRAs, the Commission, and BEREC, respectively 'take utmost account' of the opinions or recommendations of the others as foreseen in the legislation. The question whether such 'utmost account' obligations have a substantive component going beyond the procedural duty to give a reasoned justification for a difference of approach has yet to be tested.[9]

This regulatory system can claim some significant successes in respect of the liberalisation of the various national telecommunications markets in the Union. The number of markets considered to require *ex ante* regulation has diminished, and may diminish further.[10] Former telecoms incumbents have less than 50 per cent market share in most retail markets for fixed broadband connectivity, facing competition from alternative operators using regulated unbundled access as well as from cable companies, municipal utility fibre projects and others. In most mobile markets, there are three or four network operators. Additional competition comes from virtual operators.

At the same time, the market is fragmented. Alternative operators are often very localised. Multi-territorial operators (some incumbents, some mobile operators, and one major cable group) run quite distinct operations in each Member State, with few signs of price convergence. Expansion on the basis of a common business model is hampered by variations in local regulatory conditions or (in the mobile market) in spectrum-access conditions. While the construction and operation of communications networks has some inherently local elements, the procurement of equipment and the development of innovative means of commercialising data-centric network access and related services can benefit from scale. One of the objectives of the internal market in all domains is to

[8] Regulation (EC) No 1211/2009 of the European Parliament and the Council of 25 November 2009 establishing the Body of European Regulators for Electronic Communications (BEREC) and the Office [2009] OJ L337/1, Arts 1–3. BEREC replaces a previous advisory group, the ERG – see Commission Decision 2002/627/EC of 29 July 2002 establishing the European Regulators Group for Electronic Communications Networks and Services [2002] OJ L200/38.

[9] However, regarding the value of recommendations in casting light on applicable provisions of Union law, or intended to supplement such provisions, see Case C-207/01 *Altair Chimica* [2003] ECR I-8875, para 41.

[10] After a first review, the Commission Recommendation 2007/879/EC of 17 December 2007 on relevant product and service markets within the electronic communications sector susceptible to *ex ante* regulation in accordance with Directive 2002/21/EC [2007] OJ L344/65 reduced the number of such markets from 18 to 7; at the time of writing, a further review is under way and is likely to remove further markets from the list.

enable any available economies of scale to be attained – while not *imposing* scale where smaller, more geographically focused operations continue to be efficient.

Regulatory divergence is likely to be a significant factor in determining the attainability of efficient scale. The results of the current regulatory framework in terms of reducing divergence are mixed. On the one hand, there is a considerable degree of convergence regarding the (mainly wholesale) markets which are susceptible to regulation. NRA practice regarding market definition and identification of significant market power, over which the Commission has binding supervision powers, is also well aligned (benefiting also from the substantial consensus on these points under Union competition law). Even in the field of remedies, where the Commission cannot take binding decisions on individual NRAs' notifications, substantial policy consensus on a rather specific question can achieve a lot. For example, the great majority of NRAs (and thus BEREC) support the Commission's position that in the market for call termination, with each operator having virtual monopoly power for termination on its own network, regulated rates for all operators should be based on incremental costs of termination on an efficient network, and follow the Commission's recommended costing approach.[11] The Commission's approach is directly founded on the interpretation of the applicable provisions of the framework. This has resulted in very significant lowering and convergence of prices in absolute terms. In this case, a substantive orientation determined at Union level on a rather specific and one-dimensional policy matter, allied with the very intensive cost calculation work conducted by NRAs based on knowledge of local network conditions, has had tangible effects. However, even here, the NRA of one very significant Member State takes a different view (preferring to also take into account some common costs which the Commission considers can be recovered in competitive markets) and has not yet complied.[12] While either a binding general decision under Article 19 of the Framework Directive or individual infringement action may be considered, neither captures the benefits that the system of prior notification to the Commission of draft NRA remedies was meant to achieve – rapid resolution of problems and consequential market predictability. In the meantime, the operators of such outlier Member States continue to enjoy a competitive advantage over their peers in other parts of the Union.

Another area where the current institutional architecture has delivered well – subject to the inherent limitations of the substantive rules in question – is in the field of intra-Union mobile roaming. In the absence of pan-European networks, roaming by mobile customers of a given national operator on the networks of operators in other Member States requires wholesale arrangements between the operators in question for the origination and termination of calls and the provision of data connectivity. While the underlying costs of provision are not much different to those for domestic traffic, wholesale rates have historically

[11] Bottom-up long-run incremental costs (BULRIC). See Commission Recommendation 2009/396/EC of 7 May 2009 on the regulatory treatment of fixed and mobile termination rates in the EU [2009] OJ L124/67.

[12] See http://www.bundesnetzagentur.de/SharedDocs/Pressemitteilungen/EN/2013/130719_MobileTerminationRates.html.

been very expensive, and the low price sensitivity of customers (roaming is not the main determinant of operator choice) and their low price elasticity (at least as regards voice calls) led to the pass-on, with very high margins, of these expensive wholesale rates. Attempts to address this through Commission anti-trust action in respect of alleged abuse of collective dominance failed; and the problem was also judged not to be amenable to *ex ante* regulatory action by NRAs, as it had, by definition, a cross-border dimension (while the analytical tool of significant market power was, as in the anti-trust case, a difficult basis for action). The Commission finally proposed and had adopted temporary price cap legislation in 2007.[13] In this case, the legislation, in its various iterations, took the form of a regulation, with clear provisions on maximum 'euro-tariffs' at wholesale and retail level, possible opt-outs, price transparency and means of monitoring consumption. The system of national regulators has proven to be broadly effective in ensuring compliance with these rather unambiguous requirements. Moreover, in the case of the most recent roaming regulation,[14] BEREC successfully developed, in collaboration with industry and the Commission, technical guidance for the implementation of new structural measures favouring the emergence of alternative roaming providers.

Experience also shows, however, that in fields which involve more complex assessments, and in which it is difficult to lay down hard and fast rules in the legislation itself, the lack of strong Union-level tools to pursue convergence will often result in considerable regulatory fragmentation. This has been the case with the calculation of cost-oriented regulated wholesale access prices to the networks of dominant operators, on which the limited Union-level case-law has not yet given comprehensive guidance,[15] and the Commission has recently adopted a Recommendation pursuant to Article 19 of the Framework Directive[16] in order to address the very considerable variation in methodological approaches by NRAs.[17]

[13] Regulation (EC) No 717/2007 of the European Parliament and of the Council of 27 June 2007 on roaming on public mobile telephone networks within the Community and amending Directive 2002/21/EC [2007] OJ L171/32. This regulation has since been reviewed twice, and the issue is currently under discussion once more as part of the 'Connected Continent' legislative package. For an account of the background as well as an analysis of the lawfulness of the original legislation, see Case C-58/08 *The Queen, on the application of Vodafone Ltd and Others v Secretary of State for Business, Enterprise and Regulatory Reform* [2010] ECR I-4999.

[14] Regulation (EU) No 531/2012 of the European Parliament and of the Council of 13 June 2012 on roaming on public mobile communications networks within the Union, [2012] OJ L172/10.

[15] Joined Cases C-152/07, C-153/07 and C-154/07 *Arcor AG&Co KG* [2008] ECR I-5959. This judgment ruled out access charges being based exclusively on historic costs for largely depreciated networks, and largely supported use of current or forward-looking costs of replacing the network assuring a reasonable return as well as the long-term development and upgrade of networks, but did not exclude use of historic costs for some elements to avoid competition distortions, and considered that (under the earlier Regulation No 2887/2000 under consideration in that case) Union law did not dictate the precise cost accounting method (bottom-up or top-down) to be used by an NRA.

[16] Commission Recommendation 2013/466/EU of 11 September 2013 on consistent non-discrimination obligations and costing methodologies to promote competition and enhance the broadband investment environment [2013] OJ L251/13.

[17] For a comprehensive account of these divergences, see section 2.1 of the impact assessment by the Commission services accompanying the Recommendation at https://ec.europa.eu/digital-agenda/en/news/commission-recommendation-consistent-non-discrimination-obligations-and-costing-methodologies.

This recommendation extends beyond the issue of cost calculation – it also covers how to effectively assure non-discriminatory access to networks, and addresses the combination of circumstances (effective non-discrimination and the presence of significant competitive constraints from price-regulated access to copper networks or from other networks) which would justify the non-imposition of price controls for wholesale access to dominant operators' next-generation networks.

The complexity of the subject has dictated that the Commission, in line with BEREC's requests, has left within the recommended approach quite considerable scope for judgment by NRAs on how best to implement it. The process of consultation of BEREC on the draft Recommendation has contributed to development of considerable consensus on its high-level principles regarding price stability, avoidance of distortions between investment costs and rental prices ('buy or build') and the relevance of non-discrimination guarantees to the assessment of competitive constraints on the dominant network operator. Nonetheless, one would have greater assurance of effective implementation if there existed at Union level a more effective form of marginal review of individual NRAs' draft remedies than that foreseen in Article 7a of the Framework Directive. For this among other reasons, the Commission has included in its proposed 'Connected Continent' Regulation the possibility for it to require withdrawal of draft NRA remedies where these would be addressed to a European electronic communications provider, ie an undertaking active in the provision of electronic communications networks and services in more than one Member State.[18] The underlying logic is that of subsidiarity – while NRAs should in all circumstances abide by the framework, and be entrusted with the detailed and complex work of devising appropriate remedies for the networks within their jurisdiction, multi-country operators have a greater need of assurance of convergent regulatory treatment thereby justifying stronger intervention powers in the hands of the Commission. It would have been possible to argue that such powers should also accrue to the Commission to ensure convergent treatment of operators seeking access to networks in various Member States. However, this would have deprived the competence criterion of any real limiting power (any remedy addressed to any operator with market power could be said to potentially benefit an access-seeker from another Member State) and the Commission declined to go so far in its proposal. Despite this self-denial, this is among the most hotly contested provisions of the Commission proposal.

Looking beyond the case of *ex ante* market regulation based on competition principles, the case of radio spectrum management is also illustrative of the interaction between Union-level rules and supervision mechanisms designed to achieve a functioning internal market and the margin of appreciation of national competent authorities. Radio spectrum is a vital input to wireless electronic communications networks – mobile telephony, fixed and mobile wireless broadband, broadcasting – as well as to a variety of other economic and public

[18] Art 35(2), Draft Regulation of the European Parliament and of the Council laying down measures concerning the European single market for electronic communications and to achieve a Connected Continent – COM(2013) 627.

service activities (radar, GPS, short-range devices, etc.). It is acknowledged that radio spectrum constitutes a natural resource belonging to the Member States. The coordination of the use of radio spectrum is nonetheless recognised as being a matter of common interest in the internal market, to achieve a variety of objectives: interoperability of communications or other equipment using such spectrum, economies of scale for manufacture and distribution of equipment, common and favourable conditions of operation in markets which use such spectrum, avoidance of harmful interference, etc.

The current EU framework approaches the question of spectrum coordination at two operational levels, broadly speaking.[19] First, the technical harmonisation of conditions of use of certain radio spectrum bands is addressed under the Radio Spectrum Decision. This allows the Commission, typically after having given a mandate to CEPT for expert technical preparatory work,[20] to adopt, by comitology, decisions ensuring harmonised conditions for the availability and efficient use of radio spectrum – in effect, setting the technical use conditions which should prevail within a given band by a defined date. In practice, this mechanism is often used to make binding within the Union technical recommendations of CEPT, which are non-binding in character, and thus to give greater legal security to equipment manufacturers and to providers of networks and services. This mechanism has been used to specify the conditions of operation for a number of bands used for mobile telephony and wireless broadband on both an individually licensed basis (by individual mobile operators) and on an unlicensed/general authorisation basis (radio local access networks, commonly known as WiFi). While it enables the adoption of highly prescriptive binding technical rules at Union level, the circumstances under which decisions are taken under the Radio Spectrum Decision, and the substantial reliance on national expertise, ensure that potential subsidiarity concerns are effectively addressed.

The second operational level is that of authorisation or assignment of radio spectrum. Here, the current framework leaves very substantial discretion to the Member States, as regards the selection of licensees (in the case of individual authorisation) and the conditions under which authorisation takes place. The Framework Directive promotes technology neutrality subject to certain restrictions, including to achieve broadly defined general interest objectives (eg social or territorial cohesion, cultural diversity and media pluralism) and makes a rather tentative provision for transfer or lease of rights of use.[21] The Authorisation Directive provides, in cases where individual rights of use are required, for procedures to be open, objective, transparent, non-discriminatory and proportionate, with an explicit exception for cases where general interest

[19] The involvement of the Union in the upstream process of determining at international level, through the International Telecommunications Union (ITU), the permitted uses of different bands (spectrum allocation) is hampered by the fact that the Union is only an observer in the ITU. To the extent that such periodic discussions touch on the Union acquis, the Member States have to date been guided by Council conclusions.

[20] European Conference of Post and Telecommunications Administrations, operating under the aegis of the ITU and including a number of non-Member States, such as the Russian Federation.

[21] Arts 8a and 9b, Framework Directive.

objectives are at stake, such as broadcasting; it stipulates a number of procedural matters; requires national authorities to give due weight to the achievement of the objectives of the framework (promotion of competition, the internal market, end-user interests); defines in very general terms the type of conditions that can be attached to such rights of use (eg duration, coverage requirements, transfer conditions, and any commitment made in the selection procedure – which gives a rather free hand to national authorities in such negotiations); and provides, as regards fees, that they should be objectively justified and proportionate and reflect the need to ensure optimal use of these resources.[22]

These provisions have had a degree of success in ensuring procedurally fair, competitive procedures for the licensing of valuable spectrum for wireless communications. Case-law at Union level has identified a certain number of limitations on national discretion deriving from these provisions, including in the area of fees,[23] but it has also confirmed, more generally, the very wide powers of appreciation of national spectrum authorities in making such complex economic assessments, for which rigid criteria are not applicable.[24]

It should be no surprise that licensing conditions for use of spectrum in harmonised bands, including fees and licence duration, vary widely, in ways which cannot fail to have profound effects on operators' decisions (market entry; rate of investment; pricing decisions linked to recovery of investment) and on perpetuation of divergence in services, service quality and prices available to consumers, even after controlling for differences in factors such as population density and topology.

The 2009 review of the framework provided for a new tool, a multi-annual radio spectrum policy programme (RSPP), the first of which was adopted in 2012.[25] This decision identified a number of somewhat more precise regulatory principles and objectives specific to radio spectrum, including regarding flexibility of use rights, avoidance of under-use and regulatory tools to ensure that accumulation of spectrum rights does not distort competition. Article 4(8) also foresees that 'the Commission shall, in cooperation with Member States and in accordance with the principle of subsidiarity, facilitate the identification and sharing of best practices on authorisation conditions and procedures and encourage sharing of information for such spectrum to increase consistency

[22] Directive 2002/20/EC of the European Parliament and the Council of 7 March 2002 on the authorisation of electronic communications networks and services [2002] OJ L108/21 (hereafter Authorisation Directive), as amended, Arts 5(2), 7, 13, part B of the Annex.

[23] eg Case C-462/99 *Connect Austria v Telekom-Control-Kommission* [2003] ECR I-05197 regarding discriminatory spectrum fees; Joined Cases C-55/11, C-57/11 and C-58/11 *Vodafone España*, judgment of 12 July 2012; in Case C-86/10 *Telefonica Moviles* [2011] ECR I-1575, para 29, the Court of Justice indicated that either too high and too low a fee could infringe Art 13, Authorisation Directive.

[24] Case C-431/07 P *Bouygues and Bouygues Télécom v Commission* [2009] ECR I-2665, para 125. This is also illustrated in the outcome of Case C-86/10 *Telefonica Moviles* [2011] ECR I-1575, regarding the respective economic value of spectrum used for analogue and digital services, and the need for equality of opportunity for the respective users of those technologies.

[25] Art 8a(3), Framework Directive; Decision No 243/2012/EU of the European Parliament and of the Council of 14 March 2012 establishing a multiannual radio spectrum policy programme [2012] OJ L81/7.

across the Union'. However, no specific mechanism is foreseen either for consultations between Member States and the Commission, or for ensuring that best practices are in fact implemented.

The 2012 RSPP also sought to address the very fragmented picture regarding the timetable for grant of rights of use to harmonised spectrum. It laid down a common binding deadline of the end of 2012 for authorisation of all bands which had at that point been technically harmonised for wireless broadband, including the highly prized 800 MHz 'digital dividend' spectrum previously used in most Member States for broadcasting.[26] For the latter, in the presence of differing situations in Member States regarding the pace of digital transition for broadcasting and cross-border coordination needs with other Member States and third countries, the RSPP provided for a derogation mechanism. Fourteen Member States sought such derogations, for periods up to 2015, and the great majority were granted. This cannot be regarded as an unmitigated achievement of the objectives of speedy and predictable release throughout Europe of a key band for the roll-out of wireless broadband in rural as well as densely built-up areas.

The Commission considers that the solution to this degree of market fragmentation requires a number of significant changes, which must remain, however, fully respectful of the principle of subsidiarity and of radio spectrum's character as a public resource of the Member States. In its draft 'Connected Continent' Regulation,[27] at the time of writing still under negotiation with the co-legislators, the Commission has proposed, as regards radio spectrum harmonised for wireless broadband:

- more precise legislative criteria regarding the most significant authorisation conditions, reflecting best practices;[28]
- a harmonisation mechanism, by comitology, for the authorisation timetable(s) for a given harmonised band and for licence duration;[29]
- a peer-review-based coordination mechanism, whereby national authorities would notify draft spectrum authorisation conditions to the Commission; allowing the latter and the other Member States to make comments or, in cases of justified serious doubts regarding the draft's compatibility with the internal market or Union law, to require its withdrawal through a comitology procedure.[30]

In the first category, in addition to more general objectives such as maximisation of the end-user interest in network investment and competition, the efficient use of spectrum, and predictable economic conditions, the draft Regulation addresses matters such as: the assembly of complementary bands in a single assignment procedure; the criteria for specifying maximum spectrum awards ('spectrum

[26] Art 6, RSPP. This deadline was fixed at 1 January 2013 for the 800 MHz band and at 31 December 2012 for all others.

[27] Draft Regulation of the European Parliament and of the Council laying down measures concerning the European single market for electronic communications and to achieve a Connected Continent – COM(2013) 627.

[28] Arts 9–11, draft Connected Continent Regulation.

[29] Art 12, draft Connected Continent Regulation.

[30] Art 13, draft Connected Continent Regulation.

caps', often imposed on competition grounds but potentially restrictive of most efficient network management); an objective 'effective competition' test for restrictions imposed on competition grounds; criteria to minimise burden and increase efficiency in obligations related to territorial coverage; criteria for specifying conditions for transfer, lease or sharing of licensed spectrum; and, as regards spectrum usage fees, requirements that the social and economic value be reflected, including the beneficial externalities of spectrum use, that investment needs be taken into account, and that investment needs should influence the distribution between, on the one hand, (often very steep) up-front payments and, on the other, periodic fees.

In the second category, the Commission seeks to learn the lessons of the RSPP, by creating a procedure for setting sufficiently in advance the realistic Union-wide timetable for assignment of a band, for example by taking into account from the outset, through potentially staged timetables, objective difficulties that certain Member States may have (rather than an artificially common timetable whose predictive value for the market is undermined by almost a year of discussions on far-reaching derogations). At the same time, a Union-level procedure for setting the duration of licences, even with potentially different starting dates, should allow the establishment of a European spectrum renewal cycle over time, thereby favouring the integration of networks across countries; while favouring the rapid introduction of best practice regarding this variable, which is seen as especially critical to foster a positive investment environment

These two elements should have interlocking effects with the third (peer-review coordination mechanism). The common starting point is that the grant of individual rights of use for radio spectrum remains the responsibility of the competent national authorities. This is not a mere execution task – even with more granular and precise spectrum assignment principles, each national authority will retain significant powers of appreciation. These same principles should serve as criteria for the peer-review mechanism, providing a basis for constructive criticism of doubtful plans and, in extreme cases, for withdrawal and resubmission. This *ex ante* review mechanism has a number of common features with the procedure for review of the NRAs' market analysis under Article 7 of the Framework Directive, albeit the national spectrum authority would have greater 'protection' from its Member State peers through the comitology procedure – it brings with it the benefits of greater legal certainty (in those cases where a national plan is deemed compatible), in a field where national litigation is common; meanwhile, even in those cases where a national plan is condemned, the national authority remains responsible for revising and resubmitting it (as is also the case for NRAs whose market analysis is rejected). At the same time, the most vital elements for promoting rapid access to new spectrum to meet rising demand and for the facilitation in the medium-to-long term of common European wireless broadband networks, namely the authorisation timetable and duration respectively, would be subject to an efficient harmonisation mechanism in which possible variations in national circumstances are fully acknowledged in the applicable criteria and national sensitivities are protected via the comitology procedure.

Additional examples abound in other areas of electronic communications law of the need for improvement in the current balance between Union-level rules and national discretionary implementation, if a genuinely integrated internal market for electronic communications is to be achieved. These include the current level of practical variation in the implementation of basic end-user protection rules under the Universal Service Directive (the relevant provisions of which provide for minimum harmonisation only, and are sometimes merely facultative in character); or the significant differences in the commercial and technical terms of wholesale access to dominant networks under the Access Directive.[31] However, the foregoing should suffice to demonstrate the scale and difficulty of the task, as well as its importance.

The application of the subsidiarity test, as a matter of practical politics as well as of law, needs to take into account how greater substantive convergence can be achieved on matters which genuinely count in order to make economies of scale attainable in the single market, while disturbing as little as possible institutional choices in the Member States (eg the structure of national regulators) and assessments better conducted at local level, and at the same time minimising both direct bureaucratic cost and indirect bureaucratic 'drag' and uncertainty for the system in general and for market players. This inevitably involves a greater degree of precision in Union rules, wherever this can be safely done without doing violence to the underlying economic (or, in the case of end-user protection rules, socio-economic) rationale, and well scoped mechanisms for tighter coordination between the Union-level and the national-level authorities which allow judicious and effective intervention by the former but leave intact the competence of the latter in terms both of fact-finding and of judgment calls which the overarching Union rules continue to leave for case-by-case assessment within sufficiently defined parameters.

[31] Both cases are addressed by the draft Connected Continent Regulation, Arts 17–20 and 21–30 respectively – in each case, a greater level of substantive harmonisation is sought, while still leaving significant matters of implementation judgment to the NRAs at least until such time as the Commission could adopt relevant implementing acts by comitology.

PART III: ASPECTS OF IRISH LAW

12

Reconciling Ireland's Sovereignty with Membership of the European Union – the Lessons of Crotty *and* Pringle

RONAN KEANE*

THERE SEEMS TO have been a convention at one time that contributors to a *festschrift* such as this did not refer in any way in their essays to the person in whose honour it was being assembled. Since, at least in the case of members of academia, that might give rise to the unfortunate impression that they were simply finding a place for an essay which, had, for whatever reason, been gathering dust, I always had some unease in observing it and at least sought to ensure that my contribution reflected the interests of the dedicatee. In joining in the tributes to Nial Fennelly, I will happily ignore it and record my admiration for his long and distinguished career in a number of areas of the law and my appreciation of a friendship of many years. Since his tenure of the office of Advocate General of the Court of Justice of the European Union – the only Irish one so far – was a major episode in his career, I felt sure that an examination of aspects of our sometimes troubled legal relationship with the EU would be appropriate. But I am also happy to recall the all too short a time when we were fellow members of the Supreme Court and where his knowledge of European law and his great wisdom were so invaluable.

In recalling the complex history of how the Irish legal system has sought to reconcile the ceding of sovereignty mandated by our membership of the EU with the imperatives of the Constitution, I have sought to place it in the wider context of European history. When the movement to unite Europe had its first stirrings in the wake of the Second World War, the continent was not merely devastated by that appalling conflict, but was divided by the iron curtain. Its supporters knew that the historical precedents were not encouraging; unity had been brought about in the past, not by the peoples of Europe, but by the forces of imperialism and tyranny. The movement was born of a noble aspiration to consign to history the dreadful hatreds which had led, not only to two World Wars, but to the

*Former Chief Justice of Ireland

ultimate horror of the Holocaust. However, only the most optimistic would have expected that what began so modestly with the establishment of a common market in six western countries in 1957 would become the continent-wide union of 28 States stretching from the Atlantic to the frontiers of Russia, and from the Arctic to the Mediterranean coast of Africa.

For Ireland, it seemed that accession to the European Communities, as they were then called, could be a historic turning point. The protectionist policies adopted by the State in its early decades and our neutrality during the war had left us to some degree impoverished, economically and intellectually. Our ambiguous relationship with our powerful neighbour and the issues left unresolved by the partition which it imposed in 1920 had ultimately led to violence fuelled by sectarian hatred. When we became members of the Communities along with the United Kingdom and Denmark in 1973, there were good reasons for optimism; membership on our own would have been problematic, given our close trading relationship with the UK. Now there were major economic benefits to be reaped, not least from the Common Agricultural Policy. The coming of free trade with the other Member States marked the end, in the economic sphere at least, of the isolated and inward looking Ireland of previous decades. As it expanded both in membership and the reach of their policies, the requirement of the Communities that a level playing field exist throughout the single market compelled Ireland to adopt socially progressive measures, such as equal pay for equal work, anti-discrimination rules in the work place and the protection of the environment, which Irish governments might otherwise have been slow to embrace. There were, of course, negative aspects, not least the fisheries policy, which cost Ireland dearly.

But while, on balance, it seemed, as the 1980s dawned, that Irish people had benefited substantially from membership of the Communities, there had, of course, been a significant transfer of sovereignty to the Communities when we joined in 1973. This had been made possible by the amendment to Article 29 of the Constitution, which enabled us to join the Communities founded by three treaties, the most important of which was the Treaty of Rome which established the European Economic Community. The European Communities Act 1972 made those treaties part of our domestic law and thus the directives and regulations of the Council of Ministers of the Communities became as much part of our law as Acts of the Oireachtas, while the judgments of the European Court of Justice had primacy in its area of competence over decisions of Irish courts. While the architects of the Communities plainly envisaged that it would be a developing entity to which changes would be made as it embraced new areas, the extent to which such changes also required amendments to the Constitution, and hence a referendum, became a major legal issue when the Single European Act (SEA) was adopted by the Member States in 1986 and the State's capacity to ratify it without a referendum was challenged in the celebrated case of *Crotty v An Taoiseach*.[1]

[1] [1987] IR 713.

I appreciate that this is well trodden ground, but there some aspects of that case which seem to have received little attention, given its ramifications in our constitutional law.

The SEA was a treaty between the Member States of the Communities containing three titles. Titles I and II added some new areas to the areas in which the institutions of the Communities already enjoyed jurisdiction. They also altered the decision-making processes of the Council of Ministers, and these included substituting majority voting in some cases for the existing requirement of unanimity. They also provided for the establishment of a Court of Justice of First Instance in addition to the existing Court of Justice. Title III was a separate treaty requiring the Member States to take steps towards the creation of a common European foreign policy. The plaintiff claimed that some at least of these provisions would result in a transfer of sovereignty from Ireland to the Communities which was not authorised by the constitutional amendment effected in 1972.

Since the provisions of Titles I and II constituted amendments of the existing Treaties, they could not become effective in Irish law until legislation was enacted amending the European Communities Act 1972, so that the amended treaties became part of domestic law. The SEA contained its own procedure as to ratification; it would not become binding on the Member States until each of them had ratified the treaty in accordance with its own constitutional requirements and deposited the instrument of ratification with the Italian government in Rome. The amending legislation was passed by the Oireachtas and signed into law by the President in 1986; since its implementation would involve a charge on public funds, a resolution by Dáil Eireann confirming its terms was also passed in accordance with Article 29.5.2 of the Constitution. The Government intended to deposit the instrument of ratification on 1 January 1987 and thereafter to bring the amending legislation into operation, but, on 23 December 1986, the plaintiff applied to Barrington J *ex parte* at his private residence for an interim injunction restraining them from so doing unless and until the amendments were approved by the people in a referendum. Barrington J granted the relief sought on Christmas Eve and shortly afterwards an interlocutory injunction to the same effect was granted by a divisional court consisting of Hamilton P, Barrington J and Carroll J. After another short interval, there was a final hearing by the divisional court; they dismissed the plaintiff's claim for a permanent injunction, the judgment being delivered by Barrington J.

The State defendants had resisted the claims for relief on a number of grounds, one of them being that the plaintiff had no *locus standi* to bring the claim. Barrington J applied the law as recently laid down by the Supreme Court in *Cahill v Sutton*.[2] He found that, as the statute giving effect to the SEA would not take effect until the instrument of ratification was deposited and the order made bringing the legislation into operation, the plaintiff had not suffered any prejudice and was not in imminent danger of suffering any prejudice, the

[2] [1980] IR 269.

threshold laid down by O'Higgins CJ in *Cahill v Sutton* for granting *locus standi*. The plaintiff would still be in a position to challenge the legislation when it became operative.

As to the challenge to Title III, this was tersely dismissed in the following terms:

> So far as the portions of the Single European Act dealing with European Political Cooperation, and which it is not proposed to make part of the domestic law of Ireland, are concerned, this court does not consider that it has any function in relation to them.

There followed an appeal to the Supreme Court. This was complicated by the fact that, since in the case of the challenge to Titles I and II the plaintiff was questioning the validity of an Act of the Oireachtas, under the Constitution, as it then was, only one judgment could be delivered on that part of the appeal and the existence of any other opinion could not be disclosed. That did not apply to the challenge to Title III, where five judgments were delivered.

Delivering the judgment of the Court on the challenge to Title I and II, Finlay CJ had this to say on the issue of *locus standi*:

> The Court is satisfied, in accordance with the principles laid down by the Court in *Cahill v Sutton*, that in the particular circumstances of this case where the impugned legislation, namely the Act of 1986, will if made operative affect every citizen, the plaintiff has a *locus standi* to challenge the Act notwithstanding his failure to prove the threat of any special injury or prejudice to him, as distinct from any other citizen, arising from the Act.

Finlay CJ then went on to consider the merits of the plaintiff's case on Titles I and II. On this part of the case, Barrington J in the High Court, having found that the plaintiff had no *locus standi*, continued as follows:

> It is perhaps fair to say that the court is unconvinced that there is anything in the Single European Act which is outside the licence granted by the first sentence of the Third Amendment [enabling Ireland to join the Communities], extends the scope of the objectives of the [Communities], poses any threat to the rights guaranteed by our Constitution or represents anything other than an evolution of the [Communities] within the terms of its original objectives.

A broadly similar conclusion was reached in the judgment of Finlay CJ and the plaintiff's appeal on this part of the case accordingly failed.

The Court was divided on the challenge to Title III, the majority (Walsh J, Henchy J and Hederman J) holding that the nature of the provisions contained in that part of the treaty meant that the State could not ratify it unless the Constitution was amended so as to enable them to do so, which could only be done by a referendum. Finlay CJ and Griffin J dissented, holding that in agreeing to those provisions the Government was properly exercising the power conferred on it by Article 29.4.1 of the Constitution to conduct the external relations of the State.

There had been a number of cases – of which *O'Donovan*,[3] *Ryan*[4] and *McMahon*[5] are examples – in which the plaintiff had not demonstrated that he or she had or would have suffered any damage peculiar to himself or herself arising from the operation of the impugned statute, but no issue was taken by the Attorney-General as to the plaintiff's standing to bring the action. While a warning was sounded by the Supreme Court in *Cahill v Sutton* as to the undesirability of affording standing to plaintiffs who sought to rely on a possible frailty in a statute which did not affect them, it was also made clear that this should not preclude a challenge to the constitutional validity of statutes by a plaintiff, if this had the consequence of an arguably invalid statute escaping scrutiny because no other challenger was likely to emerge.

These considerations, voiced in both the High Court and the Supreme Court, led to the acceptance in the latter court in *Crotty* that the plaintiff had *locus standi* to challenge the Act giving effect to Titles I and II. That was understandable, given the provisions in the Constitution prohibiting the Oireachtas from enacting legislation repugnant to the Constitution and expressly conferring a jurisdiction on the courts to determine whether statues were constitutionally valid. These provisions were not applicable to Title III of the SEA, where legislation was neither required nor contemplated.

In the subsequent decision of *McGimpsey v Ireland*,[6] where the plaintiff, a Unionist politician from Northern Ireland, had sought to challenge the constitutional validity of the Anglo-Irish agreement which gave the Republic for the first time a role in the affairs of Northern Ireland, the defendants had disputed his *locus standi*. Although he enjoyed Irish citizenship – if that is the way to put it – by virtue of having been born in Northern Ireland, he made no secret of the fact that he was simply using the Constitution to bring an end to an agreement to which he was totally hostile. In the High Court, Barrington J was prepared to allow him *locus standi*, but dismissed his case. On appeal, his judgment was upheld, but, in the only judgments delivered in the Supreme Court, Finlay CJ and McCarthy J expressed doubts as to his *locus standi*. Since, however, there was no cross-appeal on this issue, they were prepared to consider the case on its merits.

In *Crotty*, although the majority judgments do not refer to *locus standi*, the dissenting judgments of Finlay CJ and Griffin J can be read as conflating that issue with the substantive issue as to whether the Government should be restrained from ratifying the SEA because of the provisions of Title III. Their judgments accept that, because Article 28. 1 of the Constitution provides that the executive power of the State (including its exercise in the external relations area) is to be exercised by the Government 'subject to the provisions of this Constitution', the courts have the right and duty to intervene in circumstances where its exercise of the conduct of external relations is in breach of the Constitution. In *Boland v An Taoiseach*,[7] FitzGerald CJ had said that such circumstances would have

[3] *O'Donovan v Attorney-General* [1961] IR 114.
[4] *Ryan v Attorney General* [1965] IR 294.
[5] *McMahon v. Attorney-General* [1972] IR 69.
[6] [1988] IR 567.
[7] [1974] IR 338.

to amount to 'a clear disregard' by the Government of its powers and duties under the Constitution. Both Finlay CJ and Griffin J elaborated on this by saying that, where the exercise of the power constituted 'an actual or threatened invasion or breach of the constitutional rights of an individual', the courts could and should intervene to protect those rights (Griffin J instanced a declaration of war by the Government without the assent of the Dáil contrary to Article 28.3.1 of the Constitution; another, presumably, would be implementing a treaty which involved a charge on public funds without that assent.). Since the plaintiff had not pleaded or relied on any such actual or threatened invasion of his constitutional rights, they said that his claim should be dismissed. But their judgments also make it clear that, in any event, they were satisfied that Title III did not contain any provisions necessitating a constitutional amendment.

It undoubtedly could be argued that, even in the absence of any such actual or threatened invasion of the plaintiff's rights, the courts could and should intervene at his instance in the exercise by the Government of the executive power in external relations, where it could be shown that it was not acting in accordance with the Constitution. The contrary argument would be that the Government was primarily accountable to the Oireachtas in this area and that the courts had no role, save in the limited circumstances envisaged by Finlay CJ and Griffin J, which did not arise in this case. Since there was no discussion of any sort of the issue in the majority judgments, it is difficult to avoid the conclusion that it was either overlooked or that it was erroneously assumed to be determined by the ruling on Titles I and II. Whatever the explanation, it seriously weakens the authority of the majority judgments as a binding precedent.

Title III was entitled 'Treaty Provisions on European Cooperation in the Sphere of Foreign Policy', and there is no doubt that it was intended to be an important stage in the transformation of what was still essentially an economic association of States into a European Union which would also be a political union. The SEA did not purport to create such a union, but the majority in *Crotty* took the view that the agreement by the Member States embodied in Title III to develop a 'European foreign policy' as part of the process leading to the establishment of a European Union was a constitutionally impermissible qualification of Irish sovereignty in the area of foreign policy. They regarded the obligation on the Member States to endeavour to formulate and implement such a foreign policy, to inform and consult each other in this area, and to endeavour to avoid any actions or positions which would impede a consensus as irreconcilable with the concept of Irish sovereignty enshrined in the Constitution. Walsh J and Henchy J laid particular emphasis on Article 6.1 providing that:

> All powers of government, legislative, executive and judicial, derive, under God, from the people, whose right it is to designate the rulers of the State and, in final appeal, to decide all questions of national policy, according to the requirements of the common good.

In an important passage in his judgment, Henchy J said:

> A perusal of Title III of the SEA satisfies me that each ratifying Member State will be bound to surrender part of its sovereignty in the conduct of foreign relations. That is to

> happen as part of a process designed to formulate and implement a European foreign policy. The freedom of each state is to be curtailed in the interests of the common good of the Member States as a whole. Thus, for example, in regard to Ireland, while under the Constitution the point of reference for the determination of a final position on any issue of foreign relations is the common good of the Irish people, under Title III the point of reference is to be the common position determined by Member States. *It is to be said that such a common position cannot be reached without Ireland's consent but Title III is not framed in a manner which would allow Ireland to refuse to reach a common position on the ground of its obligations under the Irish Constitution.* There is no provision in the Treaty for a derogation by Ireland where its constitutional obligations so require (emphasis added).

What does the italicised sentence mean? It appears to acknowledge that, even where all nine of the other Member States had reached a 'common position', Ireland could refuse to join that position. But the learned judge seems to have read into the treaty a requirement for Ireland to state its reasons for not joining and an implication that those reasons could not include its obligations under the Constitution. He does not elaborate on what consequences, if any, would ensue for Ireland if, through its foreign minister, it announced that it would not join 'the common position' because it was not in Ireland's interests to do so.

Let us take a concrete example. One Member State proposes to undertake military action, not as part of NATO or the Western Union, but on its own initiative, in order to avert a humanitarian catastrophe in a third country. It seeks support from the other Member States, some of whom, including Ireland, refuse to support that initiative unless it is approved by the United Nations Security Council. That body is paralysed by the veto of one of its permanent members. Six of the Member States decide to support military action, a minority, including Ireland, decide not to. The Irish foreign minister says that Ireland does not consider that peace and stability in the region affected will be helped by such an action and that it would not be in Ireland's interests, as a member of the wider international community represented by the UN, to support it. Could it be seriously suggested that Ireland was not entitled, because of Title III, to take that position?

The difficulties do not end there. Under the Constitution, according to Henchy J, the 'point of reference' (a phrase that appears nowhere in the Constitution) in arriving at a 'final position' on a foreign policy issue is the common good of the Irish people. Under Title III, the point of reference, he says, will be the common position determined by the Member States. Since, by definition, the common position cannot be determined without the consent of all the Member States, how can the 'point of reference' be determined by a common position which does not exist? In fact, Title III says something different, ie that '[t]he determination of common positions shall constitute a point of reference for the *policies* of [the Member States]' (emphasis added).

What is beyond doubt is that, if the essence of sovereignty, as succinctly defined by Finlay CJ in the judgment on Titles I and II – a definition cited by Walsh J in his judgment on Title III – is 'the right to say yes or no', that right in the area of foreign policy was not affected in any way by the provisions of Title

III. After all the talking and listening and mental processes of 'taking account' were done with, Ireland, like all the other Member States, could politely say no to joining in whatever position might be adopted by some or all of the other States. The only method by which the long term objective of establishing a meaningful political union in the area of foreign policy would be achieved was by a further amendment of the existing treaties, necessitating a referendum in Ireland. This was made clear by Finlay CJ, not merely in his dissenting judgment on Title III, but also in the judgment of the Court on Titles I and II.

It is a feature of the majority judgments that they regard the imposition on the Member States of an obligation to consult on and discuss issues of foreign policy with the other States and endeavour to arrive at a consensus in that area as of itself trenching on the sovereignty of each of the Member States. But, as Griffin J pointed out, the language of Title III had been chosen with extreme care so as to ensure that the obligations of the parties under the Treaty would permit 'the utmost freedom of action' to each of the parties in the sphere of foreign policy. The majority, however, appeared to attach no significance to what might have been thought to be the inevitable tendency of the government of any State in arriving at decisions on foreign policy to enter into discussions and consultations with other States with whom they were closely associated, and to take into account their views before arriving at a decision. Nor do they seem to have recognised that giving consideration to the views of other States did not necessarily mean adopting those views as the basis of whatever decision that government reached. Finlay CJ in his dissenting judgment observed that:

> [I]t appears probable that under modern conditions a state seeking cooperation with other states in the sphere of foreign policy must be prepared to enter into, not merely vague promises, but actual arrangements for consultation and discussion. I can find no warrant in the Constitution for suggesting that this activity would be inconsistent with the Constitution and would, as is suggested, presumably in each individual instance, require a specific amendment of the Constitution.

As we have seen, the judgments of Walsh J and Henchy J lay particular stress on the provisions of Article 6.1 of the Constitution recognising the right of the people, 'in final appeal to decide all questions of national policy according to the requirements of the common good.' It seems a surprisingly narrow construction of that provision to treat it as rendering constitutionally suspect a treaty imposing an obligation on the Irish Government to consult with and take account of the views of the other parties before arriving at decisions on foreign policy. One cannot help wondering whether that assessment of what constitutes 'the common good' of the Irish people is entirely consistent with the people, in the Preamble, seeking that 'concord [be] established with other nations', or with Article 29 which states: 'Ireland affirms its devotion to the ideal of peace and friendly cooperation amongst nations founded on international justice and morality'.

The decision of the majority on Title III in *Crotty* also raised far-reaching questions as to how the doctrine of the separation of powers operates in the context of the Irish Constitution. While some of the judgments of the five judges referred to the often-cited formulation of that doctrine by O'Byrne J, speaking for the former Supreme Court in *Buckley and Ors (Sinn Fein) v Attorney-General*,[8] they did not address the specific issue that arises in relation to judicial review of matters expressly assigned by the Constitution to one of the political arms of government, ie the legislature or the executive. Perhaps the most widely accepted statement of the criteria to be applied in determining whether such matters are, of their nature, non-justiciable is the following passage from the opinion of Brennan J in the United States Supreme Court decision, *Baker v Carr*:[9]

> Prominent on the surface of any case liable to involve a political question is found a textually demonstrable constitutional commitment of the issue to a co-ordinate political department ; or a lack of judicially discoverable and manageable standards for resolving it ; or the impossibility of deciding without an initial policy determination of a kind clearly for non-judicial discretion ; or the impossibility of the Court's undertaking independent resolution without expressing a lack of respect due to co-ordinate branches of government ;or an unusual need for unquestioning adherence to a political decision already made ; or the potentiality of embarrassment from multifarious pronouncements by various departments on one question.

In a case where what was at issue was the capacity of the executive arm to enter into an international treaty designed to promote cooperation in foreign policy, but which preserved Ireland's right as a sovereign State to refuse to accept the positions adopted by the other contracting States, it is difficult to understand how, applying these criteria, the question as to whether it was appropriate for the State to enter into contractual commitments to endeavour to reach such common positions was other than a political, and hence non-justiciable, question.

Since an almost invariable feature of international treaties is the acceptance of obligations to each other by the contracting parties, the finding of the majority in *Crotty* had serious implications for the constitutional validity of other treaties to which Ireland was a party. The first to be challenged was the Anglo-Irish agreement in *McGimpsey v Ireland*.[10] The Irish and United Kingdom governments in that agreement undertook to co-operate with each other in seeking peaceful solutions to the problems arising from the relationship between the unionist majority and the nationalist minority in Northern Ireland. One of the grounds of the challenge was that it placed constraints on the Government in its conduct of foreign policy, contrary, it was claimed, to what was decided in *Crotty*. That ground was rejected in the High Court, Barrington J distinguishing *Crotty* on the basis that it dealt with a multilateral treaty conferring powers on supra-national authorities However, the SEA did not confer any powers on the institutions of the EC, and it is difficult to see how *Crotty* could be distinguished on that ground. Finlay CJ in the Supreme Court distinguished it on the ground that it left the Irish Government free to carry out their functions under the agreement in the manner they thought most conducive to achieving its aims. That may not apply to other international agreements

[8] [1950] IR 67.
[9] (1969) 369 US 186.
[10] [1988] IR 567(HC); [1990] IR 110.

and doubts have been expressed as to whether our membership of the United Nations is compatible with *Crotty*: the Charter requires Member States to give support, including military support, to the Security Council if that body thinks it necessary for international peace and security, and in such an event Irish national interests (narrowly construed in accordance with *Crotty*) would have to be disregarded.

The Oireachtas, having passed legislation amending the Constitution so as to enable Ireland to ratify the SEA, the referendum to approve that amendment was carried.

But in its aftermath there was little if, any, progress in the formulation of a common foreign policy. The historian Tony Judt remarked of the SEA:

> [T]he signatories stepped cautiously around the embarrassing absence of any common European policy on defence and foreign affairs. At the height of the 'new Cold War' of the 1980s and on the verge of momentous developments unfolding a few dozen miles to their East, the Member States of the European Union kept their eyes resolutely fixed upon the internal business of what was still primarily a common market, albeit one encompassing well over 300 million people. [11]

Significant changes were brought about by the adoption of the Maastricht Treaty in 1992. Together with the Amsterdam Treaty of 1997, it marked the transformation of the EC into the European Union, a union which was both political and economic, and provided for the establishment of the momentous institution of a single currency, the euro. In the case of both treaties, an amendment of the Irish Constitution was obviously required, irrespective of what *Crotty* had decided, and in each case the amendments were approved by the people.

As to foreign policy, Title V of the Maastricht Treaty at least did what the SEA had so conspicuously refrained from doing: it obliged the Council of Ministers to define a common position in foreign and security policy, whenever it deemed this necessary. The Member States would then have to ensure that their foreign policy positions conformed to the common position. However, decisions of the Council had to be taken unanimously, unless the possibility of recourse to a majority vote had been agreed in advance.

Although the discretion given to the Council as to when all this was to happen and the requirement of unanimity rendered these provisions only marginally less anodyne than Title III of the SEA, they nevertheless provoked the late Lord Rees-Mogg into instituting judicial review proceedings in England claiming that they violated a fundamental feature of English constitutional law, ie that the conduct of foreign affairs was a prerogative of the Crown which only the Government could exercise and which did not even require the approval of parliament, let alone the EU. His counsel cited *Crotty* in his argument, but the Court of Appeal said it had no relevance, being concerned with the provisions of the Irish Constitution. Speaking for the Court, Lloyd LJ briskly dismissed the constitutional argument, saying that the accession by the UK to the Treaty,

[11] T Judt, *Post War: a History of Europe since 1945* (London, Pimlico, 2005) 529–30.

far from being an abandonment or transfer of the prerogative powers, was an exercise of those powers.[12]

All the judgments in *Crotty* may well have been significant in influencing the Government to hold a referendum on the Nice Treaty, a crucial step in the preparations for the major enlargement of the Union by the accession of the Eastern and Central European States which had formerly been part of the Warsaw Pact bloc, although it has been suggested that it was at least debatable whether a referendum was necessary.[13] In the event, the referendum was initially defeated, an uncomfortable reminder to the Government of the perils of the referendum process; it was carried in a second referendum after certain assurances had been given to the Government as to how the Treaty would be implemented. A referendum was also clearly unavoidable in the case of the Lisbon Treaty in 2007, which effectively replaced the proposed Constitution of the European Union, which the electorates of France and the Netherlands had declined to accept in referenda held in 2005. Again the Government suffered the embarrassment of a rejection of the Treaty which was also followed by assurances from the EU institutions as to particular aspects of the Treaty and a successful rerun, from the Government's point of view, of the referendum.

There followed the catastrophic changes in Ireland's economic fortunes with the failure of the property boom, the collapse of the leading banks and a huge deficit in the public finances. This, of course, was against the background of a worldwide recession and a threat to the existence of the euro. The Fiscal Stability Treaty,[14] adopted in 2012, which was one of the responses to the developing crisis in the eurozone, was also put to a referendum on the advice of the Attorney General. It was intended to ensure that all the Member States of the EU avoided the disregard of fiscal prudence which, in the case of some Member States, including Ireland, had been a contributory factor to the general economic crash in Europe. To that end, the Treaty replaced the largely ineffectual provisions of the Maastricht Treaty on fiscal stability by ensuring that sanctions were imposed on the non-compliant states by the institutions of the EU. Since the United Kingdom and the Czech Republic refused to accede to the Treaty, it was adopted by the other Member States as a free-standing international treaty, rather than an EU Treaty requiring amendments to the existing EU treaties. It was not clear why such a treaty required a referendum, since it did not appear to cede any powers to the EU institutions which they did not already enjoy. Despite a vigorous campaign in support of a 'no' vote, it was approved in the subsequent referendum. In accordance with normal practice, the contents of the Attorney General's advice were not disclosed, but commentators generally took the view that the almost certain invocation of the majority judgments in *Crotty* in any subsequent litigation – whether in the form of a challenge to the Treaty or a

[12] *R v Secretary of State for Foreign and Commonwealth Affairs, ex parte Rees –Mogg* [1994] QBD, 552.

[13] See G Hogan and G Whyte (eds), *J M Kelly: The Irish Constitution*, 4th edn (Bloomsbury, London, 2003), 520.

[14] Treaty on Stability, Coordination and Governance in the Economic and Monetary Union, signed at Brussels on 2 March 2012.

reference by the President to the Supreme Court of legislation giving effect to it in domestic law – was probably a crucial factor.

A challenge was, however, launched against the treaty establishing what was called the European Stability Mechanism (hereafter the ESM Treaty) and which was complementary to the Fiscal Stability Treaty, but which was not submitted to a referendum. It was a treaty signed by the seventeen members of the eurozone under which they committed themselves to the setting up of a fund from which advances could be made to those States, such as Ireland and Greece, whose economies were is such a parlous condition as to make borrowing on the markets virtually impossible. To that end, a corporate structure called the European Stability Mechanism was established, of which all the signatory States were to be the members.

The capital of this structure was to be a mind-boggling 700 billion euros, which was to be contributed by the signatory States in proportion to their size, Ireland's contribution being 11.1454 billion euros. The board was to consist of the finance ministers of the signatory states. The ESM was entitled to make advances to any of the signatory states where that was required to ensure the continued stability of the eurozone, 'subject to strict conditionality'. Such conditions could include 'a macro-economic adjustment programme.'

The challenge to the ESM Treaty was brought by a Dáil deputy, Mr Thomas Pringle. In addition to other reliefs, he sought an injunction restraining the Government from ratifying the ESM Treaty. He claimed that, in a number of respects, the decisions of the Council of Ministers which had purported to make possible the amendments to the provisions dealing with the eurozone in the existing EU treaties, required by the establishment of the ESM, and the ESM Treaty itself were contrary to the law of the EU and hence to the Constitution. In addition, citing the majority decision in *Crotty* he claimed that the vesting in an external autonomous body such as the ESM of wide ranging powers of a monetary or economic nature was an impermissible alienation to that body of powers exclusively vested in the Oireachtas and the executive, which could only be effected by an amendment of the Constitution.

In view of the far-reaching implications of the plaintiff's claim and the imminence of the scheduled entry into force of the Treaty, the proceedings were heard with great rapidity. The plaintiff's claim as to the unconstitutionality of the ESM Treaty was dismissed in the High Court and the other issues raised as to the possible invalidity of the decisions and the Treaty itself under European Union law were referred by the Supreme Court to the Court of Justice of the EU for a preliminary ruling. That Court in a ruling on the 27 November 2012 rejected the plaintiff's claim and found the decisions and the Treaty to be compatible with EU law.

The appeal to the Supreme Court on the constitutionality of the ESM Treaty was heard by seven judges, six of whom upheld the dismissal of the plaintiff's claim.[15] The *locus standi* of the plaintiff to make the claim was not disputed by the State defendants. They also accepted that the law was correctly stated by the majority in *Crotty*.

[15] *Pringle v Government of Ireland* [2012] IESC 47.

Since two Supreme Court judges and three High Court judges had taken a different view of the law in *Crotty* and the majority decision had been severely criticised, it might have been thought that the appeal in *Pringle* presented an appropriate opportunity for a decision with such wide-ranging ramifications to be at the least reviewed.[16] Speculation as to why that opportunity was not taken is pointless. In the result, and not surprisingly, the judges in the majority and the solitary dissentient, Hardiman J, concentrated in their judgments on determining what the *ratio* of the decision of the majority was, and how it should be applied to the challenged provisions of the ESM Treaty. In the result, the judgments of the minority judges in *Crotty* received little attention.

It was, of course, open to the individual judges in *Pringle* to express a view as to whether the majority decision in *Crotty* was correct, although such a view would inevitably be *obiter* and not binding on any court. A careful reading of all the majority judgments in *Pringle* – by Denham CJ, McKechnie J, O'Donnell J and Clarke J – suggest that only one of the majority, McKechnie J, expressed unqualified support of the majority decision in *Crotty*. Although the dissenting judgment of Hardiman J does not, in terms, express unqualified approval, it would seem an inescapable inference from the concern which he voiced that assigning to other bodies the right to decide all questions of national policy vested in the people by the Constitution without seeking their approval in a referendum would empty what he described as 'that great case' of all meaning.

There is in this context an interesting passage in the judgment of O'Donnell J which deserves close study. Dealing with one of the majority judgments in *Crotty*, he says:

> I very much doubt if the judgment of Henchy J can be read as suggesting that the courts can review the actions of the Government in the field of foreign relations and if appropriate restrain Governmental action on the ground that the court considers, by some standard not identified, that the action is not in pursuance of the common good of the Irish people ... I consider that this portion of the judgment of Henchy J is really an illustration of the central holding that the SEA, if enacted without constitutional amendment, would involve Ireland in an impermissible alienation or subordination of Governmental authority since the Irish Government would by definition have to take account of considerations outside Ireland's national interest. To borrow a concept from administrative law, the Irish Government would, to that extent, be making decisions by reference to a consideration which was constitutionally irrelevant and indeed impermissible. *I do not think that this could be taken, without much more elaborate and detailed argument and consideration, as an authority for the proposition that the Court can review individual decisions of the Government on the grounds that the decisions to adhere to any particular international agreement are not within the interests of the common good of the People of Ireland. Such a proposition would raise very serious issues indeed as to the standard of such review and, more fundamentally, the constitutional justification for it*' (emphasis added).

[16] For the circumstances in which the jurisdiction to review previous decisions of the court may be exercised, see the judgments of Henchy J in *Mogul of Ireland v Tipperary (NR) County Council* [1976] IR 260 and of the writer in *Society for the Protection of Unborn Children v Grogan* [1998] IR 343.

The learned judge goes on to find that the Government was fully entitled to conclude that it was in the Irish national interest to enter into an agreement providing for support of the eurozone generally.

What Henchy J said in *Crotty* on this topic was precise and unambiguous: '...the common good of the Irish people is the ultimate standard by which the constitutional validity of the conduct of foreign affairs by the Government is to be judged.'

It would seem to follow inexorably that the courts would indeed be entitled to review a decision of the Government to adhere to a particular agreement on the ground that it was not within the interests of the common good (as that expression was construed in *Crotty*) of the Irish people. While Henchy J was undoubtedly concerned with an agreement which applied to the conduct of foreign policy generally, the prohibition laid down, in the case of such an agreement, on taking into account the interests of other countries must in logic and commonsense apply to individual agreements which suffer from the same alleged frailty. How could Ireland, if the referendum in 1987 had been defeated, conceivably have entered into a whole series of agreements which did not have as their exclusive 'point of reference' the common good of the Irish people – to quote another phrase from Henchy J's judgment – if it was precluded from entering into Title III on that specific ground ?

The judgment of O'Donnell J also suggests that the differences between the majority and minority judgments in *Crotty* are relatively narrow. It has to be said, with respect, that his reasoning on this aspect is not entirely persuasive. Thus, he points out that the minority accepted that, if the SEA created a form of political union, there could be no doubt that this would be an alteration in the essential scope and objectives of the Communities which could not be achieved without an amendment of the Constitution. The learned judge thus seeks to reduce the difference in approach between the majority and minority to one of 'timing'. However, both Finlay CJ and Griffin J were emphatic that the SEA involved no transfer whatever of sovereignty to anyone and that the path of discussion and consultation which it envisaged was totally different from the partial transfer of sovereignty to the institutions of the EC in the political sphere which would necessarily be involved in the creation of a political union, a difference which was significantly more than one based on 'timing'. Nor does O'Donnell J refer to the clear view of the minority judges that the courts could intervene in the conduct of foreign affairs by the Government only where, in the words of FitzGerald CJ in *Boland,* there was 'a clear disregard' by the Government of the Constitution, which Finlay CJ and Griffin J took to mean an 'actual or threatened invasion of the constitutional rights of an individual'. We have already seen the implications this had for the *locus standi* of the plaintiff in *Crotty*, an issue which received no discussion in *Pringle*, because of the concession made by the State that the plaintiff had standing.

O'Donnell J also referred to the adoption by Walsh J in his judgment of the arresting definition by Finlay CJ in the judgment of the Court on Titles I and II of sovereignty as 'the right to say yes or no'. He says that to treat that phrase as representing the *ratio decidendi* of Walsh J's decision would be wrong, since it might give rise to what he considers would be a misleading inference, ie that Walsh J was casting doubt on the capacity of the State to enter into future international agreements that would preclude the State from saying no at some future stage, which, as he and Clarke J both emphasise, could hardly be correct, since limiting the State's freedom of action in this way is a necessary feature of virtually all such agreements.. However, while the learned judge may be correct in supposing that this was not Walsh J's intention, the fact remains that Walsh J made no attempt in his judgment to explain how the agreement in Title III offended that definition of sovereignty, although it was patent that Ireland retained the right to say 'no' to the adoption of any common position in foreign policy. How could it be argued that the State was precluded from entering into an agreement which preserved that right, but was not prevented from entering into a vast range of international agreements which, as is conceded, at the least modified that right ?

Clarke J in his judgment also suggested, somewhat more obliquely, that there were similarities between the approaches of Finlay CJ and Henchy J, but confined his comments to the judgment of Finlay CJ for the Court on Titles I and II. He referred to a passage where the Chief Justice, having said that the proposed changes from unanimity to qualified voting in those titles did not require an amendment, added: 'it does not follow that all other decisions of the Council which now require unanimity could, without a further amendment of the Constitution, be changed to decisions requiring less than unanimity.'

Clarke J treats that statement as a caution against 'what might be described as a path of gradualism', that being, of course, the expression used by Henchy J to define what he saw as the unconstitutional transition to a political union mandated by Title III. The learned judge adds: '[i]t does always need to be kept in mind that it not permissible to do by four separate small steps that which could not be done in one giant leap.'

The sentence quoted from the judgment of the Court seems, with respect, a slender foundation for concluding that Finlay CJ was lending any support to the comments of Henchy J on 'gradualism' in relation to Title III. It said no more than that, in the opinion of the Court, the question as to whether the abandonment of the unanimity principle in all cases would require a constitutional amendment remained open. It has to be remembered that a judge delivering the judgment of the Supreme Court in a case where only one judgment is permitted has the sometimes difficult task of assembling a judgment with which a majority of the court can concur, and which might be rather different in tone and content from the one he or she would deliver if freed from that constraint.[17] In the case of *Crotty*, it so happened that Finlay CJ delivered another judgment where he was under no such inhibition. There is nothing in that judgment to indicate that he agreed in any way with the comments of Henchy J as to ' gradualism' and a great deal to indicate that he took an entirely different view, as did Griffin J.

[17] The one-judgment rule was abolished by the Thirty-Third Amendment of the Constitution, save as it applied to references to the Court under Article 26.

Clarke J also indicates what he considers to be the ratio of the majority decision in *Crotty* in the following passage:

> The limit on the discretion which the Government holds arises where the relevant treaty involves Ireland in committing itself to undefined policies not specified in the treaty and in circumstances where those policies, which Ireland will be required to support, are to be determined not by the Government but by institutions or bodes not specified in the treaty. It is an abdication, alienation, or subordination of policy formation and adoption which is not permitted.

That is a possible summary of what the majority seemed to be saying in *Crotty*. A difficulty arises, however, as to what 'institutions or bodies' the majority in *Crotty* had in mind. These were certainly not the institutions of the EC, which were given no role by Title III. The ten Member States considered as a collective entity of some sort? But they could not formulate a common position unless they were all in agreement. If they were not in agreement, Ireland did not have to conform to the views of any of them. If they were all in agreement, Ireland would presumably have decided that the national interest – whether that term is used in a narrow or broad sense – would be served by adopting the common position.

All four judges who delivered judgments in *Pringle* and were in favour of dismissing the appeal drew a distinction between a treaty such as Title III of the SEA, which dealt in general with the conduct of foreign policy and, in the view of the majority in *Crotty*, impermissibly subjected its conduct to the advice or interests of other bodies, and one such as the ESM, which dealt with the single issue of the establishment by the Member States of the eurozone of a fund designed to ensure the stability of the eurozone and which, in the view of the Government, it was in the interests both of the eurozone in general and Ireland in particular for Ireland to establish. This, they concluded, was an exercise by Ireland of its sovereignty and not an abdication or surrender of sovereignty. In his dissent, Hardiman J declined to accept that this was a valid distinction, since, if anything, in his view, the abridgments of Irish sovereignty in the economic and monetary sphere effected by the treaty were more drastic than those which were found to be unconstitutional in *Crotty*.

The decision of the European Court in *Pringle* dealt with serious issues as to the legal constraints on the economic and monetary policies of the European Union which are outside the scope of this essay. The decision of the Supreme Court in the same case has, through no fault of the court, left unresolved the uncertainties as to the limitations on the conduct of foreign policy by Irish Governments which have persisted since *Crotty*. In the fourth edition of *JM Kelly: The Irish Constitution*, the learned editors said of that case:

> The breadth of the majority's reasoning is such … that it could plausibly be regarded as casting doubt on the State's general treaty-making powers. Consequently it may be appropriate to take a less than sanguine prospect of its prospects for survival.[18]

[18] Hogan and White (n 13 above) 97.

Unhappily, it still survives. At the time of writing, Ireland is about to emerge from the bail-out programme requiring close scrutiny of our domestic economic policies by the EU and the International Monetary Fund. But although the profound crisis affecting the eurozone and the wider EU has somewhat abated, further measures are contemplated with a view to ensuring financial stability and, as it is hoped, a revival of economic growth and employment. Some of these are prompted by what is seen as the need for a European banking union to ensure that there is no repetition of the recent banking crisis. But there are many economists who argue that the eurozone's problems will not be resolved until the defects are remedied which, it is said, are inevitable in a currency union which does not centralise the fiscal policies of the Member States, as well as their powers to fix interest rates and exchange rates. Of course, any transformation of the membership of the eurozone into membership of a federal state would mean referenda or plebiscites throughout the eurozone and indeed the wider EU. But as the process of resolving the present serious and fundamental problems develops, there may well be new treaties, short of so extreme a transformation, which may or may not require, in our case, amendments of the Constitution. In that event, the ghost of *Crotty* may continue to haunt us.

There are some who would consider the holding of referenda as an important and desirable feature of the Constitution. There is much to be said for the relatively rigid structure of the Constitution which makes amendment of the Constitution impossible without a referendum. But it also unquestionably has its drawbacks. Referenda are notable for their low polls and notoriously present the electorate with an opportunity to inflict a battering on an unpopular government, regardless of the merits of the particular proposal. Frequently issues become prominent in the campaign which are wholly irrelevant but may, for all one knows, prove decisive. Thus, in the case of the Maastricht Treaty, the debate was dominated by claims that passing the treaty would mean the introduction of abortion on demand (untrue) and recriminations as to how much money the then Government had secured for Ireland from the EC cohesion funds. The proposals in the treaty which laid the ground for the establishment of the single currency, and which had such momentous consequences for the Irish and wider European economy, received scant mention. There seems, however, to be little concern in Ireland with the fact that so many of our European partners, who would consider their polities perfectly democratic, do not adhere so rigidly to the principle that every constitutional amendment must receive popular approval. Would it be too much to entrust the recently established Constitutional Convention with considering possible changes to the Constitution in this area which would limit the requirement for a referendum to cases where a fundamental change in the political structures established by the Constitution or in the personal rights which it guarantees was contemplated?

As to the common European foreign policy which was, in the view of the majority in *Crotty*, to be the inevitable result of our accession to the SEA, it remains in practical terms as much of a mirage as ever. In the tumultuous decades since then, the cold war has ended and communism has collapsed throughout Eastern and Central Europe, Germany has been unified, the Balkans have been devastated by war, international terrorism has become a major threat, the Iraq and Afghanistan wars have provoked major concerns and the world wide depression has engulfed all the developed countries. Where was European foreign policy while all this was happening? In the case of the Balkan wars, the hollowness of the treaty provisions, even in their revised form post the SEA, was cruelly exposed. As one historian has put it:

> Yugoslavia was to be the first test [of the Common Foreign and Security Policy established by the Maastricht Treaty]. The Luxemburgian foreign minister, Jacques Poos, famously proclaimed it 'The Hour of Europe.' A 'troika' of foreign ministers set off to negotiate a ceasefire between Croatia and her Serb neighbours. Their efforts and all subsequent initiatives were subverted by the complete lack of consensus among EU Member States.[19]

Not that nothing was happening. In addition to the changes we have already noted which were introduced by the Maastricht Treaty, the abortive draft Constitution proposed the creation of an office of EU foreign minister, presumably as an answer to Henry Kissinger's famous question: 'whom do I call when I want to talk to Europe?'. Even that modest change was too much; instead two existing posts were merged to create the splendidly titled office of 'the High Representative of the Union for Foreign Affairs and Security Policy'. I wonder how busy her telephone is.

[19] B Simms, *Europe: the Struggle for Supremacy, 1453 to the Present* (Allen Lane, London, 2013) 493.

13

Crotty *Put to Sleep by* Pringle

HUGH GEOGHEGAN*

UNLIKE MOST MEMBER STATES of the EU, Ireland has found it necessary to hold a referendum seeking approval of the people whenever there is a proposed Treaty change or a new Treaty within the EU Membership. The Irish Constitution contains various provisions ensuring sovereignty of the State. Although the Constitution also provides for separation of powers as between the legislature, the executive and the judiciary, a purported exercise of those powers must not contravene provisions of the Constitution. Understandably, this leads to nervousness on the part of governments to proceed with new or amended treaties without the protection of an amendment of the Constitution if there is an arguable loss of sovereignty issue involved. This can only be achieved by referendum.

There has always been an element of controversy within legal circles, academic and professional, as to whether all these referendums are necessary. Blame is frequently attached to a Supreme Court decision in the case of *Crotty v An Taoiseach* [1987] I.R. 713, hereinafter referred to as '*Crotty*'. The controversial aspect of that case related to a decision by three judges to two that ratification of Title III of the Single European Act (SEA) could not be lawfully effected by Ireland without a constitutional amendment, as its provisions offended against articles in the Constitution ensuring Ireland's sovereignty.

Some referendums in relation to new or amended treaties were clearly necessary, having regard to the Constitution and for which no blame (if that is the correct word) can be attributed to *Crotty*.

It will be suggested in this chapter that the influence and effect of *Crotty* will now be considerably diminished by the majority judgments in the recent case before the Supreme Court of *Pringle v The Government of Ireland* [2012] IESC47 (*Pringle*). Hence the title of the present chapter.

Problems of reconciliation with the Constitution were naturally anticipated when Ireland joined the then three European Communities in 1973. A constitutional amendment approved by referendum effectively permitted such membership and the amendment included a provision for the validity of laws

*Former judge of the Supreme Court of Ireland

enacted acts done or measures adopted by the State and provided for laws and measures adopted by the communities to have the force of law in the State. In *Crotty*, there were two major issues. In addition to the attack on the ratification of the SEA, there was also sought a declaration that a Bill to enact domestic legislation adopting certain parts of the SEA into domestic law was repugnant to the Constitution. That last mentioned Bill was on the statute book by the time the case came before the Supreme Court and under the Constitution there had to be a single judgment only on the question of its validity. On the ratification issue, there were five separate judgments, with a three-to-two majority. That aspect of the case related to an issue not encompassed by the domestic legislation, because in Title III the SEA it introduced a new concept of a 'European foreign policy'.

The single judgment is relevant to this chapter in two respects only. First of all, it established that the Constitution permitted amendments of the Treaties but with the limitation that they 'do not alter the essential scope or objectives of the Community'. On that basis, the validity of the Act was upheld. The second relevant aspect led to surprising consequences. The single judgment of the Court delivered by Finlay CJ contained the following sentence: 'Sovereignty in this context is the unfettered right to decide to say "Yes or No".'

Despite the fact that the sentence appeared in a particular context, it was to feature quite prominently in the judgment of Mr Justice Walsh dealing with Title III (ie the foreign policy issue). As a consequence, it was discussed and, it must be suggested, put back in its rightful context by the majority of the judges in *Pringle*.

It is obviously not possible to deal at any length with the judgments of the Supreme Court in relation to Title III in *Crotty*. Broadly speaking, the majority, ie Walsh J, Henchy J and Hederman J, believed that Title III, if ratified by Ireland, offended the sovereignty provisions of the Constitution whereas the minority judgments of Finlay CJ and Griffin J concentrated on the division of powers and in particular the exclusive right of the Government, as executive, to enter into treaties.

This chapter is not concerned with whether *Crotty* was correctly decided. *Crotty* was of its time. It must surely be reasonably arguable that the development of the current European Union and Ireland's participation in it should nowadays be taken into account even in the interpretation of the Constitution. Such a viewpoint seems to have been implicitly adopted in the judgments of the majority of the judges in *Pringle*.

The issue in *Pringle* relevant to this chapter was the constitutional entitlement of the Government to enter into the European Stability Mechanism Treaty (the ESM Treaty) concluded between the Eurozone members pursuant to an amendment of the principal EU Treaty. Six of the seven judges of the Supreme Court upholding on appeal the dismissal by the High Court of the Plaintiff's case, were of the view that in doing so, the Court was not contravening the principles stated in *Crotty* which principles were not under challenge by either party. The dissenting judge, Mr Justice Hardiman, adopted a radically different view. The opinion of the majority, expounded in different ways by five separate written judgments, is encapsulated in the concluding paragraph of the judgment of Chief Justice Denham who presided over the Court. She said the following:

> On the first issue, applying the principles stated in *Crotty* to the facts of the case, I am satisfied that the Government did not abdicate, alienate, cede, or subordinate its power to another. The decision of the Government to enter into the ESM Treaty was a policy decision within its executive power, pursuant to the Constitution, and so did not involve an impermissible transfer of sovereignty.

When is a decision of a government 'a policy decision within its executive power'? There would seem to be no easy answer to that question. Ireland is now a member of the European Communities or Union for some forty years. In interpreting the Constitution, there must surely be applied an assumption of permanent membership. The longer the membership continues, the more it becomes part and parcel of the ordinary everyday governance of the State. In these circumstances, a decision of a government to allow Ireland to enter into a binding agreement with the other members in order to adopt a particular policy must not lightly be considered as infringing the sovereignty required by the Constitution. The Chief Justice can arguably be considered as having given a lead in that direction by her firm categorisation of the impugned decision of the government as a policy decision within the lawful exercise of the executive.

The position adopted by Denham CJ can be found in two successive paragraphs in her judgment which read as follows:

> 17.ii. At issue in *Crotty* was the future conduct of external relations of the State, ie the executive power of the sovereign state to decide future external relations. *Crotty* held that the Constitution provided that the Government could not dispose of its executive power by entering into an agreement with another to abdicate its powers under the Constitution, in circumstances where the interests of others may supersede the interests of the State, as the powers that are given to the organs of state under the Constitution are for the common good of the people of Ireland. Thus, if such a decision is required to be taken to relinquish the powers of an organ of state, it must be taken by the people.
> 17.iii. No such fundamental decision arises in relation to the ESM Treaty.

Mr Justice O'Donnell, in his judgment, summarises neatly what was at issue:

> The Plaintiff's case, in this regard, was that the ratification of the ESM Treaty was a momentous decision on the part of the Irish Government involving a potential liability of up to €11.1454 billion by way of contribution to a fund totalling some €700 billion for the express purpose of securing the stability of the Eurozone, or any member thereof, in circumstances where the allocations from the fund could, at least in certain circumstances, be made by a qualified majority of the contracting States which might not include Ireland, either because Ireland disagreed with the allocation or was excluded from voting.

In his judgment in *Crotty*, Walsh J had surprisingly made the following comment:

> As was pointed out in the decision of the Court in the first part of this case, the essential nature of sovereignty is the right to say yes or to say no. In the present Treaty provisions, that right is to be materially qualified.

The word 'surprisingly' is apt because the phrase had appeared in the single judgment which although delivered by Finlay CJ may well have represented a composite judgment of several or all the judges and more importantly because the phrase was used in a particular context and not as a general phrase covering 'the essential nature of sovereignty'.

O'Donnell J had this to say about the 'yes or no' sentence:

> There can be little doubt that if the essence of sovereignty, at least as contemplated by the Irish Constitution, is to be understood as meaning that Ireland fetters its sovereign right to decide by joining any organisation which acts collectively, or at least one in which Ireland does not retain a veto (and therefore the right to say No), then the ESM Treaty would be of dubious constitutional validity, along with, it must be said, many other important international agreements. However, judgments are not to be read in the same way as statutes. A single sentence in a judgment rarely encapsulates the essence of a lengthy judgment, and a judgment of one judge, even one as eminent and influential as Walsh J., is not to be taken, in isolation, as stating the *ratio decidendi* of a case. There is always a danger of substituting the invocation of a vivid and memorable phrase for the analysis of the substance of a judgment.

O'Donnell J went on to point out that the controversial sentence had been included in the judgment of Finlay CJ in a 'very specific context'. He points out that the same judgment which related to Titles I and II refers to the original licence granted by the people to join the European Communities and he characterises it as a licence 'to join a dynamic and developing entity'. He draws the conclusion that 'incremental changes' in European institutions within the scope of the existing licence 'did not require further express approval by the People'.

Within the limits of this chapter, justice cannot be done to the further detailed analysis of the sovereignty issue contained in the judgment of O'Donnell J, but it is neatly summarised in paragraph 22 which reads as follows:

> In my view, this approach also demonstrates why it is not possible to read the majority decision in *Crotty* as requiring that individual decisions made by the Government in the field of foreign policy must, if they are to be valid, make provision for future decisions to be made by unanimity or alternatively, accord to Ireland alone a veto over any such future decision. First, it is plain that no such individual decision was in issue in *Crotty;* on the contrary, the case concerned the requirement to bend Ireland's foreign policy *in general* towards a common European policy. For the reasons already set out, I do not consider that any such supposed principle could be required by the Constitution, and in my view, it is not required by *Crotty*. There is nothing in *Crotty*, or indeed in logic, to suggest that the concept of sovereignty contained in the Irish Constitution requires that Ireland, while it may enter into agreements, must insist that it retains the capacity to change its mind. Even if the judgment of Walsh J. in *Crotty* could be interpreted differently (and for the reasons already set out, I do not accept that that is the case), there is, in my view, no basis for attributing to that judgment, still less a phrase from it, a position of primacy within the case. The *ratio decidendi* of a decision made by a collegiate court is in my view to be determined by that proposition, or reason, which decides the particular case and on which, it can be said, a majority of the Court is agreed. In my view, that *ratio decidendi* is that already set out above, and as addressed in the judgments of the Chief Justice and Clarke J.

That last quotation provides a neat entry point for consideration of the judgment of Mr Justice Clarke in *Pringle*. In the limited space available, justice cannot be done to the detailed analysis contained in it, but the following significant passage must certainly be quoted:

> On a narrow reading of some of the passages cited, it might be said that this Court, in *Crotty*, came to the conclusion that the overall architecture of the Irish Constitution does not permit the Government, in exercise of its power to conduct the firm policy of the State in accordance with article 29.4.1 of the Constitution, to enter into binding arrangements with other countries which would, in any way, have the effect of circumscribing Ireland's freedom of action in the foreign policy field. For reasons which I hope to demonstrate, it does not seem to me that such a conclusion can be found in the judgments of this Court in *Crotty*. If such were to be the proper analysis of the reasoning of the majority of this Court in *Crotty*, then I would respectfully, disagree with it.

In another part of this judgment, and with reference to the wide discretion which the Government has in the conduct of the foreign policy of the State, Clarke J observes as follows:

> It would be a strange conclusion indeed if that broad discretion was to mean that the Government could not, as a means of exercising that discretion and, thus, exercising its sovereignty, enter into what must be the most usual way in which sovereign states exercise their sovereignty, ie by agreeing with other sovereign states to pursue a specified policy in a specified way. Many legitimate policy objectives which the Government in exercise of its constitutional entitlement to formulate and implement foreign policy, might wish to pursue can only, as a matter of practicality, be achieved by entering into bilateral or multi-lateral Treaty arrangements with other countries of like or similar mind with a view to securing specified ends.

The fourth of the majority judgments was that of Mr Justice McKechnie. Although one could detect rather more enthusiasm for *Crotty* than was displayed in the other written majority judgments, that judge considered Title III of SEA wholly distinguishable from the provisions of the ESM Treaty and agreed with five of his colleagues that the appeal should be dismissed. Interestingly, his judgment included strong criticism of the importance attached by Walsh J in *Crotty* to the phrase in the single judgment of the Court delivered by Finlay CJ that sovereignty meant the right to say yes or no. To quote McKechnie J's own words:

> The reason why I reject the suggested significance of the expression is, that in the first place, the judge himself expressly acknowledged that Finlay C. J. was the source of such phrase, when giving the Court's judgment on the challenge to the SEA save for Title III thereof that remark as originally made was entirely appropriate to the context then under discussion by the Chief Justice. At page 769 of the Report, the context appears: : … "*The capacity of the Council to take decisions with legislative effect is a diminution of the sovereignty of Member States, including Ireland, and this was one of the reasons why the Third Amendment to the Constitution was necessary. Sovereignty in this context is the unfettered right to decide: to say 'Yes or No'. Therefore, having transposed such remark, it is not appropriate to assign or ascribe to it, the determinative importance which has been suggested.*"

It would seem that time and circumstances have mellowed the consideration of the relationship between the Constitution and EU developments. It seems doubtful that if *Pringle* could be transposed in time back to the era when Mr Justice Walsh, Mr Justice Henchy and Mr Justice Hederman sat on the Court, the decision would be the same. Those judges would more likely have been in agreement with Mr Justice Hardiman. If that observation is correct, the title of this article is hopefully justified.

Finally, it is important to identify the two other majority judges in *Pringle.* They were the former Chief Justice, Mr Justice Murray, and the judge in whose honour this book has been published, Mr Justice Fennelly.

14

Nial Fennelly: Mallak *and the Rule of Reasons*

DONAL O'DONNELL*

WHEN IN 1995 Nial Fennelly became the first Irish person to hold the position of Advocate General of the European Court of Justice, his appointment was greeted in legal circles, and elsewhere, with universal acclaim. It was a rare piece of serendipity in Irish legal affairs that when the opportunity arose to appoint someone to a position of such importance, there was not only an identifiable candidate at the height of his professional powers with expertise in European law, but also a recognition and determination at an influential level of the importance of making appointments to such positions on the basis of demonstrable and unarguable merit.

The appointment was greeted with even greater enthusiasm, if for less worthy motives, by a small cohort of lawyers of whom I was one, junior barristers who had recently, or were about to, become senior counsel and for whom Nial's appointment meant not only the prospect of benefiting from some of the work thereby released on to the market, but also, and just as importantly, not having to face Nial Fennelly in court.

There are few vantage points which provide such a comprehensive view of an advocate's skill than the benches on the other side of the court. During my early career at the Bar, Nial Fennelly was already well established as a formidable opponent much in demand on trials which required that elusive skill set of complete knowledge of facts and law persuasively articulated with an air of irreproachable integrity. To our youthful eyes there was something almost mesmeric about the way he addressed judges. There seemed an almost unconscious assumption that both he and the judge, two persons of perception, intellect and judgement (and few judges seemed able to resist the flattery in that implicit comparison) were engaged on a common journey to find a fair, reasonable, legally correct and elegant solution to the problem posed by the case, a task that was well within their powers, but one that would only be hampered if attention was paid to the distracting sounds emanating from a, by now very

*Judge of the Supreme Court of Ireland

irritated, opponent. It was all so well mannered, authoritative and deadly. Nial's departure for Europe, if I may make an allusion that he will no doubt find distressingly lowbrow, was much like the departure more than a decade earlier of Liam Brady, then Ireland's best soccer player and arguably the best player playing soccer in Britain, for the Italian giants Juventus, where he won two consecutive Italian championships. In an era before satellite television, and the internet, information was sparse and fragmentary, and there was a nagging sense that we in Ireland did not fully appreciate the scale of achievements on the larger stage.

When he returned in 2000 he was appointed to the Supreme Court, again a creditable recognition in official circles of the demands of merit, and I had the opportunity of observing his approach to judging, first as a counsel appearing before the Supreme Court, and subsequently over the last four years, as a colleague. His judicial career has been one of astonishing productivity. He has adjudicated in, and delivered judgment upon, an extraordinarily broad range of topics ranging from areas of the criminal law such as the proper approach to sentencing in the difficult area of the offence of possession of child pornography (*D.P.P. v Loving*[1]), to almost every area of the field of torts including negligence, breach of statutory duty, misfeasance of public office and the principle of legitimate expectation (*Glencar Exploration plc v Mayo County Council (No. 2)*[2] and *Beatty v Rent Tribunal*[3]), vicarious liability (*O'Keefe v Hickey*[4]), rescuers (*O'Neill v Dunnes Stores*[5]), the law of insider trading (*Fyffes plc v DCC*[6]), endless cases on judicial review of criminal trials (*Dunne v D.P.P.*[7]), questions of contract (*Analog Devices v Zurich Insurance*[8] and *ICDL v EDCL*[9]), competition law, company law and many areas of constitutional law, libel law and cases emerging from tribunals of inquiry. His approach on almost all cases has been the same: a studied, deliberate and almost punctilious neutrality, [10] a courteous and thoughtful hearing, deep consideration, and almost always a decisive result often elegantly and persuasively explained. It is not unusual to find in his judgments a forceful expression of conclusions rarely hinted at in substance and almost never in tone during the hearing. That journey from a neutral and balanced commencement point to a decisive outcome is, or ought to be, the daily path of the judge and it seems that all of Nial Fennelly's early training, his study and career were preparation towards that journey which he has made so impressively over the last 14 years.

I have chosen to write about a recent judgment delivered by Mr Justice Fennelly on the duty to give reasons not merely because it represents a good example of his

[1] [2006] 3 IR 355.
[2] [2002] 1 IR 84.
[3] [2006] 2 IR 191.
[4] [2009] 2 IR 302.
[5] [2011] 1 IR 325.
[6] [2009] 2 IR 417.
[7] [2002] 2 IR 305.
[8] [2002] 1 IR 272.
[9] [2012] IESC 55.
[10] See eg *Kenny v Trinity College* [2008] 2 IR 40.

judicial craft, but also because it deals with a subject which is at the heart of his approach to the business of judging. The roadway from neutral starting point to decisive outcome is a road mapped by reasons and guided by reasonableness. It is not really a surprise that in *Mallak* Fennelly J observed that there is more than an etymological connection between reasons and reasonableness. There is no doubt that within their limited field of activity, all judges exercise power. At the most basic level, it is the still awesome power to determine (and, it is hoped, resolve) a dispute between citizens in a final and binding way. Especially at an appellate level, such decisions may also decide the law which is binding on all persons similarly situated, at least until the legislature speaks. If the question is one of constitutional law, then the decision in the case may determine the law affecting all citizens, at least in theory, and at least until the People themselves speak.

Viewed in a functional way from the perspective of the person or persons affected, the source of the law is irrelevant and accordingly, that part of the judicial function which makes law may appear no different to laws and decisions made by political bodies. It is, however, at the heart of the judicial process, and perhaps the reason why, despite its faults, it still captures the imagination of students and the begrudging affection of its practitioners, that decisions are made by an impartial decision maker on material which is adduced in public and that they are made by way of a reasoned judgment which explains the reasoning process by which the decision is arrived at. A reasoned judgment at best explains and may even persuade, but at worst it still facilitates the identification of errors and questionable assumptions. This is a theme explored by Professor G. Edward White in his impressive work *The American Judicial Tradition: Profiles of Leading American Judges:*

> Put another way what then seemed to me to be very important about the calculus of appellate judging in America was the extent to which judges were *constrained* in their decisions, and the constraints that I found most significant were those that seemed to stem from the nature of judging itself. Judges had an obligation to give reasons for their results; judges had an obligation not to usurp the powers of other branches of government; judges were required not to deviate too far from the consensual values of their times. Judges, thus, were not like politicians because they were constrained by the obligations of judicial reasoning. Not only must judges give reasons for their results, those reasons must at least make an effort to persuade not only those inclined to support the results, but those not inclined to. Reasoning, viewed in this fashion, becomes the vehicle by which the judge seeks to convince his or her audience that more than naked subjectivity explains the result. The reasoning offered is intended itself to serve as a constraint on that subjectivity.[11]

In that sense, judicial reasoning is closely linked to the legitimacy and enduring value of the judicial process.

Ghandi Nawak Mallak was a national of Syria qualified as a lawyer, and who arrived in Ireland with his wife in 2002. Both applied for and obtained

[11] GE White, *The American Judicial Tradition: Profiles of Leading American Judges*, 2nd edn (New York, Oxford University Press, 1988), pp ix–x.

refugee status in November of that year. The Minister for Justice Equality and Law Reform granted a declaration to Mr Mallak that he had, accordingly, the same rights as an Irish citizen to reside in the State, travel within it and to and from it, and have access to the courts. In 2005 Mr Mallak and his wife applied for a certificate of naturalisation pursuant to s. 15 of the Irish Nationality and Citizenship Act 1956 (hereinafter the "1956 Act"). In October 2008 his wife's application was granted. The following month however, Mr Mallak was notified that his application was refused. The letter informing him of this stated simply that in reaching the decision, the Minister had exercised his absolute discretion as provided for under the 1956 Act but also helpfully informing Mr Mallak that he was entitled to reapply.

Mr Mallak then sought to exercise a statutory right granted by s. 18 of the Freedom of Information Act 1997 (the 1997 Act) which provides that in certain circumstances, a head of a public body is obliged to provide reasons for a decision at which it has arrived. However, that application was refused by the departmental head pursuant to s. 18(2) of the 1997 Act which permits refusal where the provision of reasons would cause the harm envisaged by an exemption provided for in the Act. That decision was upheld on appeal by the Information Commissioner. Although the example given was the non-disclosure of a record if to do so would prejudice the conduct or outcome of contractual and other negotiations, it seems plausible to assume that the considerations at issue were related to security. Thereafter Mr Mallak also sought and obtained information pursuant to the Data Protection Acts 1988 –2003 which disclosed the existence (although not the content) of records which included a garda report and a garda request form which he speculated must be the documents deemed to be exempt records under the Freedom of Information Act and therefore must have contained the basis upon which the Minister refused his application. However it is of some significance that this was merely speculation on his part. The operation of the statutory procedures had not resulted in the provision of the information. Thereafter, Mr Mallak commenced judicial review proceedings challenging the Minister's refusal of citizenship on grounds that the failure to require reasons rendered the Act either unconstitutional or a breach of the Charter of Fundamental Rights, or both.

Section 15 of the 1956 Act undoubtedly does not provide for any express obligation to provide reasons. Furthermore, the various powers exercised by the Minister in relation to citizenship applications are expressed to be exercisable in his or her 'absolute discretion', a formula which is perhaps unsurprising at least as a matter of history since decisions in relation to citizenship and entry to the jurisdiction were important parts of the executive power before being loosely regulated by statute in the terms of the 1956 Act.

The claim failed in the High Court.[12] In a characteristically lucid and succinct judgment delivered by Nial Fennelly's much respected contemporary Cooke J, the High Court applied some classic, if classically strict, judicial review reasoning in rejecting the application. First, it was observed that there is no absolute or

[12] *Mallak v The Minister for Justice, Equality and Law Reform* [2011] IEHC 306.

general rule that reasons must be provided for a decision. Next it pointed to the entitlement to refuse a certificate of naturalisation at the Minister's 'absolute discretion'. This meant that 'quite literally ... the Minister does not need to have or to give any reason for refusing an application for a certificate'.[13] Even if the Minister did have a reason he was not required to divulge it. Consequently it would fly in the face of the unambiguous intention of the legislature to hold otherwise. Second, relying on the formidable authority of the decision of Costello J in *Pok Sun Shum v Ireland* [14] which held that since citizenship was not a right but rather a privilege to which the applicant had no right, there was no obligation of fair procedures or to state reasons. Cooke J held:

> While it might be said that the evolution of the principle of fair procedures and the obligation to state reasons over the last 25 years would have reduced the occasions when neither obligation arose in respect of a decision with adverse consequences, it remains the position in the view of this Court, that the principle of fair procedures and the requirement to state reasons can have no application where an administrative decision is wholly devoid of any detrimental or disadvantageous consequence for its addressee.[15]

The case was appealed to the Supreme Court. The decision of a unanimous court was delivered by Fennelly J.[16] It may be apparent from the very limited background already given that the case was a somewhat tangled web of fact, argument and applicable law. However, there is a confidence and clarity about the opening words of the judgment that in future years will perhaps be recognised as classic Fennelly:

> The phenomenon that is the modern law of judicial review, though rooted in history, has witnessed extraordinary development over the past thirty years. At its heart it insists that, to adapt the language of this Court in The State (Lynch) v Cooney [1982] IR 337, any administrative decision, in that case an opinion of a Minister which enabled him to make an order prohibiting broadcasts, must be 'bona fide held and factually sustainable and not unreasonable.' The underlying principles of judicial review are universal. Courts of the common law have developed and expanded the historic rules of natural justice, in more recent times with inspiration from international human-rights instruments such as the European Convention on Human Rights and, in this jurisdiction, from the Constitution. The Court of Justice of the European Union speaks of a 'complete system of legal remedies.' (Case 294/83 Parti écologiste 'Les Verts' v European Parliament [1986] ECR 1339, paragraph 23). The rules are composed of a number of inter-related features, the underlying fundamental presumption being that those to whom discretionary powers are entrusted will exercise them fairly insofar as they may affect individuals. Where fairness can be shown to be lacking, the law provides a remedy. The right of access to the courts is an indispensable cornerstone of a State governed by the rule of law.[17]

[13] Note 13, para 12.
[14] [1986] ILRM 593.
[15] N 13 above, para 15.
[16] [2012] IESC 59.
[17] N 16, para 1.

There have been other immediately engaging opening lines:

> Where, as in this case, fundamental rights are invoked as a restraint on the exercise of statutory powers, the courts are increasingly called upon to strike a balance;[18]
>
> Cases concerning the disappointment of legitimate expectations have formed part of the regular diet of the courts in judicial review matters since at least the decision of the Supreme Court in *Webb v Ireland* [1988] IR 353;[19]
>
> The cycle of continual amendment and periodic consolidation of the Social Welfare Acts inevitably throws up problems concerning the effect of legislative change on past events;[20]
>
> It used not to be considered any sort of sin to profit financially from the use of secret, private or privileged information. That was how fortunes were made. Now things are different. The trade on the use of inside information is recognised for what it is. It is a fraud on the market. The insider exploits his access to the special knowledge he enjoys for the purpose of the company in his capacity as executive or director of a company commits a crime. He may be made, additionally, to answer for the profits he has made.[21]

The recent monumental judgment in *Walsh & Anor v Sligo County Council*[22] was the combined work of three judges of the Supreme Court. Nevertheless, short odds might be offered as to the identity of the author of the opening lines:

> A public right of way is a highway. The general public has the right to pass and repass at all times across the land over which the way runs.
>
> The way may be claimed to run over the avenues of a great landed estate, such as Lissadell. It may also pass over the fields of a farm, large or small; over a suburban garden (see Bruen v Murphy and others (High Court unreported 11th March 1980)); or along a passage-way leading into a public house (see Connell v Porter [2005] 3 IR 601).
>
> Even if it is not maintained by the public road authority, a public right of way is in law a highway. It confers the unrestricted right of the general public to pass and repass at all times of the day or night, and at all seasons without notice to, or permission from, the landowner over whose land the way runs.
>
> The landowner must yield to and respect the rights of the public and must accept any consequent invasion of his right to undisturbed privacy and the enjoyment of his property.
>
> The law of public rights of way is of ancient origin.[23]

[18] *Mahon Tribunal v Keena & Kennedy* [2010] 1 IR 336, para 3.

[19] *Daly v Minister for the Marine, Ireland & the Attorney General* [2001] 3 IR 513, p. 515.

[20] *Minister for Social, Community & Family Affairs v Scanlon* [2001] 1 IR 64, p. 78.

[21] N 6 above, par 110. I admit to less enthusiasm for this passage. While undoubtedly effective in capturing attention, it may not have captured the essence of the case. The appeal proceeded on the finding of the High Court that there had been no intentional trading on insider information and the appeal dealt with the question whether there was objectively a breach of s. 108 of the Companies Act 1990 without any subjective intent. On the pleasures and perils of introductory sentences, see the entertaining essay by the late Lord Rodger of Earlsferry, 'The Form and Language of Judicial Opinions' (2002) 118 LQR 226, 244–245.

[22] [2013] IESC 48.

[23] Ibid, paras 1–5.

Style, said Edward Gibbon, is the image of character. The legal realist judge, Judge Jerome Frank, in a very backhanded compliment, said of a supreme judicial stylist, Judge Benjamin Cardozo, that given the fact that he was writing in a foreign language, namely that of an 18th century English gentleman, it was a remarkable achievement that he thought clearly at all.[24] Nial Fennelly's style is certainly more modern. The expression is clear and lucid, and the sentences and paragraphs short. Nonetheless there are perhaps, discernible in the background, the elegant cadences of the classics of English literature.

In his study of the development of judicial reputation, *Cardozo: A Study on Reputation*,[25] the distinguished scholar, Judge Richard A Posner, offered some interesting observations on the importance of style and rhetoric in judicial decisions. Notwithstanding the sometimes intense labour that goes into them and the enormous importance they carry for the individual parties, judgments, even of the highest courts, are ephemeral artefacts. Most written judgments are not reported in the official reports. Of those that are, few continue to be cited in subsequent years, being overtaken by later decisions on the same topic which cover the same ground. While the common law reveres precedent and there is a popular image of lawyers delighting in producing decisions from musty books, the truth is that the bulk of cases are, or at least could be, decided by reference to decisions which are delivered in the preceding 20 years and which almost inevitably encapsulate and repeat any of the useful learning from preceding eras. What is it then that makes some judgments by some judges survive while most others are quickly washed away by the passage of time? Posner suggests that style, or as he puts it 'rhetorical power' may be 'a more important attribute of judicial excellence than analytical power'.[26] Though Posner considers this controversial, it is perhaps not necessarily surprising. Cardozo himself observed, echoing Holmes, that there was much more to judgments than logic. He decried judges who 'marched at times to pitiless conclusions under the prod of a remorseless logic which is supposed to leave no alternative'.[27] But rhetoric, however beguiling, and language, however stylish, is not enough. As the essayist Clive James puts it, 'When we start to believe a statement must be true because it is arrestingly put we are in the first stages of being spellbound, and the later stages are a kind of slavery'.[28] Perhaps the test of a good judgment then is the extent to which rhetoric and analysis are in harmony and the extent to which it does not merely beguile but persuades.

Many judgments open with a stock unambitious and sometimes dreary banality such as 'this is a case about …' or 'in these proceedings…'. The opening passage of *Mallak* is however, simple, clear, immediately engaging, and impressive in its sweep. It seems to give a sense that the author has not only

[24] Quoted in RA Posner, *Cardozo: A Study in Reputation*, (Chicago, The University of Chicago Press, 1990), 10. Posner has also addressed the question of judicial style in *Law and Literature, A Misunderstood Relation*, 2nd edn (Cambridge MA, Harvard University Press, 1998).

[25] N 24.

[26] N 24, foreword.

[27] BN Cardozo, *The Growth of the Law* (Connecticut, Yale University Press, 1924) 66–67.

[28] C James, *Cultural Amnesia, Notes In the Margin of My Time* (London, Picador, 2007).

decided the case, but cut to the very bottom of a difficult problem, resolved it to the point where it can be clearly stated and more clearly understood, and an elegant solution placed in a wider context where it can be seen to fit with the broad pattern of the law and to achieve a result consistent with principle and an intuitive sense of justice. This sets an ambitious target and many judgments have opened with a flourish only to fall short. As Lord Devlin once observed, the first requirement of a good judgment is good judgement. The substance of the decision must persuade.

At the outset it is necessary to state the issue to be decided. To those whose knowledge of litigation in the common law world is gleaned from judgments, the stating of an issue may appear a simple task. However cases often commence without being readily categorized under the points or point of law in issue: instead they often emerge as a confused and confusing mass of fact and argumentation. By the time such cases reach the Supreme Court, the point in issue may of course have been isolated. In other cases, the process of preparation for an engaging trial, the opposing arguments advanced, the tactics employed, the manner of the cases developed, the opposing arguments which are anticipated and responded to, and the points perceived to have some fashionable appeal, can all combine to mean that the case arrives at the Supreme Court encrusted with an almost impenetrable carapace of confusion and distraction through which it is difficult to discern any issue.

Mallak was nominally a challenge to the validity of the 1956 Act by reference to provisions of the Irish Constitution, and the law of the European Union. Much learning was deployed in arguments on these points. The judgment quickly and deftly isolated the central and defining issue as to whether or not the principles of natural and constitutional justice, and fair procedures, require the giving of reasons for a refusal of citizenship. If this was required, then there was nothing in the Act which precluded reasons and reasons would have to be provided, and accordingly there could be no question of the Act being invalid having regard to the Constitution. If however, reasons were not required then there could be no question of the invalidity of the Act. The question became whether, as a matter of law, reasons were required.

In Ireland in 2012, as in many other jurisdictions, this was by no means an easy question to resolve. There was no obvious intersection between statute law and common law. Indeed, the Freedom of Information Act 1997 in providing for a general right to obtain reasons in cases captured by the Act, seemed to go further than the common law. The common law was by contrast quite confused. All cases repeated the mantra that there was no general rule that reasons were required. Inevitably cases were decided on a case by case basis with consequent uncertainty and unpredictability. In some cases reasons were found to be required: *obiter* in the Supreme Court decision of *The State (Creedon) v The Criminal Injuries Compensation Tribunal*[29], and as part of the *ratio* of the High Court in *The State (Daly) v The Minister for Agriculture,* [30]

[29] [1988] IR 51

[30] [1987] IR 165.

where the High Court went so far as to hold that the Minister's failure to give reasons meant that he had no reasons for the termination of a probationary civil servant's employment and so the decision was irrational and could be quashed. In *International Fishing Vessels Ltd v Minister for the Marine*[31] the High Court held that reasons were required for a refusal of a licence so as to facilitate appeal or review.

But other cases, particularly in the field of naturalisation and citizenship, held that no reasons were required: *Pok Sun Shum v Ireland*[32]. In yet other cases, it has been held that reasons were not required where they are self-evident or clearly discernible from the material available: *McCormack v The Garda Síochána Complaints Board*.[33] Finally, there have been cases in which the court has held that bald and laconic statements are a sufficient discharge of any obligation to provide reasons.[34] The very lack of clarity of the law was perhaps itself a sign that the area is difficult, and that there were strong competing interests at play.

The judgment in *Mallak* dealt precisely and surgically with the argument that the absolute discretion of the Minister meant that he or she did not have to have a reason and therefore did not have to give any reason for his or her decision. As the judgment observed, there was a significant difference between having a reason and disclosing it. It could not be correct to say that a discretion, even an absolute one, meant that a decision maker was not obliged to have a reason. That would be the very definition of an arbitrary power. Any power conferred by statute had to be exercised within the parameters of the statute conferring it, and for the purpose contemplated by the statute. The Minister's absolute discretion might mean that the Minister could have a bad reason in the sense that it might be a reason that might not persuade a single other person, but it had to be a citizenship related reason since it was for that purpose that the power and duty was conferred upon the Minister by the Act. This is a classic restatement of an essential principle of the rule of law laid down by Walsh J. in *East Donegal Cooperative Livestock Mart Ltd v The Attorney General*.[35]

The argument that citizenship is a privilege and not a right and therefore that reasons are not required, was also speedily dispatched. While there is a valid jurisprudential distinction between rights and privileges which may be important in some cases, it could not be the basis of a decision that reasons are not required. It could not be argued that merely because a privilege was being conferred that there could be no recourse to judicial review. If however, judicial review was available, as it plainly was, then there was no logical basis for permitting the right/privilege distinction to preclude the provision of reasons. On the contrary, such reasons would normally be required to permit review. There was a close connection between the obligation to give notice and possibly to provide access to information or have a hearing, and the obligation to give

[31] [1989] IR 149.
[32] N 14 above.
[33] [1997] 2 IR 489.
[34] See *Orange Communications Ltd v The Director of Telecommunications Regulation & Ors* [2000] 4 IR 159.
[35] [1970] IR 317.

reasons was merely one part of the process. Reasons are closely related to the ground of review and in the absence of knowing the Minister's reasons for refusal it was not possible for an applicant to ascertain whether they had grounds for applying for judicial review. By extension, it was not possible for the courts to exercise their power of judicial review effectively, something which was central to the right of a person to have access to the courts to challenge the validity of a decision, and without which the obligation on the State to act lawfully and constitutionally would be ineffective.

Accordingly, both arguments which had persuaded the High Court were carefully analysed: the precedent for them was assembled and scrutinised and the argument not merely distinguished or qualified, but rejected by reference to fundamental principles rooted in the concept of the principle of law. Once extracted, analysed and explained, the conclusion may appear obvious but it is worth recalling the confusing contradictory state of the law prior to *Mallak*, and the fact that the analysis in *Pok Sun Shum* had held sway for almost 30 years.

It is nonetheless possible to reach the right result for the wrong reasons. The very longevity of the *Pok Sun Shum* authority and the fact that it had been enunciated and applied by distinguished judges was perhaps an indicator that there were some strong considerations which made courts reluctant to insist on the elaboration of reasons for refusal of citizenship and similar decisions. While the logic of the 'absolute discretion' and 'privilege, not right' arguments might not be persuasive, the applicant did not necessarily succeed by default. It was necessary to consider whether as a matter of principle, reasons were required in this case.

The core of the decision is to be found at paragraph 66 of the judgment which deserves quotation in full:

> In the present state of evolution of our law, it is not easy to conceive of a decision-maker being dispensed from giving an explanation either of the decision or of the decision-making process at some stage. The most obvious means of achieving fairness is for reasons to accompany the decision. However, it is not a matter of complying with a formal rule: the underlying objective is the attainment of fairness in the process. If the process is fair, open and transparent and the affected person has been enabled to respond to the concerns of the decision-maker, there may be situations where the reasons for the decision are obvious and that effective judicial review is not precluded.

It is instructive that the judgment then referred to several converging legal sources which strongly suggested an emerging, commonly held view that persons affected by administrative decisions have a right to know the reasons on which they are based and indeed to understand them. First, it was pointed out that s 18(1) of the Freedom of the Information Act 1997 envisaged that a public body would give reasons for the decision at the request of an affected person. Next, the judgment referred to Article 296 of the Treaty on the Functioning of the European Union which provides that legal acts shall state the reasons on which they are based. At paragraph 69 of the judgment, the decision of the Court of Justice in Case C-417/11 *Council v Bamba* is invoked.[36] The judgment also cites with apparent approval the somewhat controversial decision of the Court of Appeal in England in *R v The Secretary of State Ex parte Al-Fayed (No. 1)*[37] which itself involved a challenge to a naturalisation decision. However, s. 44(2) of the British Nationality Act 1981 provided explicitly that the Secretary of State was not obliged to provide any reason for the grant or refusal of any application. This is no doubt reflective of the same policy which underpinned the approach of successive ministers in Ireland under the 1956 Act. There Lord Woolf explained that a decision in favour of an applicant for naturalisation conferred significant benefits and refusal could have a damaging effect on reputation. While reasons were statutorily precluded, there was a corresponding requirement to provide information in advance as to the areas of concern, and the applicant should be given an opportunity to make such submissions as he wished. These references are themselves an illustration of the breadth of knowledge and interest of the author of the judgment, but it is also not without significance that they are employed only to provide lateral support to a decision already constructed by reference to principles and precedent firmly grounded in Irish law.

It is for paragraph 66 that *Mallak* is regularly cited, and will no doubt be further cited in the future. It is an important and lucid statement of the law and one which does not purport merely to restate or synthesise existing law, but rather, to advance a principle of broad application and in doing so, significantly advances the boundaries of the territory now occupied by the duty to give reasons. That is a considerable achievement, not least when performed so elegantly. In other circumstances the analysis might end there. After all, as has been observed, the judge as superhero as presented to undergraduates is the judge who weaves his or her way skilfully past the obstacles of unhelpful precedent and achieves a result seen as progressive and desirable. This has the inestimable advantage for the law student (and lawyer) of rendering largely redundant complicated pre-existing precedent and distilling the law into a statement of such simplicity that it can readily be grasped by the most harassed student.[38] On this view, *Mallak* is a new starting point and creates a presumption of a duty to give reasons or even, if you will, a rule of reasons.

[36] Case C-417/11P, judgment of 15 November 2012.

[37] [1998] 1 WLR 763.

[38] The point is made most vividly by Antonin Scalia in *A Matter of Interpretation: Federal Courts and the Law*, University Centre for Human Values series (Princeton, Princeton University Press, 1997) 9:

> this system of making law by judicial opinion, and making law by distinguishing earlier cases, is what every American law student, what every newborn American lawyer, first sees when he opens his eyes. And the impression remains with him for life. His image of the great judge – the Holmes, the Cardozo – is the man (or woman) who has the intelligence to know what is the best rule of law to govern the case at hand, and then the skill to perform the broken-field running through earlier cases that leaves him free to impose that rule: distinguishing one prior cases on his left, straight-arming another one on his right, high-stepping away from another precedent about to tackle him from the rear, until (bravo!) he reaches his goal: good law. That image of the great judge remains with the former law student when he himself becomes a judge, and thus the common law tradition is passed on.

A good judgment is not however necessarily one which makes an easily understood generalisation. It is an interesting question whether there are fewer examples in the case law of the penetrating elucidation of a principle not previously recognised than there are of sweeping generalisations which cannot later be justified, and from which it is necessary to make a costly and sometimes undignified retreat. There is much to be said for incremental development. Looked at in this way it might be said that *Mallak* is a cautious judgment. It goes no further than saying that in citizenship decisions under the 1956 Act *some* reason must be given. Although it acknowledges the close relationship between the obligation to give fair notice to provide access to information, and even in some cases to have a hearing, and an obligation to give reasons,[39] the judgment nevertheless stops resolutely short of suggesting that any such steps are necessarily required in a decision under the 1956 Act. The judgment does not seek to determine what reasons may be given or what level of reasoning will be adequate. Indeed, paragraph 77 of the judgment contemplates that it may be possible for the Minister to refuse to disclose his reasons but provide a justification for doing so.

When set against the existing law further questions and possible qualifications arise. There are a number of cases, particularly in the field of decisions relating to prosecutions, where the court has held that the decision of the Director of Public Prosecutions will only be reviewable in exceptional cases where it can be shown to have been made *mala fide* or prompted by an improper motive, and since review is so limited, that reasons need not be required.[40] It remains to be decided if that line of authority is undermined or qualified in any way by the type of reasoning in *Mallak*. Although paragraph 66 suggests it is not easy to conceive of an area where the decision maker is dispensed from giving an explanation, that statement does not say it is impossible, perhaps paragraph 77 hints at circumstances where the duty may be significantly attenuated if not absent altogether. Furthermore, even the first sentence of paragraph 66 is qualified by reference to reasons for the decision 'or the decision-making process' which, it might be noted, should be provided 'at some stage' . The judgment itself cites with apparent approval the decision in *The State (Lynch) v Cooney*[41] which on one view not merely affected a privilege, but a right of freedom of expression, and did so without any prior notification, submissions or hearing and without the provision of any reasons until, when legal challenge was commenced, the basis of the decision was explained only in evidence produced in response to the challenge. This would not normally be sufficient in the field of what might be described as ordinary decision making, but does not appear to be inconsistent with, and is certainly not expressly disapproved of by the decision in *Mallak*. By the same token, it is instructive that the provisions of the Freedom of Information Act are invoked in support of the principle outlined in *Mallak*. Indeed, it appeared somewhat anomalous that prior to *Mallak*, although the

[39] N 16, para 52.

[40] *The State (McCormack) v Curran* [1987] ILRM 225 and *H v DPP* [1994] 2 IR 589. See also *Sharma v Browne-Antoine* [2007] 1 WLR 780, p 789.

[41] [1982] IR 337.

provision of reasons was seen as the component of the principles of natural justice, a statutory embodiment of the principle seemed to go further than was provided for by the common law. One of the benefits of *Mallak* is that it closes that gap. The Freedom of Information Act however, is not all encompassing and provides for significant, albeit tightly defined, exceptions on the basis of good public policy reasons where it is thought undesirable to provide information, and where appropriate, reasons under s.18. Inevitably a question arises whether the common law principle advanced in *Mallak* is subject to the same or similar limitations and exceptions, and the qualifications in paragraph 77 and elsewhere in the judgment might suggest that this is at least arguable.

Many of these questions, and indeed others, may arise in the years to come. For now however it is clear that *Mallak* is a significant judgment and one more component in the construction of an enviable judicial legacy. Judge Posner's study of judicial reputation in the specific context of Benjamin Cardozo, addresses the question of the impact of personality upon reputation. Posner identifies a number of traits which could without exaggeration, or undue flattery, be applied to Nial Fennelly. A gentle, diffident manner, good manners, a willingness to praise others, particularly assistants, and acknowledge the merit of their work, an essential modesty though not a false modesty, and an awareness that even an outstanding judge is prone to error and has much to learn from others including the young.[42] In the years to come, the Supreme Court may have to address the issues flowing from *Mallak*, and indeed many other complex questions. It is a matter of regret to his colleagues, I think universally shared in the Irish legal community, that when those cases arise, the Court will have to confront them without the penetrating intellect of this gentle man and gentlemanly judge.

[42] N 24, 9. In *How Judges Think* (Cambridge MA, Harvard University Press, 2008), Judge Posner has also offered a daunting definition of the concept of good judgment as, 'an elusive faculty best understood as the compound of empathy, modesty maturity, sense of proportion, balance, recognition of human limitations, saintly prudence, a sense of reality, and common sense'! (The exclamation mark is mine).

15

Declarations of Incompatibility, Inapplicability and Invalidity: Rights, Remedies and the Aftermath[1]

GERARD HOGAN*

1. Those of us who are a certain age can recall vividly the void/voidable issue which was a feature of administrative law in the 1970s and 1980s. Putting the matter as it simplest, those judges who wished to limit the potentially retroactive effect of their judgments would often say that the impugned decision was voidable only, so that the judicial decision would have only prospective effects. This rather facile approach was, of course, anathema to leading public scholars such as Professor Wade who (correctly) protested that this was simply inconsistent with the doctrine of ultra vires. The courts could only review administrative decisions for vires,[2] the logic of which necessarily implied that if the decision were adjudged to be ultra vires, then the decision-maker had no power to take the decision in question in the first place. If that were so, then it followed that an administrative decision which was bad on vires grounds must be void *ab initio*, simply because by definition the decision-maker had no power to make the decision in the first place.[3]
2. Writing in 2004, Wade and Forsyth concluded that the void/voidable distinction was now 'obsolete', the House of Lords 'having written its obituary notice decisively.'[4] That obituary notice was to be found in the elegant speech of Lord Irvine in *Boddington v British Transport Police*.[5]

*Judge of the High Court of Ireland

[1] This is a version of an earlier lecture delivered to the Public Law Discussion Group of the Law Faculty of the University of Oxford, 1 February 2013. My thanks are due to Professor Aileen Kavanagh, Fellow of St Edmund Hall, University of Oxford, who chaired the lecture and who kindly made some valuable suggestions on an earlier draft of this paper.

[2] The anomalous doctrine of error on the face of the record here excepted.

[3] 'This is a principle which is inherent in the nature of such limited powers, but it is unequivocally spelled out in some constitutions and constitutional statutes': *Murphy v Attorney General* [1982] IR 241, 309–310, per Henchy J.

[4] W Wade and C Forsyth *Administrative Law*, 9th edn (OUP, Oxford, 2004) 305.

[5] [1998] UKHL 13, [1999] 2 AC 148.

Having explained that the logic of the leading decision of *Anisminic Ltd. v Foreign Compensation Commission*[6] was that the doctrine of ultra vires had been expanded to include all errors of law – thus collapsing the theoretical distinction for the void/voidable distinction:

> [i]t is clear, in the light of *Anisminic* and the later authorities, that the Secretary of State's order in *Director of Public Prosecutions v Head*[7] would now certainly be regarded as a nullity (*ie*, as void *ab initio*), even if it were to be analysed as an error of law on the face of the record. Equally, the order would be regarded as void *ab initio* if it had been made in bad faith, or as a result of the Secretary of State taking into account an irrelevant, or ignoring a relevant, consideration – that is, matters not appearing on the face of the record, but having to be established by evidence.
>
> Subordinate legislation, or an administrative act, is sometimes said to be presumed lawful until it has been pronounced to be unlawful. This does not, however, entail that such legislation or act is valid until quashed prospectively. That would be a conclusion inconsistent with the authorities to which I have referred. In my judgment, the true effect of the presumption is that the legislation or act which is impugned is presumed to be good until pronounced to be unlawful, but is then recognised as never having had any legal effect at all.[8]

3. No one could question the logic of this conclusion. But strict legal logic is not – and cannot be – the whole story, at least when the armoury of judicial review is brought to bear not merely on administrative decisions, but on primary legislation. The legal system scarcely shudders at the quashing of a routine administrative decision or a criminal conviction – even, for example, the smoking regulations at issue in *Boddington* – but different considerations invariably come into play where primary legislation is invalidated. Here a finding of invalidity can have profound legal, political and even social consequences, as the Irish Supreme Court found out – if they did not know already – in an acute fashion in June 2006 when, following the invalidation of primary legislation governing statutory rape, it was faced with the prospect of a series of habeas corpus applications by persons convicted of sexual offences with minors whose convictions were now called into question by virtue of the fact that the legislation under which they stood convicted no longer existed. The Court's judgment in *A v Governor of Arbour Hill Prison*[9] – which, reversing the judgment of the High Court, upheld the legality of the detention – is in its own way an exquisite tribute to the complexity of these issues and how one cannot allow abstract legal logic to prevail over the dictates of justice.
4. This in itself shows the wisdom of the reservations expressed by Lord Browne-Wilkinson in *Boddington*:

[6] [1969] 2 AC 169.

[7] [1959] AC 83

[8] [1999] AC 143, 155.

[9] [2006] IESC 45, [2006] 4 IR 88. The decision itself was highly controversial at the time. It has its severest critics (R Fanning, 'Hard Case – Bad Law? A commentary on the Supreme Court decision in *A v Governor of Mountjoy Prison*' (2005) 40 *Irish Jurist* 188), as well as eloquent defenders (MW Murphy, 'The Problem of Unconstitutionality and Retroactivity in Criminal Law in Ireland, USA and Canada Compared' (2007) 42 *Irish Jurist* 63).

The Lord Chancellor attaches importance to the consideration that an invalid byelaw is and always has been a nullity. The byelaw will necessarily have been found to be *ultra vires*; therefore it is said it is a nullity having no legal effect. I adhere to my view that the juristic basis of judicial review is the doctrine of *ultra vires*. But I am far from satisfied that an *ultra vires* act is incapable of having any legal consequence during the period between the doing of that act and the recognition of its invalidity by the court. During that period people will have regulated their lives on the basis that the act is valid. The subsequent recognition of its invalidity cannot rewrite history as to all the other matters done in the meantime in reliance on its validity. The status of an unlawful act during the period before it is quashed is a matter of great contention and of great difficulty.[10]

5. All of this is by way of prelude to two themes which may now be examined. The diversity of approaches to the issue of invalidity in constitutional law and human rights adjudication in different jurisdictions can first briefly be explored. But this brings us directly to the second theme, namely, the necessity in the context of findings of invalidity to separate the remedy from the right. While this may seem at first blush to be counter-intuitive, a moment's reflection demonstrates that this is not so. If a court has no option but, for example, to confer a windfall benefit on persons deservedly serving lengthy prison sentences by releasing them from prison by reason of a finding of constitutional invalidity, or if it cannot limit the after-effects of a finding of invalidity in taxation matters, then you will find that in the end the courts will simply refuse in this type of cases to find the legislation invalid.
6. This then leads to a situation where, perversely, the very powerfulness of the remedy – including a finding of invalidity *ab initio* – has asymmetric effects on the rights which are supposed to be safeguard by a document such as a Constitution (or, for that matter, in the United Kingdom, the Human Rights Act 1998 or the ECHR), because a court will ultimately prefer to find that certain rights have not been violated by the legislation which is under challenge rather than bring about the social and political chaos which a full-blown declaration of unconstitutionality would leave in its wake. This is perhaps why courts in different jurisdictions have all developed their own ways and methods of limiting the implications of constitutional adjudication and why the second theme is inextricably linked with the first. But before examining this theme, let us first sketch out some different remedies for constitutional violations.

DIFFERENT TYPES OF INVALIDITY

7. In the field of constitutional[11] adjudication we find accordingly that there is a spectrum of possibilities ranging from the purely admonitory approach

[10] [1999] AC 143, 164.

[11] I am here including decision-making under the Human Rights Act 1998 in the United Kingdom and decisions taken by the European Court of Human Rights

at one end to the full-blown declaration of unconstitutionality with *erga omnes* effect at the other.

The Purely Admonitory Approach

8. The purely admonitory approach is, of course, typified by the innovative declaration of incompatibility procedure found in the Human Rights Act in the United Kingdom and in the jurisprudence of the European Court of Human Rights itself. Thus, for example, a particular law may be found to contravene a substantive provision of the ECHR and to be declared to be such, but the courts (whether in England and Wales or in Strasbourg) have no power to nullify the law which remains effective and good law unless there is subsequent legislative change. One could give numerous examples of this, but the following must suffice for our purposes.
9. In *V. v United Kingdom*[12] the applicant, a young teenager, had been convicted of the murder of a two year old boy following a sensational trial in the Crown Court. The European Court of Human Rights held that aspects of the trial and the setting of the sentencing tariff procedure violated Article 5 ECHR and Article 6 ECHR respectively. Yet there was not the slightest suggestion that the applicant's conviction should be quashed or that he should be released from custody, or even that the legislation under which he had been tried should be nullified.[13]
10. Some may find this approach somewhat surprising, not least given that one of the findings of the Court was that the applicant had been denied a fair trial measured by Article 5(1) ECHR. Indeed, one might go further and contend that the applicant had been denied an effective remedy (as guaranteed by Article 13 ECHR) by reason of such an omission. What, after all, was the point of going to the European Court of Human Rights to secure rulings of this far-reaching kind unless the Court was going to take active steps to ensure, for example, that the applicant be re-tried?
11. It is interesting, however, that one finds variations of this approach even in jurisdictions where constitutional courts enjoy the full power of nullification of laws. A good example here is the so-called admonitory decision (*Appellentscheidung*), a procedure created almost from thin air by the German Federal Constitutional Court and in respect of which no express constitutional grant of power by the Basic Law exists.[14] In effect, however, this procedure exists – or, at least, had to be created – in order to allow

[12] Application no 2488/94 [1999] ECHR 171, (2000) 30 EHRR 121.

[13] Compare this with the approach of the Irish Supreme Court to the same problem. In *The State (O) v O'Brien* [1973] IR 50 it was held that legislation which enabled the executive to prescribe the sentence to be served by a juvenile young offender was unconstitutional as an interference with the separation of powers and the applicant was consequently released on habeas corpus.

[14] See generally, W Rupp-von Brünneck, 'Admonitory Functions of Constitutional Courts: Germany' (1972) 20 *American Journal of Comparative Law* 387; D Ehlers, F Schock, *Rechtschutz im : Öffentlichen Recht* (de Gruyter, Berlin, 2009) at 341–342.

judicial review to be effective, precisely because the consequences of such a finding of unconstitutionality would have been socially, administratively or politically catastrophic without some mitigating measure.

12. Two examples can illustrate this point. In *The Second Apportionment Case*[15] the Constitutional Court was asked to set aside the results of 1961 federal elections. These elections had taken place on foot of unrevised constituencies and the significant demographic shifts which had taken place since the (original) 1949 electoral law was put in place. The Court side-stepped this problem by saying that the 1949 law 'has become' unconstitutional because 'it no longer corresponds to up-to-date demographic figures'. While it warned that the 1949 law could not constitutionally be used for the next election, the Court refused to annul the 1961 elections on the ground that this unconstitutionality 'was not so evident' as to invalidate the previous electoral apportionment law.
13. In the second example[16] the Constitutional Court held that legislation which considerably impeded the right of the biological father to claim paternity violated Article 6 of the Basic Law (family life). The Court, however, suspended the paternity proceedings pending before the lower courts in order to give the Bundestag the opportunity to bring the law into line with the Constitution. This, however, was no open-ended invitation; the Court gave the legislature precisely one year in order to achieve this.[17] Of course, it may be contended that in many instances the admonitory decision is simply a mere obiter dictum and there is uncertainty as to what would actually happen if the legislature actually refused to heed the judicial call for change.[18] Yet the technique is an established one which has produced real results in concrete cases. Moreover, as the Electoral Apportionment case shows, would the Constitutional Court have been willing to hold (or, at least, strongly indicate) that the constituency arrangements were actually unconstitutional unless it could de facto do so through the medium of the admonitory decision? Putting this another way, if the Court was presented

[15] BVerf GE 16: 130 (1963).

[16] BVerfGE 108 (2003) *Biologischer Vater.*

[17] Note also the comments of the European Court of Human Rights in *Walden v Lichtenstein* [2000] ECHR 710:

> [m]oreover, it has also been accepted, in view of the principle of legal certainty that a constitutional court may set a time-limit for the legislator to enact new legislation with the effect that an unconstitutional provision remains applicable for a transitional period.

Even though the Irish courts have not heretofore expressly acknowledged the existence of such an admonitory jurisdiction, one can see shades of this in *Blake v Attorney General* [1982] IR 117. Here the Irish Supreme Court held that the Rent Restrictions Act 1967 was unconstitutional since it amounted to an arbitrary interference with property rights. Conscious, however, that such an invalidation would have far-reaching consequences by eg suddenly stripping tenants of legally acquired rights of tenure etc, the Court concluded its judgment by directing the lower courts to refuse to enter applications for possession pending the enactment of new legislation by the Oireachtas (Parliament) which would regularise the position and – adapting the later language of the German Constitutional Court in *Biologischer Vater* – 'bring the law into line' with the Constitution.

[18] See, eg, D Ehlers and F Schock, *Rechtsschutz im Öffentlichen Recht* (Berlin, De Gruyter 2009) 341.

only with two choices, namely, either to find an unconstitutionality and to invalidate the election *or* uphold the constitutionality of the law, there must be a real risk that judicial concern regarding the momentous nature of the former decision would unbalance judicial decision-making and affect the substantive decision on the constitutional question.

The Declaration of Inapplicability

14. The declaration of inapplicability is the procedure utilised by the US courts in the sphere of constitutional adjudication and by the Court of Justice in pronouncing on the compatibility of national law with EU law via the *Simmenthal* doctrine.[19]
15. While only the pedantic would object to the common description of the US courts' power of judicial review as extending to the 'striking down' of unconstitutional legislation, one must not overlook the fact that the US Constitution confers no express power of judicial review of legislation. James Bryce, the noted jurist, politician and diplomat, put the matter so well in his famous work, *The American Commonwealth*: [20]

> [t]here is a story told of an intelligent Englishman who, having heard that the [US] Supreme Court was created to protect the Constitution and had authority given to it to annul bad laws, spent two days in hunting up and down the Federal Constitution for the provisions he had been told to admire. No wonder he did not find them, for there is not a word in the Constitution on the subject.

16. What happens instead under the strict theory of the *Marbury v Madison* doctrine is that, when confronted with two items of positive law which are in conflict, the court prefers to apply the higher legal instrument (namely, the Constitution) and effectively dis-applies the inferior law (ie, the item of federal or state legislation that is adjudged to be unconstitutional). In practice, of course, that finding of unconstitutionality has *erga omnes* effect, but this is again, strictly speaking, by reason of the doctrine of precedent. The reason, therefore, why a law adjudged to be unconstitutional in case A will be applied to third parties is because, should the matter be put to the test in subsequent (but sufficiently similar) case B, the court will be bound by the doctrine of precedent to follow the ruling of unconstitutionality in case A and will equally refuse to apply the ordinary statute law in respect of case B. Strictly speaking, however, the US courts do not have any power, *as such*, to annul or invalidate a law found to be unconstitutional. Such a law remains on the statute book, but it is not enforced by reason of the finding of unconstitutionality.[21]

[19] Case 106/77 *Amministrazione dello Stato delle Finanze v Simmenthal S.p.A.* [1978] ECR 629.

[20] J Bryce *The American Commonwealth* vol 1 (MacMillan, London, 1889) 246.

[21] Of course, in the event that the US Supreme Court were to reverse itself and overrule a previous decision in which a law had been judged to be unconstitutional, then in principle the earlier law would now revive, precisely because the doctrine of precedent would not now require the court in

17. It is true that the US Supreme Court has occasionally gone further. Thus, in a late 19th century decision, *Shelby v Norton County*[22] concerning the question of whether a decision of an unconstitutionally appointed bankruptcy court could create a *res judicata*, Field J emphatically rejected this contention saying in language which finds an echo in the judgment of Lord Irvine more than a century later in *Boddington*: '[a]n unconstitutional act is not a law; it confers no rights; it imposes no duties; it affords no protection; it creates no office; it is, in legal contemplation, as inoperative as though it had never been passed.'[23]
18. Yet when a similar issue was again presented to the US Supreme Court in 1940 in another bankruptcy case, *Chicot Co. Drainage District v Baxter State Bank*[24], more measured and realistic views were expressed by Hughes CJ. Here a bankruptcy court had approved the making of a composition with creditors, but the statute vesting this jurisdiction in that court was subsequently declared to be unconstitutional. Did this mean that the earlier decision no longer operated as a *res judicata*? In all but overruling the decision in *Norton v Shelby County,* the US Supreme Court held that it could, the finding of unconstitutionality notwithstanding:

> [t]he courts below have proceeded on the theory that the Act of Congress, having been found to be unconstitutional, was not a law; that it was inoperative, conferring no rights, and imposing no duties, and hence affording no basis for the challenged decree. ... It is quite clear, however, that such broad statements as to the effect of a determination of unconstitutionality must be taken with qualifications. The actual existence of a statute, prior to such a determination, is an operative fact and may have consequences which cannot justly be ignored. The past cannot always be erased by a new judicial declaration. The effect of the subsequent ruling as to invalidity may have to be considered in various aspects,— with respect to particular relations, individual and corporate, and particular conduct, private and official. Questions of rights claimed to have become vested, of status, of prior determinations deemed to have finality and acted upon accordingly, of public policy in the light of the nature both of the statute and of its previous application, demand examination. These questions are among the most difficult of those which have engaged the attention

question to dis-apply the ordinary in favour of the Constitution. While this issue never appears to have been directly put to the test, it was very much in view after 1937–1938 when the US Supreme Court abandoned its earlier views on substantive due process in the field of economic regulation. The US Attorney General advised the President that a 1923 decision on the point which was formally overruled in 1937 had simply 'suspended enforcement' of the legislation and that the legislation was now once again valid and enforceable in the light of the 1937 ruling, saying (39 Ops. Atty. Gen. 22 (1937)): '[t]he decisions are practically in accord in holding that the courts have no power to repeal or abolish a statute, and that notwithstanding a decision holding it unconstitutional a statute continues to remain on the statute books.'

[22] 118 US 425 (1886).

[23] *Cf* the comments of Latham CJ in *South Australia v Commonwealth* (1941) 65 CLR 373, 408: Common expressions, such as 'the courts have declared a statute invalid', sometimes lead to a misunderstanding. A pretended law made in excess of power is not and never has been a law at all...The law is not valid until a court pronounces against it – and thereafter invalid. If it is beyond power it is invalid *ab initio*.

[24] 307 US 371 (1940).

of courts, state and federal, and it is manifest from numerous decisions that an all-inclusive statement of a principle of absolute retroactive invalidity cannot be justified.

19. The decision in *Chicot County* paved the way for a much more nuanced view of the issue of the effect of a finding of unconstitutionality. Indeed, it has been clear since the US Supreme Court's celebrated decision in *Linkletter v Walker*[25] that the Court now asserts a complete power to determine the extent to which its decisions will have retroactive effect, declaring in the process that 'the Constitution neither prohibits nor requires retroactive effect'.[26] But if the entire doctrine of unconstitutionality of statutes itself rests on judicial decision (and, strictly speaking, by further extension, on the doctrine of precedent), then it does not seem too strange if the Court can itself assert a power to limit the retroactive effect of such judicial decisions.[27] The issue really in a way is no different in principle to the situation which obtains in many other common law jurisdictions when in case A the Supreme Court (or some other court) overrules earlier (well-established) case B.[28]
20. The same broad approach manifests itself in the *Simmenthal* line of case-law insofar as the legislation enacted by Member States is examined by reference to its compatibility with EU law. The Court of Justice does not have power as such to annul such legislation[29], but simply to declare its incompatibility with EU law. This is evident from the following passages from the judgment in *Simmenthal*:

> Furthermore, in accordance with the principles of precedence of Community law, the relationship between the provisions of the Treaty and directly applicable to measures of the institutions on the one hand and national law of the Member States on the other is such that those provisions and measures not only by their entry into force *render automatically inapplicable any conflicting provision of current national law* but – in so far as they are an integral part of, and take precedence in, the legal order applicable in the territory of each of the Member States – also preclude the valid adoption of new legislative measures to the extent that they would be incompatible with Community provisions ...
>
> It follows from the foregoing that every national court must, in a case within its jurisdiction, apply Community law in its entirety and protect rights which the latter

[25] 381 US 618 (1965).

[26] 381 US 618, 629, per Clark J.

[27] The decision in *Linkletter v Walker* has given rise to a large subsequent corpus of case-law on retroactive effects, many of which decisions are in the field of habeas corpus and turn on intricacies of civil and criminal procedure (including, in particular, whether decisions which are final can be re-opened) and of which *Griffith v Kentucky* 479 US 314 (1987) and *Teague v Lane* 489 US 288 (1989) are perhaps the most prominent: see, *eg*, S Alexander, 'Decline of the Great Writ: An Analysis of *Teague v Lane*' 31 *St. Clara Law Review* (1991). For Irish parallels to *Teague v Lane*, see *People v Cunningham* [2012] IECCA 64, [2012] 2 I.L.R.M. 406, *People v Kavanagh* [2012] IECCA 65, *People v Hughes* [2012] IECCA 69 and *People v O'Brien* [2012] IECCA 68.

[28] See, eg, *National Westminster Bank plc v Spectrum Plus Ltd* [2005] UKHL 41, [2005] 2 AC 680.

[29] Of course, completely different considerations apply in the context of EU legislation, where there is a direct power of annulment under Article 267 TFEU. This is considered below.

confers on individuals and must accordingly set aside any provision of national law which may conflict with it, whether prior or subsequent to the Community rule. Accordingly any provision of a national legal system in any legislative, administrative or judicial practice which might impair the effectiveness of Community law by withholding from the national court having jurisdiction to apply such law the power to do everything necessary at the moment of its application to set aside national legislative provisions which might prevent Community rules from having full force and effect are incompatible with those requirements which are of the very essence of Community law.[30]

21. It will be seen from the foregoing that the *Simmenthal* doctrine is really an EU version of *Marbury v Madison*, not merely in terms of its symbolic and general political significance, but at the more prosaic level we are presently discussing, in terms of the actual mechanics of the decision. In other words, faced with a conflict between two overlapping norms, in both instances the courts reach for the higher norm in the prevailing legal order, namely, the Constitution and EU law respectively.
22. This, of course, is not at all to suggest that a decision of the Court of Justice which declares an item of national law to be inapplicable does not have serious consequences, even if the law is not formally annulled. Indeed, the consequences – unless mitigated by court order – of such a finding are to all intents and purposes the same as if there had been a declaration of unconstitutionality under the *Marbury v Madison* doctrine. It cannot, therefore, be any surprise that the Court of Justice moved quickly to limit the potential *ex tunc* effect of its decisions in cases of this kind. This was made clear in at a comparatively early stage of EU law in *Defrenne v SABENA (No.2)*[31] where the Court of Justice held that by reason of the fact that numerous private undertakings in Member States had been lulled into a false sense of security regarding the applicability of the equal pay provisions of the (former) Article 119 EEC Treaty, it would be appropriate to impose temporal limits on the effect of the decision. The Court held in essence that as these undertakings (and, of course, the Member States in question) had altered their position in good faith, it would be wrong to visit them then now with potentially large claims for equal pay which they did not – and perhaps ought not – to have anticipated. The *Defrenne* approach has been adopted subsequently in a series of cases dealing with pensions, taxation and social welfare.
23. The major objection, of course, to such an explicit limitation on the scope of such a ruling is that it rather smacks of *de lege ferenda* and the arbitrary limitation of equally meritorious claims.[32] Yet the Court will invariably make an exception in favour of litigants who put forward this or other

[30] *Amministrazione dello Stato delle Finance v Simmenthal* n 19; emphasis added.

[31] Case 43/75 [1976] ECR 455.

[32] It is true that in *Murphy v Attorney General* [1982] IR 241 some members of the Irish Supreme Court expressed unease at the apparently arbitrary cut-off dates laid down by the US Supreme Court in cases such as *Linkletter v Walker*, with Griffin J expressing unease at the 'unsatisfactory and unjust results' which seemed to follow from this rule. Yet three decades later the Irish Court of

similar claims which were pending at the date of the decision. Thus, in *Sürül*[33] – a case concerning the entitlement of Turkish migrants to social security under EU law – the Court offered this practical justification:

> In those circumstances, pressing considerations of legal certainty preclude any reopening of the question of legal relationships which have been definitively determined before the delivery of this judgment, where that would retroactively throw the financing of the social security systems of the Member States into confusion.
>
> However, in order not to affect unduly the judicial protection of the rights which individuals derive from Community law, it is appropriate to make an exception to that limitation of the effects of this judgment for the benefit of those persons who, before the date of delivery hereof, initiated proceedings or made an equivalent claim.[34]

24. It may accordingly be said that this exception to the general limitation is defensible on the basis that such persons 'have invested time and money in the protection of their rights granted by Community law' and that denying them the benefit of such decision 'might unduly affect the judicial protection under Community law.'[35] Yet for all that it is impossible to disagree with the eloquent summary of *Defrenne* contained in the judgment of Henchy J in *Murphy*. While acknowledging that the arguments advanced for limited retroactivity advanced in *Defrenne* might not be easy to 'harmonize or conceptualize', he nonetheless observed:

> It would seem that the court was affected by the arguments put forward ... that full retrospective invalidation of the failure of Member States to observe the requirements of Article 119 would produce a cascade of claims that could swamp many private employers and do irreparable harm to national economies. The Court's dilemma in preserving the objectivity and paramountcy of Community law, while not applying that law to a degree that might endanger the underlying economic aims of the Treaty of Rome is evident in the following rational with which it concluded the judgment.[36]

25. Having then set out the passage from *Defrenne* just quoted, Henchy J concluded by saying that the decision stood:

> [a]s a cogent example of the principle that what has been done or left undone under a constitutionally invalid law may, in certain events, such as the evolution of

Criminal Appeal found itself de facto making the application of a rule of this nature depend on whether the accused in criminal cases had either challenged the constitutionality of a law which allowed the police to search a private dwelling without a search warrant which had been granted by a court at their trial or had raised this point on appeal prior to a decision of the Irish Supreme Court in *Damache v Director of Public Prosecutions* [2012] IESC 12, [2012] 2 I.L.R.M. 153: see, *eg*, *The People v Cunningham* [2012] IECCA 64, [2012] 2 ILRM 604.

[33] Case C-262/96 [1999] ECR I-2685.

[34] Judgment, paras 109–110.

[35] A Wiedmann, 'Non-retroactive or prospective rulings by the Court of Justice of the European Communities in preliminary rulings according to Article 234 EC' (2006) *European Law Forum* 197, 199.

[36] [1982] IR 241, 323–324.

a set of circumstances which it would be impossible, or unjust, or contrary to the common good, to attempt to reverse or undo, have to be left beyond the reach of full redressive legal proceedings and have to be treated as an exemplification of the maxim *communis error facit jus*.[37]

Declaration of Unconstitutionality

26. We may now consider the example of two common law jurisdictions – Ireland and Canada – which operate a fully-fledged declaration of unconstitutionality system. In this regard, the relevant constitutional texts are similar. Article 15.4 of the Irish Constitution (1937) provides:

    1. The Oireachtas [Parliament] shall not enact any law which is in any respect repugnant to this Constitution or to any provision thereof.
    2. Every law enacted by the Oireachtas which is in any respect repugnant to this Constitution or to any provision thereof shall, but to the extent only of such repugnancy, be invalid.

27. This may be compared with s. 52(1) of Canada's Constitution Act 1982 which provides: 'The Constitution of Canada is the supreme law of Canada, and any law that is inconsistent with the provisions of the Constitution is, to the extent of the inconsistency, of no force or effect.'
28. Although the Irish legal system has had considerable experience in dealing with the aftermath of a declaration of unconstitutionality, it still has not fully come to terms with it or perhaps completely developed the appropriate judicial response to this admittedly difficult problem. Perhaps three examples may briefly be given.

The State (Byrne) v Frawley[38]

29. Here the applicant prisoner sought habeas corpus following his conviction for robbery. During the course of the trial, however, the Irish Supreme Court had held in another case[39] that legislation providing (in effect) for all male-juries and juries composed of property owners only was unconstitutional. The Supreme Court nonetheless upheld the validity of the conviction. While the majority accepted that the conviction was notionally void by reason of the invalidity of the Juries Act, Henchy J held that by electing to proceed with his trial the finding of unconstitutionality in the *de Búrca* case notwithstanding, the applicant was now precluded by his own conduct from challenging the validity of his own conviction.

[37] [1982] IR 241, 324.
[38] [1978] IR 326.
[39] *De Búrca v Attorney General* [1976] IR 38.

Murphy v Attorney General[40]

30. The entire issue came squarely into focus in *Murphy v Attorney General*, a case where the Court had first invalidated the aggregation of income system provided for married couples because it effectively ensured that married couples paid significantly more tax than single persons living together. The Court was then required to consider the effect of the finding of unconstitutionality. A majority held that an unconstitutional law was void *ab initio*, with Henchy J observing that any contrary conclusion would:

> (1) ... fail to recognise the true nature of the constitutional limitation of the legislative power vested in the Oireachtas;
> (2) ... distort[ ] the meaning that must be given to 'invalid' in its constitutional context; and
> (3) ... fl[y] in the face of an unbroken line of judicial decisions which, expressly or by necessary implication, point to the date of enactment as the date from which invalidity is to attach to the measure which has been struck down because of its unconstitutionality.

31. He went to say that a declaration of unconstitutionality amounted to a 'judicial death certificate' for the statute, operative from the date of the enactment. This did not, however, mean that the Irish State had to repay the majority of married couples, since the Court held that all but a tiny number of litigants before them were estopped by their conduct in allowing such tax to be collected in an (as it turned out) unconstitutional fashion and to have the State alter its position by spending money which it was entitled to assume was being lawfully collected. As Henchy J put it:

> [i]t is not a universal rule that what has been done in pursuance of a law which has been held to have been invalid for constitutional or other reasons will necessarily give a good cause of action: see for example the decision of this Court in *The State (Byrne) v Frawley*. While it is central to the due administration of justice in an ordered society that one of the primary concerns of the Courts should be to see that prejudice suffered at the hands of those who act without legal justification, while legal justification is required, shall not stand beyond the reach of corrective legal proceedings, *the law has to recognise that there may be transcendent considerations which make such a course undesirable, impracticable or impossible.*
>
> Over the centuries the law has come to recognise, in one degree or another, that factors such as prescription (negative or positive), waiver, estoppel, laches, a statute of limitations, *res judicata*, or other matters (most of which may be grouped under the heading of public policy) may debar a person from obtaining a redress in the Courts for injury, pecuniary or otherwise, which would be justiciable and redressable if such considerations have not intervened ...
>
> For a variety of reasons, the law recognizes that in certain circumstances, no matter how unfounded in law certain conduct may have been, no matter how unwarranted its operation in a particular case, what has happened has happened and cannot, or should not, be undone. The irreversible progressions and bye-products of time, the compulsion of public order and of the common good, the aversion of the law

[40] [1982] IR 241.

from giving a hearing to those who have slept on their rights, the quality of legality – even irreversibility – that tends to attach to what has become inveterate or has been widely accepted or acted upon, the recognition that even in the short term the accomplished fact may sometimes acquire an inviolable sacredness, these and other factors may convert what has been done under an unconstitutional, or otherwise void, law into an acceptable part of the *corpus juris*.[41]

32. While *Murphy* certainly demonstrated that an unconstitutional law is void *ab initio* and, furthermore, that such invalidity has *erga omnes* effects,[42] in general the practical effect of the decision was to enable the courts to place effective limitations on the finding of unconstitutionality, often by reference to established doctrines such as estoppel by conduct, acquiescence and waiver. This point was stressed by Denham CJ in her judgment in *The People v Kavanagh*: [43]

> [t]he Court would further observe that it would be a fallacy to treat the issue of the consequences of a finding of unconstitutionality as if it were some form of abstract quasi-mathematical syllogism, with the courts looking on helplessly as the retroactive application of a finding of unconstitutionality worked inexorably to bring about catastrophic consequences for the legal system and ordered political society. While the first duty of the courts is to secure legal redress for those whose rights have been infringed by unconstitutional action, this duty is, as Article 40.3.1 [of the Constitution] itself recognises, tempered by considerations of feasibility and practicability. Any other conclusion would mean that the 'true social order' envisaged by the Preamble to the Constitution could not be attained.

A. v Governor of Arbour Hill Prison[44]

33. The most comprehensive analysis of this point came in the various judgments of the Irish Supreme Court in *A. v Governor of Arbour Hill Prison*. This was a habeas corpus application which arose following the invalidation of a 1935 statutory rape law, as the Court held that it was unconstitutional to create a law providing for absolute offences in cases of this seriousness.[45] In her judgment in the High Court, Laffoy J held that the applicant was entitled to be released on the basis that the offence of which he had been convicted no longer existed. This case then brought into sharp focus an issue which had been smouldering for years: how would the courts limit the effects of a finding that a particular law was unconstitutional?
34. It would be difficult to do justice to the complexity and sophistication of the judgments of the Supreme Court which allowed the appeal; it is perhaps

[41] [1982] IR 241, 340 (emphasis added).

[42] See, *eg*, *Muckley v Ireland* [1985] IR 472 (where legislation which endeavoured to provide for the collection of outstanding taxes at the date of the decision in *Murphy* itself held to be unconstitutional); *People v Cunningham* [2012] IECCA 64 (a defendant whose appeal was still outstanding at the date of a finding of unconstitutionality in another case could rely on that finding, *provided* that he had not otherwise waived or abandoned the point).

[43] [2012] IECCA 65.

[44] [2006] 4 IR 88, [2006] IESC 45.

[45] *CC v Ireland (No.2)* [2006] 4 IR 1.

sufficient to say, as Lord Rodger did in *Cadder v HM Advocate*,[46] that these 'very full judgments ... repay study.' Three general themes may nonetheless be said to emerge from these judgments. First, as all legal systems stress the finality of convictions and orders in criminal cases, such convictions are not to be re-opened lightly. Second, that all legal systems place limits on the retroactive effect of judicial decisions. Third, several judges were anxious to emphasise the chaotic – even anarchic – consequences that giving full retroactive effect to a finding of unconstitutionality would have. As Murray CJ observed:

> Only a narrow approach based on absolute and abstract formalism could suggest that all previous cases should be capable of being reopened or relitigated (even if subject to a statute of limitations). If that absolute formalism was applied to the criminal law it would in principle suggest that every final verdict of a trial or decision of a court of appeal should be set aside or, where possible, retried in the light of subsequent decisions where such subsequent decision could be claimed to provide a potential advantage to a party in such a retrial. In principle both acquittals and convictions could be open to retrial. But one has only to pose the question to see the answer. No one has ever suggested that every time there is a judicial adjudication clarifying or interpreting the law in a particular manner which could have had some bearing on previous and finally decided cases, civil or criminal, that such cases be reopened or the decisions set aside. It has not been suggested because no legal system comprehends such an absolute or complete retroactive effect of judicial decisions. To do so would render a legal system uncertain, incoherent and dysfunctional. Such consequences would cause widespread injustices.[47]

35. Geoghegan J spoke in similar terms:

> It cannot have been the intention of the draftsmen of the Constitution and more properly of the Oireachtas and perhaps more properly still of the People that if a statutory provision creating an offence was found to be unconstitutional, every past conviction and sentence, perhaps going back a large number of years were *ipso facto* nullities. In interpreting any particular provision of the Constitution it is always necessary to have regard to the general intent of the Constitution as a whole. If such was the devastating effect of a declaration of unconstitutionality in all cases, it would fly in the face of common sense, would be manifestly unjust and would be contrary to any good order in a civilised society.[48]

36. In the end the Court found against A. on a variety of grounds, but, fundamentally, however, it was held that he was precluded and estopped by his conduct in pleading guilty to the offence from asserting that his conviction was invalid, even if the law on which he had been convicted was itself unconstitutional.

[46] [2010] UK SC 43, [2010] 1 WLR 2601.
[47] [2006] 4 IR 88, 117.
[48] [2006] 4 IR 88, 197.

Separating out the Right from the Remedy

37. This brings us directly to the theme which I have been anxious to stress throughout this paper, namely, the necessity in the context of findings of invalidity to separate out the remedy from the right. Perhaps the point can best be illustrated to start with by the following comments of Lord Bingham in *Attorney General's Reference (No.2)*.[49] Here the question was whether a breach of the right to an early trial as guaranteed by Article 6(1) ECHR led *automatically* to the termination of the criminal prosecution against the accused. Lord Bingham observed in the context of a supposed automaticity rule and a breach of Article 6(1)ECHR

> *a rule of automatic termination on proof of a breach of the reasonable time requirement has been shown to have the effect in practice of emasculating the right which the guarantee is designed to protect.* .....There is, however, a very real risk that if proof of a breach is held to require automatic termination of the proceedings the judicial response will be to set the threshold unacceptably high since, as La Forest J put it in *Rahey v The Queen* (1987) 39 DLR 481, 516, "Few judges relish the prospect of unleashing dangerous criminals on the public". La Forest J drew attention to the compelling observation of Professor Amsterdam, written with reference to American experience following the Supreme Court's decisions interpreting the Sixth Amendment to the United States Constitution in *Barker v Wingo* (1972) 407 US 514 and *Strunk v United States* (1973) 412 US 434:
>
>> [T]he spectre of immunizing, of "turning loose", persons proved guilty of serious criminal offenses has been thoroughly repugnant to judges, and they have accordingly held that shockingly long delays do not "violate" the Sixth Amendment. The amendment has thereby been twisted totally out of shape – distorted from a guarantee that all accuseds will receive a speedy trial into a windfall benefit of criminal immunity for a very few accuseds in whose cases the pandemic failure of our courts to provide speedy trials has attained peculiarly outrageous proportions: Anthony G Amsterdam, "*Speedy Criminal Trial: Rights and Remedies*" (1975) 27 *Stan L Rev* 525, 539.[50]

38. As ever, Lord Bingham's comments – particularly those I have taken the liberty of highlighting – are full of wisdom and insight. Of course, it might be said that these comments were made in the context of a specific right with a peculiar importance for criminal trials, so that these comments would not necessarily have a wider application. Quite the contrary. The prospect of releasing dangerous criminals by reason of a violation of the right to an early trial may well be thoroughly unappealing to judges, but they find the prospect of Sampson-like collapsing key pillars of the legal system via a declaration of unconstitutionality even more repugnant, unless, so to speak, the building can nevertheless be kept intact while running repairs are performed either by the judiciary or (as the case may be) the legislature.
39. Indeed, in his judgment in *A.*, Geoghegan J admitted as much, because he feared that unless the courts could control the aftershocks to the legal

[49] [2003] UKHL 69, [2004] 2 AC 72.
[50] [2004] 2 AC 72, 88 (emphasis added).

system caused by a finding of unconstitutionality, fear as to the ensuring consequences could well influence any adjudication on the underlying merits of the case:

> In conclusion, I am of the view that concluded proceedings whether they be criminal or civil based on an enactment subsequently found to be unconstitutional cannot normally be reopened. As I have already indicated, I am prepared to accept that there may possibly be exceptions. But in general it cannot be done. Nor as the Chief Justice and Hardiman J. have pointed out is there any precedent for a collateral challenge of this kind. I am also firmly of the opinion that if the law were otherwise there would be a grave danger that judges considering the constitutionality or otherwise of enactments would be consciously or unconsciously affected by the consequences....[51]

40. Another contemporary example may also illustrate this point. In *Parliament v Council*,[52] the European Parliament asked the Court of Justice to annul a Council decision which supplemented the Schengen Borders Code by providing for extended marine surveillance. The Parliament contended that the contested decision should not have been adopted by the comitology procedure, but rather that it ought to have been enacted using the ordinary legislative procedure. The Grand Chamber agreed that the measure should be annulled on this ground, but there was an important coda to the judgment:

> 86. The Parliament requests the Court, should it annul the contested decision, to maintain its effects, pursuant to the second paragraph of Article 264 TFEU, until that decision is replaced.
> 87. The Parliament submits that it is necessary to maintain the effects of the contested decision, in the light of the importance of the objectives of the proposed measures in the context of the European Union's policy on border control operations.
> 88. Under the second paragraph of Article 264 TFEU, the Court may, if it considers it necessary, state which of the effects of the act which it has declared void are to be considered as definitive.
> 89. The annulment of the contested decision without maintaining its effects on a provisional basis could compromise the smooth functioning of the current and future operations coordinated by the Agency and, consequently, the surveillance of the sea external borders of the Member States.
> 90. In those circumstances, there are important grounds of legal certainty which justify the Court exercising the power conferred on it by the second paragraph of Article 264 TFEU. In the present case, the effects of the contested decision must be maintained until the entry into force, within a reasonable time, of new rules intended to replace the contested decision annulled by the present judgment.

41. Article 264 TFEU itself provides:

> If the action is well founded, the Court of Justice of the European Union shall declare the act concerned to be void. However, the Court shall, if it is to consider this necessary, state which of the effects of the act which it has declared void shall be considered as definitive.

[51] [2006] 4 IR 88, 203.
[52] Case C-355/10 [2013] 1 CMLR 1.

42. In other words, Article 264 TFEU encapsulates the classic doctrine of *vires* by providing that the contested decision or legislative act of the Union can be annulled by the Court, but it contains an express proviso which precisely enables the Court to exercise that power of annulment while these running repairs are carried out.[53] Would the Court of Justice have been so readily prepared to annul a key part of the Schengen system if it could not also control the aftermath of its decision?
43. For my part, I think that the answer has to be that, in cases with potentially enormous implications, the potential consequences of that decision can and do matter and judicial decision-making can often be affected – even distorted – as a result. This is not at all to endorse a cynical view of judicial adjudication which glibly suggests that the courts will first take whatever decision seems opportune and adventitious and then justify that decision by appropriate reasoning. It is rather to say that the precept of *fiat justitia, ruat caelum* is not – and perhaps cannot be – the only guiding consideration. In this context, the psychological pressures under which judges called upon to make momentous decisions should not be underestimated. This is perhaps especially true at appellate level where a consensus in favour of a solution which avoids difficulties or controversy may sometimes be difficult to resist. While it might be said that judges should be well capable of ignoring these pressures, they are, after all human like everyone else. I cannot help but thinking that this is an under-examined feature of the judicial process.
44. What conclusions, therefore can we draw from this general survey of findings of invalidity with potentially far-reaching consequences? First, I suggest that the classical common law of vires and voidness can only tell a part of the story, especially once this analysis is applied in the sphere of constitutional law where a declaration of invalidity will often have far-reaching consequences. Part of the problem here is that the 1970s debate was conducted in a manner which suggested the existence of some underlying inviolate and quasi-mathematical rule, to understand which clearly was the sole task of court concerned. It was true, of course, to say that the doctrine of ultra vires was at the heart of public law and that therefore every such decision was by definition void. But it did not follow that such 'void' decisions did not have real and practical effects which the courts must justly

[53] Cf the special provisions contained in s. 102 of the Scotland Act 1998 dealing with the aftermath of a finding that a legislative enactment of the Scottish Parliament is invalid:

(1) This section applies where any court or tribunal decides that–
   (a) an Act of the Scottish Parliament or any provision of such an Act is not within the legislative competence of the Parliament, or
   (b) a member of the Scottish Executive does not have the power to make, confirm or approve a provision of subordinate legislation that he has purported to make, confirm or approve.

(2) The court or tribunal may make an order–
   (a) removing or limiting any retrospective effect of the decision, or
   (b) suspending the effect of the decision for any period and on any conditions to allow the defect to be corrected.

(3) In deciding whether to make an order under this section, the court or tribunal shall (among other things) have regard to the extent to which persons who are not parties to the proceedings would otherwise be adversely affected.

recognise or that it was somehow wrong that the courts could not control the effects of such a finding of invalidity.

45. The real truth was more prosaic. Those who argued that the decision was simply 'voidable' probably wanted simply to control the consequences of their decision; if they had thought that they had the option of simply declaring that their decision would operate prospectively, it would probably have been easier to say so.

46. It is, of course, true to say that the concept of voidness is a logical corollary of ultra vires. In many ways, the legal system cannot secure an effective remedy for ultra vires unless it can guarantee that in principle decisions or laws which offend against fundamental principles can be invalidated and redress provided. It could not be correct that a legislature could, for example, promulgate some egregiously offensive law which, for example, allowed for a warrantless search of a private dwelling and which was invalidated with purely prospective effect without at least the possibility of providing retrospective redress for this wrong. That, after all, is one of the weaknesses of the declaration of incompatibility procedure. While such a declaration has, of course, great moral weight, the law remains in place and in force pending some future legislative change. It was accordingly not for nothing that Professor Marshall once famously described the declaration of incompatibility under the British Human Rights Act 1998 as a species of 'booby prize.'[54]

47. Yet the concept of full retroactive effect of invalidity cannot be allowed to hold sway as if it were some form of scientific law. If the *ultra vires* doctrine is applied with remorseless logic so as to invalidate all that went before it, then it will have chaotic and unfair effects, not least on third parties and the general orderly conduct of public administration. This would be especially true if the common law rules as to the voidness of ultra vires administrative decisions are to be applied in the context of the invalidity of legislation. The experience of jurisdictions such as Germany and Ireland shows that the courts cannot and will not tolerate a state of affairs which would involve, for example, the invalidation of a general election or the general release of prisoners or the general repayment of income tax, no matter how much some form of abstract legal logic might otherwise declare.

48. This is why the courts in these jurisdictions have all developed their own techniques for limiting the effect of a finding of invalidity. In some cases the courts have been given express powers in this regard – examples here include, as we have seen, s.102(2) of the Scotland Act 1998 and Article 264 TFEU. But even without such express enactment, the courts have found it necessary to invent or conjure up solutions to this difficult problem. Many of these solutions are innovatory such as the '*Appellentschiedung*' (or admonitory decision) in Germany or the suspended declaration of unconstitutionality

[54] G Marshall, 'Two kinds of incompatibility: more about section 3 of the Human Rights Act 1998' (1999) *Public Law* 337, 382.

which has found favour with the Canadian courts.[55] In some instances the courts have fallen back on established general principles to limit the consequences of such a decision such as *res judicata*, laches and estoppel by conduct – this has, for example, been the Irish approach. Other courts – such as the European Court of Justice and the US Supreme Court – have unblushingly placed sometimes crude and judicially-announced temporal limits on such findings of invalidity.

CONCLUSIONS

49. In the end, however, the courts have had to place such limits and place effective limits on the consequences of judicial declarations of this kind, even if in some instances the results are arbitrary and not always perfectly consistent. But if a finding of unconstitutionality had uncontrolled and devastating consequences for society in general and the legal system in particular which the courts found themselves unable to limit, then this would inevitably impact on the practical willingness of the courts to make such a finding of unconstitutionality. This would represent a form of functional asymmetry which, absent a necessary flexibility in the manner in which these remedies are administered, might well have the effect of dissuading the courts from making a finding of unconstitutionality in the first place.
50. We may thus conclude our analysis of this notoriously difficult subject by reflecting on two paradoxical truisms. First, the concept of voidness is an artificial human construct and not some scientific rule. It is simply a device to say that decisions or legislation which conflict with a higher legal norm lack formal legal validity and – depending on particular circumstances – may lack legal effectiveness. Second, there has to be a mechanism to control the aftermath of a finding of invalidity. Not only would a full finding of retrospectivity have unfair and sometimes even chaotic consequences, but the very powerfulness of the remedy would distort the courts' willingness to protect the effectiveness of the right which it was called upon to enforce and uphold.

[55] See, eg, *Schacter v Canada* [1992] 2 SCR 679 and S Shoudry and K Roach, 'Putting the Past Behind us?' (2003) 21 *Supreme Court Law Review* 205 and E Carolan, 'The Relationship between Judicial Remedies and the Separation of Powers: Collaborative Constitutionalism and the Suspended Declaration of Invalidity' (2011) 46 *Irish Jurist* 180.

16

The Case of the 'Missing Evidence'

MUIREANN NOONAN*

THE DEPARTURE OF Mr Justice Nial Fennelly from the Irish Supreme Court can only be a matter of great regret. I witnessed his hard work, methodical analysis and keen intelligence first hand when I worked with him in the Court of Justice in Luxembourg. Never a man to buy into a knee jerk reaction, every point got teased out until a logical conclusion was arrived at. In Luxembourg, he had a staff of three *référendaires* and three assistants. He made every one of us feel as if our contribution was essential in the process. I now doubt how essential we were because, suspiciously, the high standard of his work did not diminish when in 2000 he returned to the Supreme Court minus his large staff and he managed to deliver many fine judgments unaided, such as *Ryanair plc v Aer Rianta cpt,* [1] *Osayande & Lobe v Minister for Justice,* [2] *Competition Authority v O'Regan,* [3] *Mahon v Post Publications,* [4] *Hemat v The Medical Council,* [5] *Equality Authority v Portmarnock Golf Club,* [6] *Dellway v NAMA,* [7] *Mallak v Minister for Justice, Equality and Law Reform,* [8] *Thomas Pringle v The Government of Ireland, Ireland and the Attorney General* [9] and *Gallagher v ACC Bank plc,* [10] to name but a few.

A striking feature of his judicial career was his willingness to dissent from the majority view only to persuade his colleagues to come around to his point of view subsequently. A good example of this process is the course of the 'missing evidence' jurisprudence of the Superior Courts.

*Barrister-at-Law, Dublin
[1] [2003] 4 IR 264.
[2] [2003] IESC 3.
[3] [2007] 4 IR 737.
[4] [2007] 3 IR 338.
[5] [2010] IESC 24.
[6] [2010] 1 IR 671.
[7] [2011] IESC 13.
[8] [2012] IESC 59.
[9] [2012] IESC 47.
[10] [2012] IESC 35.

Although it has been claimed[11] that the foundations of this jurisprudence were laid down by Palles CB in 1887 in *Dillon v O'Brien & Davis*, [12] over a century seems to have passed without recourse being had to it, at least in a systematic fashion. The first reported judgment in the area appears to have been that of Lynch J in *Murphy v DPP*,[13] which concluded that:

> The authorities establish that evidence relevant to guilt or innocence must so far as is necessary and practicable be kept until the conclusion of the trial. These authorities also apply to the preservation of articles which may give rise to the reasonable possibility of securing relevant evidence. [14]

Irrespective of its jurisprudential antecedents, this proposition could hardly be considered revolutionary in a State bound by its Constitution to vindicate the right to a fair trial. However, it took another twelve years before the issue as to whether the duty to retain, or at least not to dispose of, material in possession of the prosecution included a duty to seek out material that might give rise to the reasonable possibility of securing relevant evidence, came up for discussion in the Superior Courts.

Braddish v DPP[15] arose out of a robbery that had been committed in a shop protected by video surveillance. A member of An Garda Síochána subsequently viewed a tape of what he understood was the robbery and formed the view that the applicant was responsible for it. On that basis he arrested and detained the applicant who, during the course of his detention, signed a statement admitting to the robbery. Having been released from custody in October 1997, in July of the following year the applicant was charged with the robbery. The applicant subsequently disputed the admissibility of the alleged confession on grounds unconnected to the absence or otherwise of the video evidence. However, his solicitor thereafter made a number of requests for any signed statements, any video footage and any stills of that video footage. In January 1999, the applicant's solicitor was informed in writing that the videos were unavailable as they had been returned to the owners of the shop after the accused had admitted his involvement in the offence.

A unanimous Supreme Court restrained the applicant's trial. Delivering a judgment with which Denham and Geoghegan JJ agreed, Hardiman J identified a net issue in the case, namely whether the fact that the video tape was unavailable because An Garda Síochána had parted with possession of it required the grant of relief in circumstances where the video allegedly showed the crime in progress and allowed the perpetrator to be identified where no other identification evidence was available. Whilst the facts thus appeared to come within the ambit of the principle established in *Murphy*, Hardiman J held that:

[11] See *Murphy v DPP* [1989] ILRM 71, 76 *per* Lynch J, applied in *Braddish v DPP* [2001] 3 IR 127, 131–132 *per* Hardiman J. However paragraphs 22 to 23 of the judgment of O'Donnell J in *Wall v DPP* [2013] IESC 56 question the soundness of this proposition.

[12] (1887) 20 LRIr 300.

[13] [1989] ILRM 71.

[14] *Murphy v DPP* [1989] ILRM 71, 76.

[15] [2001] 3 IR 127.

> This video tape was real evidence and the Gardaí were not entitled to dispose of it before the trial. It is now admitted that they should not have done so. Lest however the sentence already quoted from the State Solicitor's letter (and which can only have been based on his instructions from the Gardaí) can be read to suggest that because the prosecution was based wholly on an alleged confession, other items of evidence can be destroyed or rendered unavailable, I wish to state emphatically that this is not so. *It is the duty of the Gardaí, arising from their unique investigative role, to seek out and preserve all evidence having a bearing or potential bearing on the issue of guilt or innocence. This is so whether the prosecution proposes to rely on the evidence or not, and regardless of whether it assists the case the prosecution is advancing or not.*[16]

Although later in his judgment he qualified the application of the final two sentences of this passage by stating that the duty he had described was not absolute, did not require An Garda Síochana to make a disproportionate commitment of manpower or resources in an exhaustive search for every conceivable kind of evidence, and had to be interpreted realistically on the facts of each case, the strictly obiter observations contained in those two sentences laid the basis for a new line of authority.

In contrast with the stable state of the law up until then, development followed rapidly on the heels of *Braddish*. In *Dunne v DPP*[17] the applicant was charged with robbery of a filling station, on the basis of a written statement he had allegedly made when he had been detained on suspicion of having committed other offences.

By a majority (McGuinness and Hardiman JJ), the Supreme Court allowed the applicant's appeal and prohibited his trial. It held that it was the duty of the Gardaí to seek out and preserve all evidence having a bearing or potential bearing on the issue of guilt or innocence. This was so whether the prosecution proposed to rely on the evidence or not, and regardless of whether it assisted the case the prosecution was advancing or not. Thus, it was irrelevant whether or not the video evidence had been in the possession of An Garda Síochána.

Fennelly J did not agree with the proposition that it was irrelevant whether or not the evidence had been given to An Garda Síochána. In his dissenting judgment he stated that the evidence, which had existed, may have ceased to exist before trial for a multitude of reasons. The Court would not interfere save where the missing evidence had been in the hands of the prosecution. Had it been established that the contested video evidence had been given to An Garda Síochána, the Court could interfere.

The applicant had given evidence that the gardaí had had possession of or access to the video recordings. Detective Kenny had given evidence that a video recording was never given to any member of An Garda Síochána.

Fennelly J stated that '[t]he applicant has produced no direct evidence that the video was given to the Gardaí, but relies on inferences to be gathered from the evidence of Mr. Torley. Detective Garda Kenny, on the other hand, swears positively that it was never in his possession or of the prosecution'.

[16] *Braddish v DPP* [2001] 3 IR 127, 135, emphasis added.
[17] [2002] 2 IR 305.

He continued:

> I do not think that Mr. Torley can be said to negative the clear and repeated statements of Detective Garda Kenny that neither the video nor any record in connection with it was at any time in the possession of the prosecution. The applicant cannot simply ask the court to disregard this evidence. On the authorities, it is clear that the burden of proof is on the applicant.[18]

Although Hardiman J did not disagree with the thrust of Fennelly J's findings on the facts, he drew the opposite conclusion, namely that An Garda Síochána had in all likelihood had possession of the tapes, despite the sworn evidence of Det. Garda Kenny to the contrary.[19]

Thus, whilst on Hardiman J's view of the evidence *Dunne* and *Braddish* appear to be indistinguishable, Fennelly J drew a clear distinction between those cases. As a consequence it may be observed that, on his own analysis, Hardiman J's observations on the duty to seek out evidence were obiter, since according to him, *Dunne* was a case where An Garda Síochána had failed to retain material having a potential evidential value, whilst on Fennelly J's view his pronouncements on this point were part of the ratio of his judgment since it had never been shown that An Garda Síochána had the material in their possession but rather that they had failed to seek it out.

Hardiman J described the issue before the Court in the following terms:

> The applicant argued that the failure by the Gardaí to preserve the said video recording until the applicant had had an opportunity to inspect same amounted to a breach of the respondent's common law obligation to preserve evidence potentially relevant to the issue of the guilt or innocence of the applicant.
>
> This case does not challenge any of these developments. It seeks to take them further. It raises the question, is it open to the authorities on whom such wide powers and resources have been conferred by law or by technology, to decide in a particular case, that they will not use them? Alternatively, if for no stated reason the authorities simply do not avail of some technical assistance in the detection of crime, which might have inculpated or exculpated the suspect, is this relevant to their ability to prosecute using evidence of a more traditional sort?[20]

Hardiman J held that the duty to seek out and preserve evidence included a duty to ascertain the existence of evidence. Furthermore, to distinguish between cases where evidence had been seized and where it had not 'would constitute a positive incentive to investigators not to seize or request permission to take evidence which might contradict their suspicions or undermine the reliability of other evidence.'

This was a new departure. An Garda Síochána was henceforth under a duty to seek out evidence that might be relevant to the guilt of an accused. In this context Hardiman J laid particular emphasis on the importance of video evidence as 'real evidence' and the 'precise equivalent' of eyewitness testimony.

[18] Judgment of Fennelly J 334–336.
[19] Judgment of Hardiman J, 315.
[20] N 17 above, 310.

Hardiman J relied on *R v Swingler*, a case where an alleged rape had been committed beside a bridge.[21]

The detective constable was given to understand that the cameras on the bridge belonged to the British Transport Police. When she contacted them she was informed that the cameras in question were not switched on and were not working at the time. She therefore took no further action. The fact that the cameras were working at the material time was not discovered until a month after the alleged offence, by which time the film had been reused. The Court held that some element of bad faith, or at the very least some serious fault, on the part of the police was required in order to stay the trial.

Hardiman J had in his judgments raised objection to the requirement that bad faith or a serious fault be proven in order to establish the impossibility of a fair trial. However, in *Swingler* Rougier J also took other factors into account. He went on to consider the prospect of a fair trial in terms of the effect of the loss of the evidence and that there was a considerable body of further evidence, credible witnesses within earshot, evidence that the police found the woman in a state of distress, credible medical evidence, and so forth.

Rougier J questioned the significance of the loss of the video evidence.

> The fact of the matter is that there had been evidence of potentially great significance but that evidence had disappeared. To us there seems to be no distinction in principle between that and the situation where perhaps there was one eye witness who could have told where the truth lay but had unfortunately died before a statement could be taken from him. The evidence simply is not there. The jury had to do their best with the evidence that was there.

This is an interesting view which was reflected (albeit in the context of delay, as distinct from missing evidence) in the recent decision of *Kennedy v DPP*,[22] a case in which some witnesses were deceased. Here Clarke J held that any impairment which the applicant might suffer from in the presentation of his defence falls a long way short of the standard which would allow a court to conclude that it was not possible for him to get a fair trial. He took the view that:

> 5.6 … in balancing the public interest in stateable criminal prosecutions being tried on the merits with the entitlement of the accused to due process, it is at least arguable that a trial should only be prohibited on the basis of what I might call "no fault impossibility of fair trial" if it is clear to the court which is invited to prohibit the trial that a fair trial is not possible. My reason for suggesting that high threshold is that, in a case where the problems which the accused faces do not derive from any culpable prosecutorial delay, the public interest requires that there be a trial unless the level of impairment of the accused's ability to mount a defence is so great that the court is satisfied that a fair trial is not possible. It seems to me that it is only at that threshold that prohibition, in the absence of culpable prosecutorial delay, is a proportionate response to the difficulties of the accused.

In *Swingler*, defending the court's requirement of an element of bad faith or serious fault, Rougier J stated:

[21] Court of Appeal of England and Wales, 10th July 1998, unreported.
[22] [2012] IESC 34.

> If it were otherwise every time a significant piece of evidence by accident were not available, a defendant facing a serious charge, which might be supported by other cogent evidence, would effectively be able to avoid it on this somewhat technical ground.

Hardiman J considered the test in *Swingler* an impossible one, which in his view 'positively encourages an omission to seek objective photographic evidence if the prosecution feels they have a plausible confession or other evidence'.

Hardiman J makes a fair point, that investigators might be incentivised not to seize evidence. However it may be observed that the focus of the jurisdiction is on ensuring a fair trial, rather than disciplining the police force.[23] Moreover, as a matter of practical reality it is hard to see how an investigator could be incentivised not to seize video evidence on the grounds that it might contradict his/her suspicions, given that this could only be ascertained by acquiring and viewing the video, by which time it would already be in the investigator's possession and subject to the obligation to be preserved.

In a subsequent case, *Scully v DPP*,[24] Kearns J discusses the judgment of Geoghegan J in *Mitchell v DPP* and concludes:

> This decision confirms my own view that, where evidence has either not been obtained or been lost, which it is contended might have some relevance in establishing guilt or innocence, the Court should not too quickly yield to an application to prohibit a trial, and indeed should not accede to such an application where an explanation is forthcoming for the absence of the evidence and that explanation establishes to the satisfaction of the Court that the evidence or material could have no possible bearing on the guilt or innocence of the accused. The judgment also makes it clear that, subject to the qualifications clearly spelt out by Geoghegan J, the Gardaí must be allowed to function and perform their duties without having impossible requirements heaped upon them. In that case, as in this, the video camera could yield up nothing useful for the reasons stated. On it being established that there is no actual prejudice to an applicant there is, in my view, no basis for prohibiting a trial.

It is worth observing that in *Dunne* Hardiman J was of the view that 'where evidence has been lost to a defendant by reason of delay in prosecuting or loss or destruction by the State, one can only speculate about what its contents might have been. It is extremely difficult, perhaps impossible, to devise a basis on which this entirely speculative element can be incorporated, fairly to both sides, in a trial'. But the question is whether that loss is sufficient to stay a trial. In *Scully* Hardiman J appears to retreat from that position and instead of speculating as to what the evidence might have contained accepted the Garda evidence that the CCTV footage did not cover the area of the forecourt where the robbery had taken place, was of very poor quality and therefore of no evidential value. In like manner Fennelly J in *Dunne* stated that the applicant 'cannot simply ask the court' to disregard the clear and repeated statements on affidavit of the detective that neither the video nor any record in connection with it had been in the possession of the prosecution at any time.

[23] See Hardiman J's own comments in *Scully v DPP* [2005] IESC 11, to the effect that this was not a fault-finding exercise or disciplinary procedure for the prosecution, and what needed to be shown was a real risk of an unfair trial by engaging in a specific way with the evidence actually available.

[24] [2003] IEHC 92.

In the Supreme Court decision in *Scully*,[25] Hardiman J conceded that *Braddish* had been an exceptionally straight-forward case. He referred to Fennelly J's dissenting judgment in *Dunne* and repeated his response to it that the duty had to be interpreted realistically, but he accepted that Fennelly J's apprehension was real and serious, and that it was relevant to this case as the applicant's case was 'remote and fanciful'. On the facts of the case he believed that the CCTV footage in question would not have shown anything and found he 'would refuse relief in the present case because in the uncontroverted circumstances the relevance of the video tape is purely theoretical and the applicant's own delay in seeking it demonstrates his consciousness that this is so.'

In *McFarlane v DPP*, [26] Hardiman J overturned the High Court decision where Ó Caoimh J had felt bound by *Braddish* to grant an order of prohibition, as original fingerprints had been lost although photos of them and a report were available. Hardiman J held that the High Court had applied the test too rigidly without considering the factual differences, that, as there had been a forensic examination of the missing items prior to their disappearance and the results of the forensic analysis had been preserved, the applicant had not been deprived of the reasonable possibility of rebutting the evidence proffered against him, and he had not discharged the onus of proof that there was a real risk that he could not have obtained a fair trial.

In *Savage v DPP*, [27] Fennelly J summarized the principal points relevant to whether a court will make an order prohibiting a trial:

a. It is the duty of the prosecution authorities, in particular An Garda Síochána, to preserve and retain all evidence, which comes into their possession, having a bearing or potential bearing on the issue of guilt or innocence of the accused. This duty flows from their unique investigative role as a police force. (*Braddish* at page 133). The extent to which that duty extends to seeking out evidential material not in the possession of the Gardaí does not arise in the present case (but see *Dunne);*
b. The missing evidence in question must be such as to give rise to a real possibility that, in its absence, the accused will be unable to advance a point material to his defence. This is, like the Garda obligation to retain and preserve evidence, to be interpreted in a practical and realistic way and *"no remote, theoretical or fanciful possibility will lead to the prohibition of a trial." (Dunne* page 323);
c. The fact that the prosecution intends to rely on evidence independent of the missing evidence at issue in order to establish the guilt of the accused does not preclude the making of an order of prohibition. In *Dunne,* the prosecution intended to rely on a confession. This did not defeat the applicant's complaint of the failure of the Gardaí to take possession of a video tape covering the scene of the robbery;
d. The application is considered in the context of all the evidence likely to be put forward at the trial. The court will have regard to the extent to which aspects of the prosecution case are contested. In *Bowes,* the fact that the motor car in which the applicant was alleged to have been travelling had been lost by the Gardaí was insufficient, when the applicant did not contest the fact that he was driving it and

[25] N 23.
[26] [2006] IESC 11.
[27] [2008] IESC 39.

the charge related to possession of drugs found in the boot of the car. In *McGrath*, the court had regard to the *"circumstantial"* character of the prosecution case of dangerous driving. In *McFarlane*, the existence of photographic evidence of the missing fingerprints was highly material to the complaint that the original items had been lost by the Gardaí;

e. The applicant must show, by reference to the case to be made by the prosecution, in effect the book of evidence, how the allegedly missing evidence will affect the fairness of his trial. Hardiman J said in *McFarlane* (page 144) that:

   'In order to demonstrate that risk there is obviously a need for an applicant to engage in a specific way with the evidence actually available so as to make the risk apparent.'

f. Whether the applicant, through his solicitor or otherwise makes a timely request of the prosecution for access to or an opportunity to have the articles at issue expertly examined may be highly material. In *Bowes*, the "very belated" request was critical to the refusal of relief. On the other hand, in *Dunne*, no request was made until some five months after charge, and long after there was any possibility of producing the video tape. In that case, however, Hardiman J stated (at page 325):

   'There is......a responsibility on a defendant's advisers, with their special knowledge and information, to request material thought by them to be relevant.'

   However, a suspect or an accused person will be unable to make a timely request, if the Gardaí have destroyed or parted with possession of the material. Thus, they must give consideration to the likely interests of the defence before making such decisions;

g. The essential question, at all times, is whether there is a real risk of an unfair trial. (*Scully* page 257). The court should focus on that issue and *'not on whose fault it is that the evidence is missing, and what the degree of that fault may be.'* (*Dunne* page 322).

These principles were set out and repeated in many cases that followed, for example *CD v DPP* [28] and *Byrne v DPP*.[29]

In *CD v DPP*, Fennelly J referred to the fact that the Supreme Court had heard no less than eight missing evidence appeals in less than two years. His prediction in *Dunne* anticipating 'a rash of applications for prohibition wherever video evidence is not produced' having come to pass, he observed that '[i]t is not easy to avoid the suspicion that a practice has developed of trawling through the book of evidence in search of the silver bullet—rather the absent missing bullet—which can put a stop to any trial.'

He emphasised the jurisdiction to prohibit a trial would only be exercised exceptionally, citing a number of delay cases but saying the same principle applies, that a real risk must be shown by engaging specifically with the evidence and that the risk was one that could not be overcome by appropriate directions by the trial judge.

In *McHugh v DPP*, [30] Fennelly J held that on the particular facts, whereby a lost CCTV video formed the basis of the identification of the accused and the only evidence retained by the Gardaí were photo stills taken from the tape,

[28] [2009] IESC 70.
[29] [2010] IESC 54.
[30] [2009] IESC 15.

there was a real risk to the fairness of the trial. Noting that 'all depends on the particular facts', he emphasized that this did not mean photo stills taken from a missing video were generally inadmissible.

> Ultimately, the Court has agreed to consider the entire matter on the basis that the sole issue is whether the Respondent has established that, in the absence of any possibility of access to the original *moving* CCTV footage, there is a real risk that he will not have an [un]fair[31] trial. No other point is now raised. The Director does not contest the correctness of the basis on which judicial review was sought. Nor does he dispute – and the Court does not decide – that the Gardaí should have sought the original CCTV footage. He contests the case only on the basis that the Respondent has not demonstrated that there is a real risk to the fairness of his trial.

In *Byrne v DPP*,[32] O'Donnell J again reiterated that *Braddish* was an exceptionally straight-forward case (conceded also by Hardiman in *Scully*), and that the modern law is synthesised in the judgment of Fennelly J in *Savage* in a passage with which Hardiman J expressed agreement. He referred to Fennelly's judgment in *CD v DPP* in which he states that the jurisdiction is only exercised in exceptional circumstances, that context of the evidence is important, that evidence is never perfect and that neither prosecution nor defence can be assured that all conceivable evidence will be available. He also refers to Fennelly's suggestion there that in *McHugh* it might have been left to the trial judge to decide whether to exclude evidence rather than prohibit the trial.

The position has now been reached, he said, that other than perhaps the very straight-forward cases like *Braddish* it would require something exceptional to prohibit a trial. On reading the judgment of O'Donnell J (with whom Fennelly and Finnegan JJ agreed), one might be forgiven for thinking that the Supreme Court has tacitly abandoned the view of the majority in *Dunne.*

In the most recent judgment in this area, *Wall v DPP*, [33] O'Donnell J, with whom three of his colleagues agreed, stated:

> I am not convinced that the majority decision in *Dunne*, even as qualified by McGuinness J, should be taken merely by a process of repetition without analysis to represent an established principle of Irish law. If there is to be such a principle, then it is one which, in my view, should be deduced by a rigorous analysis of case law and a close consideration of principle. Such a process might consider if any distinction is to be drawn between cases where evidence has not been obtained, obtained but lost, obtained but not disclosed, or positively suppressed, and the role culpability on the part of the police and the materiality of any evidence lost, not found, not disclosed or even suppressed, might have in such an analysis. By referring to culpability I do not intend to suggest that a trial will only become unfair if there is deliberate wrongdoing by the police. Rather it seems to me arguable that the blameworthiness of the failure to find or retain evidence, whether deliberate, reckless negligent or careless is a factor to be taken into account together with the materiality of the evidence. Any test must carefully address the very difficult issues which arise in cases

[31] Typographical error in the original judgment.
[32] [2010] IESC 54.
[33] [2013] IESC 56.

> such as this, where there are a number of competing and sometimes irreconcilable considerations.

He continued:

> For my part I fully agree with the observations of Fennelly J in *Dunne*:
> 'All this takes place in the context of a possible trial and it is of the greatest importance that the Courts ensure that the police force behaves with impeccable fairness in its handling of evidence.'
> …
> However I am unconvinced that this proper approach should mean that cases of missing evidence should be approached on the basis of an assumption of police suppression of evidence.

This was a point made forcefully by Fennelly J in *Dunne*, when he stated that the applicant could not ask the court to disregard the evidence of the detective who stated that neither the video nor any record in connection with it was at any time in the possession of the prosecution.

O'Donnell J states of the decision in the *Dunne* case:

> McGuinness J. may have qualified the test somewhat in acknowledging that Fennelly J.'s anxieties in dissent were reasonable and dangers did exist. It was essential therefore that the duty on the part of Gardaí to seek out relevant evidence should not be too widely interpreted. Citing the judgment of Hardiman J. in Braddish, she approved the statement that "the duty must be interpreted realistically on the facts of each case" (p. 309). This qualification, understandable in itself, may risk introducing a further level of uncertainty into an already notoriously difficult test and thus increasing the chances of protracted applications for judicial review, and appeals to this court, with consequent delays. If this can be demonstrated to be an unavoidable consequence of a trial in due course of law then it must be accepted unhesitatingly, but, at a minimum, the conclusion deserves some thoughtful scrutiny.

It would appear from all that followed *Dunne* that the Supreme Court has effectively (if not formally) limited, to the point of having abandoned for all practical purposes, the imposition of a duty to 'seek out' evidence, thereby at least in practice vindicating the position adopted by Fennelly J in *Dunne*.

When considering the analysis of *Dunne*, O'Donnell J remarked:

> In my view there remains much wisdom in the observations of Chief Justice Evans Hughes when asked at an earlier fraught period in American legal history whether he was a conservative or a liberal. He replied that he set little store by such terms, saying that 'such characteristics are not infrequently used to foster prejudice. They serve as a very poor substitute for intelligent criticism. The judge who does his work in an objective spirit as a judge should, will address himself conscientiously to each case and will not trouble himself about labels'.

That in my view is what makes a great judge. Fennelly J will be sorely missed.

PART IV: TRANSVERSAL ISSUES OF NATIONAL AND EUROPEAN LAW

17

Union and Common Law: Harmony or Tension

FRANK CLARK*

UP AND UNTIL the accession of Ireland and the United Kingdom to the then European Economic Community on 1 January 1973, what has now become the European Union was exclusively a group of civil law countries. Since then, of course, two further Member States with at least significant common law influence, being Malta and Cyprus, have joined. It is also almost trite to remark that European law itself has developed extensively in the intervening period. Now may, therefore, be an appropriate point to give some consideration as to how the common law has interacted with Union law.

It is important to start by emphasising that the purpose of this article is not to compare and contrast the common law with the civil law. That is, at least in academic circles concerned with comparative law, a relatively well trodden path although it might be argued that amongst practitioners (including many judges) knowledge of the 'other' system is often highly generalised and sometimes even inaccurate. Indeed it is, perhaps, worth reflecting that the four Member States which have common law traditions are the only four Member States that consist entirely (if one disregards the vexed question of Gibraltar) of an island or islands off the European mainland. Perhaps, on both sides, there has been something of the 'fog in channel, continent cut off' mentality.

Union law is not, at least in express terms, either a civil or a common law system although it has been suggested (sometimes as a criticism) that the civil law tradition has tended to dominate in the development of European law. One particular example, to which I will return, stems from the measures adopted first in the Brussels Convention,[1] which was, of course, strictly speaking outside the ambit of Union law, and subsequently legislated for in the Brussels Regulation.[2] These measures sought to harmonise many of the rules concerning private

* Judge of the Irish Supreme Court and adjunct Professor at Trinity College, Dublin

[1] 1968 Brussels Convention on jurisdiction and the enforcement of judgments in civil and commercial matters.

[2] Council Regulation (EC) No 44/2001 of 22 December 2000 on jurisdiction and the recognition and enforcement of judgments in civil and commercial matters (OJ [2001] L12/1).

international law insofar as same applies to jurisdiction and recognition of judgments between States. Some academic commentators were particularly critical of the interpretation of those measures by the Court of Justice in cases such as *Owusu v Jackson*[3] which were suggested to represent an inappropriate ignoring of the common law position.

Furthermore, it is important to acknowledge that many who grow up in the common law system tend to see civil law jurisdictions as being all the same. That is far from the case. I was struck, on visiting in June 2013, the Naczelny Sąd Administracyjny (The Supreme Administrative Court of Poland) by an intriguing history lesson generously given to me by its president, Judge Roman Marek Hauser. President Hauser explained that, when Poland became an independent country in the immediate aftermath of the Great War (1922), a choice had to be made as to the form of administrative law to be applied. From the Polish perspective the choice was between the French model, of which Poles had experience in those parts of the then new Poland which had been part of Tsarist Russia, and to both the German and Austro-Hungarian models, which had applied in other parts of what had then become Poland. All of these were civil law jurisdictions. There were, however, radical differences involving a serious choice for those in charge of establishing an administrative law regime in the then newly independent Poland. It was a lesson for a common lawyer to learn not to treat all civil law jurisdictions as being substantively the same.

As a further example some, but not all, civil law jurisdictions require an impairment of right before a public law challenge can be maintained.[4] It is striking to note the extent to which those areas of court process which have been the subject of harmonisation by Union legislation (such as the measures implemented to comply with the Union's obligations under the Aarhus Convention[5]) have led to some problems in all countries but not necessarily the same ones in each. While the problems encountered in the common law countries (principally costs and, perhaps to a lesser extent, the intensity of review) are not necessarily mirrored in other countries, there are significant differences as and between civil law traditions with some, for example, finding it difficult to accommodate the broad standing rules required under Aarhus. Others find difficulty with remedies and still more struggle with the requirement that there be a potential for court review of both substantive and procedural legality.

It is important, therefore, in assessing how European law has itself developed and interacted with the legal traditions of its Member States, to acknowledge that such analysis is not confined simply to assessing the interaction of common law countries with a European law which has developed in a Europe

[3] Case C-281/02 *Owusu v Jackson* [2005] ECR I-1383.

[4] See, for example in the case of Germany, Case C-115/09 *Bund für Umwelt und Naturschutz Deutschland, Landesverband Nordrhein-Westfalen eV v Bezirksregierung Arnsberg* [2011] ECR I-3673; for further information, see European Network of Environmental Law Organisations, Report on Access to Justice in Environmental Matters, 2010.

[5] Directive 2003/35/EC of the European Parliament and of the Council of 26 May 2003 providing for public participation in respect of the drawing up of certain plans and programmes relating to the environment and amending with regard to public participation and access to justice Council Directives 85/337/EEC and 96/61/EC ([2003] OJ L156/17).

consisting of a significant majority of civil law jurisdictions. Those separate civil law jurisdictions have their own differences with one another. Each of those differences has had the potential to have some influence on the development of European law. Likewise, the interaction of European law with those civil law Member States is by no means uniform, not least because there are many strands to the civil law tradition operating within Europe. That is not, however, to say that the topic of this paper may not concern the most striking potential tension.

Before analysing what seems to me to be some of the more important areas of interaction it is, perhaps, also appropriate to note that the common law countries are not, in themselves, homogenous. Unlike the United Kingdom, Ireland has a written Constitution. While that Constitution indirectly recognises the common law,[6] it might, nonetheless, be argued that, as a matter of Irish constitutional theory, the common law in Ireland is not a free-standing body of law but rather one which owes its legal authority to its recognition in the Constitution. Likewise, the United Kingdom itself is not entirely a common law jurisdiction, for Scotland has a civil law system although its court processes more closely resemble those found in the common law world. Likewise, aspects of the law in Malta, such as the criminal law, are now fully codified, and thus Malta could be regarded as a civil law jurisdiction to an extent.

But the fact remains that, however analysed, there are significant features of broad difference between the common law and civil law traditions. European law seeks, within its increasing areas of competence, to impose either a uniform or at least a harmonised legal regime. The real question which this paper seeks to address is how that European legal regime, as it has evolved, interacts with common law jurisdictions. I will turn in due course to the important area of public and administrative law. There is, in my view, a strong argument for suggesting that it is in this area that there has been the greatest interaction and potential for tension. It is, of course, through administrative law that the Court of Justice[7] exercises its judicial protection role in respect of Union legislative and other measures. Given the wide range of areas where competence is jointly vested in Union institutions and those of Member States, it is hardly surprising that administrative law, as it is interpreted at the European level, has the potential to have significant influence in the very many and increasing areas in which the administration of Member States involves actions which are 'within the scope of European law' and thus subject to European law principles. However, before going on to consider how administrative law in the common law tradition has interacted with European public law some other areas are worth analysing. While many areas could be considered, I have chosen to analyse the interpretation of documents affecting legal rights; the foundations of the law

[6] Article 50.1 of Bunreacht na hÉireann provides:

Subject to this Constitution and to the extent to which they are not inconsistent therewith, the laws in force in Saorstát Éireann immediately prior to the date of the coming into operation of this Constitution shall continue to be of full force and effect until the same or any of them shall have been repealed or amended by enactment of the Oireachtas.

[7] For convenience, I will only refer to the Court of Justice, though of course my remarks apply equally to the other Union courts should they have to consider these matters.

and the codification, at EU level, of areas of law which, at common law, are exclusively or largely case-based.

TEXT AND CONTEXT

One striking and much debated area of potential difference between the approach of the civil and common law systems (at least historically) has been in relation to the proper approach to the interpretation of documents which can affect legal rights. Such documents can extend from constitutions and international treaties at one end of the spectrum, through legislative measures whether primary or secondary, to private but legally binding instruments of greater or lesser formality (stretching from complex contracts to the simple rules of a members club or organisation). At least in the past, it might be said with some force that the common law approach to interpretation was heavily text-oriented. From a common law perspective, civil law countries adopted a much more purpose-based system of interpretation. How has Union law itself approached these questions and what divergence remains between the approach of the Court of Justice and the courts of common law jurisdictions?

I think it is important to start by recognising that there has been quite a marked movement in the approach in common law countries over recent decades. While that movement is not uniform and does not necessarily apply in equal measure to the interpretation of different types of legally binding instruments, nonetheless it can, I think, be said to reflect a general movement. In Ireland, the approach to the construction of contracts and other similar documents has evolved in line with a similar change in the United Kingdom. For instance, in the Irish case of *LAC Minerals Ltd v Chevron*,[8] which concerned the interpretation of an ambiguous pre-emption clause, Keane J endorsed an approach which took into account the surrounding circumstances, ie the factual matrix in which the agreement was concluded. A similar approach can be seen in the speech of Lord Hoffman in *Investors' Compensation Scheme v West Bromich Building Society*[9], where he said:

> [S]ome general remarks about the principles by which contractual documents are nowadays construed. I do not think the fundamental change which has overtaken this branch of the law … is always sufficiently appreciated. The result has been, subject to one important exception, to assimilate the way in which such documents are interpreted by judges to the common sense principles by which any serious utterance would be interpreted in ordinary life. Almost all the old intellectual baggage of 'legal' interpretation has been discarded.

But that development is not confined to private law. The Oireachtas has enacted changes to Irish statutory interpretation law. Under section 5(1) of the Interpretation Act 2005, when construing 'a provision of any Act (other than a

[8] *LAC Minerals Ltd v Chevron Mineral Corp of Ireland (CMCI) and Ivernia West plc* (Unreported, High Court, 6 August, 1993).

[9] *Investors' Compensation Scheme v West Bromich Building Society* [1998] 1 All ER 98.

provision that relates to the imposition of a penal or other sanction)' which is obscure, ambiguous, or absurd on a literal interpretation, 'the provision shall be given a construction that reflects the plain intention of the Oireachtas or parliament concerned, as the case may be, where that intention can be ascertained from the Act as a whole'. A similar rule applies to the interpretation of statutory instruments. Section 6 is also noteworthy in this context. It provides that:

> In construing a provision of any Act or statutory instrument, a court may make allowances for any changes in the law, social conditions, technology, the meaning of words used in that Act or statutory instrument and other relevant matters, which have occurred since the date of the passing of that Act or the making of that statutory instrument, but only in so far as its text, purpose and context permit.

The position may now have been reached in Ireland where the overall approach to the construction of documents which can affect legal rights and obligations has moved a long way from a narrow textual analysis. That is not, of course, to say that text is unimportant. The text is, after all, the language in which the relevant legal rights and obligations have been defined by whatever party or parties are involved. Indeed, it has been suggested that part of the context in which the text should be viewed is the nature of the document in which the text appears. The fact that text forms part of, for example, a statute in whose drafting one would not expect loose language or error is itself part of the context by reference to which the statute should be construed. How then does this admittedly adapted form of construction, now current in the common law world, fit in with the way in which similar questions of construction would be approached by the Court of Justice?

It is perhaps appropriate to start by noting that the principal, even dominant, interpretative role of the Court of Justice is in relation to EU legal measures. While it is, of course, a well established principle of EU law that national courts should strive to construe national law so as to bring same into conformity with the obligations of the relevant Member State under EU law,[10] nonetheless the job of construing either national legal measures or private measures which may fall for interpretation as part of the underlying proceedings, lies on the national courts. The Court of Justice becomes involved when it is necessary to give a definitive interpretation of EU measures. It is, from a common law perspective, a curiosity that, in recent times, the Court of Justice has been criticised by the *Bundesverfassungsgericht* (German Constitutional Court) for adopting an excessively teleological approach[11] and has also been criticised by a number

[10] Case C-106/89 *Marleasing SA v La Comercial Internacional de Alimentacion SA* [1991] ECR I-4135.

[11] An example of this criticism can be seen in *Brunner v The European Union Treaty* [1994] 1 CMLR 57, concerning the Maastricht Treaty, where the Bundesverfassungsgericht stated at para 99:

> Whereas a dynamic extension of the existing Treaties has so far been supported on the basis of an open-handed treatment of Article 235 of the EEC Treaty as a 'competence to round off the Treaty' as a whole, and on the basis of considerations relating to the 'implied powers' of the Communities, and of Treaty interpretation as allowing maximum exploitation of Community powers (*effet utile*), in future it will have to be noted as regards interpretation of enabling provisions by Community institutions and agencies that the Union Treaty as a matter of principle

of academic commentators[12] for adopting an overly text-based approach in its construction of the Treaties in *Pringle v Ireland*.[13] The idea that academic commentators, at least some of whom come from a common law tradition, accuse the Court of Justice of an over-textual approach while civil law courts are concerned about an over-teleological approach might suggest that the Court of Justice just can't win. It may, also, however, reflect one difficulty with which the Court of Justice is faced. In most national legal systems, all of those involved are at least initially trained in accordance with their national legal culture and are brought up in that culture. Doubtless many are influenced by comparative ideas from other jurisdictions. But there is at least a national legal culture which is bound to exercise significant influence over the way in which many questions, not least the construction of legally binding documents, is to be approached. While there is a growing and substantial body of specifically EU legislation and case law, and while there are many lawyers, both academic and practitioner, who have acquired significant expertise in European law, nonetheless, it may not yet be appropriate to speak of there being an EU legal culture which has anything like the permanence and influence of many national legal cultures. The development of an EU legal culture might reasonably be described as a work in progress.

There can be little doubt that the way in which EU legal instruments are drafted appears alien to a common law eye unattuned to European law. So much was apparent from the decision of Lord Denning MR in *Bulmer Ltd v Bollinger S.A.*[14], where he discussed the interpretation of European legal instruments:

> What a task is thus set before us! The Treaty is quite unlike any of the enactments to which we have become accustomed. The draftsmen of our statutes have striven to express themselves with the utmost exactness. They have tried to foresee all possible circumstances that may arise and to provide for them. They have sacrificed style and simplicity. They have foregone brevity. They have become long and involved. In consequence, the judges have followed suit. They interpret a statute as applying only to the circumstances covered by the very words. They give them a literal interpretation. If the words of the statute do not cover a new situation – which was not foreseen – the Judges hold that they have no power to fill the gap. To do so would be a 'naked usurpation of the legislative power', ... The gap must remain open until Parliament finds time to fill it.
>
> How different is this Treaty. It lays down general principles. It expresses its aims and purposes. All in sentences of moderate length and commendable style. But it lacks

> distinguishes between the exercise of a sovereign power conferred for limited purposes and the amending of the Treaty, so that its interpretation may not have effects that are equivalent to an extension of the Treaty. Such an interpretation of enabling rules would not produce any binding effects for Germany.

This stance appears to have softened in recent years; see also in this volume W Heusel, 'Preserving national identity: the *Bundesverfassungsgericht* between national constitutional constraints and an ever closer European Union'.

[12] For example, see PP Craig (2013) '*Pringle*: Legal Reasoning, Text, Purpose and Teleology' 20 *Maastricht Journal of European and Comparative Law* 1.

[13] Case C-370/12 *Pringle v Government of Ireland, Ireland and the Attorney General*, judgment of 27 November 2012.

[14] *Bulmer Ltd v Bollinger SA* [1974] 2 All ER 1226.

> precision. It uses words and phrases without defining what they mean. An English lawyer would look for an interpretation clause, but he would look in vain. There is none. All the way through the Treaty there are gaps and lacunae. These have to be filled in by the judges, or by regulations or directives. It is the European way. …
>
> Likewise the regulations and directives. They are enacted by the Council sitting in Brussels for everyone to obey. They are quite unlike our statutory instruments. They have to give the reasons on which they are based (Article 190). So they start off with pages of preambles, 'whereas' and 'whereas' and 'whereas'. These show the purpose and intent of the regulations and directives. Then follow the provisions which are to be obeyed. Here again words and phrases are used without defining their import. … In case of difficulty, recourse is had to the preambles. These are useful to show the purpose and intent behind it all. But much is left to the judges. The enactments give only an outline plan. The details are to be filled in by the judges.
>
> Seeing these differences, what are the English courts to do when they are faced with a problem of interpretation? They must follow the European pattern. No longer must they examine the words in meticulous detail. No longer must they argue about the precise grammatical sense. They must look to the purpose or intent. To quote the words of the European Court in the Da Costa case (1963) 2 C.M.L.R. at page 237, they must limit themselves to deducing from 'the wording and the spirit of the treaty the meaning of the Community rules.' They must not confine themselves to the English text. They must consider, if need be, all the authentic texts, of which there are now eight, see Sociale Verzekeringsbank (1968) 7 C.M.L.R. 151. They must divine the spirit of the treaty and gain inspiration from it. If they find a gap, they must fill it as best they can. They must do what the framers of the instrument would have done if they had thought about it. So we must do the same. Those are the principles, as I understand it, on which the European Court acts.

To Lord Denning's common law eye, EU legal instruments were, doubtless, impossibly vague and quite likely to be interpreted in ways which a traditional common lawyer might well find strange. I think it can, perhaps, be said that EU legislation has become somewhat more specific and that there has been a broadening of everyone's understanding as to how such legislation is likely to be interpreted. But there is also a difficulty in the legislative process in the EU in ensuring that legislation is legally coherent as well as reflecting whatever political balances (whether between the representatives of the Member States on the Council of Ministers or between the Council of Ministers, the Commission and increasingly the European Parliament) may be negotiated. It may even be that the continuing problems with European legislation which concern common lawyers are now as much a problem of ensuring legal coherence in the European legislative system as ones deriving from different approaches to the construction of the legislation. That is not to say that the approach to interpreting European legislation has somehow merged with the common law approach. However, the two are not as far apart as they might once have been and, perhaps equally importantly, there is a greater understanding among common lawyers who have to deal with areas of European legislation, as to the proper approach to be taken. It might be appropriate to characterise the situation as now being one where there has been a partial narrowing of the gap at the theoretical level and a greater understanding of how to apply the different methods of interpretation at a practical level.

Two further minor points might be made. First, it must be acknowledged that, in drafting Union legislation, a problem is often encountered in providing for measures which can fit, with the minimum difficulty, into the differing legal systems of the Member States. EU measures can often be criticised, legitimately in my view, for being excessively vague and imprecise. The difficulties of interpretation which such broadly drafted measures give rise to are commonplace and may well be more extreme in the common law world where practitioners and judges alike are used to legislation which has a much greater level of specification. However, it does have to be acknowledged that the more detailed Union measures may be, the greater the risk of unintended consequences. This is all the more so where the Union measures are designed to integrate into an existing national legal regime in the area concerned rather than provide an entirely free-standing Union regime in a newly developed area. It seems likely that there will always have to be some compromise between the desire for measures to be drafted with greater specification, and thus ease of construction, on the one hand, and the need for measures which are sufficiently broad and flexible to be capable of being adapted, without too much difficulty and without risk of unintended consequences, into the disparate regimes of the Member States, on the other.

The second point is to note that there may well be an emerging trend for contractual documents with an international aspect to be drafted in what one might loosely call a common law way. The fact that many major multinational corporations operate from common law jurisdictions undoubtedly influences this fact. Thus many contracts involving corporations from civil law countries are, in their text, and as to their interpretation, capable of being described as what might loosely be called common law contracts. It seems likely, therefore, that the common law approach to construction will remain, at least in private law matters, an important international legal culture. That culture may well extend beyond the common law world. It has, for example, led to the establishment of parallel common law courts in countries such as the Emirates.[15] The extent to which that fact may have a long term influence on the approach both to drafting and construing legally binding measures within the EU raises an interesting question for the future.

FOUNDATIONS OF THE LAW

The next area of interest is, perhaps, one of fundamental theory or principle. On one view, the common law might be seen as a highly sophisticated version of customary law. The law is what judges have customarily said it to be based on the doctrine of precedent and the hierarchy of courts. On the other hand, a codified civil law system, at least in principle, treats the laws as to be found in those measures, whether constitutional, statutory, or sub-statutory, which have been

[15] See, for example, the Dubai International Financial Centre (DIFC), which is an independent jurisdiction with its own courts under the United Arab Emirates Constitution. It has its own civil and commercial laws, separate to those in force in other parts of the Emirates.

lawfully promulgated. In one sense, the distinction between the two may seem fundamental and radical. As is, however, so often the case, the distinction may be less clear cut in practice. As noted earlier, there is a sense in which the body of case law which formed the common law in Ireland at the time of the 1922 Free State Constitution and the adoption of Bunreacht na hÉireann in 1937 became part of the law of Ireland (unless inconsistent with those Constitutions) because the Constitutions said so. While the courts have recognised that the common law can evolve, there have been many cases where an over-radical alteration in the common law urged on the court has been rejected[16] precisely because it was held to amount to legislation which is, of course, the constitutional prerogative of the Oireachtas[17]. Likewise, within the national legal systems of common law countries, many areas are exclusively governed by legislation while many others, while retaining their original common law character, are increasingly influenced by legislative amendment or codification. Company law and environmental law, for example, are almost exclusively statute based. Employment law, whilst still influenced by the common law character of the contract of employment, is now heavily governed by legislation. It would not, I think, be unfair to now characterise the legal system in Ireland as one which remains loyal to its common law roots but nonetheless has both a constitutional architecture and significant legislative codification which might legitimately lead to the system being characterised as at least somewhat of a hybrid one. That is altogether separate from the influence of Union law on the Irish system.

But how then should one characterise Union law itself? In one sense it might be said that it closely resembles a civil law regime. The ultimate authority for Union law, including Union legislation and the decisions of the Court of Justice, is to be found in the treaties. The measures adopted by the Union legislature form the basis of Union law itself. However, it might also be argued that aspects of the way in which Union law has developed have characteristics in common with the common law tradition. Many of the fundamental principles of Union law are to be found in the case law of the Court of Justice and are not, at least directly, in specific and detailed legal measures. While the Court of Justice does not adopt a formal common law like doctrine of precedent, the system is, in many ways, not entirely dissimilar. The Court frequently relies on its own jurisprudence.[18] It does

[16] See for instance *L v L* [1992] 2 IR 77 where the Supreme Court considered the decision of Barr J in the High Court declaring that a wife was entitled to a 50% beneficial interest in the family home by virtue of the equality of spouses in a marriage. This was overturned on the basis that it amounted to a judicial usurpation of the legislative power. Finlay CJ, in his judgment, concluded

> that to identify this right in the circumstances set out in this case is not to develop any known principle of the common law, but is rather to identify a brand new right and to secure it to the plaintiff. Unless that is something clearly and unambiguously warranted by the Constitution or made necessary for the protection of either a specified or unspecified right under it, it must constitute legislation and be a usurpation by the courts of the function of the legislature.

[17] Article 15.2.1 of Bunreacht na hÉireann provides:

> The sole and exclusive power of making laws for the State is hereby vested in the Oireachtas: no other legislative authority has power to make laws for the State.

[18] See, for example, Joined Cases C-143/88 and C-92/89, *Zuckerfabrik Süderdithmarschen AG v Hauptzollampt Itzehoe and Zuckerfabrik Soest GmbH v Hauptzollampt Paderborn* [1991] ECR I-415 at paras 17–19, and Case C-167/01 *Inspire Art* [2003] ECR I-10155 at para 62.

not lightly depart from well settled and established principles to be found in its case law. It regards the law, as it interprets it in accordance with its case law, to be part of Union law which is required to be applied in each Member State through national courts. Thus, in practice, the decisions of the Court of Justice have a status which in many respects is not unlike the decisions of a court of final appeal in a common law system.

Indeed, aspects of the way in which the jurisprudence of the Court of Justice has evolved in this regard have sometimes been questioned in certain civil law countries, not least the Scandinavian ones. I have frequently heard it suggested at meetings of national judges that, to the eyes of those from such civil law systems, the heavy reliance on judge made law is seen to grate with their own approach which would see such an approach as inconsistent with the heavy democratic weight to be placed on legislative measures. Just as, therefore, there is a sense in which the common law in Ireland has morphed into something of a hybrid system, Union law, as it has evolved, also has material characteristics of a hybrid system.

CODIFICATION

Codification is, of course, in itself, nothing new in the common law world. As noted earlier the common law system of Malta now has a codified criminal law. From time to time various areas, previously governed by traditional case law, have been codified in one common law country or another to a greater or lesser extent. It can hardly be said, therefore, that the codification of one or more common law areas creates, of itself, any tension within the common law system.

Where the Union legislature seeks to provide a comprehensive code in an area traditionally governed, in common law countries, by judge made law, at least some potential for tension does, however, arise. In many common law systems codification represents the enactment of legislation which, at least to a large extent, broadly seeks to express in legislative form the law as it had developed in accordance with common law principles. It is true that sometimes the opportunity may be taken to bring about some change. However, in the main, codification often represents a change in the source of law (from the law reports to the statute book) rather than any major change in the substantive law itself. Codification at the EU level, however, is likely to give effect to much more significant changes of substance for it is unlikely that any scheme which emerges through the Union legislature will substantively reflect a pre-existing common law treatment of the area in question.

Perhaps one of the best examples of such a process in practice is the adoption of the Brussels Convention and its subsequent incorporation into the Brussels Regulation. Many of the traditional common law principles applicable in the areas of private international law governed by the now Brussels Regulation conferred significant discretion on the courts. On the other hand, an underlying principle behind the Brussels Regulation is to bring a much greater degree of certainty into the process of determining the identity of the courts which are to have jurisdiction.

In *Owusu v Jackson*,[19] the Court of Justice was asked on a preliminary reference by the Court of Appeal of England and Wales whether it was inconsistent with the Brussels Convention (as then governed the situation) for a court of a Contracting State to exercise a discretionary power, available under its national law, to decline to hear proceedings brought against a person domiciled in that State in favour of the courts of a non-Contracting State if the jurisdiction of no other Contracting State under the Convention was in issue and the proceedings had no connecting factors to any other Contracting State? The Court of Justice held that the effect of the Convention was to preclude a court of a Contracting State from declining the jurisdiction conferred on it by Article 2 in those circumstances. Dicey, Morris & Collins suggested that, in coming to this conclusion, the Court of Justice proceeded on a wrong footing, to the effect that 'the doctrine of forum non conveniens might routinely deprive a defendant against his will of the comfort of defending in his own courts'.[20] Some academic commentators have been even more critical, citing this judgment as another example of continental judges on the Court of Justice seeking to 'dismantle the common law' on the conflict of laws.[21]

In my decision in *Goshawk Dedicated Ltd & Ors v Life Receivables Ireland Ltd*,[22] I had to consider the effect of the decision of the Court of Justice in *Owusu* in determining whether there remained a discretion (or perhaps, indeed, an obligation) to decline jurisdiction in favour of a court of a non-Contracting State where (a) proceedings had first been commenced in the court of the non-Contracting State; and (b) the judgment of the court of that non-Contracting State was such that it would, in accordance with the terms of the Regulation, be recognised within the relevant Member State. It was necessary in the course of that decision to consider the history of the accession of Ireland and the United Kingdom to the Brussels Convention. At paragraphs 4.12 and 4.13, I observed:

> 4.12 In addition it is clear from both the judgment of the court and the opinion of Advocate General Léger that a key influence on the decision in Owusu was to be found in the intentions of the contracting parties, both as to the original Brussels Convention and the Accession Convention, whereby, amongst others, Ireland and the United Kingdom acceeded to the Brussels Convention. For the reasons very exhaustively analysed, most

[19] Case C-281/02 *Owusu v Jackson* [2005] ECR I-1383.

[20] L Collins et al *Dicey, Morris and Collins – The Conflict of Laws*, 14th ed (London, Sweet and Maxwell, 2006) at paras 12–20.

[21] See, for example, T Hartley, 'The European Union and the Systematic Dismantling of the Common Law of Conflict of Laws' (2005) 54 *ICLQ* 813:

> This judgment [*Owusu*] is remarkable for its absolute refusal to consider the requirements of reasonableness. If the United Kingdom is a member of the European Union, we obviously have to make adjustments, just like everyone else. In the legal area, this includes giving up our traditional rules in favour of continental-style rules that we may regard as inferior. However, while we have to make sacrifices in order to protect the interests of our continental partners, they should allow us to go our own way where their interests are not affected. This is what was meant above by 'the rule of reason'. The crass insistence that common law rules must be abolished even where no Community interest is at stake is the feature of this judgment that will cause most difficulty for lawyers in England. It seems that the continental judges on the European Court want to dismantle the common law as an objective in its own right. The brushing aside of all practical considerations is also disturbing.

[22] *Goshawk Dedicated Ltd & Ors v Life Receivables Ireland Ltd* [2008] IEHC 90.

particularly in the opinion of Advocate General Léger, it is clear that the original Brussels Convention followed civil law principles for the obvious enough reason that all of the countries then contracting to the Convention were civil law countries. It is also clear that detailed consideration was given to the position of Ireland and the United Kingdom (which had quite different private international law rules concerning these matters) at the time of accession of Ireland and the United Kingdom to the Convention. Notwithstanding that detailed consideration, no material changes in the Convention occurred, either at that time or later, or, indeed, when the terms of the Regulation were formulated. On that basis the obvious conclusion is that a political decision was taken at the time of the accession of Ireland and the United Kingdom to go along with the existing civil law based Brussels Convention.

To the extent that certain common law commentators are critical of the dominance of civil law over common law principles in this field, it can be said that that dominance stems from the fact that the common law jurisdictions acceded to a Convention which had been formulated on civil law principles without any material variation which would have allowed for common law principle to have an appropriate role in relation to judgment recognition after accession.

I concluded that based on the jurisprudence of the Court of Justice that I did not have jurisdiction to stay the proceedings as

> a court in Ireland retains and must exercise a jurisdiction conferred on it by Article 2, notwithstanding the fact that there may be proceedings in a non Member State which are first in time, which involve the same subject matter, and where a judgment from the court of the non Member State would be recognised in Ireland.

This decision has been followed by the High Court in England and Wales.[23]

The sequence of events thereby disclosed is perhaps a salutary lesson. The true reason why, at least in the area governed by the Brussels Convention and subsequently by the Brussels Regulation, the rules might be said to more reflect civil law rather than common law principles stems not from any imposed regime from the Court of Justice. Rather it is that those involved in the relevant negotiations on behalf of Ireland and the United Kingdom either chose not to or were unable to ensure that the harmonised regime as it was to apply after accession reflected the greater level of case by case discretion that was available in the common law system. It is difficult to avoid the conclusion that this is not an isolated case. Measures are proposed at the European legislative level which can have significant effects on common law countries. It does not seem that those effects are always identified in advance so that appropriate amendments can be suggested to enable the measures concerned to fit more readily into a common law system. In many cases a failure to identify and deal with such problems can lead to unintended consequences with which both the Court of Justice and the national courts in common law Member States have to grapple.

[23] *Catalyst Investment Group Ltd v Lewinsohn & Ors* [2009] EWHC 1964 (Ch).

ADMINISTRATIVE LAW

I propose next to turn to administrative law. Judicial review, or its equivalents in other systems, is an essential tool involved in the implementation and enforcement of Union law. Administrative litigation is, of course, also the method by which there is judicial scrutiny over EU measures. That scrutiny can occur in the courts of Member States even though a final determination of legality of EU measures is within the exclusive competence of Union judges. The question which might be asked is as to how an emerging EU administrative law has interacted with traditional common law principles in this field.

Union law, initially in the main because of developments in the jurisprudence of the Court of Justice, but more latterly because of legislative measures which require a specific approach in particular types of administrative litigation (for example, public procurement[24], environmental disputes[25] and services[26]), has forced all national systems to adapt, at least in part, their administrative law regime to the requirements of EU law.

An example, and one of particular resonance in the common law world, is *Factortame*.[27] That case, of course, provides, in its litigation history, a very good example of a common law court struggling to adapt to the requirements of European law. A divisional High Court in England and Wales referred questions concerning UK law relating to the registration of fishing vessels to the European Court of Justice. However, the immediate issue which arose was as to whether an interlocutory injunction could or should be granted which would have the affect of suspending the operation of the law concerned until its compatibility or otherwise with EU law had been determined by the Court of Justice. Such an injunction was granted by the divisional High Court, refused on appeal by the Court of Appeal and refused again on further appeal to the House of Lords although a further reference was made. It is interesting, and a point to which I will return, that Advocate General Tesauro in his opinion delivered on 17 May 1990 noted that an injunction of the type sought by Factortame would be available in all Member States except the UK and Denmark (and, by important implication, therefore, available in Ireland). In its celebrated decision, the Court of Justice held that a national court has a duty to grant interim relief to safeguard an alleged Community right until the decision of the Court of

[24] Directive 2004/17/EC of the European Parliament and of the Council of 31 March 2004 coordinating the procurement procedures of entities operating in the water, energy, transport and postal services sectors ([2004] OJ L134/1), as amended, and Directive 2004/18/EC of the European Parliament and of the Council of 31 March 2004 on the coordination of procedures for the award of public works contracts, public supply contracts and public service contracts, ([2004] OJ L134/114), as amended.

[25] Directive 2003/35/EC of the European Parliament and of the Council of 26 May 2003 providing for public participation in respect of the drawing up of certain plans and programmes relating to the environment and amending with regard to public participation and access to justice Council Directives 85/337/EEC and 96/61/EC ([2003] OJ L156/17).

[26] Directive 2006/123/EC of the European Parliament and of the Council of 12 December 2006 on services in the internal market ([2006] OJ L376/38).

[27] Case C-213/89 *R v Secretary of State for Transport, ex parte Factortame Ltd. and Others* [1990] ECR I-2433.

Justice is available and that, where a rule of national law would deny such relief, such rule must be set aside. The underlying problem was, of course, that in accordance with the common law rules applicable in the United Kingdom it was not considered possible to grant an injunction which would have the effect of disapplying an Act of Parliament on an interlocutory basis pending the result of a reference to the Court of Justice.

As a further, and perhaps striking, example of the fact that the common law as it came to be understood in Ireland (and in particular within the Irish constitutional framework) differed from that in the United Kingdom, it is necessary to emphasise that the Irish courts had come to a different view. In the 1985 case, *Pesca Valentia Ltd v Minister for Fisheries and Forestry, Ireland, and the Attorney* General,[28] fishing licences had been granted to the plaintiffs under the Fisheries Acts[29] on the condition that 75% of the crew were nationals of Member States of the European Community. The plaintiffs were later found to be in contravention of this condition and the master of the offending boat was charged with the offence of fishing otherwise than in accordance with the licence. It was then sought to challenge the underlying section permitting the inclusion of minimum nationality conditions in licences. In both the High Court and, on appeal, the Supreme Court, interlocutory injunctions were granted, restraining the enforcement of the condition attaching to the licences, pending the trial of the action.

However, it is important to emphasise that, in addition to the direct effects of Union case law and legislation, it might be suggested that the exposure which different national systems have had to the administrative law regimes in other Member States has led to some reappraisal of the principles on which judicial supervision of the administration rests.

How has the common law system fared in this interaction? Some specific aspects of deeply embedded parts of the common law system have clearly been challenged. In the environmental field the costs regime has come under detailed and frequently adverse scrutiny. Adequate solutions have yet to be found. The question of undertakings as to damages as the 'price' for interlocutory relief, a fairly fundamental aspect of the common law system, has been challenged.[30] The general discretions which common law judges frequently enjoy have been questioned on the basis of failing to bring sufficient certainty or of failing to afford persons dealing with the system a sufficient degree of predictability. For instance, in Case C-406/08 *Uniplex (UK) Ltd v NHS Business Services,*[31] the ECJ held that the requirement that judicial review proceedings in the UK be brought

[28] *Pesca Valentia Ltd v Minister for Fisheries and Forestry, Ireland, and the Attorney General* [1985] IR 193.

[29] Section 222B of the Fisheries (Consolidation) Act 1959, as inserted by s 2 of the Fisheries (Amendment) Act 1983.

[30] See the opinion of Advocate General Kokott in Case C-530/11 *European Commission v United Kingdom of Great Britain and Northern Ireland* (pending), in which she concluded that the UK had failed to fulfil its obligations under Articles 3(7) and 4(4) of Directive 2003/35 by reason of the fact that its courts may make necessary measures granting interim relief in proceedings covered by those provisions conditional on an undertaking to pay damages.

[31] Case C-406/08 *Uniplex (UK) Ltd v NHS Business Services* [2010] ECR I-817.

'promptly and in any event within three months' gave rise to uncertainty as the possibility existed that a court, in its discretion, could dismiss proceedings even though they were brought within the three month time frame. To that extent, it was held to be an ineffective transposition of Directive 89/665/EEC[32]. The Irish rule was previously in a similar form[33][34]. This has since been altered to remove the express requirement for promptness.[35] Many other examples could be quoted.

Indeed there may well be something of a misunderstanding as to what is truly meant by discretion. I have suggested in *Shell E & P Ireland Ltd v McGrath & ors*[36] that discretion may, in reality, in itself be a somewhat misleading term in so far as it suggests that 'the court is, in any real sense, at large as to whether to grant the remedy or not.' The principle of legal certainty is well recognised as a matter of EU law.[37] At first blush, a wide discretion pulls in the opposite direction to legal certainty. However, the gap may be narrower than first appears.

In *Health Service Executive v M.W. and G.L.*,[38] the Supreme Court had to consider Article 15 of Council Regulation 2201/2003/EC,[39] which provides that

[32] Council Directive of 21 December 1989 on the coordination of the laws, regulations and administrative provisions relating to the application of review procedures to the award of public supply and public works contracts ([1989] OJ L395/33).

[33] Order 84 Rule 21(1) of the Rules of the Superior Courts previously provided:

> An application for leave to apply for judicial review shall be made promptly and in any event within three months from the date when grounds for the application first arose, or six months where the relief sought is certiorari, unless the Court considers that there is good reason for extending the period within which the application shall be made.

[34] One example of where an applicant was refused certiorari for failing to act with a sufficient degree of promptness is *State (Cussen) v Brennan* [1981] IR 181, where there was a gap of four months before the initiation of the proceedings. It should be noted this case predates the six month limit included in the version of the rule quoted above.

[35] Order 84 Rule 21(1) of the Rules of the Superior Courts, as amended by SI No 691 of 2011: Rules of the Superior Courts (Judicial Review) 2011 now provides: '[a]n application for leave to apply for judicial review shall be made within three months from the date when grounds for the application first arose.

[36] *Shell E & P Ireland Ltd v McGrath & ors* [2013] IESC 1. In particular, see para 7.28 where I stated:

> In addition, it does seem to me to be appropriate to comment that the fact that a remedy may be said to be discretionary does not imply that the court is, in any real sense, at large as to whether to grant the remedy or not. Indeed, in that context, the term 'discretionary' may be somewhat misleading. In its proper context and as was pointed out by Denham J in *De Róiste v Minister for Defence* [2001] 1 IR 190 at p 209, the term simply means that the court can take into account a range of circumstances in deciding whether to make an order and if so what order should be made. In truth the term 'discretionary' simply implies that a particular remedy does not automatically follow from the establishment of a particular set of circumstances and that there may be other factors which can properly be taken into account in deciding whether to grant the remedy concerned. Amongst the circumstances that might well, on the facts of a particular case, be properly taken into account, would be the need to protect the legitimate interests of a defendant who was sued by a party placing reliance on a public law measure which the defendant wished to challenge. That factor, amongst any other relevant circumstances, would need to be taken into account by the court.

[37] Case 43/75, *Defrenne v SA Belge de Navigation Aérienne (SABENA) (No 2)* [1976] ECR 455; Case 98/78 *Firma A Racke v Hauptzollant Mainz* [1979] ECR 69.

[38] *Health Service Executive v M.W. and G.L.* [2013] IESC 38.

[39] Council Regulation (EC) No 2201/2003 of 27 November 2003 concerning jurisdiction and the recognition and enforcement of judgments in matrimonial matters and the matters of parental responsibility, repealing Regulation (EC) No 1347/2000 ([2003] OJL338/1).

a court of one Member State can request or allow a request to transfer the matter to another Member State where it believes the latter court would be in a better position to deal with the general welfare of the child.[40] When determining whether to make or permit such a request, the court is only guided by three considerations, namely the particular connection of the child with the proposed new jurisdiction, which court is best placed to hear the case, and the best interests of the child. The later two criteria, as defined by the Union legislature, seem to require the courts to exercise what, in common law terms, might be considered quite a broad discretion as to the actual factors to be taken into account. Likewise, properly defined, discretion as the term is used in common law countries is narrower than the meaning the word might sometimes convey. An oft cited example of the approach to be applied by a court in the exercise of its discretion is the judgment of Walsh J in *State (Lynch) v Cooney*,[41] where he stated in an application for certiorari:

> In Ireland it is sufficient to be 'a person aggrieved' – a term to be generously interpreted – which is generally understood to include any person who has reasonable grounds to bring the proceedings. Broadly speaking the term would be the same whether one is proceeding for certiorari or for declaratory action. Each of these is a discretionary remedy but not in the sense that the grant or refusal may be at the whim of the court. The discretion of a court to refuse either of these remedies to a person aggrieved is very limited and, normally, they will issue *ex debito justitiae*.

Be that as it may, there is no doubt that the increasing influence of Union law in procedural matters is one of the current areas giving rise to the greatest level of tension between the two systems. It also seems to me to be likely to give rise to tension within the legal systems of all Member States, not least common law countries. If, either because of specific Union legislation or because of general principles of Union law applicable to litigation which has a Union law dimension, courts in common law countries are required to apply, to a greater or lesser extent, a common Union administrative law regime, then that of itself creates a potential tension, within the jurisdiction, between the process to be followed in those areas which are subject to such 'Europeanisation' and those which are not. Will that lead to the adoption across the board of a 'European' process in common law countries so as to remove or minimise that distinction, or will there remain two, potentially significantly different, strands of judicial review applying respectively to European and national litigation? If the latter, a further tension potentially arises in that it may well, in such circumstances, matter a lot to the parties as to how the litigation is properly characterised for

[40] Article 15 (1) provides:

By way of exception, the courts of a Member State, having jurisdiction as to the substance of the matter may, if they consider that a court of another Member State with which the child has a particular connection, would be better placed to hear the case, or a specific part thereof, and where this is in the best interests of the child:

(a) stay the case or the part thereof in question and invite the parties to introduce a request before the court of that other Member State in accordance with paragraph 4; or
(b) request the court of another Member State to assume jurisdiction in accordance with paragraph 5.

[41] *State (Lynch) v Cooney* [1982] IR 337 at 368.

that may significantly influence the process. There is, in those circumstances, potential for significant debate and dispute as to whether, at least in some cases, litigation can properly be characterised as having a Union law dimension.

Where then does the common law stand in relation to an emerging Europeanisation of public and administrative law? First, it is possible to identify certain broad principles of European law which are applicable in the public law sphere. The principle of legal certainty, the concept of legitimate expectation, the requirement for proportionality and the availability of access to justice are, perhaps, amongst the most prominent. These broad principles are applied by the Court of Justice to European institutions but are also required to be applied when judicial protection is sought in national courts, either in respect of the actions of Union bodies (where such actions are amenable to litigation in national courts) or, perhaps more importantly, where national bodies are acting 'within the scope of European law'.

Many of those broad principles are, to a greater or lesser extent, imported into the common law system. While legitimate expectation has sometimes been described as the public law equivalent of estoppel[42] and while *Webb v Ireland*[43], a case which on its terms turned on estoppel, is often seen as the first case on legitimate expectation in Ireland even though the term was not used, it is fair to say that the broad concept of legitimate expectation represents, in the main, an import from Union law.[44]

Irish courts have had increasing recourse to the doctrine of proportionality over the last number of decades. The beginnings of the doctrine can be seen in *Cox v Ireland*,[45] where the Supreme Court struck down a provision of the Offences Against the State Act 1939, disqualifying automatically all those convicted of a scheduled offence under the Act from public sector employment, as being impermissibly wide and indiscriminate. The *Cox* decision was then referred to by Costello J in *Heaney v Ireland*,[46] which considered a challenge to another section of the Offences Against the State Act 1939, requiring an arrested person to give an account of their movements. In determining the constitutionality of the provision, Costello J applied a 'proportionality test', which is now well-known in Irish law. The doctrine was then applied in a number of High Court[47] cases before being expressly approved of by the Supreme Court

[42] See the comments at para 41 of my judgment in *Lett & Co Ltd v Wexford Borough Council* [2012] 2 IR 198:

> The doctrine of legitimate expectation is often seen as the public law counterpart of the equitable doctrine of estoppel. Without necessarily pushing the analogy too far it is, in my view, apposite to note that the doctrine of estoppel is designed specifically to deal with a case where it is not considered equitable to permit a party to rely on what would otherwise be their formal legal entitlements. In similar vein the doctrine of legitimate expectation is designed to ensure that a public authority may be required to deal with matters in a certain way when it would not be just to permit the public authority to rely on its strict legal rights.

[43] *Webb v Ireland* [1988] IR 353.

[44] The term 'legitimate expectation' was first used in the Irish courts in *Fakih v Minister for Justice* [1993] 2 IR 406.

[45] *Cox v Ireland* [1992] 2 IR 503.

[46] *Heaney v Ireland* [1994] 3 IR 593.

[47] See *Daly v Revenue Commissioners* [1995] 3 IR 1; and *Gallagher v Director of Central Mental Hospital (No 2)* [1996] 3 IR 10.

in *Re Article 26 and the Employment Equality Bill 1996*.[48] The doctrine has since been applied by the Supreme Court on a number of occasions.[49]

However, it is striking that the first and still most commonly used formulation of the doctrine in the Irish legal system was borrowed not from Union law (where proportionality is well established) but rather from the Canadian Supreme Court and its decisions in *R v Oakes*[50] and *Chaulk v R*.[51] In addition, the Irish Constitution and Irish law has, of course, long recognised the right of access to justice and right of access to the courts.[52]

However, it does need to be noted that not all of those terms have precisely the same meaning in differing legal systems. Is proportionality considered to be exactly the same thing by the ECJ as it would be considered by a common law supreme court? Does legitimate expectation mean the same thing in all legal systems? The public participation directive requires that there be judicial protection in the form of an ability to challenge the substantive or procedural legality of certain measures in the environmental field. However, there are real differences between jurisdictions as to what is meant by, in particular, substantive legality. The reason why common law courts have afforded a significant (some might say too great) deference to the decisions of administrative bodies is because, in the common law tradition, those bodies have the legal power to make the relevant decision and such a decision is not necessarily regarded as unlawful even if a court considers it to be wrong. A real area of tension may well derive from differences in the various traditions operating within Europe as to what degree of error or procedural irregularity renders an administrative determination actually unlawful. Case law of the Court of Justice or Union legislation which uses terminology such as substantive legality runs the risk of different interpretations in different traditions precisely because the same terminology is used with different meaning in different legal systems. The same potential tension arises from the use of terms such as legitimate expectation or proportionality which may not mean quite the same thing in separate traditions.

One of the striking features of the legislative measures adopted to date at Union level which impact on the judicial review process is how they are very much 'one-off' measures designed to have an impact only in one area of Union law. There has, as yet, been no attempt to impose, at an EU legislative level, broad principles of administrative law which are intended to have an over-arching effect across all areas where national courts are dealing with matters 'within the scope of Union law.' There have been some suggestions that such an attempt may be forthcoming in the future. The potential for significant tension thereby arising is obvious. National systems, and in particular those in common law countries, will have to come to grips with a significant adaption of their administrative law

[48] *Re Article 26 and the Employment Equality Bill 1996* [1997] 2 IR 321.

[49] See, for example, *Mahon v Post Publications Ltd* [2007] 3 IR 338; and *Re Article 26 and the Planning and Development Bill 1999* [2000] 2 IR 321 .

[50] *R v Oakes* [1986] 1 SCR 103.

[51] *Chaulk v R* [1990] 3 SCR 1303.

[52] See *The State (Quinn) v Ryan* [1965] IR 70; and *Macauley v Minister for Posts and Telegraphs* [1966] IR345.

regime in such an eventuality, and will also have to make important decisions as to whether to operate a two strand system applicable respectively to matters within or outwith the scope of European law or to seek to adapt the entirety of their national systems to any emerging European consensus.

That there is an increasing Europeanisation of public law and administrative law can hardly be doubted. That the trend is likely to continue, because of the development of the jurisprudence of the Court of Justice, the adoption of the Charter of Fundamental Rights of the European Union, and by the increasing use of legislation which requires a particular type of review or impacts on the review process, cannot be doubted. That this is an area of likely future tension equally seems almost certain. I will finally turn to further areas of potential future tension.

FUTURE AREAS OF POTENTIAL TENSION

Finally, it might be worthwhile to attempt to identify future areas of potential tension. Historically Union law, whether at the level of the jurisprudence of the Court of Justice or in its legislative measures, has not, ordinarily, sought to harmonise or interfere with national procedural law. The fundamental principle is that, in the absence of a specific Union law measure, litigation involving Union law issues is to be conducted in national courts in accordance with national procedural law subject to the principles of equivalence and effectiveness. In Case C-432/05 *Unibet (London) Ltd and Unibet (International) Ltd v Justitiekanslern*,[53] the Court of Justice stated:

> [T]he principle of effective judicial protection of an individual's rights under Community law must be interpreted as meaning that it does not require the national legal order of a Member State to provide for a free-standing action for an examination of whether national provisions are compatible with Article 49 EC, provided that other effective legal remedies, which are no less favourable than those governing similar domestic actions, make it possible for such a question of compatibility to be determined as a preliminary issue, which is a matter for the national court to establish.'

By those principles national procedural law applicable in Union law litigation is required to be equivalent to the procedural law that would be applied in like litigation involving purely national law and is required to be such as does not make the enforcement of entitlements deriving from Union law ineffective.[54]

Likewise, Union law has not had, to date, a significant influence in the field of criminal law let alone criminal procedure. The harmonisation in extradition brought about by the system of European Arrest Warrants is, perhaps, the most significant overarching measure touching on the criminal process.

However, much of that may well change with the increasing implementation of measures in the Area of Freedom, Security and Justice. While Ireland and,

[53] Case C-432/05 *Unibet (London) Ltd and Unibet (International) Ltd v Justitiekanslern* [2007] ECR I-2271.

[54] See also *Dowling & others v Minister for Finance* [2013] IESC 37.

indeed, the UK have significant derogations from aspects of the competence of the European Union in certain aspects of this area[55] nonetheless it seems likely that there will, over time, be increasing attempts to harmonise at least fundamental aspects of the court process. This seems to me to be a potential area of significant future tension.

It would be hard to disagree with the proposition that one of the more striking distinctions between the common and civil law systems is to be found in the court process, whether civil or criminal. While stemming more from the jurisprudence of the European Court of Human Rights rather than from Union law itself, the question of the delay jurisprudence in respect of civil litigation is, nonetheless, a case in point, and may provide a warning of issues to come as the EU becomes more involved in national procedural law. Ireland has been the subject of a number of adverse decisions in this field.[56] It has been suggested that the jurisprudence of the ECtHR does not adequately recognise the difference between a judge-led civil procedure and a common law party-led process. On that point I would make a number of observations.

First it is important to acknowledge that, from the perspective of the European Convention on Human Rights, the obligation to ensure the timely completion of court proceedings rests on each subscribing state and thus is an obligation of the State through all of its agencies and constitutional organs (including the courts). A finding of failure on the part of a State does not necessarily reflect on the courts themselves for the failure of obligation can arise from any or all of: a failure on the part of government to provide adequate resources, systemic failures within the court system whether by reason of legislation (the fault of the legislature) or court practice (perhaps to some extent the fault of the court) or indeed from individual failure on the part of judges or court administrators. From an ECHR perspective, it does not really matter.

Second it seems to follow that a country might legitimately be found in default if the system as a whole did not guarantee a timely conclusion of proceedings. Thus, for example, if a party in a common law process did not, either in theory or in practice, have adequate remedies available to ensure that the process was conducted in a speedy fashion, then there could be no criticism of an adverse finding.

What, however, has, in my view with some merit, been criticised from a common law perspective is an apparent failure to acknowledge that a party-led system of civil justice is as legitimate a scheme as a judge-led one. It might be said that that important fact does not always seem to have been given full recognition in some of the case law. Given that the Convention was subscribed

[55] Under Protocol (No 21) to the Treaty on European Union and the Treaty on the Functioning of the European Union on the position of the United Kingdom and Ireland in respect of the Area of Freedom, Security and Justice, Ireland may choose, within three months of a proposal being presented to the Council whether it wishes to participate in the adoption and application of any such proposed measure. However, it may, at any stage after a measure has been adopted, indicate its wish to participate. Article 8 of the Protocol provides that Ireland may notify the Council in writing that it no longer wishes to be covered by the terms of this Protocol.

[56] *McMullen v Ireland* [2004] ECHR 404; *McFarlane v Director of Public Prosecutions* [2010] ECHR 1272.

to by both civil and common law countries it can hardly have been assumed that one entirely legitimate and internationally followed system was to be regarded as inferior to another.

That does not, of course, mean that the results of many individual cases might not be the same however approached. A case can be made, on the other hand, that at least the approach and the analysis should be different. In order that there be, to use the phrase which gained such currency during the peace process, 'parity of esteem', the appropriate approach ought not, in my view, be to look at the overall delay, subtract from it any periods which might be regarded as attributable to default on the part of the complaining party, and assess whether the time taken was, on that basis, Convention-appropriate. Rather an approach which conferred parity of esteem on a party-led common law process ought assess whether the procedures available to any party whose is aggrieved by the pace of litigation are adequate to enable the litigation to progress at a speed which is Convention-compliant and to do so without placing any unreasonable burden on the party concerned. It may well be that, in some or even many cases, such an analysis would nonetheless lead to a finding of breach. But an analysis of that type would, in my view, recognise the legitimacy of party-led civil proceedings and would find breach only where the procedures, practices and resources available to the courts in a common law system were found to be inadequate to permit a party who had a grievance about the pace of litigation to have same remedied in an effective and not overly burdensome way.

Any attempt to harmonise procedure at an EU level must grapple with the need to recognise the substantial differences between civil and common law process which, at its most basic, is a distinction between a significantly court-led process in the civil law world and a party-led process in common law jurisdictions. In passing it is worth noting that there is a significant difference between the civil and common law systems in the typical number of judges and court staff and, consequently, in the cost to the tax payer of court systems. Even before recent cutbacks Ireland had, in 2006, the lowest budget allocation as a percentage of GDP (0.05%) in the members of the Council of Europe. The other common law countries were not far behind. Typically common law countries came out well below those of civil law jurisdictions. While up to date and more detailed analysis would be useful, it can be suggested that the burden on the tax payer of paying for the court system (including judges) in a typical common law country is of the order of 25%-33% of that applying in a typical civil law jurisdiction. For example, the most recent CEPEJ report[57] suggests that Ireland (at 0.14%) and the UK (at 0.16%) have expenditure on courts as a proportion of total public expenditure which is of the order of one third of the EU average (0.44%). While there are distinctions between the common law countries themselves and distinctions between the civil law countries themselves, the overall information makes clear that a highly determinative factor in the cost to the State of running a court system is as to whether it is common or civil law.

[57] European Commission for the Efficiency of Justice, 'The functioning of the judicial systems and the situation of the economy in the European Union Member States', Strasbourg, 2013.

It may well be appropriate to characterise the difference as giving rise to a cost transfer between the tax payer and the parties to litigation with the parties, in a common law jurisdiction, having a much greater role in the conduct of the case (and thus bearing much greater cost) with a corresponding saving to the tax payer.

Be that as it may, the systems are sufficiently different that harmonisation through Union measures is likely to be fraught with difficulty and the very real potential for unintended consequences and potential dissatisfaction and tension. Watch this space.

18

'Imperfect Obligations' – Constitutional Principles and the Charter of Fundamental Rights

JOHN MACMENAMIN*

I

THE TITLE OF this essay[1] is derived from an observation of Mr Justice Kingsmill Moore in the case of *Comyn v The Attorney General*,[2] wherein he referred to Article 45 of the Irish Constitution as containing Directive Principles of Social Policy which put 'the State under certain duties, but they are duties of imperfect obligation since they cannot be enforced or regarded by any Court of law, and are only directions for the guidance of the Oireachtas.' The historical process by which they came to be so characterised is briefly described later. In comparison, or least in parallel, in the subsequent sections of this essay, the socio-economic principles of the Charter of the Fundamental Rights are considered with a particular emphasis on the issue of justiciability.

The reflections contained here are best seen as comparative, and very selective, legal history. In the Irish section, I seek to outline the efforts made by a number of influential theologians to have principles with a socio-economic aspect, those 'imperfect obligations', placed in the 1937 Constitution at its drafting stage; how Eamon de Valera, the head of government, reacted to those efforts; and how the small group of lawyers and officials designated to draft the Constitution as well as some Cabinet members, adopted a solution which satisfied proponents and placated opponents of the idea. The lawyers, politicians and government officials thought that such principles had no place in the constitution of a modern republic. They set their face against the proposal for reasons based on theory and pragmatism. As to theory, they argued that placing principles, as identified from Papal encyclicals, in a modern constitution came too close to

*Judge of the Supreme Court of Ireland

[1] I take this opportunity of expressing the esteem felt by all his colleagues for Nial Fennelly as a jurist, colleague and friend.

[2] *Comyn v The Attorney General* [1950] IR 142.

making the democratic republic into a confessional state. As to pragmatism, they considered that such aspirations, written in constitutional stone, risked the consequence of creating false and unrealisable hopes, doomed to failure.

We then move forward some sixty years to the drafting of another document of a constitutional nature, the Charter of Fundamental Rights of the European Union. There, similar efforts were made, albeit by politicians. Despite opposition from representatives of some in the common law tradition, the attempt was met with success. The Charter contains a range of 'social solidarity' style, and other principles, with a socio-economic dimension.

The interactions involved on both occasions allow for some reflections on the relationship between the common law, European Union law, and the civil law of other Member States of the Union. These interactions raise the issue of 'legal pluralism,'[3] the simultaneous existence of a number of legal codes, and the pursuit of harmonised values drawn from different sources, in one constitutional document. The questions raised in the process might, some say, go to the concept of democracy itself. The challenges that these processes pose for the Court of Justice and, perhaps more remotely, for national courts are formidable, but not insurmountable. A possible risk is that, at some point, a significant constitutional crux will arise, flowing from a direct collision of different concepts of rights, justiciability, and the allocation and separation of powers. Some writers implicitly suggest that the precipitating factor for such a conflict will arise from divergent interpretations of the term 'principles' itself. These concerns derive from the fact that certain civil jurisdictions and common law states in the Union have varying concepts of what is 'justiciable', that is, a matter for the courts; how such matters are justiciable and the extent to which socio-economic concerns are matters for legislatures. This problem, in turn, connects to the concepts of liberty and equality.

The task of identifying and reconciling the means to attain the political values of liberty and equality can be traced back at least as far as Aristotle, forward through Roman law to the medieval theologians, then through the turbulent seventeenth and eighteenth centuries, and most recently to modern political theorists such as Dworkin. This more 'secular' line of theory is well traversed.

But a linked line of thought is relevant to the Ireland of 1937. It derives specifically from Roman Catholic philosophical and theological thinking. Adherents to this school of thought likewise made a distinction between different forms of justice and such thinking formed the background to the jurisprudential approach of the drafters of the Constitution.

Thomas Aquinas, interpreting Aristotle, sought to distinguish between two concepts of justice namely, 'commutative' and 'distributive' justice. He asserted that rules which appertained to the conduct of one person toward another came under the heading of commutative justice. A criminal offence also comes under that rubric, as do civil rights and duties owed by one individual to another. Distributive justice, on the other hand, relates rather to social or economic rights,

[3] For a jurisprudential exploration of this, see, generally, S Douglas-Scott, *Law after Modernity* (Oxford, Hart Publishing, 2013).

which generally require the allocation of financial resources such as food, care and housing. Within the Anglo-American politico-legal tradition, from Locke to the Founding Fathers of the United States, as much as in Thomist philosophy, the task of dispensing commutative justice fell to judges and the courts. The creation of conditions for social justice within society based on wealth allocation and taxation, however, fell to be determined by the executive and legislature. These concepts are, in turn, very closely linked to the Separation of Powers proposed by Montesquieu and Madison. On both sides of the Atlantic, both courts and legislatures in the common law tradition grew, in varying ways, to recognise the concept of 'justiciability'. Issues characterised both as 'political' or as 'socio-economic' are often seen as non-justiciable by the courts. Costello J elegantly characterised the distinction between the two concepts, as between matters to be dealt with in the Four Courts (Irish Courts) and those to be dealt with in Kildare Street (Irish Parliament).[4] What is not always recognised is that rather similar distinctions, between fundamental rights and social 'rights' and principles are observed in many civil law members of the European Union, such as the Scandinavian States. Insofar as principles are regarded as matters for the courts, such as in France and Spain, they are approached with caution and, frequently, through the prism of whether there has been a failure in the implementation of such a duty by a national legislature.

In law, principles are not always easy to define. What does the term mean? The word in the legal lexicon can vary in its significance according to context. It may, in fact, be seen as having a 'hard' connotation, meaning something fundamental and tantamount to a legal rule; or, alternatively, it may be seen as the expression of values which inform the application of a legal rule. This somewhat 'chameleon-like' character poses difficulties. A legal principle such as equality may itself embody a justiciable rule; but in other contexts, it can be seen as a form of explanation or touchstone, informing the application of a fundamental right such as property.[5] This characteristic may render a term useful for diplomacy, whose language-object is often inclusion, but it is more difficult for lawyers, or judges, who frequently use language to demarcate distinctions. In the common law tradition, one of the litmus tests of the 'hardness' of a principle is whether it is a matter appropriate to be dealt with in the courts. This is not always a 'bright-line test'(to quote a term used by the US Supreme Court); still less so in a judicial context such as that of the EU, where the ECJ has expressed reluctance to accept the notion of separation of powers.[6]

[4] *O'Reilly v Limerick Corporation* [1989] ILRM 181.

[5] *cf* the discussion in S Douglas Scott, *Constitutional Law of the European Union* (London, Longman, 2002) 452–454; and, generally, R Dworkin. I take the first as being almost contemporaneous with a promulgation of the Charter. Douglas Scott, even then, raised the question of whether 'principles' in the Charter were a conceptual guide or directly binding. She also raised the question as to the extent to which even Member States' Constitutions might be subordinated to economic interests in certain contexts of EU law. See also the discussion in R O'Connell, 'From Equality Before the Law to the Equal Benefit of the Law' in E Carolan and O Doyle (eds), *The Irish Constitution: Governance and Values* (Dublin, Thompson Round Hall, 2008).

[6] *cf* Case 188-190/80 *France, Italy and United Kingdom v Commission* [1982] ECR 2545 where it was unsuccessfully argued that all law making powers existed in the European Council, and that the Commission held powers only of implementation and monitoring.

This essay seeks later to identify some of the sources of the social principles in the Charter of Fundamental Rights and the motivation of those who proposed their inclusion in that document. It briefly describes the Charter's evolution into a constitutional document and tentatively considers the extent to which these particular principles may, in the future, be considered by courts. It seeks to describe in more detail the extent to which such principles are justiciable in some Union Member States, and considers how national courts and bodies have sought to chart this new path. This is in no way a comprehensive history, nor an essay in comparative jurisprudence, nor a learned article on European constitutional law with vast footnotes referring to the academic literature on the subject. It might best be described as a series of legal and historical snapshots, together with a short 'current' commentary on the Charter. These issues have been dealt with, in a vast array of academic commentary, which an essay such as this cannot hope to encompass.

The social principles adopted in the Charter can be located at a time when it was not precisely part of a constitution, but part of a European constitutional schema with what philosophers might call a strong constitutional 'immanence' with consequences to be realised in the future. Following the Lisbon Treaty, that potential has become reality. But, first, we must revert to the dark days of 1937.

II

The constitution of a nation state is not simply a legal document; it is a declaration of identity, containing within itself identifications of the nature of that state, its form of government, and an identification, through rights, guarantees and limitations, of the legal relationship between the citizen and the state.

But should a republican constitution merely outline a prescriptive legal rights framework? How far should it go in defining the programmatic nature of society within that framework?[7] Raising these questions in terms very redolent of that era and place, Father John Charles McQuaid, Holy Ghost priest, then President of Blackrock College, wrote in 1937 to his close friend Eamon de Valera, that a Constitution was a 'thesis of philosophy and theology.... designed to achieve

[7] This is described memorably by German jurists as '*Staatszielbestimmungen*'; the idea of a Constitution which, as well as reflecting experiences of the political past and structuring the state to enable it to cope with the present, formulates a design for the political future. See references in PJ Kabudi, 'The Directive Principles of State Policy in Tanzania' in C Finnegan and W Binchy (eds), *Human Rights, Constitutionalism and the Judiciary: Tanzanian and Irish Perspectives* (Dublin, Clarus Press, 2006). This German process of constitutional 'objective setting' is very similar to that adopted by the French Conseil Constitutionnel (described briefly later) in considering '*objectifs de valeur constitutionelle*.' In both, State agencies and institutions are committed to binding norms of constitutional value, used as a reference point for constitutional interpretation. In Germany, as well as France, such provisions as interpreted from the Basic Law, and from the French constitutional tradition, have been sometimes criticised for a lack of specificity by scholars. They are seen as objectives primarily addressed at legislators. Such values and principles are to be found in the EU Treaties, for example, in the realm of foreign relations. *cf* J Larik, 'Theoretical approaches to a peculiar norm category: shaping the international order as a Union objective' in D Kochenov and F Amtenbrink (eds), *The European Union's Shaping of the International Legal Order* (Cambridge, CUP, 2013).

the common good of the nation on Christian lines and by Christian methods.'[8] De Valera's achievement in steering a course between the Scylla of theology and the Charybdis of both republican ideals and the common law tradition was by no means insignificant.

The Roman Catholic social principles under discussion in Ireland in 1936 to 1937 will be described later. They were expressed as ideals in two Papal encyclicals.[9] They proposed the concept of a social order where dignity, justice and charity should inform all the institutions of national life, and equality between citizens. The encyclicals advocated the provision of a living wage, control of natural resources, and expressed opposition to monopolies. They advocated protection of the weaker sections of the community against the strong. In fact, as we will see later, some of these principles resonate with social principles identified in the Charter, more than sixty years later. It cannot be said they were radical even in their time. Former Chief Justice Ronan Keane described the 1937 principles as being 'mildly progressive with a leaning towards benign capitalism rather than socialism'.[10]

Some suggested to de Valera and his drafting team that these socio-economic principles be included within the rights provisions of the Constitution. The dialectic of exchange is described in detail by Mr Justice Gerard Hogan in his masterful work, *The Origins of the Irish Constitution, 1928 to 1941*.[11] Those who wish for a fuller picture of the discussion should start there, referring also to Keogh and McCarthy's interesting and pioneering work.[12]

In 1937, J.J. McElligott was the powerful and influential Secretary of the Irish Department of Finance. His comments on an early draft of the new Constitution, which contained declarations of social policy in the main body of the text, were pungent, even if they were made, as he cast himself, in the guise of a 'devil's advocate' with respect to the proposals.[13] He wrote in response to one early draft identifying social principles drawn from the encyclicals:

> These various declaratory phrases are of an idealistic tendency which while individually unobjectionable as a statement of social policy may if launched into the void in the

[8] Letter from McQuaid to de Valera on the 10 March, 1937, apparently erroneously dated 1936, cited at p 108, in D Keogh and A McCarthy, *The Making of the Irish Constitution 1937* (Cork, Mercier Press, 2007).

[9] Quadragesimo Anno (1891) and Rerum Novarum (1931); and see Denham CJ, 'Some thoughts on the Constitution of Ireland at 75' in E Carolan (ed), *The Constitution of Ireland: Perceptions and Prospects* (London, Bloomsbury, 2012). This also contains useful short biographies of the drafters of the Irish Constitution. One striking feature is the relative homogeneity of the educational background of the main authors.

[10] R Keane, 'Judges as Lawmakers', NUI Galway, 1 October, 2003.

[11] G Hogan, *The Origins of the Irish Constitution, 1928–1941* (Dublin, Royal Irish Academy, 2012).

[12] Keogh and McCarthy (n 8). One cannot ignore the republican ideals espoused by the Cabinet. In 1937, there were members of de Valera's cabinet who strongly supported ideals which necessitated a separation of Church and State. Gerry Boland, Minister for Lands, was one such politician. He said he would not live under a Constitution where an early draft had regarded Roman Catholicism as the 'true religion'. *cf* N Whelan, *Fianna Fáil: A Biography of the Party* (Dublin, Gill and MacMillan, 2011)

[13] Hogan (n 11) Document No. 104, 'Memorandum from James J. McElligott to Maurice Moynihan, Observations on the first circulated draft' 386.

> draft Constitution, recoil like a boomerang on the Government of some future day in circumstances not anticipated by the originators.[14]

He argued that such declarations were 'not of a kind usually enshrined in the Constitution. They will not be helpful to Ministers in the future but will provide a breeding ground for discontent, and so create instability and insecurity.'[15]

He added:

> They are consequently objectionable even dangerous. Their provisions are too vague to be of positive assistance to any Government and are yet sufficiently definite to afford grounds for disaffection to sections of the community, who might claim that the government were not living up to the Constitution.[16]

The departmental secretary went on to express his opposition to the constitutional expression of such ideals, especially in light of the fact that the draft Constitution was to give to the judiciary a power of judicial review. He claimed:

> The provisions are the more objectionable by reason of the earlier Articles relating to repugnance under which laws may be disallowed after reference to the Supreme Court or to a Referendum. Some of the provisions are too advanced, some too conservative and many cut across action taken daily by the Government, eg, restrictions on private property and initiative.[17]

McElligott contrasted the intended declarations with the actuality of government policy of the day. He wrote that the principles expressed opposition to 'the economic domination of the few in what pertains to the control of credit'.[18] Such an identification of social policy could be used by 'agitators' as a 'weapon of attack' on banks, credit institutions set up under the aegis of the State, or against any large joint stock concern.

His concerns included the fact that a reference to 'business monopolies', in the draft Constitution, was to be contrasted with the fact, that, by 1937, the Irish State itself, had already established monopolies on the sale of sugar, electricity, cement and car tyres. His concerns regarding entrusting judicial review to the judiciary may have been magnified by the then current controversy between Franklin Roosevelt and the United States Supreme Court.

The acerbic nature of this attack led to a parrying response from one of the drafters of the Constitution, Michael McDunphy, another senior government official.[19] He made clear that Eamon de Valera had already realised that it would be necessary to distinguish between justiciable fundamental rights, and other 'rights' which derived from socio-economic policy, which would not be so justiciable. Referring to de Valera, then President of the Executive Council, McDunphy wrote '[t]he President's intention [is] that a number of these Sections

[14] Ibid, 400.
[15] Hogan (n 11) 399.
[16] Ibid.
[17] Hogan (n 11).
[18] Ibid 400.
[19] Hogan (n 11) Document No. 105, Memorandum by Michael McDunphy, Observation on 1st circulated draft', 405.

are merely statements of moral principles and should not be created positive rights'.[20] The usage of the words 'moral principles' is strongly suggestive of their provenance from Papal encyclicals.

The drafters of the Irish Constitution arrived at a deft solution. It was to stipulate in the Constitution itself that any identification of social or moral principles therein was for the purpose of guiding the State in its general policy; but that such principles should not, of themselves, operate so as to confer rights.[21]

The importance and subtlety of this distinction was not so clear to some commentators. One, former Senator James Douglas, writing in 1937, asked what was the reason for the constitutional distinction between the Directive Principles of Social Policy and the other earlier Articles which identified fundamental rights.[22] Another, an influential, if somewhat radically minded commentator, Professor Alfred O'Rahilly of University College Cork, asked rhetorically why the courts should be bound to take cognisance of other Articles, which did address fundamental rights, but be precluded from having regard to the directives of social policy?[23] In contrast to McElligott who was concerned about judicial 'activism', O'Rahilly was concerned as to what he perceived to be the strongly conservative common law background of the judges then sitting in the Superior Courts. He thought that, to such judges, these new principles would be strange, and that the declarations of social policy might thereby be 'pared down with a knife of an alien jurisprudence'.[24] Even though O'Rahilly had reservations regarding the philosophy of the judiciary, he nonetheless objected to the idea of withdrawing 'part of the Constitution from the "cognisance" of the courts'.[25]

What was the source of all this concern? It is necessary to examine what was contained in the principles in a little more detail. The essence of the thinking behind the 1937 Constitution was the sovereignty of the independent nation-state republic. That thinking had to address political and social realities of the day. The principles ultimately contained in Article 45 of the Constitution of Ireland were very considerably circumscribed by the preamble to that Article, which stated that what was set out was to be for the general guidance of the Oireachtas, or national parliament, 'exclusively'; and not 'cognisable by any Court under the provisions of this Constitution'.

The values espoused were somewhat aspirational. They were of their time. Article 45.1 declared that the State was to 'strive to promote the welfare of the whole people by securing and protecting as effectively as it may a social order in which justice and charity shall inform all the institutions of the national life'.

Article 45.2 provided that policy should be directed towards securing equality between citizens, both men and women, and supported the ideal that, through

[20] Ibid 418.

[21] As Denham CJ (n 9) points out the idea was not new. Similar ideas were found in the Weimar Constitution of 1919. The concept was adopted and applied in former British dominions on attaining independence, or (in the case of South Africa) attaining majority rule.

[22] Irish Independent, 8 May 1937, quoted in Hogan (n 11) 330–331.

[23] Irish Independent, 15 May 1937, quoted in Hogan (n 11) 331–332. Such issues should have been clear to Professor O'Rahilly, as he had been involved the drafting of the Free State Constitution.

[24] Hogan (n 11) 332.

[25] Ibid.

their occupations, all citizens might find the means of making reasonable provision for their domestic needs. The provisions declared support for the idea that ownership and control of material resources of the community should be distributed among private individuals, in various classes, so as best to achieve the common good and espoused the ideas that free competition not be allowed to develop in such a manner so that the concentration of ownership or control of essential commodities in a few individuals would be to the common detriment; that, in the provision of credit, the constant and predominant aim should be the welfare of the people as a whole; that there might be established on the land, in economic security, as many families as in the circumstances should be practicable; that private initiative industry should be encouraged so as to ensure reasonable efficiency in the production and distribution of goods; that the public should be protected against unjust exploitation; that the economic interests of weaker sections of the community, such as the infirm, widows and orphans, be supported; that the strength of workers, men and women, and the tender age of children should not be abused, or that citizens should be forced by economic necessity to enter avocations unsuited to their sex, age or strength.

The influences giving rise to the social policy principles can be readily discerned from the archives, as both Hogan, and Keogh and McCarthy show. The primary source was undoubtedly John Charles McQuaid.[26] McQuaid frequently and privately corresponded with de Valera concerning the social content of the Papal encyclicals, '*Quadragesimo Anno*' and '*Rerum Novarum*'.

Keogh and McCarthy describe de Valera at a celebration in 1960 marking the centenary of his alma mater, Blackrock College. He remarked then that McQuaid's involvement in the drafting of portions of the Constitution had been positive: '[t]he parts he approved of then have never been questioned, the parts he disapproved of have been criticised'.[27] The two authors set out a very full comparison between the first printed draft of the Constitution, and give specific quotations from the encyclicals, which show not only a reflection of the religious principles expressed in the latter, but even a duplication of precise language in both documents.[28]

In the to and fro between 'proponents' and 'opponents' of the principles, one can detect a tension between those who wished to invest the Constitution with a religiously-based ethos which would shape the social fabric of the State, and those who adhered to the idea of identifying the republican nature of the State itself, and the rights and freedoms which citizens should enjoy within it. While it is not easy actually to discern the hand of John Hearne, the principal drafter of the Constitution, in all the documents, it would be naïve to conclude his was not a strong guiding legal influence.[29] The tension, between philosophy, social content and 'ethos', on the one hand, and rights, freedoms and duties, on the

[26] Fr McQuaid became Archbishop of Dublin in 1940.

[27] Keogh and McCarthy (n 8) 107.

[28] Ibid 117.

[29] Hogan, writing earlier, as a contributor in Keogh and McCarthy, points out that John Hearne's first draft of the Preamble to the Constitution was secular, in contrast to the final version containing religious references traceable to the Polish Constitution of 1921.

other, is readily discernible. Members of de Valera's cabinet would not have forgotten either, the role of the Roman Catholic hierarchy in opposing their stance on the Treaty of 1921, as well as their belief in the ideals of a republic derived from Tone and the United Irishmen.

John Charles McQuaid was not the only Roman Catholic influence on the Constitution. The Society of Jesus formed a committee of its members specifically to make submissions to the drafters aimed at ensuring that the Constitution would, as far as possible, espouse a Roman Catholic social ethos. One member of that committee, Father Edward Cahill S.J. expressed the hope that the Constitution should make 'a definite break with the Liberal and non-Christian type of State'.[30] He added:

> This latter, which has been forced upon us by a foreign, non-Catholic, power is exotic, unnatural and quite foreign to the native tradition. It tends in innumerable ways to cramp and paralyse the free development of the people's Catholic life and culture.[31]

In one letter, Cahill identified 'general principles' which were 'merely an application of Papal teaching and of the conclusion of Catholic philosophy'.[32] He wrote:

> They or most of them should I think be formally embodied in some shape or other in the written Constitution. *Some such series of general principles or ideals is necessary even as a means of educating the people's representatives and unifying the social outlook* (emphasis added).[33]

The correspondence shows elsewhere that other members of the Society of Jesus committee were not entirely enamoured of some of Cahill's views. But what is significant is the phraseology; Cahill's desire was that the new Constitution should constitute a 'break' or departure from an alien secular tradition, which should be supplanted with a firm Roman Catholic ethos, which would, in turn, define the social fabric of the State. More directly to the title of this essay, he wanted a statement of general *principles* or ideas 'in some shape or other'. In fact, the concepts which Cahill thought desirable were remarkably similar to those which were ultimately contained in Article 45.

Cahill's views represented those of many Irish nationalists when he wrote that the common law system was 'alien' to the 'Irish' tradition; what is noteworthy is that despite this perception, by 1937, and indeed at the time of the Irish Free State Constitution, common law ideas had grown deep roots when it came to fundamental rights and separation of powers. At those times, Ireland was an extremely homogenous, if conservative, society, where there was a broad social, legal and political consensus. Unlike the Charter of Fundamental Rights, all the contributors to the discussion came from the same tradition and the one state.[34]

[30] Hogan (n 11) Document No. 49, 'Memorandum by Fr Edward Cahill, 'Suggestions for Drafting a new Constitution' 228, 230.

[31] Ibid.

[32] Hogan (n 11) 32.

[33] Ibid.

[34] After an extensive debate in the Oireachtas, and a robust democratic campaign for and against, the Constitution was adopted by the people in a referendum on the 1 July, 1937.

To what extent did these principles of social policy subsequently enter the judicial domain?[35] In fact, the influence was limited. Essentially, they were, in fact, seen as a form of evalution or validation, informing the application of other fundamental and cognisable rights. The influences which affected the judiciary were the same three as those which permeated the drafting process. Judicial references to the principles were ancillary to the consideration of fundamental rights, such as private property or the right to earn a livelihood. The Directive Principles were referred to as a constitutional touchstone. Irish judges from a common law background were prepared only to a limited degree to have regard to Article 45 as an interpretative aid as to other Articles which were undeniably justiciable. For the first decade, the judges, very obviously, were operating within a judicial tradition where views were deeply entrenched.

Comyn concerned a claim to compensation by a judge, Michael Comyn, as a result of the compulsory purchase by the State of his phosphate mining lease in County Clare. This first, overt and direct judicial reference to the provisions of Article 45 took place some 13 years after the adoption by the people of the Constitution in 1937.

Then much time passed. But, even in the 1960s, when Ireland was exposed far more to outside and pluralistic influences, little changed. In *Murtagh Properties v Cleary*,[36] Kenny J, described by some as a judicial 'activist' dealt, as a High Court judge, with the case of a woman who was effectively excluded from employment because a trade union objected to non-male labour being used in the workplace. She claimed her right to earn a livelihood 'without discrimination of sex' associated with personal rights to be found in Article 40 of the Constitution.

Developing ideas which he had initially promulgated in *Ryan v Attorney General*[37] as to unenumerated rights in the Constitution, Kenny J stated that one of the principles upon which personal rights might be identified would be:

> ... derived from other clauses in the Constitution or from the Christian and democratic nature of the State. The right relied on in this case is derived, it was said, from Article 45... However, the defendants argued that the Court cannot have regard to this Article because it is expressed to be for the guidance of the Oireachtas only ... [The opening] passage does not mean that the courts may not have regard to the terms of the Article but that they have no jurisdiction to consider the application of the principles in it in the making of laws. *This does not involve the conclusion that the Courts may not take it into consideration when deciding whether a claim for constitutional right exists.*[38]

The final observation in the passage just quoted may be seen as the high point of the Directive Principles penetration into the identification of justiciable rights in the pre-EC membership era.

[35] See the interesting discussion on the nature and, not always foreseeable consequences, of socio-economic rights in O'Dowd, 'Social and Economic Rights', Irish Human Rights Commission, 9 December 2005.

[36] *Murtagh Properties v Cleary* [1972] IR 330.

[37] *Ryan v Attorney General* [1965] IR 294.

[38] Ibid 335 (emphasis added).

Later judgments, in the 1970s and 1980s, *Rodgers v ITGWU*[39]and *Landers v Attorney General,*[40] made passing references to Article 45, respectively in the context of right to earn a livelihood in the face of a compulsory retirement age, and a challenge to the constitutionality of a pre-Constitution statute when assessing the obligation of the State to ensure that the tender age of children should not be abused for the purpose of reaching a general conclusion of what might be embraced by the exigencies of the common good.

In *Nova Media Services v Minister for Posts and Telegraphs*,[41] and *Attorney General v Paperlink Ltd*,[42] both Murphy J and Costello J considered Article 45 of the Constitution in the context of the State monopolies. Costello J stated in *Paperlink* that the Article demonstrated

> a view, found in other Articles of the Constitution, that the social order should not be based on a system in which all the means of production are owned by the State and a preference for one in which, in the main, industry and commerce are carried on by private citizens but rather than by State agencies.[43]

However, he added:

> But it does not follow from this very general guideline that the Oireachtas could not pass laws establishing State corporations or public utilities and I do not consider that it is proper to infer from its provisions that the State is called upon at legal proceedings to justify the existence of a State monopoly either in the form of a public utility or a trading corporation.[44]

In *Kerry Co-operative Creameries v An Bord Bainne*[45], McCarthy J observed that the doctrine of restraint of trade should be read in the light of Article 45, commenting that it was desirable, from the standpoint of the public good, to protect the right to work of weaker parties from abuse, and to gain the economic benefits of preventing such abuses. His view was that the terms of the preface to Article 45 did not preclude the courts from considering that Article in the construction of the common law. He held that the construction of the doctrine of restraint of trade should be informed by the application of Article 45 of the Constitution. He referred to case law where 'some decisions have excluded the application of Article 45, others have applied the Article.'[46]

Against these somewhat tentative explorations, however, it must be said that Henchy J in *The People (Director of Public Prosecutions) v O'Shea*,[47] went so far as to pronounce that, if any person were even to institute proceedings in the High Court seeking to compel the State to give effect to any of the directives of

[39] *Rodgers v ITGWU* [1978] ILRM 51.

[40] *Landers v Attorney General* 108 ILTR 1.

[41] *Nova Media Services v Minister for Posts and Telegraphs* [1984] ILRM 161.

[42] *Attorney General v Paperlink Ltd* [1984] ILRM 373.

[43] Ibid 387.

[44] Ibid 387–388.

[45] *Kerry Co-operative Creameries v An Bord Bainne* [1991] ILRM 851.

[46] Ibid 870. He cited *Buckley v Attorney General* [1950] IR 57, *Byrne v Ireland* [1972] IR 241, *Comyn*, and *O'Brien v Manufacturing Engineering Co Ltd* [1973] IR 334 in the former category and *Murtagh Properties, Ryan, Rodgers, Landers, Nova* and *Paperlink* in the latter.

[47] *The People (Director of Public Prosecutions) v O'Shea* [1982] IR 384.

social policy, the High Court would be bound to strike out those proceedings for want of jurisdiction. In *Mhic Mathúna v Ireland*,[48] Carroll J in the High Court dismissed a claim, holding that the court could not adjudge taxation legislation to be unconstitutional in the light of the provisions of Article 45 which addressed principles of social policy. Judicial guardedness in relation to this line of jurisprudence can also be found in the observations of the Supreme Court in *Re Article 26 and Part V of the Planning and Development Bill 1999*.[49]

A consideration of the manner in which social and economic values were argued, and dealt with by the courts, would not be complete without addressing the very clear application of justiciability and the principle of separation of powers contained in the 'education cases' such as *T.D. v The Minister for Education*[50] and *Sinnott v Minister for Education*.[51] In *T.D.*, Murphy J referred to Article 45, only so as to express the view that it had not been envisaged that social welfare rights should exist at a constitutional level. In that and other subsequent cases, the majority of members of the Supreme Court (including Murphy and Hardiman JJ) expressed grave reservations on separation of powers grounds as to whether, save as specifically identified in the Constitution itself, a court could give constitutional and justiciable expression to 'socio-economic' rights or rights concerning the allocation of State resources. The strongly expressed majority view was that such were matters for the legislature rather than the judiciary; and that the identification of economic and social priorities was a matter which lay outside the purview of judges.[52] The court laid emphasis on the view that it, or any court, was ill-equipped to make determinations or choices as to social priorities, or between any one such claim and a range, or class of others, within that class.

In summary, therefore, it may be said that the impact of the 1937 social policy principles was quite limited. It cannot be said that, in themselves, they influenced the ethos and social fabric of Irish society. The Irish judges were generally profoundly respectful of the preface to Article 45. As a general proposition, the fact that these values were expressed as 'principles' was seen as a mode of distinction from 'rights', 'freedoms' and 'duties' identified elsewhere in the Constitution. The judge's interpretative role was very much influenced by the tradition of restraint; hardly surprisingly as they were products of their own politics in a nation state where separation of powers ideas had become deeply embedded.

[48] *Mhic Mathúna v Ireland* [1989] IR 504.

[49] *Re Article 26 and Part V of the Planning and Development Bill 1999* [2000] 2 IR 321.

[50] *T.D. v The Minister for Education* [2001] 4 IR 259. See the vivid exchanges on this issue in G Whyte, 'Rights and Judicial Activism' in Fanning et al (eds.) *Theorising Irish Social Policy* (Dublin, University College Dublin Press, 2004); Hardiman J, 'The Role of the Supreme Court in Our Democracy' in J Mulholland (ed.) *Political Choice and Democratic Freedom in Ireland* (Dublin, MacGill Summer School, 2004); G Whyte, 'The Role of the Supreme Court in Our Democracy: A Response to Mr. Justice Hardiman' (2006) 27 *DULJ* 1; and other articles referred to in D Kenny, 'The Separation of Powers and Remedies', in Carolan (n 9). For a very clear exposition of the arguments against rendering socio-economic rights justiciable, see the judgment of Hardiman J in *Sinnott v Minister for Education* [2001] 2 IR 545.

[51] *Sinnott* v *v Minister for Education* (n 50).

[52] For two other judgments from the common law tradition, see Brennan J's opinion in *Baker v Carr* 369 US 186 at 217, and the judgment of the Supreme Court of Canada in *Re Secession of Quebec* (1998) 161 DLR (4th) 385 at 401–402.

III

To what extent can one discern similar influences and outcomes in the drafting process of the Charter of Fundamental Rights? Just as in 1937, the intent behind the Charter was clearly to define a 'new departure' for the European Union. In *Postwar: A History of Europe since 1945*,[53] Tony Judt describes some of the challenges facing the European Union in 2000.[54] It was an era of prosperity and optimism. But, very substantial sums were being expended on agriculture. The budget process which had evolved since the formation of the EC was a 'historical relic'. The transition to the euro preoccupied the minds of every western capital. The idea of a close-knit European confederation was, Judt wrote then, 'solidifying' into 'something much more concrete'. The Member States were facing up to the issue of enlargement so as to integrate the new European democracies to the east. These states wished for full membership not some form of association. Sionaidh Douglas Scott, writing in 2002, referred, in unflattering terms, to the 'collapse and resignation' of the Commission in March 1999 as a further element of the backdrop.[55]

Judt describes the Nice Council in December 2000 as 'highly charged' as the 'leading European statesmen ... spent sleepless nights bargaining and bickering for status and influence in their common European home, illustrated the price that was now being paid for previous neglect of constitutional niceties'.[56] This gave much impetus to the establishment of a European convention to produce a system of governance for an enlarged Europe.

The initiation of, and the outcome from, the conception of a single European constitutional ideal lies a little beyond this essay.[57] Part of the process was the production of the Charter of Fundamental Rights, for a Europe that was to be much more than 'a trinity of France, England and Germany'.[58] There was undoubtedly political alienation. Judt writes of what he refers to as the 'haughty unconcern' of technocrats who had built up the new Europe being 'repaid in kind and in earnest', by perceived citizens' alienation from European institutions.[59] He quotes Clement Attlee, the British post war Prime Minister, who, in a different context, spoke of the fallacy of officials who believed

[53] Tony Judt, *Postwar: A History of Europe Since 1945* (London, Pimlico, 2005).

[54] Ibid 729.

[55] Douglas Scott, *Constitutional Law of the European Union* (London, Longman, 2002). She describes the controversy of the advocates and opponents of the Charter, quoting Joseph Weiler, writing in two years earlier, to the effect that the citizens of Europe appeared to 'suffer' from a surplus rather than a deficit of judicial protection of their fundamental rights ('Does the European Union truly need a Charter of Rights? (2000) 6 *ELJ* 95). While praising the transparency of the process, and the intent behind the Charter, she expressed strong reservations on the Charter's 'opaque language' and, specifically, its scope.

[56] Judt (n 53) 723.

[57] The Charter was contained in the main text of the draft Constitution; the explanations were included as a declaration. Under the Lisbon Treaty, the Charter has been removed from the text of the Treaties to a separate document together with explanations. See for a broader perspective, P Berman, 'From Laeken To Lisbon: The Origins and Negotiation of the Lisbon Treaty' in A Biondi et al (eds), *EU Law after Lisbon* (Oxford, OUP, 2012).

[58] Judt (n 53) 729 quoting Ortega y Gasset.

[59] Ibid 730.

that 'it is possible by the elaboration of machinery to escape the necessity of trusting one's fellow human beings.'[60]

The intent behind the Charter was to imbue the European Union, not only with a further degree of legitimacy and public acceptance by the identification of rights and freedoms, but also to promulgate social principles, which are now particularly to be found under the heading 'Solidarity' under Title IV of the Charter. Just as in 1937, there was the same dynamic between some who simply wished the Charter to be an iteration of 'rights and freedoms', on the one hand, and others who saw it as an opportunity to promulgate a new European social ethos, what is sometimes termed a 'civil religion', which would further existentially justify the European Union, and rebut criticisms that it was to be seen only as an organisation to achieve free trade, and devoid of social or human values or a full human rights dimension. Just as was the case in Ireland in 1937, the Charter expresses certain 'communitarian' ideas. Proponents of the social content of the Charter saw it as an opportunity to give further impetus and a deeper purpose to the Union; a reformulation of what the 'project' was about.

Just as in 1937, the Charter identifies a series of social principles, albeit not confined to one Article. In the Charter, the term 'principles' is to be found in close proximity to both the terms 'rights' and 'duties', where the context shows the latter two values are clearly intended to be justiciable. In fact, some principles, as defined and explained in the Charter, are said to be partly right-creating, and partly not so. The steps taken to distinguish these, both in the Charter and its explanatory memorandum, are, some commentators suggest, not always clear.

The thinking behind a Charter for Fundamental Rights can be traced back to June of 1999. Then, the Cologne European Council determined that a charter was necessary in order to identify and consolidate rights as they applied at the level of the European Union. After Cologne, the Tampere Council in October 1999 established a body consisting of representatives of the Member States, members of the Commission, members of the European Parliament and representatives of national parliaments. As well as in Berman's essay noted earlier, this process is also described in Gráinne de Búrca's prescient essay, 'The Drafting of the European Union Charter of Fundamental Rights'.[61] First, I turn briefly to consider the divergent ideas as to the Charter's purpose; then its social rights principles, and then briefly to an outline the Charter's attainment of its present status.

Space does not permit an extensive discussion of the Convention formed to draft the Charter.[62] At the initial meeting of that Convention, many representatives of constituent bodies tasked with drafting the Charter spoke. It was evident from contributions made concerning discussions as to the Convention's work

[60] Judt (n 53).

[61] G de Búrca, 'The Drafting of the European Union Charter of Fundamental Rights' (2001) 26 *EL Rev* 128.

[62] The quotations which follow are taken from CHARTE 4105/00, which is a record of the first meeting of the Convention body – available at http://www.europarl.europa.eu/charter/activities/docs/pdf/formal_cr1_en_en.pdf.

programme that there was an array of ambitions among those involved. There was disagreement as to how the topics were to be broken up into three 'working parties', namely, political and civil rights; economic and social rights; and citizen's rights. In particular, Andrew Duff, a British delegate, is recorded as expressing dissatisfaction with such a proposal, saying he would have preferred a more methodical approach 'to ensure greater consistency between the work of the rapporteurs.'[63]

The Chairman of the Convention, former German President Roman Herzog was more focused on ensuring drafting discipline than any ambition for immediate binding force:

> We are going to draft a text that will not be immediately binding as European law or Community law. Despite this, we should constantly keep the objective in mind that the Charter which we are drafting must one day, in the not too distant future, become legally binding. This calls for a little discipline on our part, as I feel we should not draft a list which will need to be curtailed or revised when the time comes to make it binding. We should therefore proceed as if we had to submit a legally binding list, and we should not forget that our mandate is in principle to draft a list addressed to the bodies of the European Union, by which they will be bound.[64]

Commissioner Vitorino, representative of the Commission, in a very carefully phrased contribution, sought to describe the intended scope of the Charter. He highlighted the necessity for the Convention to address two preliminary issues: the type of rights to be included; and the relationship between the Charter and the European Convention on Human Rights. On this first issue, he observed:

> Regarding the type of rights to be included in the Charter, thoughts should first focus on the brief adopted by the Cologne European Council. There it is stated that the Charter should contain the fundamental rights and freedoms as well as basic procedural rights guaranteed by the European Convention on Human Rights and derived from the constitutional traditions common to the Member States, as general principles of Community law.[65]

The concept of principles derived from constitutional traditions common to Member States was to become an issue of hot debate. The Commissioner continued:

> The Heads of State or Government further want the Charter to include the rights reserved for the Union's citizens and *account taken* of economic and social rights as contained in the European Social Charter and the Community Charter of the Fundamental Social Rights of Workers. Restating the point I have made about not losing sight of the ultimate aim, namely the Charter's integration into the Treaties, I believe that this body should concentrate on those fundamental rights deriving directly from the European Union's very existence.[66]

[63] Ibid 5.
[64] CHARTE 4105/00 (n 62) 9.
[65] Ibid 17.
[66] CHARTE 4105/00 (n 62) 17 (emphasis added).

He continued:

> 'In line with the wishes of the Heads of State or Government, if we follow this approach the Charter will contain civil and political rights, social rights and also rights deriving from European citizenship. However, these will be included only if – and insofar as – they are rights conferred or protected by the Union. Thus, the Union Charter of Fundamental Rights will not seek to replace national constitutions or instruments of international law, but confine itself to supplementing them from the viewpoint of the Union's legal system.'[67]

Íñigo Méndez de Vigo, a highly influential Spanish representative of the European Parliament and a leading member of the European People's Party, was, however, definite in his idea of what the Parliament's aspirations for the Charter. He said:

> I would like to make it quite clear that for us a mere declaration is not enough, and this being the case we would like to work as you yourself said, Chairman, 'bearing in mind' the second hypothesis sketched out in Tampere. The Charter of Fundamental Rights must be binding and must be incorporated into the Treaty. To the extent that the Treaties constitute the Constitutional Charter of the European Union, as reaffirmed by the case-law of the Court of Justice, the Charter of Fundamental Rights should be a part of it.[68]

As we will see, the Charter contained resonances of the Spanish Constitution of 1978, as well as French constitutional thinking.

De Búrca writes that, when the work of drafting was completed, it was difficult to avoid the conclusion that the political participants in the Nice Council, which was to adopt and promulgate the Charter, were not entirely convinced as to the jurisprudential nature of the document which had been created. The Charter was 'proclaimed'. Speeches of those involved in its inception were curtailed. At the outset it was hardly seen as a legal document at all. Many saw the Charter as being unexceptionable as a purely political document that did not then have any legal consequence or effect.

But as de Búrca comments, elements of the British media thought otherwise. They portrayed the Charter as being a Trojan horse, carrying within it dark implications. Paul Craig describes some of the press coverage as painting a picture of expansionism by 'some reified entity called the EU, with the Commission playing a Machiavellian role in the process.'[69] De Búrca rebuts such a scenario however. She comments that it was the Member States, and not the Commission, which set the terms of reference for the Charter, and that, if anything, the Commission's legal advisors sought to be restraining influences.[70]

But what was the nature of the agreed document? Did the language deployed demonstrate consensus or conceal division? One commentator, Miguel Poiares Maduro, commented that the Charter reflected 'an emerging trend to agree on

[67] Ibid 18.

[68] CHARTE 4105/00 (n 62) 12.

[69] P Craig, *EU Administrative Law* (Oxford, OUP, 2006).

[70] Even in 2014, at the time of writing, the range and effect of the Charter is a highly controversial issue in the United Kingdom media.

the language of constitutionalism in European integration without agreeing on the conception of constitutionalism underlying such language.'[71]

Another commentator, Professor Conor Gearty, commented that there was something suggestive of 'Platonic guardianship' about the Convention process, in the sense of its relative absence of democratic legitimation, and the fact that, despite inviting and listening to various interest groups from civil society, the Convention did not submit the Charter to democratic ratification in the preponderance of Member States.[72] The Lisbon Treaty recognising the Charter was, of course, passed by referendum in Ireland.

One of De Búrca's observations, written as long ago as 2000, deserves reiteration in the context of the process of legal integration and constitutionality of the Charter which followed over the next decade. She wrote then:

> [T]he grand moments of legal and constitutional change in the European Union have long been characterised by precisely the kind of deeply ambivalent process represented by the drafting of the E.U. Charter, a compromise which bridges sharp divisions of political opinion about the nature, role and future of the European Union, as well as the relationship between the European Union and its Member States.[73]

She continued: '[t]he fact that a number of the central actors involved in the Charter process have been capable … of providing entirely different accounts of the nature of the undertaking in which they are engaged, illustrates this feature sharply.'[74]

What was the Convention process intended to achieve? Roman Herzog referred to it as simply a 'consciousness-raising public relations exercise'.[75] Some espoused the view that the body had no constitutional mandate.[76]

At the conclusion of her Article, de Búrca wrote:

> Yet the very act of opening up of a new forum of this kind is suggestive of the potential for newer and more experimental forms of constitutional development in the European Union. As Ulrich Preuss has commented, we should not underestimate 'the cunning of reason' and the likelihood of such a process, albeit developed on an ad hoc basis and entirely outside the terms of the European Union Treaties, outgrowing the limited intentions and design of the heads of state who established it, and acquiring an independent constitutional significance which could ultimately threaten their status as Herren der Verträge [Masters of the Treaties].[77]

From participants, one can glean that the debates at the Convention involved different concepts of democracy, different notions of the separation of powers,

[71] M Poiares Maduro, 'The Double Life of the Charter of Fundamental Rights' in T Hervey and J Kenner (eds), *Economic and Social Rights under the EU Charter of Fundamental Rights: A Legal Perspective* (Oxford, Hart Publishing, 2003).

[72] C Gearty, Conference on the Charter, King's College London, October 2000, referred to in Douglas Scott (n 55).

[73] de Búrca (n 61) 127.

[74] Ibid.

[75] de Búrca (n 61).

[76] See 'Vers une charte des droits fondamentaux de l'Union européene' (Paris, *La documentation Française*, 2000) referenced in de Búrca, ibid.

[77] de Búrca (n 61) 138.

different ideas of justiciability, and that these very differences were particularly evident in the resolution of the concept of 'principles' as outlined in the Charter.

Writing in 2001, Lord Goldsmith, then the leading British representative at the Convention, identified the treatment of social and economic rights in the Charter as having been an area of 'great difficulty' in the negotiations, along with the Charter's relationship with the European Convention on Human Rights.[78]

He considered the concept of justiciable *principles* was per se objectionable, and wrote later:

> It is to be doubted that judges have any mandate or special expertise to determine how national resources shall be allocated between different priorities. These are decisions to be made by governments chosen through the ballot box.[79]

He emphasised that in the common law tradition, social and economic rights are usually not justiciable, but rather inform the legislator in policy making.

Again echoing McElligott, Goldsmith then wrote: '[m]oreover, at the very least to include such rights will raise expectations that the Charter was giving rights which the EU, the principal addressee, was in no position to deliver, having neither the competence nor the budget.' [80]

But he added:

> Others, however, had greater ambitions for the Charter. The debate was long and difficult. The ultimate solution to this problem emerged in the recognition of these differences through a new concept: that these 'rights' essentially took the form of principles which, whilst common to Member States, are implemented differently in the national laws and practices; and that the principles only give rise to rights to the extent that they are implemented by national law or, in those areas where there is such competence, by Community law.[81]

At that time, Goldsmith wrote quite accurately, that the Charter was then neither 'embryo Constitution' nor 'law of binding rights', but rather that it put human rights at the heart of Europe, which had been seen too often as a 'cold place' concerned more with economic integration and red tape.[82] Was it envisaged in 2000 that the Charter would in time become a constitutional document? The quotation from President Herzog indicates that, for some at least, it was.

In *EU Law after Lisbon*, Anderson and Murphy write in an illuminating essay that leading British politicians disavowed any notion that the Charter would be justiciable in English courts.[83] Seen from today's standpoint such remarks might

[78] P Goldsmith, 'A Charter of Rights, Freedoms and Principles', (2001) 38 *CML Rev* 1201.

[79] Ibid 1212.

[80] Goldsmith (n 78).

[81] Goldsmith (n 78) 1212–1213.

[82] Ibid 1216.

[83] D Anderson and C Murphy, 'The Charter of Fundamental Rights' in A Biondi et al (n 57). These clear statements must be seen in the context of the UK Protocol to the Charter (Protocol on the application of the Charter of Fundamental Rights of the European Union to Poland and to the United Kingdom). Article 1 of the Protocol provides:

1. The Charter does not extend the ability of the Court of Justice of the European Union, or any court or tribunal of Poland or of the United Kingdom, to find that the laws, regulations

be seen as rather erroneous. They must be seen in the context of the time they were made and the extreme scrutiny given to the Charter by the UK Parliament, as well as the various United Kingdom 'opt-outs'. But it cannot be said any longer that the Charter is merely a political document. In the successive decade, it began to be mentioned in judgments and opinions of the Court of Justice; ultimately, it became law with the adoption of the Lisbon Treaty.

The Charter's legal status is now firmly established in Article 6(1) of the Treaty of European Union which provides:

> The Union recognises the rights, freedoms and principles set out in the Charter of Fundamental Rights of the European Union of 7 December 2000, as adopted at Strasbourg, on 12 December 2007, which shall have the same legal value as the Treaties.

In general, it is binding on all Member States. It is clear that the Charter does not purport to abrogate pre-existing general fundamental rights principles of law which had been regarded as human rights protections in the EU for some decades, but rather pronounces values with a social or economic dimension. The latter socio-economic values are now the focus of the essay.

In what follows, I quote from the Charter itself, or, alternatively, outline some concerns expressed by learned commentators. Interpretation of the Charter's provisions can only be made in the context of specific cases and specific facts. Some judicial prudence is a necessary constraint here.

IV

The difficulty which the negotiators encountered at the Convention can still be traced in some of the phraseology of the Charter.[84] As we will now see, there is some acknowledgment that there is no, one, dividing line between 'rights' and 'principles', which can be found in the Charter itself. While some might have thought that 'rights' should be justiciable, and 'principles' available for the guidance of legislators, such a line of demarcation was not, apparently, always observed consistently. Title VII, 'General Provisions Governing the Interpretation and Application of the Charter', is of considerable interpretative significance. It seeks to address the question by stating that Article 52(5) of the Charter clarifies the distinction between rights and principles. That sub-Article provides:

or administrative provisions, practices or action of Poland or of the United Kingdom are inconsistent with the fundamental rights, freedoms and principles that it reaffirms.

2. In particular, and for the avoidance of doubt, nothing in Title IV of the Charter creates justiciable rights applicable to Poland or the United Kingdom except in so far as Poland or the United Kingdom has provided for such rights in its national law.

This must also, of course, be seen as well prior to the adoption of the Lisbon Treaty and Charter. The interpretation of this Protocol has caused much controversy in the United Kingdom. See *The Queen (A.B) v Home Secretary* [2013] EWHC 3453 (Admin); and Case C-411/10 *N.S. v Secretary of State for the Home Department* (Unreported, Court of Justice, 21st November 2011).

[84] See F Jacobs, 'The Lisbon Treaty and the Court of Justice' in Biondi (n 57) and particularly, the concerns expressed as to the Charter, 207.

5. The provisions of this Charter which contain principles may be implemented by legislative and executive acts taken by institutions, bodies, offices and agencies of the Union, and by acts of Member States when they are implementing Union law, in the exercise of their respective powers. They shall be judicially cognisable only in the interpretation of such acts and in the ruling on their legality.

It might be thought that, on its face, these words seek to reflect a concept of non-justiciability analogous to what is contained in the preface to Article 45 of the Irish Constitution regarding the non-justiciability of the Directive Principles of Social Policy.[85]

The Explanation relating to the text of the Charter[86] goes on to state that the distinction between rights and principles is to be based on the fact that subjective rights shall be respected, whereas principles shall be observed. The memorandum refers to Article 51(1), which sets out to whom the Charter is addressed:

> The provisions of this Charter are addressed to the institutions, bodies, offices and agencies of the Union with due regard for the principle of subsidiarity and to the Member States only when they are implementing Union law. They shall therefore respect the rights, observe the principles and promote the application thereof in accordance with their respective powers and respecting the limits of the powers of the Union as conferred on it in the Treaties.

In relation to Article 52(5), the Explanation states:

> Principles may be implemented through legislative or executive acts (adopted by the Union in accordance with its powers, and by the Member States only when they implement Union law); accordingly, they become significant for the Courts only when such acts are interpreted or reviewed. They do not however give rise to direct claims for positive action by the Union's institutions or Member States' authorities. This is consistent both with case-law of the Court of Justice[87] … and with the approach of

[85] A very succinct and powerful description of concerns as to the scope of the Charter can be found in P Gallagher, 'The Limits of Constitutionalism', in Carolan (2012) (n 9), particularly from p. 182 onwards. The author draws attention to the fact that Article 51(1) of the Charter is, inter alia, addressed to the institutions of the Union, as well as its bodies, offices and agencies. He draws attention to the fact that Union courts are Union institutions (Article 13 TEU) and are bound to respect the rights, observe the principles and provide the application thereof in accordance with their respective roles and respecting the powers of the Union, as expressed in the Treaties. He writes, '[t]here is nothing that expressly limits this obligation to cases brought against political authorities, whether Union or national ones.' While expressing disagreement, the author refers in detail to Professor Paul Craig's 'radical' analysis of Article 51(1) of the Charter, which might allow for a horizontal application of a Charter right and, perhaps, principle against another individual provided the subject matter falls within EU law. The former Attorney General draws attention also to the impact of Article 52(3) of the Charter which provides that, in the areas where the Charter applies, the ECHR will operate at a constitutional level. The author writes: '…it is difficult to believe that the development and identification of rights under the Charter will not ultimately have an enormous impact on the development of rights under the [Irish] Constitution.' He also describes the wide range of 'third generation' rights also to be found in the Charter, such as the protection of the environment.

[86] Explanations relating to the Charter of Fundamental Rights ([2007] OJ C303/02).

[87] The omitted portion reads: (*cf* the case-law on the 'precautionary principle' in Article 191(2) of the Treaty on the Functioning of the European Union: judgment of the CFI of 11 September 2002, Case T-13/99 *Pfizer v Council*, with numerous references to earlier case-law; and a series of judgments on Article 33 (ex-39) on the principles of agricultural law, eg judgment of the Court of Justice in Case 265/85 *Van den Berg* [1987] ECR 1155: scrutiny of the principle of market stabilisation and of reasonable expectations).

> the Member States' constitutional systems to 'principles', particularly in the field of social law. For illustration, examples for principles, recognised in the Charter include eg Articles 25, 26 and 37. In some cases, an Article of the Charter may contain both elements of a right and of a principle, eg Articles 23, 33 and 34.[88]

These and other provisions deserve further consideration.

Article 23, 'Equality between women and men' provides:

> Equality between women and men must be ensured in all areas, including employment, work and pay.

Then it provides:

> The principle of equality shall not prevent the maintenance or adoption of measures providing for specific advantages in favour of the under-represented sex.

Anderson and Murphy comment that Article 23 describes the already judicially enforceable right to equality between women and men as 'the *principle* of equality'(emphasis added).[89]

Article 25 is headed 'The rights of the elderly'. It states:

> The Union recognises and respects the rights of the elderly to lead a life of dignity and independence and to participate in social and cultural life.

Article 26 is headed 'Integration of persons with disabilities'. It states:

> The Union recognises and respects the right of persons with disabilities to benefit from measures designed to ensure their independence, social and occupational integration and participation in the life of the community.

Article 37 addresses environmental protection. It guarantees:

> A high level of environmental protection and the improvement of the quality of the environment must be integrated into the policies of the Union and ensured in accordance with the principle of sustainable development.

Articles 25, 26 and 37, by their phraseology, might be taken as being purely principles. But Article 25 refers to the recognition and respect for *rights* of the elderly. The explanatory memorandum states that 'rights shall be respected, whereas principles shall be observed'. This is a provision which the memorandum says contains a principle, yet, commentators say, adopts the phraseology and terms used in the context of rights, a term which is itself used in the Article.[90] Discerning the distinctions will pose challenges to legal minds.

The Explanation states that there are Articles which contain elements of both a right and a principle,[91] for example Article 23, 'Equality between women and men', referred to earlier. This provides equality between women and men must be ensured in all areas including employment, work and pay. It goes on to state the *principle* of equality shall not prevent the maintenance or adoption

[88] Explanations (n 86) 19.
[89] Anderson and Murphy (n 83) 162.
[90] See the Note to Article 52(5), quoted above.
[91] See the Note to Article 52(5), quoted above.

of measures providing for specific advantages in favour of the unrepresented sex. The value of equality itself is a justiciable value, routinely engaged in ECJ case-law.[92]

Article 33 addresses family and professional life. It states:

> 1. The family shall enjoy legal, economic and social protection.
> 2. To reconcile family and professional life, everyone shall have the right to protection from dismissal for a reason connected with maternity and the right to paid maternity leave and to parental leave following the birth or adoption of a child.

Here, one might comment that the demarcation line between right and principle is again yet to be defined. The usage of the word 'shall' occurs in Article 33(1) and Article 33(2). This term ('shall') is often used in conferring a right. The rights contained in Article 33(2) are justiciable and have been identified in ECJ case law.

Article 34(1) provides for 'the entitlement to social security benefits and social services providing protection in cases such as maternity, illness, industrial accidents, dependency or old age, and in the case of loss of employment, in accordance with the rules laid down by Union law and national laws and practices'. This is the language which the explanatory memorandum might indicate, should, in accordance with Article 52, be used in the context of principles.

A leading writer on the subject, Professor Paul Craig, has recently commentated on this issue in *The Lisbon Treaty: Law of Politics and Treaty Reform*.[93] Craig's view is that many of the Charter provisions dealing with social matters may actually be properly thought of as rights capable of individual legal enforcement.[94] He instances the right in Article 29 to free placement services, and the right to an injunction against unfair dismissal under Article 30. Craig points out that these provisions, like others, stipulate that the protection operates in accordance with 'Union law and national law and practices.' However, he adds, this does not preclude interpretation of the relevant Article as an enforceable right, and affirms that the utilisation in the Charter of the phrase 'Union law and national law and practices' cannot be seen as an infallible guide as to whether, what is in question is a right or a principle.

Craig rejects any demarcation based on an equation between rights and prohibitions on the one hand, and principles and positive action on the other. He points out that a right can be infringed by inaction as well as action, and that the protection of a right can require positive action by the State or other public body.

Anderson and Murphy draw attention to the fact that Article 52(5) provides that the provisions of the Charter which contain principles 'may be implemented' by Union institutions and Member States, and that 'they shall be judicially cognisable only in the interpretation of such acts and in the ruling

[92] Gallagher (n 85) observes that, pursuant to Article 157 TFEU, the principle of equal pay has both vertical and horizontal effect.

[93] P Craig, *The Lisbon Treaty: Law of Politics and Treaty Reform* (Oxford, OUP, 2010).

[94] Ibid 218.

on their legality'. No such restriction is placed on the 'rights and freedoms' or 'rights' referred to elsewhere in Article 52.' The authors express the view that:

> The distinction is evidently intended to be a significant one, given that principles do not give rise to direct claims for positive action by the Union's institutions or Member States.[95] However, it depends on the existence of a dividing line between provisions of the Charter that contain 'rights' and those that contain 'principles'.

To this they add, 'the Charter was not drafted with such a distinction in mind'.[96]

Those authors refer to principles in the Charter which, in their view, appear unenforceable in the absence of implementing measures, but which are expressly described in the title or their texts as rights, 'for example, the Article 27 principle that workers must be guaranteed information "under the conditions provided for by Union law and national laws and practices", and the Article 30 provision for protection in the event of unjustified dismissal.'[97]

Conversely, they state, the 'only provision referring to "principles" in its title is Article 49: "Principles of legality and proportionality of criminal offences and penalties". Yet that Article confers rights that the Court of Justice has long felt able to apply without the need for implementing legislation'.[98]

They comment it is not plain whether, what they describe as 'these hybrid Articles' 'contain separate rights and principles or whether the concept of rights and principles are blended in a single provision'.[99] They write that one of the six examples identified in the explanatory memorandum (Article 34, which deals with social security and social assistance) actually uses the terminology 'in accordance with the rules laid down by Union law and national law and practices', which, they write, might have been thought a good indicator of a principle requiring implementation. However, this Article, despite being qualified in all respects by that apparently key phrase, is said in the Explanations to include elements of a right. Those authors contend that '[i]n the absence of precise guidance, the distinction between rights and principles, though important, seems set to remain obscure and unpredictable.'[100]

Craig contends there is an ambiguity latent in Article 52(5).[101] He comments that a narrow interpretation would dictate that the courts can only take cognisance of such principles when interpreting a ruling on the legality of acts that directly seek to implement such principles. He writes that, if this view were to be adopted, such cognisance could only be taken when a Union or Member State measure could be said to implement directly the Charter itself. However,

[95] The footnote to this states:
As stated in the explanations with regard to Article 52 by reference, inter alia, to existing case law on the principle. If taken literally, however, the curious result will ensue that the misimplementation of a principle could be condemned as invalid, whereas in the event that a 'principle' is not implemented, that principle would apparently not be allowable even as an aid to the interpretation of related provisions of law.

[96] Anderson and Murphy (n 83) 161.

[97] Ibid 162.

[98] Anderson and Murphy (n 83); see also Case C-63/83 *R v Kent Kirk* [1984] ECR 2899.

[99] Anderson and Murphy (n 83).

[100] Ibid.

[101] Craig (n 93) 220.

he suggests that such a reading would not fit with the explanatory memorandum which, he writes, exemplifies the judicial role in relation to Charter principles by analogy to existing jurisprudence on the precautionary principle and principles used in agricultural law. He then states that '[t]hese principles, however, do not apply when the challenged act is designed directly to implement those principles'.[102] His view is that Charter provisions regarded as principles could be given cognisance when interpreting a ruling on the legality of Union acts, irrespective of whether the Union act was directly implementing the relevant principle or not. How these various views will resolve themselves must await developments, specifically in the CJEU.

V

Those who come from a common law background can sometimes hold an oversimplified view as to the homogeneity of civil law jurisdictions. As a consequence, common lawyers sometimes labour under the misperception that all continental European jurisdictions do not distinguish, or sufficiently distinguish between socio-economic, and other rights. However, when one looks to other jurisdictions, one becomes aware of the uniqueness of each jurisdiction, despite common background in the civil law.[103] These differences are also apparent in how different jurisdictions deal with the rights-principles 'dichotomy,' where it is recognised. This has helpfully been addressed in a very recent publication.

In 2012, the Association of the Councils of State and Supreme Administrative Jurisdictions of the European Union sought to address the question of whether the differentiation between 'rights' and 'principles' is 'totally alien' to national political systems, or whether, on the contrary, such systems do, in fact, feature something similar.[104] In a questionnaire used to compile a final report[105], Member States were asked whether they recognised rights which were directly applicable and others which were not. The authors found a distinction such as that to be found in Article 52(5) of the Charter in the case of Spain, France, Poland, Germany, Austria, Italy, Greece, Switzerland, Portugal, Denmark, Slovakia, the Czech Republic and Slovenia. They note:

> What these provisions have in common is that they a) cannot give rise in and of themselves to action before a court but, rather, they are applied only when law makers

[102] Ibid.

[103] *cf* A Ben-Basset and M Dahan, 'Social Rights in the Constitution and in Practice', (2008) 36 *Journal of Comparative Economics* 103. This paper identifies two clear groups when it comes to social rights, those sharing the French civil law tradition on the one hand, and those with an English common law basis, with the former typically showing a higher commitment to social rights. Countries with a German or Scandinavian tradition are said to more closely resemble the common law position. See also in this volume, F Clarke, 'Union and Common Law : Harmony or Tension'.

[104] The Association of the Councils of State and Supreme Administrative Jurisdictions of the European Union, *Application of the Charter of Fundamental Rights of the European Union by national courts: the experience of administrative court* (Brussels, 2012).

[105] Final Report by LMª Díez-Picazo and M Fraile Ortiz.

> embrace them, or (b) constitute rules of interpretation of other norms; and (c) in many cases refer to social rights.[106]

The report adds other States do not make a distinction between rights and principles. These include Belgium, the Netherlands, Finland, Lithuania, Hungary, Sweden, Romania, Bulgaria, Cyprus, Estonia and Latvia. One might add that the common law countries undoubtedly make such distinctions.

In the same report, President of the Fifth Chamber of the ECJ, Judge Von Danwitz, expressed his personal view that Spain and France probably served as a source of inspiration as to the distinctions between principles and rights in the Charter. The accuracy of Judge Von Danwitz's observation can be seen from a brief consideration of the text of the Spanish Constitution, and in particular Chapter 2, 'Rights and Liberties', and Chapter 3, 'Principles governing Economic and Social Policy'. The latter contains provisions related to 'Redistribution of income', 'Full employment', 'Good working conditions',[107] 'Social Security,'[108] 'Quality of life,'[109] 'Housing,'[110] 'Disabled Persons,'[111] those in 'Old age,'[112] and 'Consumer protection.'[113] But the Report states that, in Spanish jurisprudence, the distinctions and application are clear because the idea underlying the inclusion of principles in the Spanish Constitution 'was to include social rights without affecting the legislator's freedom in the achievement of social policies. Principles in the Spanish Constitution had the same binding force as rights … *but they do not normally constitute autonomous legal foundation for claiming subjective rights*' (emphasis added).[114] They must first be developed by legislators.

In the case of France, it is said 'the Constitution distinguishes between *droits-libertés* and *droits-créances*; the latter are those which would seem to be like principles'.[115] This distinction is not expressly provided for, but arises out of rulings of the Conseil Constitutionnel in 1970 and 1971[116], and subsequent

[106] Ibid 38.
[107] Section 40.
[108] Section 42.
[109] Section 45.
[110] Section 47.
[111] Section 49.
[112] Section 50.
[113] Section 51.
[114] Díez-Picazo and Ortiz (n 105) 38.
[115] Ibid.
[116] See Décision n° 70-39 du 19 juin 1970 and Décision n° 71-44 DC du 16 juillet 1971. In J Bell, *French Constitutional Law* (Oxford, OUP, 1995) at 56 et seq, the author discusses the contrast between the individualistic values of the Declaration of the Rights of Man in 1789 and the social values espoused in the Preamble to the Constitution of 1946. These latter were adopted by the Constitutional Assembly in 1946 after an effort to draft a new Declaration of Rights was rejected by referendum in 1946. Failing a radical revision the Assembly listed additional fundamental political, economic and social rights 'that were particularly necessary for our times'. These contained provisions on equality of the sexes (§ 3), equal access to education and training (§13), the right to work (§5), the right to collective bargaining and participation in the management of a company (§8) as well as rights of asylum (§ 4) and health (§ 11). The State also has a duty to provide the conditions necessary for individual and family development (§ 10). On this Bell comments,

> To see in this Preamble a set of rights is problematic. It is very much a set of pious hopes and objectives lacking in specificity. These are matters of interest in that the Preamble to the current 1958 Constitution declares for a commitment to the rights of man and principles of national sovereignty to be found in the 1946 Constitution.

judicial interpretation thereof, on the status of the 1789 *Declaration of the Rights of Man* and the Preamble to the 1946 Constitution, both of which are recognised in the Preamble to the 1958 Constitution.

The 1789 Declaration incorporates what may now be seen as traditional rights, such as liberty, the right to hold property, freedom of expression, the presumption of innocence, non-retroactivity of punishments, etc. These are what are termed above '*droits-libertés*'. On the other hand, the 1946 Preamble also focuses on certain social values. In principle, these '*droits-créances*' can only be invoked against the legislator for failing to take them in account. It would also seem that a stricter test is applied when assessing a legislative provision against a '*droit-liberté*' rather than a '*droit-créance*'.[117]

The 2012 report goes on to deal with what it describes as the 'uncertain' situation as to the legal consequences for legal systems if an issue involves a right or a principle. If a principle is not directly applicable, does that mean it is not binding? Not all Member States make such a distinction; it may depend on the consequences. Two of the cases where the issue had arisen thus far (in Slovenia and Estonia), have revealed difficulties in identifying the nature of distinction and, therefore, *the need to find rules to determine when one is dealing with a right or principle.* The report points out that the task of distinction will not be easy, or at least not as easy as in Spain, where principles are grouped together in a specific chapter of the Constitution. The Dutch report to the Association said that 'not even the terms of the Charter or its Explanations will always be conclusive, as their use in the texts is not necessarily rigorous'.[118] The Finnish courts adhere first to the literal wording of the precept, and thereafter go to the Explanations, taking into account the circumstances of the case.

The report goes on to state that the task of such identification will devolve upon the CJEU, and also cites extensive case law from that Court, but it says

The Preamble to the 1946 Constitution also contained a series of fundamental principles recognised by the Republic such as freedom of the press (1881), freedom of association (1901) and freedom of religion (1905). Bell comments that the intent behind the term 'fundamental principle recognised by the laws of the Republic' was to 'smuggle in certain values such as freedom of education about which there was considerable disagreement in the Second Constitutional Assembly of 1946': 67–69. The careful 'sifting process' in which the Conseil Constitutionnel engages in recognising this open-ended category of fundamental principles is described in Bell, 69–70.

As well as freedom of association, the Conseil has recognised fundamental rights such as the independence of administrative judges, due process, freedom of movement and privacy as well as respect for all human beings from the beginning of life. However, not all values in the French republican tradition have been constitutional. In the Amnesty Law of 1988, Bell writes, the Conseil stated that the breach of the breach of the republican tradition could only provide the basis for the argument that a provision was unconstitutional 'to the extent that this tradition has given rise to a fundamental tradition recognised by the laws of the Republic.' Other values such as Mitterand's 'social acquisitions' may be contained in the republican tradition but give rise to political and not legal obligations. One might comment that there again can be seen here some reflection of the language of the Charter and its explanatory memorandum.

[117] F Rangeon, 'Droits-Libertés et Droits-Créances: Les Contradictions du Préambule de la Constitution de 1946' in *Le Préambule de la Constitution de 1946* (Paris, Presses Universitaires de France, 1996).

[118] The Association of the Councils of State and Supreme Administrative Jurisdictions of the European Union (n 104) 39.

the distinction between 'rights' and 'principles' has yet to be identified. More complex still is the issue of the manner in which courts are to examine the compatibility of an Act with a principle that is similar to those mentioned in Article 52(5) in the Charter, and the legal consequences of a violation of a principle as opposed to that of a right.[119]

One might comment that the CJEU competence in this area is developing. Suffice it to say that, thus far, the CJEU has adopted a careful, conservative and pragmatic approach, and has addressed any questions arising by a strict adherence to the literal words of Article 52(5).[120]

Some suggest that more fundamental may be the permanence or otherwise of the distinction between EU competence and national competence. Can the CJEU recognise an EU competence, even if has not hitherto been exercised by the Union or its institutions? This question arose in the opinion of Advocate General Sharpston in Case C-34/09 *Zambrano Ruiz.*[121] From paragraph 163 of the Opinion onwards, the Advocate General addressed what she considered to be the need to determine with certainty the meaning of the term 'the scope of Union law', deployed when fundamental rights are at issue. She suggested that the scope should depend on the applicability of the Charter to the acts of the Member States, and on the existence of a material EU competence; even if that competence has not yet been exercised. This suggestion is not supported by CJEU jurisprudence to date. Similarly, the question may arise whether principles give rise to horizontally effective rights between private parties. There is no suggestion to date that the CJEU is disposed to develop its jurisprudence in this way insofar as concerns principles.

VI

It might be thought that concern regarding this distinction is merely one of characterisation; that ultimately it will be 'a matter for the courts'. However, some commentators suggest the task of distinguishing between rights and principles having a socio-economic background is potentially a highly charged one, raising issues regarding concepts of democracy. There may arise questions as to the extent to which the Court of Justice has developed doctrines regarding the issues of justiciablity and competence. It is suggested that these are at an

[119] The issue of accession of the EU to membership of the Council of Europe is outside the scope of this essay.

[120] For an indication as to the manner in which the CJEU will process in future, one need look no further than the *Åkerburg Fransson* (Case C-617(10) [2013] 2 CML Rev 46. There the CJEU captured the scope of application of EU fundamental rights to Member States' actions in a single sentence, 'the applicability of EU law entails applicability of the fundamental rights guaranteed by the Charter'. It confirms that the CJEU will not interpret the phrase 'implementing Union Law' in Article 51 of the Charter narrowly, but more broadly, as 'in all situations governed by EU law'. *Åkerburg Fransson* also implies that the CJEU will make no distinction between the scope of Charter rights and those rights developed in the case law on general principles on EU law. cf B van Bockel and D Wattell, 'New Wine into Old Wineskins: The Scope of the Charter of Fundamental Rights of the EU after Åkerburg Fransson', (2013) 38 EL Rev 866.

[121] Case C-34/09 *Zambrano Ruiz* [2011] ECR I-1177.

embryonic stage, and that, in that context, the potential extension principles is not sufficiently limited or defined.[122] There is no indication of such a tendency from the judgments of the Court. There may arise questions of how the separation of powers is to be applied within the European Union in its application to the Court of Justice. Clearly, this is the more difficult because of the very *sui generis* nature of the European Union itself. It is not simply one nation-state but an association of twenty-eight Member States. One might mention here that further and deeper discussion is necessary as to what lies within the traditions of the Member States of the Union.

It is not impossible that the CJEU may be called on to make difficult choices. Can a clear distinction now be drawn between what is justiciable per se and what may not be? Can distinctions be drawn between principles which are not the affair of the courts on the basis of category alone; or because to answer the question would take a court beyond its own area of competence within its conceptual framework; or because the question does not lie within its own area of expertise; or because it trespasses on the domain of other EU or national organs of government?[123] If, hypothetically, a court is asked to take on a broad role of arbiter of social change, to what extent can it engage in a broader range of fact-finding, rather than confining itself within the facts of a particular case, perhaps a very emotive one? How far can the broader social context or effect of the application of a principle, or a right, be contextualised? Depending on the range and reach of the Charter, one might envisage that this task of classification may give rise to an increased case load on the CJEU and national courts, especially where it might be thought that for national courts the safer course will be to refer such a matter to the Court of Justice. Cases of this type can have the effect of placing courts under a constraint to issue a judgment rapidly rather than allowing it the task of engaging in reasoned explanation. Niamh Nic Shuibhne contends that the CJEU faces challenges in fulfilling its duties to provide clear reasoned judgments raising questions as to legitimacy.[124]

VII

One wonders how JJ McElligott would regard this changed jurisprudential world and how common law judges of past eras would view the idea of justiciable principles. By coincidence, the 'Lochner era' of the United States Supreme Court ended in the same year as the adoption of the Irish Constitution.[125] Despite its troubled history, the Ireland of 1937 was, generally speaking, a remarkably

[122] The Court has traditionally shown great reluctance to strike down a measure as a breach of the principle of subsidiarity.

[123] *cf Baker v Carr* and *Re Secession of Quebec*, cited earlier.

[124] N Nic Shuibhne, Inaugural Lecture, 'The Lawless Science of EU Law: Constitutional Responsibility and the Court of Justice', Edinburgh University, 9 November 2012. Nic Shuibhne criticises the ECJ for insufficiently reasoned judgments. She claims that such judgments run the risk of depriving the ECJ of its legitimacy as a court.

[125] *West Coast Hotel Co v Parrish*, 300 US 379 (1937).

homogenous, if conservative, State. The observations of all those engaged in the process were very much of their time and place. It is doubtful whether many would now disagree with the content of the principles actually identified in the 1937 Constitution. O'Rahilly's concern was what conservative judges would make of the Irish principles. Some courts nowadays, both national and international, are criticised for excessive activism.

One idea which may present challenges is the common law principle of 'separation of powers'. As matters stand, responsibility for legislative and executive matters lies with the Council of the European Union. The Commission enjoys executive, legislative and quasi-judicial powers. The Parliament holds legislative power. The Court of Auditors addresses audit matters. The Court of Justice addresses itself to the interpretation of the EU treaties and matters of Union law. That task involves the equal application of EU law across all Member States. How is the Court to perform that task in the context of social and economic principles? These are quite profound issues.

To what extent will the Charter, in the future, enjoy a form of direct or indirect effect? To what extent will the Charter, as recognised by the TEU, supersede national laws, inform their interpretation, or acquire horizontal effect? These, also, are deep questions. It is ironic that despite criticisms of activism, the CJEU has often adapted a remarkably cautious 'common law' approach to developing its own jurisprudence and powers, approaching each issue carefully on a case-by-case basis, especially in this sensitive area.

Writing in 2011, Weiler criticised what he perceived as a form of 'political messianism' derived from the Schuman Declaration and, traceable through developments in the 1950s and later.[126] He contrasted the desire for true democracies within the Member States to the onset of what he saw as 'political messianism' in pursuit of the European ideal, a form of process where the pursuit of the ideal (the means) was placing at risk the objective of democratic political integration (the end). Might the CJEU be accused of 'judicial messianism' at some future time? It is undoubtedly a charge the Court will seek to guard itself against.

As a general observation, some writers, such as Nic Shuibhne, suggest the ascription of a political or executive role to judges can come at a cost of judicial legitimacy; and that the identification of judges as 'drivers' of the social direction of the Charter may raise challenges for the future.

VIII

But, perhaps, in the end, it is necessary to stand back a little and take a more historical perspective. It is possible to over-dramatise the interaction between the common law and the various systems of civil law as some form of 'clash of legal civilisations'. The situation is far more nuanced and multi-textured than

[126] J Weiler, '60 Years since the first European Community – reflections on political messianism', (2011) 22 *European Journal of International Law* 303.

that caricature. Some of the commentary would suggest that what is occurring is some subterranean grinding of tectonic plates between irreconcilable legal cultures, resulting in some future yet to be defined legal earthquake or political schism. In the law, life is not often like that. The process of harmonisation is designed to avoid such an eventuality.

Seen through the lens of history, can it now be said there is anything jurisprudentially objectionable about any of the Directive Principles of Social Policy contained in the 1937 Constitution? It might be thought that, with the passage of time, these distributive 'principles', have become so universally accepted so as to be uncontroversial. Seen from the perspective of thirteen years, to what extent are the Charter 'principles', the identification of which caused so much controversy in 2000, already uncontroversial? This remains to be seen. Much will depend on how the Court of Justice sees its role.

There is undoubtedly a need to identify criteria for the harmonisation, or prioritisation, of rights, freedoms, duties and principles in the Charter. It is in the nature of many legal systems that some issues are such that while the general guidelines are set out in legislation or in constitutions, it is left to the judges to fill in the interstices.

To observe that the task of judges frequently involves the reconciliation or prioritisation of rights is not new. This fundamentally engages Rawls' two principles of liberty and equality. How they are reconciled, and the principled and rational basis for doing so, is often part of a judge's job description. Even in the common law, a judge's task, even in an individual inter partes matter, has broader dimensions, of making 'fair choices' for society, as well as the parties.

For judges, the task is to address a series of new challenges. In many senses, Lisbon and the Charter constitute a new departure. Will the Charter follow the general trend of harmonisation in EU law? One can anticipate extreme caution in this area. Will there be, at some stage, further discussion of what properly lies in the province of the courts, as opposed to other bodies, organs of state or legislatures? It is to be hoped so. How will our jurisprudence evolve so that 'principle based' decisions accord with some pre-identified and general set of criteria? The identification of such processes is by no means alien to the common law or to civil law traditions, nor to the judicial cultures of the Union's Member States. But one imagines that the Charter will broaden the role the CJEU as a fundamental 'rights' court, whether or not the Union accedes to the ECHR.

It requires no feat of imagination to conclude that the precise meaning of Article 51(1) and Article 52(5) of the Charter will be a subject that will continue to exercise many legal minds. Like the principle of subsidiarity, will the role of those principles be subordinated as an interpretive aid?[127] Courts will have regard to the meaning and intent of the Charter as explained in its own Explanatory Memorandum. In particular, one may speculate that a particular focus will lie on the meaning to be imparted to the statement in the Explanation that

[127] See *Commission v Germany* [2003] ECR I-5369.

principles become significant for the courts only when legislative or executive acts are adopted by the Union and are being interpreted by Member States; to which is added the words 'they do not however give rise to direct claims for positive actions by the Union's institutions or Member State's authorities.' This is to be seen in the context of the approach of each Member State to 'principles'. What is clear from this essay is that the questions raised could occupy a book or books, and that Member States, each in their own way, have sought to avoid any suggestion of 'government by judges'. What is necessary perhaps is a clear 'principled' approach to addressing principles.

Here, as in so many other areas, history will be the ultimate arbiter, but bearing in mind OW Holmes' comment that the life of the law has not been logic, it has been experience.[128]

[128] OW Holmes Jr, *The Common Law* (Boston, Little, Brown and Company, 1881) 1.

19

The Role of National Courts in the Enforcement of EU Competition Law

AINDRIAS Ó CAOIMH*

THE ROLE OF national courts in the enforcement of EU competition law has evolved over time and is essential for the future development of competition law in the European Union. This role has to be seen further in the protection of individual rights within the European Union. It is now 10 years since the entry into force of Regulation No 1/2003, providing for greater enforcement of European competition rules at the national level, and accordingly it is appropriate to have regard to developments in the past 10 years.

Since the coming into being of the European Economic Community under the Treaty of Rome of 1957, national courts or tribunals have made almost 200 preliminary references in the field of competition law dealing with the areas covered by Articles 101 and 102 TFEU, which have resulted in judgments of the Court of Justice.[1] From the earliest days of the then EEC, the Court of Justice recognised the role of national courts in the enforcement of the competition law rules under the Treaties.

In its seminal judgment in *BRT v SABAM*,[2] the Court of Justice indicated that as the prohibitions of Articles 85(1) and 86 EEC[3] 'tend by their very nature to produce direct effects in relations between individuals, these Articles create direct rights in respect of the individuals concerned which national courts must safeguard'. This clearly indicated that individuals and indeed companies could invoke the Treaty provisions in question before national courts. In theory this enabled those adversely affected by anti-competitive agreements and practices in breach of the Treaty provisions to take actions before the national courts to enforce their rights, including seeking damages. In practice there were a number of obstacles to having recourse to national courts in order to enforce these rights.

* Judge of the European Court of Justice

[1] In the areas in question, 194 judgments were delivered by the Court of Justice in the period to 31 December 2013.

[2] Case 127/73 *BRT v SABAM* [1974] ECR 51.

[3] Now Articles 101(1) and 102 TFEU respectively.

The judgment in *BRT v SABAM* followed upon the celebrated case of *Van Gend en Loos*,[4] where the Court in a judgment delivered on 5 February 1963 recognised for the first time that Treaty provisions of European law could produce direct rights in favour of individuals which national courts must protect.

Regulation 17/62[5] ('Regulation 17') was adopted by the Council on 6 February 1962, and was the first regulation implementing Articles 85 and 86 EEC. It is of some significance that it predated the Court's decision in *Van Gend en Loos*. The wording of Regulation 17 envisaged public enforcement of the competition rules by the Commission and by the competent authorities of the Member States. There is no mention whatsoever in the Regulation of actions being taken before the national courts in the context of private enforcement.

Questions on the interpretation of the Treaty provisions on competition were referred to the Court of Justice from as early as 10 July 1961, when the Court of Appeal of The Hague made the first reference ever to the Court of Justice for a preliminary ruling under what was then Article 177 of the EEC Treaty. This was in the case of *Bosch v Van Rijn*,[6] in which Advocate General Lagrange delivered his opinion on 27 February 1962, some 6 days after the publication of Regulation 17 in the Official Journal. The Court of Justice indicated that Article 85 had been applicable from the time of the entry into force of the Treaty.[7] However, it is clear that the Court ruled on the case before it with the benefit of Regulation 17, even though that regulation had not yet entered into force at the time when the reference was made by the national court.

Following the initial judgment in *Bosch v Van Rijn* in 1962, 52 references for preliminary rulings from national courts in the fields covered by Articles 85 and 86 EEC resulted in a judgment in the 25 years that followed. The issues of competition arose on occasion in the context of a defence to an action at the national level, as in *Bosch v Van Rijn*, and not necessarily in the context of what is now referred to as private enforcement at the national level. Enforcement at national level was beset by a number of problems, not least the provisional validity of agreements notified to the European Commission under Regulation 17.

Regulation 17 provided for a centralised notification and authorisation system by which undertakings had to notify agreements to the Commission to benefit from the exemption provided for in Article 85(3) EEC,[8] since the Commission had exclusive competence to apply this provision by adopting formal exemption decisions.

Agreements which were notified to the Commission in accordance with Regulation 17 obtained provisional validity upon due notification and the parties to such agreements benefited from exemption from fines.[9]

[4] Case 26/62 *Van Gend en Loos v Nederlandse Administratie der Belastingen* [1963] ECR 1.

[5] EEC Council Regulation No 17: First Regulation implementing Articles 85 and 86 of the Treaty [1962] OJ 13/204 (OJ English special edition: Series I, vol 1959–1962, 87).

[6] Case 13/61 *Bosch v Van Rijn* [1962] ECR 45.

[7] Idem, 51.

[8] Subsequently Article 81(3) EC and now Article 101 (3) TFEU.

[9] Article 15 (5) of Regulation 17.

The problems faced in the private enforcement of the then European Community's competition rules were addressed by the European Commission in April 1999 in its White Paper on 'Modernisation of the Rules Implementing Articles 85 and 86 of the EC Treaty'[10] (the 'White Paper'), which highlighted the shortcomings of the then system and outlined the Commission's thinking for the future. The White Paper noted that Regulation 17 had established a system of supervision and enforcement that the Commission had applied for over 35 years without any significant change. It noted that the system had led undertakings to notify large numbers of restrictive practices, not only to get legal certainty but also to block private actions before national courts and national competition authorities. This had undermined efforts to promote the decentralised application of EC competition rules. The White Paper also noted that 'the rigorous enforcement of competition law had suffered and efforts to decentralise the implementation of Community law have been thwarted'.[11] The Commission proposed the abolition of the notification and exemption system and its replacement by a Council Regulation which would render the exemption rule of Article 85(3) EC directly applicable without prior decision by the Commission. It envisaged that Article 85 EC as a whole would be applied by the Commission, national competition authorities and national courts. The White Paper envisaged the enlargement of the Community to include the countries of central and eastern Europe and Cyprus and noted that the system that then existed had been designed to deal with a Community of six Member States, wherease there were 15 Member States.

The White Paper noted that at the time of the adoption of Regulation 17 'national laws, which either did not exist or were heterogeneous, were unable to guide undertakings or courts in their interpretation of Community law'.[12] The system introduced by Regulation 17 resulted, within four years, in the notification of thousands of cases such that, as early as 1967, the Commission was faced with a mass of 37,450 cases that had accumulated since the entry into force of the Regulation.[13] This forced the Commission to adopt a number of measures. In its first formal decision under Article 85 EEC,[14] the Commission introduced the concept of appreciable effect on competition, which allowed for minor cases to be removed from the scope of Article 85 (1) EEC. This interpretation of Article 85 (1) EEC was upheld by the Court of Justice in *Völk v Vervaeke* in 1969.[15] This enabled the Commission to publish a notice on agreements of minor importance, which it published in 1970[16] and updated in 1977, 1986 and 1997.

From 1962, the Commission published a number of general notices, which were intended to allow undertakings to determine themselves whether the restrictive

[10] Commission Programme No 99/027, available at http://europa.eu/documents/comm/white_papers/pdf/com99_101_en.pdf.

[11] Ibid, para 6.

[12] White Paper n 10 above, para 18.

[13] White Paper, n 10 above, para 25.

[14] Commission Decision 64/344/EEC of 1 June 1964 concerning a request for negative clearance pursuant to Article 2 of Regulation 17 (Grosfillex-Fillistorf case) [1964] OJ L64/1426.

[15] Case 5/69 *Frans Völk v SPRL Ets Vervaecke* [1969] ECR 297 para 7.

[16] [1970] OJ C 64/1.

practices to which they were parties were compatible with Community law. These commenced with a notice on exclusive dealing contracts with commercial agents, which was followed by a notice concerning agreements, decisions and concerted practices in the field of cooperation between enterprises,[17] a notice concerning the assessment of certain subcontracting agreements in relation to Article 85(1) EEC[18] and thereafter by a notice concerning the assessment of cooperative joint ventures pursuant to Article 85 EEC.[19] This had the effect of somewhat limiting the number of applications for negative clearance under Article 2 of Regulation 17.[20]

Thereafter the Commission was enabled by the Council under Regulation No 19/65/EEC[21] to adopt a number of 'block exemption regulations' with a view to reducing the number of applications for exemption.[22] These block exemption regulations enabled the Commission to declare the prohibition in Article 85(1) EEC inapplicable to certain categories of agreements. There were five such block exemption regulations for vertical and technology transfer agreements in force at the time of the publication of the Commission's White Paper in April 1999.[23] Under Regulation (EEC) No 2821/71, the Commission adopted two block exemption regulations for horizontal agreements.[24] Regulation (EEC) No 1534/91 enabled the Commission to adopt a block exemption regulation for categories of agreements, decisions and concerted practices in the insurance sector.[25]

The Commission has estimated that these block exemption regulations resulted in a considerable reduction in the number of individual applications for exemption.[26]

[17] [1968] OJ C75/ 3, corrected by [1968] OJ C 84/14.

[18] [1979] OJ C1/2.

[19] [1993] OJ C43/2.

[20] White Paper, n 10 above, para 28.

[21] [1965] OJ 36/533.

[22] Regulation No. 19/65/EEC [1965] OJ 36/533 (OJ English special edition: Series I, vol 1965–1966, 35–37), Regulation No. 2821/71/EEC [1971] OJ L285/46 (OJ English special edition: Series I vol 1971(III), 1032–1034) and Regulation (EEC) No. 1534/91 [1991] OJ L143/1.)

[23] – Regulation (EEC) No 1983/83 of 22 June 1983 on the application of Article 85(3) to categories of exclusive distribution agreements [1983] OJ L 173/1, as amended by Commission Regulation (EC) No 1582/97 of 30 July 1997 [1997] OJ L 214/2.

– Regulation (EEC) No 1984/83 of 22 June 1983 on the application of Article 85(3) to categories of exclusive purchasing agreements [1983] OJ L173/7, as amended by Commission Regulation (EC) No 1582/97 of 30 July 1997 [1997] OJ L 214/2.

– Regulation (EC) No 1475/95 of 28 June 1995 on the application of Article 85(3) to certain categories of motor vehicle distribution and servicing agreements [1995] OJ L 145/25.

– Regulation (EEC) No 4087/88 of 30 November 1988 on the application of Article 85(3) to categories of franchise agreements [1988] OJ L 359/46.

– Regulation (EC) No 240/96 of 31 January 1996 on the application of Article 85(3) to certain categories of technology transfer agreements [1996] OJ L 31/2.

[24] Regulation (EEC) No 417/85 of 19 December 1984 on the application of Article 85(3) to categories of specialisation agreements [1985] OJ L53/1, as amended by Commission Regulation (EC) No 2236/97 of 10 November 1997 [1997] OJ L 306/12, and Regulation (EEC) No 418/85 of 19 December 1984 on the application of Article 85(3) to categories of research and development agreements [1985] OJ L53/5, as amended by Commission Regulation (EC) No 2236/97 of 10 November 1997 [1997] OJ L 306/12.

[25] Regulation (EEC) No 3932/92 of 21 December 1992 [1992] OJ L392/7.

[26] White Paper, n 10 above, para 33.

At the same time the Commission was confronted with particularly cumbersome procedures in the adoption of formal decisions arising from individual notifications, which resulted in the Commission using the technique of 'comfort letters', which informed undertakings that, according to information in the Commission's possession, the notified agreement either did not meet the conditions for the application of Article 85(1) (negative clearance letter) or qualified for exemption (exemption letter). These comfort letters helped to speed up the processing of cases considerably by avoiding the cumbersome procedures of publication and formal consultation as well as translations. This led the Commission to reach a point where 90% of notifications were closed informally.

As these informal procedures constituted neither a decision granting negative clearance nor a decision applying Article 85(3) of the Treaty, they lacked binding effect on national courts before whom such agreements and restrictive practices were alleged to be incompatible with Article 85. National courts and authorities could take them into account as elements of fact.[27]

Following *BRT v SABAM*, the Court of Justice indicated in *Delimitis*[28] in 1991 that national courts could directly apply Article 85(1) EEC if it were beyond doubt that Article 85(3) EEC was not applicable to the case in question and furthermore that they could adopt interim measures pursuant to national rules of procedure. The Court further acknowledged that national courts could apply to the Commission for information on the state of any procedure which the Commission might have set in motion and where the concrete application of Article 85(1) EEC or Article 86 EEC raised particular difficulties, in order to obtain the economic and legal information which the Commission could supply it. The Court clearly recognised the division of competences between the Commission and national courts. It indicated that

> account should here be taken of the risk of national courts taking decisions which conflict with those taken or envisaged by the Commission in the implementation of Articles 85(1) and 86, and also of Article 85(3). Such conflicting decisions would be contrary to the general principle of legal certainty and must, therefore, be avoided when national courts give decisions on agreements or practices which may subsequently be the subject of a decision by the Commission. [29]

Following the publication of the White Paper, the Court of Appeal (England and Wales) made a reference to the Court of Justice for a preliminary ruling in the case of *Courage v Crehan* in July 1999.[30] The Court of Justice indicated the importance of private claims for damages for loss caused by conduct liable to restrict or distort competition. It stated that 'any individual can rely on a breach of Article 85(1) of the Treaty before a national court even where he is a party to a contract that is liable to restrict or distort competition within the

[27] Case 99/79 *SA Lancôme and Cosparfrance Nederland BV v Etos BV and Albert Heyn Supermart BV* [1980] ECR 2511, paras 10–11.

[28] Case C-234/89 *Stergios Delimitis v Henninger Bräu AG* [1991] ECR I-935.

[29] Ibid, para 47.

[30] Case C-453/99 *Courage v Crehan* [2001] ECR I-6297.

meaning of that provision'.[31] The Court later indicated in the same judgment that

> The full effectiveness of Article 85 of the Treaty and, in particular, the practical effect of the prohibition laid down in Article 85(1) would be put at risk if it were not open to *any individual* to claim damages for loss caused to him by a contract or by conduct liable to restrict or distort competition'[32] (emphasis added).

While these statements were particularly important in the recognition of the right to damages in the field of competition, the subsequent case of *Manfredi* [33] enabled the Court to go further in light of the legislative developments since *Courage v Crehan*.

In its White Paper, the Commission favoured the option of what it described as a directly applicable exemption system in which the competition authorities and courts of the Member States would have the power to apply not only Article 85(1) and 86 of the Treaty but also Article 85(3).

On 16 December 2002, the Council adopted Regulation No 1/2003 to provide essentially for the system envisaged by the Commission in its White Paper. The Regulation entered into force on 1 May 2004, on which date 10 new Member States acceded to the Union. The Regulation established a decentralised system of enforcement of European competition law at the national level, while retaining the central role of the Community bodies, such that the Member States were associated more closely with the application of the Union competition rules. It was provided that, in accordance with the principles of subsidiarity and proportionality set out in the Treaty, the Regulation does not go beyond what is necessary in order to achieve its objective, which is to allow the Union's competition rules to be applied effectively. The Regulation regulated the burden of proof under the Treaty provisions which now, following the entry into force of the Treaty of Lisbon in 2009, are Articles 101 and 102 TFEU. It was provided that the Regulation affects neither national rules on the standard of proof nor obligations of competition authorities and courts of the Member States to ascertain the relevant facts of a case, provided that the rules and obligations are compatible with general principles of Community law.

The seventh recital in the preamble to the Regulation indicates that national courts have

> an essential part of play in applying the [Union's] competition rules. When deciding disputes between private individuals, they protect the subjective rights under [Union] law, for example by awarding damages to the victims of infringements. The role of the national courts here complements that of the competition authorities of the Member States. They should therefore be allowed to apply Articles [101 and 102] of the Treaty in full.

While its 37th recital stated that the 'Regulation respects the fundamental rights and observes the principles recognised in particular by the Charter of

[31] Ibid, para 24.
[32] *Courage v Crehan*, n 30 above, para 26.
[33] Joined Cases C-295/04 to C-298/04 *Manfredi and others* [2006] ECR I-6619.

Fundamental Rights of the European Union', it was then indicated that the Regulation should be interpreted and applied with respect to those rights and principles.

Following the coming into effect of Regulation No 1/2003, the Commission issued its Green Paper on damages actions for breach of the EU competition rules in December 2005,[34] in which it described the law in the then 25 Member States as presenting a picture of 'total underdevelopment'. The Commission identified what it described as 'significant obstacles' which exist in the Member States to the effective operation of damages actions for infringement of Community antitrust law. These relate to (i) obtaining the evidence needed to prove a case; (ii) the lack of effective collective redress mechanisms, especially for consumers and SMEs; (iii) the absence of clear rules on the passing-on defence; (iv) the absence of a clear probative value of decisions by national competition authorities; (v) the possibility to bring an action for damages after a competition authority has found an infringement; and (vi) the quantification of antitrust harm.

Among the obstacles identified was the difficulty for a claimant to have access to evidence both in the context of stand-alone actions and in the context of follow-on cases where the Commission or a national competition authority has undertaken an investigation. Associated with the issue of access to evidence is that of the evidentiary value of national competition authority decisions. The Green Paper raised questions in relation to disclosure of evidence including documents held by national competition authorities. Further to this, the Commission raised questions relating to the burden of proof in damages actions.

The Commission also raised questions on the defences that should be open to a party infringing the EU competition rules, the onus of proof, the need to prove fault and the passing-on defence.

Finally, the Commission raised questions in regard to the costs of such actions and the co-ordination of public and private enforcement.

While the Court's recognition in *Courage v Crehan* of the right to claim damages for infringement of the Treaty rules on competition was particularly important, the subsequent case of *Manfredi* enabled the Court to go further in light of the legislative developments since *Courage v Crehan*. Advocate General Geelhoed made express reference in his Opinion in *Manfredi* to speeches of successive members of the Commission with regard to damages actions for breaches of EU competition rules and to the Commission's Green Paper on 'Damages actions for breaches of the EC antitrust rules'.[35] The Advocate General referred to the growing importance that had been attached to private enforcement since the introduction of Regulation No 1/2003.[36]

Having referred to *BRT v SABAM* and *Courage v Crehan* amongst other cases, Advocate General Geelhoed stated clearly his view that third parties with a relevant legal interest may rely on the invalidity of an agreement which is prohibited under Article 81 EC and may claim damages if there is a causal

[34] COM(2005) 672 final, 'Damages actions for breach of EC antitrust rules'.
[35] Opinion in *Manfredi* (n 33 above) fn 13.
[36] Ibid, para 27.

relationship between the prohibited agreement or concerted practice and the harm suffered.

In its judgment the Court recalled, referring to *Eco Swiss*,[37] that Articles 81 EC and 82 EC are a matter of public policy which must be automatically applied by national courts.

With regard to claiming damages, the Court reiterated what it had said in *Courage v Crehan* but went somewhat further in specifying, with regard to the entitlement to damages, that it follows from the principle of effectiveness and the right of any individual to seek compensation for loss caused by a contract or by conduct liable to restrict or distort competition that injured persons must be able to seek compensation not only for actual loss (*damnum emergens*) but also for loss of profit (*lucrum cessans*) plus interest.[38] The Court added that total exclusion of loss of profit as a head of damage for which compensation may be awarded cannot be accepted in the case of a breach of Community law since, especially in the context of economic or commercial litigation, such a total exclusion of loss of profit would make reparation of damage practically impossible.[39]

While Regulation No 1/2003 has now been in force for approximately 10 years, experience shows that the task of the national courts in applying the Union's competition rules is not an easy one and that, while those affected by infringement of the Union's competition rules can rely on the direct applicability of the Treaty provisions to seek damages, there remain many obstacles in practice which may render actions aimed at recovering damages particularly difficult and costly.

By the end of 2013, the Court of Justice had delivered 16 judgments in references from the courts of the Member States relating to Regulation No 1/2003. However, only half of these cases raised directly or implicitly the interpretation of the Regulation.

This leads one to bear in mind the words of Advocate General Geelhoed in *Manfredi,* where he stated, *inter alia*, that 'despite that case-law, private enforcement in Europe is still in its infancy, or at least it is clearly not practised on the scale familiar from other jurisdictions, especially that of the United States, where some 90% of antitrust proceedings are initiated by private parties'.[40] He added that in the European Union, the emphasis has traditionally lain on public enforcement, both by the European Commission and by national authorities.[41]

Advocate General Geelhoed recognised the potential benefits of Regulation No 1/2003 in providing for private enforcement. He added, that 'civil actions may have a deterrent effect on (potential) offenders against the prohibition of cartels and so contribute to the enforcement of that prohibition and to the development of a culture of competition among market operators'.[42]

[37] Case C-126/97 *Eco Swiss* [1999] ECR I-3055, paras 39 and 40.
[38] *Manfredi* (n 33 above), para 95.
[39] Ibid, par 96.
[40] *Manfredi* (n 33 above), para 29 of the Opinion.
[41] Ibid.
[42] *Manfredi* (n 33 above), para 30.

He further opined that the initiative for private actions must come primarily from those whose interests are protected by competition law. He noted that the actions themselves are governed, subject to a number of general conditions laid down by Community law, by national procedural and private law. He foresaw the possibility of an uneven playing pitch in the divergent procedures existing in the Member States when he added that

> The growth in private enforcement may, however, vary from one Member State to another, depending on procedural culture, the restrictions imposed on jurisdiction, rules on the burden of proof, the possibility of class actions, etc. The effectiveness of that enforcement is, of course, partly determined by the accessibility of the national courts.[43]

After inviting submissions in the area the Commission published a White Paper on Damages Actions in April, 2008.[44] Thereafter in June 2013 the Commission, having engaged in extensive consultation on its White Paper, published its proposal for a Directive to be adopted by the European Parliament and the Council.[45] While experience to date with regard to the public enforcement of the Union's competition law rules at national level has been positive, the experience with regard to private enforcement has been more problematic. The Commission's proposal for a Directive constitutes a radical proposal to move matters on from being simply governed by national procedural rules, to a point where it is proposed to require Member States to change their law to reach minimum standards to facilitate private enforcement of EU competition law.

This will help to ensure a level playing field within the European Union whereby actions for damages against undertakings infringing competition law will be facilitated throughout the Union and no competitive advantage will ensue for certain undertakings which may have infringed Articles 101 or 102 TFEU.

Insofar as Article 3(1) of Regulation No 1/2003 requires national competition authorities to apply Articles 101 and 102 TFEU where they are applying national competition rules to agreements, decisions by associations of undertakings or concerted practices which may affect trade between Member States within the meaning of Article 101(1) or any abuse prohibited by Article 102 of the Treaty, the proposed new procedural rules will apply to such actions.

While at present, in the absence of Union law, actions for damages are governed by the national rules and procedures of the Member States, they must comply with the principles of equivalence and effectiveness. In this way the rules must be no less favourable than those applying at the national level to similar domestic actions and must not be such as to render excessively difficult or impossible in practice the pursuit of a claim for damages.

The Commission's proposed Directive is predicated upon the view that it is necessary to establish Union-wide procedures to be applied at the national level to ensure a greater opportunity for claimants to bring claims for damages in the context of an alleged infringement of the Treaty competition rules.

[43] Ibid, para 31.
[44] COM (2008) 165 final.
[45] COM (2013) 404 final.

The proposal aims to enhance the entitlement to disclosure of evidence/discovery of documents.

A significant aspect of the proposal is a limitation on disclosure of evidence from the file of a competition authority. This relates in particular to (a) leniency corporate statements and (b) settlement submissions. This restriction must be seen in the light of the judgment of the Court of Justice of 14 June 2011 in *Pfleiderer*,[46] where the Court was asked to rule on the entitlement to access to leniency documents filed with the German national competition authority. While the Amtsgericht in Bonn had ordered access both to the leniency documents in the possession of the competition authority and to incriminating evidence collected, this order was stayed by the same court pending a ruling from the Court of Justice.

In its ruling the Court recognised that the matter had not been regulated at the Union level. The Court indicated, following its earlier judgment in *Courage v Crehan*, that the applicable national rules must fulfil the requirements of the principles of equivalence and effectiveness. The Court indicated that it was for the national courts and tribunals to weigh the respective interests in favour of disclosure of the information and in favour of the protection of the information provided voluntarily by the applicant for leniency. This weighing exercise had to be conducted by the national courts and tribunals only on a case-by-case basis, according to national law, taking into account all the relevant factors in the case. The Court recognised that Union competition law, and in particular Regulation No 1/2003, could not be interpreted as precluding access to leniency documents. On the other hand the Court recognised the importance of leniency programmes and the deterrent effect on such programmes if such leniency documents were disclosed.

The proposed Directive, if adopted, will fill a lacuna noted in *Pfleiderer* insofar as it will provide a legal basis for the protection of leniency programmes operated both at national level and by the European Commission and will further provide such protection for documentation provided in the context of settlement submissions. It may also address the concerns of the Court of Justice with regard to the principle of effectiveness in the context of refusal of disclosure to third parties seeking to bring an action for damages in the field of competition as expressed on 6 June 2013 in *Donau Chemie AG*.[47]

With regard to limitation periods, the proposed Directive sets out specific rules which may have the effect of extending the limitation periods currently available under the national law of a Member State. The essential element is that it will allow actions to be brought after proceedings by a competition authority.

Another important aspect of the proposal is the availability of the 'passing-on defence' to defendants who can show that the claimant for damages has passed on the whole or part of the overcharge resulting from the infringement. This

[46] Case C-360/09 *Pfleiderer* [2011] ECR I-5161.

[47] Case C-536/11 *Bundeswettbewerbsbehörde v Donau Chemie AG and others*, judgment of 6 June 2013. See also Case C-139/07P *Commission v Technische Glaswerke Ilmenau* [2010] ECR I-5885; Case C-404/10P *Commission v Editions Odile Jacob* judgment of 28 June 2013; and Case C-477/10P *Commission v Agrofert Holding* judgment of 28 June 2013.

will avoid the unjust enrichment of a party who may have been overcharged for goods or services. This is in line with what the Court indicated in *Courage v Crehan* and in *Manfredi,* where it stated that 'Community law does not prevent national courts from taking steps to ensure that the protection of the rights guaranteed by Community law does not entail the unjust enrichment of those who enjoy them'.

The proposal also recognises that third parties may maintain claims for damages, in line with what the Court indicated in *Courage v Crehan* and in *Manfredi,* where it referred to the fact that 'any individual' can rely upon a breach of Article 101 TFEU before a national court.[48] Thus claims can be maintained by direct and indirect purchasers.

The proposed Directive, insofar as it may represent a significant change for certain legal systems, must be seen in the context of the second paragraph of Article 19 (1) TEU which provides that 'Member States shall provide remedies sufficient to ensure effective legal protection in the fields covered by Union law' which repeats in essence what was stated by the Court of Justice in its judgment in *Unión de Pequeños Agricultores.*[49] Implicit in the proposal is the belief that in many cases, national law fails to afford effective protection to the victims of anti-competitive behaviour.

It should be noted that the proposed Directive does not address the issue of collective action. The Commission, influenced by the European Parliament, appears to be in the process of providing for a horizontal approach to collective redress common to all fields of law.[50]

CONCLUSION

It is now over 12 years since the Court of Justice indicated that the Treaty had to be interpreted as meaning that any individual can rely on the invalidity of an agreement or practice prohibited under Article 101 TFEU and claim compensation for harm resulting from such invalidity. The Court then stressed the importance of the requirements of equivalence and effectiveness for the domestic legal systems of the Member States 'in the absence of Community rules governing the matter'. It is clear that to date the absence of Union rules has resulted in divergent treatment between the Member States, with the result that parties harmed by infringement of the Union's competition rules are faced with considerable difficulty in bringing claims for damages under the rules applicable in certain Member States. Whether this situation represents a failure on the part of those Member States to have sufficient regard for the principle of effectiveness or to honour their obligations under Article 19(1) TEU or otherwise, it is clearly a matter of particular importance in the context of the rights recognised by the Court for the victims of anti-competitive behaviour. It is in this context that

[48] See *Courage v Crehan* , n 30 above, para 24; *Manfredi,* n 33 above, para 59.
[49] Case C-50/00 *Unión de Pequeños Agricultores v Council* [2002] ECR I-6677, para 41.
[50] Commission Staff Working Document, SWD (2013) final, 11 June 2013, para 22.

one may opine that the time has come for the establishment of Union rules to overcome the deficiencies in the domestic legal systems of Member States and to ensure that victims have available to them effective mechanisms to ensure the protection of their rights to damages. The adoption of Union rules will ensure that infringing undertakings may have to bear the consequences of their actions throughout the Union and will not be able to shelter in Member States where the right of action is difficult to realise, such that the objectives of the Treaty rules on competition will be more effectively attained.

20

The Italian Model of a Dualist Approach to the Multilevel Protection of Human Rights

GIUSEPPE TESAURO*

1. MULTILEVEL PROTECTION OF HUMAN RIGHTS AND THE ITALIAN LEGAL SYSTEM: THE 1948 CONSTITUTION

HUMAN RIGHTS ARE an area in which the contribution of courts has always been very important. Indeed, judges play a key role whenever there are provisions granting rights or imposing duties which can be enforced directly. Nowadays, however, the scenario in which judges operate and the parameters of legality according to which they have to evaluate individual behavior and/or the applicable law have changed. Norms granting fundamental rights are no longer just national, constitutional or statutory, since judges have to take into consideration international law and, for EU Member States, European Union law. This means that fundamental rights are protected through different, albeit complementary, levels of legality, according to the rules of the national, international or European Union legal orders. The presence of two courts, respectively the European Court of Justice (ECJ) and the European Court of Human Rights (ECtHR or Strasbourg Court), in addition to the national courts, contributes to creating a common space for the interpretation and enforcement of the relevant rules, both national and external. This means that when, for a particular case, Union law and/or the European Convention on Human Rights (ECHR) are relevant, the national judge has to define his role and the boundaries of his jurisdiction in relation to the role and jurisdiction of the ECJ, the ECHR and with respect to his 'own' constitutional judge.

For the protection of fundamental rights, the choice of the competent legal order, and therefore of the applicable law, has some similarities with the equivalent choice in private international law, since judges are called on to consider and possibly apply rules which are implemented, modified and abrogated outside

*Judge of the Italian Constitutional Court

the national legislative processes, in short, which are external to the national legal system. The application by the judge of external norms is of course regulated by his own legal order, with some compliance requirements, normally at the constitutional or statutory level, with international and European Union principles and norms.

I will examine in particular the Italian legal order. The Constitution of 1948 provides for the automatic adaptation of Italian law to the generally recognized rules of international law (Article 10, paragraph 1), and allows such limitations on national sovereignty as are required by participation in international organizations which have been set up to ensure peace and justice among nations (Article 11). After the Constitution was drafted, the idea prevailed, in case law and in the literature, that the automatic adaptation did not concern treaties, but only general, ie customary, international law. The adaptation of the Italian legal system to treaties was ensured and is ensured by a special procedure, that is, an ordinary law which, apart from authorising ratification of the treaty, requires its implementation in the national legal system. In short, in case of a conflict between national and external law, only customary international law may prevail. In case of a conflict between national law and a treaty, the traditional principle *lex posterior derogat priori* had to be applied, with the result that a national statute approved the day after the entry into force of a treaty should prevail.

This solution applied to all international treaties, including the ECHR and the European Community Treaties. The effect was obviously critical, because of the old and well-established principle that States may not justify the violation of international norms, either general or conventional, on the ground of a conflicting internal rule. For this reason judges, including constitutional ones, had to find practical remedies.

2. NATIONAL LAW AND EU LAW: A QUESTION OF DISTRIBUTION OF COMPETENCES

As for EC Law, a practical solution was found after a 20-year dialogue between the Italian Constitutional Court and the ECJ. In the first step of this dialogue, a profound difference of opinion emerged in *Costa v ENEL*[1] regarding the primacy of the subsequent national norm as opposed to the EC Treaty. This conflict was partially limited by the Constitutional Court with the *Frontini*[2] and *Industrie Chimiche*[3] judgments of 1973 and 1975. The Court of Justice, with *Simmenthal*,[4] led the Italian Court to further reflection, the result of which was the *Granital* judgment of 1984.[5]

[1] Case 6/64 [1964] ECR 585.
[2] Judgment no 183, 1973.
[3] Judgment no 232, 1975.
[4] Case 70/77 *Simmenthal SpA v Amministrazione delle Finanze* [1978] ECR1453.
[5] Judgment no 170, 1984.

This decision, which is still good law today, is based on the delegation of legislative powers to the European Union allowed by Article 11 of the Constitution. The judgment analysed the relationship of Italian law with EU rules having direct effect in terms of the competence of one or of the other legal order, so as to give to the national judge the power to set aside, in short, to disapply, internal provisions conflicting with Union law which had been adopted within its proper sphere of competence. The conflict with EU rules lacking direct effect was instead considered to be a matter of constitutionality, and thus left to the scrutiny of the Constitutional Court. The dialogue between the latter and the ECJ, therefore, produced good results, at least on a practical level, which is in fact the most salient point in the context of an issue of decisive importance, namely the primacy of Union law.

The questions put by the Italian Constitutional Court to the Court of Justice on matters relating to the protection of fundamental rights are also quite important. The 1965 *Acciaierie San Michele* case[6] produced a number of comments on the EC system of judicial review. The Italian Constitutional Court subsequently drew attention to a number of problems regarding effective judicial protection raised by certain decisions of the Court of Justice concerning the temporal effects of its judgments.[7] It is also worth mentioning the repeated calls by the German Constitutional Court to the ECJ for the protection of fundamental rights (*Solange I*[8] *and II*[9]), which, together with those of the Italian Court, contributed to changing Luxembourg case law in the early seventies, specifically with the famous statement that

> in fact, respect for fundamental rights forms an integral part of the general principles of law protected by the Court of Justice. The protection of such rights, whilst inspired by constitutional traditions common to the Member States, must be ensured within the framework of the structure and objectives of the Community.[10]

It should be recalled that in 2008, the Italian Constitutional Court changed its position and utilised for the first time the mechanism of the preliminary ruling, and hence the possibility of direct dialogue with the Court of Justice;[11] the overruling was also stimulated by the great attention paid at EU level to fundamental rights - it is sufficient to consider the importance that the Nice Charter of Fundamental Rights of the EU had even before the Lisbon Treaty - a significant field of activity common to the two courts.

[6] Corte Costituzionale, Judgment no 98, 1965; ECJ, Joined Cases 9 and 58/65 [1967] ECR 1.

[7] Corte Costituzionale, Judgment no 232, 1989; ECJ, Case 145/79 *Roquette Frères v French State – Customs Administration* [1980] ECR 2917.

[8] *Solange I - Internationale Handelsgesellschaft von Einfuhr- und Vorratsstelle für Getreide und Futtermittel*, decision of 29 May 1974, BVerfGE 37, 271 [1974] CMLR 540.

[9] *Solange II - Wünsche Handelsgesellschaft*, decision of 22 October 1986, BVerfGE 73, 339, [1987] 3 CMLR 225.

[10] Case 11/70 *Internationale Handellsgesellschaft* [1970] ECR 1115, para 4; see also Case 29/69 *Stauder v City of Ulm* [1969] ECR 419; Case C-260/89 *ERT v DEP* [1991] ECR I-2925, para 41.

[11] Order no 203, 2008; see more recently Order no 207, 2013.

3. ECHR AND NATIONAL LAW AFTER THE 2001 REFORM

As far as international treaties were concerned, including the ECHR, different remedies were used whenever possible to ensure their de facto primacy: first, interpreting the national legislation consistently with international rules, even when a consistent interpretation was difficult to achieve; second, using the specialty criterion; third, simply applying de facto the conventional provisions on the basis of their particular characteristics, sometimes connecting them to different international sources, particularly those granting fundamental rights. These remedies made it possible, in most cases, to ensure at least de facto the priority of the treaties, particularly the ECHR, even as regards later conflicting national legislation.[12]

The reform of 2001 introduced into the Italian Constitution (Article 117, paragraph 1) the express duty of the national legislator to respect international obligations, a duty which has been interpreted as including treaties. As a result, there is now a reference to the external relevant rules, which are integrated on a case by case basis into the content of the constitutional norm. The parameter of constitutionality of domestic statutes is therefore formally the constitutional norm, in reality the external one.

With regard to the ECHR, the Constitutional Court, with its judgments No 348 and No 349 of 2007, instigated an important dialogue with the European Court of Human Rights on a typical constitutional topic, that is, the protection of fundamental rights. Both decisions, identical in many substantive respects, though not so much in other points, focused attention on the different roles that ordinary and constitutional national judges respectively play in the enforcement of national and international rules concerning human rights, in particular the ECHR, and on the role of the Strasbourg court too.

First of all, the Court rejected the argument put forward mainly by non-specialist academic writers in the fields of national and comparative law, and by some judges, according to which the ECHR had been transformed into European law through Article 6 of the Treaty on European Union. According to this idea, such a rule would have given ECHR norms direct effect, such as many EU norms enjoy, thereby enabling the ordinary judge to dis-apply the conflicting national provision.

It is useful to dwell on this point. Article 6 TEU, in the original version of the Maastricht Treaty, which recalls the fundamental rights of the ECHR and national constitutions and includes them among the general principles guaranteed by the European Court of Justice, reproduced the formula established in the ECJ case-law mentioned above. However, in forty years of EU case law no-one ever considered that the commitment to the respect of fundamental rights, as guaranteed by the ECHR and the constitutional traditions of the Member States, might transform the ECHR into Community law. Those conventional norms stay outside the EU system, and indeed the legal orders of the Member States. This also applies to the new wording of Article 6 TEU following the

[12] Corte Costituzionale, judgments no 310, 1996; no 342,1999; no 26, 2000; no 29, 2003.

Lisbon reform, which equally has certainly not produced any transformation of ECHR provisions into EU law, as certain non-specialist legal writing and at least some judgments have asserted based on a superficial reading of this provision:

> Fundamental rights, as guaranteed by the European Convention for the Protection of Human Rights and Fundamental Freedoms and as they result from the constitutional traditions common to the Member States, shall constitute general principles of the Union's law.[13]

I shall consider this point further below.

The Italian Constitutional Court ruled that the judge, irrespective of the supposed 'communitarisation' of the ECHR, does not have the power to dis-apply a domestic-law provision which conflicts with the norms of the Convention, since neither the character nor structure and objectives of the ECHR taken as a whole could allow it to do so.[14] That said, the Constitutional Court did not, however, deny the self-executing nature of certain ECHR provisions in general. On the contrary, by referring to the ECJ's approach regarding the conditions for the direct effect of EU provisions, the Court excluded the application to ECHR provisions of the so-called '*Simmental-Granital* effect'. Any hypothesis of conflict between national law and ECHR provisions that cannot be solved by interpretative means is therefore an issue of constitutionality with respect to Article 117, paragraph 1, of the Italian Constitution, into which the relevant ECHR provision is incorporated; this is an issue which may only be referred to the Constitutional Court.

EU provisions which have direct effect, expressing the full exercise of legislative powers delegated to the Union, are immediately and directly applied in the internal legal order because the latter 'is not relevant'. In short, this does not give rise to a question of hierarchy of norms, with the primacy of the rule of Community law, but rather it raises the question of the competence of the European Union legal order. On the procedural level, the question of constitutionality raised by the ordinary judge would be inadmissible. The power to dis-apply national laws conflicting with EU norms is not a consequence of the direct effect of the norm, but reflects the full exercise of European competence as established by the Treaty. This direct effect merely provides the condition for the internal legal system to withdraw, and for the national court to apply in its place the only 'competent rule', ie the Union one.

As for the ECHR, this problem does not arise, because there has been no delegation of legislative powers. Therefore, any conflict with ECHR provisions raises a simple question related to infringement of Article 117, paragraph 1, of the Constitution, which requires the legislator to comply with international treaties.

In short, unlike the conflict with EU law having direct effect, the conflict between an internal norm and an ECHR provision results in an issue of constitutionality of laws, and not of competence between legal orders. The consequence is that,

[13] Tribunale Amministrativo di Lazio, no 11984/2010; Consiglio di Stato, IV Sez, no 1220/2010.
[14] Judgment no 349, 2007.

in a centralised system of constitutional review, only the Constitutional Court is entitled to annul any internal norm breaching the constitutional provision into which the ECHR rule has been incorporated. Here, it should also be stressed that it is necessary to guarantee precise, reliable and stable compliance with the obligations laid down by the ECHR system of protection of human rights. The desire of the ordinary judge to verify for himself the compatibility of ECHR provisions with the Constitution is strong, as can be seen in a small part of the literature and case-law, but it surely collides with the competence reserved exclusively to the Constitutional Court.

4. THE ROLE OF THE JUDGES: STRASBOURG, LUXEMBOURG AND ROME

The scenario of relations between the three instruments of protection of fundamental rights, namely the Constitution, EU law and the ECHR, as well as relations between the judges called upon to enforce such protection, has been presented schematically. It transpires from this that the Italian system is not very different from the legal orders of any other European country.

The national judge, who is the natural or normal or first[15] judge of European Union law and of compliance with the ECHR, has the task of interpreting the applicable national provision, consistently with the relevant external provision of the ECHR or EU law, as interpreted by the courts of Strasbourg and Luxembourg respectively, within the limits - and there are not so many - of a reasonable reading of the legislative text. As such, the conformity criterion operates, according to which the external rule has to be applied as it is interpreted and applied in its own legal system and by its own judges, and hence in accordance with its own dynamics and effectiveness. In other words, the national judge is required to interpret national law in conformity with external law. Moreover, it must be emphasised that, even though the interpretation by judges concerns only one specific case, this usually affects one or more norms. As a result, even though not in absolute terms, the interpretation can have legal repercussions beyond the particular case. That is especially so of an interpretation given by the Court of Justice in a preliminary ruling or even in infringement proceedings, but it also affects the judgments of the Strasbourg Court which go beyond the formal boundary of Article 46 ECHR.

The scope of the functions of the ordinary judge, then, is quite broad and the intervention of the Constitutional Court quite exceptional. It is only when no solution by means of interpretation can be found for a conflict between the national provision and the ECHR that the ordinary judge, in a system of centralised control of constitutionality (for instance in Germany, Austria, Italy, Spain, and nowadays also in France), is not in a position to solve the case autonomously, in contrast to a conflict with an EU provision having

[15] N Fennelly, 'The National Judge as Judge of the European Union', in A Rosas et al (eds), *The Court of Justice and the Construction of Europe, Analyses and Perspectives on Sixty Years of Case-Law* (The Hague, Asser Press, 2013), 61.

direct effect. Now, because of the conflict between the national provision and that of the ECHR, the national judge will not be able to apply the national law, nor will he be able to dis-apply the national rule, since it is tied to an issue of constitutionality, which falls under the exclusive competence of the Constitutional Court, the only court competent to annul the national provision.[16] The Constitutional Court must verify whether or not applying the external provision may be impeded by another relevant constitutional principle. To this end, it is necessary to find the right balance between constitutional values, and proceed to an assessment of the degree of protection guaranteed by internal norms and that guaranteed by the ECHR provision. The Constitutional Court will decide whether or not to exclude the reference to the external source when the level of protection provided by the ECHR is considered to be lower than that provided for in the national legal system. This is what Article 53 of the European Convention provides, in stipulating that no provision of the Convention may be interpreted as limiting human rights and fundamental freedoms as they are recognised by national law.

It follows that the Constitutional Court is entitled to verify whether or not the ECHR norm, as interpreted by the Strasbourg Court, is in violation of another relevant constitutional norm. This verification, which is reserved exclusively to the Constitutional Court, recalls the category of counter-limits in relation to the application of EU Law. Whilst for EU Law such verification is conducted with reference to the fundamental principles of the constitutional legal order, in the context of ECHR provisions this verification is conducted with respect to any relevant provision of the Constitution.

5. WILL ECHR NORMS NO LONGER BE EXTERNAL AFTER THE ACCESSION OF THE EU TO THE ECHR?

In analyzing where the external law is to be located in domestic law, academic writing refers to the nationalisation of the international norm or to its transformation, incorporation or other equivalent formulae, into a national norm. In reality, the international norm, for each modification and its possible extinction, remains subject to the rules of international law, without any impact from the national law. Therefore, a conventional international norm, generated outside the domestic legal system, will remain external even when the national legal system refers to it in order to regulate certain relations and thus to impact on certain subjective legal positions. The internal legal order provides for the application and observance of the external norm in conjunction with its own rules, to the extent national law provides, including any changes or even the abrogation of the norm, regulated by international law. In short, the adaptation and/or application of an external norm does not imply its 'nationalisation,' which, on the contrary, only occurs when the rules are reproduced in a national statute. In the latter case, the external norm will remain valid irrespective of

[16] Judgments Nos 348 and 349 of 2007, and No 78 of 2012.

any change or settlement that might intervene in its original legal order (general international law or treaty), and of course with possible further problems.

Precisely to prevent such problems and possible overlaps, case-law has clarified this point, especially when it criticised the practice adopted by some Member States of reproducing in a national law EU regulations, which had already been published in the Official Journal of the EU. Italian case-law has put an end to this practice of internal repetition of regulations, and has clarified precisely the separate and autonomous character of the EU legal order with respect to the national one, even if they are coordinated. The same considerations also apply to the ECHR, both with respect to the laws of the Member States and to the European Union legal system considered as a whole. The commitment to the respect of fundamental rights as guaranteed by the ECHR and the constitutional traditions of the Member States, expressly stated by the Court since the early 1970s and confirmed by Article 6 of the EU Treaty before and after Lisbon, does not convert ECHR provisions into EU Law. Those conventional rules remain external to both the EU system and the legal orders of Member States. It is therefore clear that ECHR provisions have not acquired the characteristics of EU rules with regard to the relationship between such provisions and the domestic laws of Member States, or even with regard to the scope of Article 11 of the Italian Constitution.

The most widely-debated issue remains whether or not the scenario just outlined has somehow changed or is destined to change in the future. The Nice Charter (Charter of Fundamental Rights of the European Union) has now formally been attributed the same rank as the Treaties, even though the Charter corresponds in fact to a significant extent to the case-law of the Court of Justice. Another new outcome of the Lisbon Treaty was the possibility, and substantially the commitment formalised in Article 6 TEU, of achieving the old dream of EU accession to the ECHR.

A small part of the case-law and especially of academic literature, because of an excess of enthusiasm and too rapid a reading of the texts, first considered that accession had already occurred with the entry into force of the Lisbon reform. But it was not so. The negotiations were and are neither swift nor easy, and most Member States must now deal with other and more complicated questions. In the meantime, an Opinion on the proposed accession agreement has been asked of the Court of Justice; [17]we are looking forward to it.

Furthermore, it is not even sure that the Union's accession to the ECHR would in itself change the relationship between the ECHR, EU law and national law. In this regard, as has just been pointed out in terms of general legal theory, the accession of a State or an international organisation to a treaty does not in itself automatically entail the inclusion of the treaty in the internal legal system of that State or of that international entity. The external life of those rules remains unchanged, unless the content of external norms is formally reproduced in a national statute.

The rules of the Convention, to which the European Union made a commitment to accede, cannot become EU law with all the features that they

[17] Opinion 2/13 (pending).

possess in their relations with EU Member States, just because of accession. In short, what the Italian Constitutional Court and the ECJ have clearly and correctly determined would still be valid notwithstanding the accession to the Convention. Moreover, it is true that ECHR provisions as interpreted and applied by the Strasbourg Court bind the State in all its branches, including the courts at all levels and not only the Constitutional Court, but it is the State which regulates the different competences of its bodies with regard to their relationship with external sources, and it is free to find the appropriate remedy to solve any possible conflict. This point in the judgment no 349/07 of the Italian Constitutional Court was confirmed a few years later in very similar terms by the Court of Justice in the *Kamberaj* case.[18]

The rank of international or EU norms within the national system of sources of law has been a matter of some debate. Even in this regard, especially in light of the foregoing considerations, it does not seem appropriate to pose the problem of the rank of the external provision in the internal legal system. For example, with regard to the Italian legal order, it is now widely recognised, and it was specifically stated by the Italian Constitutional Court, that international norms, in particular the ECHR, are integrated into the content of Article 117, first paragraph, of the Constitution, and thereby become the parameter for constitutionality, as well as for the compatibility of the internal law with conventional norms. The Italian Constitutional Court has sometimes, however, asserted the sub-constitutional rank of ECHR provisions,[19] while at other times it has accorded such provisions the same rank as constitutional provisions.[20] In my view, beyond any systematic rigour, the second construction clarifies to the interpreter, in particular to the judge, the impact of the external provision. Furthermore, such a construction is coherent with the unchallenged idea that the external norm is integrated into the content of the constitutional provision.

Let us finally consider more generally the EU accession to the ECHR. The documents which have been disseminated over the years that the negotiations have painted a picture which is open potential criticisms, confirming the doubts concerning accession felt by even the most fervent proponents of the Community integration process. The Court's Opinion No 2/94,[21] even though it only concerned the issue of competence, should have led to wider reflection, not just superficial criticism of the institutional defence of the Courts of Luxembourg. Since the *Internationale Handelsgesellschaft* judgment,[22]the protection of fundamental rights has achieved a very high level and a significant degree of modernity. With the adoption of the Nice Charter, the need to fill the alleged gap due to the absence of a Bill of Rights is no longer present.

[18] Case C-571/10, *Servet Karmberaj v Istituto per l'Edilizia sociale della Provincia autonoma de Bolzano*, judgment of 24 April 2012; see also Case C-61/10, *Åklageren v Hans Åkerberg Fransson,* judgment of 26 February 2013, para 44.

[19] Judgment no 348, 2007.

[20] Judgment no 236, 2011.

[21] *Draft Agreement on Accession of European Community to the ECHR* [1996] ECR I-1759

[22] N 10 above.

It is true that there are many problems still to be solved and this is not the place to list them all. However, it would be sufficient, for example, to think of the possible overlap and conflict between the interpretation of the Strasbourg and Luxembourg courts and the capitals of the Member States. Or to think about the doubts cast on the competence of Strasbourg Court to evaluate acts of the Union in the field of the Common Foreign and Security Policy (CFSP). Or, even Protocol 16 on the optional and non-binding preliminary ruling, which I believe is a real parody of the preliminary ruling, which is a mark of a Community of law, pride of the European Union legal system: we remember Opinion 1/91 of the Court of Justice.[23] Dialogue between judges is a serious matter and does not allow minor solutions, designed only to enrich the literature and to create confusion in practice.

[23] *EEA Agreement* [1991] ECR I-6079, esp para 61.

21

Damages in Public Procurement – An Illusory Remedy?

ANTHONY M COLLINS*

SCOPE AND PURPOSE

THE PURPOSE OF this contribution is to inquire into the nature, availability and appropriateness of the damages remedy for breaches of the Procurement Rules.[1] It thus does not consider damages as a remedy for acts in the course of a contract award procedure that are equivalent to, or constitutive of, misfeasance in public office, fraud, conspiracy or an abuse of power.

By way of introduction it may be observed that the aim of the Remedies Directive,[2] which imposes obligations upon the Member States in the implementation of the Procurement Directive, is to ensure that the decisions of contracting authorities are reviewed 'effectively and, in particular, as rapidly

* Judge of the General Court of the EU. The author thanks Mr Peter Cronin-Burbridge BL for his assistance in the preparation of this contribution. The views expressed are personal to the author and do not purport to represent any position adopted or to be adopted by the General Court.

[1] For the purposes of this contribution, 'the Procurement Rules' is shorthand for Directive 2004/18/EC of the European Parliament and of the Council of 31 March 2004 on the coordination of procedures for the award of public works contracts, public supply contracts and public service contracts (([2004] OJ L134/114), hereafter the 'Procurement Directive'), Directive 2004/17/EC of the European Parliament and of the Council of 31 March 2004 coordinating the procurement procedures of entities operating in the water, energy, transport and postal services sectors (([2004] OJ L134/1), hereafter the 'Utilities Directive'), all national rules transposing and implementing those directives and the regulations governing the award of contracts by the EU Institutions, consisting of Regulation (EU, Euratom) No 966/2012 of the European Parliament and of the Council of 25 October 2012 on the financial rules applicable to the general budget of the Union and repealing Council Regulation (EC, Euratom) No 1605/2002 ([2012] OJ L298/1) and Commission Delegated Regulation (EU) No 1268/2012 of 29 October 2012 on the rules of application of Regulation (EU, Euratom) No 966/2012 of the European Parliament and of the Council on the financial rules applicable to the general budget of the Union ([2012] OJ L362/1).

[2] Council Directive 89/665/EEC of 21 December 1989 on the coordination of the laws, regulations and administrative provisions relating to the application of review procedures to the award of public supply and public works contracts ([1989] OJ L395/33), as amended by Council Directive 92/50/EEC of 18 June 1992 ([1992] OJ L209/1) and Directive 2007/66/EC of the European Parliament and of the Council of 11 December 2007 ([2007] OJ L335/31).

as possible'. Articles 2 to 2f of the Remedies Directive prescribe minimum standards for the conduct of that review,[3] whilst conceding that the Member States enjoy a significant degree of autonomy when applying those standards.[4] Article 2.1 of the Remedies Directive requires the provision of three categories of remedies: interim measures, the power to set aside decisions and the award of damages.

NATURE OF DAMAGES AS A REMEDY FOR BREACHES OF THE PROCUREMENT RULES

Damages as a remedy for breaches of the Procurement Rules can be said to have three sources. The second paragraph of Article 340 TFEU provides that the Union is liable for real damage to an individual or to an undertaking caused by the unlawful conduct of an EU Institution.[5] Member States may be liable in damages for breaches of EU law in the circumstances described at paragraphs 40 and 41 of the celebrated *Francovich*[6] judgment. Finally, Article 2(1)(c) of the Remedies Directive requires Member States to ensure that their procedures for the review of contract awards include a power to award damages for harm caused by an infringement of the Procurement Directive.

Given these different origins, it may be asked whether the conditions governing the availability of damages as a remedy for a breach of the Procurement Rules are the same irrespective of the identity of the author of the alleged illegality. In *Spijker* the Court of Justice was of the view that Article 2(1)(c) of the Remedies Directive 'clearly indicates that Member States must make provision for the possibility of awarding damages in the case of infringement of EU law on the award of public contracts'.[7] In complying with this obligation, Member States were not required to go beyond the conditions for establishing non-contractual liability for breaches of EU law, observing that Article 2(1)(c) gives 'concrete expression to the principle of State liability for loss and damage caused to individuals as a result of breaches of EU law for which the State can be held responsible'. Thus in order to obtain reparation for such losses three conditions had to be met: the rule infringed must be intended to confer rights on individuals; the breach of that rule must be sufficiently serious; and there must be a direct causal link between the breach and the alleged loss.[8] This statement of the law prompts four observations on the nature of the damages remedy for breaches of the Procurement Rules.

First, since Article 2(1)(c) of the Remedies Directive gives 'concrete expression' to the existing rules governing the liability of contracting authorities for breaches

[3] Remedies Directive, Article 1(1).

[4] Remedies Directive, Articles 1(3)–(5), 2(5)–(7), 2b, 2c, 2d(2)–(3), 2e(1) and 2f (2).

[5] By way of example, see Case T-39/08 *Evropaiki Dynamiki v Commission* [2011] ECR II-437, para 45.

[6] Joined Cases C-6/90 and C-9/90 *Francovich and Others* [1991] ECR I-5357.

[7] Case C-568/08 *Combinatie Spijker Infrabouw v Provincie Drenthe* [2010] ECR I-12655, para 86.

[8] Ibid, para 87.

of the Procurement Rules, that provision is declaratory, rather than constitutive, of the law. It follows that Article 2(1)(c) does not require that damages for breaches of the Procurement Rules be available in circumstances other than those envisaged under the Court's case-law on the non-contractual liability of Member States and EU Institutions for breaches of EU law.

Second, by requiring that any breach grounding an action in damages be 'sufficiently serious', the Court cut down the rule in *Francovich*, which did not make that requirement of litigants seeking compensation for losses caused by a Member State's failure to take the measures necessary to achieve a result prescribed by a directive. In that respect *Spijker* follows the judgment of the Court of Justice in *Bergaderm*[9] where, after finding that the nature of a measure is not a decisive criterion in order to identify the extent of the discretion exercised by an institution,[10] it held that identical conditions govern the availability of damages for a breach of a rule of EU law whether by a Member State or by a Union institution.

Third, the requirements that the rule breached must be intended to confer rights on individuals and that the breach of such a rule must be "*sufficiently serious*", means that not every legal error in the course of an award procedure can ground an action in damages. In its judgment in *Bergaderm*, the Court observed that the system of rules it had worked out with regard to Article 215(2) of the EC Treaty[11] took account, *inter alia*, of 'the complexity of the situations to be regulated, difficulties in the application or interpretation of the texts and, more particularly, the margin of discretion available to the author of the act in question'[12], and concluded that 'the decisive test for finding that a breach of Community law is sufficiently serious is whether the Member State or the Community institution concerned manifestly and gravely disregarded the limits on its discretion'.[13] Whilst a simple infringement of the law may constitute a sufficiently serious breach where a Member State or Union institution exercises a limited discretion,[14] the technical nature of the Procurement Rules, coupled with the elements of discretion that Member States enjoy in transposing the Procurement Directive and contracting authorities require to operate them, means that not every such infringement will constitute a 'sufficiently serious' breach of EU law. An examination of the exercise conducted by the EU Courts in adjudicating upon challenges to contract awards by the Union institutions supports this conclusion. At paragraph 56 of its judgment in *VIP Car Solutions*,[15] the General Court[16] observed that since the Community Institutions had a broad discretion as regards the factors to be taken into account in the award of a contract, the review of the exercise of that discretion is limited to checking compliance with the rules governing the procedure and statement of reasons, the correctness of the facts, and the absence of a manifest error of

[9] Case C-352/98 *Bergaderm v Commission* [2000] ECR I-5291.
[10] Ibid, para 46.
[11] Now Article 340, 2nd para, TFEU.
[12] N 9, para 40.
[13] N 9, para 43.
[14] N 9, para 44
[15] Case T-89/07 *VIP Car Solutions sarl v Parliament* [2009] ECR II-1043.
[16] Then the Court of First Instance, hereinafter 'General Court'.

assessment or a misuse of powers. Thus not every error of law is a manifest and grave disregard of the limits upon a contracting authority's discretion such as will ground a damages action.

Fourth, *Spijker* also makes it clear that the Member States enjoy some latitude in making damages available for breaches of national rules transposing the Procurement Directive. Paragraphs 88 and 89 of the judgment observe that the Court's case-law does not prescribe more detailed criteria for the assessment of damage than those enunciated in *Bergaderm* and that the Union legislature did not take the opportunity to alter that state of affairs on the last occasion it amended the Remedies Directive. Each Member State is thus free to determine the criteria for the assessment of such damages provided they respect the principles of equivalence and effectiveness.[17] The Court's judgment in *Stadt Graz v Strabag AG* contains a further gloss on the limits of Member State discretion, since it held that the availability of damages could not be the subject of restrictions that did not apply to the other remedies envisaged by Article 2(1) of the Remedies Directive.[18] Since Member States are required to ensure that the other remedies envisaged by the Remedies Directive are effective and rapid, it seems to follow that they may subject to actions for damages caused by breaches of the Procurement Directive to considerably shorter limitation periods than those generally applicable actions for damages for State liability.[19]

By reason of the foregoing it seems that whilst a decision to award a contract can, at least in principle, be set aside on the basis of any illegality in the procedure leading to its adoption, damages are unavailable as a remedy for every breach of the Procurement Rules. Accordingly, of its nature, damages are a supplementary remedy for breaches of the Procurement Rules.

THE AVAILABILITY OF DAMAGES IN PRACTICE

In those cases where the availability of as a remedy for a breach of the Procurement Rules has been considered, a distinction has been made between 'direct' and 'contingent' loss.

The costs of participation in an award procedure have been deemed to be a direct loss on the basis that they were incurred as a direct consequence of the illegal act. This categorization may be questioned, particularly where more than one party seeks compensation as a result of an illegality, since all of those parties could not have benefited from the award of the contract at issue. The General Court has, in principle, declined to treat such costs as direct losses,

[17] N 7, para 90.

[18] Case C-314/09 *Stadt Graz v Strabag AG* [2010] ECR I-8769, paras 37–39. This appears to be the ratio of the earlier judgment in Case C-70/06 *Commission v Portugal* [2008] ECR I-1.

[19] See *Dekra Éireann Teo v Minister for the Environment and Local Government* [2003] 2 IR 270, 304–305 *per* Fennelly J, which rejected the argument that a more liberal application of the time limits contained in RSC O 84A was warranted by the fact that the applicant had limited its claim to damages.

expressing the view that, in the usual course of events, economic operators must bear the economic risks inherent in their activities. Since the outcome of a competition for a contract is, of its nature, uncertain, charges and expenses incurred by reason of participation in a tendering procedure cannot, in principle, be recouped by way of damages.[20] The General Court has also pointed out that the absence of any legal obligation in a contracting authority to enter into a contract on foot of an award procedure severs the causal link between an illegality in that procedure and the loss of an opportunity to have obtained the benefit of any contract that might have been awarded as a result thereof.[21] Since award procedures conducted under the Procurement Rules usually do not impose an obligation upon contracting authorities to conclude a contract, the causality necessary to establish a direct loss appears to be absent.

Nevertheless the General Court has not always consistently followed this position, and has held that damages may be available where a disappointed tenderer can show that a contracting authority's breach of the principle of equal treatment 'directly prejudiced' its chances of obtaining the contract.[22] This approach may be explained by reference to Article 2(7) of Directive 92/13[23], which has no counterpart in the other Procurement Rules[24] and which provides that:

> Where a claim is made for damages representing the costs of preparing a bid or participating in an award procedure, the person making the claim shall be required only to prove an infringement of Community law in the field of procurement or national rules implementing that law and that he would have had a real chance of winning the contract and that, as a consequence of that infringement, that chance was adversely affected.

Whatever the state of the law regarding the availability of damages for 'direct' losses, it is doubtful if compensation is available by way of damages for what are regarded as 'contingent' losses. In his Opinion in *Spijker*, Advocate General Cruz Villalón observed that, whilst it might give rise to difficulties, there was no reason why courts could not assess the probability of a tenderer obtaining a contract, since similar assessments were regularly conducted in other fields of law.[25] However, it is suggested that the issue is not the complexity of the exercise a court may be asked to carry out, but rather whether such contingent loss is simply too remote from the alleged unlawful act. In that regard it must be kept in mind

[20] Case T-160/03 *AFCon Management Consultants v Commission* [2005] ECR II-981, para 98. See also Case T-247/08 *C-Content BV v Commission* [2010] ECR II-205, para 86.

[21] Case T-461/08 *Evropaïki Dynamiki v EIB* [2011] ECR II-6367, paras 211–212.

[22] *AFCon*, n 20, para 102; *C-Content BV*, n 20, para 87.

[23] Directive 92/13 co-ordinating the laws, regulations and administrative provisions relating to the application of Community rules on the procurement procedures of entities operating in the water, energy, transport and telecommunications sectors ([1992] OJ L76/14).

[24] At para 95 of his Opinion in *Spijker*, n 7, Cruz Villalón AG observed that this absence appeared to be intentional.

[25] *Spijker*, n 7, paras 85–86. Examples of such assessments in the United Kingdom and Ireland include *Chaplin v Hicks* [1911] 2 KB 786; *Hawkins v Rodgers* (1950) 85 ILTR 128; *Allied Maples Group v Simmons and Simmons* [1995] 1 WLR 1602; *Philp v Ryan* [2004] 4 IR 241; *Lett and Co Ltd v Wexford Borough Council* [2012] 2 IR 198.

that profit (which is the basis upon which any damages fall to be calculated) is generated not from the entry into a contract (which is not, as we have already seen, in any way guaranteed), but from the execution of that contract.[26] It may be asked why an illegality by a contracting authority in an award process should make it an insurer for the successful execution of a contract in circumstances where it never had any control over that outcome?

The General Court has taken a consistently sceptical view of actions seeking compensation for loss of profits resulting from the unlawful conduct of an award procedure. In *AFCon* it pithily dismissed this heading of loss on the grounds that it presupposed an entitlement to have obtained the contract the subject matter of the unlawful award and was, accordingly, 'not real and certain but conjectural.'[27] Similarly, at paragraphs 46 and 47 of its judgment in Case T-39/08 *Evropaïki Dynamiki v Commission*, it observed that:

> The condition relating to damage requires that the damage for which compensation is sought be actual and certain, which it is for the applicant to prove (Case C-243/05 P Agraz and Others v Commission [2006] ECR I-10833, paragraph 27, and judgment of 16 July 2009 in Case C-481/07 P SELEX Sistemi Integrati v Commission, [2009] I-127, paragraph 36). It is for the applicant to adduce conclusive proof as to the existence and extent of the damage it alleges (Case C-362/95 Blackspur DIY and Others v Council and Commission [1997] ECR I-4775, paragraph 31, and SELEX Sistemi Integrati v Commission, paragraph 36).
>
> In that regard, it follows from the case-law that the action in support of which damage resulting from loss of profit is claimed must be dismissed, because the damage at issue is not real and existing, but future and hypothetical. Indeed, the success of such an action presupposes that, in the absence of the unlawful conduct alleged against the Commission, the tenderer whose tender was rejected was entitled to be awarded the contract. However, even if the evaluation committee proposed to award that tenderer the contract, the contracting authority is not bound by the evaluation committee's proposal but has a broad discretion in assessing the factors to be taken into account for the purpose of deciding to award a contract (see, to that effect, Case T-13/96 TEAM v Commission [1998] ECR II-4073, paragraph 76 and the case-law cited, and Case T-160/03 AFCon Management Consultants and Others v Commission [2005] ECR II-981, paragraph 113).[28]

It follows that, in a claim for damages against a contracting authority arising out of a breach of the Procurement Rules, compensation for loss of profit is unavailable.

As a matter of Irish law, it might be argued that such a claim could be advanced in reliance upon the principle of equivalence. The resolution of that issue depends on the answer to the question as to whether a breach of a similar nature by a public authority sounds in damages at Irish law. That question

[26] As O'Donnell J observed in *Lett and Co Ltd v Wexford Borough Council* [2012] 2 IR 198, 262, '[b]usiness is rarely as easy, or as profitable, as it is made to appear on projections produced in court.'

[27] *AFCon*, n 20, paras 112–114.

[28] [2011] ECR II-437. See, in the same vein, Case T-461/08, *Evropaïki Dynamiki v EIB* [2011] ECR II-6367, paras 209–212.

may be sub-divided into two parts: are breaches of the Procurement Directive in the nature of an ultra vires act or a breach of a statutory duty and, if they are regarded as falling within the latter category, does such a breach of statutory duty sound in damages?

Losses arising as a consequence of *ultra vires* acts are recoverable in damages under Irish law only where the act is tainted by an additional element of illegality. In *Pine Valley Developments v The Minister for Environment* [29], Finlay CJ cited with approval the following passage from Wade on *Administrative Law* (5th edn) at p 673:

> The present position seems to be that administrative action which is ultra vires but not actionable merely as a breach of duty will found an action for damages in any of the following situations:
> 1. If it involved the commission of a recognised tort, such as trespass, false imprisonment or negligence.
> 2. If it is actuated by malice, e.g. a personal spite or a desire to injure for improper reasons.
> 3. If the authority knows that it does not possess the power which it purports to exercise.[30]

In *Glencar Exploration plc v Mayo Co Co (No 2)* Fennelly J justified this approach on two grounds. As a matter of principle, he observed that:

> As the trial judge correctly pointed out, "there is no direct relationship between the doing of an *ultra vires* act and the recovery of damages for that act." This fundamental proposition can be underlined in two ways.
>
> Firstly, an individual needs no power to perform a wide range of actions which affect others and with the potential to affect them adversely. An individual's activity is not actionable, however, unless it consists of the commission of some civil wrong, most usually a breach of contract or a tort. The fact that a public authority must act within the scope of the powers conferred upon it has no necessary connection with loss which may be suffered by persons affected by it. Many people or bodies corporate are affected for better or worse by the actions of public authorities in the performance of their statutory functions. However, the incidence of gain or loss to individuals is unrelated to the validity of the decisions made. A valid decision is no more or less likely to cause loss than an invalid one. Breach of a specific statutory duty is, of course, a special case, to which I will return.
>
> Secondly, the nature of the tort of misfeasance in public office emphasises that lack of *vires* is insufficient on its own to ground a cause of action sounding in damages.[31]

From the procedural standpoint, he observed that while

> the sufferer of loss from a lawful but non-tortious private act is entirely without a remedy, a similarly positioned victim of an ultra vires act of a public authority, by way of contrast, has at his disposal the increasingly powerful weapon of judicial review. Thus, he may be able to secure, as in this case, an order annulling the offending act. In

[29] [1987] I.R. 23, 36.
[30] Applied in *Glencar Exploration plc v Mayo Co Co (No 2)* [2002] 1 IR 84, 127 *per* Keane CJ.
[31] N 30, 148.

> appropriate cases, a court may be able to grant an interlocutory injunction against its continued operation.[32]

The award of a contract has the consequence that the unsuccessful tenderers lose the opportunity to perform that contact. Contractors that can point to an illegality in the conduct of an award process are entitled to seek to have it re-run in order to be put in the position they would have been had that procedure been conducted in accordance with law. But why should they be able to obtain damages for a 'loss' that they might never have suffered, and moreover for reasons that are, at their height, only indirectly attributable to the contracting authority? As Fennelly J put it, 'the incidence of gain or loss is unrelated to the validity of the decisions made'.[33] Of greatest importance is the fact that the effective and rapid remedy envisaged by the Remedies Directive is provided by way of judicial review. When account is taken of the subsidiary nature of the damages remedy for breaches of Procurement Rules, it can be contended that breaches of the rules transposing the Procurement Directive into Irish law are closer in character to *ultra vires* acts than breaches of statutory duty. In any event there is persuasive authority for the proposition that a failure by the State to implement (and, it is submitted, to apply) a directive is not a breach of statutory duty, although that does not mean that loss caused by such a failure may not be remediable by way of damages.[34]

If, notwithstanding the foregoing, breaches of the Procurement Rules are assimilated to breaches of statutory duty, the inquiry turns as to whether such breaches can sound in damages. At Irish law a breach of a duty imposed by statute for the specific protection of particular categories of persons may confer on those individuals a right to damages provided they can show that they suffered loss as a consequence of that breach. In this context a litigant may not rely upon a general expectation that the public body would act in accordance with law.[35] As Fennelly J made clear in his analysis of the issue in *Glencar Exploration plc v Mayo Co. Co. (No. 2)*, it is in limited circumstances only that a breach of statutory duty can successfully ground an action in damages:

> As a matter of principle, it would not be wise to rule out the possibility that a case may in the future present itself where the relationship between a person liable to be affected by a ministerial or other public law decision is entitled to expect that care will be exercised in and about the decision to take legal advice and the manner of its taking. At the least, I think it would have to be shown that the statutory power in question was of the type which is designed to protect particular interests and that the plaintiff comes within its scope. In addition, it would probably be necessary for the claim to arise from the context of the type of individual transaction which was the subject-matter of *Ward v McMaster* [1988] I.R. 337 or perhaps from the sort of reliance on the expertise of another which formed the background to *Hedley Byrne v Heller and Partners Ltd* [1964] A.C. 465. I do not consider, however, that this is such a case. There is, of course, no doubt that the applicants' interests were well known to

[32] N 30, 149–150. See also Keane CJ, 128.
[33] N 30, 148
[34] *Tate v Minister for Social Welfare* [1995] 1 ILRM 507, 522 and 525 *per* Carroll J.
[35] N 30, 141 *per* Keane CJ.

> the respondent at the time the decision was in contemplation. The applicants could scarcely have made their interest more clear or their complaint more insistent. The respondent was fully aware that the applicants would be affected by a mining ban. But that is not enough to take them out of a class of mining enterprises, actual and potential, similarly affected. They were not engaged in any direct legal relationship with the respondent. Their prospecting licences had been granted by the State. They had not made any application for planning permission, not that that would necessarily alter the position.[36]

The power to award contracts is conferred to assist the contracting authority in discharging its functions, not to protect the interests of undertakings that might supply it with goods or services. Moreover, it is suggested that in the normal course of events it is hard to see how suppliers of goods or services could successfully assert that they relied upon a contracting authority in a manner similar to the plaintiffs in *Ward v McMaster* or in *Hedley Byrne v Heller and Partners Ltd*. The act of submitting a tender in response to a call for tenders, a step which any supplier of the relevant goods or services can take, does not distinguish that supplier from other suppliers so as to entitle it to recover damages for a breach of statutory duty in the course of an award procedure. It follows that even if, as a matter of Irish law, an infringement of the Procurement Directive could be assimilated to a breach of statutory duty, damages are unavailable for such losses as might result therefrom because a breach of a similar character committed at Irish law would not give rise to an entitlement to such compensation.

In this context, it is of interest to observe how Fennelly J considered the argument to the effect that, in prohibiting the recovery of damages allegedly caused by an illegal act on the part of a public authority, Irish law was out of step with EC law, holding that:

> The notion of a protective norm is familiar to many systems of law. For example, the applicants have cited *Francovich v Italy* (Case C-6/90 & C-9/90) [1991] E.C.R. I-5357, the decision which first established the principle and then laid down the criteria for establishing state liability for breach of a provision of European Community law. The first condition enunciated by the Court of Justice is that the Community act which is invoked – in that case a directive – "should entail the grant of rights to individuals" (para. 40 of the judgment). A duty imposed by statute on a public body will not be held to create a right to damages for its breach unless it can be shown to have within the scope of its intendment a reasonably identifiable protective purpose and identifiable class intended to benefit.[37]

Moreover, the manner in which the Court of Justice applied the somewhat laconic statement at paragraph 40 of its judgment in *Francovich* bears further examination. At paragraph 44 of that judgment, the Court observed that it was clear from an examination of the first part of the first question that the content of the right granted to the employees could be identified on the basis of the directive's provisions. Turning to that part of the judgment one finds that

[36] N 30, 159.
[37] N 30, 150.

the Court of Justice held that the directive contained precise and unconditional provisions identifying both the beneficiaries of the directive[38] and the content of those rights.[39] It follows that the directive considered in *Francovich* had 'within the scope of its intendment a reasonably identifiable protective purpose and identifiable class intended to benefit.' It is submitted that the approach of the Court of Justice, which echoes that adopted by the Supreme Court in *Ward v McMaster*, does not apply to tenderers for public contracts, in like manner as the licence holders in *Glencar* could not rely upon that line of authority in order to obtain compensation from Mayo County Council.

It follows that, so far as damages are concerned, contracting authorities are not required to compensate tenderers for the costs of participating in an unlawfully conducted award procedure unless the latter can demonstrate that (a) the conduct of the procedure contravened a legal right or duty owed to the tenderer; (b) the tenderer had a real chance of winning the contract and (c) the illegality directly prejudiced the realisation of that opportunity. A breach of a procedural rule will not establish such an entitlement. A breach of a substantive rule must have had a direct impact on the claimant's opportunity of obtaining the contract. If those conditions are met, the General Court may also award compensation for losses incurred in challenging the legality of an award over and above those recoverable by way of costs in any proceedings.[40] Compensation is unavailable under any other head of damage.

APPROPRIATENESS OF THE DAMAGES REMEDY

By reason of these limitations, it should come as no surprise that many tenderers do not consider damages to be an effective remedy for breaches of the Procurement Rules. A Staff Working Document prepared by the European Commission prior to the enactment of Directive 2007/66[41] describes three principal reasons for the reluctance of disappointed tenderers to commence damages actions. First, such actions were perceived to have no corrective effect, as the challenged contract remained extant. Second, the evidential burden of showing that the unsuccessful tenderer had a serious chance of winning the contract was too difficult, if not impossible, to discharge in practice, particularly where the allegations consisted of breaches of transparency. Third, damages actions were lengthy and costly. Any compensation as might be available was not guaranteed to cover the costs of the proceedings and did not compensate for any injury to the tenderer's future relationship with the contracting authority. The first of these complaints reflects the subsidiary nature of the damages remedy for breaches of the Procurement

[38] N 6, paras 13 and 14.

[39] N 6, paras 15–22.

[40] *AfCon*, n 20, para 104.

[41] Annex to the Proposal for a Directive of the European Parliament and of the Council amending Council Directives 89/665/EEC and 92/13/EEC with regard to improving the effectiveness of review procedures concerning the award of public contracts: Impact Assessment Report – Remedies in the field of public procurement: June 4 2006 SEC(2006) 557, para 4.3.

Rules. The second and third reflect the practical limitations upon its availability. The authors of the Staff Working Document concluded that

> it would seem that damages, in the specific context of public procurement procedures, present a less attractive or efficient means of sanction than pre-contractual Remedies – the work and costs involved are often disproportionate to the outcome, deterring bidders from using damages.

It might therefore be contended that greater use would be made of damages as a remedy if the legal and evidential requirements imposed on applicants were relaxed, thereby facilitating a rise in the level and frequency of awards, and a consequent increase in its deterrent effect. It is submitted that there is no evidence that such a consequence would necessarily ensue. Indeed the suggested approach is more likely to encourage speculative claims, particularly since the public purse would become an insurer for the profits of unsuccessful tenderers who were able to identify a legal error in the course of an award procedure, a benefit unavailable to tenderers who obtained contract awards as a result of procedures conducted in accordance with law. The capricious consequences of such an approach are revealed by the observation that, where a contracting authority declines to enter a contract upon the conclusion of an award procedure, a tenderer will incur the same 'loss', irrespective of the reasons for the contracting authority's decision.

In this context the observations of Deeny J at paragraph 21 of his judgment in *McLaughlin & Harvey Ltd v Department of Finance & Personnel (No. 3)* may be apposite:[42]

> Which is the most appropriate remedy to grant to the plaintiff, it having succeeded in proving a breach of duty? The assessment of the loss of profits might well have to wait for some time, perhaps years, to allow the court to make a reasonable estimate of the profits which the successful economic operators will enjoy from the Framework Agreement. I consider that would be necessary here and clearly it is not ideal. The profits of the economic operators who are given contracts under the Framework Agreement (or who are not) will not necessarily be publicly available, particularly as they apply to each contract. Indeed as some of these contracts are of a very substantial nature it may take years for them to work out before one would know what profit, if any, the economic operator made out of a particular contract. As indicated earlier the court would have to value the percentage of any profits which the plaintiff here should recover i.e. the value of the loss of its chance consistent with the principles laid down in *Chaplin v Hicks* [1911] 2 KB 786. But reliably fixing the value of that percentage loss of chance would take time, face difficulties and be costly. Mr. Bowsher made the point at this hearing that there could be very live arguments as to what margins any particular contractor might charge or might recover. So I acknowledge that the defendant is entitled to say that damages could be an adequate remedy. However in my view they are manifestly an inferior remedy here to that of setting aside the Framework Agreement. I say that not only for the reasons set out above but for public policy reasons. At the present time there is a question mark over whether the best five economic operators were selected under this Framework Agreement. Given that some £800m of works are said by the Department to be at stake here it must be in the public

[42] [2008] NIQB 122.

> interest to try and ensure that the best five, whether or not that includes the plaintiff, are in fact selected. Secondly it cannot be in the public interest for the public to pay for these new buildings and to pay the plaintiff again a percentage of the profits of the contractor who actually builds the new buildings. That is in the most literal sense of the word a waste of money. It may be that in some circumstances there is no alternative to such an award being made, but where, as here, there is a much better alternative I consider it preferable to opt for it.

Moreover, the availability of damages in actions challenging the validity of public contract awards has had the unintended consequence of undermining the effectiveness of the other remedies provided for.

The Remedies Directive envisages that Member States confer a jurisdiction upon review bodies to grant interim relief after the expiry of the standstill period either to restrain contracting authorities from entering into contracts the subject matter of review or to lift any statutory impediment to the conclusion of those contracts. In so doing, Member States may provide that the review body take into account the probable consequences of such measures for all of the interests likely to be harmed thereby, including the public interest, and may decide not to grant such measures when their negative consequences could exceed their benefits.[43] Any application for interim measures of its nature requires an inquiry into the adequacy of damages as a remedy for the asserted illegality. Since in the vast majority of cases tenderers compete for public contracts in order to make profits and contracting authorities are a mark for damages, contracting authorities can rely upon the availability of damages in order to defeat applications for interim measures or to prevent them from entering into a contract the subject matter of an allegedly unlawful award.[44] A contention on behalf of an applicant that damages may be an inadequate remedy encounters two principal difficulties. First, as already discussed, the level of damages which are available is likely to be low and, in any event, will be almost certainly be well within the ability of the contracting authority to meet. The availability of damages thus allows contacting authorities to satisfy one of the critical tests for defeating or succeeding in an application for interim measures. Second, should it contend that damages are inadequate, an applicant undermines any action for damages it might seek to advance at a later stage in the proceedings.

It is suggested that this is an unsatisfactory state of affairs. A clear recognition by courts of the supplementary and limited nature of the damages remedy for breaches of the Procurement Rules would allow the financial balance of convenience element in the adjudication of applications for interim remedies to be considered in a manner more favourable to tenderers who assert that the law has been infringed, thereby strengthening the effectiveness of the principal remedies designed to remedy such infringements. Indeed might it not be simpler to remove damages entirely from the remedies available for breaches of the Procurement Rules? Such a limitation in the range of the remedies available in

[43] Remedies Directive, Article 2(5).

[44] By way of example, see *McLaughlin and Harvey Ltd v Department of Finance and Personnel (No 1)* [2008] NIQB 25.

this sphere could help to focus the attention of the courts on the real issue at stake in such proceedings, namely the integrity of the award process, without doing any substantive injustice to the interests concerned.

22

Transparency, Reasons and the Europeanisation of Public Law

CATHERINE DONNELLY*

I. INTRODUCTION

PERHAPS ONE OF the most interesting and notable developments in public law in recent years at both national and European Union (EU) level has been the increased focus on transparency and openness in government[1] and on the evolving duty on decision-makers to provide reasons for their decisions. As has been observed, '[t]ransparency is a fashionable term'.[2] It is manifested in a number of Treaty and legislative provisions at EU level,[3] and promoted by, inter alia, freedom of information legislation at national level.[4] The principle is used both to guarantee access to documents and, as developed in the case law of the European Court of Justice since the leading *Telaustria* case[5] – in which Advocate General Fennelly gave the Opinion – to require advance disclosure of the criteria guiding the exercise of discretion. The duty to provide reasons, while most usually, in the common law at least, located in the duty to provide procedural fairness, also obviously

*Barrister in the Law Library, Dublin and Blackstone Chambers, London. Associate Professor and Fellow of Trinity College, Dublin.

[1] See, H Woolf, J Jowell, A Le Sueur, C Donnelly and I Hare, *De Smith's Judicial Review*, 7th edn (London, Sweet and Maxwell, 2013), para 7-089 (referring to a 'strong momentum recently in favour of greater openness in decision-making); see also *R v Ministry for Defence, Ex p Murray* [1998] COD 134 (Hooper J referring to the 'perceptible trend towards an insistence on greater openness in the making of administrative decisions').

[2] J Howell, 'Is There a General Principle Requiring Transparency about How Decisions will be Taken?' (2011) 16 *Judicial Review* 322, para 1.

[3] See, eg, Articles 1 and 10, Treaty on European Union (TEU); Article 15, Treaty on the Functioning of the European Union (TFEU); Regulation No. 1049/2001 regarding public access to European Parliament, Council and Commission documents [2001] OJ L145/43.

[4] See, eg, Freedom of Information Acts 2007 to 2003 (Ireland); Freedom of Information Act 2000 (United Kingdom). See M McDonagh, *Freedom of Information Law* 2nd edn (Dublin, Round Hall, 2006). In the United Kingdom, see generally, P Coppel, *Information Rights: Law and Practice* 3rd edn (Oxford, Hart, 2010).

[5] Case C-324/98 *Telaustria Verlags GmbH and Telefonadress GmbH v Telekom Austria AG* [2000] ECR I-10745.

promotes and is bolstered by the ever-increasing emphasis on transparency in governance. This is evidenced by the welcome recent Irish Supreme Court judgment in *Mallak v Minister for Justice, Equality and Law Reform*[6] – written by Fennelly J for the Court – in which the duty to give reasons was promoted and strengthened in national law.

Against the background of the increasing focus on transparency, this chapter will examine the duty to provide reasons at EU and national level, in terms of the scope of the duty, its content and the remedies for its breach. This review will also be used to comment on the impact of EU law on domestic law and to consider potential future development of the principle of transparency at both EU and national level. It will be contended that transparency and reason-giving demonstrate what may be described as the 'cross-fertilising'[7] or 'spill-over' effect of EU law on national public law, forming, over time, part of a trend described by some commentators as an increasing convergence of public law standards across Europe.[8] It will also be observed that the EU principle of transparency, although currently most often invoked in the context of public procurement law and administrative authorisations, has significant potential to prompt the future evolution of public law standards more generally and to provide further opportunities for the Europeanisation of national public law.

II. THE INCREASING EMPHASIS ON TRANSPARENCY

A. The Emphasis on Transparency at EU Level

(i) The Evolution of the Principle of Transparency

Lenaerts has observed that growing distrust of government by citizens and the emergence of civil society and non-governmental organisations required those in political power to increase the transparency of decision-making processes, not only at national level, but also at Union level, starting with Declaration No 17 on the right of access to information annexed to the Maastricht Treaty in 1992.[9] Since then, the principle of transparency has evolved through both legal

[6] [2012] IESC 59; see in this volume, D O'Donnell, 'Nial Fennelly: *Mallak* and the Rule of Reasons'.

[7] J Bell, 'Mechanisms for Cross-fertilization of Administrative Law in Europe' in J Beatson and T Tridimas (eds), *New Directions in European Public Law* (Oxford, Hart, 1998) 147.

[8] Ibid; G de Búrca, 'Proportionality and *Wednesbury* Unreasonableness: The Influence of European Legal Concepts on UK Law' (1997) 3 *European Public Law* 561; P Birkinshaw, *European Public Law* (London, Butterworths, 2003); G Anthony, 'Community Law and the Development of UK Administrative Law: Delimiting the Spill-Over Effect' (1998) 4 *European Public Law* 253; J Schwarze (ed), *Administrative Law under European Influence* (London, Sweet and Maxwell, 1996). The term 'cross-fertilisation' derives from the comparative law tradition; the term 'spill-over' derives from the wider literature on EU integration and, in particular, from the neo-functionalist paradigm of regional integration: Anthony, 254, fn 6. While perhaps not strictly correct, the terms are sufficiently close in meaning to be used interchangeably for present purposes.

[9] K Lenaerts, '"In the Union we trust": Trust-enhancing principles of Community law' (2004) 41 *CML Rev* 317, 318.

and policy initiatives.[10] Policy initiatives have included significant Commission papers, such as *European Governance: A White Paper.*[11]

In the legal context, since the Amsterdam Treaty of 1997,[12] transparency has been identified as a general objective of the Union, with Article 1 TEU stating that the Treaty 'marks a new stage in the process of creating an ever closer union among the peoples of Europe, in which decisions are taken as openly as possible and as closely as possible to the citizen'. Article 10(3) TEU – a new provision introduced by the Lisbon Treaty – links transparency with democratic participation, noting that '[e]very citizen shall have the right to participate in the democratic life of the Union. Decisions shall be taken as openly and as closely as possible to the citizen'. As Craig has noted,[13] transparency is also associated with dialogue and consultation,[14] features in the legislative process,[15] is linked to access to documents[16] and is imposed as an obligation on EU institutions and Member States.[17]

The Lisbon Treaty reforms have also continued to promote transparency, with Article 15(3) TFEU extending beyond its predecessor (Article 253 EC) by providing that, in addition to EU institutions, the right of access to documents applies more broadly to EU 'bodies, offices and agencies'.[18] This provision is also protected by Article 42 of the Charter of Fundamental Rights of the European Union (the Charter) and thereby takes on the status of a fundamental right, the limitations to which must comply with Article 52 of the Charter.[19] Moreover, transparency in its role of granting access to documents is regulated by Regulation 1049/2001.[20]

In the case law too, transparency has been evolving quickly, in particular since the 'landmark' *Telaustria* case,[21] a case on the duty to advertise contracts falling

[10] D Curtin and AJ Meijer, 'Does transparency strengthen legitimacy? A critical analysis of European Union policy documents' (2006) 11 *Information Polity* 109.

[11] COM(2001) 428 final, 25 July 2001.

[12] Treaty of Amsterdam Amending the Treaty on European Union, Article 1(4).

[13] P Craig, *EU Administrative Law*, 2nd edn (Oxford, Oxford University Press, 2012), 358–359.

[14] Article 11(2) TEU states that the EU institutions shall maintain an open, transparent, and regular dialogue with representative associations and civil society. Article 15(1) of the Treaty on the Functioning of the European Union (TFEU) states that in order to promote good governance and ensure the participation of civil society, the Union's institutions, bodies, offices, and agencies shall conduct their work as openly as possible. Article 11(3) TEU requires the Commission to carry out broad consultations with parties concerned in order to ensure that the Union's actions are coherent and transparent.

[15] Article 16(8) TEU imposes an obligation on the Council to meet in public when it deliberates and votes on a draft legislative act. Article 15(2) TFEU renders the European Parliament subject to the same duty.

[16] Article 15(3) TFEU sets out the right of Union citizens and any natural or legal person residing or having its registered office in a Member State of access to documents to the Union's institutions, bodies, offices and agencies.

[17] Craig (n 13 above) 359 (citing Case C-260/04 *Commission v Italy* [2007] ECR I-7083; Case C-203/08 *Sporting Exchange Ltd v Minister van Justitie,* 3 June 2010).

[18] See K Lenaerts, 'The principle of democracy in the case law of the European Court of Justice' (2013) *ICLQ* 271, 301.

[19] Ibid.

[20] See n 3 above.

[21] A Brown, 'Seeing through transparency: the requirement to advertise public contracts and concessions under the EC Treaty' (2007) *Public Procurement Law Review* 1, 3. See also Howell (n

outside the scope of the publication duty in the Procurement Directives.[22] While there had been previous references to a general obligation of transparency in the context of public procurement,[23] it was not until *Telaustria* that the general obligation was concretised into a specific requirement to advertise public contracts to enhance competition from potential bidders across the EU. The Court of Justice held that even though public service concessions are excluded from the scope of the Procurement Directives, when awarding such concessions, it is nonetheless necessary to comply with the fundamental rules of the Treaty, in general, and the principle of non-discrimination and equal treatment on grounds of nationality, which non-discrimination principle implied an obligation of transparency.[24] The Court also held that the obligation of transparency consisted in ensuring 'for the benefit of any potential tenderer, a degree of advertising sufficient to enable the services market to be opened up to competition and the impartiality of procurement procedures to be reviewed'.[25]

In his opinion in *Telaustria*, Advocate General Fennelly had established a strong foundation for the principle of transparency, on which the Court built in its judgment, observing that 'substantive compliance with the principle of non-discrimination on grounds of nationality requires that the award of concessions respect a minimum degree of publicity and transparency' and agreeing with the Commission that 'what must at all costs be avoided is that their grant be shrouded in secrecy or opacity'.[26]

(ii) The Application of the Principle of Transparency at EU Level

Turning to the application of transparency, while a 'flexible notion' with many functions in different contexts,[27] performs two particularly important roles in EU law: first, what could be described **as *an access-providing role*** insofar as the

2 above), para 11, describing *Telaustria* as the 'practical starting point' of the development of the principle of transparency in the context of public procurement.

[22] The Directives applicable at the time were: Council Directive 92/50/EEC of 18 June 1992 relating to the coordination of procedures for the award of public service contracts [1992] OJ L209/1 and Council Directive 93/38/EEC of 14 June 1993 coordinating the procurement procedures of entities operating in the water, energy, transport and telecommunications sectors [1993] OJ L199/84.

[23] Case C-108/98 *RI.SAN. Srl v Comune di Ischia, Italia Lavoro SpA and Ischia Ambiente SpA* [1999] ECR I-5219, para 20 and Case C-275/98 *Unitron Scandinavia A/S and 3-S A/S, Danske Svineproducenters Serviceselskab v Ministeriet for Fødevarer, Landbrug og Fiskeri* [1999] ECR I-8291, para 31.

[24] Case C-324/98 (n 5 above), para 61.

[25] Ibid, para 62.

[26] Ibid, para 43. In this respect, there was a slight difference between the approach of the CJEU and the Advocate General, who, relying on the Commission's submission at the hearing, required publicity but not necessarily publication (Opinion, para 42). The CJEU took the obligation of transparency as developed by Advocate General Fennelly to the further stage of requiring advertising of the competition in advance (Judgment, para 62).

[27] See S Prechal and ME de Leeuw, 'Transparency: A General Principle of EU Law?' in U Bernitz, J Nergelius and C Cardner (eds), *General Principles of European Community Law in a Process of Development* (Alphen aan den Rijn, Kluwer Law International, 2008) 201, 202. Prechal and Leeuw provide an excellent and comprehensive overview of the many uses of transparency beyond what is possible here.

principle serves to facilitate access to documentation[28] and, second, ***a discretion-constraining role*** reflecting the development of the principle from the *Telaustria* case.

In its access-providing role, transparency is regarded as 'derived from the most essential political foundations of the Member States of the Community'[29] and is considered by the Court of Justice as bolstering the democratic values of the Union.[30] This aspect of transparency is also, as described above, strongly promoted by Treaty provisions and secondary legislation, and has been invoked by the Court of Justice to interpret secondary legislation.[31]

Following *Telaustria*, the discretion-constraining role of transparency has been developed in the procurement context to require prior publication of the criteria which will guide the exercise of discretion. Thus, the principle of transparency has been used not only to support the non-discrimination principle – which was its starting point in *Telaustria* – but has served as the source of a separate obligation to publish matters which were not specifically required to be published by the Procurement Directives;[32] the emphasis has been on ensuring that the discretion of the decision-maker is regulated and constrained in accordance with pre-determined criteria. This use of transparency to regulate the exercise of discretion follows naturally from the role attributed to the principle by Advocate General Fennelly in *Telaustria* itself, namely, of 'ensuring the *fundamental fairness and openness* of the award procedures'[33] (emphasis added).

The link drawn between transparency and fairness in *Telaustria* has also been evident in a number of cases at EU level. For example, in *SIAC Construction Limited v County of Mayo*,[34] the CJEU found that the principle of transparency meant that an award criterion could not have the effect of conferring an unrestricted freedom of choice on the contracting authority when awarding any contract: it required such criteria to be formulated 'in such a way as to allow all reasonably well-informed and normally diligent tenderers to interpret them in the same way' and that they must be capable of being applied objectively.[35] It has also been observed that the principle of transparency is 'essentially intended to

[28] For comment on the access-providing role of transparency, see: Lenaerts, '"In the Union we trust"' (n 9 above) 318–324; M Broberg, 'Access to documents: a general principle of Community Law?' (2002) 27 *EL Rev* 194. Prechal and Leeuw describe this role as constituting a 'relatively well-defined notion of transparency': Prechal and Leeuw (n 27 above) 201; see also 205 and 208–212, 214–215.

[29] Case C-353/99 P *Council v Hautala* [2001] ECR I-9565, Opinion of Advocate General Léger, para 47.

[30] See Lenaerts, '"In the Union we trust"' (n 9 above) 320.

[31] *De Smith's Judicial Review* (n 1 above), para 14-118; Cases C-154 and 155/04 *The Queen on the application of Alliance for Natural Health and Nutri-Link Ltd v Secretary of State for Health* [2005] ECR I–6451, paras 81– 82.

[32] Case C-470/99 *Universale-Bau AG* [2002] ECR I-11617; Case C-331/04 *ATI EAC Srl v ACTV Venezia Spa* [2005] ECR I-10109; Case C-532/06 *Lianakis AE v Dimos Alexandroupolis* [2008] ECR I-251.

[33] Case C-324/98 (n 5 above), para 43.

[34] Case C-19/00 [2001] ECR I-7725.

[35] See Howell (n 2 above), para 8. See also Case C-368/10 *Commission v Netherlands*, judgment of 10 May 2012, para 110.

preclude any risk of favouritism or arbitrariness on the part of the contracting authority'.[36]

Similar use of the principle of transparency can be found in the context of schemes that require prior administrative authorisations before services may be or are to be provided where restrictions on the free movements arise, such as the freedom to provide services.[37] Howell gives the example of a case considering a scheme affecting the freedom to provide maritime transport, in which the Court of Justice stated that:

> if a prior administrative authorisation scheme is to be justified even though it derogates from a fundamental freedom, it must, in any event, be based on objective, non-discriminatory criteria which are known in advance to the undertakings concerned, in such a way as to circumscribe the exercise of the national authorities' discretion, so that it is not used arbitrarily.[38]

In *Sporting Exchange Ltd v Minister van Justitie*, it was held that 'compliance with the principle of equal treatment and with the consequent obligation of transparency necessarily means that the objective criteria enabling the Member States' competent authorities' discretion to be circumscribed must be sufficiently advertised'.[39] Howell has also identified a similar link between transparency and constraint of arbitrary discretion in the Grand Chamber judgment in the *Carmen Media Group* case, in respect of a restriction on the freedom to provide services, in which the Court observed that discretionary conduct on the part of national authorities could not negate the effectiveness of provisions of EU law, such that any prior administrative authorisation scheme must be 'based on objective, non-discriminatory criteria known in advance, in such a way as to circumscribe the exercise of the authorities' discretion so that it is not used arbitrarily.'[40]

Perhaps the most useful summary of the principle of transparency as it operates in its discretion-constraining role is found in Commission guidance in the procurement context, in which it is stated that those affected by a decision 'must be able to know the applicable rules in advance and must have the certainty that these rules apply to everybody in the same way'.[41]

B. Transparency at the National Level

At the national level in Ireland, the most obvious manifestation of the principle of transparency has been in an access-providing role, as implemented through

[36] Case T-476/07 *Europaïki Dynamiki v European Agency for the Management of Operational Cooperation at the External Borders of the European Union*, judgment of 12 July 2012, para 76.

[37] Howell (n 2 above), para 13.

[38] Case C-205/99 *Analir v Administración General del Estado* [2001] ECR I-1271, para 38.

[39] See n 17 above.

[40] Howell (n 2 above), para 15; Case C-46/08 *Carmen Media Group v Land Schleswig-Holstein* [2011] 1 CMLR 19, paras 86–87. See also Case C-62/09 *R (ABPI) v Medicines and Healthcare Products Regulatory Agency* [2011] PTSR 391; Case C-280/00 *Altmark Transport GmbH v Nahverkehrsgesellschaft Altmark GmbH* [2003] ECR I-7747, paras 90 and 95.

[41] Commission Interpretative Communication on the Community law applicable to contract awards not or not fully subject to the provisions of the Public Procurement Directives, 23 June 2006, Section 2.2.1.

statutory measures, and in particular, through the Freedom of Information Acts 1997 to 2003 (the 1997 Act). Further amendments to the 1997 Act to extend the range of bodies bound by freedom of information legislation are anticipated.[42] Significantly, for present purposes, Section 18 of the 1997 Act imposes an obligation on a public body, on request, to provide a statement of the reasons for any act to any person affected by the act and who has a material interest in the matter affected by the act or to which it relates.[43] Section 18 is regarded as having had a very significant impact,[44] however, it must not be overlooked that the provision is limited by the overall scheme of exemptions in the legislation,[45] which as will be seen from the facts in the *Mallak* case discussed below, may be significant.

In the case law, apart from being applied in those areas of EU law in which it is compulsory,[46] there is no independent principle of transparency in domestic public law. However, as will be seen below,[47] the ***value*** of transparency is increasingly invoked in many contexts in justification for particular reasoning and conclusions.[48]

III. THE RELATIONSHIP BETWEEN THE PRINCIPLE OF TRANSPARENCY AND THE DUTY TO PROVIDE REASONS

A. The Allied Purposes of Transparency and Reason-Giving

The links between the principle of transparency and the duty to provide reasons are in many respects obvious and, for example, the two are frequently allied in public discourse. For example, as Curtin and Meijer point out,[49] in 1998, the European Ombudsman, Jacob Söderman defined the term transparency as requiring that 'the process through which public authorities make decisions should be understandable and open; the decisions themselves should be reasoned; as far as possible, the information on which the decisions are based should be available to the public.'[50] Meanwhile, according to Lord Nolan, transparency

[42] See, eg: N Whelan, 'Freedom of Information Bill suggests we are still stuck with old-world attitudes', *Irish Times*, 16 November 2013.

[43] For a useful overview of the impact of this provision, see H Biehler, *Judicial Review of Administrative Action: A Comparative Analysis*, 3rd edn (Dublin, Round Hall, 2013), 354–356; G Hogan and DG Morgan, *Administrative Law in Ireland*, 4th edn (Dublin, Round Hall, 2010), paras 14-123 and 14-124.

[44] Ibid.

[45] 1997 Act, s 18(2).

[46] See, eg: *Baxter Healthcare Ltd v Health Service Executive* [2013] IEHC 413; *Fresenius Medical Care (Ireland) Ltd v Health Service Executive* [2013] IEHC 414; *O'Kelly Brothers Civil Engineering Company Ltd v Cork City Council* [2013] IEHC 159; *Vodafone Ireland Ltd v Commissioner for Communications Regulation* [2013] IEHC 382.

[47] See eg: *Mallak* (n 6 above).

[48] See eg: *Callan v Ireland* [2013] IESC 35 (Hardiman J); *Burke v South Dublin County Council* [2013] IEHC 185, para 4.4.

[49] Curtin and Meijer (n 10 above) 111.

[50] J Söderman, 'The Citizen, the Administration and Community Law', General report for the 1998 FIDE Congress, Stockholm, 1998, 6.

requires that 'holders of public office should be as open as possible about all decisions and actions they take', including giving reasons for their decisions.[51]

The principle of transparency and the duty to give reasons also pursue similar goals. At one level, transparency can, as observed by Advocate General Fennelly in *Telaustria*, promote the goal of openness. Transparency is also invoked, as in the post-*Telaustria* case law described above, to deliver fairness by ensuring that individuals are aware in advance of the criteria pursuant to which decisions affecting them will be made. As already outlined, and following from the notification of advance criteria, transparency obligations ensure that discretion is not exercised arbitrarily; the exercise of the discretion will be constrained by the pre-notified criteria. In addition, transparency, at least in its inception in *Telaustria* and a number of other early cases,[52] was concerned with allowing a mechanism by which there could be effective review of whether there had been compliance with the principle of equal treatment.

At a more general level, transparency obligations – particularly in their access-providing role – can be regarded as enhancing democratic participation and trust in public institutions. Lenaerts has noted in the EU context that:

> The emergence of the principle of transparency illustrates this change of perspective: from a basic guarantee founded on the right to defend oneself in situations where one is directly and adversely affected, it became over time a general principle aimed at 'strengthening the democratic character of the institutions and the trust of the public in the administration'.[53]

Like transparency, reason-giving promotes fairness.[54] It too serves a discretion-constraining role and seeks to eliminate arbitrariness in decision-making. As the authors of De Smith observe, '[t]o have to provide an explanation of the basis for their decision is a salutary discipline for those who have to decide anything that adversely affects others', which, in turn, 'encourages a careful examination of the relevant issues, the elimination of extraneous considerations, and consistency in decision-making'.[55] Reason-giving may be regarded as increasing public confidence in the decision-making process.[56] It also promotes effective remedies, by facilitating assessment of whether there are grounds for appeal or review.[57] The link between reason-giving and effective judicial review has

[51] Lord Nolan, *First Report of the Committee on Standards in Public Life*, Cm 2850, HMSO, London, 1995.

[52] See n 23 above.

[53] '"In the Union we trust"' (n 9 above) (citing from Case T-14/98 *Hautala* [1999] ECR II-2489, para 83; Case C-353/99 P *Hautala* (n 29 above), para 25).

[54] See, eg: *McAlister v Minister for Justice, Equality and Law Reform* [2003] 4 IR 35, 44 ([i]t is important that justice should be seen to be done and this will very often require that a person affected by a decision should know why that particular decision has been taken). The duty to give reasons is usually regarded as located in Irish law in the guarantee of fair procedures: Biehler (n 43 above), 343–348; *State (Creedon) v Criminal Injuries Compensation Tribunal* [1988] IR 51, 55

[55] *De Smith's Judicial Review* (n 1 above), para 7-090. See also *Re Northwestern Utilities and the City of Edmonton* (1978) 89 DLR (3d) 161, 175

[56] *Stefan v General Medical Council (No 1)* [1999] 1 WLR 1293, 1300.

[57] *De Smith's Judicial Review* (n 1 above), para 7-091. The link between reason-giving and effective judicial review has been given particular emphasis in Irish law: Biehler (n 43 above), 356–360. See also *Rawson v Minister for Defence* [2012] IESC 26.

been emphasised in both the EU context and in the national context, as without reasons, errors may be extremely difficult to detect.[58]

Beyond the perspective of the individual, like transparency, reason-giving can also promote democratic government. Indeed, Higgins has observed that one of the most significant justifications for requiring reasons is that reason-giving is central to democratic government, which necessitates the practices and policies of the public decision-makers to be transparent if the public is to fully participate in the democratic process. She also suggests that the public can only consent to the exercise of public power when it understands the rationale for it.[59]

It is also the case that the purpose of reason-giving can simply be to promote transparency, as an important goal in itself, and 'the duty to notify reasons … is dictated precisely by concern to ensure a minimum level of transparency'.[60] In this regard, failure to provide reasons will result in a failure to provide transparency, in particular, as neither the party affected, nor the reviewing court, will be able to determine the basis on which the decision has been taken.[61]

B. The Differing Functions of Transparency and Reason-Giving

While pursuing similar goals and objectives however, it is important to note that transparency and reason-giving – at least as developed to date – perform different, perhaps corollary, functions. For example, the discretion-constraining roles of transparency and reason-giving are performed differently: while the principle of transparency in the EU procurement and prior authorisation case law requires administrators to identify in advance how they will exercise their discretion, the duty to give reasons provides an indication of how the discretion has been exercised. In this way, the principle of transparency imposes an ex ante constraint on arbitrary discretion and the duty to give reasons an ex post facto constraint.

The principle of transparency also goes further than the duty of reason-giving in a number of respects. As Howell explains – in its discretion-constraining role – transparency performs two functions which are not currently performed by English (or Irish) domestic administrative law: first, reasons do not allow a full analysis of the rationality of the decision under scrutiny, as even when reasons are provided, it will not be evident for example whether similar cases have been or

[58] See *Mallak* (n 6 above); *McAlister* (n 54 above). In the English context, see *O'Reilly v Mackman* [1983] 2 AC 237, 277 (Lord Diplock noting that judicial review for error of law on the face of the record 'was liable to be defeated by the decision-making body if it gave no reasons for its determination).

[59] I Higgins, 'The Duty to Give Reasons in Irish Law: Is it Time to Recognise a General Duty' (2011) 23 *Dublin University Law Journal* 23.

[60] Case C-92/00 *Hospital Ingenieure Krankenhaustechnik Planungs-Gesellschaft mbH (HI)* [2002] ECR I-5553, para 46.

[61] B Vesterdorf, 'Transparency – Not Just a Vogue Word' (1999) 22 *Fordham International Law Journal* 902, 906; see also Cases T–246 and 332/08 *Melli Bank Plc v Council* [2009] ECR II–2629, para 146 for an example of breaches of transparency and reason-giving being aligned.

would be treated similarly; second, reason-giving does not promote predictability by allowing those subject to the law to plan their activities in the way that the transparency obligation might.[62] In addition, transparency – in its access-providing guise – goes further than reasons insofar as it requires access to the contemporaneous record of the deliberations, which is not provided by reasons.

Thus, while closely linked in their objectives, transparency and reason-giving are not perfectly correlated in their operation. This lack of correlation raises the question, considered below, of the extent to which the broader transparency principle may be used to bolster the duty to provide reasons, and indeed, other aspects of national public law.

IV. THE DUTY TO GIVE REASONS AT NATIONAL AND EU LEVEL

A. The Existence of the Duty to Give Reasons

(i) EU Level

At EU level, the existence of the duty to give reasons is uncontentious. Article 296 TFEU provides that '[l]egal acts shall state the reasons on which they are based', while Article 41 of the Charter provides that every person benefits from the right to good administration, which includes, pursuant to Article 41(2), 'the obligation of the administration to give reasons for its decisions.' As such, there is a fundamental right to reasons, enforceable against all institutions and bodies of the Union. There is also a duty on national authorities making decisions affecting Union rights to provide reasons, although this duty, unlike at EU level itself, does not extend to measures of general application.[63]

(ii) National Level

a. The Holding in the *Mallak* Case

By contrast, the question of the existence of reason-giving duty has proved difficult in Irish and English administrative law, with the traditional common law position being that there is no over-arching duty on administrative decision-makers to provide reasons. While a robust case law on reason-giving has been evolving in Ireland for some time[64] – assisted by the statutory intervention of Section 18 of the 1997 Act – the position has generally been regarded as being as set out in the case of *McCormack v Garda Síochána Complaints Board*, namely, that 'it is not the law of this country that procedural fairness requires that in

[62] Howell (n 2 above), para 32.

[63] Case C-70/95 *Sodemare SA v Fédération de Maisons de Repos Privés de Belgique (Femarbel) ASBL and Regione Lombardia* [1997] ECR I-3395 (in which Advocate General Fennelly delivered the Opinion).

[64] See, eg: *State (Daly) v Minister for Agriculture* [1987] IR 165; *Creedon* (n 54 above); *McCormack v Garda Síochána Complaints Board* [1997] 2 IR 489; *Flood v Garda Síochána Complaints Board* [1997] 3 IR 321.

every case an administrative decision-making authority must give reasons for its decisions'.[65] A similar statement is made by Barron J in *Manning v Shackleton*, who premised the duty to provide reasons on the avoidance of injustice and observed that the duty 'is not an essential obligation and arises only when required to prevent an injustice or to ensure that not only has justice been done but is seen to have been done'.[66]

In what is now the leading case on the issue in Ireland, *Mallak*, this traditional position arose for the consideration of the Supreme Court.[67] The applicant had applied for a certificate of naturalisation with a view to obtaining citizenship pursuant to Section 15 of the Irish Nationality and Citizenship Act 1956 (the 1956 Act).[68] This application had been refused and no reasons had been furnished by the Minister, who relied on the provision in Section 15 for the Minister to grant a certificate in his 'absolute discretion'. The appellant had sought initially to rely on Section 18 of the 1997 Act, as amended, for a statement of the reasons for the refusal of his application, but the Minister was able to rely on an exception to the duty in Section 18(2), which applies where the non-disclosure of the existence or non-existence of the record was required by the exemptions to access identified in the 1997 Act. The Minister's reliance on the exception was upheld by the Office of the Information Commissioner, but the difficulties created for the appellant were acknowledged and the Office noted that the circumstances were 'such that the appellant was left none the wiser as to why his naturalisation request and subsequent request for reasons were refused'.[69]

In his legal challenge, the appellant made three arguments: first, insofar as Section 15 of the 1956 Act permitted the Minister to refuse to grant a certificate of naturalisation in his absolute discretion, namely, without providing reasons, it was unconstitutional; second, the section should be interpreted such that the Minister was obliged to give reasons; third, the decision of the Minister to grant or refuse a certificate of naturalisation was a decision regarding the acquisition of citizenship of the EU to which general principles of EU law applied, in particular Article 41 of the Charter, such that the Minister was obliged to give reasons.

In accordance with its usual practice of only resolving constitutional matters where necessary, the Supreme Court considered the second issue first, namely, whether Section 15 could be interpreted to impose an obligation to provide reasons. Fennelly J had no difficulty concluding that Section 15 could be so interpreted. In so doing, while not endorsing an over-arching and automatically-applying duty to provide reasons, as found in Article 296 TFEU for example, Fennelly J can be regarded as having moved Irish law significantly closer to the EU position and, more particularly, as having altered the balance of the previous

[65] *McCormack* (n 64 above) 500 (Costello P). For the similar English position, see *R (on the application of Hasan) v Secretary of State for Trade and Industry* [2008] EWCA Civ 1312; [2009] 3 All ER 539, paras 19 and 21.

[66] [1994] 1 ILRM 346. For the Supreme Court, see [1997] 2 ILRM 26 (SC).

[67] See *Mallak* (n 6 above), para 4.

[68] Ibid, para 8.

[69] Ibid, para 11.

Irish case law. The crucial holding in the judgment is found towards the end and, after examining the judgment of the English Court of Appeal in one of the most important cases on reason-giving in England, *R v Secretary for State ex parte Fayed*,[70] Fennelly J reached the following conclusion:

> It might be thought unnecessary to call in aid this parallel development of the law in the United Kingdom. The developing jurisprudence of our own courts provides compelling evidence that, at this point, it must be unusual for a decision maker to be permitted to refuse to give reasons. The reason is obvious. In the absence of any reasons, it is simply not possible for the applicant to make a judgment as to whether he has a ground for applying for a judicial review of the substance of the decision and, for the same reason, for the court to exercise its power. At the very least, the decision maker must be able to justify the refusal. No attempt has been made to do so in the present case and I believe it would be wrong to speculate about cases in which the courts might be persuaded to accept such justification.[71]

The effect of this language clearly alters the traditional legal position in Ireland, as described above and as formulated by Barron J in the *Manning* case. As articulated in *Manning*, the duty to provide reasons arises in Irish law when it can be justified as being required to prevent injustice; as articulated by Fennelly J, the duty to provide reasons arises unless the decision-maker can justify not providing reasons. In other words, the burden of justification appears to have shifted. It is not necessary to justify imposing an obligation to provide reasons; rather, it is necessary to justify not imposing such an obligation.[72]

Moreover, while Fennelly J indicated that he did not wish to speculate as to when a refusal to provide reasons might be justified, his judgment suggests that the range of such justifications is limited; the only scenarios expressly contemplated in the judgment as excusing a failure to provide reasons are those in which the process is fair, open and transparent, the affected person has been enabled to respond to the concerns of the decision-maker, the reasons for the decision are obvious and effective judicial review is not precluded.[73]

In light of the increasing emphasis on transparency and the hugely important goals and objectives of reason-giving, considered above, the holding in *Mallak* can only be welcomed. The judgment is however also notable for three particular aspects of its analysis, namely, its invocation of transparency, its reliance on the accepted rationales discussed above for reason-giving, and its use of EU law.

b. The Invocation of Transparency

While the principle of transparency does not form the basis for the Court's conclusion in the *Mallak* judgment, it does receive one important mention. As noted above, Fennelly J observed that if the process is 'fair, open and transparent' and the reasons obvious, effective judicial review may not be precluded.[74] In

[70] [1998] 1 WLR 763, considered in *Mallak* (n 6 above), paras 70–73.
[71] *Mallak* (n 6 above), para 74; see also para 77.
[72] See also F McDonagh, 'The Duty to Give Reasons', Bar Council CPD Seminar, 13 March 2013, 5.
[73] *Mallak* (n 6 above), para 66.
[74] Ibid.

articulating this point, Fennelly J develops two of the observations made above regarding transparency: first, a link between transparency and reason-giving is identified insofar as it is envisaged that it may be possible for the effects of a failure to provide reasons to be mitigated or indeed removed by transparency in the process and, secondly, Fennelly J explores the link between transparency and effective judicial review. Thus, a transparent process will render the reasons for the decision obvious without any formal provision of reasons and in this way, effective judicial review will not be precluded.

c. The Rationales for Reason-Giving

The importance of effective judicial review was given particular emphasis by Fennelly J to support his reasoning in *Mallak*, with the Court observing that the absence of a statement may render a right of appeal nugatory and that it may also render it impossible for an applicant to ascertain whether he has a ground for applying for judicial review and, by extension, for the courts effectively to exercise their power of judicial review.[75] The link between reason-giving and fairness was also identified, and it was noted that the question of the obligation on decision-makers to disclose the reasons for their decisions was closely related to other features of the rules of natural justice covered by the broad principle of *audi alteram partem*.[76]

Interestingly also, in light of the discussion above of the principle of transparency in its discretion-constraining role, on the facts of the case and given that it appeared to be open to the applicant to reapply for a certificate of naturalisation, Fennelly J identified a link between the duty to give reasons and the exercise of the Minister's discretion in a subsequent application: as Fennelly J observed, '[w]hile, therefore, the invitation is, to some extent, in ease of the appellant, it is impossible for the appellant to address the Minister's concerns and thus to make an effective application when he is in complete ignorance of the Minister's concerns.'[77]

These three rationales – effective review, fairness and discretion-constraining – are fused and interlinked in the following statement:

> In the present state of evolution of our law, it is not easy to conceive of a decision-maker being dispensed from giving an explanation either of the decision or of the decision-making process at some stage. The most obvious means of achieving fairness is for reasons to accompany the decision. However, it is not a matter of complying with a formal rule: the underlying objective is the attainment of fairness in the process. If the process is fair, open and transparent and the affected person has been enabled to respond to the concerns of the decision-maker, there may be situations where the reasons for the decision are obvious and that effective judicial review is not precluded.[78]

[75] Ibid, paras 63, 65 and 74.
[76] Ibid, para 2.
[77] Ibid, para 64.
[78] Ibid, para 66.

d. The Use of EU Law

Turning to the Court's use of EU law, Fennelly J referred to EU law in two contexts, both with the same overarching purpose: namely, to influence and bolster the approach being adopted by the Court.

At the outset, Fennelly J used EU law to support the fundamental proposition that the courts must be capable of providing effective judicial review, as required by reason-giving. Referring comparatively to the common law and the European Convention on Human Rights in his opening paragraph, Fennelly J placed significant weight on the requirement for the law to provide a remedy where fairness can be shown to be lacking. In this regard, he noted the important reference of the CJEU in *Parti écologiste 'Les Verts' v European Parliament*,[79] to the need for a 'complete system of legal remedies'.

In its second invocation, EU law was relied upon more specifically to bolster the position taken by the Court in its imposition of a duty to provide reasons. The Court referred to both Article 296 TFEU and Article 41 of the Charter, and to recent jurisprudence of the Court of Justice in the *Bamba* case,[80] in which the Court had located the duty to provide reasons in the rights of the defence, and in the need to ensure that a person is provided with sufficient information to assess the soundness of any decision taken affecting him or her and to enable the judiciary to review the legality of the act. In this way, EU law was identified as one of several converging legal sources which 'strongly suggest an emerging commonly held view that persons affected by administrative decisions have a right to know the reasons on which they are based, in short to understand them'.[81]

d. The Significance of the *Mallak* Judgment

The *Mallak* judgment is significant for at least four reasons. First, as explained above, the judgment has strengthened the obligation to provide reasons and Irish law has now evolved closer to the situation where an over-arching duty applies; at the very least, the decision maker must be able to justify any refusal to provide reasons.

Secondly, the case has arguably invigorated Irish case law more generally on the duty to give reasons. For example, in the case of *EMI Records (Ireland) Ltd v Data Protection Commissioner*,[82] Clarke J relied upon the *Mallak* judgment and the principle of legal certainty to hold that there should not be any doubt as to where the reasons for a decision could be found.[83] In the same judgment, Clarke J also rejected the contention of a respondent that an applicant was not entitled to complain of lack of reasons in circumstances in which it had managed to otherwise construct a challenge to an administrative decision. As

[79] Case 294/83 [1986] ECR 1339, para 23.

[80] Case C-417/11 *Council v Bamba*, judgment of 15 November 2012.

[81] *Mallak* (n 6 above), para 67.

[82] [2013] IESC 34.

[83] Ibid, para 6.9.

the learned judge observed: '[t]he fact that a party may, in many circumstances, be able to make a good fist of inferring the reasons does not meet the legal obligation of a statutory decision maker to ensure that the reasons can be determined with adequate certainty.'[84] This particular holding in *EMI* may be significant in future case law insofar as it suggests a slight weakening of the link between reason-giving and effective judicial review and identifies the importance of simply having adequate certainty as to the reasons, a rationale which could perhaps be regarded as closer to promotion of transparency as a goal in itself.[85]

Thirdly, the *Mallak* case is also significant as, often, notwithstanding the rich constitutional tradition in this jurisdiction, Irish courts can occasionally be slower to expand the realms of public law than their English counterparts;[86] in contrast to that usual position, the statement of the Supreme Court in *Mallak* is arguably more robust than any statement on reason-giving found in the English context.

Fourthly, the case also demonstrates the openness of Irish public law to comparative influence and in particular, through its reliance upon EU standards, exemplifies the phenomenon, noted above, of cross-fertilisation and spill-over of legal concepts, and in particular, of cross-fertilisation and spill-over of EU law into national public law, which aspect of the judgment will be considered further below.

B. The Content of the Duty to Give Reasons

On the content of the reason-giving duty, it is impossible in the limited space available to provide a comprehensive review of the content of the reason-giving duty at EU and national level. However, identified against a number of core indicators, a comparison of the duty reveals strong similarities between the two legal systems.

First, the touchstone for assessing the adequacy of reasons is generally regarded as being twofold. In EU law – both insofar as the reason-giving duty applies to EU institutions and to national authorities making decisions affecting Union rights – it has been held that the reasons given must 'enable ... the persons concerned to be aware of the reasons for the measure in order to assert their rights' and that they must enable the Court to exercise its review.[87]

[84] Ibid, para 7.7.

[85] For a further example of the influence of *Mallak*, see: *Wicklow County Council v Fortune (No 3)* [2013] IEHC 397, paras 17–18.

[86] For example, Irish courts have been slower than their English counterparts to reject the distinction between jurisdictional and non-jurisdictional errors (contrast *Anisminic Ltd v Foreign Compensation Commission* [1969] 2 AC 147 and *State (Abenglen Properties Ltd) v Dublin Corporation* [1984] IR 381); slower to accept a role for error of fact in judicial review (contrast *E v Secretary of State for the Home Department* [2004] QB 1044 with *R v Refugee Appeals Tribunal* [2011] IEHC 151) and slower to incorporate proportionality into review of decisions affecting fundamental rights (*R (Daly) v Secretary of State for the Home Department* [2001] 2 AC 532 and *Meadows v Minister for Justice, Equality and Law Reform* [2010] 2 IR 701).

[87] See, eg: Case C-333/07 *Société Régie Networks v Direction de contrôle fiscal Rhône-Alpes Bourgogne* [2008] ECR I–10807 (Grand Chamber), paras 62–63; Case T-17/09 *Evropaïki Dynamiki*

Similarly, in the national context, as Finlay CJ has observed, the unsuccessful applicant should be made aware 'in general and broad terms of the grounds'.[88] Likewise, in *Mulholland v An Bord Pleanála (No 2)*,[89] Kelly J cited the following passage from *State (Sweeney) v Minister for the Environment*,[90] holding that the adequacy of reasons had to be determined on the basis that the obligation is:

> to give ... [to an] applicant such information as may be necessary and appropriate for him, firstly, to consider whether he has got a reasonable chance of succeeding in appealing against the decision of the planning authority and secondly to enable him to arm himself for the hearing of such an appeal.[91]

Secondly, the reasons must also be 'clear and cogent',[92] 'intelligible' and identify 'what conclusions were reached on the "principal important controversial issues", disclosing how any issue of law or fact was resolved'.[93]

Thirdly, it appears that reasons cannot be issued retrospectively to justify the decision and must be issued prior to the initiation of proceedings. EU law is particularly robust on the importance of the reasons being furnished at the outset and prior to the initiation of proceedings. For example, in the procurement law context, the adequacy of reasons can only be assessed on the basis of the reasons provided ***prior*** to the initiation of proceeding.[94] In the national law context, the position is not so clear. In the case of *McAlister v Minister for Justice, Equality and Law Reform*,[95] Finnegan P refused an application where a prisoner discovered the reasons for the Minister's failure to allow him temporary from a policy document exhibited to an affidavit in the proceedings. By contrast, in the

v Commission, 22 May 2012, para 45; Case T-554/08 *Evropaïki Dynamiki v Commission*, 26 April 2012, para 137; Case 108/81 *Amylum v Council* [1982] ECR 3107, para 19; Case 222/86 *UNECTEF v Heylens* [1987] ECR 4097, para 15; Case C-340/89 *Vlassopoulou v Ministerium für Justiz, Bundes- und Europaangelegenheiten Baden-Wurttemberg* [1991] ECR I-2357, para 22. With respect to the general obligation in Article 296 TFEU, a third objective of enabling third persons to ascertain the circumstances in which an enacting institution has applied the Treaty is also cited: Case 24/62 *Germany v Commission* [1963] ECR 63, 69.

[88] *Creedon* (n 54 above) 55. See also *O'Donoghue v Bord Pleanála* [1991] ILRM 750, 757.

[89] [2006] 1 IR 453, 464.

[90] [1979] ILRM 35, 37.

[91] See also *Grealish v An Bord Pleanála* [2006] IEHC 310, in which O'Neill J observed that the reasons must 'provide sufficient information to enable somebody in the position of the applicant in this case to consider whether he has a reasonable chance of succeeding in judicially reviewing the decision; can arm himself for such a review; can know if the respondent has directed its mind adequately to the issues it had to consider; and finally give sufficient information to enable the court to review the decision.'

[92] *Mulholland v An Bord Pleanála (No 2)* [2006] 1 IR 453, 464.

[93] *South Bucks County Council v Porter* [2004] 1 WLR 1953 (cited in *Deerland Construction Limited v the Aquaculture Licences Appeals Board* [2008] IEHC 289); *Meadows* (n 86 above), para 93 (the decision 'should at least disclose the essential rationale on foot of which the decision is taken'). For similar articulations of the duty in EU law, see Case 322/81 *Michelin v Commission* [1983] ECR 3461, para 14; Case T-95/94 *Sytraval and Brink's France SARL v Commission* [1995] ECR II-2651, para 52; Case T-36/06 *Bundesverband deutscher Banken v Commission* [2010] ECR II-537, para 45.

[94] See, eg: Case T-50/05 *Evropaïki Dynamiki v Commission*, 19 March 2010 (General Court) (appeal dismissed, Case C-289/10 P), para 135; Case T-387/08 *Evropaïki Dynamiki v Commission* (General Court) 9 September 2010, para 36 (appeal dismissed: Case C-561/10 P); Case T-89/07 *VIP Car Solutions SARL v Parliament* [2009] ECR II-1403, para 73.

[95] *McAlister* (n 54 above).

Deerland case, Kelly J expressed concern that the respondent had 'sought to fill the material gaps by affidavit evidence'.[96] The EU position, and that adopted by Kelly J in *Deerland*, is to be preferred: caution should be exercised where reasons are furnished after the initiation of proceedings.[97]

C. The Remedy for Breach of the Duty to Provide Reasons

Where there has been a defective statement of reasons, the remedy in the EU context is generally annulment of the decision.[98] This is also in accordance with the view expressed by Kelly J in *Deerland*,[99] in which Kelly J approved the view of Simons,[100] that ' [t]he better view is that a failure to state reasons at the time of the decision invalidates the decision under Irish law, and same should be set aside in judicial review proceedings'. It is suggested that this remedy is to be preferred – rather than, for example, an order directing that reasons be provided, which is the solution sometimes adopted by the Irish courts[101] – given the concern stated above about reasons furnished after the initiation of proceedings.[102]

D. Summary on Review of Reason-Giving at EU and National Level

Clearly, the case study of reason-giving demonstrates an element of convergence of national and EU standards. While there are broad parallels between the content of the reason-giving duty and in the remedies for its breach in the national and EU frameworks, there had been a greater gap in terms of the fundamental prior question of the extent of the existence of a duty to provide reasons. That gap has now been reduced, with, as observed above, the EU law position providing support and corroboration for the development of national law.

V. THE EUROPEANISATION OF PUBLIC LAW

Turning then to the last theme of this Chapter, Europeanisation of public law, it is useful to first consider the process of Europeanisation of law, and then, in what will hopefully draw together all the themes explored above, consider the potential for future Europeanisation in the context of transparency and reason-giving.

[96] *Deerland Construction Limited v the Aquaculture Licences Appeals Board* [2009] 1 IR 673, 691.

[97] The English approach in this regard is preferred: see *Nash v Chelsea College of Art and Design* [2001] EWHC Admin 538.

[98] See, eg: Case T-300/07 *Evropaïki Dynamiki v Commission*, 9 September 2010, paras 74–75.

[99] See also: *De Smith's Judicial Review* (n 1 above), paras 7-112–7-113.

[100] G Simons, *Planning and Development Law* 2nd edn (Dublin, Round Hall, 2007), paras 12-161 and 12-162.

[101] *Hurley v Motor Insurers' Bureau of Ireland* [1993] ILRM 886.

[102] See also *De Smith's Judicial Review* (n 1 above), paras 7-112–7-113.

A. The Process of Europeanisation

(i) Use of Comparative Law Generally

The use of EU law to develop national law can be considered within the more general and well-rehearsed debate as to the appropriate use of comparative law.[103] Comparative law is 'a diverse tradition, riven by methodological disagreements and differences of emphasis and style'.[104] Broadly, however, for some, legal concepts may be simply transplanted from one system to another, on the assumption that, as Watson puts it, 'legal rules move easily and are accepted into the system without too great difficulty'.[105] For others however, such as Montesquieu and Kahn-Freund,[106] caution should be exercised against the '*très grand hasard*' of transplantation.[107] The risks of comparative law derive largely from the concern, as articulated by Legrand, that rules and concepts alone actually reveal very little about a given legal system, providing a 'thin' rather than a 'thick' description[108] and failing to account for the '*mentalité*'[109] or 'mindset'[110] of each individual legal system. In short, context is all, whether it be cultural,[111] political[112] or environmental.[113] The perils of the comparative method are often regarded as being particularly marked in the public law context since public law is often considered to have such 'particularly deep roots inside a cultural and political framework'[114] as to render it peculiarly unsuited to benefit from comparative concepts.

While transplantation constitutes one method of developing national law through use of comparative law, other theorists have identified more incremental and gradual processes, sometimes described as 'fertilization' and 'cross-fertilization'. As Beatson has explained, these concepts 'involve an external stimulus promoting a careful internal evolution within the receiving

[103] For further analysis of these ideas, see C Donnelly, *Delegation of Governmental Power to Private Parties: A Comparative Perspective* (Oxford, Oxford University Press, 2007), 10–18.

[104] D Kennedy, 'New Approaches to Comparative Law: Comparativism and International Governance' (1997) *Utah Law Review* 545, 581.

[105] A Watson, *Legal Transplants: An Approach to Comparative Law*, 2nd edn (London, University of Georgia Press, 1993), 95–6.

[106] O Kahn-Freund, 'On Uses and Misuses of Comparative Law' (1974) 37 *Modern Law Review* 1; see also G Teubner, 'Legal Irritants: Good Faith in British Law or How Unifying Law Ends Up in New Divergences' (1998) 61 *Modern Law Review* 11, 12.

[107] Montesquieu, *De l'Esprit des Lois* (J Brèthe de la Gressaye, ed) (Paris, Société Les Belles Letters, 1950) Book 1, 26.

[108] P Legrand, 'European Legal Systems Are Not Converging' (1996) 45 *ICLQ* 52, 56.

[109] Ibid, 60.

[110] C Harlow, 'Changing the Mindset: The Place of Theory in English Administrative Law' (1994) 14 *OJLS* 419.

[111] P Legrand, 'Public Law, Europeanization, and Convergence: Can Comparatists Contribute?' in P Beaumont, C Lyons, and N Walker (eds), *Convergence and Divergence in European Public Law* (Oxford, Hart, 2002) 227.

[112] O Kahn-Freund (n 106) 11–12 (referring to distinctions between communist and non-communist countries, and dictatorships and democracies).

[113] Montesquieu (AM Cohler, BC Miller, and HS Stone, trs and eds), *The Spirit of the Laws* (Cambridge, Cambridge University Press, 1989) 1, 8–9.

[114] C Harlow, 'Voices of Difference in a Plural Community' in Beaumont, Lyons, and Walker (n 111) 199, 208; see also Legrand (n 111) 246.

legal system'.[115] This stimulus will then be accommodated to a greater or lesser degree, depending on existing domestic tradition.[116] To some extent, a search for fertilization accommodates the opposing views of both Watson and Kahn-Freund[117] and, in this way, comparative law can be used to provide a 'stimulus'[118] which generates new techniques of problem-solving within the national legal order.[119]

(ii) Use of EU Law in National Public Law

The evolution of the reason-giving duty, as informed by the principle of transparency and as demonstrated by the *Mallak* case, arguably constitutes an example of cross-fertilisation. The very strong duty of reason-giving in the EU context was used to support a strengthening of the reason-giving duty in the national context. Moreover, rather than a direct transplantation of a duty equivalent to that found in Article 296 TFEU, Fennelly J opted for a slightly more nuanced duty, which imposed a reason-giving obligation, unless the decision-maker could provide a justification for not providing reasons. In this way, what arose was an example of what Beatson would describe as a 'careful internal evolution' of Irish law, by reference to the 'stimulus' of EU law.

While it is not intended here to examine more broadly how Irish courts make use of EU law in their development of national law, it is worth noting in passing that this approach is not dissimilar from that which has also been used by the Irish courts in the context of proportionality. Rather than simply transplanting the doctrine of proportionality into national administrative law, Irish courts have implemented it by incorporating it into pre-existing national doctrines. Thus, in the *Meadows* case, the Supreme Court held that, when reviewing the exercise of discretion having an impact on fundamental rights, it was necessary to apply the well-established standard of review identified in *State (Keegan) v Stardust Victims' Compensation Tribunal*,[120] namely, that unreasonableness arises if the impugned decision plainly and unambiguously flies in the face of fundamental reason and common sense. However, the Court concluded that this test permits the court to 'have recourse to the principle of proportionality in determining' whether the threshold for unreasonableness has been met.[121]

[115] J Beatson and T Tridimas, 'Introduction' in Beatson and Tridimas (n 7 above) 1, 1.

[116] Ibid 9; see also J Bell, 'Mechanisms for Cross-fertilization of Administrative Law in Europe' in Beatson and Tridimas (n 7 above) 147.

[117] JWF Allison, 'Transplantation and Cross-fertilization' in Beatson and Tridimas (n 7 above) 169, 171.

[118] K Schiemann, 'German Law of Obligations. Vol 1: The Law of Contracts and Restitution: A Comparative Introduction' (1998) *Law Quarterly Review* 515, 523.

[119] Legrand (n 111) 241.

[120] [1986] IR 642.

[121] See n 86 above, para 57.

B. Future Possibilities for the Europeanisation of National Public Law

The review of transparency and reason-giving undertaken above suggests that at the intersection of the principle of transparency and the duty to provide reasons, there are rich possibilities for cross-fertilisation and spill-over and for prompting 'careful internal evolution' of national public law by reference to EU law.

The first obvious source of potential cross-fertilisation – albeit one that would involve quite a significant development of current national law – would be the recognition of a general principle of transparency in national public law.

Secondly, the discretion-constraining obligation of transparency as developed in the procurement and administrative authorisation context could be developed more widely to require prior publication of unambiguous, objective criteria on which any administrative discretion will be exercised.[122] Such an obligation would go beyond the existing constitutional requirement for *audi alteram partem,* insofar as it would require specification of the factors affecting the exercise of discretion not just with respect to a particular individual, but the factors guiding the exercise of the discretion more generally.[123] As Howell has noted, there is currently no obligation on administrative decision-makers to publish policies or criteria guiding their discretionary powers.[124] That such an obligation could potentially be contemplated by the Irish courts is suggested, interestingly, in a case on reason-giving. In *Hurley v Motor Insurance Bureau of Ireland,*[125] reasons were found inadequate in circumstances in which the Bureau has rejected a claim referring to the MIBI Agreement which required it to make a payment only where there was serious and permanent disablement. Carroll J considered the information the applicant would have needed in order to challenge the MIBI's decision, and summarised the requirement for reasons as including a requirement to disclose the criteria applying to the discretion in the following terms:

> [I]t seems to me that the applicant was not given sufficiently clear reasons to enable this Court to determine how the MIBI came to its decision. It should: (1) Give their definition of disablement (2) Give the criteria they apply to decide whether a disability is serious or not serious. (3) Say whether the applicant qualifies under these definitions.

Thirdly, the value of transparency could be used to bolster the content of the reason-giving obligation even further. This could occur in a number of ways. One interesting example of an attempt to use transparency to bolster reason-giving is found in the procurement case, *bpost NV van publiek recht v Commission.*[126] The applicant sought to expand the reason-giving duty of Article 100(2) of the Regulation 1605/2002[127] to require disclosure of the evaluation report of

[122] Howell (n 2 above), paras 28–38 (arguing against such an obligation).

[123] Careful consideration would be required in respect of the interaction between such an obligation and the non-fettering principle: see *McCarron v Superintendent Peadar Kearney* [2010] 3 IR 302.

[124] Howell (n 2 above), para 32.

[125] See n 101 above.

[126] Case T-514/09 *bpost NV van publiek recht v Commission*, 23 November 2011, para 116.

[127] Council Regulation (EC, Euratom) No 1605/2002 of 25 June 2002 on the Financial Regulation applicable to the general budget of the European Communities [2002] OJ L248/1.

the competition by relying on the principle of transparency. This attempt to bolster the reason-giving duty using transparency was unsuccessful but the case nonetheless demonstrates the way in which transparency could be invoked to require the provision of more expansive reasons.

Fourthly, the principle of transparency could also be used to strengthen those aspects of the national reason-giving duty which are perhaps less well-established, and, in particular, to support the position adopted by Kelly J in the *Deerland* case with respect to reasons provided after the initiation of proceedings and the available remedies for a failure to provide reasons: scepticism about late reasons and a preference for annulment of decisions not providing reasons safeguards transparency more effectively.

VI. CONCLUSION

As indicated at the outset, this Chapter has sought to explore the increasing emphasis on transparency in governance at both national and EU level, its relationship to the duty of reason-giving and how this relationship reflects upon the impact of EU law on national public law. It has been argued that transparency and reason-giving pursue similar objectives and goals, while operating in different ways; the principle of transparency goes further than the reason-giving obligation and, in so doing, also has the potential to bolster the duty to provide reasons. The recent welcome strengthening of the duty to provide reasons in Irish law mirrors the increasing emphasis on transparency and demonstrates the primary manner in which EU law influences the development of Irish law, namely, through providing 'stimulus' for internal evolution. To date, the development of the law from the seminal statement on transparency in the Advocate General's opinion in *Telaustria* to the judgment of the Supreme Court in *Mallak* has been impressive. Yet, as suggested here, the possibilities for future development are also notable and interesting.

23

Preserving National Identity: The Bundesverfassungsgericht *between National Constitutional Constraints and an Ever Closer European Union*

A Tribute to Nial Fennelly

WOLFGANG HEUSEL*

ACCEPTING IN SUMMER a friendly invitation to deliver an article by the end of the year can be a risky commitment, and while Christmas is approaching I feel like Robert Frost when *Stopping by woods on a snowy evening*:

> *The woods are lovely, dark and deep.*
> *But I have promises to keep,*
> *And miles to go before I sleep...*[1]

However, being invited to write in honour of Nial Fennelly is not only an honour for the author but also joy, at least in Tagore's sense,[2] as it allows me to pay a public tribute to an old friend and active supporter of the Academy of European Law (ERA). Nial Fennelly has not only made lasting contributions to the development of European and Irish law in the course of his distinguished career as a Barrister, as Advocate General of the European Court of Justice and as Justice of the Irish Supreme Court; for many years he has also served as an active member of ERA's Board of Trustees. We are profoundly grateful for his generous friendship, his sound advice and his committed support.

* Director, Academy of European Law, Trier

[1] Robert Frost, *Selected Poems*, I Hamilton (ed) (London, Penguin, 1973).

[2] 'I slept and dreamt that life was joy. / I awoke and saw that life was service. / I acted and behold, service was joy' (Rabindranath Tagore).

I. INTRODUCTION

For some forty years, since its famous 1974 *Solange I* ruling, the *Bundesverfassungsgericht* (hereinafter 'BVerfG') or, in the literal translation of its name, the 'German Federal Constitutional Tribunal,' has been at the forefront of constitutional resistance to an unconditional and unlimited advancement of European integration: unconditional, as *Solange I* and *Solange II* specifically made clear that, at least from the point of view of the German Constitution,[3] European integration measures would be allowed to restrict fundamental rights in Germany only if they respect a standard of Human Rights protection equivalent to that of the Basic Law; unlimited, as the *Lisbon* judgment formulates constitutional limits to integration which must not (or, from a constitutional point of view, cannot) be surpassed without involving the *pouvoir constituant*, ie the German People by way of referendum.

Every time a new judgment in this line was pronounced, the jurisprudence of the BVerfG has caused much excitement in and outside Germany.[4] It has been berated for being nationalist and anti-integrationist by fervent partisans of the 'United States of Europe' project, and praised by the defenders of national sovereignty and identity for building dams against an alleged creeping federalisation driven beyond the limits of conferred competences by the EU institutions, notably the Court of Justice (ECJ). The BVerfG has even been criticised for not following up its strong '*non ultra vires*' admonition by restricting or not applying certain EU rules or decisions of the ECJ in its concrete case law.[5]

The BVerfG's jurisprudence on the status of EU law and European integration under national constitutional law has found parallels in the case law of the constitutional courts of other Member States of the EU, notably the Italian, Spanish, Polish and Czech constitutional courts.[6] This contribution however is exclusively concerned with the stance taken by the German court and undertakes to examine to which extent the claim of the BVerfG to have its own final say in conflicts of competence is compatible with the current state of Union law, the

[3] *Grundgesetz* of 23 May 1949 (Basic Law, or 'GG'), as last amended by Art 1 of the Act of 11 July 2012 (BGBl I, 1478).

[4] The BVerfG itself lists critical comments on its Lisbon judgment in its subsequent judgment on Germany's participation in the European Stabilisation Mechanism, 2 BvR 987/10 of 7 September 2011, at § 101. See also C Tomuschat, 'The Defence of National Identity by the German Constitutional Court, in A Saiz Arnaiz and C Alcoberro Llivina (eds), *National Constitutional Identity and European Integration* (Cambridge/Antwerp/Portland, Intersentia, 2013), 205; T Stein, *Always Steering a Straight Course? The German Federal Constitutional Court and European Integration*; in W Heusel (ed), *A European Law Practitioner, Liber Amicorum John Toulmin*, (2011) 12 *ERA Forum* suppl. 1, 219.

[5] Stein (n 4).

[6] Cf H López Bofill, What is not Constitutional Pluralism in the EU: National Constitutional Identity in the German Lisbon judgment, in Saiz Arnaiz/Alcoberro Llivina, (n 4), 221 (with references to France, Spain, the Czech Republic, Latvia and Poland); J Rideau, 'The Case law of the Polish, Hungarian and Czech Constitutional Courts on National Identity and the 'German Model', ibid 243. On the jurisprudence of the Polish Constitutional Court, see also W Czapliński, 'Recent Constitutional Jurisprudence Concerning the European Union: Some Remarks on 2010 Judgments of the Polish Constitutional Court' in Heusel (ed), *A European Law Practitioner* (n 4), 197, and A Wróbel, 'Die Grenzen der europäischen Integration im Lichte jüngerer Entscheidungen des polnischen Verfassungsgerichts', (2013) *ERA Forum* 491.

perspective of national constitutional law being left for debate among German scholars. The focal point of the discussion will be the concept of national constitutional identity as recognised by Art 4(2) TEU.[7]

II. THE *LISBON* JUDGMENT

The most recent fundamental ruling of the BVerfG on the relationship between EU law and the constitutional position of Germany, the *Lisbon* judgment of 30 June 2009,[8] offers a fairly complete and systematic set of the arguments developed by the Court in its jurisprudence on integration issues. It seems appropriate to start our analysis of the compatibility of the BVerfG jurisprudence with EU law there and, first of all, to take stock of the main reasoning and conclusions of the *Lisbon* judgment.

The BVerfG had been seised – unsuccessfully by way of an *Organstreit* proceeding[9] and partly successfully by way of constitutional complaint (*Verfassungsbeschwerde*) – which aimed to block ratification of the Lisbon Treaty and to annul the corresponding implementing legislation in Germany. The first ground of review, which alone opened the appellants' access to the Court, was their right to vote, which the BVerfG considers equal to a fundamental right.[10] In its judgment, the BVerfG draws three main conclusions determining the German attitude towards the Lisbon Treaty and further integration measures:

- First, the BVerfG instructs the German legislature to introduce specific procedural safeguards for any future transfers of competence on the basis of the Lisbon Treaty, in particular with regard to the *passerelle* clauses;[11] and provided such procedural safeguards have been introduced by law, it clears the way for ratification of the Treaty.
- Second, the BVerfG defines abstract constitutional limits to an ever progressing transfer of sovereignty to the EU.
- Third, it states its firm intention to examine, even after ratification, 'whether legal instruments of the European institutions and bodies keep within the boundaries of the sovereign powers accorded to them by way of conferral.'[12]

[7] 'The Union shall respect the equality of Member States before the Treaties as well as their national identities, inherent in their fundamental structures, political and constitutional, inclusive of regional and local self-government. It shall respect their essential State functions, including ensuring the territorial integrity of the State, maintaining law and order and safeguarding national security. In particular, national security remains the sole responsibility of each Member State.' The concept was first introduced by Art F of the Maastricht Treaty. For a methodological approach, see C Grewe, 'Methods of Identification of National Constitutional Identity', in Saiz Arnaiz/Alcoberro Llivina (n 4), 37.

[8] BVerfG, 2 BvE 2/08, 30 June 2009, authentic German version at http://www.bverfg.de/entscheidungen/es20090630_2bve000208.html, English translation at http://www.bverfg.de/entscheidungen/es20090630_2bve000208en.html

[9] Litigation between organs of state, Art 93.1.1 GG.

[10] Art 38.1.1 in conjunction with Art 93.1.4a GG.

[11] These are Treaty provisions which allow limited amendments to specified Treaty provisions without recourse to the normal Treaty revision procedures. The term comes from the French for 'footbridge'.

[12] Headnote 5 of the *Lisbon* judgment (n 8).

The reasoning underlying these conclusions is the following:

1. Compatibility of Germany's Obligations under the Lisbon Treaty with the Basic Law

Starting from the appellants' right to vote, which for the Court is *the* fundamental expression of democratic participation at federal level in Germany (bearing in mind that for the time being the Basic Law does not offer the option of referenda or other elements of direct democracy at federal level),[13] it emphasises the importance of democracy as one of the structural principles of the German State enshrined in Article 20 GG. The Constitution puts these principles (as well as democracy, the rule of law, the principle of the social State, the Republican and the federal principles and finally the core of fundamental rights) beyond the reach of the constitutional legislature; Article 79.3 of the Basic Law shields them from any constitutional amendment so that they may only be overturned if the German People as *pouvoir constituant* adopts a new Constitution.[14] As the Basic Law itself declares these principles unamendable, the BVerfG considers them as 'the inviolable constitutional identity' of the German State, which at the same time defines the abstract and absolute limit to any transfer of sovereignty to the EU.[15]

In stating this, the BVerfG sees no conflict with the Basic Law's openness to European integration (Article 23 GG) and its 'constitutional mandate to realise a united Europe', which it even considers a constitutional obligation.[16] However, given the compelling character of Articles 79.3 and 20 GG, the BVerfG holds that the German institutions are not empowered

> to abandon the right to self-determination of the German people in the form of Germany's sovereignty under international law by joining a federal State. Due to the irrevocable transfer of sovereignty to a new subject of legitimation that goes with it, this step is reserved to the directly declared will of the German people alone.[17]

The BVerfG considers that Article 23 GG only allows for Germany's integration into a European Union 'designed as an association of sovereign States (*Staatenverbund*) to which sovereign powers are transferred ... but ... in which the peoples ... of the Member States remain the subjects of democratic legitimation'.[18] The Court makes very clear where it sees the borderline:

[13] 'The right to vote establishes a right to democratic self-determination, to free and equal participation in the state authority exercised in Germany and to compliance with the principle of democracy including the respect of the constituent power of the people', *Lisbon* judgment (n 8) § 208; in parallel the BVerfG clarifies obiter dictum that the Basic Law could also be amended to introduce referenda at federal level (ibid § 270).

[14] Art 79.3 GG.

[15] *Lisbon* judgment (n 8) §§ 217, 219.

[16] The BVerfG refers to Art 23.1 and the preamble of the GG, ibid § 225.

[17] *Lisbon* judgment (n 8) § 228.

[18] Ibid § 229. Art 23.1 indeed expressly calls for Germany's participation in a 'united Europe', to which end 'the Federation may transfer sovereign powers by a law with the consent of the Bundesrat'. It has to be noted however that the following sentence in the same paragraph expressly refers to Art 79.3 as the ultimate limit to any transfer of sovereign powers.

> The Basic Law does not authorise the German State bodies to transfer sovereign powers in such a way that their exercise can independently establish other competences for the European Union. It prohibits the transfer of competence to decide on its own competence (*Kompetenz-Kompetenz*).[19]

Checking the Lisbon Treaty against these criteria and principles, the BVerfG notes that the Treaty does not cross the border where the Union would be constituted as a federal State.[20] The transfer of sovereignty to the European Union is not irrevocable, as is already illustrated by the Member State's right to decide unilaterally to leave the Union.[21] Another argument in this context is that seats in the European Parliament continue to be allocated by Member State, and that consequently the Parliament remains a representation of the peoples of the Member States and not of a yet-to-be-constituted European People.[22] However, a number of Treaty provisions are perceived as *potentially* infringing the principle of democracy in the sense of the Basic Law, that is, the core sovereignty attributed to the German People.

It is far from surprising that these provisions considered critically by the BVerfG include all 'dynamic Treaty provisions with a blanket character', and in this regard it asks the German legislature for 'suitable national safeguards' to guarantee that European integration continues to take place 'without the possibility for the European Union of taking possession of *Kompetenz-Kompetenz* or to violate the Member States' constitutional identity, which is not open to integration.'[23] These provisions include in particular the general and special *passerelle* clauses which allow the Union to move on to qualified majority voting where the Treaty still foresees unanimous decision-making in the Council, or to the ordinary legislative procedure with QMV in areas which so far are subject to a special legislative procedure again requiring unanimity in the Council.[24] Waiving the Member State's right of veto by using a *passerelle* clause is perceived by the BVerfG as a serious encroachment on the powers of national parliaments which, in the case of Germany, requires the participation of these competent legislative bodies 'even as regards subject-areas which have already been factually defined in the treaties.'[25] Such participation may not always need to take the form of a formal law, but the *express prior* consent of the legislative bodies affected by the *passerelle* decision will be required in each individual case a *passerelle* clause is activated, regardless of the fact that in some

[19] *Lisbon* judgment (n 8) § 233.

[20] Ibid §§ 276: '[a] will aiming at founding a state cannot be ascertained' (ibid § 277).

[21] Art 50(1) and (3) TEU; according to the BVerfG the exercise of this right is not justiciable at EU level, *Lisbon* judgment (n 8) § 330.

[22] *Lisbon* judgment (n 8) § 284. Ironically, the BVerfG criticises the EU for contradicting one of its own core values – the principle of non-discrimination on grounds of nationality – when graduating the political influence of EU citizens in the EU by their nationality:

> 'The European Union thus shows an assessment of values in contradiction to the basic concept of a citizens' Union, as it regards itself; this contradiction can only be explained by the character of the European Union as an association of sovereign states' (ibid § 287).

[23] *Lisbon* judgment (n 8) § 239.

[24] See the general *passerelle* clause in Art 48(7) TEU; § 316 *Lisbon* judgment (n 8) lists the special *passerelle* clauses such as Art 81(3), second subpara, TFEU in the area of family law.

[25] *Lisbon* judgment (n 8) §§ 293, 320.

cases the Treaty itself grants national parliaments an express right to veto a *passerelle* decision.[26]

The BVerfG expresses similar concern with regard to the flexibility clause of Article 352 TFEU which allows the Union to adjust scope of its activities to the objectives of the Treaty, should the Treaty not provide elsewhere the powers of action necessary to attain these objectives. Although this principle existed in primary law long before the Lisbon Treaty, the BVerfG finds its relevance considerably enlarged as it is no longer limited to achieving the objectives of the Single Market but now applies to all policies defined in the Treaties (with the exception of the Common Foreign and Security Policy). Consequently, to ensure 'the ban on transferring blanket empowerments or on transferring Kompetenz-Kompetenz' is respected, no German consent may be given to any proposal based on Article 352 TFEU unless the legislative bodies (*Bundestag* and *Bundesrat*) have formally ratified it.[27]

A third area which the BVerfG characterises as particularly sensitive is the 'supranationalisation' by the Lisbon Treaty of the remaining third pillar competences, as it considers substantive criminal law and criminal procedure profoundly to affect democratic self-determination in that they set minimum ethical standards by law.[28] It argues that the Treaty itself recognises this sensitivity by introducing the so-called 'emergency brake' procedure (Articles 82(3) and 83(3) TFEU). The Court holds it all the more important that any enlargement of the Union's competences in this area require formal ratification by the German legislature:

> The use of the dynamic blanket empowerment pursuant to Article 83.1(3) TFEU, to extend the list of particularly serious criminal offences with a cross-border dimension, 'on the basis of developments in crime', is factually tantamount to an extension of the codified competences of the Union, and it is therefore subject to the requirement of the enactment of a statute under Article 23.1 second sentence, of the Basic Law.[29]

2. Abstract Limits to Transfers of Sovereignty

Although it was not required to decide the matter in the instant dispute, the BVerfG used the opportunity to outline the absolute limits which, according to its interpretation, the Basic Law imposes on the transfer of powers to the European Union even if the latter is not constituted as a federal state with *Kompetenz-Kompetenz*. In the Court's view, these limits again derive from the unalterable core of the Constitution defined by Articles 79.3 and 20. Set in context with the right to vote (Article 38) as the central expression of the democratic principle, the Court considers that the German Bundestag must retain its 'own responsibilities and competences of substantial political importance', and that 'the Federal

[26] Any Member State parliament may veto – within six months following the submission of such proposal – a *passerelle* decision based on Art 48(7) TEU or on Art 81(3)3rd subpara, TFEU.

[27] *Lisbon* judgment (n 8) §§ 325 ss., 328.

[28] Ibid §§ 293 and 358.

[29] *Lisbon* judgment (n 8) § 363.

Government, which is answerable to it politically,' must be 'in a position to exert a decisive influence on European decision-making procedures'.[30]

The BVerfG goes on to list in detail those policy areas where 'sufficient space' needs to be left for the German political institutions to form 'the economic, cultural and social living conditions' in Germany. Along with language, culture, education, family, the freedom of opinion and media, and religion, these areas include

> citizenship, the civil and the military monopoly on the use of force, revenue and expenditure including external financing and all elements of encroachment that are decisive for the realisation of fundamental rights, above all in major encroachments on fundamental rights such as deprivation of liberty in the administration of criminal law or placement in an institution.[31]

While the list of areas where the German institutions must retain their own *substantial* competences might seem quite comprehensive, the concrete limits to further transfers of sovereignty in these areas are left somewhat obscure. In most cases the BVerfG limits its holding to repeating the general formula that the State must retain substantial freedom of action[32] or that the State must remain the subject of democratic legitimation.[33] The borderline seems sharper with regard to the armed forces, where 'supranationalisation involving primacy of application with a view to the specific deployment of German armed forces' is declared 'inadmissible'. At the same time the Court does not see an insurmountable constitutional barrier to any other forms of military integration, including the 'technical integration of a European deployment of armed forces via joint general staffs'.[34]

Finally, with regard to budget policy the BVerfG concedes that the financial effects of EU membership have to be catered for by the national budget legislature even if it cannot directly influence them. It postulates however that the overall responsibility for the budget, 'with sufficient political discretion regarding revenue and expenditure' has to rest with the German Bundestag.[35] The BVerfG has developed this principle further in its subsequent jurisprudence on the currency stabilisation measures since 2011.[36]

3. Continued Right of Control after Ratification

Having established the constitutional limits to the transfer of competences to the European Union, the BVerfG does not confine its judgment to ascertaining

[30] Ibid §§ 244 and 246. This requirement was already expressed in its *Maastricht* judgment, 1993 *Neue Juristische Wochenschrift* 3047.

[31] *Lisbon* judgment (n 8) §§ 249–260.

[32] For criminal justice policy at § 253 and for social policy at § 259, *Lisbon* judgment (n 8).

[33] In the area of cultural, educational or religion policy at § 260, ibid.

[34] *Lisbon* judgment (n 8) § 255: 'The constitutive requirement of parliamentary approval for the deployment of the Bundeswehr abroad is not open to integration.'

[35] Ibid § 256.

[36] See III 2c below.

that the ratification of the Lisbon Treaty does not infringe these limits as long as the national implementing legislation provides the required safeguards with regard to Treaty-based transfers of sovereignty. In the tradition of its *Maastricht* judgment, the Court again claims the right to examine whether these limits are respected by the EU institutions post ratification:

> The obligation under European law to respect the constituent power of the Member States as the masters of the Treaties corresponds to the non-transferable identity of the constitution (Article 79.3 of the Basic Law), which is not open to integration in this respect. Within the boundaries of its competences, the Federal Constitutional Court must review, where necessary, whether these principles are adhered to.[37]

The starting point of the BVerfG's reasoning is the recognition of the inherent dynamic of a supranational system vested with its own competences which is designed to develop independently on the basis of principles such as *effet utile* or the implied powers doctrine. This institutional setting however also implies the risk of transgression of the principle of conferred powers which for the BVerfG is the decisive element for the respect of constitutional or national identity protected by both Union law (Article 4(2) TEU) and the German Constitution (Article 79.3 GG).[38] Consequently the Court feels compelled to exercise its jurisdiction with regard to EU acts which do not respect these boundaries; by a process of elimination, these can only be legislation or sub-legisative acts or, in the last resort, judgments of the Court of Justice interpreting primary or secondary EU law.

The BVerfG refers expressly to its *Maastricht* judgment which had for the first time introduced the concept of a general ultra vires review by the BVerfG, should the EC or EU institutions transgress the limits of their conferred competences.[39] In its *Lisbon* ruling, it adds that it will also guarantee respect of the 'core content of the constitutional identity' by the appropriate review procedure. The BVerfG emphasises that the exercise of this review power is not in conflict with the Basic Law's openness towards EU integration nor with the EU law principle of sincere cooperation (Article 4(3) TEU), as it is inspired by the same principles whilst ensuring respect for the equally relevant principles of conferral (Article 5(2) TEU) and national constitutional identity (Article 4(2) TEU).[40] The BVerfG concludes that its review of an alleged transgression of their competences by EU institutions might result in declaring Union law inapplicable in Germany.

[37] *Lisbon* judgment (n 8) § 235.

[38] Ibid §§ 237: the EU institutions 'are moving on a road at the end of which there is the power of disposition of their foundations laid down in the treaties, ie the competence of freely disposing of their competences. There is a risk of transgression of the constitutive principle of conferral ... if institutions of the European Union can decide without restriction, without any outside control ... how treaty law is to be interpreted' (ibid § 238).

[39] So-called '*ausbrechende Rechtsakte*', headnote 5 of the *Maastricht* judgment, 1993 NJW 3047.

[40] *Lisbon* judgment (n 8) § 240.

III. PRE-RATIFICATION REVIEW AND IMPLEMENTATION REQUIREMENTS IMPOSED BY THE CONSTITUTION

There is no reason or argument why the pre-ratification review of a new Treaty provision with regard to its compatibility with a Member State's Constitution could infringe on any EU law obligation of that Member State. As long as the State has not ratified the provision, it cannot be bound by its content beyond the limits of Article 24 of the 1969 Vienna Convention on the Law of Treaties. There is no duty under EU law to participate in Treaty amendments either; as any amendment of the Treaties by way of ordinary or simplified revision (with the exception of the general and special *passerelle* clauses)[41] requires ratification by all the Member States in accordance with their respective constitutional procedures, Member States remain free not to ratify. This is the reason the BVerfG repeatedly emphasises that the Member States remain the masters of the Treaties.[42] Consequently, if a Member State court vetoes the ratification of a Treaty amendment because it considers the amendment incompatible with its Constitution, such a ruling may be criticised for impeding further integration but it cannot in itself constitute a violation of EU law.[43]

The same must be true as regards requirements which a national court defines for implementing EU law in a way which is compatible with the national Constitution, provided these requirements stay in line with the EU legislation to be implemented. If EU law leaves Member States a margin of discretion for its implementation, a decision of a national court declaring only one of several ways of implementation to be constitutional cannot be in conflict with EU law. The mechanism is a reverse form of the principle of interpreting national law in conformity with EU law.

1. *Lisbon* Judgment

Hence, from a point of view of EU law the *Lisbon* ruling of the BVerfG is unproblematic in so far as it examines the compatibility of Germany's ratification of the Lisbon Treaty with the requirements of the German Constitution, and calls for specific national procedural safeguards before further competences are conferred to the European Union by activating certain provisions of the Treaty. Checking the envisaged transfer of additional competences to the Union against the core identity of the Constitution or other constitutional requirements is a judicial act of national sovereignty which complies with EU law for the simple reason that this part of sovereignty has not yet been transferred. The safeguards called for by the BVerfG in future uses of the *passerelle* clauses or of Article 352 TFEU may be cumbersome for the German government but this is not of legal concern at EU level, as EU law leaves Member States full discretion on how to exercise their right of veto.

[41] Article 48 TEU.

[42] *Lisbon* judgment (n 8) §§ 235 and 298.

[43] The same applies mutatis mutandis if a national court vetoes the activation of a *passerelle* clause to which the representative of that Member State has consented in the (European) Council.

The same is true for the absolute limits to European integration which the BVerfG distils from Articles 79.3 and 20 GG, and defines as the constitutional identity of the German State. As long as these principles of the German Constitution are presented as ultimate limits to possible future transfers of power to the European Union, they are irrelevant from the point of view of EU law in force. In this perspective it is a matter of domestic concern only whether German scholars and politicians agree or disagree, for legal or for political reasons, with the stance taken by the BVerfG.

2. Other BVerfG Case Law

Constitutional concerns or objections of this type which do not affect EU law have also been raised in other BVerfG rulings. They have not only concerned new primary law but also secondary legislation. The following decisions might be worth mentioning:

a) The EAW Judgment[44]

In this case the BVerfG had been seised by a German citizen facing surrender to the Spanish authorities on the basis of a European arrest warrant (EAW). The Court declared the German Act implementing the Framework Decision on the EAW void and incompatible with fundamental rights protected by the Basic Law, in particular with the Constitution's ban in principle on the extradition of German nationals (Article 16.2 GG). Although this ban had been loosened by a constitutional amendment to allow for the implementation of the EAW, the BVerfG states that the legislature does not have an unrestricted discretion to depart from it; in implementing the EAW legislation, the legislature was under an obligation to use the margin left by the EAW Framework Decision to the maximum extent if so required by the effective protection of fundamental rights.[45] According to the Court, the implementing legislation had 'failed to take sufficient account of the especially protected interests of German citizens.'[46]

The approach of the judgment is in line with EU law, as it is limited to instructing the implementing legislature to use the scope of discretion left by EU law in a certain way determined by the Constitution and fully respecting the provisions of the Framework Decision.

[44] 2 BvR 2236/04, 18 July 2005, http://www.bverfg.de/entscheidungen/rs20050718_2bvr223604.html (German version), http://www.bverfg.de/entscheidungen/rs20050718_2bvr223604en.html (English).

[45] Ibid §§ 79, 82 (§§ 76, 80 of the German version).

[46] Ibid § 92 (§ 90 of the German version).

b) Judgment on the German Act on the Elections to the EP[47]

With this judgment the BVerfG quashed the clause in the electoral Act barring access to the European Parliament for parties scoring less than 5 % of the votes at national level. In 1979 the Court had held this clause – which also applies to elections to the Bundestag – constitutional. It bases its new reasoning on the fact that EU law leaves the introduction of barring clauses to the discretion of the national legislature,[48] and that such clauses infringe on the equality of votes to an extent which at national level may be justified to ensure stable majorities. The Court however concluded that at EU level no compelling grounds exist to justify such an encroachment on voting equality, as the EP does not elect a government which would depend on the continued support of a parliamentary majority.[49]

The judgment was handed down almost two years after the entry into force of the Lisbon Treaty.[50] It is open to criticism on the ground that it does not sufficiently take account of the strengthened position of the European Parliament, but it remains within the margins of discretion left by EU law to national regulation of the European elections and represents a typical case of a constitutional implementation requirement accepted by EU law. Incidentally, the Court's change of approach since its 1979 judgment might have been motivated by its repeated criticism of the principle of degressive proportionality (Article 14(2) TEU), which it considers cannot be reconciled with the constitutional principle of electoral equality.[51]

c) Interim Judgment of 12 September 2012 in the ESM Case[52]

This most recent ruling of the BVerfG in European matters allowed Germany to ratify a number of measures[53] to establish the European Stability Mechanism (ESM), though only on condition that Germany make two binding reservations

[47] 2 BvC 4/10 of 9 November 2011, (no English translation is available), German version at http://www.bverfg.de/entscheidungen/cs20111109_2bvc000410.html.

[48] The EU legal framework for the EP elections is Art 14.3 TEU and the so-called Direct Elections Act (Act concerning the election of representatives of the European Parliament by direct universal suffrage of 20 September 1976, as last amended by Council Decision of 25 June and 23 September 2002, [2002] OJ L283/1).

[49] Ibid (n 47) § 118.

[50] At the time of writing this contribution another case (2 BvE 2/13) is pending before the BVerfG on the new German Act on EP elections which has replaced the 5% threshold by a 3% clause (Europawahlgesetz of 7 October 2013, BGBl. I 3749). The hearing took place on 18 December 2013, judgment is due well ahead of the May 2014 EP elections.

[51] See above n 22.

[52] 2 BvR 1390/12, http://www.bverfg.de/entscheidungen/rs20120912_2bvr139012.html (German version), http://www.bverfg.de/entscheidungen/rs20120912_2bvr139012en.html (English). See in this context also BVerfG judgments 2 BvE 4/11 of 19 June 2012 on the Bundestag's right under Art 23.2 GG to be informed on EU matters, here again in the context of the ESM; 2 BvE 8/11 of 28 February 2012 on the (limited) right of the Bundestag to delegate its budgetary control competences in the context of the European Stabilisation Mechanism to a committee; 2 BvR 987/10 of 7 September 2011 on Germany's participation in the EFSF and in financial aid programmes for Greece, where the BVerfG again emphasises that 'The decision on public revenue and public expenditure is a fundamental part of the ability of a constitutional state to democratically shape itself' (Headnote 2a).

[53] In particular the European Council Decision of 25 March 2011 to amend Art 136 TFEU; Treaty of 2 February 2012 establishing the ESM; Act for Germany's financial participation in the ESM.

under public international law to ensure that an absolute ceiling to Germany's financial obligations under the ESM Treaty would be respected, and that no provision of the ESM Treaty could be interpreted in a way to prevent at any time the provision of full and comprehensive information to the German Parliament.[54] The Court's reasoning draws on one of the elements of national sovereignty which in its *Lisbon* judgment it had defined as part of the unalterable core of German Statehood under the Basic Law; the Parliament's responsibility and right to decide on the budget as a 'central element of the democratic development of informed opinion'. This excludes the creation of any mechanism under international law which would be 'tantamount to accepting liability for decisions by free will of other states, above all if they entail consequences which are hard to calculate'.[55]

The requirement under public international law to ensure a certain interpretation of new Treaty obligations is the standard constellation of pre-ratification review and perfectly in line with EU law. But this ruling is also remarkable insofar as, with the main proceedings still pending, it emphasises the design of the Monetary Union as a 'stability community' – in the Court's view a precondition of German participation – which implies 'in particular … the prohibition of monetary financing by the European Central Bank, the prohibition of accepting liability (bailout clause) and the stability criteria for sound budget management (Articles 123 to 126, Article 136 TFEU).'[56] It seems inevitable that in the main proceedings the BVerfG will have to assess the ECB's sovereign debt purchases against these requirements, as the Court explicitly states that 'an acquisition of government bonds on the secondary market by the European Central Bank aiming at financing the Members' budgets independently of the capital markets is prohibited as well, as it would circumvent the prohibition of monetary financing.'[57] This would, however, fall into the category of post-ratification review.

[54] Operative provision of the judgment:

[T]he Treaty establishing the European Stability Mechanism (Bundestag printed paper 17/9045, pages 6 ff.) may only be ratified if at the same time it is ensured under international law that (1) the provision under Art 8 § 5 sentence 1 of the Treaty establishing the ESM limits the amount of all payment obligations arising to … Germany from this Treaty to the amount stipulated in Annex II to the Treaty …; (2) the provisions under Art 32 § 5, Art 34 and Art 35 § 1 of the Treaty establishing the ESM do not stand in the way of the comprehensive information of the Bundestag and of the Bundesrat.

[55] Ibid §§ 210, 214 (quote); in the German original §§ 106, 110. The same formula appears in headnote 3b of judgment 2 BvR 987/10 (n 52).

[56] Ibid § 219 (in the German version § 115). In its prior judgment 2 BvR 987/10 the BVerfG had refused to examine the purchase of sovereign bonds by the ECB in the framework of a constitutional complaint procedure, as these measures 'are not sovereign acts of German State authority … which may be challenged by the complainants.' (§ 116).

[57] Ibid § 278 (in the German version § 174). Judgment in the main proceedings is now expected for spring 2014.

IV. CONSTITUTIONALITY REVIEW OF EU LAW POST-RATIFICATION

While the possible rejection by a national court of EU law for alleged incompatibility with national constitutional law before entry into force is not problematic under EU law, the matter is quite other when the EU law at stake has acquired the status of *lex lata*. Two fundamental principles of EU law seem to exclude this possibility: the primacy of EU law, and the monopoly of the Court of Justice to interpret EU law (Article 19(3)(b) TEU and Article 263 TFEU). A claim by a national court, even the supreme constitutional court of a Member State, to review EU law as interpreted by the ECJ with regard to its compatibility with the national Constitution will almost inevitably lead to frictions between the two courts and, should their conclusions in a concrete case diverge, to a confrontation which could create a major institutional crisis for the EU. For this reason, the relationship between the BVerfG and the ECJ is probably one of the most delicate conceivable between courts, as it incarnates at court level the unavoidable tension between two fundamental legal principles in a multi-layer system of supranational integration – national sovereignty and the supremacy of supranational law.[58]

One might think that this antagonism would be obviated in federal States which have a clear rule on the precedence of federal law, such as Article 31 of the German Basic Law:[59] but even in the German system this rule only applies to federal law which has been validly enacted in line with the Constitution, and in particular with its allocation of competences.[60] Hence a conflict between the federation and a State concerning the validity of federal law on the ground that the federal legislature has not respected the limits on its competences is a standard constellation, and only the *Federal* Constitutional Court is entitled to resolve such a dispute; no court of a German State has ever challenged the ultimate jurisdiction of the BVerfG.

At first glance, the EU system looks very similar; the fundamental principle of the supremacy of EU law as developed by the ECJ since its *Costa v ENEL* ruling in 1964[61] works essentially the same way in the legal system of the European Union[62] as it does, mutatis mutandis, within the German federal system. By contrast with national practice in Germany however, the ECJ has to face national constitutional courts reserving their right to review any alleged ultra vires act adopted by the EU institutions, including the ECJ itself.

While conflicts of competence within a federal system like the German usually do not give rise to fundamental disputes about ultra vires activism and

[58] Monica Claes, *National Identity: Trump Card or Up for Negotiations?*, in Saiz Arnaiz/Alcoberro Llivina (n 4) 109, 110, rightly emphasises that the core question is fairly common to any divided powers system, be it federal or supranational: 'who gets to decide what …?'

[59] 'Federal law strikes down state law' (*Bundesrecht bricht Landesrecht*), Art 31 GG.

[60] Not unlike the EU, in the German federal system all state competences (= sovereignty) belong to the States *unless* the Constitution confers a competence on the federation.

[61] Case 6/64 [1964] ECR 585.

[62] Even the BVerfG admits in its *Lisbon* judgment (see n 8, § 336) that, although national law in conflict with EU law will only be set aside and may still apply in areas not governed by EU law, the difference between that and Art 31 GG which voids conflicting state law is rather theoretical.

the limits to the ultimate objectives of the federal entity, this is different within the supranational system of the EU, and we can see political and legal reasons for this difference which are intertwined; politically, at least in Germany and despite a subsidiarity clause in the Constitution,[63] there is no popular support for limiting the legislative competencies of the federal State but rather a desire for ever more uniformity in regulation. The political situation is different in the EU, where the Member States remain jealous of their 'sovereign' competences, where criticism of legislative activism by the Union is pervasive and where Eurosceptical forces are growing. Legally (or constitutionally), the ultimate reason for this difference is the same as that which separates the concept of a State from that of the Union; in the Union system, it is still Member States that confer powers on the Union, while in the federal State it is the federal institutions which enact transfers of power. Hence the legitimacy and the role of the BVerfG as the single and final arbiter of any competence dispute within the German system are uncontested, while the ECJ is confronted with national constitutional courts claiming their own final say on whether a particular competence has been conferred or not.

The first question is hence whether the mere claim by a Member State's constitutional court of a right to review the constitutionality of EU law as interpreted by the ECJ is compatible with EU law. The second question will be how this right – if recognised by EU law – can be exercised and what would be the legal consequences of divergent rulings by the two courts.

Starting from the principal legal difference between the supranational system of the Union and the federal system in a State like Germany, it is pertinent to conclude that the primacy of EU law and the interpretation of EU law by the ECJ can only go as far as the validity of EU law stretches and as far as competences have been conferred (Article 5.2 TEU). Logically, there is no contradiction between the exclusive jurisdiction of the ECJ to interpret EU law, including its validity, and the right claimed by a national court to check whether the exercise of a presumptive EU prerogative is still within the constitutional limits of the powers conferred; powers not conferred cannot be subject to an interpretation by the ECJ. EU law based on a competence not transferred cannot limit the competences of a national constitutional court, as by definition such EU law is not valid.[64]

While in an ideal world both courts will come to congruent conclusions on the scope and validity of the transferred competences which are the alleged basis of the EU act at stake, it would be naïve to assume that the problem is merely theoretical. However, even if the world is far from ideal and conflicts of competence easily conceivable, the BVerfG and the ECJ have so far avoided any direct confrontation.

[63] Cf Art 72.2 GG.

[64] In this sense also R Bustos Gisbert, 'National Constitutional Identity in European Constitutionalism: Revisiting the Tale of the Emperor's New Clothes in Spain?' in Saiz Arnaiz/ Alcoberro Llivina, (n 4), 75 (76); cf. G Martinico, What Lies Behind Article 4(2) TEU?, ibid 93, who sees the risk of 'interpretative anarchy' (97).

1. The *Lisbon* ruling and the *Honeywell* test

Like the *Maastricht* judgment in 1993, the *Lisbon* judgment reserves the right of the BVerfG to examine 'whether legal instruments of the European institutions and bodies keep within the boundaries of the sovereign powers accorded to them by way of conferral'[65] in rather general terms, which as such do not give rise to concerns under EU law, even if the BVerfG's reasoning here is not particularly strong; it does not discuss the problem of the ECJ's exclusive competence to rule on the validity of EU law and confines its argumentation to contending that 'it must be possible within the German jurisdiction to assert the responsibility for integration if obvious transgressions of the boundaries occur when the European Union claims competences'.[66] This is presented as a consequence of the continuing sovereignty of the Member States which 'remain the masters of the Treaties.'[67]

The exercise of this right has been put to the test in the 2010 *Honeywell* decision of the BVerfG,[68] which followed the *Mangold* judgment of the ECJ.[69] The cases were factually almost identical and concerned the prohibition of age discrimination under Directive 2000/78/EC and German labour legislation which allowed the conclusion of fix-term labour contracts with employees aged 52 or older under certain conditions. Although at the time of the *Mangold* ruling the deadline for implementing the Directive had not yet expired, the ECJ found a general principle of Community law prohibiting age discrimination which it distilled from international covenants and the common constitutional traditions of the Member States. The judgment caused popular outrage in Germany, as in fact the principle is not mentioned in any international covenant and is absent from almost the totality of the Constitutions of the Member States.[70] Many therefore expected the BVerfG to declare the ECJ ruling to be ultra vires and inapplicable in Germany when, following the non-application of the German law by German labour courts in line with *Mangold*, Honeywell seised the BVerfG of the question in 2006.

Although the BVerfG expresses serious doubts with regard to the deduction by the ECJ of a common constitutional principle prohibiting discrimination on grounds of age,[71] it does not declare the *Mangold* conclusions inapplicable. Instead it restricts its own right to review ultra vires acts of the EU to transgressions of competence which are 'sufficiently qualified,' ie which are 'manifestly in violation of competences' and 'highly significant ... with regard

[65] Headnote 5 of the *Lisbon* judgment (n 8).

[66] Ibid § 240. The frequent use of the term 'responsibility for integration' ('*Integrationsverantwortung*') by the BVerfG seems either ironic or euphemistic, as it rather stipulates a duty to defend national competences against transgressive integration measures and not a responsibility to facilitate integration.

[67] Ibid §§ 334, 336.

[68] 2 BvR 2661/06 of 6.7.2010, http://www.bverfg.de/entscheidungen/rs20100706_2bvr266106.html (German version), http://www.bverfg.de/entscheidungen/rs20100706_2bvr266106en.html (English).

[69] C-144/04, ECR I-9981.

[70] For a detailed review of both judgments see Stein (n 4), 225–227.

[71] *Honeywell* judgment (n 68) § 78.

to the principle of conferral.'[72] It emphasises the need to exercise its ultra vires review 'reservedly' in order not to damage the unity of EU law and the role of the ECJ; it even accords the ECJ 'a right to tolerance of error.'[73] Misinterpretations of EU law in individual cases which do not involve 'a considerable shift in the structure of competences' do not qualify as manifest violations of competence.

The *Honeywell* decision is an extremely important concrete application of the right of post-ratification review which the BVerfG continues to claim. It not only clarifies the narrow limits within which such review is exercised, but it also emphasises that the BVerfG 'must comply with the rulings of the Court of Justice in principle as a binding interpretation of Union law' and for this reason afford the ECJ

> the opportunity to interpret the Treaties, as well as to rule on the validity and interpretation of the legal acts in question, ... according to Article 267 TFEU. As long as the Court of Justice did not have an opportunity to rule on the questions of Union law which have arisen, the [BVerfG] may not find any inapplicability of Union law for Germany.[74]

In practice, this narrows further down the potential for a competence conflict between the two courts, even if this possibility remains a reality.

2. Other BVerfG case law

a) The Solange *Jurisprudence of 1974 and 1986*

The so-called *Solange I* decision of 29 May 1974[75] was the first ruling in which the BVerfG declared its competence to review EU acts issued on the basis of primary law in force with a view to ensuring a level of protection of fundamental rights equivalent to the standard of protection granted by the Basic Law, 'as long as' ('*solange*') Community law lacked a catalogue of fundamental rights. In a nutshell, the decision already lists a number of key considerations which would determine its subsequent *Maastricht* and *Lisbon* judgments; the Court states first of all that the EC is not a federal State, so that the BVerfG's competence to rule on the compatibility of secondary EC law with core constitutional principles remains unaffected.[76] The BVerfG adds that the Treaties do not unilaterally bind the Member States vis-à-vis the Community, but also oblige the latter to respect

[72] Ibid. § 61; the BVerfG refers expressly to the ECJ definition of a 'sufficiently qualified' breach in its liability jurisprudence. This is the official translation by the BVerfG of the German 'hinreichend qualifiziert', which corresponds to 'sufficiently serious' in the English terms of the ECJ jurisprudence on Member State liability.

[73] Ibid § 66.

[74] Ibid § 60. – In this sense the BVerfG seems to be on the good track of 'negotiations' on the substance of national identity with the ECJ called for by Claes (n 58), 134, 137. In favour of a 'pluralistic conception of the relationship between EU law and national constitutional law' also A von Bogdandy/S Schill, 'Overcoming Absolute Primacy: Respect for National Identity under the Lisbon Treaty', (2011) 48 *CML Rev* 1417, 1452.

[75] 2 BvL 52/71, online version at http://www.servat.unibe.ch/dfr/bv037271.html.

[76] Ibid §§ 40–42.

compelling principles of a national – in this case the German – Constitution (which make up its core identity), of which the catalogue of fundamental rights is a main component. For the Court, the fundamental rights guarantee must prevail in a case of conflict (which *in concreto* was not assumed).[77] At the same time, the BVerfG acknowledges the exclusive jurisdiction of the ECJ in the interpretation of EU law and requests the German courts to refer a matter to the ECJ before they ask the BVerfG whether the secondary act as interpreted by the ECJ is compatible with fundamental rights.[78]

The most heavily criticised element in the Court's argumentation was its conclusion that by applying an EC secondary act in Germany, the German administration and courts would exercise German State authority which is always bound by the Constitution.[79] But this was just the flipside of its principal assumption that the EC was not entitled to encroach on the constitutional identity of a Member State which in the supranational system of the EC the constitutional court has the lasting duty to review.[80]

It is important to note that the subsequent *Solange II* decision of 22 October 1986[81] was no revocation of the *Solange I* principle. Following the development of the ECJ jurisprudence acknowledging fundamental rights as an emanation of common fundamental principles of the legal orders of the Member States, the BVerfG did not in any way give up its proclaimed right to review the compatibility of secondary EC legislation with a fundamental rights standard equivalent to that of the Basic Law; it only decided to refrain from exercising this right 'as long as' EC law ensured a sufficient protection level of fundamental rights.[82]

b) The Maastricht *judgment of 12 October 1993*[83]

The *Maastricht* judgment is in many regards a precursor of the BVerfG's *Lisbon* judgment. It accepts the right to vote (Article 38 GG) as the legal basis for constitutional complaints challenging the transfer of sovereignty to the EC; it emphasises the principle of democracy from which it deducts absolute limits for transfers of competences under Article 79.3 GG; it underlines the principle of conferred powers, objects to blanket empowerments and reserves the right to review whether legal acts of the EU remain within the limits of transferred powers and to declare them inapplicable if they do not. It also formulates specific requirements for Germany's participation in Monetary Union. The issues raised by the Maastricht judgment were very much in parallel to those raised by the *Lisbon* judgment, even if its tough language after the conciliatory wording of *Solange II* was perceived as being particularly critical of the integration process.

[77] Ibid § 45.

[78] Ibid § 48. The BVerfG underlines that it has no power to decide on the validity of an act of EC law but will only rule on its applicability in Germany, § 49.

[79] Ibid § 54.

[80] The Court does not yet expressly use the term 'constitutional identity' in *Solange I*.

[81] 2 BvR 197/83, online version at http://www.servat.unibe.ch/dfr/bv073339.html.

[82] Ibid headnote 2.

[83] 2 BvR 2134/92, NJW 1993, 3047 ss.

From an EU law perspective, the problematic part of the judgment is the assumed right to review the applicability of EU acts in Germany post-ratification of the Treaty, a concept which already underlay the *Solange* jurisprudence and has not been ceded since.

3. Conflict Resolution in case of a 'Manifest Violation of Competence'

Conflicting decisions on the validity of an EU competence which the BVerfG would consider as 'sufficiently qualified' may not be likely, and both courts seem to be avoiding an open conflict as long as possible. However, the pending BVerfG ruling on the ESM and the ECB purchases of sovereign bonds might bring about the concrete scenario for such a conflict to arise. It is therefore not just a theoretical exercise to examine whether and how such conflict could be resolved in accordance with EU law.

Using the example of the *ESM* case, a first consequence of the *Honeywell* decision is to create the expectation that the BVerfG refer to the ECJ the question of a transgression of competence (Article 267 TFEU) before taking its own final stance, highlighting in its referring decision the incompatibilities of the EU action at stake (eg the ECB's policy of purchasing sovereign bonds) with primary law, and in particular with the principle of conferred competences. It is assumed that the BVerfG would explain in detail to the ECJ where it sees the dividing line between further developing the law by jurisprudence (*Rechtsfortbildung*), which in its view is an uncontested competence of the ECJ as part of the powers conferred to the EU, and the changing by the ECJ case law of primary law, or the creation by the ECJ of new provisions of a fundamental character, which would cause structural shifts in the system of competences between EU and Member States.[84]

Assuming for the sake of argument that the ECJ will rule that the *ESM* case is in line with the Treaty, this interpretation of the Treaty will be binding on the BVerfG. From the point of view of German constitutional law however, this cannot mean that the ECJ ruling would preclude the BVerfG from exercising its right to review whether the ECJ ruling in itself constitutes a 'manifest violation of competence' in the sense of *Honeywell*, as such a manifest violation would

[84] *Honeywell* judgment (n 68) § 64. As it happens, just at the time of proofreading this contribution (7 February 2014) the BVerfG published a press release on its decision to separate the issue of the ECB's *OMT* decision of 6 September 2012 from the remainder of the pending ESM cases (see n 52) and to pronounce its judgment on the latter on 19 March 2014. More excitingly, fully in line with its *Honeywell* judgment and with express reference to it, the BVerfG for the first time in history adopted a decision to transfer the now separated *OMT* case to the ECJ for a preliminary ruling on the grounds of an assumed ultra vires act of the ECB. In its decision (2 BvR 2728/13 of 14 January 2014 (https://www.bundesverfassungsgericht.de/entscheidungen/rs20140114_2bvr272813.html – German version; English translation: https://www.bundesverfassungsgericht.de/entscheidungen/rs20140114_2bvr272813en.html), the Court sets out the reasons why the *OMT*decision should be considered as a manifest violation of the EU competence order. At the same time the BVerfG refers the ECJ to the possibility to heal such transgressive effect by means of a restrictive interpretation of the *OMT* decision (§ 99). The BVergG expressly leaves the question open whether the *OMT* decision and its possible execution could infringe Germany's constitutional identity; the answer will depend on its interpretation by the ECJ (§§ 102, 103).

constitute a transgression of conferred competences and could hence not bind the BVerfG. Conversely, from the point of view of EU law, the exercise of such a national competence review in a case where an ECJ ruling has already been delivered seems hardly admissible. It can only be justified in the light of the EU's obligation to respect the national constitutional identity (Article 4(2) TEU), which includes the constitutional competences of a constitutional court, together with the distant possibility for that Court to reconcile a possibly conflicting conclusion with EU law.

Again there is, of course, no problem if the BVerfG also accepts the ruling of the ECJ with regard to German constitutional law and disregards its own former ultra vires concerns. But assuming that the BVerfG finds a manifest transgression of competence in both the practice of the ECB and the ruling of the ECJ confirming this practice, it would have a number of options, of which two could be considered as compatible with EU law:

(1) It could simply rule that the EU act at issue is not valid for Germany and that German institutions are not allowed to participate in, or contribute to, its adoption;
(2) It could rule that, as the EU act at issue infringes the core of Germany's constitutional identity, it is not valid for Germany and that German institutions are not allowed to participate in, or contribute to, its adoption:
    (a) until the German People has consented to it by way of referendum; or
    (b) that the German government was constitutionally obliged either to seek an amendment of EU primary law within an appropriate time-limit which would bring a unconstitutional situation to an end or, if a Treaty amendment is out of reach, to terminate Germany's membership of the EU;
(3) It could also rule that, despite ultra vires being established under German constitutional law, the EU act at issue would continue to have effect in and on Germany for a limited period in which alternatively:
    (a) the German government would have to seek an amendment of EU primary law to terminate the EU act considered unconstitutional, or
    (b) the German People would be invited to ratify the EU act at stake by way of referendum;

    and order Germany's withdrawal from the EU at the end of such period if a Treaty amendment was not available or a referendum fails.

It is difficult to see how ruling (1) could be reconciled with EU law. From an EU law point of view, the judgment of the ECJ is the final interpretation of whether, and to which extent, a competence exercised has been validly transferred to the Union. The mere statement of a national constitutional court that in its view the EU acted ultra vires can hardly suffice to allow that State not to apply the contested EU act.

This could be different if the national court makes clear that the EU act at issue encroaches on the core of the Member State's constitutional identity and orders its inapplicability (option (2)). While it is true that the concept of 'national' or 'constitutional identity' enshrined in Article 4(2) TEU is a concept of EU law and has to be interpreted autonomously, it is also true that the definition of this core identity belongs to the Member State's supreme jurisdiction. While EU law may autonomously restrict the criteria determining the concept of national identity, it is for the BVerfG to fill these criteria and define their content. As it can hardly be argued that provisions of a Constitution which this Constitution declares unamendable do not qualify under EU law as criteria for determining the constitutional identity of the country, it is for the BVerfG alone to decide whether a specific EU act infringes on this constitutional identity.[85]

In this context the BVerfG's argument is of interest, given that the ECJ itself in its *Kadi* judgment accepted the principle that binding international law (in this case a Resolution by the UN Security Council) may be disregarded by EU institutions if otherwise fundamental legal principles of the EU cannot be respected.[86] According to the BVerfG, the same must apply within the legal system of the EU if 'exceptionally, and under special and narrow conditions', the BVerfG declares EU law inapplicable in Germany as being the 'only way in which a violation of fundamental principles of the Constitution can be averted.'[87]

If EU law is rather open to references to the national *ordre public* (public policy) in general,[88] this reservation must all the more be admissible in a context which aims at the core of national constitutional identity. Again, it will be for the ECJ alone to determine the limits and conditions for invoking this right in detail,[89] but it seems that Article 4(2) TEU provides a principal basis for the Member State – and in our case for the BVerfG – to rely on.

It is thus conceivable that a declaration of inapplicability of a specific EU act in Germany is in line with EU law because it is deemed to infringe on the core of Germany's constitutional identity, either for an unlimited period or until the constitutional conflict is resolved by amending the Basic Law by way of referendum or by amending the Treaty (option (2)).

There is, however, the possibility of an ultimate culmination of the conflict if the ECJ states that a declaration of non-application in Germany is in breach of EU law

[85] In this sense the BVerfG's argument in the *Lisbon* judgment (n 8), § 332, that EU law may not claim primacy over the constitutional identity of the Member States protected by Art: 4(2) TEU. Cf Grewe (n 7), 37, 40 who argues that the constitutional core in the sense of Art 4(2) TEU is 'obviously concerned' with 'intangible' provisions of a constitution such as Art 79.3 GG and lists seven further Member States with such constitutional clauses (Cyprus, the Czech Republic, France, Greece, Italy, Portugal, Romania). In the same publication, Bustos Gisbert (n 64) concludes that the lack of any 'intangible' clause in the Spanish Constitution makes Art 4(2) ineffective for Spain (90). Cf also N Jääskinen, *Constitutions in the European Union – Some Questions of Conflict and Convergence*, in Heusel (n 4), for whom this fundamental conflict between the two legal orders is not resolvable with legal means (212).

[86] Joint cases C-402/05 and C-415/05 [2008] ECR I–6351, in particular par 285.

[87] *Lisbon* judgment (n 8) § 340.

[88] All four freedoms of the Single Market are subject to public order reservations (cf. Arts. 36 for the free movement of goods, 52, 62 for the freedom of establishment and of services; 65 I b for the free movement of capital), even if the jurisprudence of the ECJ has developed criteria and limits for the use of these provisions. Cf. C Kessedjan, 'Public Order in European Law,' (2007) *Erasmus Law Review*, 25.

[89] Claes (n 58) rightly emphasises that it is for the ECJ to decide whether a claim based on national identity can justify non-compliance with EU law (112).

because the conditions for invoking the *ordre public* argument of Article 4(2) TEU are not met. In this case, the only stance by the BVerfG in line with EU law would be option (3); the EU act considered ultra vires under the German Constitution has to be respected by the German institutions as long as Germany is a member of the EU. The German Constitution will, however, oblige the German institutions in this case to achieve constitutionality either by amending the conflicting legal rules in accordance with the Constitution, or to leave the supranational order which in its view has ceased to respect the rule of law.[90]

V. CONCLUSION

This analysis of the BVerfG's jurisprudence on the relationship between EU law and the German Constitution shows a fairly consistent approach of the Court since the early days of the *Solange* rulings. While it is true that the strength of its rhetoric varies, this oscillation between *cris de guerre* and 'a high degree of harmony between Karlsruhe and Luxemburg'[91] has often concealed the fact that substantially the position of the BVerfG has always followed the same course; to preserve the core principles of the Basic Law which make up its identity within the meaning of Article 4(2) TEU. To this end, the BVerfG has not given up one iota of its principal claim since *Solange I* to review EU acts for infringing on this core of the German Constitution, a claim it upheld even in times of utmost harmony with Luxembourg. On the other hand, it was precisely the rhetoric of the *Maastricht* and *Lisbon* judgments which made some partisans of State sovereignty hope that the BVerfG would use the next suitable opportunity to show the ECJ the limits of its jurisdiction, disregarding the fact that in *Solange I* the BVerfG had already made clear that such conflict of jurisdictions would only be an *ultima ratio* decision in the case of a really serious infringement.

In a supranational system governed by the constitutional principle that Member States alone decide on the conferral of competences on the Union, the right of the constitutional courts of the Member States to examine from their constitutional point of view whether a competence has been conferred must be in line with Union law. On this assumption, conflicts of jurisdiction cannot be excluded, but they can be resolved in a way which is compatible with both legal orders.

[90] The BVerfG refers to this option in its *Lisbon* judgment (n 8), § 264.
[91] Tomuschat (n 4), 219.

24

The Weakening of Allegiance to the Polity in the Institutional Practices of European Judges and Courts

DIARMUID ROSSA PHELAN*

INTRODUCTION: THE ISSUE TO BE ADDRESSED

WHAT TO GIVE a lawyer on retirement who, professionally, has done it all? Something more to read? What to write for Nial Fennelly, Senior Counsel, Advocate General and currently judge of the Supreme Court of Ireland. Our genial editor planned ahead and allowed us time to contemplate. The topic of the impact on the concept of allegiance of judge's switching positions, from the Court of Justice of the European Union to the court of a Member State, may have enough echo, whilst not biographical, in the structure of his extraordinary career to entice his readership of one more legal article.

The salient, simplified fact pattern is that a judge may find himself appointed under the Constitution of a Member State, taking the oath and assuming the constitutional duties of that office, then resign or suspend that office and be appointed to the Court of Justice of the European Union, taking the oath or affirmation and assuming the obligations of that office, then resign or come to end of term in that office and be appointed as a judge of the Member State, taking whatever oath and assuming the constitutional duties of that office. Judges switch allegiance. This is interesting. The reader may differ in identification of the issues posited in the analysis below. But ponder the problematic: judges switch allegiance, bind themselves to uphold one system, and then another

* Diarmuid Rossa Phelan practices as Senior Counsel at the Bar of Ireland and lectures in Trinity College Dublin. The author thanks Judit Beke-Martes, Sarah Cronin, David Kenny, David Prendergast , Christine Ryan and Declan O'Keeffe for their comments, and the members of the Jean Monnet Centre of the Friedrich-Schiller-Universität Jena where the ideas herewith were presented in a guest lecture.

which may be in opposition, each time bound by duty to obey, like any subject of the law, and to uphold, like any officer of the law, and to judge, the epitome of fidelity to the legal order, and to apply the law in judgments which continue to bind its subjects, well after the judge has switched allegiance.

One could spend many paragraphs teasing out variants; suspension or resignation of national judicial office; reappointment to a different court level; conceivably appointment post CJEU to the court of a different Member State, or another European or international body; oath or affirmation etc.. The reader may select the most interesting.

The concepts of allegiance, fidelity and loyalty imply continuity. For the concept of loyalty, any thesaurus will identify the characteristic of constancy, and dependability. In some examinations of the concept of loyalty, the characteristic of devotion is identified.[1] In common understanding, betwixt friend and friend, man and woman, employer and employee, citizen and Republic, judge and the Constitution, the concept is meaningless (or, certainly, not focally present) without duration in time. It is the durability of the relationship which partially defines it. For example, switching loyalties in war is the antithesis of loyalty – betrayal; switching loyalties in life is at least fickle; at its extreme even a soccer player switching clubs may be criticized by fans, in whom allegiance is more strongly rooted.

THE SCOPE OF THE INQUIRY

The scope is limited to judges in the EU but in principle extends to other officials and times. For example, there were lawyers who served as judges in the Weimar Republic, the Third Reich, and the post-unification German Federal Republic, where the conceptions of law in each were different. [2]

This article identifies the phenomenon of judicial switching of allegiance, gives some limited detail of the law and literature for the reader's contextualization, explores some refutations, and makes some suggestions of its impact. Only one core thesis is maintained: the institutionalization of the switching of allegiances at the highest judicial level changes the concept of allegiance. This point is not *his loyalty has changed* but *Loyalty has changed*. The first point is summarised by J. Habermas: '[o]ld loyalties fade, new loyalties develop, traditions change and nations, like all other comparable references, are not

[1] J Royce,*The Philosophy of Loyalty* (London, Macmillan, 1908). Royce is one of a line of theorists who argue for the pivotal moral value of loyalty, eg op cit 14–15: '[i]n loyalty, when loyalty properly defined, is the fulfilment of the whole moral law. You can truthfully centre your entire moral world about a rational conception of loyalty. Justice, charity, industry, wisdom, spirituality, are all definable in terms of enlightened loyalty'. John Ladd, 'Loyalty' in P Edwards (ed), *The Encyclopaedia of Philosophy* (London, Macmillan, 1967), 97, argues that the notion of loyalty is 'an essential ingredient in any civilized and humane system of morals.'

[2] This observation must be credited to Professor M Ruffert of the Friedrich-Schiller Universitat Jena on the occasion of the presentation of a trial run of this article, in *über*draft, to their Jean Monnet Centre.

natural givens either'.[3] The second point is a change in concept, which this article attempts to summarise.

The taking of the oath is not a *sine qua non* of the thesis advanced here on the switching of allegiance. There is much study on this subject in its own right (including, in this jurisdiction, by the Law Reform Commission *Report on Oaths and Affirmations*).[4] The judicial oath is to be distinguished from the oath taken by witnesses to tell the truth. Aquinas distinguishes between an oath of asservation, calling God to witness about things present or past, and a promissory oath in confirmation of future performance.[5] The judicial oath is both at the institutional core of the law – the assumption of office of the judiciary – and the most acute and personal concretisation of loyalty. Aquinas distinguishes between an oath *tout court* and a vow:

> Article VIII.—*Is the obligation of an oath greater than that of a vow?*
>
> *R.* Both obligations, that of an oath and that of a vow, are caused by something referring to God, but not in the same way. The obligation of a vow is caused by the fidelity which we owe to God, to discharge our promise to Him; while the obligation of an oath is caused by the reverence that we owe Him, which binds us to make true whatever we promise by His name. Now every violation of fidelity involves irreverence, but it is not every irreverence that contains a violation of fidelity. A subject's violation of the fidelity that he owes his lord, is reckoned the greatest irreverence. And therefore a vow in its own nature is more binding than an oath.[6]

Certain oaths, such as oaths of allegiance, oaths to uphold a Constitution, are oath-bound vows of fidelity. The importance of this loyalty goes beyond morality: the internal attitude of officials, and certainly of judges, to the law, is an existential requirement of law in many common explanations of law, such as HLA Hart, *The Concept of Law*.[7] The oath is an expression of allegiance.

This article does not evaluate whether or not switching of allegiance is good or bad or pretend to enquire exhaustively. It endeavours to photograph the shadow concept by looking at its most institutionalized, systemic form, in the following stages:

- immediate objections to the issues posed,
- the obligations of a national judge (taking Ireland and the United Kingdom),
- the obligations of a judge of the CJEU,
- comparatively, the obligations of a judge in the United States,
- God, history, bases of allegiance, and treason,
- implications.

[3] 'The Crisis of the European Union in the Light of a Constitutionalization of International Law', (2012) 23 *European Journal of International Law* 335, 346.

[4] Dublin, LRC 34-1990.

[5] Summa Theologica – Secunda Secundae Pt 2 [1274] (trans J Rickaby), (Online Library of Liberty – http://oll.libertyfund.org), Question LXXXIX, of Oaths, Article I.

[6] Ibid.

[7] 3rd edn (Oxford, OUP, 2012).

OBJECTIONS

(i) Indeterminacy

The concepts of allegiance, fidelity, loyalty, are of course both indeterminate and contestable. One immediate objection to this article, therefore, is that one is speaking of a shift in indeterminacies, and therefore necessarily nebulously.

However, one may point to shifting shadows, and say with certainty that the shadows shift, without delineating the shadows precisely.

Furthermore, allegiance is given precise formulation in both words (for example, the oath of office), and fact (the making of the oath or affirmation). Allegiance is institutionalized in the operation of the appointment as judge.

(ii) Objection – False Premise

One could argue that the legal systems of the European Union and its Member States are not in any opposition, or even that the contribution to EU institutions is a patriotic extension of duty to nation given the Member States' commitments to the EU, the reception of EU law in national law, the foundation of EU citizenship on national citizenship and the expression in some Constitutions of the participation of the State in the EU. Some even argue that the EU is a *Verfassungsverbund* (an alliance of [national] Constitutions). Others argue that European allegiance originates in national allegiance.[8] With no tension in law or loyalties, the premise for the inquiry vanishes. There is no switching of allegiances.

Whilst it is true that constitutional systems can co-exist in a state of tension and politic ambiguity, and that there is no current overt state of crisis in the legal system(s) in Europe, it is taken as the case that the claims of the Member States legal systems and of the EU are still in part incompatible. This article is not about this debate.[9]

Moreover, the direction of the allegiance (in an EU or national institution) is not the same. Whilst judges are not roaming Europe like Hessians or Gallowglass, the subtleties and complexities of the modern arrangements do not erase the switch. To claim switching of allegiances in judicial offices in the EU was betrayal would be as inaccurate as claiming that there was no switch. Indeed, the EU and the Member States insist on it: a judge who moves between systems does not take one oath, or make a single commitment, or retain a single judicial office.

[8] K van Kersbergen, 'Double Allegiance in European Integration: Publics, Nation-States, and Social Policy' (European University Institute, Working Paper RSC No 97/15, February 1997); 'Political Allegiance and European Integration' (2000) 37 *European Journal of Political Research* 1.

[9] My own views on the matter when last addressed are set out elsewhere, eg 'Two Hats, One Wig, No Halo' (1995) *Doctrine and Life* 130; *Revolt or Revolution: The Constitutional Boundaries of the European Community* (Dublin, Roundhall Sweet & Maxwell, 1997); 'Monism in International Relations, Dualism in International Law, Trinitarianism in Legal Theory – An Irish Crossroads' in M Novacovik (ed), *Basic Concepts of Public International Law – Monism & Dualism,* (Faculty of Law of the University of Belgrade, Belgrade, March 2013).

(iii) Objection – Oath in Lieu of Contract

Judges in some systems, such as Ireland, are the holders of constitutional office, and as such do not have contracts of employment. Consequently it is necessary to mark the relationship with an oath.

However the oath is not a substitute for a contract in either form, purpose, or effect.

Even without an oath, the central thesis of this article regarding the impact of switching office on the concept of allegiance could be pursued. A Constitution binds, like all law, without any self-expression of its binding. Indeed such an expression would be not only otiose, but also weakening, for the binding of that expression of binding would have to rest on the same unexpressed binding of the expressing law. To put the point out of its syntactical misery: if the law did not bind, then the law stating that the law bound would have no effect.

It may be possible in some jurisdictions to assume judicial office without an oath. However there remain the acts of assumption of office and switching of office.

An office holder – an official – has an obligation to obey the law as does any other citizen. People are supposed to do their jobs without swearing they will. Further, treason is proscribed by the operation of law. But the office holder, with or without oath, enters into a closer relationship with the State, and a closer reciprocity of benefit. Normally, but not necessarily, persons appointed as judges will have through their formations absorbed the concepts, values, duties on which the office depends.

The oath is more than a contract. Whilst oaths of office are substantively different to oaths of witnesses, both share the operational significance of securing the promise by invoking divine retribution in this life-time in the event of breach. The oath is peculiarly solemn,[10] and invokes its own enforcement.[11]

(iv) Objection – Political Theory Requires Allegiance to the EU

Allegiance is owed in return for the successful coordination by the polity of distributive justice, and the European Union is the successful coordinator due to the transnational nature of world economy and, increasingly, society, or some such. There is no new concept of duty, but just the old concept applied to the new circumstances which require a bigger coordinating entity such as the EU.

However, this objection does not address the switching of allegiance (including the switching back to national judicial office).

[10] '*Judgment* is wanting in an incautious oath; *truth* in a lying oath; and *justice* in an iniquitous or unlawful oath' St T Aquinas, n 7 above, Article II.

[11] The Law Reform Commission, *Report on Oaths and Affirmations* (LRC 34-1990), at p 11, referring to the oath in judicial proceedings, states that it is rooted in the concept of *judicium dei*, and in the Anglo-Saxon forms of proof 'the oath was a traditional self-curse, which could be used as security for a promise.' *The Shorter Oxford English Dictionary* 3rd (Oxford, OUP, 1944) defines 'oath' as '[a] solemn appeal to God (or to something sacred) in witness that a statement is true, or a promise binding.'

It may be that the concept of allegiance is linked to the concept of nation and now, linked to a different entity, has a different meaning. The strong (not good, or bad) sense of the concept dwindles with the nation; just as the concept differed when the sovereign was God's anointed, and duty to the sovereign was owed because of duty to God – a different kind of duty than that owed to a secular State.[12] Indeed, to continue the historical recession, the duty was love to a God who commanded that He be loved.

OBLIGATIONS OF A NATIONAL JUDGE

(i) Ireland

The High and Supreme Court are established by the Constitution. The judges of the High and Supreme Court are holders of constitutional office – positions established by the Constitution. The judicial oath requirement extends to all judges (Article 34.5.2: 'the judges of every other Court').

Article 34.5.1 of the Constitution provides:

> Every person appointed a judge under this Constitution shall make and subscribe the following declaration:
>
> 'In the presence of Almighty God I, ___________, do solemnly and sincerely promise and declare that I will duly and faithfully and to the best of my knowledge and power execute the office of Chief Justice (or as the case may be) without fear or favour, affection or ill-will towards any man, and that I will uphold the Constitution and the laws. May God direct and sustain me.'

Article 34.5 was most recently amended in November 2013 (Thirty-third Amendment of the Constitution (Court of Appeal) Act 2013) by the addition of a Court of Appeal (Article 34.5.2 specifies that judges of the Court of Appeal must take this oath). No amendment was made to allow for affirmation, or to excise God from the text of the oath. The substance of the text requires fulfillment of office and upholding the Constitution.

No oath is taken by natural citizens to uphold the law. This is the same in the United Kingdom and the United States. It was not always thus. In Ancient Athens, young citizens to be had to take the Ephebic Oath.[13]

However, naturalizing citizens must make a declaration in the following form:[14]

> Declaration of fidelity to the nation and loyalty to the State
>
> I , (name in full) of (place) having applied to the Minister for Justice and Equality for a certificate of naturalisation, hereby solemnly declare my fidelity to the Irish nation and my loyalty to the State.

[12] HS Maine, *Ancient Law: its connection with the early history of society, and its relation to modern* ideas (London, John Murray, 1861, 398–399) points out that everything could be settled in Arthurian criminal law except cases of treason.

[13] On the oath taken by the 6,000 annually elected Athenian judges, see EM Harris, 'The Rule of Law in Athenian Democracy: Reflections on the Judicial Oath' (2007) IX *Ethics & Politics* 55.

[14] Form 6 in the Irish Nationality and Citizenship (Amendment) Regulations 2011 (SI 569 of 2011).

The distinction between fidelity to the Irish nation and loyalty to the State is striking. There is no mention of the Constitution. In gross approximation, the nation has replaced the king, and it is fidelity to the nation but loyalty to the State. The distinction goes back to negotiation over the form of oath for members of the First Dáil, a matter of Treaty negotiation, and one of the issues which led to the Civil War (1922–1923). No oath is now taken by Irish members of parliament or senators (since the Constitution (Removal of Oath) Act, 1933.) No oath was constitutionally required or specified for the judiciary. The cultural and moral difference in the importance placed in an oath between the Civil War and now is itself noteworthy.

The war Oath was included in Article 17 of the Free State's Constitution of 1922

> I (name) do solemnly swear true faith and allegiance to the Constitution of the Irish Free State as by law established, and that I will be faithful to H.M. King George V, his heirs and successors by law in virtue of the common citizenship of Ireland with Great Britain and her adherence to and membership of the group of nations forming the British Commonwealth of Nations.

This oath was repeated verbatim in the Articles of Agreement for a Treaty between Great Britain and Ireland (Article 4) contained in the Second Schedule to the Constitution of the Irish Free State (Saorstát Éireann) Act 1922. The text argued for by the Republican side (to simplify) was

> I (name) do solemnly swear true faith and allegiance to the constitution of the Irish Free State, to the Treaty of Association, and to recognize the King of Great Britain as Head of Associated States.[15]

(ii) United Kingdom

Two separate oaths are taken, an oath of allegiance and an oath of office.

> I, __________, do swear by Almighty God that I will be faithful and bear true allegiance to Her Majesty Queen Elizabeth the Second, her heirs and successors, according to law.

> I, __________, do swear by Almighty God that I will well and truly serve our Sovereign Lady Queen Elizabeth the Second in the office of ________, and I will do right to all manner of people after the laws and usages of this realm, without fear or favour, affection or ill will.

[15] President De Valera, in the Dáil Éireann debate on the Treaty (Volume 3, 19 December 1921, 26–27: http://historical-debates.oireachtas.ie/D/DT/D.T.192112190002.html) made an interesting observation, not apposite to the issues discussed in this article but of interest to issues of reception of EU law:

> If you accept it [the Treaty], time will tell; it cannot be one way in this assembly and another way in the British House of Commons. The Treaty is an agreed document, and there ought to be pretty fairly common interpretation of it. If there are differences of interpretation we know who will get the best of them.

These can also be taken as affirmations,[16] or sworn by Gita, Allah, or Guru Nanak.

In contrast to Ireland, an oath of allegiance is required of judges and many other office holders, including Members of Parliament (Parliamentary Oaths Act, 1866) before they take their seat. In keeping with the Republican stance on the Treaty of 1922, Members of parliament of the Sinn Féin Party elected in Northern Ireland refused to take the oath and were prevented from taking their seat.[17]

EUROPEAN UNION

Protocol (No 3) to the Treaty on European Union and to the Treaty on the Functioning of the European Union on the Statute of the Court of Justice of the European Union provides in Article 2:

> Before taking up his duties each Judge shall, in open court, take an oath to perform his duties impartially and conscientiously and to preserve the secrecy of the deliberations of the Court.[18]

This insistence on a secrecy oath is not sinister; while alien to common law countries it is well known to civil law countries. For example, in France, at the time of entrance into the national magistracy school, students swear to keep professional secrecy *réligieusement*.

Protocols have the same status as Treaty articles (Article 51 (TEU)). Consequently the rules in the Statute are equivalent in the hierarchy of norms to the rules of the constituent Treaties.

Article 4 of the Statute provides:

> The Judges may not hold any political or administrative office.
>
> They may not engage in any occupation, whether gainful or not, unless exemption is exceptionally granted by the Council, acting by a simple majority.
>
> When taking up their duties, they shall give a solemn undertaking that, both during and after their term of office, they will respect the obligations arising therefrom, in particular the duty to behave with integrity and discretion as regards the acceptance, after they have ceased to hold office, of certain appointments or benefits.
>
> Any doubt on this point shall be settled by decision of the Court of Justice. If the decision concerns a member of the General Court or of a specialised court, the Court shall decide after consulting the court concerned.

[16] Aquinas, n 5 above, Article VII:
§ 1. The case of a simple affirmation is different from that of an oath, in which the witness of God is invoked. For the truth of a simple affirmation it is enough that the person says what he intends to do, because that is true at the time in his case, or in the purpose of the doer. But an oath ought not to come in except upon a matter on which the person's mind is immovably made up. And therefore if an oath is used, then for reverence of the witness of God that is invoked, the man is bound to make true what he has sworn to, to the best of his power, unless the issue is for the worse.

[17] A challenge of incompatability of the oath with the European Convention on the Protection of Human Rights and Fundamental Freedoms failed as manifestly unfounded: *McGuinness v United Kingdom* [1999] ECtHR (No. 39511/98).

[18] [2010] OJ C83/210.

Consequently, the Treaty provides in its protocol that the solemn undertakings of judges of the CJEU bind them to their obligations arising from their term of office. These include but are not limited to professional secrecy, their duty to behave with integrity, their discretion in accepting regarding appointments and benefits. The obligations extend beyond their term of office. Notably, the obligations relate to their term of office, not to the office. The European law therefore does not make the assumption of subsequent national office unlawful, but clashes with any national duty to breach the obligations of the term of office in the CJEU, for example if a case involving the national interest or constitutional order would be affected by a secret held from a time in the CJEU.

The Rules of Procedure of the Court of Justice[19] provide:

> Article 4 – Taking of the oath:
> Before taking up his duties, a Judge or Advocate General shall, at the first public sitting of the Court which he attends after his appointment, take the following oath provided for in Article 2 of the Statute:
> 'I swear that I will perform my duties impartially and conscientiously; I swear that I will preserve the secrecy of the deliberations of the Court.'
>
> Article 5 – Solemn undertaking:
> Immediately after taking the oath, a Judge or Advocate General shall sign a declaration by which he gives the solemn undertaking provided for in the third paragraph of Article 4 of the Statute.

Annex 1 of the Statute of the CJEU provides in Article 5 that:

> Articles 2 to 6, 14, 15, the first, second and fifth paragraphs of Article 17, and Article 18 of the Statute of the Court of Justice of the European Union shall apply to the Civil Service Tribunal and its members.
> The oath referred to in Article 2 of the Statute shall be taken before the Court of Justice, and the decisions referred to in Articles 3, 4 and 6 thereof shall be adopted by the Court of Justice after consulting the Civil Service Tribunal.

Therefore members of all the EU Courts, including the Civil Service Tribunal, all take the same oath.

UNITED STATES OF AMERICA

Article VI of the Constitution of the United States provides:

> All debts contracted and engagements entered into, before the adoption of this Constitution, shall be as valid against the United States under this Constitution, as under the Confederation.
> This Constitution, and the laws of the United States which shall be made in pursuance thereof; and all treaties made, or which shall be made, under the authority of the United States, shall be the supreme law of the land; and the judges in every state shall be bound thereby, anything in the Constitution or laws of any State to the contrary notwithstanding.

[19] [2012] OJ L265/1.

> The Senators and Representatives before mentioned, and the members of the several state legislatures, and all executive and judicial officers, both of the United States and of the several states, shall be bound by oath or affirmation, to support this Constitution; but no religious test shall ever be required as a qualification to any office or public trust under the United States.

As HJ Vogel points out, clause 3 requires all officials to bind themselves by oath to support the Constitution. But clause 2 singles out judges in every state as the class who 'shall be bound.'[20] (This is probably explicable by what the Constitution sought to achieve in structuring the US federation).

Article VI(2) can be contrasted to EU Treaties, where there is no specific expression of 'bindingness' in the EU Treaties of EU law on national judges.

There is no EU law obligation requiring national judges to take any oath to be bound by the EU treaties, nor to my knowledge any national oath of same effect (perhaps there is an exception among the 28 Member States). The reception of EU law and obligation in the Member States rests, so far as national law is concerned, on national law.

The First Act of the United States Congress was An Act to Regulate the Time and Manner of Administering Certain Oaths (1789).[21] There is a deal of literature on oaths in the United States system, but not, perhaps naturally given the extent of federation and the provisions of clause 2 of Article VI, on the topic of focus here.

GOD, HISTORY, BASES OF ALLEGIANCE AND TREASON

(i) God

Even if one does not believe in God, He arises religiously.

The United States Constitution prohibits religious tests for office. Therefore it is illegitimate to deny office to someone because of beliefs. How far then can one deny office to someone lest they act in office in accordance with their core beliefs? There is literature in the United States on the compatibility of the practice of Senate scrutiny of religious appointees with the prohibition of a religious test for office.[22]

The common denominators of the oaths at national and at EU level is that they are required, and that they are *sworn*. At EU level and probably in most Member States they can be affirmed. But where they are sworn, which is probably still the norm, they are sworn before God, using language such as 'may God direct and sustain me'. Curiously, then, one might venture that the common substantive denominator, the thing which is not switched, is not any political

[20] HJ Vogel, 'The Judicial Oath and the American Creed: Comments on Sanford Levinson's *The Confrontation of Religious Faith and Civil Religion: Catholics Becoming Justices*' (1989–1990) 39 *DePaul Law Review* 1107, fn 1.

[21] S Levinson, 'Taking Oaths Seriously: A Comment on Carter and Sunstein' (1990) 2 *Yale Journal of Law & the Humanities* 113, 116.

[22] S Levinson, 'The Confrontation of Religious Faith and Civil Religion: Catholics Becoming Justices' (1989–1990) 39 *De Paul Law Review* 1047; Vogel (n 21 above).

or legal concept, but God. However the possibility of affirmation removes the necessity to track this further.

(ii) History

HS Maine's thesis, taking Status to mean the powers and privileges residing in the family, excluding those resulting from agreement, maintained 'that the movement of the progressive societies has hitherto been a movement *from Status to Contract*.'[23]

The relationship of subject to sovereign was based on duty, not contract. The emergence of the social contract as a political theory is pegged generally to the Enlightenment.[24] Most important relationships were on duty, not contract.

Nation comes from *natio* ('that which has been born'). There is a link between nation and race, and later to genealogy of parents as citizens (irrespective of race) and even to territory of birth (irrespective of genealogy). Neither race, genealogy, nor territory of birth is dependent on the choice, will, or contract of the citizen. Allegiance owed in law of a subject or citizen to the sovereign or State does not originate in consent.

Whatever about the rise since Rousseau of the social contractarian model for the self-understanding of societies, that model as explanation of society is not the same as the model of private law contract determining the allegiance of an individual official to the nation.

(iii) Bases of Allegiance

Various bases of allegiance are offered in the literature. Of these, four are commonly referred to:[25]

- *(i)* *Ligeantia naturalis, absoluta, pura et indefinita*, by birth
- *(ii)* *Ligeantia acquisita*, by acquisition or denization
- *(iii)* *Ligeantia localis*, due for example by entering a sovereign territory
- (iv) Legal obedience, due where the law requires an oath ((iv) may be combined with (i)–(iii)).

J Waldron has written subtly on the topic[26] highlighting the distinction between insiders and outsiders to explain the specialness of an individual's relation to certain institutions, such as those of this own country. He draws the distinction between two main accounts of citizen obligation to State, theories of acquired obligation and theories of natural duty. Whilst Waldron addresses these issues in the abstract. Applying the insider analysis language here, one

[23] Maine (n 12 above) 170 (emphasis in the original).

[24] Although there were strains prior to that – JM Kelly, *A Short History of Western Legal Theory* (Oxford, OUP, 1992).

[25] A useful accessible summary is in Wikipedia http://en.wikipedia.org/wiki/Allegiance .

[26] J Waldron, 'Special Ties and Natural Duties' (1993) 22 *Philosophy and Public Affairs* 3.

may comment that judges are not just inside, but the core of, the legal *system* (not, of course, of the law).

Reciprocity is both central to the history of the concept of allegiance (for example, in feudalism) and to its theoretical analysis (for example, by Waldron, and by Habermas[27]).

The fundamental distinction in analyses of the basis of allegiance is whether or not it may be acquired, or disposed of, by act of individual will, or is conferred by status independent of expressions of will.

The principle *nemo potest exuere patriam* has held sway for most of civilization. Exceptions have been introduced in Europe since the late nineteenth century, for example by the Naturalisation Act of 1870 which allowed British subjects to renounce their nationality and allegiance, and earlier in the United States.[28]

In his trial for treason, counsel on behalf of William Joyce, known as 'Lord Haw-Haw', submitted:

> Apart from the Naturalization Act, 1870, the general principle still holds good. *Nemo potest exuere patriam*. Nothing a man does can make him a British subject and nothing he can omit to do can prevent him from being a British subject if he was so born.[29]

Lord Jowitt LC (for the 4:1 majority of the House of Lords) held:

> Whether you look to the feudal law for the origin of this conception or find it in the elementary necessities of any political society, it is clear that fundamentally it recognizes the need of the man for protection and of the sovereign lord for service. "*Protectio trahit subjectionem et subjectio protectionem*." All who were brought within the King's protection were ad fidem regis: all owed him allegiance. The topic is discussed with much learning in *Calvin's case* [footnote omitted]. The natural-born subject owes allegiance from his birth, the naturalized subject from his naturalization, the alien from the day when he comes within the realm. By what means and when can they cast off allegiance? The natural-born subject cannot at common law at any time cast it off. "*Nemo potest exuere patriam*" is a fundamental maxim of the law from which relief was given only by recent statutes. Nor can the naturalized subjects at common law. It is in regard to the alien resident within the realm that the controversy in this case arises.[30]

And further:

> The principle which runs through feudal law and what I may perhaps call constitutional law requires on the one hand protection, on the other fidelity: a duty of the sovereign lord to protect, a duty of the liege or subject to be faithful. Treason, "*trahison*," is the betrayal of a trust: to be faithful to the trust is the counterpart of the duty to protect.[31]

[27] J Habermas, (n 3 above) 346: '[a] measure of the *relative* weights attached to loyalties, and thus of a stronger identification with one social unit rather than another, is the willingness to make sacrifices based on long-term relations of reciprocity.'

[28] The Expatriation Act of 1868; in *Talbot v Jansen* (1795) 3 US 133, the Supreme Court held that a man (Talbot, a citizen of both France and the US) could enjoy the rights of dual citizenship.

[29] *DPP v Joyce* [1946] AC 347, 355.

[30] Ibid at 366.

[31] *DPP v Joyce* (n 29 above) 367.

The case concerned the interpretation and application of the Treason Act 1351 (25 Edw S St c2) which is also the model for Section 3 of Article III of the Constitution of the United States. Interestingly, Article III Sections 1 and 3 concern the judicial power of the United States. The last section of the judicial power article deals with treason. It provides in part:

> Treason against the United States, shall consist only in levying war against them, or in adhering to their enemies, giving them aid and comfort. No person shall be convicted of treason unless on the testimony of two witnesses to the same overt act, or on confession in open court.

What may constitute treason is the subject of ongoing interpretation. The concept of adhering to the enemy is exemplified by giving aid or comfort. There is no indication that an oath might itself constitute an act of treason. It is noteworthy that one of the ways which treason is proved is by admission in Court.

IMPLICATIONS

(i) Voluntarist Concept of Allegiance and Duty to Obey Law

The EU has changed the concept of allegiance. In the EU, notions of allegiance, duty, and fidelity, are consensual, transient, reversible, and dependent on reciprocity of benefit. The fact that allegiance in the EU, in its epitome of judicial office, is contingent, transient, and consensual, is itself an important realization.

At the highest level of the EU legal system, the concept of allegiance to the EU and duty to the legal system is dependent on individual will. The system of rotation of judges entrenches this. The core value then is will. There is no real community, where that would bring with it any obligation inhering in membership, but rather a temporary contract contingent on ongoing satisfaction with benefits. For example, social identification is dependent on opportunism.

The concept of duty has a subjective element. Without subjective intention, there is a lack of duty. A polity demands a sense of duty towards it. Whereas this is demonstrated by external acts consistent with duties, these acts are required because an internal commitment is expected. For a judge, there is not just the obligation to respect the law by external conformity, but the obligation to actually respect the law.

What does it mean when a judge transfers from upholding the Constitution of a country to upholding the European Constitution above the national Constitution, to back again? One might argue that lawyers draw on concepts of law and professional responsibility which overarches both the legal systems. This would lead to an inquiry into the origin of such concepts, into whether a judge has a concept of law and legal duty which is not based on or indeed defined by the national law or the European law, and into a concept of duty and allegiance which is detached from both. Or that judges in different systems differ in their understanding of what they are swearing to do, dependent on their constitutional order's understanding of the EU.

(ii) Inequality in Basis and Extent of Allegiance Expected of Different Classes

One of the recurring analyses of loyalty, and one of the recurring historical manifestations of loyalty, is that of reciprocal exchange: fealty for benefits. This is not the only understanding of loyalty, but it has echoes with both the practices of high office in Europe, and the orientation of the welfare dependent. The most 'pro EU' groups are EU officials, whose lives are sustained by their employment arrangements and for whom a transnational feudalism of service and protection makes sense. A national judge, and an EU judge, and any national or EU office holder or legislator derive significant benefits from their office of salary, pension, and conditions, and may switch loyalty as opportunity arises.

Loyalty for this class of persons rests on a different calculation than that of the private sector citizen in no special relationship to the State, either as employee, office holder, or welfare dependent. A new classification of Europeans emerges.[32] One class is the State benefit class, which encompasses both public officials and those dependent on state welfare. For this class, allegiance remains grounded in reward, current (in salary etc.) and promised (pension etc.). Another class consists of capitalists whom the financial system rewards. The third class in Europe is the private sector tax-paying segment of 'the coping class', living in an extractive State, on the one hand part of the '99 percent', in the phraseology of the Occupy Wall Street movement, on the other hand winners neither from the market of capital, nor from the State of benefits which equate with the level of tax and regulatory obligation. This is a class who contribute their labour and custom to the market and their tax to the State,[33] sustaining the other two classes. Formerly known as citizens of a republic, this class is now known to their polity as potential tax evaders or émigrés, and to the markets as debtors, on a theory of contract they have been defrauded by a State which has forced them to assume the obligations of other classes, the bloating of the public sector, the welfare of the non-contributor, and the debts of failed banks.

If at the core of European law and institutions, fidelity, allegiance, and duty, rests on individual contract based on reciprocity of benefit, on what can the allegiance of this most populous third class in the EU be presumed? On a concept of natural non-consensual allegiance, differing from the voluntarist allegiance of the classes such natural allegiance supports.

[32] See Phelan, in Novacovik (n 9 above): '[m]onism in practice; a new dualism of public / private replacing the dualism of national / international?'

[33] The effective tax rate in Ireland is circa 55% for citizens and less than 1% for some foreign corporations. Whilst public sector employees pay tax, the tax operates as a deduction from what the State pays them, rather than as an expropriation of what they have generated.

25

Child Citizens and De Facto Deportation: Tender Years, Fragile Ties and Security of Residence

CATHRYN COSTELLO*

I. INTRODUCTION

CITIZENS MAY NOT be deported. That proposition is today axiomatic – the age of banishment is no more. Non-deportability is not just a hallmark of citizenship, but constitutive thereof.[1] Not being deportable means to enjoy security of residence in the polity, to belong legally. Taking that as given, when may the foreign parents of citizens of 'tender years' be deported? This question has been subject of much constitutional controversy in Ireland and at supranational level. Under some approaches, to remove the parents of a young citizen-child is acknowledged as 'de facto deportation'[2] of the children, as it means that the child's right of residence is ineffective or at best only to be exercised under conditions that are themselves a denial of rights. Yet, that approach is permitted under many Constitutions.[3] The present contribution examines this issue, illustrating the wax and wane of domestic constitutional,

* Andrew W Mellon University Lecturer in International Human Rights and Refugee Law, Refugee Studies Centre and St Antony's College, University of Oxford. The author thanks profusely John Stanley BL and Bríd Moriarty BL for sharing their knowledge and insights into the Irish jurisprudence, and provision of references to important unreported judgments.

[1] See generally B Anderson, M Gibney, E Paoletti (eds) 'Boundaries of Belonging: Deportation and the Constitution and Contestation of Citizenship', (2011) 15 *Citizenship Studies: Special Edition* 1.

[2] See, for example, United States Court of Appeals, Seventh Circuit in *Schleiffer v Myers* (1981) 644 F.2d 656, stating that:

> Many courts of appeal have concluded that the constitutional rights of such citizen-children are not violated when the deportation of their parents necessitates *de facto* deportation. In such cases, it has been noted that the child's return to the foreign country will merely postpone, but not bar, his (or her) residence in the United States if he or she should ultimately choose to live here.

[3] See J Bhabha 'The "Mere Fortuity of Birth"? Children, Mothers, Borders, and the Meaning of Citizenship' in S Benhabib and J Resnik (eds), *Migrations and Mobilities* (New York, New York University Press, 2009) 192.

EU and ECHR protections. Its purpose is not an exhaustive survey of the case law, but rather to identify the different approaches within and across the different systems.

As readers will be aware, for some time the Irish Constitution was deemed to give strong protection against removal for families of Irish Citizens, based on the Supreme Court's ruling in *Fajujonu*.[4] In a later Supreme Court ruling, which did not overrule the former case, a different approach emerged. Under *Lobe and Osayande*,[5] the State was permitted to deport families of Irish citizen children of 'tender years', not because the families posed a particular demonstrated threat to the 'common good', but on immigration law grounds alone. Kevin Lobe and Osaze Joshua Osayande were born about month apart in 2001 in the Ireland that granted automatic *jus soli* citizenship to children born on the territory. Kevin's family were Czech Roma, while Osaze's were from Nigeria. Both sets of parents were rejected asylum seekers, who had previously sought protection in the UK. To put it somewhat crudely and harshly, the majority in *Lobe and Osayande* did not balance the right to reside of the child with the States' right to deport non-citizens, but rather defined the residence rights of the citizen-child out of existence. The dissenting judgment of Fennelly J in *Lobe and Osayande,* with which McGuinness J concurred, is the inspiration for this contribution.

At the time of *Lobe and Osayande,* the ECHR standards were not part of Irish law.[6] Moreover, at that time, the European Court of Human Rights ('ECtHR' or 'Strasbourg') standards were not so clearly articulated, particularly as regards child-migrants. The role of the 'best interests' standard in such cases had not been developed.[7] The Strasbourg standards are the pan-European minimum, aiming to protect all children across the Council of Europe, not just citizens. The development of these standards is traced in Part II below.

When *Lobe and Osayande* was decided, the deportation of the third country national parents (TCN) of an Irish citizen from Ireland did not raise questions of EU law. Now, since the revolutionary ruling in *Zambrano*,[8] there is an EU dimension, so Irish citizen-children may invoke EU law against their own State. Yet, we should pause. Were Kevin and Osaze born in Ireland today, they would

[4] *Fajujonu v Minister for Justice and Another* [1990] 2 IR 151.

[5] *Lobe and Osayande v Minister for Justice, Equality and Law Reform* [2003] IESC 3 (23 January 2003).

[6] The European Convention on Human Rights Act 2003 postdates the litigation. The Supreme Court gave some consideration to the Strasbourg case law, but it was not decisive in the analysis.

[7] Although the importance of drawing on the 'best interests' standard from the UN Convention on the Rights of the Child was evident for some time. See further U Kilkelly, *The Child and the European Convention on Human Rights* (Aldershot, Ashgate Publishers, 1999).

[8] Case C-34/09 *Ruiz Zambrano v Office national de l'emploi* (ONEm) [2011] ECR I-1177. The case has been the subject of much academic commentary. See N Nic Shuibhne 'Seven Questions for Seven Paragraphs' (2011) 36 *ELRev* 161; D Kochenov 'A Real European Citizenship, A New Jurisdiction Test, A Novel Chapter of the Development of the Union in Europe', (2011) 18 *CJEL* 56; A Lansbergen and N Miller 'European Citizenship Rights in Internal Situations: An Ambiguous Revolution?' (2011) 7 *EuConst* 287; P Van Elsuwege and D Kochenov 'On The Limits of Judicial Intervention: EU Citizenship and Family Reunification Rights' (2011) 13 *EJML* 443; T Kostakopoulou 'Co-Creating European Union Citizenship: Institutional Process and Crescive Norms' (27 August 2013), forthcoming (2014) 15 *Cambridge Yearbook of European Legal Studies*; Warwick School of Law Research Paper No. 2013–24, available at SSRN: http://ssrn.com/abstract=2316839.

be unlikely to become Irish citizens by birth, following the Irish constitutional referendum removing automatic *jus soli* citizenship in 2004.[9] EU law would, in likelihood, treat them starkly differently: Kevin would be an EU citizen, the Czech Republic having become an EU Member State on 1 May 2004, just three years after the Supreme Court ruling in *Lobe and Osayande*. Assuming he would acquire Czech nationality by descent, the legal situation of children like him is also examined. Assuming that Osaze today would not be Irish, but derive Nigerian nationality from his parents, he would have difficulty relying on EU law. The most relevant measure, the Family Reunification Directive,[10] only applies to TCNs who have a reasonable prospect of a right to permanent residence. Ireland has not opted in to this Directive. It appears he would have to rely on the protections of the ECHR and the Irish Constitution only. The diverse standards which apply to EU citizens at home, migrant EU citizens, and TCNs, are examined in Part III.

Part IV turns to the challenges facing the national judge. National judges now must regularly apply at least three sets of protections, national constitutional, ECHR and EU law.[11] In so doing, they must keep these different strands distinct, as while they may sometimes overlap and cohere, they have distinct purviews and purposes. The development of domestic constitutional law is for national judges, but there are good reasons to develop domestic constitutional standards in a frank and open engagement with supranational ones. A suggested framework for approaching claims for protection against removal for citizen- and migrant-children is set out, which seeks to overcome some of the difficulties of balancing the competing rights and interests in these cases. In particular, the difficulty of assessing the 'weight' to be accorded to the prerogatives of the State in relation to migration control is addressed.

II. THE ECHR AND MIGRANT CHILDREN

1. Article 8(1) ECHR: Identifying the Interference with Family Life

Strasbourg case law is informed by the statist assumption, which is the assumption that States have an intrinsic right to control admission and stay in their territory by non-citizens.[12] The ECtHR repeatedly asserts that

[9] For analysis of the debate and outcome, see C Costello 'Accidents of Place and Parentage: Birthright Citizenship and Border Crossings' in *The Citizenship Referendum: Implications for the Constitution and Human Rights* (Law School TCD, Dublin, 2004) 5; B Ryan 'The Celtic Cubs: The Controversy over Birthright Citizenship in Ireland' (2004) 6 EJML 173; I Honohan 'Citizenship Attribution on a Country of New Immigration: Ireland' (2010) 36 *Journal of Ethnic and Migration Studies* 811.

[10] Council Directive 2003/86 of 22 September 2003 on the right to family reunification [2003] OJ L251/12.

[11] Mr Justice Fennelly has himself described this as a 'brave new world' in N Fennelly 'Human Rights and the National Judge: His Constitution; The European Union; the European Convention' (2011)12 *ERA Forum* 87, 92. See also in this volume, G Tesauro 'The Italian Model of a dualist approach to multilevel protection of human rights' .

[12] For an overview, see M Bruins and P Boeles *Case law on Article 8 of the European Convention on Human Rights: A Survey* (Institute of Immigration Law, Leiden, November 2006); MB Dembour

> a State is entitled, as a matter of well-established international law and subject to its treaty obligations, to control the entry of aliens into its territory and their residence there. The Convention does not guarantee the right of an alien to enter or to reside in a particular country.[13]

Article 8(1) permits settled migrants to resist removal, or seek regularisation in recognition of their de facto ties with host countries. However, it is not concerned with vindicating the residence rights of citizens as such, rather with ensuring that families can enjoy family life together. Deportations, or refusals to admit family members, are regarded as an interference with human rights only exceptionally, if families cannot relocate together to enjoy family life elsewhere. This feature of the case law, I refer to as the 'elsewhere' test or approach.[14] The cases considered deal variously with first admissions, refusals to renew residence permits and actual removals. While we might expect to find a difference in treatment between admission and removal, in *Gül*,[15] the ECtHR refused to draw a sharp distinction between the negative obligation not to deport, and the positive obligation to admit. Spijkerboer suggests that the

> effect of the Court's approximation of negative and positive obligations is that the Court does not get caught in clear-cut criteria which it has to apply. ... The result of this anti-formal attitude is that the Court can assess the facts of each case separately, and minimise the precedential value of its judgments.[16]

The claims are framed under Article 8 ECHR, which requires first of all a demonstration of the connection between the migrant and the host State. The various connections and relationships of long-term residents in the country of residence warrant protection as 'private life', irrespective of whether family ties have been developed,[17] as confirmed by the Grand Chamber in *Üner.*[18] A further development is the acknowledgement that a State's failure to provide a secure right of residence may itself violate Article 8 ECHR,[19] in effect meaning that

'Human rights law and national sovereignty in collusion: The plight of quasi-nationals at Strasbourg' (2003) 21 *Netherlands Quarterly of Human Rights* 63.

[13] See, for example, Application No 265/07 *Omoregie v Norway*, judgment of 31 July 2008, para 54, citing 'among many other authorities' Applications No 9214/80, 9473/81, 9474/81 *Abdulaziz, Cabales and Balkandalo v UK* (1985) EHRR 471, para 67; Application No 25404/94 *Boujlifa v France*, judgment of 21 October 1997, para 42.

[14] Drawing on S Peers 'Family Reunion and Community Law' in N Walker (ed) *Towards an Area of Freedom, Security and Justice* (OUP, Oxford, 2004), 143. For a recent, typical, application, see Application No 11243/13 *Muradi and Alieva v Sweden*, judgment of 23 June 2013.

[15] Application No 559845/93 *Gül v Switzerland* (1996) 22 EHRR 93.

[16] T Spijkerboer 'Structural Instability: Strasbourg Case Law on Children's Family Reunion' (2009) 11 *EJML* 271, 291.

[17] Application No 48321/99 *Slivenko v Latvia*, judgment of 9 October 2003.

[18] Application No 46410/99 *Üner v the Netherlands* [GC], judgment of 18 October 2006, para 59. For comments, see P Boeles and M Bruins (2005) 7 *EJML* 321; C Steinorth '*Üner v the Netherlands:* Expulsion of Long-Term Immigrants and the Right to Respect for Private and Family Life' (2008) 8 *HRLRev* 185.

[19] See Application No 51431/99 *Mendizabal v France*, judgment of 17 January 2006; Application No 60654/00 *Sisojeva et al v Latvia*, chamber, judgment of 16 June 2005; [GC] judgment of 15 January 2007; Application No 50435/99 *Rodrigues da Silva / Hoogkamer v the Netherlands*, judgment of 31 January 2006.

irregular migrants may invoke Article 8 ECHR to regularise their stay. These cases seem to suggest a new approach, at least when children are involved, as may be seen in *Nunez v Norway,* discussed in the next section.[20] Nonetheless, the Strasbourg Court's general deference to the State's prerogative to authorise entry and presence remains the dominant theme, in particular in cases concerning adults only, as exemplified in *Omoregie,*[21] discussed below.

Concerning spouses, the Strasbourg case law explicitly privileges the prerogatives of the State in relation to admission control, over individual autonomy in the choice of life-partner. In *Abdulaziz, Balkandali and Cabales* the ECtHR expressly rejected any 'general obligation ... to respect the choice by married couples of the country of their matrimonial residence and to accept the non-national spouses for settlement in that country.'[22] This proposition applied even though the sponsors were clearly 'insiders', nationals or long-settled migrants in the UK.

The ECtHR has explicitly tempered the 'elsewhere test' in cases on the admission of children. Initially it required applicants to demonstrate that admission was the 'only way' they could enjoy family life together, the standard in the background of the Supreme Court's *Lobe and Osayande* ruling. *Sen v Netherlands*[23] lowered the requirement to showing that admission was the 'most adequate way' of developing family life. *Sen* concerned the admission of a 12 year-old child of Turkish parents, who were legally resident in the Netherlands. Mr Sen had lived in the Netherlands since he was a child, returning in 1982 to Turkey to get married there and then returning to the Netherlands leaving his wife in Turkey. In 1986 Mrs Sen moved to the Netherlands also, leaving their three year-old daughter with family members. The couple had two further children who were born in the Netherlands. The Court concluded that the 'best way of developing family life with the family as it existed' would be for that child to be admitted, unanimously finding an Article 8 violation. A key factor seems to have been the fact that the two younger Sen children were born in the Netherlands and had never lived anywhere else.

Subsequent cases entail diverse assessments of similar facts. The general approach though examines the family unit as a whole, rather than starting from the premise of the residence rights of the citizen-children. The ECtHR rejected several similar claims as inadmissible for lack of distinguishing features,[24] suggesting that *Sen* did not herald any significant change, until in *Tuquabo-Tekle*[25] it found an Article 8 violation, in part based on the conditions the child would face were she to remain away from her family.

[20] Application No 55597/09 *Nunez v Norway*, judgment of 28 June 2011. The line of reasoning is pursued further in Application No 47017/09 *Butt v Norway*, judgment of 4 December 2012.

[21] *Omoregie,* above n 13.

[22] *Abdulaziz,* above n 13, para 68.

[23] Application No 31465/96 *Sen v Netherlands,* judgment of 21 December 2001 (2003) 36 EHRR 7.

[24] Application No 41226/98 *IM v Netherlands,* judgment of 25 March 2003; Application No 59186/00 *Ebrahim and Ebrahim v the Netherlands,* judgment of 18 March 2003; Application No 53675/00 *Andradev v Netherlands* 6 July 2004; Application No 53102/99 *Chandra v Netherlands,* judgment of 13 May 2003.

[25] Application No 60665/00 *Tuquabo-Tekle v Netherlands*, judgment of 1 December 2005. See casenote P Boeles and M Bruins (2006) 8 *EJML* 372.

2. Article 8(2) ECHR: Public Policy Grounds

Establishing that removal or non-authorisation of residence will interfere with Article 8(1) rights is only the first hurdle. Once that is established, the Court will examine the legality and proportionality of the interference. Interferences must be 'in accordance with law', so removal without clear legal authority will violate Article 8 ECHR.[26] Notwithstanding the statement in *Gül*[27] that the treatment of positive and negative obligations is similar, in cases concerning the legality of removal of settled migrants, the ECtHR often finds an interference with Article 8(1) rights, so that it falls on the State to justify removal under Article 8(2). Article 8(2) lists various justificatory grounds, being 'national security, public safety or the economic well-being of the country, for the prevention of disorder or crime, for the protection of health or morals, or for the protection of the rights and freedoms of others.'

The ECtHR tends to assume that States pursue a legitimate aim when refusing admission or deporting. Yet, just as the Court will not accept bare assertions that removal is necessary for 'national security' reasons,[28] similarly migration control should not be assimilated in itself to a legitimate aim per se. In that respect, Fennelly J's reading of the Strasbourg case law in *Lobe and Osayande* is faithful to the logic of proportionality assessment, when he notes that:

> It seems probable – I would not go further – that the ECHR would not accept as a reason for expulsion, which had disruptive effect on family life, an abstract argument, unrelated to some concrete need of the State, but based simply on the general need to maintain the integrity of the immigration system.[29]

In *Berrehab*,[30] the ECtHR examined immigration law enforcement in so far as it demonstrated genuine concern for population density and labour market regulation, which in turn fell under the aim of 'preservation of the country's economic well-being'.[31] In contrast, in cases where migrants have never been afforded a stable right of residence, the ECtHR seems to treat migration control as a 'pressing social need' in itself. When the State is not required to articulate the aim of its actions clearly, the proportionality assessment is weakened. *Omoregie*[32] illustrates: Mr Omoregie was a rejected Nigerian asylum seeker, married to a Norwegian woman. Together they had a young child. The ECtHR had no difficulty recognising that his proposed deportation was an interference with family life. The State simply relied on its migration control prerogative as embodying a 'pressing social need' justifying removal. The crux of the matter

[26] See, for example, Application no 58149/08 *Amie and others v Bulgaria*, judgment of 12 February 2013.

[27] N 15 above.

[28] Application No 1365/07 *CG and Others v Bulgaria*, judgment of 24 April 2008, para 49.

[29] N 5 above.

[30] Application No 10730/84 *Berrehab v Netherlands*, judgment of 21 June 1988 (1988) EHRR 322. Concerning divorced couples, see further Application No 29192/95 *Ciliz v The Netherlands*, judgment of 11 July 2000.

[31] *Ibid*, para 26.

[32] N 13, above.

was the ECtHR's view that where family life was created when the persons involved knew of one partner's questionable immigration status, no right to family life in the host State arose.[33] In sharp contrast, the Dissenting Opinion of Judge Malinverni (joined by Judge Kovler) stressed the issue of proportionality. The applicant had not committed a criminal offence, but merely breached immigration law. For the dissenting judges, this act was 'purely administrative and in no sense criminal', so the State's justification was weak.

Nunez v Norway[34] provides a sharp contrast with *Omoregie*. Mirtha Nunez was a Dominican national, who first entered Norway in 1996 on a tourist visa. She was deported having been convicted of theft, and re-entered on a different passport in defiance of a two-year ban. She then promptly married a Norwegian national, and obtained a residence permit, stating in her application that she had not previously entered Norway. After their divorce, she had two daughters with a settled immigrant of Dominican origin in Norway. The Court found that at no time had her residence in Norway been lawful,[35] and the expulsion was an appropriate remedy for breach of immigration law, in particular given the aggravated character of the applicant's breaches.[36] Nor did she have any reasonable expectation of being able to remain in the country.[37] Nonetheless, the Court held that as expulsion would deprive the children of contact with their mother for two years,[38] and that Norway had not acted promptly in removing her,[39] expulsion with a two-year re-entry ban was disproportionate.

Berrehab, *Omeregie* and *Nunez* deal with removals on immigration control grounds alone. Also prevalent are cases where long-settled migrants commit criminal offences, so that their removal is amenable to justification as necessary to 'prevent disorder or crime.' The ECtHR set out criteria in *Boultif*[40] for assessing the justifiability of removal under Article 8(2) where the migrant has committed criminal offences, with an important addition in *Üner*, namely:

- the best interests and well-being of the children, in particular the seriousness of the difficulties which any children of the applicant are likely to encounter in the country to which the applicant is to be expelled; and
- the solidity of social, cultural and family ties with the host country and with the country of destination.[41]

Omoregie suggested that migration status is decisive in spousal cases, yet *Nunez* introduces an important qualification when the children's best interests are at stake. Recall that in *Omoregie,* the migrant had committed no crime, yet the State's generic migration control prerogatives were taken to amount to a 'pressing social need.' Although proportionality takes many guises under the ECHR, its

[33] *Ibid*, para 57.
[34] N 20, above.
[35] *Ibid,* para 67.
[36] *Ibid*, paras 71–72.
[37] *Ibid,* para 67.
[38] *Ibid*, para 81.
[39] *Ibid,* para 82.
[40] Application No 54273/00 *Boultif v Switzerland*, judgment of 2 August 2001, para 40.
[41] *Üner*, n 18 above, para 58.

typical structure builds on the textual reference to necessity, often amounting to a less or even least restrictive means test. However, if enforcement of immigration law is taken as both the means and an end in itself, the proportionality test loses traction, and fails to restrict the State's writ. In contrast, *Nunez v Norway* suggests that the 'best interests' standard is gaining additional weight in cases concerning young children.

In *ZH (Tanzania)*,[42] the UK Supreme Court developed the Article 8 ECHR standards in cases concerning the deportation of families of UK Citizens, in light of the 'best interests' standard. The Court identified the diverse interests of the child that would be adversely affected by having to leave their State of nationality.[43] Importantly, the child's best interests and the wishes of her parents may not always be the same, so it cannot simply be assumed that the parents can speak for the child. Importantly too, in *ZH* it was noted that although the mother had committed serious infractions of immigration law, her children were not to blame for these. Indeed, her immigration history was characterized as 'appalling,' but nonetheless, the best interests assessment tilted the balance in favour of permitting her to reside in the UK.

III. THE DIVERSE EU STANDARDS

EU law has long provided protection against deportation for EU migrants.[44] Their rights to move and reside freely throughout the EU include a right to be joined or accompanied by their family members, irrespective of their nationality. These standards are now set out in the 2004 Citizenship Directive.[45] The Court of Justice has notably held that that Directive provides a right to enter and reside in the EU for third country national family members of EU citizens.[46] By expanding the scope of protection of EU citizenship to at least some scenarios where EU citizens remain in their country of nationality in *Zambrano*,[47] the Court of Justice has created a new route to protect residence rights of EU citizens and their TCN families. These two co-existing sources of EU protection are examined below.

[42] *ZH (Tanzania) v SSHD* [2011] UKSC 4.

[43] Indeed, a criticism may be leveled at bringing the matter of citizenship into the 'best interests' analysis, for the facts that would determine that a citizen-child would be better off staying in her country of nationality could equally militate in favour of a non-citizen-child staying in her country of residence. See further, J Fortin 'Are Children's Best Interests Really Best? *ZH (Tanzania) (FC) v Secretary of State for the Home Department*' (2011) 74 *MLR* 947.

[44] For an overview of the foundational case law, see N Fennelly 'The European Union and the Protection of Aliens from Expulsion' (1999) 1 *EJML* 313. Regrettably, in some recent cases, the Court of Justice seems to have departed from the values and principles of its traditional approach. See D Kochenov and B Pirker 'Deporting the Citizens within the European Union: A Counter-intuitive Trend in Case C-348/09 *PI v Boderbürgermeisterin der Stadt Remscheid*' (2013) 19 *Colum J Eur Law* 369.

[45] Parliament and Council Directive 2004/58/EC of 29 April 2004 on the right of citizens of the Union and their family members to move and reside freely within the territory of the Member States [2004] OJ L229/45.

[46] Case C-127/08 *Metock* [2008] ECR I-6241. See further, C Costello '*Metock*: Free Movement and "Normal Family Life" in the Union' (2009) 46 *CMLRev* 587.

[47] N 8 above.

The Family Reunification Directive[48] has set out minimum standards for the entry of family members of third country national migrants who have a 'reasonable prospect' of acquiring a right of permanent residence. Ireland has not opted in to that measure, so it is not considered in detail here. Nonetheless, it is important to note that this Directive is not, in any event, all-embracing. Most notably and unfairly, those recognized as refugees under the Refugee Convention enjoy family reunification rights under EU law, while those who get 'subsidiary protection' do not.[49] There is often little difference between their predicaments, so such a sharp distinction in their rights is indefensible.

1. Third Country National Family Members of EU Citizens, Pre-*Zambrano*

At the time the *Lobe and Osayande* case was decided, there was no obvious EU dimension to the case. Back then, EU citizenship rights were mainly applicable when EU citizens had exercised free movement transnationally.

EU law has long provided economic migration rights for EU nationals, but even after the inclusion of the status of citizenship of the Union in the EU Treaties, EU citizenship remained predominantly a transnational status. Yet, from the outset, families of migrant workers were entitled to accompany the migrant worker, irrespective of their nationality.[50] Family reunification for migrant EU citizens is a right, not a privilege.[51] The citizenship case law goes beyond the letter of the legislation, permitting EU citizens, even in infancy,[52] to be joined by family members. In *Carpenter*,[53] *Baumbast*,[54] and *Chen*,[55] the Court of Justice recognised as bearers of EU rights to reside, various TCN family members of migrant EU citizens. The residence rights were rationalised as necessary to avoid barriers to free movement for the EU citizen, which required that the EU citizen be able to live a 'normal family life.' The Court stated in *Metock* that 'if Union citizens were not allowed to lead a normal family life in the host Member State, the exercise of the freedoms they are guaranteed by the Treaty would be seriously obstructed.'[56]

Carpenter and *Metock* illustrate the added value of EU rights over and above the ECHR standards. As illustrated in Part II above, the ECHR approach is informed by the statist assumption, resulting in the 'elsewhere test'. In contrast, EU citizenship entails a stable right of residence, which protects the family's right

[48] Council Directive 2003/86 of 22 September 2003 on the right to family reunification [2003] OJ L251/12.

[49] Ibid, Chapter V.

[50] Article 10 of Regulation 1612/68 [1968] OJ SpEd L257/2.

[51] The original legislation imposed a condition that workers must possess accommodation considered as normal by national standards. This potential limitation has been interpreted restrictively, as only applying a condition at the time of initial entry. Case 249/86 *Commission v Germany* [1989] ECR 1263.

[52] Case C-200/02 *Chen* [2004] ECR I-9925.

[53] Case C-60/00 *Carpenter v Secretary of State for the Home Department* [2002] ECR I-6279.

[54] Case C-413/99 *Baumbast* [2002] ECR I-7091.

[55] Above n 52.

[56] Above n 46, para 62.

to live together with the EU citizen. Had the *Carpenter* family sought protection under the ECHR, the decision would have turned on whether the entire family could relocate to Mrs Carpenter's country of origin, the Philippines. Perhaps on the facts the UK authorities would have deemed relocation overly burdensome. However, the structure of the EU law enquiry seeks to protect Mr Carpenter's right to reside within the EU. Consequently, denial of Mrs Carpenter's right of residence would have created an 'obstacle' (broadly defined) to living in the UK. Absent strong justification, this obstacle would be a violation of Mr Carpenter's EU Citizenship *and* EU human rights.[57]

In *Metock*, the Court of Justice stated that the citizenship right to 'normal family life' precluded Member States from encouraging blended TCN/EU Citizen families to make their home elsewhere. This passing statement invites interpretation as a tacit criticism of the approach of the ECHR to family reunification matters.[58] Yet, rather than explicitly engage with the Strasbourg case law, in *Metock* the Court was curiously reticent on the issue of the human right to family reunification, confining its analysis to EU citizenship and free movement. The strict separation of human rights and EU citizenship rights is also evident in the Opinion of AG Kokott in the case on the validity of the Family Reunification Directive. She drew a sharp distinction between the two, her starting premise being that 'protection of the family as a *human right* [was] something distinct from the fundamental rights of citizens of the Union, that is to say is typically less extensive than citizens' rights.'[59]

Whether the law on Citizenship of the Union is applicable to a given situation depends, under the pre-*Zambrano* approach, on whether that scenario falls within the personal *and* material scope of EU law. Traditionally, that required a transborder context. This requirement created much-litigated anomalies in the family migration context, which national governments systematically sustained. In response, individuals deliberately engaged in transborder activity, because, to paraphrase the applicants in *Akrich*, they had heard about EU rights.[60]

Various forms of transborder movement are sufficient. For instance, leaving the home State and returning after a period is sufficient, and EU rights endure on return.[61] In *Akrich*,[62] the TCN family member had avoided the impact of a UK deportation order by moving to Ireland with his British spouse. On return to the UK, the authorities resisted the application of the *Surinder Singh* principle. The Court attempted an awkward reconciliation of domestic immigration law

[57] Above n 53, para 39–45.

[58] Costello, above n 46, 603–604. Cited in agreement by S Peers 'Free Movement, Immigration Control and Constitutional Conflict' (2009) *European Constitutional Law Review* 173, 191.

[59] Case C-540/03 *Parliament v Council* [2006] ECR I-5769, para 63 (emphasis in the original).

[60] Case C-109/01 *Secretary of State for the Home Department v Hacene Akrich* [2003] ECR I-9607, para 36.

[61] Case C-370/90 *Surinder Singh* [1992] ECR I-4265; Case C-291/05 *Minister voor Vreemdelingenzaken en Integratie v Eind* [2007] ECR I-10719. A case is currently before the Court of Justice on the scope of these rulings. See the Opinion of AG Sharpston in Cases C-456/12 and C-457/12 *Minister voor Immigratie, Integratie en Asiel v O, and Minister voor Immigratie, Integratie en Asiel v S*, 12 December 2013.

[62] N 60, above.

prerogatives and EC rights by deeming the right to move to another Member State to be dependent on 'prior lawful residence' in a first EU State. However, that criterion proved unworkable, and the Court unequivocally overruled that aspect of *Akrich* in *Metock*.[63] In some contexts, a transborder element may emerge through the interaction of national systems, without actual transborder movement. In *Chen*,[64] baby Chen had not moved from one Member State to another at all, her entire life having been spent in the UK. However, due to her birth in Northern Ireland, she was an Irish citizen. The Court accepted that there was a sufficient transborder element in the case. Dual citizenship can also create transborder issues, as is evident in *Garcia-Avello*,[65] although in itself is not sufficient, as *McCarthy* illustrates.[66] *Carpenter*[67] remains the ruling where the Court's finding of cross-border activity seems most tenuous, with Mr Carpenter's occasional service-provision outside the UK sufficient to allow him to rely on EU law.

These tenuously cross-border cases made the position of static EU Citizens look even more troubling. Given the evident inconsistencies in the case law, there was growing scholarly support for a rethink of the approach to purely internal situations in light of the Citizenship provisions.[68] Some Advocates General suggested an interim approach, allowing EU scrutiny of the anomalies that result from the rule in individual cases.[69] I have argued elsewhere that TCN residence rights provide an example where the rationale underlying the concept of 'purely internal situations' is not borne out, so that in this particular context at the least, EU law should embrace internal situations.[70] That move came in *Zambrano*.

2. The *Zambrano* Revolution

The revolution of *Zambrano* means that Irish citizens can invoke EU law against their home State, in order to prevent the 'denial of the genuine enjoyment of the substance of the rights conferred by virtue of their status as citizens of the Union.' In that case, the Court of Justice deemed to have such an effect the Member State's refusal to grant a right of residence to a third country national

[63] *Metock*, n 46 above, para. 58.

[64] N 52, above.

[65] Case C-148/02 *Garcia-Avello v Belgian State* [2003] ECR I-11613.

[66] Case C-434/09 *McCarthy v Secretary of State for the Home Department*

[67] N 53, above.

[68] For a detailed examination in the context of family reunification, see A Walter *Reverse Discrimination and Family Reunification* (Wolf Legal Publishers, Nijmegen, 2008). For general criticisms of the 'purely internal rule' see N Nic Shuibhne 'Free Movement of Persons and the Wholly Internal Rule: Time to Move On?' (2002) 39 *CMLRev* 731; E Spaventa 'Seeing the Wood Despite the Trees? On the Scope of Union Citizenship and its Constitutional Effects' (2008) 45 *CMLRev* 13.

[69] Opinion of AG Maduro in Case C-72/03 *Carbonati* [2004] ECR I-8027. The Opinion reflects his position in 'The scope of European Remedies: The Case of Purely Internal Situations and Reverse Discrimination' in B Fitzpatrick, T Novitz and P Skidmore *The Future of Remedies in Europe* (Hart Publishing Oxford 2000) 117. See also, Opinion of AG Sharpston in Case C-212/06 *Government of the French Community and Walloon Government* [2007] ECR I-5305.

[70] Costello, n 46 above, 619–621.

with dependent minor children in the Member State where those children were nationals and were resident. The ruling was jurisgenerative: it created a right to live and work in the Member State concerned for Mr Ruiz Zambrano. The roots of *Zambrano* lie in *Rottmann*, which established that EU Citizens may invoke EU law to prevent their denaturalisation.[71]

The Grand Chamber ruling in *Zambrano* heralds a new era in EU Citizenship law. The Zambranos and their child fled violence in Columbia and sought asylum in Belgium. Their asylum application was refused, but a *non-refoulement* clause granted them a precarious right of residence there. They remained in Belgium and had two further children, Diego and Jessica, who had Belgian nationality by operation of law. They sought to assert their rights as EU Citizens, in order to establish a derivative right of residence for their father, Geraldo. The powerful Opinion of AG Sharpston sets out various options for the Court to overcome the strictures and inconsistencies of its previous case law, in order to vindicate the rights of the EU Citizen. The Opinion clearly influenced the Court, though its terse, elliptical ruling leaves much to be clarified. Drawing on *Rottmann*, the Court held that deprivation of the father's right to reside and right to work was such as to deprive the EU citizen children 'of the genuine enjoyment of the substance of the rights conferred by virtue of their status as citizens of the Union.'[72] The reason for this characterization was the Court's assumption that denying the father a right to reside and work would lead to a situation where the children 'would have to leave the territory of the Union in order to accompany their parents.'[73]

Shirley McCarthy[74] held dual UK and Irish nationality, but had always lived in the UK. She sought to rely on her EU Citizenship, in light of *Zambrano*, in order to establish an EU right of residence for her TCN husband. The Opinion of AG Kokott, in sharp contrast to that of AG Sharpston in *Zambrano*, is a reassertion of the orthodoxies of EU law on internal situations. Perhaps in light thereof, the Court (Third Chamber) held that in contrast to Zambrano, the denial of a right of residence to Mrs McCarthy's husband did not have the effect of obliging her to leave the territory of the European Union.[75] This is assumed rather than analysed. The next reference, *Dereci*, was a joint case concerning five different TCN applicants, each in a distinctive family relationship with Austrian nationals resident in Austria.[76] The Court interpreted *Zambrano* as only applying where the effect of the impugned national measure was to oblige the EU citizens 'in fact, to leave not only the territory of the Member State of which he is a national but also the territory of the Union as a whole.'[77] This 'exceptional' protection was to ensure the effectiveness of EU citizenship.[78] In contrast, 'the mere fact that it might appear desirable to a national of a

[71] This is the implication of Case C-135/08 *Rottmann v Freistaat Bayern* [2010] ECR I-1449.
[72] *Zambrano*, para 42, citing *Rottmann*, para 42.
[73] *Ibid*, para 44.
[74] Case C-434/09 *McCarthy* [2011] ECR I-3375.
[75] *McCarthy*, para 50.
[76] Case C-256/11 *Dereci v Bundesministerium für Inneres*, judgment of 15 November 2011.
[77] *Ibid*, para 66.
[78] *Ibid*, para 67.

Member State, for economic reasons or in order to keep his family together in the territory of the Union, for the members of his family who do not have nationality of a Member State to be able to reside with him in the territory of the Union, is not sufficient in itself to support the view that the Union citizen will be forced to leave Union territory if such a right is not granted.'[79] The Court of Justice left this to the national court to verify.[80] The Court reasserted the orthodox position that EU fundamental rights would only be applicable if the matter fell within the scope of EU law, which was dependent on finding a prior infringement of EU law.[81]

Dereci appears to limit *Zambrano* in two ways. First, it emphasises the 'exceptional' nature of the *Zambrano* residence rights. Second, it states that 'genuine enjoyment' test will be met only when the citizen is in effect obliged to leave the territory of the Union as a whole, not merely only her own Member State, by the denial of the family member's residence rights. This is somewhat puzzling, as the novel reference in *Zambrano* to the 'territory of the Union' had the purpose of diminishing the importance of cross-border movement. If the EU citizen moves to another Member State, she brings herself within the protections of the Citizenship Directive, so in that way, can secure a right of residence for her TCN family member, provided the conditions in that Directive are fulfilled, which include having sufficient resources and health insurance. By implicitly suggesting that the 'hop' to another Member State should be exercised, the Court seems to reassert the importance of the transnational dimension of Union Citizenship. It also, as Kochenov and Pirker point out, obscures the harm of deportation: only deportation from the EU is deemed to impair the core of EU citizenship, while intra-EU deportation is treated implicitly as less serious.[82]

In another respect though, *Dereci* confirms the breadth of *Zambrano* as a residual protection for residence rights. While *McCarthy* was read by some as suggesting that the *Zambrano* ruling would only come to the assistance of minors, the, admittedly terse, ruling in *Dereci,* lends no support to that view. In contrast, whether the EU Citizen would have to leave 'territory of the Union' is open for assessment in all situations. The AG's Opinion casts some light on the scenarios where it would be accepted that residence in the territory of the Union was imperilled. AG Mengozzi opined that in none of the five applicants' cases was the EU citizen being compelled to leave to the territory of the Union (the trigger for the *Zambrano* genuine enjoyment tests) or experiencing an impediment to her free movement (as under the traditional test).[83] Yet, he also admitted that examining the possibility of moving to another EU Member State may put families with one EU Citizen parent at a disadvantage in contrast to the Zambrano family, as the option to move to another Member State would be open in the former case. However, if that were not possible, for instance if the EU Citizen parent was for whatever reason, 'unable to work and thus to

[79] *Ibid*, para 68.
[80] *Ibid*, para 74.
[81] *Ibid*, paras 70–74.
[82] Kochenov and Pirker, above n 44.
[83] Opinion of AG Mengozzi in *Dereci,* paras 33–37.

provide for the needs of her children,' then the TCN parent's residence might be protected in order to maintain the children's residence in the EU.[84] The notion of dependency informing the Opinion is broad, encompassing 'legal, administrative or emotional dependency.'[85] Accordingly, the Opinion also countenances the situation whereby a TCN child derives a *Zambrano* right of residence in order to maintain the residence rights of a dependent EU Citizen parent.[86]

Thus far, the 'genuine enjoyment' test protects Citizenship itself (as in *Rottmann*) and rights of residence (as in *Zambrano*). The difficulty with *McCarthy* and *Dereci* is that, while in *Zambrano*, the Court establishes an assumption that the family would have to leave Belgium were Mr Ruiz Zambrano not to be accorded a right to reside and work, in *McCarthy* the Court assumes the converse: that Mrs McCarthy will not be compelled to leave the UK to be with her husband. In contrast in *Dereci*, the Court delegates the assessment of the 'genuine enjoyment' test to the national courts, in recognition of its fact-specific character. In subsequent cases, it has provided some guidance to national judges, deciding in two such cases that the *Zambrano* threshold was not met. In *Iida v Ulm*,[87] the Japanese father sought to assert an EU right to reside in Germany, while his German family lived in Austria. The Court clarified that the Citizenship Directive was inapplicable, and also found that the 'genuine enjoyment' threshold was not met. In *Ymeraga*,[88] the applicant had Luxembourg nationality, and sought to have his parents and brothers join him from Kosovo. His case was not covered by the Citizenship Directive or Family Reunification Directive. Nor did he meet the *Zambrano* test.

O, S and L[89] concerned the rights of residence of two TCN men, both married to women who had been lawfully resident in Finland for considerable periods. The women were both mothers and primary caregivers of Finnish children, having previously been married to Finnish nationals. In the second case, the couple also had a child together, who was a TCN. The husbands' applications had been rejected for lack of stable means. It was also emphasised that they were not the custodial parents of the EU citizen children. The intervening governments (Finnish, Danish, German, Italian, Netherlands and Polish) and the European Commission all argued that Article 20 TFEU did not apply. The Court again distilled the *Zambrano* ruling, in light of *Dereci*, into the question of whether the EU citizen would have to leave not only the Member State, but the territory of the EU as a whole,[90] a test it deemed 'specific in character'[91]. Leaving the matter to the referring court to determine, it nonetheless required the former to take into account the right to permanent residence of the mothers

[84] *Ibid*, paras 47.
[85] *Ibid*, para 48.
[86] *Ibid*.
[87] Case C-40/11 *Iida v Stadt Ulm*, judgment of 8 November 2012.
[88] Case C-87/12 *Ymeraga v Ministre du Travail, de l'Emploi et de l'Immigration*, judgment of 8 May 2013.
[89] Joined Cases C-356/11 and C-357/11 *O, S v Maahanmuuttovirasto and Maahanmuuttovirasto v L*, judgment of 6 December 2011.
[90] Para 47.
[91] Para 48.

in Finland,[92] and suggested that on the basis of the limited evidence before it, there seemed to be no 'dependency' between the EU citizens and the men in question.[93] It noted too that even if the *Zambrano* test was not met, the right to family life would have to be addressed 'in the framework of the provisions on the protection of fundamental rights which are applicable in each case.'[94] This formulation leaves open the question as to which human rights standards (EU and ECHR, or ECHR alone) are applicable. The former only apply if the matter falls within the scope of EU law, while the latter apply due to the Member States' international obligations. The Family Reunification Directive was applicable, as the women were TCN sponsors residing lawfully in Finland, and so the Court also provided important guidance on that measure.

Most recently in *Alokpa*,[95] a Togolese woman sought a derivative right of residence in Luxembourg. Her twins were born in Luxembourg in 2008, but had French nationality due to their paternity. The twins were premature, and had needed hospital care. They had lived their entire lives in Luxembourg, and never had a relationship with their father. Mrs Alokpa was accepted as having sole responsibility for their care. She could not be regarded as a dependent TCN family member, but based on *Chen,* provided they met the resource sufficiency test in the Citizenship Directive, Mrs Alokpa would derive a right of residence from them. The Court noted that

> the refusal by the Luxembourg authorities to grant Mrs Alokpa a right of residence cannot result in her children being obliged to leave the territory of the European Union altogether. It is, however, for the referring court to determine whether, in light of the facts of the main proceedings, that is in fact the case.

In contrast, AG Mengozzi took this view that it was 'inconceivable' that Mrs Alokpa would not have been allowed to live in France with her children.[96] Indeed, he even went so far as to suggest that she would be permitted to work in Luxembourg as a frontier worker if needs be.

Thus far, the scope of the *Zambrano* ruling has been limited to cases where EU Citizen-children depend on their TCN family members to such a degree that without their presence, the EU citizens would be forced to leave the territory of the Union. In so confirming and confining *Zambrano*, the best reading of the case is that it establishes a form of residual EU jurisdiction to ensure that EU citizenship is a meaningful status, but one which applies *in extremis*.[97]

Applying the ruling to the *Lobe and Osayande* scenario illustrates the distinctive features of EU rights. If it can be demonstrated that without the parent(s), the children will not be able to live in Ireland, the parents acquire an EU right to live and work. Their previous immigration status is of no significance. However, triggering *Zambrano* protections will be difficult if the

[92] Para 50.

[93] Para 57.

[94] Para 59, citing *Dereci and Others*, n 76, para 69.

[95] Case C-86/12 *Alokpa v Ministre du Travail, de l'Emploi and de l'Immigration*, judgment of 10 October 2013.

[96] Opinion, para 56.

[97] Kochenov, n 8 above.

family enjoy residence rights elsewhere in the EU. It appears that immediately post-*Zambrano*, the Irish government granted parents of Irish citizen children rights to reside in Ireland, or even permitted some to return to Ireland post-deportation, based on a then appropriately expansive reading of the case.[98] However, with the ECJ's clarification in *Dereci*, a line of cases emerged which rejected applications where it was not clear that the Irish citizen would be required to leave the territory of the Union, if the TCN family member were not granted an EU right of residence.[99] Yet, the unreported judgments suggest that there has been greater attention accorded to the rights of the citizen-child post-*Zambrano*, even under domestic constitutional law alone. [100] If that is so, the new EU jusrisdiction is serving an important corrective function, opening up space for improvements in national constitutional standards.

IV. APPLYING EU AND ECHR STANDARDS IN THE NATIONAL COURTS

The application of diverse, potentially overlapping standards is a challenge for national litigants and judges. The standards should not be conflated, so their respective scope needs to be clarified. Nonetheless, in order for any rights protection to be meaningful, limitations on rights must be scrutinized carefully. No matter what the source of the right in question (constitutional, ECHR or EU), this demands a proportionality assessment. While the intensity of proportionality review varies from context to context, and the factors that are to be balanced vary too, proportionality's structure demands careful articulation and evaluation of the competing rights and interests at stake.

1. The Scope of ECHR and EU Protections

The first task is to determine which standards apply. The ECHR standards apply to all actions of the Irish State, so are in that sense all-embracing. The Strasbourg case law is highly fact-specific, even casuistic at times. It can be difficult to summarise or derive principles of general application therefrom, and sometimes difficult to apply. Nonetheless, there has been a clear shift in the cases on children, which seek to ensure that the consequences of their parents' immigration law infractions do not undermine their best interests. When

[98] See, for example, *Amobi v Minister for Justice* Unreported, Clark J, judgment of 8 February 2013.

[99] *Okunade v Minister for Justice Equality and Law Reform and the Attorney General* [2012] IESC 49; *Gilani v The Minister for Justice And Equality* Unreported, Cooke J, 14 May 2012; *A.O v Minister for Justice, Equality and Law Reform (No. 2)* Unreported, Hogan J, 17 January 2012; *E.A. v Minister for Justice* Unreported, Hogan J, 7 September 2012; *Wang (A minor) v Minister for Justice and Law Reform* Unreported, Cooke J, 23 July 2012; *Troci v The Minister for Justice and Equality* Unreported, O'Keeffe J, 7 December 2012.

[100] See, for example, *S v Minister for Justice, Equality and Law Reform,* Unreported, Clark J, 13 October 2012. With particular thanks to John Stanley BL for sharing his at yet unpublished work on this topic. See J Stanley *Immigration and Citizenship Law in Ireland* (Dublin, Round Hall Thompson Reuters, *forthcoming*).

national judges apply the ECHR case law, they should treat it as the articulation of a pan-European minimum human rights standard. The 'elsewhere approach', which permeates the Strasbourg case law, is open to criticism as undermining the rights in question. In addition, where the ECtHR grants States a wide margin of appreciation, it should be recalled that this institutional device reflects the ECtHR's position as a subsidiary protector of rights. When national courts scrutinise their own executives, such a margin is not appropriate. Bearing in mind these institutional features, it is certainly appropriate for national constitutional and EU standards to be higher than the Strasbourg minimum.

In contrast, EU standards are of limited scope and internally differentiated. To illustrate, let's return to Kevin Lobe's case with its contemporary twist. If we imagine his claim as a Czech citizen-child in Ireland, he may invoke the protection of transnational EU Citizenship, as a national of one Member State, resident in another. However, as a 'child of tender years', while not economically active, he is held to the resource conditions in the Citizenship Directive. As in *Chen* and *Alokpa*, he would have to demonstrate that the primary caregiver has sufficient resources, in order to secure her right of residence. If the family does meet these conditions, the Citizenship Directive provides strong protections against removal. The alternative approach is to invoke the protective *Zambrano* jurisdiction. However, as a Czech national, any removals from Ireland will be mitigated (under the current approach) by the possibility of moving back to the Czech Republic. On the current case law, he fails to trigger *Zambrano* protections, even if he is entirely dependent on the family member in question. If either method of triggering EU law succeeds, this brings with it EU fundamental rights protections, including the EU Charter of Fundamental Rights, and the general principle of proportionality.

2. Rights Protection and Proportionality

i. The Ubiquity of Proportionality

As discussed above, the Strasbourg case law requires a proportionality assessment. Indeed, proportionality is also a general principle of EU law, so will be relevant if EU law applies to any purported deportation. The perfunctory proportionality analysis in some of the case law on Irish citizen-children suggests that something has gone awry.[101] For proportionality to work meaningfully, we must develop a metric to value the rights at stake, the seriousness of the rights infringement in contemplation, and the competing State's interests being invoked to justify that infringement. This basic structure of enquiry applies across constitutional, ECHR and EU law. In some of the Irish case law since *Lobe and Osayande,* two restrictive moves occur, which when taken together, weaken the proportionality assessment, in my view excessively. This account

[101] For a similar critique of the case law, see S Mullally 'Citizen Children, 'impossible subjects' and the limits of migrant family rights in Ireland' (2011) *European Human Rights Law Review* 43.

does not purport to an exhaustive summary. Indeed, there is considerable variation within the judicial reviews on this topic over time. Rather, I seek to identify the moves that lead to very weak protections in a constitutional system that claims to value the residence rights of the citizen-child.

ii. Valuing Rights: Citizens' and Human Rights Contrasted

The first move is to diminish the significance of the right of residence of the citizen-child, pointing out the remaining rights that will accrue to her *qua* citizen, even if she has to leave her country of citizenship for her formative years. US Constitutional jurisprudence, while of course a useful source of comparative constitutional wisdom for any liberal democracy,[102] is an outlier in the global conversation on constitutional rights, in particular in not embracing proportionality as the appropriate rights vindicating standard of review.[103] In *Lobe and Osayande,* its citation seems to have contributed to the diminution of the Irish citizens' rights.

So, to take an example of this approach, in *Alli*,[104] Clark J located the 'real difference' between citizen and foreigner not in the non-deportability of the citizen, but rather in other rights citizens may enjoy, which are not dependent on continuity of residence.[105] That move seems unconvincing. While residence rights are certainly not the only rights of citizens, without residence, citizenship is hollow. Moreover, non-deportability is not merely an idiosyncratic constitutional guarantee – it is a ubiquitous feature of nationality as understood in the international system, and reflects the nature of the bond between citizen and State. Deportability is a defining feature of alienage, while non-deportability defines citizenship.[106] The non-deportability of citizens is both constitutive and consequential. Rather than playing this down, we must accord it significant weight. To de facto deport a citizen is to treat her as if she is not a citizen at all. Moreover, it impairs the effectiveness of most other citizenship rights, including the right which turns citizenship from a legal status into an affective one, namely the possibility to grow up within the polity, participate and interact in its life. In this respect, Fennelly J in *Lobe and Osayande* is correct that 'the most natural right, one which inheres in citizenship, is the right to reside in the State of that citizenship.'[107]

[102] Although of course US courts do not routinely look outside for inspiration as to how to develop their constitutional jurisprudence.

[103] K Möller, *The Global Model of Constitutional Rights* (Oxford, OUP, 2012) 17–20.

[104] *Alli v Minister for Justice, Equality and Law Reform* [2010] 4 IR 45.

[105] These rights were said to include the 'lifelong rights to hold an Irish passport, to enter and leave the State at will; to apply for employment and to vote in constitutional referendums. A citizen applicant to university and third level courses will not normally face discrimination in entry eligibility or the payment of fees nor will that citizen be affected by entry into those courses operating restricted entry to foreign nationals. A citizen child who lives abroad can return to avail of his/her privileges in further education, in unimpeded entry into the other EU States, and in access to that large labour market. The removal of the citizen child's parents and the consequent following of that child do not strip the child of citizenship rights and privileges as those rights can be enjoyed fully when the child is of age if he/she seeks to return to the birth country. However, the birthright of an Irish citizen child does not extend to an unrestricted right to reside here with his/her foreign national family.'

[106] B Anderson et al, n 1 above; Kochenov and Pirker, n 44 above.

[107] N 5 above.

It may be helpful to draw out the contrast between the two sets of rights, citizens' rights and human rights. A citizenship approach values security of residence both intrinsically, for it defines what it is to be a citizen, and instrumentally, for it makes possible participation in the polity and the collective interactions of citizenry. A human rights approach, in contrast, will focus on interests, and the interests that are impaired in a particular case if a child can no longer live in the country of her nationality. The citizenship inquiry and the human rights inquiry may overlap in some respects, but not completely. For instance, a citizenship approach will not be concerned with duration of residence in the country of nationality, for the status of citizenship is unaffected by that fact. Yet, a human rights approach will consider the duration of residence to assess the strength of de facto ties.[108] Importantly, a human rights approach will be attuned to the various real-world consequences, personal, developmental, social, economic, and cultural, of deportation, and require comparison between the conditions in the country of nationality and the country to which return is in contemplation. In contrast, the citizenship assessment is more focused in that principally it demands that the residence rights of the citizen at home be accorded considerable weight in the analysis, demanding strong justification for the deportation of the family members.

iii. Assessing Claims Relating to the State's Migration Control Prerogatives

The other side of the 'balance' is the State's interest. Here, we must examine the reasons for the attempted deportation of the family members. For that balancing process to be meaningful, there must be an articulation of the reasons for deportation, not merely an assertion that immigration law requires it. A proportionality analysis requires articulation of the reasons behind the State's decisions, not merely an assertion of that the law requires a particular act.[109] Deportation is not the sine qua non of immigration law, but rather, one of the State's most coercive acts. If parents lack stable residence rights in the country of nationality of their child or children, the causes for that predicament should be examined. Moreover, as was emphasised in *ZH*, even if the parents have egregiously flouted immigration law, that wrong-doing is not attributable to the citizen-child.

There is quite a range of situations in which TCNs may find themselves without secure rights of residence. Take two examples. Firstly, *Zambrano* itself: the *Zambrano* case prompted a telling scholarly spat between some

[108] This may help explain why Fennelly J was not able to distinguish *Lobe and Osayande* from *Fajujonu* on this basis. While duration of residence may make the removal more harmful to the interests of the citizen-child and her family, and so is relevant to the human rights analysis, it does not alter the nature of the rupture of the citizen-state bond, which was the focus of his assessment.

[109] To give two straightforward examples, assessing the proportionality of a limitation of any fundamental right requires an assessment of the legitimate aim behind the limitation, not merely an assertion that the limitation in enshrined law. Similarly, in considering whether incarceration is a proportionate punishment for wrong-doing, it says nothing to assert that the law imposes a term of imprisonment. A proportionality assessment means looking at the rationale for imprisonment, not merely asserting that the law demands it.

commentators who characterized the parents as 'illegals' in the EU,[110] and others who emphasised the family's repeated attempts to regularize their precarious status in Belgium, and generally law-abiding behaviour. The latter account was more accurate, in that the *Zambrano* parents fell into the category of being non-removable (given the human rights concerns about the risks they faced if returned to Columbia), but without a secure right of residence in Belgium. Secondly, consider overstayers under temporary migration programmes, which only permit renewal of work visas on the employers' application. Workers under such systems do not control their migration status in the manner that debates over 'illegal immigration' tend to suppose. Rather, 'illegality' may be produced and exploited by employers.[111]

It cannot be assumed in all cases of irregular or insecure migration status that deportation is the legally appropriate response. Rather, rule of law arguments may militate in favour of regularization of migrants with insecure statuses.[112] The 'integrity of the legal system' is a helpfully broad term, as it focuses not only on any irregularity or illegality on the part of the parents, but also on the State's conduct, in terms of both the quality of its immigration laws, whether their enforcement is coherent with stated law and policy, and whether in failing to provide secure statuses for migrants, the State itself is creating conditions which undermine legality.[113] Some of the Irish case law post-*Lobe and Osayande* seems to treat deportation as the only way to demonstrate legal integrity, a deeply troubling proposition.[114] Proportionality means scrutinising the reasons behind official action, not merely its formal legality. Such scrutinity will reveal that migrants may come to face removal for many reasons, some of which are legally convincing, while others are not. Whether those official reasons outweigh the rights of the child, *qua* citizen or simply in virtue of her humanity, is the task that falls to national judges. In *Lobe and Osayande*, Fennelly J insisted that only 'grave and substantive reasons associated with the common good' would justify the de facto deportation of the citizen-child. This chimes with the approach advocated here.

[110] K Hailbronner and D Thym 'Annotation of Case C-34/09 *Ruiz Zambrano* (2011) 48 *CMLRev* 1253 and the reply thereto, M Olivas and D Kochenov 'Case C- 34/09 *Ruiz Zambrano*: A Respectful Rejoinder' *University of Houston Public Law and Legal Theory Series 2012-W-1*.

[111] B Anderson and M Ruhs 'Researching illegality in the migrant labour market' (2010) 16 *Population, Space and Place* 175.

[112] See, A Ellerman 'The Rule of Law and The Right to Stay: The Moral Claims of Undocumented Migrants' *Politics and Society (forthcoming)*. Some commentators develop analogies with adverse possession: A Shachar *The Birthright Lottery: Citizenship and Global Inequality* (Cambridge Mss., Harvard University Press, 2009) 185–188; M Risse 'On the Morality of Immigration' (2008) 22 *Ethics and International Affairs* 25.

[113] R Rubio-Marín *Immigration as a Democratic Challenge,* (Cambridge, CUP, 2000) 95.

[114] The High Court (Clark J) in *Alli,* above n 101, held that the following recital in a deportation decision was a substantial reason for deportation of the parent of an Irish child: 'there is no less restrictive process available which would achieve the legitimate aim of the State to maintain control of its own borders and operate a regulated system for control, processing and monitoring of non-national persons in the State.' This finding is particularly troubling deportation orders in Ireland usually include non-return obligations. See Section 3(1) Immigration Act 1999.

V. CONCLUSION

To conclude, let me return to the various sources of the inspiration for this piece in the judgment of Mr Justice Fennelly in *Lobe and Osayande*. That judgment is infused with humanity. Its opening reference, to the Biblical injunction 'thou shalt not oppress a stranger', reminds us that it is in how we treat the 'other' that we find our common humanity.[115] It seeks consistency with constitutional authority and principle, demanding that only 'grave and substantive reasons associated with the common good' would justify deportation of the parents of citizen-children, the standard articulated in *Fajujonu*, a case the majority in *Lobe and Osayande* does not purport to overrule. There is also a deep concern to ensure proper accountability of the executive in immigration and citizenship matters, with an insightful acknowledgment that 'the routine application of the unmodified *Wednesbury* test … makes decisions of the Minister virtually immune from review.'[116] Relatedly, the judgment probes the underlying official rationales, to place the claims in the appropriate context. In order to judge the cogency of the State's claims that deportation was necessary, Mr Justice Fennelly examined the policy and practice towards other families in the same legal predicament, a matter the majority deemed irrelevant to the inquiry.[117] Most importantly, the judgment takes seriously the residence rights of the citizen-child, and so is prescient of the EU developments in *Zambrano* and on the 'best interests' of children in Strasbourg.

[115] For an inspirational analysis, cited by Mr Justice Fennelly (above n 44) see JHH Weiler 'Thou Shalt Not Oppress a Stranger: On the Judicial Protection of the Human Rights of Non-EC Nationals – A Critique' (1992) 3 *EJIL* 65.

[116] N 5 above.

[117] The case could have gone in a different direction had this point been fully argued. If it was demonstrable that the deportations at issue and the articulated policy were not congruent, this should be a basis for judicial review in and of itself. For an analogous argument on immigration detention in the UK, where lack of coherence between stated policy and actual practice was the basis for judicial review, see *Walumba Lumba v Secretary of State for the Home Department* [2011] UKSC 12.

Index